GENERALIST SOCIAL WORK PRACTICE

John Poulin, PhD, MSW, is a professor emeritus and adjunct professor at Widener University's Center for Social Work Education in Chester, Pennsylvania, currently teaching the foundation field seminar in Widener's online MSW program. In 2016, he retired from Widener University, where he taught generalist practice, research, and policy courses for 32 years. Dr. Poulin received a BA from the University of Southern Maine, an MSW from the University of Michigan, and a PhD from the University of Chicago's School of Social Service Administration. As a former director of Widener's BSW program, he founded its MSW program and served as the dean and director for 13 years. He also served for 10 years as the executive director of Social Work Consultation Services (SWCS), an innovative community-based field placement agency developed by the school of social work in collaboration with local community human services organizations. SWCS provides a wide range of free social work services to low-income community residents as well as free capacity-building services to underresourced community-based human services organizations. SWCS has served as a field placement site for hundreds of BSW and MSW students. Dr. Poulin has published numerous journal articles and book chapters and three editions of a generalist social work practice textbook. He also has many national and international conference presentations to his credit. (Orcid ID: https://orcid.org/0000-0003-2165-8242)

Selina Matis, PhD, LCSW, LICSW, is a licensed clinical social worker and assistant professor at Capella University. She received her doctoral degree in social work from Widener University. Additionally, she has an MSW, BS in elementary education, and an MS in school psychology, all from PennWest University (formerly California University of Pennsylvania). Clinically, she has worked primarily in the mental health arena supporting children and their families in a variety of settings. She has specialized in treating trauma across the life span. She currently runs a private practice providing counseling, consultation, and supervision services. Dr. Matis has taught at both the BSW and MSW levels in a variety of subject areas including practice education, clinical practice, research, policy, human behavior in the social environment, child welfare, and program evaluation. She has experience supporting students through the social work practice internships in a variety of ways as well, including as a practice coordinator, practice faculty liaison, and as MSW supervisor. Dr. Matis has been published and presented on a variety of topics including resilience, self-care and burnout, ethics, trauma-informed social work, working with families, helping students succeed, and the social work competencies. She has two current social work textbooks in print: *Social Work Practice* and *The Social Work Field Placement*.

Heather Witt, PhD, LMSW, MEd, is a licensed social worker, associate professor of social work, and BSW coordinator at Boise State University. She received her PhD and MSW from Widener University in Chester, Pennsylvania. As a clinical social worker, she worked with children, adolescents, adults, and older adults providing individual, group, family, and relationship therapy. This work focused on a variety of issues including sexual trauma, infertility, depression, anxiety, and sexual functioning difficulties. Additionally, Professor Witt provided psychoeducational sex education groups for families. Professor Witt has experience in administration in community health and nonprofit education settings, which informs her approach to policy and macrolevel social work practice. Her current research focus is on human rights and policy practice, with an additional focus on social justice related to human sexuality. Her past scholarship topics include infertility; trauma-informed approaches in the classroom; and cross-cultural research on body image, fear of intimacy, psychological well-being, and sexual anxiety. She recently published *The Social Work Field Placement: A Competency-Based Approach* and contributed chapters to *Handbook on Social Work Ethics and Values* and *Sexuality Concepts for Social Workers and Human Service Professionals*.

GENERALIST SOCIAL WORK PRACTICE
A Competency-Based Approach

Second Edition

John Poulin, PhD, MSW
Selina Matis, PhD, LCSW, LICSW
Heather Witt, PhD, LMSW, MEd

Copyright © 2026 Springer Publishing Company, LLC
All rights reserved.

First Springer Publishing edition 978-0-8261-7852-7 (2021)

No part of this publication may be reproduced, stored in a retrieval system, or transmitted in any form or by any means, electronic, mechanical, photocopying, recording, or otherwise, without the prior permission of Springer Publishing Company, LLC, or authorization through payment of the appropriate fees to the Copyright Clearance Center, Inc., 222 Rosewood Drive, Danvers, MA 01923, 978-750-8400, fax 978-646-8600, info@copyright.com or at www.copyright.com.

Springer Publishing Company, LLC
902 Carnegie Center/Suite 140, Princeton, NJ 08540
www.springerpub.com
connect.springerpub.com

Acquisitions Editor: Mindy Okura-Marszycki
Production Editor: Diana Osborne
Compositor: S4Carlisle Publishing Services

ISBN: 978-0-8261-6682-1
e-book ISBN: 978-0-8261-6683-8
DOI: 10.1891/9780826166838

SUPPLEMENTS:

 A robust set of instructor resources designed to supplement this text is located at http://connect.springerpub.com/content/book/978-0-8261-6683-8. Qualifying instructors may request access by emailing textbook@springerpub.com.

Instructor Materials:
LMS Common Cartridge—All Instructor Resources ISBN: 978-0-8261-6688-3
Instructor Manual ISBN: 978-0-8261-6684-5
Instructor Test Bank ISBN: 978-0-8261-6685-2
Instructor PowerPoints ISBN: 978-0-8261-6686-9
Sample Syllabi ISBN: 978-0-8261-5379-1
Transition Guide to Second Edition ISBN: 978-0-8261-5688-4

Student Materials:
Student Resources ISBN: 978-0-8261-6687-6

25 26 27 28 / 5 4 3 2 1

The author and the publisher of this Work have made every effort to use reliable and current sources to provide information that is accurate and compatible with the standards generally accepted at the time of publication. Nevertheless, the authors and publisher are not responsible for any errors or omissions or any consequence from application of the information in this book and make no warranty, expressed or implied, with respect to the content of this publication. Because science and knowledge are continually advancing, readers therefore should always consult current research and specific institutional policies before performing any clinical procedure and should carefully check the manufacturer's package insert before delivering medication. The author and publisher shall not be liable for any special, consequential, or exemplary damages resulting, in whole or in part, from readers' use of, or reliance on, the information contained in this book. The publisher has no responsibility for the persistence or accuracy of URLs for external or third-party internet websites referred to in this publication and does not guarantee that any content on such websites is, or will remain, accurate or appropriate. Similarly, Springer Publishing recognizes that cultural and social language preferences may change and that there may be disagreement on what is considered appropriate terminology within the context of the content. We strive for inclusivity and representation in all our content but must rely on the author's knowledge and interpretation of what is appropriate for the subject matter at the time of writing.

Library of Congress Cataloging-in-Publication Data

Names: Poulin, John, author. | Matis, Selina, author. | Witt, Heather, author.
Title: Generalist social work practice : a competency-based approach / John Poulin, PhD, MSW, Selina Matis, PhD, LCSW, LICSW, Heather Witt, PhD, LMSW, MEd.
Other titles: Social work practice
Identifiers: LCCN 2024049731 (print) | LCCN 2024049732 (ebook) | ISBN 9780826166821 (paperback) | ISBN 9780826166838 (ebook)
Subjects: LCSH: Social service—Practice. | Social work education.
Classification: LCC HV10.5 .P684 2026 (print) | LCC HV10.5 (ebook) | DDC 361.3/2—dc23/eng/20241223
LC record available at https://lccn.loc.gov/2024049731
LC ebook record available at https://lccn.loc.gov/2024049732

Contact sales@springerpub.com to receive discount rates on bulk purchases.

Publisher's Note: New and used products purchased from third-party sellers are not guaranteed for quality, authenticity, or access to any included digital components.

Printed in the United States of America by Gasch Printing.

This book is dedicated to the social workers, social work students, and others who are fighting for the rights of women, LGBTQIA+ individuals, immigrants, refugees, and all other oppressed, targeted, and excluded people in the United States and throughout the world. Social workers combat social and economic injustice daily and are on the front lines in the struggle for equality and social justice in these troubling times.

Contents

Additional Contributors   xvii
Preface   xix
Resources   xxi

1. Social Work Concepts, Theories, and Paradigms   1
Learning Objectives   1
About This Book   2
Anti-Oppressive Practice and Antiracism, Diversity, Equity, and Inclusion Concepts   2
   Power   3
   Privilege   4
   Oppression   4
   Intersectionality   4
Paradigms, Theories, Perspectives, and Practice Models   5
   The Positivist Paradigm   7
Summary   20
Discussion Questions   22
Key References   23

2. Generalist Social Work Practice: Incorporating an Antiracist and Anti-Oppressive Perspective   25
Learning Objectives   25
Generalist Social Work Practice   26
   Definition of Generalist Social Work Practice   26
   Generalist Interventions   27
Anti-Oppressive Generalist Social Work Practice   30
   Core Anti-Oppressive Practice Principles   31
   The Helping Process   35
Client Change Process   39
   Working With Clients Who Have Experienced Discrimination and Oppression   40
   The Experience of Being a Client   40
   Expectations About the Helping Experience   41
Professional Social Work Competencies   41
   Accreditation and Social Work Competencies: Educational Policy and Accreditation Standards 2022   42
Holistic Competency   44
   Knowledge   44
   Values   44
   Skills   44
   Cognitive Processes and Affective Reactions   45
Interrelationships Among the Competencies   45
Summary   46
Discussion Questions   48
Key References   49

3. Ethical and Professional Behavior   51

Learning Objectives   51
Competency 1: Demonstrate Ethical and Professional Behavior   52
Social Work Values and Ethics   53
Core Social Work Values   53
   Service Value   53
   Social Justice Value   53
   Dignity and Worth of the Person's Value   55
   Importance of Human Relationships Value   56
   Integrity Value   57
   Competence Value   57
Ethical Standards   58
Ethical Dilemmas   58
   Ethical Guidelines   59
Value Conflicts   61
Interprofessional Collaboration   64
Interprofessional Collaboration Competencies   65
   Values and Ethics for Interprofessional Practice   65
   Roles and Responsibilities   66
   Teams and Teamwork   66
Mechanisms That Support Interprofessional
   Collaborative Practice   67
   Institutional Supports   67
   Working Culture   67
Supervision   69
Trust, Sharing, and Vulnerability   71
Self-Reflection   73
Self-Awareness   73
Professional Development   74
Professional and Ethical Use of Technology   75
Professional Online Identity   76
Confidentiality and Privacy   76
Summary   76
Discussion Questions   79
Key References   79

4. Advancing Human Rights and Social, Racial, Economic, and Environmental Justice   81

Learning Objectives   81
Competency 2: Advancing Human Rights and Social, Racial, Economic,
   and Environmental Justice   82
National Association of Social Workers *Code of Ethics*   82
Maslow's Theory of Motivation (Human Need)   83
Theories of Social Justice   84
   Distributive Justice   84
Oppression and Human Rights Violations   85
Global Interconnections   88
Forms of Oppression   89
   Racism   90
   Xenophobia and Ethnocentrism   90

    Classism   91
    Religious Oppression   91
    Sexism   91
    Homophobia, Biphobia, and Heterosexism   92
    Transgender Oppression   92
    Ableism   93
    Ageism   93
Types and Sources of Power   94
Social Processes   95
Conflict   95
Justice-Informed Practice   96
Anti-Oppressive Practice, Human Rights, and Social Justice   99
Policy Issue   105
Summary   106
Discussion Questions   109
Key References   110

5. Antiracism, Diversity, Equity, and Inclusion   *111*

Learning Objectives   111
Competency 3: Engage Antiracism, Diversity, Equity, and Inclusion in Practice   112
National Association of Social Workers *Code of Ethics*   112
Conflict Theory   115
Critical Race Theory   116
Intersectionality   117
Compa Love   120
Racial Triangulation Theory   121
Cultural Wealth   121
Oppression Theory   122
Forms and Mechanisms of Oppression and Discrimination   122
    Microaggressions   123
Engaging Antiracism, Diversity, Equity, and Inclusion in Social Work Practice   125
    Self-Awareness   126
    Personal Values and Biases   128
    Constituents as Experts   130
    Cultural Competence Standards   130
    Empowerment   132
    Empathy   133
    Humility   133
    Rural Diversity   134
    Practice Recommendations   135
    Education Recommendations   136
    Training Recommendations   136
    Policy Recommendations   136
    Research Recommendations   136
    Workforce Recommendations   136
Policy Issue   137
Social Justice Issue   138
Summary   139
Discussion Questions   141
Key References   141

6. Research-Informed Social Work Practice   143

    Learning Objectives   *143*
    Competency 4: Engage in Practice-Informed Research and Research-Informed Practice   *144*
    Competency 9: Evaluate Practice With Individuals, Families, Groups, Organizations, and Communities   *144*
    National Association of Social Workers *Code of Ethics*   *145*
    Positivism   *148*
    Empiricism   *148*
    Scientific Inquiry   *149*
    Role of Research in Social Work Practice   *150*
    Research-Informed Practice   *151*
    Critiquing Existing Research   *152*
    Culturally Responsive Research   *153*
    Evidence-Based Practice   *154*
    Multiple Ways of Knowing   *155*
    Translating Findings Into Practice   *158*
    Evaluating Micropractice Effectiveness: Informal Approaches   *158*
        Supervision and Self-Reflection   *158*
        Ongoing Client Feedback   *159*
        Measurement Tools   *160*
    Social Justice Considerations   *166*
    Summary   *168*
    Discussion Questions   *170*
    Key References   *171*

7. Policy-Informed Practice   173
Stephen Kauffman and Heather Witt

    Learning Objectives   *173*
    Competency 5: Engage in Policy Practice   *174*
    National Association of Social Workers *Code of Ethics*   *174*
    Social Welfare Policies: What They Are and Why We Care   *175*
        Definition of Policies: What Are Policies?   *175*
        What Are Social Welfare Policies?   *176*
        What Are the Important Components of Social Welfare Policies?   *178*
        Why Should We Care: The Social Work Role in Policy and Policy Practice   *182*
    Policy Formation: Why Do We Choose the Social Welfare Policies We Do?   *183*
        Social Structure and Power   *187*
    What Is Policy Practice?   *188*
        Stages of the Policy Process and the Associated Primary Tasks   *188*
    Policy Stages: Problem Identification and Characterization   *190*
        Problem Identification   *190*
        Problem Characterization   *191*
        Political Mobilization and Political Advocacy   *194*
    Policy Implementation   *202*
        Regulatory Actions   *202*
        Organizational Practice   *203*
        Types of Policy Analysis   *206*
    Summary   *207*
    Discussion Questions   *210*
    Key References   *210*

8. Engagement and Social Work Practice   213

Learning Objectives   *213*
Competency 6: Engage With Individuals, Families, Groups, Organizations, and Communities   *214*
National Association of Social Workers *Code of Ethics*   *214*
Theories Related to Engagement   *217*
   Psychodynamic Theories   217
   Humanistic Theory   218
   Maslow's Theory of Motivation   219
   Personality Theory and Client-Centered Therapy   220
Social Constructivism and Conflict Theories   *221*
   Feminist Standpoint Theory   221
   Oppression Theory   222
   Trauma Theory   222
Person-in-Environment Perspective   *224*
Engagement With Different Client Systems   *226*
   Commonalities   226
   Differences   227
Building Relationships   *227*
   Affective Reactions   228
   Self-Reflection and Biases   229
   Trust Building   229
The Helping Relationship Inventory   *230*
The Helping Process   *232*
   Engage   232
   Assess   233
   Intervene   233
   Terminate   234
Interprofessional   *234*
   Collaboration   234
   Building Professional Relationships   236
   Working on a Team   236
Policy Issues   *237*
Social Justice Issues   *239*
Summary   *241*
Discussion Questions   *243*
Key Reference   *243*

9. Generalist Practice With Individuals: Assessment and Intervention   245

Learning Objectives   *245*
Competency 7: Assessment With Individuals, Families, Groups, Organizations, and Communities   *246*
Competency 8: Intervene With Individuals, Families, Groups, Organizations, and Communities   *247*
National Association of Social Workers *Code of Ethics*   *247*
Assessment   *249*
Human Development Theories   *250*
   Psychosocial Theories   250
   Psychosocial Development Theory   252
   Stage Theory   258

Psychodynamic Theories   *260*
   Ego Psychology   *261*
   Object Relations Theory   *261*
   Self-Psychology   *262*
Intervention   *263*
Stages of Change   *263*
Generalist Practice Interventions   *266*
   Case Management   *266*
   Supportive Counseling   *266*
Clinical Practice Models   *267*
   Ecological Perspective   *267*
   Life Model   *267*
   Strengths Perspective   *269*
   Narrative Therapy   *271*
   Task-Centered Practice   *273*
   Solution-Focused Brief Therapy   *273*
   Social Learning Theory   *274*
   Cognitive Behavioral Therapy   *275*
   Motivational Interviewing   *277*
   Rational Emotive Behavioral Therapy   *278*
   Empowerment Therapy   *278*
   Conflict Theory   *279*
   Feminist Therapy   *279*
   Anti-Oppressive Practice   *279*
Transitions and Endings   *280*
Policy Issues   *280*
Social Justice Issues   *282*
Summary   *282*
Discussion Questions   *284*
Key References   *285*

10. Generalist Practice With Families: Assessment and Intervention   *287*

Learning Objectives   *287*
Competency 7: Assessment With Individuals, Families, Groups, Organizations, and Communities   *288*
Competency 8: Intervene With Individuals, Families, Groups, Organizations, and Communities   *288*
National Association of Social Workers *Code of Ethics*   *289*
Practice With Families   *290*
Systems Theory   *291*
Family Systems Theory   *291*
Family Assessment   *294*
   Use of Self   *294*
   Affective Reactions   *295*
   Value Conflicts   *295*
   Person-in-Environment Perspective in Assessment   *296*
   Strengths-Based Assessment   *296*
   Strengths Perspective Principles   *296*
   Ecomaps   *298*
   Genograms   *302*

Family Interventions   305
   Family Systems Therapy   305
   Functional Family Therapy   305
   Multisystemic Therapy   307
   Brief Structural Family Therapy   307
Policy Issues   308
Social Justice Issues   309
Summary   309
Discussion Questions   312
Key References   312

11. Generalist Practice With Groups: Assessment and Intervention   313

Learning Objectives   313
Competency 7: Assess Individuals, Families, Groups, Organizations, and Communities   314
Competency 8: Intervene With Individuals, Families, Groups, Organizations, and Communities   314
National Association of Social Workers *Code of Ethics*   315
Social Work Practice With Groups   316
Theories Related to Social Work Practice With Groups   317
   Systems Theory   317
   Psychodynamic Theory   318
   Cognitive Theory   318
   Humanism   319
   Mutual Aid   319
   Empowerment   319
Types of Groups   320
Group Development   320
   Tuckman's Five Stages of Group Development   321
   The Social Justice Model   323
Group Structure   324
Group Dynamics   325
   Communication Processes and Interaction Patterns   325
   Interpersonal Attraction and Cohesion   325
   Social Integration and Influence   325
   Power and Control   326
   Culture   326
Assessment Process in Group Work   327
Person-in-Environment Perspective in Assessment   327
   Strengths Perspective Principles   327
Strengths-Based Assessment: Groups   328
   Assessing the Group as a Whole   328
   Assessing Individual Group Members   328
   Strengths-Based Group Assessment   329
   Assessment in Group Therapy   329
Group Interventions   330
   Psychoeducational Groups   330
   Prevention Groups   331
   Mental and Physical Health Groups   331

       Interactional Group Psychotherapy   *332*
       Social Skills Training Groups   *332*
       Group Cognitive Behavioral Therapy   *332*
Group Skills   *333*
Social Action Groups   *334*
Policy Issues   *335*
Social Justice Issues   *336*
Summary   *336*
Discussion Questions   *339*
Key References   *339*

12. Generalist Practice With Organizations: Assessment and Intervention   341
Stephen Kauffman and John Poulin

Learning Objectives   *341*
Competency 7: Assess Individuals, Families, Groups, Organizations, and Communities   *342*
Competency 8: Intervene With Individuals, Families, Groups, Organizations, and Communities   *342*
National Association of Social Workers *Code of Ethics*   *343*
Organizational Theories   *343*
    Rational Decision-Making Theory   *343*
    Organizational Development Theory   *345*
    Change Theory   *346*
Anti-Oppressive Generalist Practice With Organizations   *348*
    Engagement   *348*
    Assessment   *348*
    Intervention   *353*
    Community Education   *361*
    Evaluation   *371*
Summary   *372*
Discussion Questions   *374*
Key References   *375*

13. Generalist Practice With Communities: Assessment and Intervention   377
Marina Barnett and John Poulin

Learning Objectives   *377*
Competency 7: Assessment With Individuals, Families, Groups, Organizations, and Communities   *378*
Competency 8: Intervene With Individuals, Families, Groups, Organizations, and Communities   *378*
National Association of Social Workers *Code of Ethics*   *379*
Community Theories   *379*
    Community Development Theory   *379*
    Conflict Theory   *380*
    Structural Functionalism   *381*
    Critical Race Theory   *383*
Anti-Oppressive Generalist Practice With Communities   *383*
    Engagement   *383*
    Intervention   *398*

      Evaluation   *405*
      Termination   *405*
Summary   *406*
Discussion Questions   *408*
Key References   *409*

14. Evaluation in Generalist Social Work Practice   *411*

Learning Objectives   *411*
Competency 9: Evaluate Practice With Individuals, Families, Groups, Organizations, and Communities   *412*
National Association of Social Workers *Code of Ethics*   *412*
Applied Research   *413*
    Action Research and Anti-Oppressive Practice Social Work Research   *413*
Practice-Informed Research and Evaluation   *414*
    Quantitative Research   *414*
Evaluating Practice Effectiveness   *416*
    Measurement Guidelines   *417*
    Standardized Measures   *421*
    Designing the Evaluation   *422*
    Components of Single-System Designs   *423*
    Analyzing Single-System Data   *425*
Program Evaluations   *428*
    Logic Models   *428*
    Process Evaluations   *429*
    Outcome Evaluations   *433*
Dissemination   *435*
    Conference Presentations   *436*
    Journal Articles   *436*
    Research Reports   *437*
Summary   *438*
Discussion Questions   *440*
Key References   *440*

Index   *443*

Additional Contributors

Marina Barnett, DSW, is the assistant provost for civic engagement and an associate professor at Widener University's Center for Social Work Education. Marina has taught social welfare policy, organizational practice and grant writing, and community organization at the BSW, MSW, and PhD levels and is the codirector of the Academic Service-Learning Fellows program.

Marina has more than 30 years of organizational and community development expertise, collaborating with nonprofit agencies to develop organizational capacity through strategic planning, program evaluation, and funding strategies to ensure organizational sustainability. As a grant writer, she has secured more than 3 million dollars to fund programs that address local community needs, create opportunities that prepare youth to become 21st-century leaders, and build coalitions to create sustainable strategies to address health disparities and end youth violence in Delaware and Philadelphia counties. Her research interests include conducting community-based participatory research, using geographic information system (GIS) software to map community assets, and developing a model to train residents and local leaders to understand and conduct research in their communities.

Stephen Kauffman, PhD, is a professor at Widener University's Center for Social Work, where he has taught community practice, program evaluation, research, and policy since 1991. Since receiving his PhD from Bryn Mawr College and his MSW from Washington University in St. Louis, his research and practice have focused on citizen participation and community and organizational responses to global problems, environmental decay, poverty (in all its dimensions), organizational trauma, and education.

With this focus, major research projects have included program evaluations of U.S. Department of Justice (DOJ) violence prevention programs, U.S. Department of Health and Human Services (DHHS) housing programs, Century 21 school performance studies, lead abatement, and teenage pregnancy prevention. His work has also examined the relationship between universities and their surrounding environments. The programs (and evaluations) have received funding from the DOJ, the U.S. Department of Housing and Urban Development, the state of Pennsylvania, and several private foundations.

Most recently, his work has targeted the assessment of trauma informed organizations. He has published in *Social Work, Journal of Social Work Education, Journal of Community Practice, Journal of Baccalaureate Social Work,* and elsewhere.

Preface

This generalist social work practice textbook is designed and structured around the nine professional social work competencies as defined by the Council on Social Work Education's 2022 Educational Policy and Accreditation Standards (EPAS), with one or two chapters devoted to each professional competency. The chapter content covers all the components and topics described in the 2022 EPAS. The textbook's coverage of the professional social work competencies helps students develop the knowledge and skills needed to become effective social workers. Each chapter provides a comprehensive overview of the theories, concepts, and practice components of a competency.

In addition to providing detailed content related to the professional competencies, this generalist social work practice text provides a model of generalist practice that incorporates anti-oppressive social work practice principles. Attention to anti-oppressive practice and diversity, equity, and inclusion is stressed throughout the book. There are numerous case examples throughout each chapter as well as a detailed case summary that will help students develop a deeper understanding of the application of the social work competencies from an anti-oppressive practice perspective. The textbook focuses on mastering the professional competencies rather than just presenting content on social work practice. This approach helps students expand their competency knowledge, application, and integration by creating a purposeful approach to the development of the professional competencies that must be mastered by today's social work students.

This textbook is designed for use in undergraduate and graduate social work practice courses. It can be used in two-semester or one-semester practice courses that target upper-level BSW and foundation-level MSW students. It differs from other practice textbooks in that it is designed to fully cover the nine professional social work competencies. It is the only textbook currently available that approaches social work practice from the perspective of the 2022 EPAS social work competencies. The existing texts typically have charts that point to content related to the social work competencies. They apply the competencies to their existing textbooks. This generalist textbook uses the professional competencies as the structure of the book. The chapters cover all components of the professional competencies described in EPAS 2022. This approach ensures that the professional competencies are covered in the social practice course(s) and that students experience the relationships among the competencies and social work practice. The book is also designed to increase students' awareness and understanding of antiracism, diversity, equity, and inclusion with detailed content on anti-oppressive generalist social work practice with individuals, families, groups, organizations, and communities.

KEY FEATURES

Each chapter of this textbook begins with opening vignettes to help engage students in the chapter content, followed by chapter objectives that outline key concepts to be reviewed. In addition, each chapter has multiple case examples, reflection questions, and a detailed case summary with anti-oppressive–focused discussion questions. Answers to the questions are available on Springer Publishing CourseConnect. See inside front cover and tear-out card for CourseConnect details. The numerous case examples throughout the book bring to life the application of social work competencies in actual case situations. The same case summary is used in each chapter, providing students with an opportunity to reflect upon a case situation and describe how they would respond from the perspective of each competency. It is designed to engage students' critical thinking and decision-making skills in relation to the identified social work competency. Using the same case summary in each chapter illustrates the complexity of social work practice and the interconnections among the professional competencies.

Other key features of this book are the instructor and student supplementary resources. The Student Resources provide students with electronic access to all of the tools discussed in this book. Each chapter has QR codes linking to digital resources to aid student learning. The instructor resources include an instructor manual with critical thinking questions, a test bank, PowerPoint presentations, and sample syllabi for each chapter. The critical thinking questions in the Instructor Manual can be used for classroom discussion or for small group exercises. The PowerPoint presentations cover the key points in each chapter and provide a structured guide for presenting the chapter content to students. Sample MSW syllabi are provided for one-semester practice courses: one with a concurrent field placement and one without a concurrent field placement. There is also a sample syllabus for a 7-week online course.

The authors are experienced social workers and social work educators. This book is designed as a companion to the authors' textbook *The Social Work Field Placement: A Competency-Based Approach* published by Springer Publishing Company in the fall of 2022.

John Poulin
Selina Matis
Heather Witt

Resources

All purchasers of this text have access to the following resource at http://connect.springerpub.com/content/book/978-0-8261-6683-8:

- Student Resources
  - Templates, forms, scales, worksheets, sample logs, sample evaluation plans, and exercises

INSTRUCTOR RESOURCES

 A robust set of instructor resources designed to supplement this text is located at http://connect.springerpub.com/content/book/978-0-8261-6683-8. Qualifying instructors may request access by emailing textbook@springerpub.com.

- LMS Common Cartridge—All Instructor Resources
- Instructor Manual
  - Learning objectives
  - Critical thinking questions with more than 70 short-answer questions
- Instructor Test Bank with more than 250 multiple-choice questions (including full rationales)
- Instructor PowerPoints summarizing chapter content
- Sample Syllabi containing two sample course syllabi (one for a 7-week MSW online course and one for a 14-week MSW course with field placement) with recommended and additional readings
- Transition Guide: First Edition to Second Edition

Visit https://connect.springerpub.com/ and look for the "**Show Supplementary**" button on the **book homepage**.

1 Social Work Concepts, Theories, and Paradigms

Karen is a first-year master of social work (MSW) student who had recently graduated from college with no prior social work experience. Her field placement was with a family service agency that provided individual and family counseling. During her first week, she observed her field instructor conduct three intake assessments. After each assessment, she and her field instructor debriefed and discussed the process and the case recommendations. During her second week, Karen's field instructor told her that she thought Karen was ready to take the lead in conducting an intake assessment. Her field instructor would sit in, but Karen would conduct the interview. The intake was scheduled for that afternoon. Karen took a couple of hours in the morning to review the assessment form and prepare for the assessment. She was excited and felt comfortable doing the assessment.

At the beginning of the interview, Karen was nervous and anxious about meeting with a client. The client was not very forthcoming with her responses and appeared angry about something. Karen found it challenging to ask all the questions and get the information recorded accurately. She became more comfortable as the interview proceeded. She was familiar with many of the terms on the assessment form, and getting her client to respond became easier. The assessment instrument had many open-ended questions and asked her to describe, among other things, the client's ecosystem, social supports, presenting problems that needed to be addressed, strengths and challenges, and potential factors that might influence the client's capacity to engage in a helping relationship and the treatment program. Karen met with her field instructor to debrief after she completed the assessment. Her field instructor gave her some constructive feedback on her documentation, but for the most part, she was very pleased with Karen's performance. Karen left her field placement that day feeling excited about her chosen career path and the learning opportunities she will have in her field placement. Although she was pleased with her first client assessment, she recognized that she had a long way to go in developing her professional social work competencies.

LEARNING OBJECTIVES

This chapter introduces some of the key social work practice concepts. It begins with a brief overview of the focus of the book. This is followed by a summary of the concepts used in anti-oppressive practice (AOP) and the major overarching theoretical foundations of generalist social work practice. The chapter ends with a detailed case summary with discussion questions. By the end of this chapter, you will be able to:

- Describe the differences among paradigms, metatheories, perspectives, midlevel theories, and practice models.

- Describe the ecosystems perspective and its role in social work practice.
- Describe the strengths perspective and its role in social work practice.
- Describe AOP and its role in social work practice.
- Describe power, oppression, privilege, and intersectionality and their relationship to AOP.
- Describe conflict perspective and its role in social work practice.
- Describe critical race theory and its role in social work practice.

ABOUT THIS BOOK

This textbook is organized around the nine professional social work competencies developed by the Council on Social Work Education (CSWE) Commission on Educational Policy (COEP) and presented in the *Educational Policy and Accreditation Standards* (EPAS; CSWE, 2022). The COEP develops curriculum policies for social work education. The EPAS are the guidelines social work programs must comply with to become and maintain their status as a CSWE-accredited program. The 2022 EPAS define the core professional competencies for social workers. Except for the first two chapters, each chapter in this textbook is devoted to a professional competency. Our goal is to provide social work students with a comprehensive understanding of each competency and the knowledge and skills to develop their professional competence.

Second, we will be examining the social work concepts and generalist social work practice from an AOP perspective. Antiracism, diversity, equity, and inclusion (ADEI) is a major theme in social work practice and a primary component of the 2023 EPAS and professional competencies.

ANTI-OPPRESSIVE PRACTICE AND ANTIRACISM, DIVERSITY, EQUITY, AND INCLUSION CONCEPTS

We believe that it is ethically necessary to view the entire generalist intervention model from an AOP perspective. AOP is a lens from which social workers can identify and challenge forms of oppression at micro, mezzo, and macro levels, while critically considering their own role in oppressive practices and systems. AOP requires the social worker to simultaneously look out at social justice issues while looking inward and exploring personal power, privilege, and biases (both conscious and unconscious). We will define AOP as "a critical framework that guides us in challenging and dismantling oppressive structures and practices. It requires social workers to critically reflect on their values, beliefs, and biases and actively work to eliminate oppressive systems and practices" (Baylor School of Social Work Team, 2023, para. 6).

It is important that we acknowledge another term used frequently is *antiracist practice*. For the purposes of this text, as a generalist introduction to the social work profession, we will use the term *anti-oppressive* to include all forms of oppression including racism as well as others which include (but are not limited to)

sexism, ableism, heterosexism, classism, ageism, and antisemitism. This is in no way intended to minimize the experience of racism that individuals have experienced. Rather, we are collectively considering oppression and how that impacts clients and client systems based on their identity and intersectionality of identities.

The 2022 CSWE EPAS highlight the important of ADEI in social work practice. There are many concepts and dimensions of ADEI—some of these include power, privilege, oppression, and intersectionality, which are defined later. Vital to competent social work practice is the understanding that the injustices that clients and communities experience are rooted in historical and contemporary discrimination and oppression based on a multitude of intersecting identities and experiences. Lasting significant change requires social workers to address systemic issues that perpetuate inequalities, not simply focusing concerns on an individual level.

There has been a movement that calls for deprofessionalization of several professions. We see the deprofessionalization of the medical model of care. In this context, the term *deprofessionalization* seeks to deconstruct the current view of the established professional system and seeks to balance power between the profession and the recipient. In a deprofessionalized model, the client is the expert. In social work, we often lean into that sentiment, but what does that really look like? Through our AOP, we will attempt to define what that looks like throughout the generalist intervention model. To be clear, deprofessionalization does not mean that there is no value in the profession of social work—absolutely not! We view deprofessionalization as a call to be mindful of the hierarchical relationship that exists between the social worker and the client system. Further we recognize that it is impossible to fully eliminate the hierarchical relationship between the social worker and client. For example, as a mandated reporter, the social worker holds power to break confidentiality and share information related to such incidents of abuse or harm. Though it is important and necessary that social workers do make reports when mandated, it does illustrate the power differential. One way that the social worker could potentially address this is through open and honest communication with the client and collaborating with the client through the process when possible. Though it cannot be eliminated, it must be considered, and the social worker must be aware of this imbalance and how it could show up throughout the helping process.

Power

Important for an understanding of privilege, oppression, and AOP is the concept of power. Understanding power relationships is important for social workers, as power exists in all relationships (Karim, 2023). Lukes (2005) defines power as possessing the capacity or ability to exert influence. While power can be conceptualized in how it is held in institutions and macrolevel power structures, it is also important to consider how power impacts individuals and social workers in their everyday practice (Hafford-Letchfield, 2015). Power can have both positive and negative implications, and social workers "exercise power by virtue of our professional standing . . . and epitomize the professional exercise of power" in positive, negative, or limiting ways by the choices we make in our practice (Karim, 2023, p. 1078). Additionally, power is essential in the perpetuation of social injustices, as the multiple dimensions of power (such as social, economic, and political) allow those in power to control resources, the creation and enforcement of laws and policies, access to opportunities, and more. Oppression is created and perpetuated when specific groups are denied access to resources, opportunities, and decision-making spaces. Social workers cannot work to dismantle social injustice without a recognition of power and a commitment to challenging and reshaping power structures for more equitable outcomes.

Privilege

Privilege is a form of power. Williams and Franks define privilege as "advantages across multiple dimensions of identity, race, class, gender, sexual orientation, sexual identity, age, ability status and more" (2013, para. 1). Examples of privilege include access to cleaner environments with less pollution, safer neighborhoods, better-funded schools, and more. Additionally, privilege offers protection, advantage, access to resources, and limited surveillance. Privilege acknowledges the fact that some social groups have advantages and others have disadvantages. Privilege contributes to the oppression of individuals who belong to disadvantaged social groups, as one of the driving perpetuators of privilege is social hierarchies. Based on the identities and characteristics explained earlier, hierarchies allow some groups to be considered better than others and allow groups to be treated differently based on this belief. Privilege relates to social workers in similar ways to power: it is both something social workers have that can impact everyday practice, and it impacts our clients in their lived experience. Hillock (2012) explains that social workers who practice without examining their own privilege will contribute to the oppression of their clients. An example of this is the social worker who dominates the helping relationship or the social worker who engages in practices with assumptions steeped in White supremacist culture.

Oppression

Young defines oppression as a "structural phenomena that immobilize[s] or diminish[es] a group" (2004, p. 40). It results in restrictions on individuals, groups, or institutions and thrives due to bias, social norms, and personal beliefs. Young (2004) argues that this takes the form of violence, exploitation, marginalization, powerlessness, and cultural imperialism. All forms of oppression are interconnected in some way (Aquil et al., 2021). Scammell (2016) explains that oppression can occur on personal, cultural and structural levels. Examples include microaggressions based on bias (personal), dominant cultural values accepted as the default and superior to others (cultural), and policies that distribute resources in inequitable ways (structural). Social workers recognize that power, privilege, and the resulting oppression create and perpetuate problems that may otherwise be viewed as individual issues (Garcia et al., 2022). As discussed earlier, AOP aims to dismantle oppression at all levels of society through the development and implementation of tools, practices, programs, and policies that move societal dynamics toward equalizing power (Aquil et al., 2021).

Intersectionality

Legal scholar Kimberlé Crenshaw coined the term *intersectionality* in response to her observation that, within the legal system, racial discrimination was believed to occur in the same way regardless of gender, and discrimination based on gender happened in the same way to all women. This view allowed for a misunderstanding of the unique experiences of women of color. Plainly, intersectionality explains that different identities, group memberships, and individual characteristics intertwine and intersect, resulting in different experiences with discrimination and privilege. This can include race, gender, sexuality, age, class, ability/disability status, and others (Mattsson, 2014). Intersectionality can be seen as a tool of AOP for social workers. Centering the combination of clients' identities allows social workers to better meet their needs and provide support. For example, only focusing on a client's unique needs as a queer individual can result in the social worker ignoring the implications of the client's unique needs as someone with an invisible disability. Additionally, not all individuals with a specific disability will have the same barriers as an individual with that disability who is also a member of the LGBTQ+ community. Intersectionality also allows us to recognize how an individual can have privilege in some realms and experience marginalization in others. Also important to social work practice is the way that intersectionality highlights the unique strengths each person brings because of their varied identities. Incorporating intersectionality into practice is vital to a strengths-based, person-centered approach. It requires you to ask questions that relate to the client as a whole, complex person and to tailor the work you are doing to that unique individual.

We want to address that we recognize that when using an AOP lens, we are looking at large influences and thinking about changes at the system level that need to occur. Though this may feel overwhelming, know that system change can start at the individual level. We recognize that in the field of social work, we hold to values that are well aligned with AOP, including social justice, the dignity and worth of all people, the importance of human relationships, and service. We invite you to take the AOP lens and use it in your practice, and through that, we can influence great change.

PARADIGMS, THEORIES, PERSPECTIVES, AND PRACTICE MODELS

Several theories influence the practice of social work with individual, families, groups, organizations, and communities. To most beginning social work students, the numerous theories and practice models are overwhelming and confusing. Adding to the confusion is a lack of standardization in terminology. Sometimes they are referred to as theories and other times as perspectives or paradigms. Sometimes an approach is called a theory, and other times it is a model. In this text, we use the terms *paradigms*, *metatheories*, *perspectives*, and *midlevel theories*. Figures 1.1 and 1.2 show a classification of the paradigms and theories discussed in this book.

Paradigms are the broadest level of theory conceptualization. A paradigm is a distinct set of concepts, theories, and postulates that constitute a philosophical or theoretical framework. The two dominant paradigms in social work are positivism and constructivism. Within these two paradigms, there are a number of theories that help shape the practice of social work.

Metatheories in social work are broad general theories about concepts and propositions about what can or might happen in certain situations, given certain circumstances (Teater, 2014). As shown in Figure 1.1, there are seven metatheories reviewed in this book: systems theory, social constructivism, conflict theory, psychosocial theory, psychodynamic theory, social learning theory, and humanistic theory. These metatheories provide theoretical

Generalist Social Work Practice

FIGURE 1.1 Social work paradigms and theories.

FIGURE 1.2 Social work theories and mezzolevel practice.

conceptualizations for social work practice with individuals, families, groups, organizations, and communities.

Perspectives are broad frameworks for practice. They provide a structure for approaching social work practice. A perspective is different from a theory, as it does not necessarily predict but describes a way of viewing and understanding situations (Teater, 2014). Two major perspectives used in social work practice in the United States are the ecosystems perspective and the strengths perspective. A third perspective that is becoming more widely used in social work practice is the Afrocentric perspective.

Midlevel theories are theoretical propositions that fall under the broader metatheories. Several midlevel theories influence social work practice. As shown in Figures 1.1 and 1.2, numerous midlevel theories are associated with the metatheories discussed in this book. The midlevel theories are reviewed in subsequent chapters.

> ▶ **Reflection Question**
>
> In what ways do theories impact your social work practice?

The Positivist Paradigm

Positivism has been one of the dominant paradigms in social work and the social sciences of this century (Peile & McCouat, 1997). Positivism is associated with a period of philosophical thought generally referred to as modernism. Positivists believe that knowledge grows out of careful observation and empirical verification. Positivists break down social phenomena into parts so that the causal connections can be empirically verified. The positivist paradigm assumes that there is an objective reality that can be scientifically tested and verified.

The social work profession is deeply rooted in positivism (Irving & Young, 2002). Until the mid-1990s, empiricism and the scientific approach dominated the social work profession (Dybicz, 2015). The early history of social work is characterized by a consistent adherence to the scientific model of knowledge (Montano, 2012). Social work's adherence to the scientific method began with the publication of Mary Richmond's *Social Diagnosis* in 1917. Richmond viewed "social diagnosis" as a scientific process of gathering facts and testing hypotheses about clients' social functioning. The psychoanalytic-oriented casework movement that began in the 1920s was also based on scientific principles of study, diagnosis, and treatment. In the 1960s, the empirical practice movement evolved (Reid, 1994). The empirical practice model stresses the application of scientific research methods to social work practice in assessing client situations, specifying goals, formulating solution-focused interventions, and evaluating their effectiveness. The positivist approach focuses on the assessment of relevant facts, the specification of the problem in measurable terms, and the objective assessment of outcomes.

Systems Theory

Social work practice has a long tradition of helping individuals and promoting healthy environments (Gitterman & Germain, 2008). The focus on the person and the environment is a core defining feature of social work, and the person-in-environment approach has been a widely accepted principle of social work practice since its inception (Rothery, 2016). The theoretical perspective shaping the person-in-environment approach is the ecosystems perspective. This perspective is derived from the metatheory known as systems theory. Therefore, before we delve into the ecosystems perspective, a review of the origins and basic principles of systems theory is warranted.

Systems theory and its application to the social sciences is generally attributed to von Bertalanffy, who proposed the idea of general systems theory (1968). Von Bertalanffy postulated that systems are holistic and that they contain properties that are not found within its separate parts. In other words, systems have their own characteristics that are separate and distinct from the individual components that make up the system. It is the interaction of the elements within the system that together form the entity (Bowers & Bowers, 2017). Systems theory provides a lens to view problems within a context and examine how the interactions of the various components create and/or maintain problems (Smith-Acuna, 2011). The elements in a system can be examined separately, but it is the interactions among and between the elements that create the system.

System components can also be composed of subsystems. For example, a family system could be composed of a parent subsystem, a child subsystem, a mother/daughter subsystem, and so on. Thus, in systems theory, there is the main system with multiple components and various subsystems within each of the main system components (Teater, 2014).

Systems theorists have developed language to describe the characteristics of a system. One characteristic is the degree openness. An open system allows information to flow in and out of the system. On the other hand, a closed system is one that is unresponsive or unaffected by outside stimuli (Teater, 2014). Closely associated with open and closed systems are system boundaries. A system boundary may be thought of as the point at which data flow from one system to another. The degree to which data are free to flow is known as the permeability of the boundary. A permeable boundary allows data to flow freely, resulting in an open system. An impermeable boundary is one that strictly controls (or even restricts) the acceptance or dispensing of data, resulting in a closed system. System boundaries may be physical or psychological, and they can vary in their degree of permeability.

Four other terms used to describe the characteristics of systems are *homeostasis, equilibrium, disequilibrium,* and *steady state*. Homeostasis is the tendency of a system to be resilient in terms of external factors and maintain its key characteristics. Equilibrium and disequilibrium are closely related to the concept of homeostasis. A system responding to conflicting messages from the environment and maintaining its internal sense of balance is considered to be in equilibrium. Disequilibrium is the opposite. The system is off balance, and the responses to and from the environment are negatively affecting the system. Systems are in a steady state when they are responding to the environment and experiencing positive growth and development.

Systems theory was conceptualized by von Bertalanffy as a way of understanding biology as an organized system of interrelated parts of a whole (Langer & Lietz, 2015). Ecological theory, an offshoot of systems theory, developed from the field of ecology. Ecological theory added the environment to systems theory. In addition to examining the relationships among organisms, ecological theory examines their interactions with the environment. The application of systems theory and ecological theory to social work gained popularity through the work of Gitterman and Germain (1976) with their publication of the life model of social work practice, which incorporates ecological theory as its framework. The combination of systems and ecological theory is now commonly referred to in social work as the ecosystems perspective.

Thus, systems theory and ecological theory together provide a lens to assess individuals' behaviors and interactions within systems and between systems, as well as the fit and effectiveness in achieving a steady state with growth and development. These two theories are consistent with social work's early focus on people and their environments. They also formed the basis for the development of the ecosystems perspective, which has been a widely adopted framework for the practice of social work in the United States (Payne, 2016).

Ecosystems Perspective

The ecosystems perspective has been the dominant framework of social work practice since the mid-1970s. The ecosystems perspective fits in well with social work's long-standing mission to address the situational and environmental factors that negatively affect disadvantaged persons.

The heart of the ecosystems perspective is the *person-in-environment concept*, which views individuals and their environments as an interrelated whole (Gitterman & Germain, 2008). Individuals are perceived as interacting with a variety of external systems, such as immediate family, extended family, peers, work or school, and community. The foci are on the interactions between the individual and the systems in their environment and on improving the interactions and transactions between individuals and the various systems in their environment (Teater, 2014). Figure 1.3 shows the potential systems in a typical person-in-environment system at the micro, mezzo, and macro levels. It is important to remember that

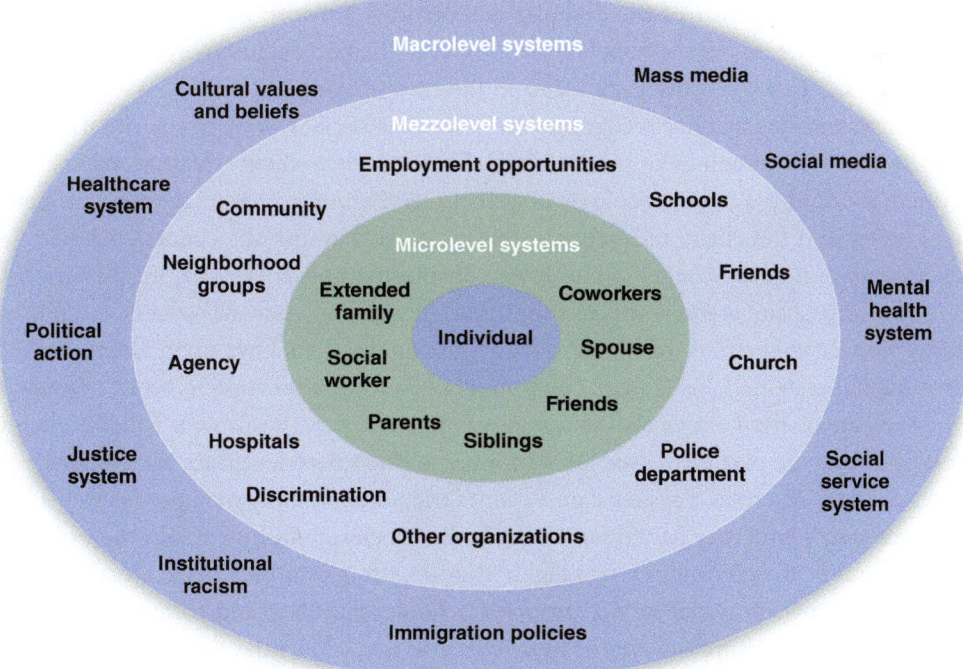

FIGURE 1.3 Typical person-in-environment systems.

each system in the figure is potentially composed of several subsystems. Also keep in mind that each person's environmental system will be different for all three system levels and that those shown in Figure 1.3 are just examples that may or may not be part of a client's environmental system. It is also very likely that other micro, mezzo, and macro systems could be part of a client's social environment.

The person-in-environment perspective recognizes the interdependence of these various systems. The relationship between individuals and their social environment is reciprocal, with each component in the client's system affecting and being affected by the others. The social environment influences individuals' perceptions of themselves and their interactions with others. Individuals, in turn, influence their environmental systems. Thus, the intervention might be focused on the individual, a system(s) within the person's environment, or both.

In the ecosystems perspective, understanding the person-in-environment fit is key. Assessing a person's needs, capacities, and aspirations and their environmental interactions is a core concept in the use of the ecosystems perspective in social work practice (Gitterman & Germain, 2008). The ecosystems perspective "helps the practitioner to see that all aspects of an individual's problem involve circular connections between the individual and environment, leading to a 'transactional focus' for practice that is consistent with social work's dual concern with person and environment" (Wakefield, 1996, p. 6).

A defining characteristic of the ecosystems perspective in social work practice is the importance given to improving clients' person-in-environment transactions to facilitate their growth, health, and social functioning. The focus is on the interactions and the fit for the individual. It is not an assessment of the individual and an assessment of the environment. Rather, it is an assessment of the complex interactions between an individual and all the systems and subsystems in their social environment. The person-in-environment and the fit concepts are key to social work practice from the ecosystems perspective.

The ecosystems perspective recognizes the role of the social worker in the client's environmental system (Gitterman & Germain, 2008). Social worker–client transactions are viewed as a component of the client's ecological system (see Figure 1.3). Interactions between the social worker and the client and between the social worker and the client's social environment become part of the client's dynamic person-in-environment system. In this important system, you, the social worker, are often omitted from the assessment process. Do not overlook the impact the helping relationship and your interactions have upon clients and their environmental systems. This is a key component of AOP generalist social work practice.

The ecosystems perspective also recognizes different system levels with which individuals interact and that are part of the social environment. The micro levels are the systems closest to the individual. Microlevel systems are a client's friends and family members as well as other individuals with whom they have interactions in their social environment. The mezzolevel systems are those in the community or neighborhood with whom the client interacts. Possible mezzolevel systems are social service agencies, schools, churches, and community organizations as well as the community and/or neighborhood itself. Macrolevel systems are the larger systems that impact the client. They include state and national policies and programs, social service systems, healthcare systems, and the clients' cultural values and beliefs. Client interactions with systems at all three levels are all part of the ecosystems perspective in social work.

There are three possible ways in which individual clients can change the person-in-environment fit. The first is for the individual client to change and meet expectations or demands. The second is to change the environment to make it more responsive to client needs or demands, and the third is to change the person/environment transactions (Gitterman & Germain, 2008). The ecosystems perspective provides a lens to assess person-in-environment fit issues to identify the appropriate intervention targets and intervention strategies (see Case 1.1). It is not a practice model or an intervention. It does not address how to make the needed changes in the individual, the environment, or both, but rather it helps identify where change is needed to promote positive growth and functioning.

The Constructivist Paradigm, Social Constructivism, and the Strengths Perspective

Postmodernism is a more recent period of philosophical thought that assumes that language is used to construct our perceptions of reality (Greene et al., 1996). Two of the dominant postmodern paradigms are constructionism and constructivism. Simply put, constructionism

---

CASE 1.1 NO TIME FOR ME: APPLYING THE ECOSYSTEMS PERSPECTIVE IN SOCIAL WORK PRACTICE

John R is an 11-year-old boy with behavior management problems. He has attention deficit hyperactivity disorder and has a great deal of difficulty controlling his impulses. He is socially immature. His peers usually make fun of him and reject him. He usually plays with much younger children. In addition to his behavior problems, he has a very difficult family situation. His mother lives out of state. He lives with his father, stepmother, and 18-month-old stepsister. His stepmother resents his presence in the family and the difficulties he causes her.

John is a student at an alternative school, where he is in a special behavior modification program. Dawn W is John's social worker at the school and is also assigned to work with the family. The behavior management program is working well, but John's relationship with his stepmother is undermining his progress at home. The stepmother refuses to follow the treatment plan and is very rejecting. In fact, she openly tells John that he is bad and that she does not want him anywhere near his stepsister. When at home, John is generally either being punished or is alone in his room. John's father defers to his wife and pretty much lets her discipline John as she sees fit.

Dawn is approaching her work with John from an ecosystems perspective. One of the treatment goals is to improve the interactions between John and his stepmother. Dawn recognized that John is good with young children. He is thoughtful and caring and has a nice way of engaging them in play. Dawn suggested that John take care of his little sister for 1 hour a day. Her hope was that by having John demonstrate responsibility to his stepmother, the interactions between them would improve.

The intervention was successful. John took good care of his little sister, and his appreciation of being allowed to play with and care for her was evident. His stepmother's confidence in and patience with him improved. What other systems and/or subsystems in John's social environment could also be targeted to improve the person-in-environment fit?

emphasizes the use of internal processes to understand the world and make meaning of one's reality. Constructivism also emphasizes internal processes as well as interactions with others and objects in the environment. The two terms are often used interchangeably. *Constructivism* is the term and concept used in this book.

While the modern period of thought stressed objective knowledge and verifiable facts, postmodern thought and constructivism stress the creation of knowledge and the relativity of truth (Carpenter & Brownlee, 2017). Knowledge is constructed and not discovered. Within this paradigm, there are multiple realities based on peoples' perceptions and constructions of their thought processes and experiences. There is less emphasis on the validity of knowledge and more on the variability of knowledge and subjective experiences.

A number of metatheories evolved out of the constructivist paradigm. They include relational, communal, radical, and social constructivism. Social constructivism is the metatheory that informed the development of the strengths perspective in social work and a number of midlevel theories and practice models. Social constructivism and the strengths perspective are discussed next.

Social Constructivism

Social constructivism emphasizes the importance of culture and context in the construction of one's perceptions of knowledge and reality. Reality is constructed through human activity and interactions. Individuals create meaning through their interactions with each other and with the environment they live in (Teater, 2014). People construct their reality through their interactions with people, organizations, and institutions. These experiences are different from person to person (Greene & Lee, 2002). No two people experience an event or interaction the same. Each person's perception of reality is unique. Social constructivists value "each person's life experiences and acknowledge that each individual can experience situations very differently, particularly when one is influenced by social and/or cultural values" (Teater, 2014, pp. 76–77). Thus, "social constructivism takes the view that both individual and social processes are involved in the social construction of reality; it is not a matter of 'either/or' but rather 'both/and'" (Greene & Lee, 2002, p. 179).

Acknowledging that everyone has a different social construction of reality means that language must be used to begin to understand another's view of reality. In a world where individuals construct their own realities and the objective external world can only be viewed indirectly through perception, belief systems, and language, truth becomes what is agreed on. The agreement can be between two or more people or among larger social units. The agreed-on truth is usually determined by the dominant group within a culture. It is often not the truth for disadvantaged individuals and communities. In summary, the basic premises of social constructivism are as follows:

- Individuals have their own reality and their own way of viewing the world.
- People are active participants in developing their own knowledge of the world, rather than passive recipients of stimulus-response interaction with their environment.
- An individual's reality and knowledge are placed in a historical and cultural context, and the reality is developed through social interactions within these historical and cultural contexts.

- Language is used to express an individual's reality.
- Reality is what we agree on; truth is agreement. (Teater, 2014, pp. 77–78)

Strengths Perspective

The strengths perspective draws heavily from social constructivism theory and its emphasis on individuals' subjective perceptions of reality based on social interactions within their social environment, the historical context, and their culture. The strengths perspective in social work provides a framework from which to approach practice with clients. It is a lens from which to view a client's perception of their reality and a set of guiding principles for interacting with clients. The strengths perspective is not a specific practice model. It is a framework or perspective that can be applied to a variety of practice models and/or interventions.

The idea of building on clients' strengths has received a lot of attention in social work. Most social work agencies now claim adherence to "the strengths perspective." A strengths-based approach is very different from those that focus on client problems and history taking (Hepworth et al., 2017). Social work has a long history of helping disadvantaged clients overcome individual problems and problem situations. Clients come to us with problems, and there is a natural tendency to attempt to resolve the problems and to view the clients from a deficit perspective. Often social workers' perceptions are different from their clients' self-perceptions. The clients view themselves as proactive, autonomous human beings who are using counseling services to enhance their functioning and competence. In contrast, social workers working from a medical model tend to focus on client problems and deficits that need to be addressed.

When social workers focus on problems, they tend to perceive clients in essentially negative terms, as a collection of problems and diagnostic labels. This negative perception may lower expectations for positive change. More likely than not, clients are seen as diagnostic categories or their presenting problems, or both. These labels may create distance between clients and helpers (Saleebey, 2013). They also create pessimism in both parties. Negative labels and expectations obscure the unique capabilities of clients. The social worker's ability to recognize and promote a client's potential for change is markedly reduced. The focus is on what is wrong and the client's inability to cope with their life situation. Saleebey (2013) suggests that instead of focusing on problems, we should focus on possibilities.

The pathologic problem approach searches the past for causes. How did the client get into this situation? Why is the client experiencing these difficulties? The search for causes and rational explanations assumes a direct link between cause, disease, and cure (Saleebey, 2013). Human experience is rarely that simple. Often, it is uncertain and tremendously complex. In addition, looking to the past diverts attention away from exploring the present. The shift from problems to strengths moves the focus from the past to the present and future. Strengths-oriented social workers seek to discover the resources clients currently have that can be used to change their futures. The past cannot be completely dismissed because it provides a context for the present. However, in strengths-based practice, the focus is on the present and the future. Rather than focusing on why clients are having problems, social workers who have adopted a strengths perspective focus on what clients want, what they need, and how they have managed to survive (Saleebey, 2013). A strengths-based approach to social work practice emphasizes basic dignity and the resilience of people in overcoming challenging obstacles (Birkenmaier et al., 2014).

Adopting a strengths perspective does not mean that social problems such as domestic violence, child abuse and neglect, poverty, discrimination, and opioid addiction do not have devastating effects on many individuals, families, and communities. They do, and programs and policies to address these and other pressing social problems are needed. What the strengths perspective provides is a way of viewing and interacting with the individuals, families, and communities that balances the focus between the presenting problem and client strengths (Langer & Lietz, 2015).

The strengths perspective's fundamental belief is that all clients have strengths (Kondrat, 2014). Strengths can be internal and external. Internal strengths are internal qualities that help clients cope with the challenges they face and may include resilience, hope, determination, and motivation. External strengths are resources that can be used to support the client. External strengths may include extended family members, faith communities, community services, and informal support networks.

Saleebey conceptualized a "CPR" strengths triangle (2013). The C stands for competence, capacities, and courage. The P refers to promise, possibility, and positive expectations. The R signifies resilience, reserves, and resources (Saleebey, 2013). The CPR triangle helps focus the identification of client strengths beyond the obvious personal strengths to the subtler internal capacities and external resources (Kondrat, 2014).

Strengths Perspective Principles

Saleebey (1992) identified six principles to guide strengths-based generalist practice. They also link the strengths perspective to the core values of the profession. Social work practice is not only about whether and how to intervene or about skills and techniques but also about our profession's core values.

Principle 1: Every Individual, Group, Family, and Community Has Strengths

Regardless of the situation, every person, family, and community possesses assets, resources, wisdom, and knowledge that you need to discover (Saleebey, 2013). To become aware of these strengths, you need to be genuinely interested in your clients and respectful of their perceptions of their own experiences. The ultimate key to identifying client strengths is your belief in the clients and their possibilities. Adopting a strengths perspective requires you to view your clients as underused sources of knowledge and untapped resources.

Principle 2: Trauma, Abuse, Illness, and Struggle May Be Injurious, But They May Also Be Sources of Challenge and Opportunity

Dwelling on clients' pasts and hardships promotes an image of themselves as helpless. Focusing on past hurts and deficits leads to discouragement and pessimism. What is more extraordinary is that your clients have survived and that they are working with you to bring about changes in their lives. There is dignity and affirmation in having prevailed over trauma, abuse, illness, and other difficult situations. Posttraumatic growth illustrates the capacity for resilience and growth despite previous adversity. The strength of having survived and coped with numerous obstacles is often lost on clients who are struggling to meet life's daily challenges. A strengths approach recognizes clients' inherent competencies, resilience, and resourcefulness in having survived past difficulties as well as their current motivation for growth and development.

Principle 3: Assume That You Do Not Know the Upper Limits of the Capacity to Grow and Change, and Take Individual, Group, and Community Aspirations Seriously

Simply put, this means that you should set high expectations for your clients and help expand their hopes, visions, and aspirations. The strengths perspective is the perspective of hope and possibilities. Believe in clients' capacities for change, growth, and self-actualization. If you do not believe in their abilities and motivation, you really do not believe in the possibility of change. Creating hope where there is little to hope for, strengthening belief when there is little to believe in, and creating aspirations where there are none are the essence of social work practice from a strengths perspective.

Principle 4: We Best Serve Clients by Collaborating With Them

The strengths perspective calls for a partnership characterized by reciprocity and mutual respect between you and your client. There should be a sharing of knowledge and resources. You are not the sole expert or the only one with specialized information; your clients are experts who know more about coping with their situations than you do (Saleebey, 2013).

Take advantage of the wisdom, insights, and understanding your clients bring to the helping process by entering into a collaborative partnership with them. The strengths approach to social work practice requires it. Work with your clients in partnership. Do not presume to work on your clients or to do the work for them.

Principle 5: Every Environment Is Full of Resources

No matter how deprived a client's community, neighborhood, or family system, each has an abundance of untapped resources. "In every environment, there are individuals, associations, groups, and institutions who have something that can help" (Saleebey, 2013). Looking to these untapped resources does not negate our responsibility to work for social and economic justice, and it does not mean that we accept the notion that a disadvantaged person should assume sole responsibility for their situation and its amelioration. It does mean, however, that the possibilities for identifying and arranging needed resources for clients from within their own environment are more numerous than you would expect.

Principle 6: Caring, Caretaking, and Context Are Important

Caring for others and being cared for is a basic human right. Families can assist in caring for their members (Saleebey, 2013). Caring strengthens our social web, our interconnectedness. Social work is a caring profession, and the strengths perspective recognizes and embraces our dependence on others for our well-being.

Strengths Perspective Practice Principles

Rapp et al. (2005) developed six standards that could be used to judge whether an intervention was strengths based or not (see also Case 1.2). The motivation for this was that the

> **CASE 1.2 ALWAYS ANGRY AND ISOLATED: APPLYING THE STRENGTHS PERSPECTIVE IN SOCIAL WORK PRACTICE**
>
> Jim is a 15-year-old sophomore previously diagnosed as having a moderate learning disability. He takes regular college preparation courses and has managed to maintain a "B" average. He receives tutoring in math and science and uses the writing center at the school to help him write all of his papers. Although he struggles academically, he has been relatively successful in school.
>
> Jim has no close friends and very few friendly acquaintances. His peers view him as odd and as a "loser." His attempts to fit in and make friends have met with rejection and ridicule, and he has withdrawn socially and makes no attempt to interact with classmates. He appears to have low self-esteem. Jim spends all of his free time at home watching television and playing computer games.
>
> While at home, Jim appears to take out his frustration on his family. He is very demanding of his parents and causes many disturbances within the family. He gets angry quickly and lashes out at his parents over little things. He constantly picks on his younger sister, puts her down in front of her friends, criticizes her looks and abilities, and treats her with general disrespect.
>
> Jim's parents are concerned about his lack of peer relationships and his behavior at home. They contacted the school social worker to inquire about help for their son.
>
> You are the school social worker, and you approach your cases from a strengths perspective. Based on the aforementioned information, what are Jim's strengths? How would you go about applying the strengths perspective in your work with Jim?

authors felt that while the original strengths perspective principles were being widely adopted in social work, much of the practice claiming to be strengths based was actually functioning from a deficit model (Simmons et al., 2016). The six practice standards that define strengths-based social work practice are as follows:

- *It is goal oriented.* Clients set the goals they would like to achieve. Social workers help clients define their goals. Clients are encouraged to consider the hopes and possibilities they have for the future (Saleebey, 2013).
- *There is a systematic assessment of strengths.* Strengths-based practice includes a systematic set of protocols for assessing and documenting strengths. The assessment focus is on understanding internal and external factors that help overcome barriers. The assessment searches for what is working well, instances when barriers are not present, and untapped coping strategies and skills.
- *The environment is seen as rich in resources.* The client's natural community is seen as a principal source for resources, supportive relationships, and opportunities (Rapp et al., 2005).
- *Explicit methods are used to leverage client and environment strengths for goal attainment.* Strengths-based practice entails matching a client's goals and strengths with resources. Assessing client strengths alone is insufficient. In strengths-based practice, the social worker helps the client mobilize their internal and environmental strengths (Simmons et al., 2016).

- *The relationship is hope inducing.* In strengths-based practice, the helping relationship is explicitly focused on increasing the client's sense of hopefulness. Building a positive helping relationship is a key component of the helping process that empowers the client to increase positive perceptions of their choices, abilities, and capacities (Saleebey, 2013).
- *The provision of meaningful choices is central, and individuals have the authority to choose.* In strengths-based practice, the social worker helps clients make choices and explore their options. Clients are seen as the experts in their own lives and are encouraged to assume the authority in directing the process.

Ecosystems and Strengths Perspectives Together

The ecosystems perspective and the strengths perspective are two frameworks that guide social work practice with individuals, families, groups, organizations, and communities. Although each perspective is derived from a different metatheory, they work well together in actual practice with a variety of different practice models. The ecosystems perspective focuses on the interactions between an individual and their social environment. The strengths perspective focuses on clients' internal and environmental strengths. The two perspectives can easily be utilized together in social work practice. For example, social workers often use ecomaps and the ecosystems perspective to assess a client's interaction and fit within their social environment. The same social worker can also employ a strengths perspective in helping the client identify internal and external strengths as well as use the helping relationship to inspire hope and encourage client autonomy in making goal and intervention decisions. Neither perspective is an actual practice model or intervention. They are frameworks from which several specific practice models or interventions can be used to help individuals, families, groups, organizations, and communities.

Critical Theories Paradigm

Neutrality in social work is equivalent to the support of oppressive systems. The critical theories paradigm is vital for social workers engaging in AOP. This paradigm allows us to view human experience through the lens of power, inequity, and social change (DeCarlo, 2018). These frameworks provide us with a practice structure that places justice at the center of the work because it emphasizes that without social change at the heart of practice, it will not naturally occur. The frameworks seek to highlight, not ignore, the intricacy involved in working with diverse populations and striving for cultural competence and AOP with all. The frameworks lay the foundation for developing the knowledge, skills, and values that are anti-oppressive in nature, as they provide practice lenses that emphasize distinctiveness in experience, worldview, and access. Social workers operating from this paradigm understand that critical social work practice requires us to critique and transform both social work and society (Campbell & Baikie, 2012). This is more challenging than it sounds. Consider social work research, which is rooted in the notion of neutrality. The unfortunate impact of overemphasizing neutrality is the minimizing of the true impacts of research. Critical research emphasizes the consideration and understanding of the reality that oppression is pervasive and works toward the development of knowledge that dismantles oppression and injustice.

Conflict Perspective

Social workers have a long history of recognizing structural inequality and oppression (Campbell & Baikie, 2012). Conflict perspective is an important perspective from sociology, commonly attributed to Karl Marx and his focus on class struggles, that explains structural inequalities and oppression through the recognition that social systems are divided and reflect differences in social power. This perspective acknowledges that limited resources exist and groups are constantly battling for access to those resources (Kendall, 2018). This approach can be useful for social workers because it explains why social problems and inequities exist and helps identify potential ways to push back against them. When examining problems, conflict perspective requires that we view the structural issues contributing to the creation and perpetuation of the issue. Solutions to issues must be addressed through societal and structural change. Through this lens social workers can see that focusing solely on individual adaptation to inequitable systems perpetuates oppression of the very clients we are striving to assist. It requires the social worker to consider the external causes of the individual issue, including discrimination or poverty. Identifying these origins can allow clients and social workers to identify interventions that allow them to seek justice. Additionally, use of this perspective elucidates structural inequalities for the social worker, allowing them to have a stronger focus on how to focus energies for social changes through AOP in advocacy. Critiques of the conflict perspective include the risk of oversimplifying social issues, emphasizing differences, being too radical or pessimistic for some contexts, and increasing polarization or a victim mentality (Robbins et al., 2006).

Critical Race Theory

Another important framework for AOP is critical race theory (CRT). Though it draws on multiple disciplines, CRT was developed by several legal scholars including Kimberlé Crenshaw, Derrick Bell, Richard Delgado, and Alan Freeman. Legal scholars developed CRT as a way to understand the stoppage and reversal of civil right advances in the 1970s and 1980s. Important principles of CRT include the following (Abrams & Moio, 2009; Demaske, 2023):

- Race and racism are fundamental pieces of society in the United States.
- Racism cannot be easily corrected by law.
- Race is socially constructed, and classification by race is determined by those in power to meet specific economic, historical, or social needs. This is evidenced in how racial categories have changed over time in the United States. This classification is the basis of racism and has real, negative impacts on people of color.
- The current system only allows racial progress if it promotes the interest of those in power—White elites. This is due to the fact that the racism does provide tangible benefits to those in the dominant racial/ethnic group.
- Race is acknowledged as a focal point of oppression; however, other forms of oppression exist, and individuals have membership in multiple social groups. This relates to intersectionality, explained earlier.

Good-faith critiques of CRT argue that the theory does not provide specific ways to address intersectionality and that the theory emphasizes oppression on race at the expense of other forms of oppression (Constance-Huggins, 2019). More broadly, CRT has been used as a stand-in term for programs and curricula that have a focus on diversity and inclusion, even if those programs are not actually grounded in CRT as a framework, and as such, opponents of those programs have sought to ban the use of CRT in K–12 education (Sawchuk, 2021).

Queer Theory

Queer theory is a critical analysis of social constructions of deviance. This theory asserts that "normal" is socially constructed, changes, and is used as a way to oppress those who do not fit into that context's version of normal. The term *queer* was once considered a homophobic slur, but has since been reclaimed by the LGBTQ+ community. Infusing this term in the title of a theory that seeks to call attention to how dominant beliefs around sexuality are used to center heterosexuality and cisgender individuals at the expense of all others only further emphasizes the importance of its reclamation. Queer theory not only challenges dominant ideals around gender and sexuality but also highlights the pervasiveness of heterosexism (devaluing of all nonheterosexual orientations), heteronormativity (centering and privileging heterosexuality as the norm or ideal), and cisgender normativity (centering and privileging cisgender identities as the norm or ideal).

Queer theory critiques ideas around categorization and fixedness of individuals and their identities (Halperin, 2003; LeFrançois, 2013). While queer theory emphasizes critical analysis of sexuality related concepts and identities, its application goes beyond these topics. It can be used to understand how race, class, and other identities intersect with gender, sexuality and more, as it emphasizes the deconstructions of dominant conceptualizations around identity and challenges the centering of the nonnormative or dominant identities. Critiques of queer theory argue that it is too abstract, it is disconnected from the real, lived experiences of queer people, and that it does not sufficiently address persistent inequalities (Gambino, 2020; Heinz, 2003). Queer theory can be useful for social work practice, because it, like other critical paradigms, emphasizes critical thinking in such areas as policing identity, identifying and questioning privilege, and idealizing heterosexual and cisgender identities.

Feminist Perspectives

Feminist perspectives seek to clarify how societal and power structures affect women's experiences (Saulnier, 2000) and to eradicate oppression of women and girls. These perspectives are based in feminism, a social movement for equality for women focused on oppressive experiences including violence against women and employment discrimination. There multiple feminist perspectives, including liberal feminism, which focuses on equal opportunities (Vogel, 1990); radical feminism, which focuses on the harms and damages caused by patriarchy, including violence against women (Ortner, 2014); socialist feminism, which argues that economic inequality is the cause of oppression of women (Mandel & Shalev, 2009); Black feminism, which addresses how racism intersects with sexism and how Black women experience unique challenges (Few, 2007); and postmodern feminism, which questions the idea of universal experiences and focuses on individual differences (Fawcett & Featherstone, 2000). What links them all as feminist theories is that they seek to examine the relationship between cultural and societal structures and norms that result in inequities and oppression of women and girls. Critiques of feminist perspectives vary depending on which perspective is under consideration but can include overgeneralization of individual experiences of women and men, not operating from a strengths-based perspective, and, for some feminist perspectives, a lack of focus on power. While there are differences in feminist perspectives, they can still be useful for social workers to gain a better understanding of and empathy for clients, especially in circumstances such as navigating familial dynamics and situations involving intimate partner violence.

SUMMARY

In this chapter, we have reviewed the differences among paradigms, metatheories, theories, perspectives, and practice models. Positivism, systems theory, and the ecosystems perspective were described and compared with constructivism theories and the strengths perspective. We introduced AOP and its role in social work practice. Additionally, we included information about power, oppression, privilege, and intersectionality and how those relate to anti-oppressive social work practice. Critical paradigms, including conflict perspective and CRT, were explored, along with information as to how those can be used to better understand the clients we serve and their experiences in the systems they encounter.

CASE SUMMARY | UNDOCUMENTED AND HOMELESS

Practice Setting Description

Jackie is a first-year MSW student completing an internship at an inner-city family service agency in the Southwest. The agency is in a section of the city that has a high crime rate, gang activity, and failing schools. The area has a diverse population with many immigrants from Central and South America and a substantial African American population. The agency provides individual and family counseling services on a sliding fee scale. The agency also runs several educational and treatment groups as well as a temporary shelter for women and their children. Jackie has been assigned to work with the women and their children in the shelter. Her primary tasks are to provide concrete services and supportive counseling to the shelter residents.

Background Information

Elicia and her daughter, Maria, are undocumented immigrants from Mexico. They have been in the United States for 5 years. Elicia and Maria fled to the area from another southwestern city to escape her abusive husband approximately 2 months ago. Elicia is 25 years old and Maria 8 years old. Elicia has a 2-year-old daughter, Sarah, who was placed in foster care because of suspected abuse in the home. Sarah is in a foster home in a small rural community in the state hundreds of miles from Elicia's current residence. Since moving to the area, Maria has not been attending school.

Elicia and Maria are currently residing in the agency's temporary shelter for families. They have been at the shelter for 2 weeks, and the agency has a 90-day limit. Prior to arriving at the shelter, Elicia and Maria were homeless and living on the streets.

(continued)

CASE SUMMARY: UNDOCUMENTED AND HOMELESS (*CONTINUED*)

Elicia is a high-school dropout and was a stay-at-home mother prior to leaving her husband and moving to a different part of the state. She chose to move there because she has two female cousins living in the area who are also undocumented immigrants. Elicia's native language is Spanish. She speaks some English but is not as comfortable speaking in English. Her English comprehension appears to be good. Maria speaks both English and Spanish well. When communicating with the staff, Maria acts as Elicia's interpreter since none of the staff at the shelter speak Spanish.

Maria appears to be behind academically. She struggles reading simple children's books written in English. It is unknown if her ability to read in Spanish is better than her English reading skills.

Other than her two cousins, Elicia has no other sources of support in the community. Her cousins have young families and limited resources but are well established and connected to a Latino community in the city and the local Catholic church. Her cousins refused to let Elicia and Maria live with them while she was trying to find her own place and a job. They stated that they did not have enough room and are concerned they would get in trouble with their landlord if it was found out that they were letting people stay with them. They sent her to the local church for help, and she was given the address for the agency's shelter by the priest.

Elicia has been looking for housing in the Latino community. The housing market is tight with limited options, and she has been unable to find anything that she could possibly afford. The only affordable housing she found was a room in a rundown motel that rents by the hour or by the month. It is in an area of town known for drug dealing and sex work.

On arrival in the community, Elicia found occasional work for a house cleaning company. The company hires undocumented workers, pays them very low cash wages, and threatens to turn them in to Immigration and Customs Enforcement (ICE) if they complain. The job bosses also exploit their female workers sexually, threatening to turn them in if they do not comply. Elicia was fearful about applying for other jobs because of her illegal status. She considered turning to sex work to be able to take care of her child, but her Catholic upbringing and thoughts of how doing so would shame her family have kept her from doing so. She is in constant fear of being detained, separated from Maria, and having her placed in foster care. She is also afraid that she will end up homeless again and forced to live on the streets or return to her abusive husband.

Elicia is extremely reluctant to sign up for any federally funded services, even those that she and her child are entitled to receive. On the suggestion that she enroll for supplemental food through Supplemental Nutrition Assistance Program (SNAP), Elicia became nervous and refused, as she has heard that participation in SNAP services, and others like them, would draw the attention of ICE, and she had heard stories on the news of individuals being deported after signing up for such programs.

Presenting Problems

Elicia and her child are facing multiple obstacles. They need to find permanent, affordable housing and a job that pays enough to cover her housing and living expenses. In addition, Maria needs to be enrolled in school.

(*continued*)

CASE SUMMARY: UNDOCUMENTED AND HOMELESS (*CONTINUED*)

Additionally, Elicia is experiencing an immense amount of stress, anxiety, and possibly post-traumatic stress disorder (PTSD). She described an instance where she could not calm down her breathing, and she felt lightheaded. She is very fearful of men and tries to avoid all contact with men in the community. She reports difficulty sleeping at night and feeling exhausted most of the time.

She is concerned about Maria. She has started acting out at the shelter, getting into fights with the other children, disobeying her mother, and being disrespectful and defiant to the staff and other adults. Elicia and Maria fight frequently, and when Elicia tries to discipline Maria, she throws a temper tantrum until Elicia gives up.

Elicia has many strengths. She had the strength to leave her abusive husband and move to a different city. She loves her daughter and wants desperately to keep Maria with her. She is resilient and has managed to survive and keep her daughter safe despite not having a place to stay, a job, and a limited support network. Elicia feels safe in the shelter, but she is very fearful of being caught as an illegal immigrant and is generally mistrustful of helping professionals and persons of authority.

DISCUSSION QUESTIONS

1. What are the social justice issues affecting Elicia's case situation at the micro, mezzo, and macro levels?
2. What are the micro, mezzo, and macro systems that are in Elicia's person-in-environment? If you were her social worker, what systems or subsystems would you target for intervention and why?
3. What are the mechanisms of oppression and discrimination that exist in the systems and subsystems you identified in the previous question?
4. Elicia has many strengths. How would you incorporate the strengths perspective in helping Elicia?
5. What client factors do you think will help you in developing a positive helping relationship with Elicia? What factors do you think will hinder the helping relationship? What would you do to try and build trust with Elicia?
6. What existing social divisions (which exist across various social categories such as race, class, gender, etc.) might affect your ability to meet the client's needs?

A robust set of instructor resources designed to supplement this text is located at http://connect.springerpub.com/content/book/978-0-8261-6683-8. Qualifying instructors may request access by emailing textbook@springerpub.com.

KEY REFERENCES

Only key references appear in the print edition. To access the full reference list, visit www.springerpub.com/courseconnect. See inside front cover and tear-out card for CourseConnect details.

Baylor School of Social Work Team. (2023). *5 things to know about anti-oppressive practice in social work.* https://socialwork.web.baylor.edu/5-things-to-know-about-anti-oppressive-practice-in-social-work

Constance-Huggins, M. (2019). Critical race theory in social work education: A framework for addressing racial disparities. *Critical Social Work: An Interdisciplinary Journal Dedicated to Social Justice, 13*(2). https://doi.org/10.22329/csw.v13i2.5861

Garcia, B., Van Soest, D., & Jayasundara, D. (2022). Oppression. *Encyclopedia of Social Work.* https://doi.org/10.1093/acrefore/9780199975839.013.271

Gitterman, A., & Germain, C. B. (2008). *The life model of social work practice: Advances in theory and practice* (3rd ed.). Columbia University Press.

Payne, M. (2016). *Modern social work theory* (4th ed.). Oxford University Press.

Saleebey, D. (2013). *The strengths perspective in social work practice* (6th ed.). Pearson.

...graduated from college with
...service agency that provides
...ved her field instructor's ses-
...debriefed and discussed the
...uld build rapport with her cli-
...er that she thought
...uled for that afternoon.
...sment and her case file. She
...g a good job and not being
...lient and possible solutions.
...ngry about something. Karen
...client's past experiences with
...egative. Karen focused more
...rsation, and by the end Karen
and her client had only explored how they would work together. It was a positive start.

LEARNING OBJECTIVES

This chapter focuses on generalist social work practice concepts and presents a model of anti-oppressive generalist practice. A definition of generalist social work practice is presented, and the range of generalist practice interventions are discussed. The core anti-oppressive practice (AOP) principles are reviewed, an AOP model of generalist practice is presented, the generalist social work practice helping process is discussed, and the client change process is described. A review of the professional social work competencies and their dimensions is followed by a description of the interrelationships among the competencies. By the end of this chapter, you will be able to:

- Define generalist social work practice.
- Provide examples of generalist practice with individuals, families, groups, organizations, and communities.
- Identify the five core AOP principles.
- Describe the four components of generalist practice and their different stages.
- Identify the stages of the client change process.

- Identify the professional social work competencies and their dimensions.
- Describe the interrelationships among the social work competencies.

GENERALIST SOCIAL WORK PRACTICE

Definition of Generalist Social Work Practice

Generalist social work practice is the foundational level of social work practice. Accredited baccalaureate social work (BSW) programs prepare students to become professional generalist social work practitioners. An accredited MSW program's curriculum typically devotes the first year of the program to generalist social work practice and the second year to the program's specialization(s). The Council on Social Work Education's definition of generalist social work practice is adopted by all accredited BSW and MSW programs in the United States.

Generalist social work practitioners work with individuals, families, groups, communities, and organizations in a variety of social work and host settings. Generalist practitioners view clients and client systems from the ecosystems and strengths perspectives. They engage, assess, broker services, advocate, counsel, educate, and organize with and on behalf of clients and client systems. In addition, generalist practitioners engage in community and organizational development. Finally, generalist practitioners evaluate social policies service outcomes to continually improve the provision and quality of services most appropriate to the client's needs (Poulin, 2010).

Generalist social work practice is guided by the National Association of Social Workers' (NASW) *Code of Ethics* (2021) and is committed to improving the well-being of individuals, families, groups, communities, and organizations and to furthering the goals of social justice (Association of Baccalaureate Social Work Program Directors [BPD], 2023). The Council on Social Work Education (CSWE) states the following:

> Generalist practice is grounded in the liberal arts and the person-in-environment framework. To promote human and social well-being, generalist practitioners use a range of prevention and intervention methods in their practice with diverse individuals, families, groups, organizations, and communities, based on scientific inquiry and best practices. The generalist practitioner identifies with the social work profession and applies ethical principles and critical thinking in practice at the micro, mezzo, and macro levels. Generalist practitioners engage diversity in their practice and advocate for human rights and social, racial, economic, and environmental justice. They recognize, support, and build on the strengths and resiliency of all human beings. They engage in research-informed practice and are proactive in responding to the impact of context on professional practice. (CSWE, 2022, p. 17)

The CSWE specifies the phases of the generalist practice in its Educational Policy and Accreditation Standards (EPAS; CSWE, 2022). The components of generalist practice, as defined by the 2022 EPAS, are engagement, assessment, intervention, and evaluation.

We find that this model has limitations, which we will attempt to address in this text. First, we believe that there is a phase prior to engagement, which we refer to as pre-engagement. This is a critically necessary part of the helping process where the attention is on the social worker. During the pre-engagement phase, the social worker is practicing ongoing self-reflection and self-awareness, paying particular attention to considerations related to topics such as current societal happenings and their implication on clients or client systems, potential countertransference concerns, and the appropriate use of self from an anti-oppressive perspective.

Second, we believe that the generalist intervention model is a fluid experience rather than distinct, linear stages. The four components of generalist practice are interconnected and inform one another continuously throughout the helping process. This bidirectional relationship is an important consideration for social workers as we move through the helping process with clients. The bidirectional relationships are described and illustrated in Figure 2.1 later in this chapter.

Generalist Interventions

A classification of generalist social work practice interventions is shown in Exhibit 2.1. In this conceptualization, intervention tasks are categorized by practice level (micro, mezzo, and macro) and system level (individual, family, group, organization, or community). Generalist practice often requires simultaneous interventions on multiple levels. In any case situation or practice setting, you might be involved in several interventions on different practice and systems levels.

As Exhibit 2.1 indicates, generalist social work practice entails change activities at the micro, mezzo, and macro levels. Micro social work practice is interventions with individuals, couples, and families (Poulin & Matis, 2021). The term *direct practice* is used to refer to work done with client systems. Helping relationships with individual, family, and small group client

FIGURE 2.1 AOP generalist practice model.
AOP, anti-oppressive practice.

Exhibit 2.1 Generalist Practice Interventions

System Level	Client System	Generalist Interventions
Micro		
Individual	Individuals	Counseling
Family	Families/couples	Assessment
Group	Small groups	Supportive counseling
		Education and training
		Case management
		Service linkage
		Service coordination
		Service negotiation
		Resource mobilization
		Client advocacy
Mezzo		
Organization	Administrators	Education and training
Community/	Task forces	Strategic planning
neighborhood	Committees	Program development and grant writing
	Advisory boards	Program evaluation
	Community groups	Needs assessments
	Professional task forces	Policy analysis
	Community coalitions	Community organizing
	Neighborhood groups	Community development
		Cause advocacy
		Resource coordination
Macro		
Municipality	Governmental bodies	Policy analysis
County	Advocacy groups	Policy proposals
State	Professional organizations	Advocacy
National	Policy think tanks	Basic research
International	Foundations	Program evaluation
	Research institutes	Needs assessments
	Intergovernmental organizations	

systems share common purposes, this book treats social work practice with small groups as a form of micro practice. Regardless of the client system, the purpose of microlevel practice is to enhance functioning and empower the client. Mezzolevel practice involves interventions with organizations and communities or neighborhoods. The purpose of mezzolevel practice is to improve organizational functioning and service delivery and community well-being for vulnerable populations. Macrolevel practice involves change efforts at the municipality, county, state, national, or international level, whereas the purpose of macrolevel practice is to help vulnerable populations indirectly through policy change, program development, and advocacy.

Generalist social workers engage in a wide range of client system change activities with individuals, families, and small groups. Micro interventions commonly used by generalist social workers are divided into two broad groups: counseling and case management (Exhibit 2.1). Counseling interventions include supportive counseling as well as education and training. Case management includes service linkage, service coordination, service negotiation, resource mobilization, and client advocacy.

Mezzolevel interventions focus on organizational and community change. As shown in Exhibit 2.1, typical client systems at the organizational level are organizational leaders, task forces, and committees. The system level is the organization, and the client systems that the social worker engages with are the decision-makers and decision-making structures of the organization. The worker usually participates in formally organized work groups, such as agency task forces or committees, often to develop new services or improve existing services. The client system might also be the organization's decision-makers—that is, administrators and supervisors. Thus, a generalist social worker seeking to change an organization may view the decision-makers or the decision-making structures as the client system when trying to improve how decisions are made or how the organization communicates about decisions, activities, or services. Addressing these client systems is often of the greatest importance because micro systems (individual clients) tend to turn to these organizations for help. An organization that does not function well may not serve its clients or even the very staff who work within those organizations. Thus, at the organizational level, the purpose of macrolevel practice is to improve the functioning of the organization, improve services and service delivery, or develop new services through program development and/or grant writing. All three purposes involve change of the organization or agency. Generalist social workers tend to be agency based and work within an organizational framework.

Typical client systems at the community level are professional task forces, community coalitions, and neighborhood or community citizens' groups. Often, the purpose of community practice is to improve community or neighborhood conditions, empower residents, develop resources, increase community awareness of social and economic problems, and mobilize people to advocate for needed resources and changes. Generalist social workers engaged in community change usually work with professional or community groups. Some groups have both professional and citizen members. Social workers engaged in community practice may view the group they are working with as the client system. In other words, the client system may be a professional task force, neighborhood group, or community coalition that is seeking to change or improve the community. Alternatively, the client system may be the residents of the community.

▶ **Reflection Questions**

1. Which client systems do you feel most comfortable with? Why?
2. Which client systems are you most uncomfortable with? Why?
3. Which microlevel interventions do you need to strengthen?
4. Which mezzolevel interventions do you need to strengthen?
5. How comfortable would you be implementing macrolevel interventions?

Macrolevel generalist social work practice focuses on larger system change. As shown in Exhibit 2.1, macrolevel client systems typically include governmental bodies, advocacy groups, intergovernmental organizations, professional organizations, and other entities focused on larger system change to improve the well-being of individuals, families, and communities. Macro interventions include policy analysis, development of policy proposals, cause advocacy, basic research, program evaluations, and needs assessments. There are even roles for international collaboration. In recent years, more and more social problems have begun to cross borders. Such issues as globalization, immigration, and climate change often require social workers to dialogue and work with international partners.

Importantly, all the microlevel skills generalist social workers develop may well be needed when working with mezzolevel and macrolevel client systems. Effective communication, goal setting, and sensitivity to the needs of individuals in some ways become even more important when working with the (often) large and complex client systems that are found at the organizational, community, and national levels. For an example of multileveled generalist social work, see Case 2.1.

CASE 2.1   SO MANY LEVELS

Shelia is a 30-year-old African American single mother who has been on and off public assistance since the birth of her daughter when she was a junior in high school. She dropped out of school and never returned. Over the past 10 years she has had three low-paying service-type jobs but was fired from each because of childcare issues. When she was 20, she was arrested and received a felony conviction for drug distribution. Her criminal record has made finding employment very difficult even though she has not had any further arrests or drug involvement. As a requirement of receiving public assistance, she was mandated to attend a life skills and job readiness program called Circle for Change.

Tracy is a first-year MSW student doing her generalist field placement with the Circle for Change program. Circle for Change is an intensive 12-week program with the participants attending 5 days a week from 9:00 a.m. to 4:00 p.m. The program has a morning support group circle, General Educational Development (GED) prep, individual counseling, life skills, and job readiness training. Tracy was assigned to work with Shelia as her case manager. She cofacilitated Shelia's support group, provided individual counseling, and cofacilitated the job readiness training classes.

During support group and in her individual sessions, Shelia identified several issues of concern. Shelia's primary concern was getting her criminal record expunged. She felt that her biggest obstacle to employment was her felony conviction. She also expressed interest in finding stable housing for her daughter and herself. Her difficulty in paying her rent has resulted in frequent apartment changes. The lack of stability has been difficult for her daughter's schooling and friendships. In addition, Shelia has had difficulty dealing with her public assistance case worker, who consistently schedules meetings without taking Shelia's availability into consideration. Finally, Shelia's daughter has had behavioral issues at home and in school. Shelia is concerned that her daughter is beginning to associate with a group of teens who appear to be headed toward drug use and criminal activity.

With what client systems will Tracy possibly be working? What possible generalist interventions will Tracy need to employ?

ANTI-OPPRESSIVE GENERALIST SOCIAL WORK PRACTICE

Anti-oppressive practice (AOP) is a framework that is used to challenge oppression at all levels. AOP requires social workers to engage in critical reflection and the examination of their values, beliefs and biases. This book presents a model that expands the conceptualization of generalist social work practice to include the core principles of AOP. The foundational perspectives of person-in-environment and the strengths perspective are embedded in our model and are assumed to be fundamental frameworks for generalist social work practice. CSWE identifies four major components of social work practice—engagement, assessment, intervention, and evaluation (CSWE, 2022).

Our model of AOP generalist social work practice expands on the four components to include the different stages of the helping process for each component. Our model also views the helping process as nonlinear. The relationships between and among the engagement, assessment, intervention, and evaluation components are bidirectional. For example, the engagement process informs assessment, and in turn the assessment process impacts client engagement. The bidirectional nature of the helping process applies to all the components in our AOP model of generalist social work practice. Figure 2.1 shows our AOP model. The various components are described in the following sections.

Core Anti-Oppressive Practice Principles

We have identified five core AOP practice principles. These practice principles, shown in Figure 2.1, are critical self-reflection, empowerment, collaboration, critically assess experiences of oppression, and minimal intervention. The AOP practice principles all impact the helping process, and taken together, they provide a perspective that informs AOP generalist social work practice with individuals, families, groups, organizations, and communities.

Critical Self-Reflection

The CSWE (2022) engagement competency states that "social workers are self-reflective and understand how bias, power, and privilege as well as their personal values and personal experiences may affect their ability to engage effectively with diverse clients and constituencies" (p. 11). Self-reflection is a critical component of AOP generalist practice. To be a competent professional social worker, you will need to engage in self-reflection and self-regulation. AOP social workers self-reflect to identify and challenge their biases, assumptions, and privileges. This entails examining how their identities and experiences shape their worldview and how they interact with clients.

Professional social workers must be reflective and possess self-awareness skills. Self-awareness refers to social workers' ability to reflect upon and consider their own thoughts, beliefs, and reactions. Social workers utilize self-awareness to monitor their use of *self* in practice. Effective use of self requires social workers to consider how and why they are experiencing what they are because of their current situation and circumstances. Social workers can utilize supervision to assist them in finding meanings and connections that assist in an increased level of self-awareness. Social workers must possess self-awareness to be fully able to attend to the needs of clients and ensure that their own issues are not interfering with the helping process. Yet we fully understand and appreciate that social workers are human and as a result have their own experiences. However, professional social workers must be diligent to not allow their own issues to interfere with the helping process and work for the client. If social workers cannot contain themselves or lack self-awareness, they should seek support immediately, as the well-being of clients is of paramount concern.

As we have noted, self-awareness is necessary for professional practice. Whether working with clients of dissimilar or the same cultures, it is necessary for social workers to be aware of different experiences of culture and challenges that could potentially occur. Self-awareness leads to a social worker's ability to understand and work from a multicultural perspective.

Social workers must first be self-reflective regarding their own cultural experience as well as their personal values and any potential biases that may exist. Social workers should honestly reflect upon experiences and interactions that have been positive, negative, and indifferent. Then the social worker should consider mitigating circumstances to those situations and consider why and how they informed the experience on both sides of the interaction (see Case 2.2).

Empowerment

Empowerment is defined as the "process of increasing personal, interpersonal or political power so that individuals can take action to improve their life situations" (Gutierrez, 1990, p. 149). The process of empowerment emphasizes the acquisition of power. Empowerment is a key practice principle of AOP generalist social work practice. Anti-oppressive social work aims to empower clients by recognizing and building on their strengths, skills, and knowledge and by openly acknowledging the power and privilege of the service providers. AOP social workers strive to empower individuals, families, groups, organizations, and communities. Social workers may empower service users at the micro level by helping enhance self-efficacy or boosting self-confidence in clients. Empowerment may flourish out of a positive helping relationship. At the macro level, the social worker may assist in community organizing to give the community members a chance to advocate for themselves.

Empowerment theory is an advocacy-based approach used by social workers to promote social justice and bring about change at various levels while addressing differences in social power (Congress & González, 2020). Payne (2021) asserts that empowerment is a process.

CASE 2.2   SELF-REFLECTION

As noted in Case 2.1, Shelia identified several issues of concern. Her primary concerns were getting her criminal record expunged, finding stable housing, difficulty dealing with her public assistance case worker, and her daughter's behavioral issues.

Tracy was feeling somewhat overwhelmed and uncomfortable having to deal with so many difficult issues. In supervision with her field instructor, she shared her concerns. Her field instructor asked Tracy to engage in critical self-refection and make a list of some possible reasons for her discomfort in working with Shelia. Her field instructor also asked her to reflect on possible values conflicts, biases, privilege, and power. Her self-reflection helped Tracy realize that she had strong feelings about the choices Shelia had made that negatively impacted her education and ability to gain stable employment. Tracy's family background emphasized the value of education and hard work. Tracy also identified her discomfort with the power dynamic between her and Shelia. She felt that Shelia wanted her to fix her problems, which made her very uncomfortable since she felt overwhelmed and powerless. Discussing her critical self-reflection with her field instructor helped Tracy put her biases aside to focus on Shelia's needs, and it helped her realize that she needed to clarify with Shelia how they would work together.

You have been assigned to work with Sheila and have been asked by your field instructor to do a critical self-reflection. Reflect on your values and biases in relation to Shelia's situation. In what ways have you experienced privilege compared to Shelia?

Throughout the process of empowerment, social workers assist clients in identifying and ameliorating circumstances, conditions, and situations.

The focus of AOP social work practice should be on the reduction of the power imbalance between social workers and clients (Karim, 2023). The balance of power between the social worker and the client is inherently unequal. Traditional approaches to social work practice do not adequately address this power differential. AOP social work practice is based on acknowledgement of the power and privilege differentials between the service provider and the service user (see Case 2.3).

Collaboration

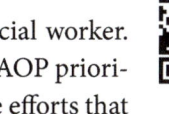

Collaboration is a partnership between the service user and the social worker. It is a fundamental practice principle of AOP generalist social work. AOP prioritizes working in partnership with service users through collaborative efforts that position the service user as the expert in their own life (Matthews et al., 2020).

Collaboration is closely tied to self-determination. The NASW *Code of Ethics* states that "the social worker should make every effort to foster maximum self-determination on the part of clients" (NASW, 2021, para. 1.02). Self-determination is achieved when the client is fully involved and participating in all the case decisions. The social worker is not making decisions independently. You and your clients are partners in the decision-making process.

Self-determination is often a challenge. Achieving it is difficult when your client makes choices that you do not support. In these situations, your task is to resolve the conflict between your values and the value choices of your client while continuing to honor their self-determination. Critical self-reflection and self-awareness of your values and biases is a critical first step. The AOP practice principle of collaboration suggests that the social worker and the client openly discuss the value conflict to help the client review alternative pathways. The ultimate decision rests with the client. AOP generalist practice is based on the belief that clients are the experts and that they ultimately know what is best for themselves.

CASE 2.3 EMPOWERMENT

As noted in Case 2.1, Shelia has almost no power in her relationship with her public assistance case manager. To continue receiving public assistance, Shelia must do whatever her case manager tells her. Her case manager decides when they will meet, what she must do to find employment, and ultimately if she will receive her public assistance. It appears that Shelia's experiences with helping processionals have primarily been disempowering. Tracy her social work intern at the Circle for Change program expressed concern that Sheila wanted Tracy to fix her concerns and that Shelia would not be taking responsibility for change. Tracy feared that because of her past experiences, Shelia would assume a powerlessness role in their helping relationship.

If you were assigned to work with Shelia, how would you address the power imbalance? What steps would you take to empower Shelia in your helping relationship? How would you begin to empower someone who does not expect and perhaps not want to take responsibility for addressing her identified concerns?

Critically Assess Experiences of Oppression

CSWE's competency on antiracism, diversity, equity, and inclusion (ADEI) states that "social workers understand cultural humility and recognize the extent to which a culture's structures and values, including social, economic, political, racial, technological, and cultural exclusions, may create privilege and power resulting in systemic oppression" (CSWE, 2022, pp. 9–10). A fundamental practice principle of AOP generalist social work is to collaboratively explore and critically assess the service users' experiences of oppression, power, and privilege. One purpose of this critical assessment is to help the service users reframe the narrative from that of being the "problem" to that of recognizing the personal, cultural, and structural factors that have contributed to their experiences of oppression (Baines, 2017). A second purpose is to help service users understand the intersectionality of their experiences of oppression and that life experiences may include oppression, poverty, marginalization, and alienation as well as privilege and power. The multiple intersectionality dimensions include but are not limited to "age, caste, class, color, culture, disability and ability, ethnicity, gender, gender identity and expression, generational status, immigration status, legal status, marital status, political ideology, race, nationality, religion and spirituality, sex, sexual orientation, and tribal sovereign status" (CSWE, 2022, p. 9).

Exploring the service users' experiences of the different types of oppression helps reframe the problem from a client-based problem to systems-level issues related to equity, inclusion, power, and privilege. Analyzing the interactions of the various factors that contribute to the service users' experiences of oppression, discrimination, power, and privilege helps them understand various ways oppression has affected their life experiences. It also helps broaden the focus to include macro change.

Another component of critically assessing experiences of oppression is to explore with the service users their experiences with social service agencies and social work professionals. Acknowledging your power and privilege as a professional social worker and how the power imbalance impacts the helping process is an important component of critically assessing the service users' experiences of oppression. This conversation also contributes to the development of a collaborative relationship and to client empowerment (see Case 2.4).

CASE 2.4 — EXPERIENCES OF OPPRESSION

As noted in Case 2.1, Shelia is an African American single mother with a felony conviction with a sporadic work history. She is also a high school dropout and long-term public assistance recipient.

You have been asked to conduct a critical assessment of Shelia's experiences of oppression. Your field instructor suggested that before meeting with Shelia you reflect upon her experiences of oppression and discrimination. In what possible ways has Shelia experienced discrimination? How might the intersectionality of Shelia's class, race, gender, legal status, educational status, and marital status have impacted her experiences of oppression? How would you approach analyzing with Shelia her experiences of oppression and discrimination? What impact do you think Shelia's past experiences will have on your work together?

Minimal Intervention

The fifth AOP practice principle calls for minimal intervention or intrusion in the service user's life (Healy, 2014). The aim is to reduce oppression and increase empowerment. Social services and programs, by their nature, exert social control, and many have extraordinary power over the service users' lives. AOP generalist social work seeks to reduce this imbalance by strategically intervening in the least intrusive way possible in service users' lives (Matthews et al., 2020). Minimal interventions include early intervention and preventive services as well other types of generalist practice. The guiding AOP principle is to collaboratively determine the most empowering and least restrictive intervention available to address the target problem. In AOP generalist social work practice, this usually entails having the service users identify possible solutions and plans of action.

The Helping Process

As defined in the CSWE (2022) EPAS professional competencies, the practice of social work with individuals, families, groups, organizations, and communities has four major components—engagement, assessment, intervention, and evaluation. These are the fundamental helping processes of generalist social work practice.

As shown in Figure 2.2, the relationships among the engagement, assessment, intervention, and evaluation components are bidirectional. It is not a linear process. For example, the engagement process helps inform your assessment, and the assessment process impacts your relationship with the service user. This circular process takes place among the four

FIGURE 2.2 Interrelationships of social work competencies.

components of generalist social work practice. In what follows we briefly describe the four components of the helping process. They are each described individually in a sequential order. It is important, however, to keep in mind that in actual practice you rarely proceed simply from one component to the next. There is a great deal of back and forth between each component of the helping process.

Engagement

Successful engagement involves establishing trust and developing a bond between the social worker and the client (Berg-Weger & Tyuse, 2023). It requires effective communication and the ability to communicate empathy and understanding. Without trust and understanding, the relationship will not develop, and hence the client will not truly engage in the helping process.

Client engagement is the cornerstone of the helping process. We have identified three stages of client engagement—preengagement, establishing a collaborative helping relationship, and maintaining the relationship. Without client engagement, change does not occur. The service users must be active participants in the helping process. The key to client engagement is a collaborative helping relationship. The key to developing a collaborative helping relationship is developing trust.

As noted earlier, the engagement component of generalist social work practice is composed of three stages—preengagement, establishing the helping relationship, and maintaining the helping relationship. Each stage is briefly described next.

> ▶ **Reflection Questions**
>
> 1. To what extent are you a trusting person? What makes you think so?
> 2. How do you communicate your trustworthiness?

Pre-Engagement Stage

The pre-engagement stage occurs ideally before your initial meeting with the service user. Two primary tasks are involved in AOP pre-engagement—research and self-reflection. Your research task is to learn as much as you can about your clients' experiences, values, and beliefs. Each service user will be unique and should not be stereotyped. However, before your initial meeting, you should become familiar with the cultural traditions, values, beliefs, and lifestyles of your client's population group. You should also try to find out as much as you can about the specific life experiences of your individual client. In addition to educating yourself about the client population and your client, you should educate yourself about the community, local service network, and resources available.

Being knowledgeable about your client's culture, values and beliefs, experiences, life stage, and community increases your cultural competence and your potential understanding of your clients' unique experiences and beliefs. Clients who feel understood and experience you as being aware of and sensitive to their situation, life experience, culture, traditions, and belief systems are more likely to be open and take appropriate risks than those who experience you as culturally unaware and insensitive. Cultural competence does not guarantee a client's willingness to take risks. However, being culturally incompetent and insensitive does guarantee mistrust and risk aversion, especially if clients come from ethnic or racial backgrounds that differ from your own.

Critical self-reflection is a core AOP practice principle. It is important to engage in self-reflection prior to meeting with your service user. What are your values and biases? How does your privilege and power impact your work with the service user? How are your values potentially different from your client's? How will you deal with your value differences? How can you minimize the impact of your biases on your helping relationship? How have the dominant cultural structures and beliefs contributed to their experiences of oppression? How have the client's intersectionality of their experiences contributed to their oppression? The process of self-reflection decreases the impact of your biases, privilege, and power and increases your chances of developing an empowering, collaborative helping relationship.

Establishing the Helping Relationship

The second stage of engagement is developing a collaborative helping relationship. Clients who have experienced discrimination and oppression often mistrust helping professionals. Alienation theory provides an explanation for the reluctance of oppressed and disadvantaged clients to fully engage in a helping relationship with social work professionals (Ferguson & Lavalette, 2004). People who are stigmatized and discriminated against on a continuous and systematic basis feel devalued by people who have power and occupy positions of authority in society. A natural response to feelings of powerlessness, oppression, and devaluation is to distance oneself physically and emotionally from the oppressors. This sense of separateness or alienation can be viewed as a normal response or as a coping mechanism that helps protect the oppressed. Therefore, people who have experienced racism, discrimination, and other forms of oppression are unlikely to be willing to engage in an open and trusting relationship with a helping professional who, by virtue of their authority, has power and influence over their lives and well-being.

A key to developing a strong positive collaborative relationship is establishing some level of trust. The client must be able to trust the social worker. Relationships cannot be built in the absence of trust. A certain degree of trust must be established between the client and the social worker for the client to engage in a collaborative helping process. Trust is essential for relationships to develop and grow between social workers and their clients.

Maintaining the Helping Relationship

The third stage of engagement is sustainment. The helping relationship needs to be nurtured to survive. The trust must be maintained and allowed to grow. This is done through ongoing interactions with your client. Trust is difficult to establish and easily broken. Always take care to be honest and trustworthy in all aspects of your work together. This is especially important in the practice of AOP generalist social work with disadvantaged and oppressed clients.

Assessment

Assessment is an ongoing interactive process. The first stage of this generalist practice component is the initial assessment process. Your initial assessment entails a collaborative exploration of the client's internal and environmental challenges and strengths. In AOP practice, this includes conversations about the service user's experiences with oppression and discrimination as well as an exploration of the intersectionality of those experiences. The aim here is to help the client view their current situation from a structural and cultural perspective rather than just an individual or personal problem.

The initial assessment should focus on asking your client to tell their story, including experiences, beliefs, expectations, concerns, strengths, coping abilities, and, most importantly, hopes and dreams. The asking approach contrasts sharply with the telling approach that most disadvantaged clients have experienced in their prior interactions with helping professionals and other people in authority. Being asked about your hopes and concerns is empowering. Being told what your problem is and what you need to do is disempowering.

The AOP model of generalist social work places a great deal of emphasis on allowing the client to be in charge of the helping process. This begins when the worker simply asks the client to tell their story. You should approach this task from a position of curiosity or not knowing (Gottlieb, 2021). Show an interest in hearing what your client has to say. Do not make assumptions about the client's situation and perceptions. Be open and encourage exploration. Ask for specifics, explore the meaning of silences, summarize when appropriate, reframe, and, most importantly, contain yourself. Containing oneself is critical at this point in the helping relationship. The focus must be on having clients tell their story and helping them see the connection between their story and the structural, social, and cultural sources of oppression.

> **Reflection Questions**
> 1. What are your strengths in conducting initial assessments?
> 2. What do you need to do to improve your assessment skills?
> 3. How comfortable are you to listening to your clients' stories instead of wanting to offer solutions?

Assessment is not limited to the intake process. You and your clients should continuously gather and analyze information to better understand their needs, challenges, and progress. The initial assessment should be thought of as a starting point, and new insights and information are added to the assessment as the work progresses. It is an ongoing process of assessment throughout the helping relationship.

Intervention

Intervention is the third component of generalist practice. It is the actual work the client and social worker do to address the client's identified needs and challenges. The intervention stage is an ongoing interactive process with the engagement, assessment, and evaluation components of generalist social work practice. You and your client continue to engage and build trust as well as continue to assess your client's needs and the effectiveness of the intervention.

In our AOP model, the intervention component has four stages—developing the plan, implementing the plan, adjusting the intervention, and termination. In AOP generalist social work practice, the guiding principle is minimal intervention. Collaboratively develop a plan that incorporates the least invasive intervention. Put the plan into action. Continually evaluate the effectiveness of the intervention and revise as needed. The final stage of the intervention component is the termination of the helping process. This is based on your ongoing evaluation. It is a collaborative decision made between you and your client.

Evaluation

The fourth generalist practice component is evaluation. In our AOP model of generalist practice, there are two evaluation stages—ongoing process evaluation and an outcome evaluation. Generally, the ongoing evaluation assesses the client's progress on the goals identified during the assessment component and development of the intervention plan. Its purpose is to obtain information on the effectiveness of the intervention in helping the client address the identified needs and challenges. Conducting ongoing evaluations is important in that doing so enables the social worker and client to adjust the interventions if progress is not taking place. To be consistent with the AOP practice principles of empowerment and collaboration, we recommend qualitative approaches to conducting ongoing process evaluations that elicit service users' perceptions on progress and the helping process.

Outcome evaluations usually take place as part of the termination process. In AOP generalist social work, the process is the same as the ongoing process evaluations. The purpose, however, is different. The outcome evaluation provides you and your client an opportunity to review your work together to identify progress, what worked, and what did not work as well as what still needs to be done. This process will help your client plan their next steps and help them prepare for ending the helping relationship.

> **Reflection Questions**
>
> 1. How comfortable are you in assessing the effectiveness of your work with your clients?
> 2. What do you need to do to improve your ongoing process evaluations?

CLIENT CHANGE PROCESS

Prochaska et al. (1992) identified five stages of client change: precontemplation, contemplation, preparation, action, and maintenance. "*Precontemplation* is the stage at which there is no intention to change in the foreseeable future" (p. 1103). Clients at this stage are often unaware of their problems and are not seriously considering getting help. They are reluctant participants in the helping process. They have not chosen to seek help and probably are unhappy about the prospect of being helped. "*Contemplation* is the stage in which clients are aware that a problem exists and are seriously thinking about overcoming it but have not yet made a commitment to take action" (p. 1103). The key here is the lack of commitment to change. Many clients recognize the need to address concerns or problems but need help in making a genuine commitment to bring the change about. "*Preparation* is the stage that combines intention and behavioral criteria" (p. 1104). Clients at this stage have started to address the problem and are motivated to make the necessary changes. "*Action* is the stage in which individuals modify their behavior, experiences, or environment in order to overcome their problems" (p. 1104). During the action stage, clients are engaged in the helping process and are taking necessary steps to achieve the desired changes. "*Maintenance* is the stage in which people work to prevent relapse and consolidate the gains attained during action" (p. 1104). In a way, maintenance is a continuation of the action phase. The client is actively trying to prevent a relapse.

The five stages of change highlight client differences in readiness to engage in the helping process. It is important to recognize these individual differences. Not all potential clients have reached the stage of contemplation or action. Many clients who are referred or have a mandate for service are in the precontemplation or contemplation stage. To become true clients, they must make a commitment to change. In the end, only those who willingly agree to work with the social worker to achieve a specified outcome can engage in a collaborative helping relationship. Nonvoluntary and involuntary clients might go through the motions because they are required to do so, but they will not truly become clients until they decide on their own to engage in a helping relationship. We believe the AOP approach to generalist practice is especially effective in engaging clients who have experienced discrimination and oppression and as a result are often in the precontemplation stage of change.

Working With Clients Who Have Experienced Discrimination and Oppression

Social workers often work with clients who are in the precontemplation stage and are not interested in getting help. In the past, these clients were viewed as "resistant" and often blamed for not cooperating with their social workers (Anderson & Stewart, 1983). Many clients, at best, are going to be reluctant to engage in a helping relationship (Rooney & Mirick, 2018). The following discussion reviews some factors that affect clients' willingness and ability to move beyond the precontemplation stage in the helping process.

> ▶ **Reflection Questions**
>
> 1. Have you experienced working with a client in the precontemplation stage? How did that make you feel?
> 2. What was your reaction to the client's unwillingness to engage in a helping relationship?
> 3. What would you do differently?

The Experience of Being a Client

Several factors impact a person's willingness to become a client and engage in a professional helping relationship. AOP generalist practice emphasizes understanding these factors and exploring them with the client. Understanding the client's feelings about needing and asking for help as well as their perceptions of what it means to be a client facilitates the helping process of engagement.

Most discriminated and oppressed clients will have received social services in the past and have had numerous prior contacts with helping professionals. Ignoring the possibility of prior negative experiences or assuming that all prior experiences were positive is a mistake. Clients' expectations about receiving help from a professional are influenced by their past experiences (Gambrill, 2013). Were they treated with respect? Were they given a voice in the decision-making process? Were the services helpful? Were their prior experiences with helping professionals satisfactory or unsatisfactory? Clients whose prior experiences were negative may expect more of the same and approach your work together with reservations, whereas those who enjoyed more positive experiences might be much more willing to engage in the helping process.

Early in the working relationship, preferably during the pre-engagement stage, the social worker should explore the client's perceptions of prior experiences. The social worker may not change these perceptions, but recognizing them and learning what clients liked and did not like about earlier experiences is an important step in the helping process. It is also important to explore power and privilege experiences in prior interactions with helping professionals.

Clients' perceptions of the agency may also influence their approach to service (Seabury et al., 2011). Does the agency have a negative or positive reputation in the community? Does the agency communicate respect for clients and their cultures in its physical appearance and decor? Are clients greeted at the agency in a courteous and respectful manner? Is the waiting area pleasant and comfortable? Negative agency perceptions can impede the development of a helping relationship and the client's receptiveness to the helping process.

Understanding clients' perceptions of their prior experiences with helping professionals and their expectations for upcoming experiences with the agency is a critical step in the engagement process. Being sensitive to the possibilities of both positive and negative prior experiences enables you to directly address concerns. Communicating empathy about negative experiences and perceptions validates clients' experiences and perceptions. This validation begins the process of co-constructing a more positive mindset regarding the helping process and a willingness to engage in a collaborative helping relationship.

Expectations About the Helping Experience

Social workers also need to be sensitive to clients' expectations about the helping process and their role as client. Ignoring or misunderstanding client expectations may result in the client dropping out prematurely (Gambrill, 2013). Client expectations about changes or outcomes should match those of their helpers. Different expectations will affect outcome and client retention (Gambrill, 2013).

Clients come to the helping process with various expectations. Some may have little or no hope of making any meaningful change in their lives, whereas others may expect a miracle. Some might be aware of the collaborative nature of the helping process, and others might expect the social worker to fix the problem. As an AOP generalist social worker, it is important to discuss how you will work together and what your respective roles will be. This is part of the broader discussion of power and privilege in the helping relationship. Clients need to clearly understand the helping process as well as their roles and responsibilities in it. Inappropriate expectations and misunderstandings about how the work will proceed can lead to disillusionment and dissatisfaction. It is important to share your vision of the helping process. It is probably wise to assume that you and your clients have different visions and expectations. These differences need to be reconciled before meaningful work can begin.

PROFESSIONAL SOCIAL WORK COMPETENCIES

For social work education programs in the United States, the accrediting body is the CSWE Board of Accreditation (BOA). The CSWE Commission on Educational Policy (COEP) creates educational policy for social work education, and the BOA creates accreditation standards. The educational policy and accreditation standards together form the EPAS, which guide the accreditation of baccalaureate and master's-level social work educational programs (CSWE, 2022).

Accreditation and Social Work Competencies: Educational Policy and Accreditation Standards 2022

The 2022 EPAS describe the knowledge, values, skills, and cognitive and affective processes that comprise the nice professional social work competencies at the generalist level of practice (CSWE, 2022). Exhibit 2.2 lists the nine competencies and summarizes the content areas covered in each competency. To review the complete competency descriptions, go to www.cswe.org.

Exhibit 2.2 Social Work Competencies

Competency	Content Areas
Competency 1: Demonstrate Ethical and Professional Behavior	• Professional values • Ethical standards • Human rights, social, racial, economic, and environmental justice • Ethical decision-making • Personal and professional values • Professional judgment and behavior • Self-care • Antiracist and anti-oppressive lenses • Historical and current contexts of oppression • Interprofessional practice • Lifelong learning • Digital technology • Ethical use of technology
Competency 2: Advance Human Rights and Social, Racial, Economic, and Environmental Justice	• Human rights • Injustice • Oppression • Racism • Power and privilege • Social, racial, economic, and environmental justice • Oppressive structural barriers • Protection of civil, political, economic, social, and cultural human rights
Competency 3: Engage Antiracism, Diversity, Equity, and Inclusion (ADEI) in Practice	• Racism and oppression • White supremacy • Antiracist practice • Diversity and intersectionality • Equity and inclusion • Discrimination • Alienation • Privilege and power • Social and racial injustices • Cultural humility • Culture structures and systemic oppression

(continued)

Exhibit 2.2 Social Work Competencies (*continued*)

Competency	Content Areas
Competency 4: Engage in Practice-Informed Research and Research-Informed Practice	• Antiracist and anti-oppressive research • Research-informed practice decisions • Practice-informed research and evaluation • Critical evaluation • Research bias • Qualitative research • Quantitative research • Data analysis • Reliability and validity • Dissemination of findings • Interprofessional collaboration
Competency 5: Engage in Policy Practice	• Social policy • Human rights and justice • Service delivery • Social policy analysis • Policy formulation • Antiracist and anti-oppressive policy practice
Competency 6: Engage With Individuals, Families, Groups, Organizations, and Communities	• Dynamic and interactive process • Importance of human relationships • Theories of human behavior • Person-in-environment • Self-reflection • Bias • Power and privilege • Personal values and experiences • Interprofessional collaboration
Competency 7: Assess Individuals, Families, Groups, Organizations, and Communities	• Dynamic and interactive process • Theories of human behavior • Person-in-environment • Interprofessional conceptual frameworks • Culturally responsive • Collaboration • Client strengths • Plan of action • Self-reflection • Bias • Power and privilege • Personal values and experiences • Interprofessional collaboration
Competency 8: Intervene With Individuals, Families, Groups, Organizations, and Communities	• Dynamic and interactive process • Theories of human behavior • Person-in-environment • Interprofessional conceptual frameworks • Culturally responsive • Evidence-informed interventions • Interprofessional collaboration • Transitions and endings

(*continued*)

Exhibit 2.2 Social Work Competencies (*continued*)

Competency	Content Areas
Competency 9: Evaluate Practice With Individuals, Families, Groups, Organizations, and Communities	• Dynamic and interactive process • Process evaluation • Outcome evaluation • Antiracist and anti-oppressive perspectives • Theories of human behavior • Person-in-environment • Interprofessional conceptual frameworks • Qualitative methods • Quantitative methods • Practice effectiveness

Source: Data from Council on Social Work Education. (2022). *Educational policy and accreditation standards.* https://www.cswe.org/getmedia/bb5d8afe-7680-42dc-a332-a6e6103f4998/2022-EPAS.pdf

HOLISTIC COMPETENCY

McKnight (2013) proposes that competence is an "ongoing ability" to "integrate knowledge, skills, judgment, and professional attributes in order to practice safely and ethically" within one's professional scope (p. 460). The CSWE defines holistic competence as the "demonstration of knowledge, values, skills, and cognitive and affective processes that include the social worker's critical thinking, affective reactions, and exercise of judgment in regard to unique practice situations" (CSWE, 2022, p. 7).

Knowledge

The knowledge dimension is your mastery of the substantive content of the competency. Social work curricula are constructed to provide students with coursework that includes readings, assignments, and discussions that educate students on the current knowledge related to each competency. Students also increase their competency knowledge through their own research on the topics that comprise the underlying content and processes of each competency. A prerequisite of one's ability to demonstrate competence is a solid understanding and knowledge of the literature that comprises the competency.

Values

The value dimension is less clear than the knowledge dimension. Although Competency 1 focuses on values, ethics, and professional behavior, the other eight competencies all have social work value dimensions as well. The value dimensions can have knowledge (social work values) as well as skill (ethical behavior and decision-making) components. Understanding the values and ethics associated with the application of the different social work competencies in unique practice situations is the fundamental aspect of ethical decision-making and professional social work competence.

Skills

The skills dimension refers to your ability to apply social work knowledge and values in your social work practice. Numerous skills are associated with each professional competency.

Your field placement experience provides you with an opportunity to apply, refine, and learn social work skills in practice situations. Your skill is your ability to apply social work theories, concepts, and techniques in your practice with clients or client systems.

Cognitive Processes and Affective Reactions

This dimension has three associated subdimensions—critical thinking, affective reactions, and professional judgment. Critical thinking is the open-minded search for understanding. It is a process focused on explaining the why. The process includes "providing evidence, examining the implications of the evidence, recognizing any potential contradictions and examining alternative explanations" (Heron, 2006, p. 221). The CSWE (2022) defines critical thinking as an intellectual, disciplined process of conceptualizing, analyzing, evaluating, and synthesizing multiple sources of information generated by observation, reaction, and reasoning.

Critical thinking is a crucial component of professional competence because it ensures that your social work practice is reasoned and thoughtful and not the rote application of social work techniques. Affective reaction, on the other hand, generally refers to the affective component of social work practice with clients (Rubaltelli & Slovic, 2008). It is the social worker's emotional response to the client's presentation and situation. It is tied to empathy and other affective processes. Affective reaction has relevance for social work competency in that effective social work practice requires cognitive and affective understanding of the client as well as one's own feelings, emotions, and reactions (Poulin & Matis, 2015).

Professional judgment is about decision-making in social work practice. A key issue debated in relation this is the extent to which social workers use analytical versus intuitive reasoning styles (Collins & Daly, 2011). Thus, professional judgment is reasoned decision-making based on evidence, knowledge, analytical reasoning, and practice wisdom. It is a process of examining all facets of the case and making a reasoned decision supported by both objective and subjective evidence. Exercising informed professional judgment is a critical component of professional social work competence (Poulin & Matis, 2015).

INTERRELATIONSHIPS AMONG THE COMPETENCIES

The nine social work competencies and the associated dimensions are the interrelated components of professional social work practice. The competencies are interconnected. They do not stand alone. Holistic competency is social work practice utilizing multiple professional competencies in each practice activity or client interaction. Figure 2.2 shows a conceptualization of the interrelationships among the nine professional social work competencies. The competencies in the two outer bands are those that apply broadly to all practice situations. The ethical and professional behavior; diversity and difference; and social, economic, and environmental justice competencies are fundamental components of effective social work practice at all levels (Poulin et al., 2024).

The competencies in the middle band of Figure 2.2 are the two areas of social work practice that are not client based—policy practice and research. These competencies are informed by the ethical behavior, diversity, and justice competencies and in turn inform social work practice with clients and constituencies competencies. The center band represents the engagement, assessment, intervention, and evaluation competencies in social practice with individuals, families, groups, organizations, and communities. Thus, the ethical behavior, diversity, social justice, policy practice, and research competencies all inform the practice competencies of engagement, assessment, intervention, and evaluation with individuals, families, groups, organizations, and communities (Poulin & Matis, 2015).

The nine professional competencies are interconnected in the delivery of social work practice with clients and constituencies. For example, a social worker's ability to engage with an individual client is influenced by their ethical and professional behavior competency; diversity and difference competency; social, economic, and environmental justice competency; and possibly their policy practice and research competencies. In short, most social work practice situations require the use of all or most of the nine professional competencies. Thus, to be a competent social work practitioner, you must develop knowledge, values, skill, cognitive process, and affective reaction competencies for each professional competency and be able to apply multiple competencies in a variety of practice situations.

SUMMARY

This chapter began with a definition of generalist social work practice and a classification of generalist interventions at the micro, mezzo, and macro levels of practice. This was followed by a review of the five core practice principles of AOP. We presented our model of anti-oppressive generalist social work practice. The four major components and their associated stages of the helping process were reviewed. The chapter concluded with a discussion of client change, the CSWE (2022) professional competencies, holistic competency, the four competency dimensions, and a discussion of the interrelationships among the nine professional competencies.

CASE SUMMARY   UNDOCUMENTED AND HOMELESS

Practice Setting Description

Jackie is a first-year MSW student completing an internship at an inner-city family service agency in the Southwest. The agency is in a section of the city that has a high crime rate, gang activity, and failing schools. The area has a diverse population with many immigrants from Central and South America and a substantial African American population. The agency provides individual and family counseling services on a sliding fee scale. The agency also runs several educational and treatment groups as well as a temporary shelter for women and their children. Jackie has been assigned to work with the women and their children in the shelter. Her primary tasks are to provide concrete services and supportive counseling to the shelter residents.

Background Information

Elicia and her daughter, Maria, are undocumented immigrants from Mexico. They have been in the United States for 5 years. Elicia and Maria fled to the area from another southwestern city to escape

(continued)

CASE SUMMARY   UNDOCUMENTED AND HOMELESS (*CONTINUED*)

her abusive husband approximately 2 months ago. Elicia is 25 years old and Maria 8 years old. Elicia has a 2-year-old daughter, Sarah, who was placed in foster care because of suspected abuse in the home. Sarah is in a foster home in a small rural community in the state hundreds of miles from Elicia's current residence. Since moving to the area, Maria has not been attending school.

Elicia and Maria are currently residing in the agency's temporary shelter for families. They have been at the shelter for 2 weeks, and the agency has a 90-day limit. Prior to arriving at the shelter, Elicia and Maria were homeless and living on the streets.

Elicia is a high school dropout and was a stay-at-home mother prior to leaving her husband and moving to a different part of the state. She chose to move there because she has two female cousins living in the area who are also undocumented immigrants. Elicia's native language is Spanish. She speaks some English but is not as comfortable speaking in English. Her English comprehension appears to be good. Maria speaks both English and Spanish well. When communicating with the staff, Maria acts as Elicia's interpreter since none of the staff at the shelter speak Spanish.

Maria appears to be behind academically. She struggles reading simple children's books written in English. It is unknown if her ability to read in Spanish is better than her English reading skills.

Other than her two cousins, Elicia has no other sources of support in the community. Her cousins have young families and limited resources but are well established and connected to a Latino community in the city and the local Catholic church. Her cousins refused to let Elicia and Maria live with them while she was trying to find her own place and a job. They stated that they did not have enough room and are concerned they would get in trouble with their landlord if it was found out that they were letting people stay with them. They sent her to the local church for help, and she was given the address for the agency's shelter by the priest.

Elicia has been looking for housing in the Latino community. The housing market is tight with limited options, and she has been unable to find anything that she could possibly afford. The only affordable housing she found was a room in a rundown motel that rents by the hour or by the month. It is in an area of town known for drug dealing and sex work.

On arrival in the community, Elicia found occasional work for a house cleaning company. The company hires undocumented workers, pays them very low cash wages, and threatens to turn them in to Immigration and Customs Enforcement (ICE) if they complain. The job bosses also exploit their female workers sexually, threatening to turn them in if they do not comply. Elicia was fearful about applying for other jobs because of her illegal status. She considered turning to sex work to be able to take care of her child, but her Catholic upbringing and thoughts of how doing so would shame her family have kept her from doing so. She is in constant fear of being detained, separated from Maria, and having her placed in foster care. She is also afraid that she will end up homeless again and forced to live on the streets or return to her abusive husband.

Elicia is extremely reluctant to sign up for any federally funded services, even those that she and her child are entitled to receive. On the suggestion that she enroll for supplemental food through Supplemental Nutrition Assistance Program (SNAP), Elicia became nervous and refused, as she has heard that participation in SNAP services, and others like them, would draw the

(*continued*)

CASE SUMMARY: UNDOCUMENTED AND HOMELESS (*CONTINUED*)

attention of ICE, and she had heard stories on the news of individuals being deported after signing up for such programs.

Presenting Problems

Elicia and her child are facing multiple obstacles. They need to find permanent, affordable housing and a job that pays enough to cover her housing and living expenses. In addition, Maria needs to be enrolled in school.

Additionally, Elicia is experiencing an immense amount of stress, anxiety, and possibly post-traumatic stress disorder (PTSD). She described an instance where she could not calm down her breathing and she felt lightheaded. She is very fearful of men and tries to avoid all contact with men in the community. She reports difficulty sleeping at night and feeling exhausted most of the time.

She is concerned about Maria. Maria has started acting out at the shelter, getting into fights with the other children, disobeying her mother, and being disrespectful and defiant to the staff and other adults. Elicia and Maria fight frequently, and when Elicia tries to discipline Maria, she throws a temper tantrum until Elicia gives up.

Elicia has many strengths. She had the strength to leave her abusive husband and move to a different city. She loves her daughter and wants desperately to keep Maria with her. She is resilient and has managed to survive and keep her daughter safe despite not having a place to stay or a job and a limited support network. Elicia feels safe in the shelter, but she is very fearful of being caught as an illegal immigrant and is generally mistrustful of helping professionals and persons of authority.

DISCUSSION QUESTIONS

1. What types of oppression has Elicia experienced?
2. If you were assigned to work with Elicia, how would you address the power and privilege differentials?
3. How might your values, biases, and experiences affect your work with Elicia? How would you address potential value conflicts?
4. How would you approach developing a helping relationship with Elicia?
5. What system factors have contributed to Elicia's experiences of oppression? How would you begin to address the system or structural sources of oppression?

A robust set of instructor resources designed to supplement this text is located at http://connect.springerpub.com/content/book/978-0-8261-6683-8. Qualifying instructors may request access by emailing textbook@springerpub.com.

KEY REFERENCES

Only key references appear in the print edition. To access the full reference list, visit www.springerpub.com/courseconnect. See inside front cover and tear-out card for CourseConnect details.

Baines, D. (2017). *Doing anti-oppressive practice: Social justice social work*. Fernwood Publishing.

Council on Social Work Education. (2022). *Educational policy and accreditation standards*. https://www.cswe.org/getmedia/bb5d8afe-7680-42dc-a332-a6e6103f4998/2022-EPAS.pdf

Gottlieb, M. (2021). The case for a cultural humility framework in social work practice. *Journal of Ethnic & Cultural Diversity in Social Work*, *30*(6), 463–481. https://doi.org/10.1080/15313204.2020.1753615

Gutierrez, L. (1990). Working with women of color: An empowerment perspective. *Social Work*, *35*, 149–153. http://www.jstor.org/stable/23715256

Healy, K. (2014). *Social work theories in context: Creating frameworks for practice*. Bloomsbury Publishing.

Karim, S. (2023). Power-informed practice in social work. *Journal of Social Work*, *23*(6), 1062–1079. https://doi.org/10.1177/14680173231180307

Matthews, H., Sibbald, S., Szoke, T., & Varela, T. S. (2020). *Anti-oppressive practice*. Critically Infused Social Work. https://www.criticallyinfusedsw.com/antioppressive-practice

National Association of Social Workers. (2021). *Code of ethics*. https://www.socialworkers.org/About/Ethics/Code-of-Ethics/Code-of-Ethics-English

Payne, M. (2021). *Modern social work theory* (5th ed.). Oxford University Press.

Prochaska, J. O., DiClemente, C. C., & Norcross, J. C. (1992). In search of how people change: Applications to addictive behaviors. *American Psychologist*, *47*(9), 1102–1114. https://doi.org/10.1037/0003-066X.47.9.1102

3 Ethical and Professional Behavior

Jill is a first-year master of social work (MSW) student who is completing her generalist field placement in a shelter serving homeless families in an economically disadvantaged urban community. The shelter has a full-time staff of five professionals plus Jill and another intern. The shelter serves four families at a time and collaborates with other service agencies in the community and surrounding areas.

Lisa is a 25-year-old African American single mother of two children ages 1 and 3. Lisa has been off and on public assistance since the birth of her first child. She has been unsuccessful in finding employment. Her biggest obstacle to finding full-time employment has been her criminal record for drug possession. She also has had difficulty in keeping her low-paying part-time service jobs. She often must miss work due to required visits to the public assistance office and because of doctor appointments for her children. She has no support network. She is estranged from her mother because of her drug use. An elderly neighbor occasionally helped with the children but was unable to take them to appointments. Lisa lost her most recent part-time job in a supermarket due to missing work multiple times. Lisa was unable keep up with her rent and was evicted. She and her two children lived in her car until there was space for them in the shelter.

Jill was assigned to work with Lisa. As she reflected upon Lisa's situation, she tried to identify the social justice issues as well as Lisa's experiences of oppression. Jill also reflected upon how social work values and ethics as well as her own personal values and biases will impact her work with Lisa.

LEARNING OBJECTIVES

This chapter focuses on the social work competency related to ethical and professional behavior. The competency and National Association of Social Workers (NASW) *Code of Ethics* (2021) are reviewed in relation to the anti-oppressive practice (AOP) core practice principles. Ethical decision-making is reviewed and guidelines for resolving ethical dilemmas, interprofessional collaboration, and social work supervision are discussed.

By the end of this chapter, you will be able to:

- Describe the various components of the ethical and professional behavior competency.
- Identify the NASW ethical principles and ethical standards for social work practice.
- Describe the similarities among the ethical and professional behavior competency, the NASW *Code of Ethics,* and the AOP core practice principles.
- Apply a framework for approaching and resolving ethical dilemmas.
- Describe the differences and relationships between personal and professional values.

- Apply guidelines for resolving value conflicts.
- Identify the challenges and strengths of interprofessional collaboration.
- Describe the role supervision and self-reflection play in upholding the NASW *Code of Ethics* and the Council on Social Work Education (CSWE) ethical and professional behavior competency.
- Discuss how professional development and the use of technology are related to ethical and professional behavior.

COMPETENCY 1: DEMONSTRATE ETHICAL AND PROFESSIONAL BEHAVIOR

Social workers understand the value base of the profession and its ethical standards, as well as relevant policies, laws, and regulations that may affect practice with individuals, families, groups, organizations, and communities. Social workers understand that ethics are informed by principles of human rights and apply them toward realizing social, racial, economic, and environmental justice in their practice. Social workers understand frameworks of ethical decision-making and apply principles of critical thinking to those frameworks in practice, research, and policy arenas. Social workers recognize and manage personal values and the distinction between personal and professional values. Social workers understand how their evolving worldview, personal experiences, and affective reactions influence their professional judgment and behavior. Social workers take measures to care for themselves professionally and personally, understanding that self-care is paramount for competent and ethical social work practice. Social workers use rights-based, antiracist, and anti-oppressive lenses to understand and critique the profession's history, mission, roles, and responsibilities and recognize historical and current contexts of oppression in shaping institutions and social work. Social workers understand the role of other professionals when engaged in interprofessional practice. Social workers recognize the importance of lifelong learning and are committed to continually updating their skills to ensure relevant and effective practice. Social workers understand digital technology and the ethical use of technology in social work practice.

Social workers:

- make ethical decisions by applying the standards of the NASW *Code of Ethics*, relevant laws and regulations, models for ethical decision-making, ethical conduct of research, and additional codes of ethics within the profession as appropriate to the context;
- demonstrate professional behavior, appearance, and oral, written, and electronic communication;
- use technology ethically and appropriately to facilitate practice outcomes; and
- use supervision and consultation to guide professional judgment and behavior (Council on Social Work Education [CSWE], 2022, p. 7).

The ethical and professional behavior competency, as shown in Figure 2.2 in Chapter 2, is a broad overarching competency that impacts the application of the other professional competencies in social work practice at all levels. This chapter covers the professional values and ethics, resolving ethical dilemmas, personal and professional values, professional judgment and behavior, interprofessional practice, ethical use of technology, digital technology, personal reflection, and supervision components of Competency 1 using an antiracist and anti-oppressive lens.

SOCIAL WORK VALUES AND ETHICS

The practice of social work is based on a number of value positions and principles that guide the work with clients irrespective of the approach used, the presenting client problem, the client population, or the setting in which services are provided. These values and principles apply to all forms of social work practice (Poulin et al., 2019).

CORE SOCIAL WORK VALUES

Social work is a value-based profession (Beckett & Maynard, 2005; Reamer, 2013). Values provide the basis for professional social work practice (Congress & McAuliffe, 2006; Gumpert & Black, 2006). They guide the actions we take and our evaluations of what is "good" (DuBois & Miley, 2014). Social work has a rich tradition of principles and beliefs. The heart of these is reflected in the NASW *Code of Ethics* (National Association of Social Workers [NASW], 2021), which identifies core social work values, which are referred to as ethical principles. The core professional values are service to others, social justice, dignity and worth of the person, the importance of human relationships, integrity, and competence. These values and their associated ethical standards all play a critical role in social work practice. The NASW *Code of Ethics* is available online (www.socialworkers.org/About/Ethics/Code-of-Ethics/Code-of-Ethics-English).

Service Value

The ethical principle related to the service value is that social workers help people in need. This ethical principle emphasizes serving others and the fact that social work is a service profession dedicated to providing help to individuals, families, and groups in need and to improving community and social conditions (NASW, 2021). Helping those in need and seeking to improve community and social conditions are fundamental concepts of anti-oppressive generalist practice. The service value aligns closely with the AOP focus on helping individuals and families who have experienced oppression and discrimination as well as targeting larger social change at the organizational, community, and societal levels.

Social Justice Value

The NASW's second ethical principle focuses on challenging social injustice (NASW, 2021). Social justice has long been valued in social work. Concern with social justice and inequality in the profession goes back to the advocacy efforts of Jane Addams and the settlement house movement of the early 1900s. Additionally, social justice is the heart and soul of AOP generalist social work practice.

Social workers traditionally work with people who are victims of discrimination and prejudice. Many of our clients are unemployed or underemployed, have limited access to resources, have received inadequate education and training, and are among the most disadvantaged members of society. They often face prejudicial attitudes and are identified as lesser persons (DuBois & Miley, 2014). Social injustice is manifested in discrimination on the basis of race, gender, social class, sexual orientation, age, and disability. Prejudicial attitudes provide justification for social structures that provide fewer prospects—fewer opportunities, fewer possibilities, and fewer resources—for those with lower status (DuBois & Miley, 2014).

Social workers' commitment to social justice is based on concern about the negative effect of discrimination and prejudice on disadvantaged populations. We often work with clients who have been denied basic rights and opportunities. We are called on to challenge social injustice and to increase the opportunities, possibilities, and resources of our clients. We have an ethical responsibility to address the social, economic, and environmental injustices experienced by our clients as well as their experiences of oppression and discrimination.

At least two of the NASW ethical standards connect the professional behavior of social workers with social justice issues. The first concerns ethical responsibilities to the profession and not engaging in or tolerating any form of discrimination (NASW, 2021). The other ethical standard related to social justice is under ethical responsibilities to society and advocating for changes in policy and legislation to promote social justice (NASW, 2021).

Clearly, the ethical standards on discrimination and social and political action call for social workers as professionals to engage in actions and activities that address social justice–type issues in organizations, institutions, communities, and society. Our professional values and ethics define professional behavior and the expectation that social workers be active participants in the promotion of social justice and in change efforts to address social injustice.

Unfortunately, today in the United States and in many other countries, a number of social justice issues are in the news on a weekly basis, if not daily. It appears that tolerance of others is declining and divisions are increasing. In our opinion, the need for social action to fight injustice is as great now as it was a century ago. In the United States alone, transgendered persons are being denied the right to use bathrooms of their choice, and school bullying is still an issue in many communities. According to the U.S. Department of Health and Human Services website on bullying, almost 30% of students aged 6 to 12 have been bullied, and over 55% of LGBT youth have experienced cyberbullying (StopBullying.gov, 2018). Human trafficking for the sex trade and some other industries is an ongoing problem. In a 2017 report from the International Labour Organization and the Walk Free Foundation, an estimated 24.9 million victims are trapped in modern-day slavery. Of these, 16 million (64%) were exploited for labor, 4.8 million (19%) were sexually exploited, and 4.1 million (17%) were exploited in state-imposed forced labor (Human Rights First, 2017). Discrimination against people of color, LGBT persons, immigrants, persons with physical and mental challenges, Jews, Muslims, and women has not abated. Persons seeking asylum at our borders are being arrested, and families are separated and children detained separately from their parents. Hate crimes have risen for 3 straight years, with a 17% rise between 2016 and 2017 (Eligon, 2018). The majority of violent attacks on people were based on their race, ethnicity, religion, and sexual orientation (Eligon, 2018). These are but a few of the social injustices that occur all too frequently in the United States and globally.

> **CASE 3.1** **PROTECTING THE RIGHTS OF LGBT PERSONS IN SOCIAL WORK PRACTICE**
>
> Bill is a social worker employed at a service center for LGBT youth in Boston. In 2016, the State of Massachusetts passed a law protecting the rights of LGBT persons from discrimination based on their sexual orientation or identity. A group of conservative Christians obtained the necessary signatures on a petition to have the law repealed as a referendum question in the 2018 midterm elections. The referendum question called for the repeal of the Massachusetts 2016 law banning discrimination against LGBT persons.
>
> Bill joined a citizens group organized to turn out the vote against repealing the ban. It was a statewide effort, with committees operating in almost every municipality in the state. Bill took a leadership position in his community. It was a grassroots effort with almost no funding. They used a committee structure to organize their tasks. One committee raised funds for lawn signs urging votes against the repeal, another committee organized a door-to-door campaign to encourage residents to vote and to vote against the repeal, and a third committee solicited volunteers to staff polling places to encourage voters. Bill volunteered his time to help defeat the referendum question. He felt it was his ethical responsibility to fight to protect the rights of his clients and other LGBT persons in his community and state.

The NASW *Code of Ethics* and the CSWE professional competencies make addressing these human rights issues part of what it means to be a social worker. There are many ways this could be accomplished. AOP social workers can engage in social and political action at the neighborhood or community level. They can become active in addressing injustice at the organizational level and at all levels of government. Case 3.1 describes a social worker's involvement in social action to address potential discrimination against LGBT persons in the state of Massachusetts.

Dignity and Worth of the Person's Value

NASW's third ethical principle focuses on a person's individual worth and dignity (NASW, 2021). This entails treating our clients in a caring and respectful fashion, being mindful of individual differences and cultural and ethnic diversity. The underlying assumption of this value is that all human beings have intrinsic worth, irrespective of their past or present behavior, beliefs, lifestyle, race, or status in life (Hepworth et al., 2017). As a social worker, you are expected to treat your clients with respect and dignity. They deserve respect by virtue of their humanness. This does not mean that you have to agree with your clients' life choices or decisions. It does mean that you should strive to affirm their dignity and self-worth. Not doing so can have profound negative effects on the helping process, and doing nothing could potentially cause harm.

Before clients are willing to risk and trust, they need to feel accepted and valued. Doing so is even more important when clients' problematic behaviors involve moral, social, or legal infractions. A client whose behavior has violated social and cultural norms is not likely to engage in a collaborative helping relationship with a professional who communicates disapproval and condemnation.

Closely associated with respect for the individual is a nonjudgmental attitude. As a social worker, you must not blame the client in either your attitude or behavior. Focus on understanding your clients and their difficulties and on helping them find solutions or alternative ways of behaving. If you blame them for their difficulties and assign pejorative labels, most will become defensive and unwilling to trust you. The more you understand the life experience of your clients, no matter how personally distressing their behavior or beliefs may be, the more likely it is that you will be able to accept them as human beings (Hepworth et al., 2017).

Many of our clients' behaviors conflict with our personal values and beliefs. More often than not, there will be a clash of values between you and your clients. These differences should be viewed as a normal part of generalist social work practice. Expect them and accept them. There are going to be differences; in fact, there are going to be major differences. If you focus on your values and assign blame to clients for adopting behaviors or attitudes with which you disagree, you will not be able to help them.

Adopting nonjudgmental attitudes is a prerequisite for developing effective working relationships (Poulin, 2010). The challenge is to maintain your own values without imposing them on others and without judging those whose behavior and beliefs are in conflict with your belief system. To accomplish this, you need to be open to others and treat everyone with respect and dignity. This is difficult when you have negative feelings about your client. You are human, and you will have negative feelings about some clients. Pretending that you do not have these feelings will not work; clients will sense insincerity and negative reactions. The best approach is to try to understand your client and to communicate that understanding in a caring and nonjudgmental manner. Clients are not seeking your approval; they are seeking your help. They need to feel that they have been heard and that you understand them and their situations. They need to feel that you care and that you want to work with them. Communicating care and concern facilitates the helping process. If clients perceive you as judging and blaming them, they are not likely to accept help from you.

Overall, the social work value of dignity and worth of the person is consistent with AOP generalist practice. Being mindful of individual, cultural, and ethnic diversity is achieved through the AOP practice principles of empowerment and collaboration as well as by critically assessing your client's experiences of oppression and discrimination. Empowering clients to be in control of the helping process communicates respect. Engaging in a collaborative helping process also enhances the dignity of your clients by reducing the power differential. Finally, critically assessing past experiences of oppression gives clients a voice and an experience of being heard. It validates their experiences, which communicates respect, which in turn enhances the dignity and worth of your clients.

Importance of Human Relationships Value

NASW's fourth ethical principle focuses on relationships (NASW, 2021). Focusing on the relationship issues of clients is common in generalist social work. Many clients need help in improving their human relationships and interpersonal interactions.

Historically, the helping relationship has been given a central role in the helping process (Perlman, 1979). The *Code of Ethics* states that "social workers engage people as partners in the helping process" (NASW, 2021). The word *relationship* implies that there is a reciprocal interactive process between two people. In social work, the helping relationship is a partnership. You and the client both have input and make decisions together. You are joint participants. Social workers do not solve problems for their clients; they work with clients and help them solve their own problems.

> ▶ **Reflection Questions**
> 1. Which social work value do you identify with most strongly? Why?
> 2. Are there any social work values that you feel are less important than the others? Why?

Beginning social workers often feel that unless they are doing something specific and concrete for their clients, they are not being helpful. You will be tempted to do things for clients, using your skills and abilities to get the task done and hand over the results to clients. It will make you feel useful and productive. Avoid the temptation because it is a trap. More often than not, clients will not appreciate your generous efforts on their behalf. By doing work for them, you will put them in a dependent position, highlighting their inability to manage their lives. No one likes feeling incompetent and dependent. Rather than making your clients dependent on you, empower them. Help them help themselves. Help them do whatever they need to do to manage their own lives as best they can. Ultimately, your clients must become confident and learn to do tasks for themselves. The helping relationship in social work is a collaborative partnership. Social workers do not work for clients; rather, they work with clients.

The social work value of the importance of human relationship is also consistent with AOP generalist practice. The AOP practice principles of critical self-reflection, empowerment, collaboration, assessing past experiences of oppression and minimal intervention all indirectly contribute to strengthening the helping relationship, which is a key component of generalist social work practice.

Integrity Value

NASW's fifth ethical principle focuses on being trustworthy (NASW, 2021). You have probably heard the sentiment that honesty is the best policy; in the social work profession, we value honesty very much. Social workers should demonstrate integrity at all times through honesty, sincerity, and responsibility. This is the key to developing trust and a positive helping relationship. Be open and honest. It is okay to admit that you do not know or are unsure about something. If that happens, let your clients know that you will find out and then follow through and get back to your clients with the information.

Competence Value

NASW's sixth ethical principle focuses on competence and professional expertise (NASW, 2021). Social workers are to practice within their areas of training and seek ongoing supervision, education, and support on a regular basis. As social work students, the primary learning objective is to become a competent generalist social worker. This is done by demonstrating proficiency through your practice experiences as they relate to the nine professional competencies defined by the CSWE (2022). The development of competence is a lifelong undertaking that involves critical thinking, reflection, and ongoing professional development.

ETHICAL STANDARDS

The core social work values and ethical principles embody the ideals to which all social workers should aspire. The NASW *Code of Ethics* sets specific standards and explains how the core values and principles influence the actions of professional social workers. The NASW *Code of Ethics* (2021) identifies the six areas of professional behavior: responsibilities to clients, to colleagues, to practice settings, as professionals, to the profession, and to the broader society. Each area of responsibility includes a number of subareas. They are detailed, comprehensive guidelines for professional behavior. It is important that you carefully review the detailed descriptions of the standards found in the NASW *Code of Ethics* available online (www.socialworkers.org/About/Ethics/Code-of-Ethics/Code-of-Ethics-English).

> ▶ **Reflection Questions**
>
> 1. How will your ethical responsibilities to the broader society affect your professional life?
> 2. Which of the six areas of ethical responsibilities do you think will be most difficult to implement? Why?

ETHICAL DILEMMAS

Social workers frequently have ethical obligations to several parties at the same time. For example, we have ethical obligations to both our clients and our employing organizations. This creates the possibility of conflict or ethical dilemmas. An ethical dilemma occurs when one or more social work values are in conflict. In these situations, you are forced to choose between two competing values or undesirable courses of action. Because we have ethical responsibilities to our clients, our colleagues, our practice settings, the profession, and the broader society, value conflicts and ethical dilemmas occur often within and among the six areas of professional responsibilities.

Resolving ethical dilemmas is never easy or straightforward. Rarely is there a clear-cut right or wrong choice. The choice is between two seeming "rights"; the task is to determine which "right" is more so given the circumstances.

The first step in addressing ethical dilemmas is to refer to the *Code of Ethics* for clarification of the standards of practice. The code, however, does not offer bases for choosing between two or more conflicting standards. A number of guidelines have been developed to help resolve ethical dilemmas. A hierarchy of value assumptions is the basis for decision-making. The hierarchy developed by Reamer (1990) is shown in the following.

Ethical Guidelines

1. The rights to life, health, well-being, and necessities of life are superordinate and take precedence over rights to confidentiality and opportunities for additive "goods" such as wealth, education, and recreation.
2. An individual's basic right to well-being takes precedence over another person's right to privacy, freedom, or self-determination.
3. People's right to self-determination takes precedence over their right to basic well-being, provided they are competent to make informed and voluntary decisions with consideration of relevant knowledge and as long as the consequences of their decisions do not threaten the well-being of others.
4. People's rights to well-being may override laws, policies, and arrangements of organizations.

The first guideline proposes that a person's right to health and well-being takes precedence over the right of confidentiality. If you had to choose between protecting a person's health and well-being and violating a client's confidentiality, you would choose health and well-being. For example, the right of neglected and abused children to protection takes precedence over their parents' rights to confidentiality.

The second guideline proposes that a person's right to health and well-being takes precedence over another person's right to privacy, freedom, or self-determination. When you must choose between protecting a person's freedom and protecting another person from harm, the choice is to protect the person from harm. For example, if a client reveals plans to seek physical revenge on their former spouse, you should warn the former spouse.

The third guideline states that a person's right to self-determination takes precedence over their own right to well-being. That is, an individual's self-determination supersedes that person's well-being. The principle promotes freedom to choose and possibly fail or make mistakes. It protects the right of people to carry out actions that do not appear to be in their own best interests, as long as they are competent to make informed and voluntary decisions. However, the first guideline takes precedence if the individual's decision might result in death or serious harm. For example, you must act to protect a client who is at risk of committing suicide.

The final guideline proposes that the right to well-being may override agency policies and procedural rules. Social workers are obligated to follow the policies and procedures of social work agencies, voluntary associations, and organizations. When agency policy has a negative effect on a client's well-being, however, violating the policy or procedure may be justified.

Congress (1999) developed another model of ethical decision-making to help social workers make ethical decisions quickly. The model's acronym ETHIC stands for the following:

E	**E**xamine relevant personal, societal, agency, client, and professional values.
T	**T**hink about what ethical standard of the NASW *Code of Ethics* applies as well as relevant laws and case decisions.
H	**H**ypothesize about possible consequences of different decisions.
I	**I**dentify who will benefit and who will be harmed in view of social work's commitment to the most vulnerable.
C	**C**onsult with supervisor and colleagues about the most ethical choice. (Congress, 2000, p. 10)

The guidelines described previously—or any other guidelines—will not always provide clear-cut courses of action. They will, however, help you prioritize values to help clarify your thinking about an ethical issue. Resolving ethical dilemmas almost always entails making value judgments and subjective interpretations. For example, Reamer's third guideline states that a person's right to self-determination takes precedence over their right to basic well-being, provided they are competent to make an informed decision. A social worker may have to apply this guideline to a person who is mentally ill and homeless, who prefers to remain on the street, and who has little or no interest in participating in a treatment program. Does this person have the right to refuse treatment as well as the right to live wherever they want? The complicating factor in this situation is determining the person's competence and the degree of physical or mental harm that is likely to ensue. Can a person who is mentally ill, delusional, and exhibiting psychotic behavior make informed decisions? At what point does refusing shelter or treatment create a serious risk of physical and mental harm? Clearly, the answers to these questions are subjective and open to value judgments.

In attempting to resolve ethical dilemmas, always invoke the concept of shared responsibility and decision-making (Reamer, 2013). Do not make the decision on your own; enlist others in the process. Get your supervisor's or administrator's advice and approval before you act on an ethical dilemma. Case 3.2 illustrates the difficult decisions involved in resolving ethical dilemmas.

CASE 3.2 AN ETHICAL DILEMMA IN SOCIAL WORK PRACTICE

Desiree is a first-year MSW student who has been placed in an after-school program for emotionally disturbed children. The program is run by a comprehensive mental health agency that offers a wide range of services for children and adults. The agency is a subsidiary of a larger organization that owns and operates a number of inpatient and outpatient mental health facilities. The after-school program has two full-time social workers, a case aide, a half-time supervisor, and a quarter-time program administrator.

Approximately 20 children with emotional and behavioral problems are provided with on-site services 5 days a week and in-home services once a week. Because of a technicality, the program lost its primary source of funding and was slated to close. Desiree found out about the pending closing of the program from her supervisor. She was told not to tell the other staff or the children. The program administrator had decided that it was best for the children, their parents, and the staff not to know in advance about the closing.

Desiree was concerned about the children's need to have enough time to deal with their feelings about leaving the program and about the parents' needs to have time to make other arrangements for the treatment and after-school care of their children. She also wondered how the lack of process about closing the program would affect the staff and their morale. Desiree believed that the well-being of the children was being subjugated to the perceived needs of the agency. She suspected that the agency administrator felt that telling the children and their parents would upset them and that the children would act out more than usual during the time remaining in the program.

(continued)

> ### CASE 3.2 AN ETHICAL DILEMMA IN SOCIAL WORK PRACTICE (*CONTINUED*)
>
> She also suspected that her supervisor wanted to avoid having the parents put pressure on the agency to continue the program. It appeared to her that the closing policy was designed to protect the agency from disruption at the expense of the children and their parents.
>
> Desiree is faced with an ethical dilemma. She has been told by her supervisor to follow an agency policy that she believes is not in the best interests of her clients. Does she advocate for changing the agency's policy? What are the consequences for the children of following the agency's policies? For their parents? Using Reamer's guidelines or Congress's ETHIC model, assess Desiree's ethical dilemma, propose a case decision, and provide an explanation for your decision.

VALUE CONFLICTS

"Value conflicts occur when an individual's personal values clash with those of another person or system" (Birkenmaier et al., 2014, p. 54). Ethical dilemmas, on the other hand, occur when a social worker must choose between two contradictory ethical principles or standards. Value conflicts occur when your personal values are different from the values of the profession, clients, or colleagues. Value conflicts in social work practice occur when the actions taken by your agency, colleagues, or your clients go against your personal values (Reamer, 2013). See Case 3.3 for an example of a value conflict.

There are five types of values: social, cultural, religious, professional, and personal. Social values are generally accepted norms, customs, and beliefs of a particular society. These types of values are regulated by social pressure rather than public policy (Edwards & Seek, 2018). For example, beliefs about individual responsibility, competition, and hard work are social values associated with the United States. Social values can vary from society to society. In contrast to the United States, common social values in Japanese society include harmony, obligation to the group, and collective responsibility.

Cultural values are similar to social values. The difference is that cultural values are beliefs that are integrated into public policy (Edwards, 2014). They are institutionalized as standards for the culture. An example of a cultural value is our laws regarding education. Our beliefs about education have been codified into laws that require young children to attend school. Another American cultural value is the belief in self-government. The idea that Americans have a say in how and who runs their government is institutionalized through voting laws and regulations.

Religious values are those associated with specific faith communities. These values can vary from religion to religion. They tend to be doctrinal statements about behaviors, such as sexual behavior, interpersonal behavior, dietary restrictions, and religious practices. Professional values are those designed to regulate behavior of people within a profession. In social work, the NASW *Code of Ethics* spells out the expected professional behavior for social workers. The final type of values is personal values. These are the values individuals adopt from the previous four value categories as guiding principles for their lives. Individuals have a core

CASE 3.3 GET A JOB: EXAMPLE OF A VALUE CONFLICT IN SOCIAL WORK PRACTICE

Shureka is a first-year MSW student completing her foundation field placement in a shelter for women and children in Georgia. The shelter's mission is to help homeless women find employment, permanent housing, and the resources they need to care for their children. Trish is a 20-year-old single mother with a 2-year-old child. She moved from South Carolina to the area with her boyfriend, Carl, when her daughter was born because of a work opportunity for her boyfriend. She has no family in the area. Four months ago, Carl lost his job and left for somewhere out West. Carl was the wage earner in the family, and after he left, Trish was not able to pay her rent and became homeless. She moved into the shelter shortly after Shureka started her internship.

Trish had completed high school and had become pregnant shortly thereafter. She has never really worked at a full-time job. Her only work experience was some part-time employment at a supermarket when she was in high school. Shureka conducted Trish's intake assessment and had been meeting with her twice a week as her social worker. Trish liked meeting with Shureka and talking about her hopes and dreams. Together they established Trish's treatment goals, which were to find employment and then permanent housing. Each week they would set tasks and weekly goals. Each week Trish, for one reason or another, would not complete her tasks or goals. Trish seemed happy in the shelter. She had childcare and did not have to look after her 2-year-old daughter all the time; she had food for her and her daughter as well as a place to live. She also liked the attention she got in talking with Shureka and the other staff members.

Shureka was frustrated in her work with Trish and found that she was losing her patience and willingness to try to help her. She was beginning to avoid Trish, which was difficult to do in the shelter, and she was finding excuses to cancel their scheduled meetings. Shureka's field instructor and supervisor noticed the change in her behavior and brought it up in supervision. As Shureka reflected upon her change in behavior toward Trish, she realized that she had been raised in a family with a strong work ethic that valued independence and hard work. She also realized that she is most comfortable in helping clients who want to help themselves and that she is less comfortable with clients who are content to rely on the services provided and not become self-sufficient. Shureka's supervisor pointed out that her personal values around work and independence were probably the cause of her behavior toward Trish. She was experiencing a value conflict with her client's behavior and actions or lack of actions. Shureka and her supervisor talked about ways she could address her value conflict. They both agreed that her awareness and understanding of how her personal values were affecting her work with Trish was an important first step. What are the next steps Shureka should take to resolve her value conflict? What ethical principles and standards are relevant in this situation?

---

set of principles or a core belief system. Thus, one's core beliefs can conflict with the values of the profession, one's organization or agency, peers and professional colleagues, and clients.

There are personal and professional value conflicts in social work practice (Osteen, 2011; Valutis & Rubin, 2016). Gough and Spencer (2014) found in a survey of 1,800 Canadian social workers that 53% had experienced a conflict between their personal values and the profession, 82% between their personal values and their organizational workplace, and 75% between their personal values and a client. Clearly, even though a student's motivation for choosing a social work career has been found to be a desire to help others and make positive contributions to society (Osteen, 2011) and that their personal values are aligned with the professional values of social work, conflicts between personal values and the values of the profession, employers, colleagues, and clients will arise.

Resolving value conflicts is never easy. By definition, values are beliefs that we hold dearly. They help define who we are and how we behave. When a conflict arises, it is natural to feel that your belief and values are correct and that the conflict value or behavior is not. Valutis and Rubin (2016) found that the vast majority of social workers in their study indicated that they use professional values as a decision-making guide when faced with a value conflict. Chechak (2015) suggested that social workers must conform personal values to the profession's values and that ethical codes and practice guidelines cannot be made to conform to individual belief systems. Social work's values and ethics have always been the cornerstone of social work practice (Reamer, 2013). Gough and Spencer (2014), however, found in their survey of Canadian social workers that the most common approach to dealing with value conflicts was to consult with colleagues and supervisors. We believe that both approaches should be used in addressing value conflicts in your social work practice. The following lists the steps for addressing value conflicts in your practice:

- Identify your own value that is causing the conflict. Determine if it is a social, cultural, religious, or personal value. Assess the importance of the value to your sense of self-worth and identity.
- Identify the behavior, action, or decision that is in conflict with your value. Determine if it is a social, cultural, religious, professional, or personal value. Assess the importance of the value to your agency, colleague, or client.
- Determine the consequences of choosing one value over the other. What are the benefits of each and for whom? What are the possible negative consequences and for whom?
- Review the values' positions from the perspective of the NASW *Code of Ethics* ethical principles and ethical standards. How does each value position correlate with social work values and principles? Are the values in conflict with the values and principles of the profession?
- Discuss your value conflict with colleagues and your supervisor. Get other professionals' opinions and thinking about your course of action. Is there a consensus about how to deal with your value conflict? How do others see the pros and cons of your options?
- Make the decision on how to resolve your value conflict a shared decision with your supervisor and/or agency administrators.

These guidelines are consistent with AOP generalist practice. A core AOP practice principle is critical self-reflection. This involves a reflection on your personal values and how they might bias work with the client and any potential value conflicts. The self-reflection process also entails assessment of potential values between your personal values,

> **Reflection Questions**
>
> 1. What are three personal values that are very important to you? How do they fit with core social work values?
> 2. What are some potential value conflicts you might encounter in your social work practice?

the client situation, and agency policies and regulations. The AOP practice principle of empowerment entails a discussion of power and the power imbalance in the helping relationship. This discussion helps set the stage for dealing with value conflicts between you and your client through a collaborative helping process.

INTERPROFESSIONAL COLLABORATION

Both the CSWE competency on ethical and professional behavior and the NASW *Code of Ethics* identify interprofessional collaboration as a component of social work practice. The competency on ethical and professional behavior states that "social workers also understand the role of other professions when engaged in interprofessional teams" (CSWE, 2022, p. 7). The NASW *Code of Ethics* Ethical Standard 2.03 addresses interdisciplinary collaboration. The standard has two subsections. The first states that social workers who are members of an interdisciplinary team should participate in and contribute to decisions that affect the well-being of clients by drawing on the perspectives, values, and experiences of the social work profession. Professional and ethical obligations of the interdisciplinary team as a whole and of its individual members should be clearly established (NASW, 2021, Ethical Standards, Interdisciplinary Collaboration, para. 1).

The second states that "social workers for whom a team decision raises ethical concerns should attempt to resolve the disagreement through appropriate channels. If the disagreement cannot be resolved, social workers should pursue other avenues to address their concerns consistent with client well-being" (NASW, 2021, para. 2). CSWE and NASW recognize the importance of interprofessional collaboration in the provision of social work services.

There has been an increase in recent years in the use of interprofessional teams in the provision of healthcare services and in other areas of practice in the United States and globally (Bayne-Smith et al., 2014; West et al., 2016). The World Health Organization (WHO, 2010) recognized the importance of interprofessional collaboration in addressing the global health crisis. Similarly, the Institute of Medicine (2003), the American Public Health Association (2008), and the CSWE (2016) all have issued statements in support of interprofessional collaboration in education and practice.

Interprofessional collaboration is the process of bringing together professionals from different disciplines, such as nursing, medicine, physical therapy, psychologists, and/or social workers, to provide team-based care. WHO defines interprofessional collaborative practice as "when multiple health workers from different professional backgrounds work together with patients, families, carers, and communities to deliver the highest quality of care" (2010, p. 7).

The movement toward interprofessional care is driven by the belief that solutions to complex health and social problems need the coordinated interventions of more than single disciplines (Perreault & Careau, 2012). There is growing evidence that interprofessional collaborations result in more positive patient outcomes in healthcare and other service areas (WHO, 2010). WHO, summarizing existing research, reported that interprofessional collaborative practice increased patient access, made better use of specialists, improved patient outcomes, increased caregiver and patient satisfaction, had greater acceptance of treatment, reduced costs, and resulted in shorter treatments than noncollaborative approaches to the delivery of healthcare services (WHO, 2010, pp. 18–19). The Institute of Medicine (2003) also reported improved patient outcomes and more effective service delivery with interprofessional collaboration approaches. Similar results have been found in nursing, social work, and other allied health disciplines (Caven & Bland, 2013; Freshman et al., 2010). Conversely, lack of collaboration and poor communication have been found to negatively affect outcomes and reduce patient satisfaction (Fewster-Thuente & Velsor-Friedrich, 2008).

A challenge for AOP generalist social workers is collaborating with professionals from other disciplines who approach their work from a medical model or a noncollaborative expert approach. These situations require you to assume the role of advocate. Advocate for increased client participation and power in the helping process. Advocate to include the client in a collaborative decision-making process. Additionally, the social worker can help the client advocate for themselves. As part of an interprofessional team, the social worker also needs to assume the role of broker between the team members and the client. This entails a delicate balance between being a good team member and serving the client. The following section discusses guidelines for successful interprofessional collaboration.

> ▶ **Reflection Questions**
>
> 1. How might interprofessional collaboration affect your identity as a social worker?
> 2. What do you see as a benefit of interprofessional collaboration to your development as a social worker?

INTERPROFESSIONAL COLLABORATION COMPETENCIES

In 2011, the Interprofessional Education Collaborative (IPEC) issued a report of an expert panel that outlines four core competencies for interprofessional collaborative practice. The four competencies are (a) adopting values/ethics for interprofessional practice, (b) understanding interprofessional roles/responsibilities, (c) enhancing interprofessional communication, and (d) facilitating teams and teamwork (IPEC, 2011).

Values and Ethics for Interprofessional Practice

Each discipline brings to the team its own set of professional values and ethics. Competency is the interprofessional collaborative practice required for the development of a professional identity that includes interprofessional ethics.

> Mutual respect and trust are foundational to effective interprofessional working relationships for collaborative care delivery across the health professions. At the same time, collaborative care honors the diversity that is reflected in the individual expertise each profession brings to care delivery. (IPEC, 2011, p. 17)

This philosophy is reflected in IPEC's general competency statement for values and ethics, which states that interprofessional collaborative team members "work with individuals of other professions to maintain a climate of mutual respect and shared values" (IPEC, 2011, p. 19).

Roles and Responsibilities

Interprofessional collaborative practice requires an understanding of the roles and responsibilities of each member/discipline on the team. Team members need to be able to clearly describe their own professional roles and responsibilities and understand others' roles and responsibilities in relation to their own roles. Understanding your role and how your role interfaces with the other team members' roles is a critical component of effective interprofessional collaboration. Doing so also requires you to have a clear understanding of the other team members' roles and responsibilities. All team members need to understand their roles and responsibilities, with a clear understanding of the roles and responsibilities of the other team members and a clear understanding of how the various roles and responsibilities interface among and between each other. This concept is reflected in IPEC's general competency statement for roles and responsibilities, which states that interprofessional collaborative team members "use the knowledge of one's own role and those of other professions to appropriately assess and address the healthcare needs of the patients and populations served" (IPEC, 2011, p. 21).

Interprofessional Communication

Developing effective communication skills is a core competence for all professional disciplines, but communication skills across disciplines are often problematic. Professional jargon creates a barrier to effective interprofessional collaboration. Communicating readiness to work together and finding a common language for the collaborating team members are important steps in developing effective communication among and between interprofessional collaborative teams. This concept is reflected in IPEC's general competency statement for interprofessional communication, which states that interprofessional collaborative team members "communicate with patients, families, communities, and other health professionals in a responsive and responsible manner that supports a team approach to the maintenance of health and the treatment of disease" (IPEC, 2011, p. 23).

Teams and Teamwork

Being on an interprofessional collaborative team requires teamwork and being a good team player.

> Teamwork behaviors involve cooperating in the patient-centered delivery of care; coordinating one's care with other health professionals so that gaps, redundancies, and errors are avoided; and collaborating with others through shared problem-solving and shared decision-making, especially in circumstances of uncertainty. (IPEC, 2011, p. 24)

Understanding group dynamics and team functioning is important to becoming an effective team member. Conflict resolution skills are also important. Conflicts will arise, and being skilled in resolving misunderstandings and differences requires effective interprofessional communication and a shared commitment to improved client outcomes. "Staying focused on patient-centered goals and dealing with the conflict openly and constructively through effective interprofessional communication and shared problem-solving strengthen the ability to work together and create a more effective team" (IPEC, 2011, p. 24). The concept of teamwork is reflected in IPEC's general competency statement, which states that interprofessional collaborative team members "apply relationship-building values and the principles of team dynamics to perform effectively in different team roles to plan and deliver patient-/population-centered care that is safe, timely, efficient, effective, and equitable" (IPEC, 2011, p. 25).

MECHANISMS THAT SUPPORT INTERPROFESSIONAL COLLABORATIVE PRACTICE

WHO identified three practice-level mechanisms that influence the effectiveness of interprofessional collaborative practice. The three mechanisms are institutional supports, working culture, and the environment. These three factors support successful interprofessional team collaboration.

Institutional Supports

Institutional supports shape the way collaborative teams can function. "Staff participating in collaborative practice need clear governance models, structured protocols and shared operating procedures" (WHO, 2010, p. 28). They need administrative support and the organization's commitment to the collaborative model. Collaboration, by definition, means giving up some autonomy and sharing resources. The organization's leadership and the leadership of the participating partners all need to support the collaboration conceptually and through the development of supportive management practices and the sharing of operating resources. Adequate time and space need to be provided to support collaboration. Without strong institutional support, interprofessional collaborations are doomed to failure.

Working Culture

Interprofessional collaborative practice needs opportunities for shared decision-making and regular ongoing team meetings. Getting together to share perspectives, viewpoints, and ideas as a team is critical to effective collaboration. This process in itself helps build a collaborative culture of respect and helps keep the focus on client goals and outcomes. "Structured information systems and processes, effective communication strategies, strong conflict resolution policies and regular dialogue among team and community members play an important role in establishing a good working culture" (WHO, 2010, p. 29).

Environment

Another factor affecting collaboration is the physical environment. Having team members housed in different physical locations can hinder the effectiveness of the collaboration and the development of a working culture (West et al., 2016). The physical space can also enhance or detract from effective collaboration. "Most notably, physical space should not reflect a hierarchy of positions. Additional considerations could include developing a shared space to better facilitate communication or organizing spaces and rooms in ways that eliminate barriers to effective collaboration" (WHO, 2010, p. 29). Refer to Case 3.4 for an example of a successful interprofessional collaborative team.

> ▶ **Reflection Questions**
> 1. In your experience, how does the physical environment affect communication patterns?
> 2. How has the use of digital forms of communication affected team building and collaboration?

CASE 3.4 INTERPROFESSIONAL COLLABORATION OF THE HOSPICE TEAM

Gail is a social worker employed by a nonprofit agency providing hospice and bereavement services. The agency serves approximately 400 individuals and families daily. The hospice services are all provided by interprofessional teams. The teams are composed of a physician, nurse, pharmacist, social worker, chaplain, and volunteer coordinator. The nurse on the team functions as the case manager for all the patients assigned to the teams. The team meets weekly to review the patients and to make case treatment decisions. All the team members provide input on the patient from their discipline perspectives, and the team collectively decides the respective tasks of each team member.

The roles and responsibilities of each team member are clearly defined and understood by the other team members. Gail's responsibilities included conducting biopsychosocial assessments, helping the patient and/or family obtain needed resources, and making referrals to other community service providers. The chaplain provides spiritual counseling to the patient and family members and works closely with Gail in terms of assessing the patient's and family's social/emotional needs. The nurse, who functions as the case manager, oversees the patient's medical needs in consultation with the physician and pharmacist as well as input from the volunteer coordinator, who has patient information via volunteer visitor reports, Gail, and the chaplain. This structure ensures that patient information from all the different perspectives is taken into consideration on a weekly basis.

The team members' offices are all located in the same building and in close proximity to one another. The physical arrangement of the team members' offices helps facilitate informal and formal communication. Program policies and procedures all support the functioning of the collaborative teams, and the agency has a strong culture of mutual respect and collaboration. Gail loves her job and being part of a well-functioning interprofessional team.

In summary, WHO recommends the following action steps to advance interprofessional collaborations:

- Structure processes that promote shared decision-making, regular communication and community involvement.
- Design a built environment that promotes, fosters, and extends interprofessional collaborative practice both within and across service agencies.
- Develop personnel policies that recognize and support collaborative practice and offer fair and equitable remuneration models.
- Develop a delivery model that allows adequate time and space for staff to focus on interprofessional collaboration and delivery of care.
- Develop governance models that establish teamwork and shared responsibility for healthcare service delivery between team members as the normative practice. (WHO, 2010, p. 30)

SUPERVISION

As with interprofessional practice, supervision is recognized as a component of the ethical and professional behavior competency defined by CSWE (2022) and an ethical standard specified in the NASW *Code of Ethics*. The competency on ethical and professional behavior states that social workers use supervision and consultation to guide professional judgment and behavior (CSWE, 2022, p. 7). The NASW *Code of Ethics* Ethical Standard 3.01 addresses supervision and consultation. The standard has four subsections. The first states that social workers providing supervision should have the necessary knowledge and skills. The second indicates that social workers providing supervision set clear, appropriate, and culturally sensitive boundaries. The third subsection is about not engaging in any dual or multiple relationships with supervisees, and the fourth is about providing fair and respectful evaluations of supervisees. Thus, the CSWE competency focuses on how to use supervision, and the NASW ethical standard focuses on the provision of supervision. Both are important components of ethical and professional behavior in social work practice. In this context, we are referring to clinical supervision that focuses on your work with clients and your social work competencies.

Social work supervision can be traced back to the beginning of the profession in the early 20th century as it was described and used with charity workers in New York (Kadushin & Harkness, 2014). Supervision within social work has long been a means to pass along practice wisdom from the trained professional social worker to the learner. It is through social work supervision that you can hone your social work skills based on your work with clients and constituencies. Social work supervision is a collaborative process where both you and the supervisor work together in order to enhance your practice skills and develop your professional self (NASW & Association of Social Work Boards [ASWB], 2013). Through social work supervision, your professional social work identity can mature (Field, 2016). Social work supervision serves to ensure that you are developing the appropriate skills necessary to be an ethical and competent social work practice professional (Caras, 2013).

To supervise is to direct, watch over, or keep an eye on the work of another. In supervision, the supervisor monitors the actions of the supervisee. Social work supervision goes beyond this basic definition. Social work supervision involves a dynamic engagement between the supervisor and supervisee. High-quality supervision provides a foundation for the developing social worker. As a social work student, we encourage you to make the most of your weekly supervisions during your field placements in order to set a strong foundation for your future as a professional social worker (Poulin et al., 2019).

A supervision agreement both clarifies the process and helps define the supervisor/supervisee relationship. Caras and Sandu (2014) set forth that "supervision requires a learning alliance, which empowers the person to acquire relevant skills and knowledge for his profession. This alliance aims to develop interpersonal skills in supervision relationship" (p. 76). Since social work supervision is multidimensional and can have multiple functions or purposes, it is important to be clear on what to expect out of supervision. Social work supervision can serve many purposes, including:

- developing and assessing your professional social work competencies;
- developing your professional self and increasing a sense of professional autonomy;
- promoting personal development by exploring how personal values and beliefs align and merge with those of the profession;
- promoting professional values within all elements of practice; and
- reflecting upon ethical considerations related to your social work practice.

Social work supervision consists of three primary domains: support, administration, and education (Kadushin & Harkness, 2014; NASW & ASWB, 2013). Figure 3.1 illustrates the three domains and their interrelationships.

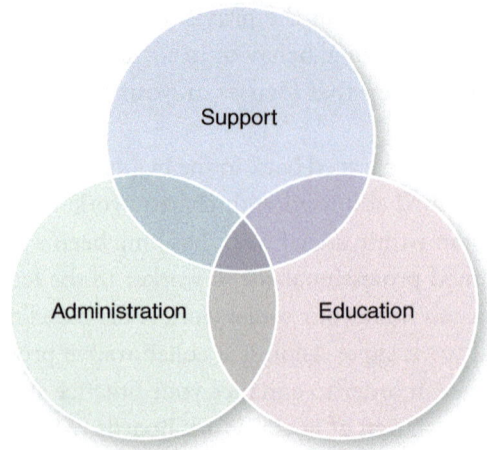

FIGURE 3.1 Three domains of social work supervision.

Supervision serves to support your work as a social worker. Support is very important within the profession of social work. At times, this profession can be quite demanding and stressful. It is important to learn ways to diminish and manage stress whenever possible. Through supportive supervision, you, as the developing social worker, can address situations, experiences, or processes that are difficult for you. Together with the support of your supervisor, you can brainstorm and problem-solve potential solutions in order to ameliorate such conditions. There may be simple changes that you are able to make that your supervisor can help you see. In the event that it is something beyond your control, your supervisor may be able to provide you with suggestions for ways to cope or better manage the stressor.

Social work supervision covers administrative processes. Through supervision, you can review agency policies and procedures. You can review macrolevel policies that relate to your practice as well. Reviewing professional ethical values and standards is also a part of administrative supervision. Administrative supervision is often a central component to employment supervision, which we discuss later in this chapter. Within administrative supervision, work tasks and assignments are often explored in order to ensure that agency mission, goals, and objectives are being met and clients are being served appropriately, both effectively and efficiently.

Last, social work supervision can serve as an educational process. Educational supervision seeks to increase your knowledge, skills, and training and help push you toward mastery of the social work competencies. Educational supervision is a pivotal aspect of clinical supervision and your development as a professional social worker. It is necessary to understand not just what to do in a situation with a client but also why you are doing it. The why is often connected to theories, perspectives, models, or evidence-based practices that have been found to be well suited for the situation you are experiencing as a social worker. Good social work practice is grounded in the research and derived from the wealth of practice knowledge available to us.

TRUST, SHARING, AND VULNERABILITY

In order for social work supervision to be most beneficial, it is important that there is trust between the supervisor and supervisee. Trust involves many factors but ties closely to the social work value of integrity. Related to the value of integrity, we can increase trust by being honest and truthful. We can follow through with what we say we are going to do and be dependable and reliable (Poulin et al., 2019).

Open, honest sharing is important in social work supervision. It is important to use your time in supervision not as a time to try and impress your supervisor by saying what you think the "right thing" is, but rather as a time to sort through your thoughts and feelings in order to become a competent social work professional. At times, you may need to explore your own personal thoughts, feelings, and beliefs in supervision regarding how they are impacting your practice as a social worker. You may also need to discuss situations or experiences with clients or systems that you work with during your placement that are triggering to you. Though social work supervision often involves discussing personal issues, it is not to be confused with personal therapy. Unguru and Sandu (2017) put forward the following distinction between counseling and supervision:

> While counseling involves the direct relationship between the social worker and the beneficiary, the reflection on the problem being the responsibility of the beneficiary guided by the counselor, within the supervision the social worker is the one who reflects upon his own practice, with the beneficiaries, identifying the best professional solutions he approached/is about to approach in working with his customers. (p. 18)

Social work supervision requires self-reflection not only on elements of social work practice but also on the practitioner's thoughts, feelings, and behaviors. Effective social work professionals must engage in continuous self-reflection. We must be mindful of how our thoughts, feelings, and behaviors influence our practice. Self-reflection is discussed in more detail in the following section.

> ▶ **Reflection Questions**
>
> 1. How does clinical supervision differ from supervision in a nonsocial work setting?
> 2. In what ways would your behavior as a supervisee differ in a social work setting versus a nonsocial work setting?

Brown (2017) puts forth the acronym BRAVING in order to better understand trust. In this acronym, the B stands for maintaining **B**oundaries. As we know as social workers, boundaries are very important. We talk about having healthy boundaries with our clients quite often. Regarding social work supervision, it is important to also have boundaries. One way to have clear boundaries in your field supervision is to maintain a professional relationship and be clear on each other's roles and responsibilities in the supervisory process. The R stands for **R**eliability. As you may recall from a research course you have taken, being reliable refers to consistency. We can develop trust by being consistent. As we have discussed, one way we can do this is to demonstrate the social work value of integrity. We can do what we say we are going to do. By following through on our words with actions, we are demonstrating integrity and that we are reliable. **A**ccountability is what the A stands for in the acronym. Being accountable requires that you are responsible for what you have done (or maybe did not do). The V represents the concept of **V**ault. By its definition, a vault is a storage compartment. In Brown's analogy, the vault refers to holding information as secret or in confidence. In order to have a relationship of trust, we should not share things that are meant to be held in confidence. The I represents **I**ntegrity. As social workers, through the NASW *Code of Ethics* (2021), we understand integrity as being "continually aware of the profession's mission, values, ethical principles, and ethical standards and practice in a manner consistent with them" while being honest and responsible (p. 6). The N stands for **N**onjudgment. Trust requires that we integrate a nonjudgmental stance and attitude. Last, the G stands for **G**enerosity. Brown suggests that generosity means that we give the benefit of the doubt to the person we are in a relationship with. By being generous, we assume goodwill toward the person and try not to take offense or become defensive.

Once you have a foundation of trust in your supervisory relationship, you can proceed with sharing and vulnerability. Sharing is a necessary aspect of supervision. Sometimes it can be difficult to determine what to share. Sometimes we may not want to share certain things because they make us feel vulnerable. Vulnerability refers to a state of being open or exposed in which we could possibly get attacked. Vulnerability can be scary. Despite that, vulnerability is necessary for many things in life, including true connection and in order to feel emotions such as joy. Brown (2012) defines vulnerability as "uncertainty, risk, and emotional exposure" (p. 34). Vulnerability is connected to having the courage to speak our truth (Brown, 2012). As a social work student, you may at times feel vulnerable during your field placements. For example, if you are presented with a task to complete at the agency and you do not know how to do it, you may feel vulnerable to say you do not know and ask for help. We encourage you to remember that during your field placement (and throughout your social work career), it is okay to be vulnerable. It is okay not to have all of the answers. It is okay to ask for help. In fact, the NASW *Code of Ethics* lists competence as one of our values—it is our duty to ask for help when it is needed to ensure we are meeting the expectation of competence in our work.

SELF-REFLECTION

The CSWE (2022) ethical and professional behavior competency states that social workers understand how their evolving worldview, personal experiences, and affective reactions influence their professional judgment and behavior. As discussed earlier, to be a competent AOP generalist social worker, you will need to engage in critical self-reflection.

When we are thinking deeply or carefully about something, we are engaging in reflection. Self-regulation is our ability to maintain or control ourselves regarding our thoughts, feelings, and behaviors. Successful reflection and self-regulation require self-awareness. It is impossible to engage in reflection and self-regulation if you are unaware of your thoughts, feelings, and behaviors. Effective social workers are self-aware and continually examine their own selves so that they can be more effective helping professionals (Poulin et al., 2019).

SELF-AWARENESS

Self-awareness is a term used to describe the recognition of personal thoughts, feelings, and behaviors. When your stomach growls and feels the sensation of hunger, that is self-awareness. Another example would be when you are texting with someone you are interested in and you feel butterflies in your stomach—that is self-awareness. Any time that you can recognize your thoughts, feelings, and behaviors, you are being aware of your *self*. Some people naturally seem to do a better job at self-awareness than others, but do not worry; self-awareness is something that you can practice and improve. Being present in the moment and practicing mindfulness are ways that you can improve your self-awareness.

Self-awareness is critical and necessary in social work practice. Social workers often use their *self* in helping clients. Just as accountants would use a calculator to do their job, social workers use their self to do their job. A big piece of social work is being present with the client. In order to be fully present with the client, we must be present with ourselves.

How do we get to know our *self* better? Hopefully, your education, especially your social work courses, has served as a catalyst for self-exploration and critical thinking. Throughout your social work education, you have learned about the use of self in your practice classes. In addition to what you learn in the classroom, you may also gain insights into yourself from a variety of other sources. Maybe you have received feedback from people you are close to, or maybe you have sought your own avenues to get to know yourself better through books, groups, or activities designed with such a purpose. Self-awareness, or personal knowledge about the social worker's self and needs, can be achieved in a variety of ways (Bogo, 2010). Throughout your field experiences, you can explore your self-awareness and use of self in the following ways: field supervision, process recordings, feedback from others (including field supervisors, faculty members, colleagues, peers, and clients), and personal reflection.

Focusing on self-awareness as a component of AOP generalist social work practice is critical. In order to provide sound, ethical social work services, social workers need to be aware of their biases, beliefs, and values and how these are connected to their personal experiences, feelings, and reactions. Throughout your social work education, you have learned to pay attention to your verbal and nonverbal behaviors (making eye contact, nodding, etc.) to demonstrate to the client that you are concerned and listening. In a similar way, you also need to turn your attention inward and pay attention to your thoughts and feelings while working with others. Though it is important that you are aware of what is going on with you, you cannot allow that to be the focus of the session. It is a delicate balance and requires some practice in order to be able to be reflective while still focusing on the clients in front of you. As you develop this skill, you will become a more effective social work professional.

PROFESSIONAL DEVELOPMENT

The CSWE (2022) ethical and professional behavior competency states that social workers "recognize the importance of life-long learning and are committed to continually updating their skills to ensure they are relevant and effective" (CSWE, 2022, p. 7). The NASW Ethical Standard 1.04, Competence, also addresses the importance of ongoing professional development. Subsection (c) states that social workers take "responsible steps (including appropriate education, research, training, consultation, and supervision) to ensure the competence of their work and to protect clients from harm" (NASW, 2021, Ethical Standards, Competence, para. 3). Also, state licensing requirements for social workers all need a specified annual number of continuing education hours to maintain a social work license. The continuing education workshops, conferences, and trainings have to be approved for credit by the state authority in charge of licensure. Licensed social workers are required to engage in professional development activities by their state licensing boards and are encouraged by the NASW *Code of Ethics* and the CSWE competency on ethics and professional behavior.

Updating your social work skills and knowledge can take many forms. Attending professional conferences is an excellent way to stay current on a number of topics in a short period of time. The CSWE, the Association of Baccalaureate Social Work Program Directors, and the Society for Social Work and Research all hold annual conferences on a variety of social work topics. There are also a number of social work–related national conferences on specialized topics, such as aging, health, addictions, trauma, and other topics. Additionally, NASW holds regional and state conferences.

In addition to conferences, social workers can attend local, state, national, and international training workshops in person or online. Training workshops can cover the whole range of topics relevant to social work. Many social workers' places of employment also provide workshops and trainings related to the populations they serve.

Finally, many graduate social work programs hold symposia and lectures on current best practices in social work and other topics. Many schools of social work also offer certificate programs for advanced training on a range of specialized topics.

> **Reflection Question**
>
> As a social work student and future social worker, how will you have to change your use of social media and electronic communications? Why?

PROFESSIONAL AND ETHICAL USE OF TECHNOLOGY

The CSWE (2022) ethical and professional behavior competency states that social workers "understand emerging forms of technology and the ethical use of technology in social work practice" and they "use technology ethically and appropriately to facilitate practice outcomes" (CSWE, 2022, p. 7).

It is important that as professional social workers, we are caring and genuine with our clients. In demonstrating that connection, we may be friendly toward our clients, but we must be clear that though we are friendly, we are not our clients' friends. Establishing and maintaining appropriate boundaries is a critical component of competent social work practice. The responsibility for the development and maintenance of boundaries falls totally on the social worker. So, as the social worker, you need to establish and be clear about these professional boundaries with your clients. It is inappropriate to be friends with clients on social media. Social work professionals should not accept requests and invitations from clients on social media platforms in order "to prevent boundary confusion, inappropriate dual relationships, or harm to clients" (NASW, 2021, p. 11). Furthermore, social workers should not engage in personal communication with clients through any electronic forum.

According to Loue (2016), "social workers are increasingly relying on the Internet to provide information to clients/patients, to seek advice about patients, to provide mental health treatment, and as part of an ongoing supervisory or consultant relationship" (p. 1). With a growing focus on telehealth services and a rise in app-based video conferencing as a way to connect with helping professionals, social workers must be aware of the benefits and potential limitations of such advances. Furthermore, several social work professional organizations came together recently to release technology standards for social workers. The NASW, Association of Social Work Boards (ASWB), CSWE, and Clinical Social Work Association (2017) clearly set forth that social workers must continue to practice within the guidelines of the NASW *Code of Ethics* as well as:

> [w]hen using technology to provide services, practitioner competence and the well-being of the client remain primary. Social workers who use technology to provide services should evaluate their ability to assess the relative benefits and risks of providing social work services using technology . . . reasonably ensure that electronic social work services can be kept confidential . . . reasonably ensure that they maintain clear professional boundaries . . . confirm the identity of the client to whom services are provided electronically at the onset of each contact with the client . . . assess individuals'

familiarity and comfort with technology, access to the Internet, language translation software, and the use of technology to meet the needs of diverse populations, such as people with differing physical abilities. (pp. 11–12)

PROFESSIONAL ONLINE IDENTITY

Developing a professional online identity is another important step to consider. For some social workers, developing this professional online identity is necessary (especially if they deliver services electronically). Curington and Hitchcock (2017) suggest that professional social workers who utilize social media for professional purposes should create a professional online identity, post for professional reasons, and create a social media policy. Your professional online identity is different from your personal online identity that we have previously discussed in this chapter. Your professional online identity may utilize social media platforms, blogs, business websites, or other online forums. Through these forums, you are clearly identifying yourself as a professional social worker. Since this is a professional presentation, your postings should be aligned with social work values and principles while following guidelines set forth by professional organizations. As this is a professional presentation, you should develop a social media policy regarding how you utilize technology and your response to various situations.

CONFIDENTIALITY AND PRIVACY

As professionals, we must always consider the intended and unintended consequences of behaviors. When utilizing electronic communication and the assistance of technology, we must be aware of our limitations to safeguard information. In this day and age, it is common to hear about hackings and data breaches, but we must never get accustomed to these terms to forget what that means for us as social workers and for the clients we serve. When serving vulnerable populations and dealing with sensitive and confidential information, we must take all of the steps possible to protect the information of our clients. We should follow all state and federal guidelines related to privacy and compliance. There are many considerations in ensuring confidentiality while using technology-driven social work practices (Groshong & Phillips, 2015). We should ensure that we are compliant with the Health Insurance Portability and Accountability Act (HIPAA) when using technology that often involves levels of encryption and agreements with servers. HIPAA was passed into law in 1996 in the United States and serves to safeguard protected health information (PHI). The act also has provisions to ensure that any PHI that is transmitted electronically (ePHI) is safeguarded to ensure confidentiality and privacy.

SUMMARY

This chapter focused on the various components of the ethical and professional behavior competency. The competency and the NASW *Code of Ethics* (2021) were reviewed in relation to the core AOP practice principles. The *Code of Ethics* describes the core social work values, which are called ethical principles. The ethical principles are social justice, dignity and worth of the individual, importance of human relationships, integrity, and competence. These are the guiding principles for social work practice. The *Code of Ethics* Ethical Standards specifies ethical behaviors in six domains. The domains are ethical responsibilities to clients, ethical responsibilities to colleagues, ethical responsibilities in practice settings, ethical responsibilities as professionals, ethical responsibilities to the social work profession, and ethical responsibilities to the broader society. These ethical standards, taken together, define ethical behaviors and responsibilities for social workers in all practice settings and as a professional social worker. The discussion of ethical principles and standards was followed by a review of ethical dilemmas and frameworks for resolving ethical dilemmas and a review of personal and professional values and approaches to resolving value conflicts.

The chapter then reviewed interprofessional collaboration, interprofessional collaboration competencies, and mechanisms that support effective interprofessional collaboration. This was followed with discussions on supervision, self-reflection, professional development, and the ethical use of technology in social work practice.

CASE SUMMARY: UNDOCUMENTED AND HOMELESS

Practice Setting Description

Jackie is a first-year MSW student completing an internship at an inner-city family service agency in the Southwest. The agency is in a section of the city that has a high crime rate, gang activity, and failing schools. The area has a diverse population with many immigrants from Central and South America and a substantial African American population. The agency provides individual and family counseling services on a sliding fee scale. The agency also runs several educational and treatment groups as well as a temporary shelter for women and their children. Jackie has been assigned to work with the women and their children in the shelter. Her primary tasks are to provide concrete services and supportive counseling to the shelter residents.

Background Information

Elicia and her daughter, Maria, are undocumented immigrants from Mexico. They have been in the United States for 5 years. Elicia and Maria fled to the area from another southwestern city to escape Elicia's abusive husband approximately 2 months ago. Elicia is 25 years old and Maria 8 years old. Elicia has a 2-year-old daughter, Sarah, who was placed in foster care because of suspected abuse in the home. Sarah is in a foster home in a small rural community in the state hundreds of miles from Elicia's current residence. Since moving to the area, Maria has not been attending school.

Elicia and Maria are currently residing in the agency's temporary shelter for families. They have been at the shelter for 2 weeks, and the agency has a 90-day limit. Prior to arriving at the shelter, Elicia and Maria were homeless and living on the streets.

Elicia is a high-school dropout and was a stay-at-home mother prior to leaving her husband and moving to a different part of the state. She chose to move there because she has two female cousins living in the area who are also undocumented immigrants. Elicia's native language is Spanish. She speaks some English but is not as comfortable speaking in English. Her English comprehension appears to be good. Maria speaks both English and Spanish well. When

(continued)

| CASE SUMMARY | UNDOCUMENTED AND HOMELESS (*CONTINUED*) |

communicating with the staff, Maria acts as Elicia's interpreter since none of the staff at the shelter speak Spanish.

Maria appears to be behind academically. She struggles reading simple children's books written in English. It is unknown if her ability to read in Spanish is better than her English reading skills.

Other than her two cousins, Elicia has no other sources of support in the community. Her cousins have young families and limited resources but are well established and connected to a Latino community in the city and the local Catholic church. Her cousins refused to let Elicia and Maria live with them while she was trying to find her own place and a job. They stated that they did not have enough room and are concerned they would get in trouble with their landlord if it was found out that they were letting people stay with them. They sent her to the local church for help, and she was given the address for the agency's shelter by the priest.

Elicia has been looking for housing in the Latino community. The housing market is tight with limited options, and she has been unable to find anything that she could possibly afford. The only affordable housing she found was a room in a rundown motel that rents by the hour or by the month. It is in an area of town known for drug dealing and sex work.

On arrival in the community, Elicia found occasional work for a house cleaning company. The company hires undocumented workers, pays them very low cash wages, and threatens to turn them in to Immigration and Customs Enforcement (ICE) if they complain. The job bosses also exploit their female workers sexually, threatening to turn them in if they do not comply. Elicia was fearful about applying for other jobs because of her illegal status. She considered turning to sex work to be able to take care of her children, but her Catholic upbringing and thoughts of how doing so would shame her family have kept her from doing so. She is in constant fear of being detained, separated from Maria, and having her placed in foster care. She is also afraid that she will end up homeless again and forced to live on the streets or return to her abusive husband.

Elicia is extremely reluctant to sign up for any federally funded services, even those that she and her child are entitled to receive. On the suggestion that she enroll for supplemental food through Supplemental Nutrition Assistance Program (SNAP), Elicia became nervous and refused, as she has heard that participation in SNAP services, and others like them, would draw the attention of ICE, and she had heard stories on the news of individuals being deported after signing up for such programs.

Presenting Problems

Elicia and her child are facing multiple obstacles. They need to find permanent, affordable housing and a job that pays enough to cover her housing and living expenses. In addition, Maria needs to be enrolled in school.

Additionally, Elicia is experiencing an immense amount of stress, anxiety, and possibly post-traumatic stress disorder (PTSD). She described an instance where she could not calm down her breathing and she felt lightheaded. She is very fearful of men and tries to avoid all contact with men in the community. She reports difficulty sleeping at night and feeling exhausted most of the time.

(continued)

> **CASE SUMMARY UNDOCUMENTED AND HOMELESS (*CONTINUED*)**
>
> She is concerned about Maria. Maria has started acting out at the shelter, getting into fights with the other children, disobeying her mother, and being disrespectful and defiant to the staff and other adults. Elicia and Maria fight frequently, and when Elicia tries to discipline Maria, she throws a temper tantrum until Elicia gives up.
>
> Elicia has many strengths. She had the strength to leave her abusive husband and move to a different city. She loves her daughter and wants desperately to keep Maria with her. She is resilient and has managed to survive and keep her daughter safe despite not having a place to stay or a job and a limited support network. Elicia feels safe in the shelter, but she is very fearful of being caught as an illegal immigrant and is generally mistrustful of helping professionals and persons of authority.

DISCUSSION QUESTIONS

1. What is a possible issue facing Jackie that comes under ethical responsibilities to clients?
2. What is a possible issue facing Jackie that comes under ethical responsibilities as a professional?
3. What is a possible issue facing Jackie that comes under ethical responsibilities to the broader society?
4. What is a possible ethical dilemma facing Jackie, and how would you resolve it?
5. What social justice issues are relevant to Elicia's case?

A robust set of instructor resources designed to supplement this text is located at http://connect.springerpub.com/content/book/978-0-8261-6683-8. Qualifying instructors may request access by emailing textbook@springerpub.com.

KEY REFERENCES

Only key references appear in the print edition. To access the full reference list, visit www.springerpub.com/courseconnect. See inside front cover and tear-out card for CourseConnect details.

Bayne-Smith, M., Mizrahi, T., Korazim-Kőrösy, Y., & Garcia, M. (2014). Professional identity and participation in interprofessional community collaboration. *Issues in Interdisciplinary Studies, 32*, 103–133.

Caras, A. (2013). Ethics and supervision process: Fundamentals of social work practice. *Procedia – Social and Behavioral Sciences, 92*(10), 133–141. https://doi.org/10.1016/j.sbspro.2013.08.649

Caras, A., & Sandu, A. (2014). The role of supervision in professional development of social work specialists. *Journal of Social Work Practice, 28*(1), 75–94. https://doi.org/10.1080/02650533.2012.763024

Chechak, D. (2015). Social work as a value-based profession: Value conflicts and implications for practitioner's self-concepts. *Journal of Values and Ethics, 12*(2), 41–48. https://www.jswve.org/wp-content/uploads/2015/12/10-012-206-JSWVE-2015.pdf

Congress, E. (2000). What social workers should know about ethics: Understanding and resolving practice dilemmas. *Advances in Social Work, 1*(1), 1–25. https://doi.org/10.18060/124

Gough, J., & Spencer, E. (2014). Ethics in action: An exploratory survey of social worker's ethical decision making and value conflicts. *Journal of Social Work Values and Ethics, 11*(2), 23–40. https://api.semanticscholar.org/CorpusID:155030834

Loue, S. (2016). Ethical use of electronic media in social work practice. *Romanian Journal for Multidimensional Education, 8*(2), 21–30. https://doi.org/10.18662/rrem/2016.0802.02

Osteen, P. J. (2011). Motivations, values, and conflict resolution: Student's integration of personal and professional identities. *Journal of Social Work Education, 47*(3), 423–444. https://doi.org/10.5175/JSWE.2011.200900131

Valutis, S., & Rubin, D. (2016). Value conflicts in social work: Categories and correlates. *Journal of Social Work Values and Ethics, 13*(1), 11–24. https://www.jswve.org/wp-content/uploads/2016/01/10-013-104-JSWVE-2016.pdf

West, A., Miller, S., & Leitch, J. (2016). Professional socialization and attitudes towards interprofessional collaboration among graduate social work and health professionals. *Advances in Social Work, 17*(2), 134–150. https://doi.org/10.18060/19809

4   Advancing Human Rights and Social, Racial, Economic, and Environmental Justice

Frankie was a second-year master of social work (MSW) student doing her placement at a community action agency in a small eastern city that has high levels of poverty and a large minority population. A few months in to her placement, Frankie began to hear complaints from her clients about health issues that were cropping up within families and the community. The school health nurse was raising concerns about the number of children she was seeing who had asthma as well as the number of children with learning difficulties and exhibiting sluggishness and fatigue. The residents were concerned about the waste treatment plant that processed all the garbage and waste for all the surrounding communities and about the presence of lead paint in most of the aging housing stock, which might be causing the health and behavioral issues with their children. Based on her clients' concerns, Frankie decided to do a little research to gather recent health data from the community to try and see if there was a link between the environmental issues and health problems in the community.

Frankie's initial research found some public health data that showed higher rates of asthma in the city than in the surrounding, more affluent communities. She also found data that indicated that a very large percentage of the residences in the city had been built in the 1940s, which pointed to the presence of lead paint in many of the homes. Frankie and her field instructor concluded that there was sufficient evidence proving there was an environmental justice issue that needed to be addressed. They decided to begin organizing a community group of residents and service providers to address the community health concerns and their possible environmental causes.

LEARNING OBJECTIVES

This chapter focuses on Competency 2: Advance Human Rights and Social, Racial, Economic, and Environmental Justice. The chapter begins with a review of the National Association of Social Workers (NASW) ethical principles and standards that address human rights and social justice. This is followed by a discussion of Maslow's theory of motivation and hierarchy of need. We then review theories of justice and Rawls's theory of distributive justice. Discussion of universal human rights and human rights violations is followed by a review of the various forms of oppressions and the types and sources of power, social processes, and conflicts. The chapter concludes with a discussion of justice-informed practice, anti-oppressive practice (AOP) and a human rights policy issue. By the end of this chapter, you will be able to:

- Connect social justice issues with the NASW *Code of Ethics* (2021).
- Recognize the importance of advancing social, racial, economic, and environmental justice.
- Understand the conceptual theories and frameworks for social justice work.

- Describe the various forms of oppression.
- Understand the facets of power and social aspects that contribute to injustices in these areas.
- Utilize change strategies to implement social justice and anti-oppressive approaches in your social work practice.
- Explain how AOP intersects with human rights and social justice.

COMPETENCY 2: ADVANCING HUMAN RIGHTS AND SOCIAL, RACIAL, ECONOMIC, AND ENVIRONMENTAL JUSTICE

Social workers understand that every person regardless of position in society has fundamental human rights such as freedom, safety, privacy, an adequate standard of living, healthcare, and education. Social workers understand the global interconnections of oppression and human rights violations and are knowledgeable about theories of human need and social justice and strategies to promote social, racial, and economic justice and human rights. Social workers understand strategies designed to eliminate oppressive structural barriers to ensure that social goods, rights, and responsibilities are distributed equitably and that civil, political, environmental, economic, social, and cultural human rights are protected. Social workers:

- apply their understanding of social, racial, economic, and environmental justice to advocate for human rights at the individual and system levels; and
- engage in practices that advance social, racial, economic, and environmental justice.

This chapter focuses on human rights issues, justice issues, and social work practice from a social justice and anti-oppressive perspective.

NATIONAL ASSOCIATION OF SOCIAL WORKERS *CODE OF ETHICS*

The NASW *Code of Ethics* (2021) has three ethical principles and two ethical standards that address human rights and social, racial, economic, and environmental justice. The first value is service and its associated ethical principle of addressing social problems. The second is social justice and its associated ethical principle of challenging injustice. The third is dignity and worth of the person and its associated ethical principle of respecting the inherent dignity and worth of the person (NASW, 2021). The ethical standards come under responsibilities to clients and the call for cultural competence, as well as the responsibilities to the broader society and the call for social and political action (NASW, 2021).

The social, racial, and political focuses on equal access to resources, employment, services and opportunities to meet basic human needs; expanding choice and opportunity for all people; promoting policies that safeguard peoples' rights; and preventing exploitation and discrimination against anyone based on their race, ethnicity, national origin, color, sex, sexual orientation, gender identity or expression, age, marital status, political belief, religion, immigration status, or mental or physical ability (NASW, 2021).

4: Advancing Human Rights and Social, Racial, Economic, and Environmental Justice

Clearly, the NASW *Code of Ethics* addresses the social work competency on advancing human rights and social, racial, economic and environmental justice. Social justice is a core social work value and an important component of social work practice. It is impossible to truly practice in line with these ethical principles and standards without utilizing an AOP framework at every level. This is because this competency explicitly names an understanding of AOP-related concepts of position in society, oppression, racism, power, and privilege as necessary components of achieving these aims. In fact, ". . . eliminat[ing] oppressive structural barriers. . ." is explicitly named as well (Council on Social Work Education [CSWE], 2022, p. 9).

MASLOW'S THEORY OF MOTIVATION (HUMAN NEED)

Maslow's theory of motivation (1943) is applicable to any discussion of human rights and social, racial, economic, and environmental justice. His hierarchy of human needs is shown in Figure 4.1.

There are five levels of need. The first four levels (lower-order needs) are considered physiological needs, while the top fifth level of the pyramid is considered growth needs. The needs are hierarchical. Lower-level needs must be satisfied before the next level of need or needs can influence behavior. The two lowest levels of need are physiological and safety. Physiological includes air, food, water, shelter, and sleep. Safety needs include security and stability. Security and safety include personal, emotional, and financial security as well as health and well-being. These two basic levels of need are survival needs and as such are fundamental human rights. People for whom these needs are not adequately met often face

FIGURE 4.1 Maslow's hierarchy of human needs.

overwhelming social, racial, economic, and/or environmental injustice. Not being able to satisfy these basic human needs is a violation of a person's human rights and an act of oppression by those with the power and resources to correct the injustice.

THEORIES OF SOCIAL JUSTICE

Social justice is a broad concept that encompasses fair and unbiased treatment of all individuals, eradication of discriminatory practices and institutionalized oppression, and establishment of equality for members of historically marginalized and oppressed groups—achieved through the establishment of truly equal opportunity and access to resources (Barsky, 2010; Reisch, 2002; Young, 2001). The CSWE addresses the social justice mandate by stating that "the purpose of social work is actualized through its quest for social, racial, economic, and environmental justice; the creation of conditions that facilitate the realization of human rights; the elimination of poverty; and the enhancement of life for all people, locally and globally" (2022, p. 14), and specifically calls upon all social workers to address "the global intersecting and ongoing injustices throughout history that result in oppression and racism, including social work's role and response; advocate for and engage in strategies . . . to ensure that social resources, rights, and responsibilities are distributed equitably and that civil, political, economic, social, and cultural human rights are protected [. . .]; and engage in practices that advance social, racial, economic, and environmental justice" (2022, p. 9).

The meanings of social justice have wide implications, yet can be ambiguous, and interpretation into practice is challenging. It is important to remember that the concept of social justice is bound by context and history. Attempts to define the correct relationship between individuals, communities, states, and countries have been explored for centuries by philosophers, political theorists, and social workers (Finn & Jacobson, 2017). The notion of social justice within the field of social work is generally based on Western ideologies and the Judeo-Christian religious tradition (Finn & Jacobson, 2017). Beliefs around social justice are generally abstract and are in line with what is moral and/or right—with a specific focus on the notion that all citizens are equal and have the right to meet their basic needs, the desire to share opportunities as equitably as possible, and the obligation to work toward eliminating unjustified inequalities. Caputo (2002) points out that while many notions of social justice within social work actually maintain the status quo, it still remains important as a goal of social work.

Some scholars examine social justice through the always-present tension that exists between individual liberty and the common good. These scholars would argue that social justice is endorsed to the degree that we can promote collective good without violating basic individual freedoms (Finn & Jacobson, 2017). Others contend that social justice incorporates fairness within fundamental rights and duties, economic opportunities, and social conditions (Miller, 1976).

Distributive Justice

A perspective often utilized by social work and in line with AOP is that of a distributive approach to social justice—advocating for an organization of societal institutions that assures human rights and access to meaningful social participation, as well as equitable distribution of resources. Distributive justice focuses on what society owes an individual. Other frameworks focus on what people owe society—legal justice, and what individuals owe one another—commutative justice (Reichert, 2003; Van Soest, 1995).

Social work generally addresses the conflicting philosophical frameworks used to explain choices in the realm of social justice using three dominant theories: utilitarian, libertarian, and egalitarian (Finn & Jacobson, 2017). Utilitarian theories consider decisions that result in greater good and less harm for the most people to be the appropriate course of action. The right of the individual is deemed less important than the needs of the community or society at large, and as such, those rights may be infringed upon if a particular decision results in assisting the greater good (McCormick, 2003). Libertarian perspectives focus on individual freedom from external control or influence. This framework rejects the concept of equitable resource distribution, instead arguing that individuals have the right to any resources they acquire as long as no law is broken (Nozick, 1974). Clearly, this is in direct contrast to the utilitarian perspective, as the obligation to society lies in the protection of individual freedoms. Finally, egalitarian theoretical frameworks argue that everyone should be guaranteed the same rights, opportunities, and access to goods and resources (Rawls, 1971). This approach is in line with AOP, as it advocates for the redistribution of resources to the vulnerable, oppressed, or disadvantaged in society to guarantee that unmet needs are rectified (Rawls, 1971).

Political philosopher Rawls (2001) examines what would need to be present in a society that meets basic human needs, reduces excessive stress, encourages individuals' abilities, and reduces threats to well-being. Rawls advocates for an equal distribution of resources and burdens from tangible resources (good and services) and intangible resources (power and opportunity). Social justice comes down to two principles (Rawls, 2001, pp. 42–43):

- Each person has the same indefeasible claim to a fully adequate scheme of equal basic liberties, which is compatible with the same scheme of liberties for all; and
- Social and economic inequalities are to satisfy two conditions: First, they are to be attached to offices and positions open to all under conditions of fair equality of opportunity, and second, they are to be to the greatest benefit of the least advantaged members of society (the difference principle).

Distributive justice as defined by Rawls helps the field of social work to integrate social justice and AOP approaches in both micro- and macrolevel practice settings (Wakefield, 1988). This theoretical framework focuses on counteracting inequalities by advocating for unequal distribution of resources only if it is done to advance the least advantaged groups in society (Reisch, 1998).

OPPRESSION AND HUMAN RIGHTS VIOLATIONS

Unfortunately, in the United States and throughout the world, there are large numbers of homeless people, people with insufficient food, people with inadequate and unsafe drinking water, people living with dangerous air pollution, and people living in environmentally unsafe areas. Also, large numbers of people are unsafe in their homes and neighborhoods, living in poverty with inadequate incomes as well as inadequate access to healthcare.

Article 25 of The Universal Declaration of Human Rights (UDHR) states that "everyone has the right to a standard of living adequate for the health and well-being of himself and of his family, including food, clothing, housing and medical care and necessary social services, and the right to security in the event of unemployment, sickness, disability, widowhood, old age or other lack of livelihood in circumstances beyond his control" (United Nations, 2018a, Article 25, para. 1). These fundamental human rights are not being met for a large number of people here and around the globe. This is a humanitarian and human rights crisis in the midst of unprecedented wealth and prosperity. "The best survey data show that the share of wealth held by the top 1% rose from just under 30% in 1989 to nearly 39% in 2016, while the share held by the bottom 90% fell from just over 33% to less than 23% over the same period" (Stone et al., 2018, para. 1). The income/wealth gap between the very wealthy and the rest of the population has widened, increasing inequality and social, economic, and environmental injustice. In fact, an even greater increase in the overall wealth of the 1% began during the COVID-19 pandemic, with this segment of society accumulating an additional $15 trillion since that time (Frank, 2024).

In addition to the large numbers of people lacking the minimum standard of living, many other human rights violations are occurring globally. Some examples from the Amnesty International's 2009 *World Report* are shown here for five regions of the world:

- *Africa:* Armed conflict and insecurity in several African countries forced hundreds of thousands of people to flee from their homes, trying to find international protection across borders or some form of security within their own country. In some of the worst armed conflicts still affecting the region, government forces and armed groups completely disregarded the dignity and physical integrity of the population. The civilian population was routinely the object of attacks by parties to the conflict; rape and other forms of sexual violence remained widespread; children were often recruited to take part in hostilities; and humanitarian workers were targeted (p. 3).
- *The Americas:* Laws to improve respect for women's rights and, in particular, the right to freedom from violence in the home, community, and workplace, exist in most countries in the region, with the notable exceptions of Haiti and some other Caribbean countries. Nicaragua and Haiti stood out in the region as two countries where more than 50% of all reported victims of sexual abuse were 18 years old or younger. In the vast majority of cases, the perpetrators were adult men, many holding positions of power. The sexual abuse of girls, some as young as 9 or 10, was intrinsically linked to poverty, deprivation, and exclusion, which left the girls at risk of sexual exploitation as their only means of survival. Despite the widespread nature of the problem, the stigma associated with sexual violence condemned many survivors to silence (p. 13).
- *The Asia-Pacific region:* Even where ethnic discrimination did not give rise to armed conflict, it remained a common feature of the social landscape in the Asia-Pacific region, from the wealthiest societies to the most impoverished. For example, China's large ethnic minorities in the west of the country, in Tibetan-populated areas, and the predominantly Muslim province of the Xinjiang Uighur Autonomous Region continued to suffer systematic discrimination (pp. 26–27).

- *Europe and Central Asia:* Those already in poverty continued to lack access to many basic needs. Despite the festering economic crisis, Europe was home to some of the wealthiest countries in the world in 2008. It also, however, housed serious failings in the implementation of its inhabitants' rights to education, healthcare, and secure housing and livelihoods. Across the region, the divide between rich and poor remained gaping, and from either side of that divide, the experience of accessing human rights was markedly different (p. 31).
- *Middle East and North Africa:* Women within the region faced additional insecurity through discrimination under the law and in practice, and violence, often at the hands of their male relatives. At its most acute, such violence saw women killed in so-called honor crimes, as in Iraq, Jordan, the Palestinian Authority, and Syria. Women migrant domestic workers were particularly vulnerable to sexual and other abuse by employers, as they were often unprotected by labor laws (p. 43).

In the United States, Amnesty International (2009, p. 348) reported:

- Racial, ethnic and national minorities, especially Latino and African American people, were disproportionately concentrated in poor residential areas characterized by substandard housing conditions, limited employment opportunities, inadequate access to healthcare facilities, underresourced schools, and high exposure to crime and violence.
- Marginalized and poor women were at higher risk of death and complications from pregnancy and childbirth, with the maternal mortality rate among African American women three times higher than that of White women.
- Native American and Alaska Native women continued to experience disproportionately high levels of sexual violence and inadequate access to support and justice. There were some welcome measures to address this issue.

These examples are just a few of the many human rights violations that are occurring around the world. Most, if not all, human rights violations involve some form of oppression of vulnerable people at the hands of more powerful individuals or groups. It is beyond the scope of this textbook to detail all the types of human rights violations that occur on a daily basis in the United States and around the globe.

> The UDHR resolution was approved by the United Nations in 1948. Since its passage, the UDHR has spawned many other international treaties, including the International Convention on the Elimination of All Forms of Racial Discrimination (179 [states]); the International Convention on the Elimination of All Forms of Discrimination Against Women (189 [states]); the United Nations Convention on the Rights of the Child (196 [states]); and the United Nations Convention Against Torture (162 [states]). (United Nations, 2018b, para. 4)

While there has been some progress during the past 70-plus years, human rights violations continue to be a significant issue for millions of people worldwide. The United Nations Human Rights Office's 70th Anniversary Report on the UDHR highlighted the following ongoing human rights challenges:

- 880 million people today live in urban slums.
- 1 in 10 children worldwide are still engaged in child labor.

- 65 million men, women, and children were forced from their homes by war and persecution in 2015, which is 1 in every 113 people.
- 101 journalists were killed in 2016: 1 death every 4 days.
- Almost 1 in 3 people in detention are held without being tried or sentenced for a crime.
- 59 million children were not in primary school in 2014; 52% of these were girls.
- Women represent only 24% of national parliaments.
- 700 million women today were married before age 18; 250 million were married before age 15. (United Nations, 2018b, para. 5)

GLOBAL INTERCONNECTIONS

The world has become increasingly interconnected. Events that happen in one part of the world are known instantly throughout the rest of the world. Social media connects people in many different ways and platforms. The flow of news media is constant, going 24/7, and the number of media outlets is constantly expanding. However, in terms of human rights and oppression, the biggest threat comes from business and the global economy.

We live in a global economy. For the most part, countries trade with each other, and businesses can operate where they want. Many would agree that this globalized world has created jobs and helped grow the economy as a whole. However, certain economic decisions can violate human rights and increase oppression. For example, if a business decides to expand internationally and invest in projects that enforce child labor or utilize sweatshops with dangerous working conditions that do not pay workers a livable wage, that business is responsible for the violation of human rights. This situation is not uncommon, and many corporations have come under scrutiny for supporting unjust, unsafe, and oppressive working environments.

"Although many governments and people have benefited from globalization, the key human rights issue is who benefits the most from globalization and who defines its goals or rules" (Reichert, 2011, p. 184). If a company closes a factory in the United States and shifts production to China, where it is cheaper to produce the product with fewer regulations, who benefits? The winners in this case are the company executives and shareholders and those in China who receive profits from the investment. The Chinese workers benefited from having jobs, but they may also be experiencing oppression with nonlivable wages and hazardous working environments. The factory operating with few regulations may be contributing to air and water pollution, which affects all the residents of the area. Also, the U.S. employees are losers in that they have lost their means of employment, healthcare, and other benefits. The closing of the factory also negatively impacted the economic and social well-being of the community.

On the question of who defines the goals or rules, in this case it is the Chinese government and the executives of the U.S. company. They define the goals, and they are the beneficiaries of the decision to move the production operations. The workers from both countries do not play any role in the decision, yet their lives are greatly impacted.

The human rights argument is that the globalization of the economy has created human rights violations and increased oppression. In the previous example, the U.S. workers experience economic hardships and the community where the factory was located also experiences economic and social challenges. Articles 23 and 25 of the UDHR address the situation described. Article 23 states that "everyone has the right to work, to free choice of employment, to just and favorable conditions of work and to protection against unemployment" (United Nations, 2018a, Article 23, para. 1). Article 25 states that "everyone has the right to a standard of living adequate for the health and well-being of himself and of his family, including food, clothing, housing and medical care and necessary social services, and the right to security in the event of unemployment, sickness, disability, widowhood, old age or other lack of livelihood in circumstances beyond his control" (United Nations, 2018a, Article 25, para. 1). Both of these human rights would have been violated by the company's decision to close the U.S. factory and move its production facility to a county with lower wages and fewer regulations. Both articles also apply to the Chinese government's approval of the factory, the working conditions, and the negative impact the factory has on the environment and living conditions of the community.

The interconnectedness of the global economy has created numerous human rights violations worldwide. Another significant form of oppression and global human rights violation is human trafficking. Data on the extent of international trafficking of women and young girls are difficult to obtain. The United Nations Office on Drugs and Crime (UNODC) 2009 *Global Report on Trafficking in Persons* found that the most common form of human trafficking is sexual exploitation (79%), followed by forced labor (18%); about 66% of the victims were women and about 13% were girls (p. 11). "Much of the cross-border trafficking activity was between countries of the same general region, particularly between neighboring countries. But there was also evidence of intercontinental trafficking" (UNODC, 2009, p. 11). Long-distance trafficking included:

> the trafficking of African victims to locations in Europe and North America; the trafficking of Latin American victims to North America and Europe; the trafficking of Central European, Eastern European and Central Asian victims to Europe and the Middle East; and the trafficking of South Asian victims to the Middle East. (p. 11)

In the United States "in 2006 victims originated mainly from Latin America and the Caribbean (62%), Africa, Asia, Europe and the Pacific Islands. In 2007 certified victims originated mainly from Latin America and the Caribbean (41%), Asia (41%), Europe and the Pacific Islands" (UNODC, 2009, p. 137).

FORMS OF OPPRESSION

As discussed earlier in the chapter, oppression is the result of inequities in power that allow groups in power to act out their biases, prejudices, and stereotypes in ways that deprive those not in power full access to resources, self-actualization, and autonomy (Thomas & Schwartzbaum, 2017).

There are many ways in which oppression, discrimination, and prejudice are seen in everyday life: prejudicial talk, avoidance of certain groups or individuals, segregation or exclusion in social systems (e.g., employment, education), violence to person or property, exploitation, marginalization (exclusion from social life), cultural imperialism (repressing the nondominant groups norms and values), and organized extermination of a group of people based on their membership (Allport, 1954, as cited in Thomas & Schwartzbaum, 2017; Young, 1990). Social workers will be able to identify the ways that these oppressive actions take place on micro, mezzo, and macro levels. Daily microaggressions (common, regularly occurring humiliations—intentional or not, based on stereotypes and prejudices as defined by Sue et al., 2007), imbalances of power within interpersonal relationships, and systemic institutional and cultural discrimination and exclusions deny individuals the ability to be seen, and see themselves, as spiritually, mentally, and emotionally whole.

The damaging effects of oppression reach their height when individuals begin to internalize the negative stereotypes about the group they have membership in (Sue & Sue, 2012). Internalization of oppression can manifest itself in a variety of ways that can include self-hatred, engaging in self-harming behaviors, and acting in ways that are in accordance with the stereotypical messages they have received, among others. Kagan and Burton (2005) argue that the helplessness that many oppressed individuals feel is also a form of internalized oppression—they have internalized the dominance of those in power and are rendered incapable, helpless, and powerless. While some are able to prevent this internalization through the coping skills they have developed, others are overwhelmed by the ongoing assault on their sense of self. Because of this, social workers must remember to utilize an ever-present lens of culture and oppression when working with clients. The next section will define the ways in which individuals are often targets for oppression—this list is not exhaustive.

Racism

Racism is pervasive, is rooted in assumptions of superiority based on race, is deeply infused in the history of the United States, and requires the critical attention of all social workers (Rodgers, 2015). As overt racism (legalized segregation, lynching, etc.) became less acceptable during the civil rights era, the acting out of racist ideologies evolved into a more concealed form of racism that is persistent in the institutions of society. The resulting policies create unequal outcomes for people of color, including higher rates of incarceration; unequal access to financial, employment, and educational resources; inequity in representation; disparities in health outcomes; and more (Rodgers, 2015). A very important and often confusing concept is color-blind racism (Bonilla-Silva, 2003). Perhaps some of you reading this passage were even coached as children to "see people, not color." While regularly well-intentioned, claiming to not see people with regard to their race is actually an exceptionally damaging approach—not acknowledging and celebrating the differences in culture imposes the dominant (White) culture on everyone, robs people of color of their cultural uniqueness and pride, and assumes that everyone has the privilege of moving through the world in the same way, with a total disregard for the impact of discrimination, oppression, and ongoing microaggression (Bonilla-Silva, 2003). Recently, the United States has experienced a significant increase in the expression of overt forms of racism, including the use of brazenly racist slogans aligned with belief systems of the Ku Klux Klan and Nazism, with the intention of inciting violence and discrimination toward people of color (Siddique & Laughland, 2017).

Xenophobia and Ethnocentrism

Often fueled by racism, xenophobia is the fear or hatred of other countries and individuals from other countries. This is often seen in conjunction with ethnocentrism—the belief that one group (ethnic, religious, or specific culture) is superior to others—and often leads to prejudice and oppression based on ethnicity, religion, or country of origin (Sue & Sue, 2012). This greatly impacts beliefs and policies around immigration and globalization. Targeting immigrants as the cause of society's ills has long been a practice in the history of the United States. Which groups of immigrants are targeted and what those forms of discrimination look like fluctuates significantly based on political and economic factors (Thomas & Schwartzbaum, 2017). However, racism often plays a role in who is most often targeted, with people of color at a greater risk of discrimination due to racial profiling. An example of this is the ongoing targeting, since the attacks of September 11, 2001, of Arab individuals, Muslim individuals, and South Asian individuals for questioning related to immigration violations (American Civil Liberties Union, 2017).

Classism

Classism is the differential treatment based on (actual or perceived) social class. Lott and Bullock (2007) point out that classism occurs both individually and institutionally. Individual classism refers to the stereotypes and prejudices that are believed about individuals living in poverty, as well as working-class individuals. Institutional classism refers to the social institutions that enact policies and procedures that negatively impact, marginalize, and harm individuals living in poverty. This can be seen in the education system, legal system, political system, and beyond. Additionally, denying the fact that class difference has systemic roots and blaming the poor for their poverty are also forms of classism (Thomas & Schwartzbaum, 2017).

Religious Oppression

The pervasive oppression based on minority religious status is the product of the intersection of the historical tradition of Christian hegemony in the United States, the unequal power relationships of minority religious groups with the Christian majority, and the often-held belief of "One True Religion." Christian beliefs and norms are hegemonic in that they are assumed status and are interwoven into society. Some examples are the addition of "In God We Trust" and the observance of Christian holidays by governmental agencies. Religious persecution based on these beliefs has resulted in violence and religious cleansing (systematic extermination of groups based on religious belief).

Sexism

Sexism is the discrimination on the basis of gender, most commonly occurring by men toward women. This form of discrimination is often rooted in a belief that women should be subservient to men and that men are superior to women intellectually (Thomas & Schwartzbaum, 2017). Traditional notions of gender link behavioral, cultural, and social characteristics to an individual's gender. Sexism and gender-based discrimination and inequality include violence; restricted access to education, economic, and governmental opportunities; resource restriction that results in health disparities; and others (Littlefield et al., 2015). Moral, religious, and cultural practices often reinforce traditional gender roles and attitudes. These beliefs are so strongly held that violence is perpetrated against those who violate them.

Challenging traditional beliefs of gender and advocating for policies that decrease gender discrimination and sexual harassment are some of the ways that discrimination based on gender can be confronted (Littlefield et al., 2015).

Homophobia, Biphobia, and Heterosexism

Homophobia is the intense fear, hatred, or dread of homosexuals and homosexuality (Moses, 1982). Biphobia is an aversion to bisexuals and bisexuality. It is important to remember that individuals of any sexual orientation can hold homophobic and biphobic beliefs. Similar to other forms of oppression, homophobia and biphobia can manifest in a variety of ways, including violence and discrimination in education, employment, and housing. State-sponsored homophobia includes practices and policies that criminalize homosexuality; governmental figures engaging in hate speech toward gay, lesbian, and bisexual individuals; and withholding certain rights and privileges (e.g., marriage, healthcare decision-making capacity) from same-sex couples. Often, many homophobic and biphobic beliefs are rooted in heterosexism (sometimes referred to as heterocentrism)—the systematic preferencing of opposite-sex sexuality and relationships (Jung & Smith, 1993). Heterosexism is pervasive in societal customs and institutions by keeping homosexuality and bisexuality invisible. Some examples include denial that bisexuality and homosexuality exist, the assumption that sexual orientation can and should be changed, hostility toward same-sex relationships (with same-sex marriage only recently becoming legally recognized nationally), the existence of sodomy laws in a third of states, and resistance to the addition of sexual orientation to nondiscrimination statutes resulting in a lack of legal protection from discrimination based on sexual orientation. Additionally, social workers often unintentionally utilize heterosexist language in service delivery to clients, such as asking a female client if she has a boyfriend or husband. Evaluating service delivery for inclusion and making changes, such as moving away from exclusive language, take intention and practice for social workers.

Transgender Oppression

Transgender oppression refers to the devaluing, discrimination, stereotyping, and violence that individuals face when their appearance or identity does not conform to conventional beliefs of gender—namely, that only two genders exist, that they are fixed at birth, and that they are determined solely by the chromosomal and anatomical sex of an individual. Common beliefs tied to transgender oppression include that transgender individuals do not actually exist, individuals presenting as gender nonconforming are doing so for an ulterior motive (e.g., attention, political motivation), and that transgender individuals are defying nature and/or are acting against the will of God. These beliefs are tied to transphobia—the disgust, fear, hatred, and disbelief in the existence of transgender and gender-nonconforming individuals (Chakraborti & Garland, 2009). Transgender oppression includes bullying, physical violence, harassment, false arrest, and sexual assault. Transgender and gender-nonconforming individuals are often discriminated against in employment, education, and healthcare settings and lack legal protection from discrimination based on the absence of gender identity in many nondiscrimination statutes. Data collected by the Federal Bureau of Investigation

(FBI) concluded that lesbian, gay, bisexual, and transgender individuals are more likely to be targets of hate crimes than any other minority group—with transgender women of color being the most frequent targets of violence (Park & Mykhyalyshyn, 2016). Transgender oppression is further reinforced throughout the social systems in the United States, most notably through transgender and gender-nonconforming invisibility. One obvious example is that most federal, state, institutional, organization, and agency forms only provide two options for gender or sex: male or female.

Ableism

Ableism is discrimination in favor of able-bodied people, the negative judgment about the capabilities of individuals with disabilities, the expression of hate for people with disabilities, and the denial of accessibility and resources (Smith et al., 2008; Thomas & Schwartzbaum, 2017). Smith et al. (2008) aptly point out that discrimination against individuals with disabilities is often characterized by the belief that they are abnormal, have some sort of deficit, need to be fixed, and cannot fully function in society. This framing of disability as deficient as opposed to difference has resulted in the ignoring of this dimension of cultural competence (Smith et al., 2008). Discrimination based on ableism manifests as discrimination in employment (most specifically, the rejection of disabled applicants for housing and jobs), failing to provide accessibility at all or beyond wheelchair ramps, using ableist language, individuals without disabilities utilizing resources allocated for those with disabilities (e.g., parking spaces, restrooms), making assumptions about an individual's disability status based on the visibility (or invisibility) of their disability, and policies and systems that, intentionally or not, keep people with disabilities in poverty.

Ageism

Ageism refers to stereotypes, prejudices, and discrimination based on age. While ageism impacts all people, older adults are greatly impacted by discrimination and prejudices around aging. Children and adolescents also experience oppression due to their age. The privileged age groups in the United States tend to be individuals in early and middle adulthood. A key aspect of ageism relates to an assumption that the privileged age group is the default, thereby structuring society around those individuals. This results in the need of the older and younger individuals in society to be ignored. It is considered one of the socially acceptable prejudices (Weir, 2023) and is not taken as seriously as other forms of discrimination even though it has the capacity to cause the same social oppression and negative impacts as other forms of oppression. Ageism is prevalent in everyday interactions, in media, in institutions, and even our own vision of ourselves. Capitalism is tied to ageism in multiple ways. First, the elevation of the Protestant work ethic and prioritization of productivity naturally result in an inferior status of children and older adults (Morelock, 2021). Second, capitalism exploits fears around aging, with the United States seeing an anti-aging market growing into a $4.9 billion industry as of 2021 (Eisenberg, 2023). What does oppression based on age look like? A significant impact of age discrimination is economic—this can look like being denied a job, being fired, being overlooked for a promotion, and experiencing workplace harassment all based on age.

In healthcare, prejudices and stereotypes impact treatment decisions, and some healthcare policies support rationing healthcare due to age. Young people are disallowed voting rights, have employment opportunities restricted, and are subjected to additional laws to limit certain activities (e.g., status offenses), regardless of their individual capacity. While there is a legitimate interest in protecting children from harm, as they are a vulnerable population, some laws go beyond what is necessary for protective measures (Todres, 2022).

TYPES AND SOURCES OF POWER

Earlier we discussed forms of oppression that exist due to inequities in power that allow dominant groups to act out their biases, prejudices, and stereotypes in ways that deprive those not in power full access to resources, self-actualization, and autonomy (Thomas & Schwartzbaum, 2017). An understanding of power is essential to AOP. Power was discussed briefly in Chapter 1, but in this section we will do a deeper dive into the types of power that exist, as well as social dimensions that contribute to these power differences.

While power is a complex term with multiple meanings depending on context, the type of power we are focused on in regard to social justice refers to power within social structure and systems. Legitimately or otherwise, certain individuals and groups have power, and with that power utilize force (of varying types) to exploit others for their own gain. The purpose of focusing on power within social relationships and societal structures is to better understand how we, as social workers, can better understand social justice advocacy and can attempt to address the connections between privilege and exploitation.

Three different types of power exist (Dobratz et al., 2012):

- *Coercive and dominant power*: Likely the most obvious use of power, coercive power uses the command of resources to dominate others into submission. For example, coercive power in the form of physical force could include military strength, brute force, violence, and so forth.
- *Authority and legitimate power*: Society creates order by acknowledging power based on tradition, norms, and laws. Authority and legitimate power is the form that arises from this acknowledgment. Members of society accept that specific individuals or groups have power based on a sense of legitimacy and obedience or duty. This type of power is able to be obtained because individuals believe that placing power in states offers protection to members of society and preserves community interests.
- *Privileged and interdependent power*: This type of power tends to be subtler, but still results in dramatic implications for social interactions and distribution of power in society. This type of power focuses specifically on the power relationship between two actors. Often, the actors do not realize exactly how much influence they have in a given situation. Piven and Cloward (2005) point out that people have potential power when others depend on them for the contributions they make to interdependent relationships that make up society. Johnson (2006) also points out that privilege links to the ways society makes differences important or significant. These include unearned advantages (one specific group is rewarded) and conferred dominance (when one group pressures another group, or groups, into conforming to that privilege) as ways that privilege is created in society.

When framing societal power within your social work practice experience, it is important to recognize that power is the ability of individuals, groups, and/or structures to attain a plan through authority, influence, or even force (Dobratz et al., 2012). This is important because it recognizes that power exists on the micro level as well as the macro level. When we are thinking about social justice and human rights, we are particularly concerned with the ways that dominant power, individually or collectively, is exploited by privileged individuals or groups. Often within the guise of preserving societal interests, certain groups end up marginalized, scapegoated, and exploited for the benefit of more powerful groups.

> ▶ **Reflection Questions**
>
> Advancing social justice and engaging in AOP requires critical self-reflection, practitioner transparency, collaboration, and respectful curiosity and humility in work with clients. It also requires that you consider the social justice implications of your interactions with clients. In reflecting upon your work with clients, describe an experience in which you identified a potential abuse of power, either by yourself, someone else, or the agency as a whole.
> 1. What were your affective reactions to this experience?
> 2. What ethical principles and standards apply to this situation?
> 3. How would you approach or respond to this situation if it were to happen again?

SOCIAL PROCESSES

Originating from sociology theories, social processes refer to the various patterns of social interactions in which individuals and groups interact and establish social relationships. Examples of different forms of social interaction include competition, cooperation, conflict, assimilation, exploitation, accommodation, and others (Ginsberg, 1956). While there are a large number of social processes (e.g., education, political, religious, economic), Ruhela (2005) argues that within the vast array of social processes, there are really only two categories they can all fall under:

- Integrative, conjunctive, or associative processes—social processes that bring the individuals and groups together to produce unity among members of a group or society. These processes take the interests of all members into account. Examples of this are cooperation and accommodation.
- Disintegrative, disjunctive, or dissociative processes—social processes that produce hatred and tension and bring disagreement among the members of a group or society. Competition, rivalry, and conflict are the main disintegrative processes.

Oppression and discrimination are embedded in the complexity of ever-changing and constant social processes.

CONFLICT

Conflict is an important social process that is a huge part of society as a whole. It is a codified form of struggle that is deliberate in its attempt to oppose or resist the will of others. Conflict is universal, ever present, and personal. While there are a multitude of theories on the origin of conflict, we do know that social change can be a direct cause of conflict, and conflict can result in social change. Conflict may seem overwhelmingly negative, due to the fact that it resists cooperation and can cause chaos, however, conflict can perform positive functions as well. It can result in a redefinition of circumstances by the conflicting individuals or groups. Generally, the groups in conflict have to give up outdated value systems and accept new value systems at the end of the conflict—this may result in new efforts of cooperation and accommodation.

There is perhaps no better-known example of using conflict in the pursuit of social justice than that documented in a passage from Martin Luther King Jr.'s *Letter From Birmingham Jail* (1963, para. 12) in which King states:

> You express a great deal of anxiety over our willingness to break laws. This is certainly a legitimate concern. Since we so diligently urge people to obey the Supreme Court's decision of 1954 outlawing segregation in the public schools, it is rather strange and paradoxical to find us consciously breaking laws. One may well ask, "How can you advocate breaking some laws and obeying others?" The answer is found in the fact that there are two types of laws: there are just laws, and there are unjust laws. I would agree with St. Augustine that "An unjust law is no law at all."

JUSTICE-INFORMED PRACTICE

So often, social justice is considered something that a social worker simply carves time out for (for instance, on something like an advocacy day), as opposed to being a framework for practice. It can be challenging to envision a practice philosophy that infuses these theories in an effort to have a human rights and social justice focus in daily work as a social worker. For example, traditional assessments in clinical practice often focus on problems, which a social construction framework will remind you are culturally and relationally bound. This opens up the possibility of seemingly endless interpretations with no one interpretation as the truth. However, the social worker can utilize collaborative approaches to seek to understand the client's theory of the problem, which helps the social worker toward collaborative solutions.

Within practice, these lenses provide the social context necessary to recognize the impacts of oppression and economic disadvantages experienced by clients. Social justice requires practitioner transparency, collaboration, and respectful curiosity and humility in work with clients. Major (2011) emphasizes how social constructions are well suited for practice with families in the child welfare system due to their emphasis on contextual meanings—so often families are judged according to the same standards as those with significantly more opportunities and resources.

Harrison et al. (2016) identify three strategies for implementing a social justice–infused practice framework even in micro-level social work practice. The first of these is increased self-awareness. Bonnycastle (2011) provides a helpful continuum for examining this critical theme of the

> ▶ **Reflection Questions**
>
> Concepts of social constructions encourage us to be critically self-reflective of the language used with clients.
>
> 1. What problematic language have you heard used with clients? Why was it problematic?
> 2. How could the situation have been approached in a justice-informed way?

self-awareness needed for effective justice-focused micro practice. This includes moving from a simple recognition that discrimination is bad to a full confrontation of the privilege the social worker holds and the impact of the social worker's practice in relation to the social locations of the clients served. This process involves overcoming the social worker's denial and struggle to change.

The second strategy discussed by Harrison et al. (2016) is justice-informed engagement, assessment, and intervention. Because of the person-in-environment perspective, social workers are better prepared to infuse justice through their micropractice skills. This includes a focus on enhancing individuals' economic, psychological, and social conditions through collaborative approaches. The quest of social justice within micropractice can be infused into many theoretical approaches and intervention models. Examples of this include client-centered and collaborative approaches; strengths-based and empowerment approaches; biopsychosocial assessment that includes a historical and political basis for social constructions; and a focus on the ways in which oppression, discrimination, and historical trauma can contribute to the development of individual difficulties.

The final strategy discussed by Harrison et al. (2016) is justice-informed policy and systems advocacy. Social workers must infuse social justice in their microlevel work by addressing social and organizational policies that perpetuate inequities. Similarly, social workers work in concert with their client toward social and economic justice, as they may begin to strive to address inequities in their own lives as their awareness of such inequities arises in their therapeutic experience (Moradi, 2012).

Reisch and Garvin (2016) stress the importance of utilizing social justice–infused approaches, especially as it relates to processes and outcomes. While you are unable to deeply scrutinize every action you take, every facial expression, every word decision, and so on, it benefits you to critically self-reflect on the implications of these social interactions with clients. You need to consider the social justice implications of such a process, including how each part of the process reveals information about power differentials; how the actions reflect considerations for the empowerment of clients and oppressive social conditions; how you have informed your work through critical self-reflection on sources of injustice; what roles you are fulfilling in your social interactions with clients and whether those are reflective of the needs and rights of others; and finally, a critical self-reflection of the potential of abuse of power.

In thinking about social justice implications in mezzo and macro levels of practice, it is important to relate the personal and the political. The concerns that clients bring in to their work with you are not due solely to individual shortcomings but also to unjust policies and practices that occur within agencies and the larger society. The driving force for social justice–infused social work practice is the skill of challenging inequalities, which creates opportunities for change. You must understand that not every mezzo and macro challenge you attempt will be successful, and the process of challenging oppressive practices and policies can be uncomfortable and tedious as you attempt to institute the challenge. The most effective and appropriate challenges need to be person-centered; use an egalitarian value approach; use empowerment approaches to assist individuals in reducing unjust policies; and, like microlevel work, focus on process and outcome (see also Case 4.1).

As an example of challenging a potential abuse of power, consider this experience. In your placement with child protection services, one of your clients, a 17-year-old foster youth, was denied a request to begin attending an after-school church youth group. The agency made this decision based on some bullying experiences the client had experienced. Upon reflection, you recognize that the agency you are working within may have misused their power under the guise of "protecting" the client from harm. You decide to challenge this decision by approaching your supervisor and explaining that you appreciate the agency's concern for the client's safety; however, you are concerned about the organization taking away the client's right to self-determination. You share with your supervisor the importance of this client,

CASE 4.1   IT'S A SHAME, REALLY: EXAMPLE OF BIAS AND INEQUITIES IN AN INSTITUTION

Bianca is a senior bachelor of social work (BSW) student completing her field placement at Prairie View Middle School, located in a low-income area in a Mid-Atlantic state. Bianca was pulled aside by Mrs. Iverson, a science teacher at the school. Mrs. Iverson has concerns about a student named Andrea, a seventh-grader who is having a difficult time turning in her homework, even though she is one of the top-performing students on the tests and in-class activities. Mrs. Iverson has tried to reach out to Andrea's parents by phone and email but has never gotten a response. Mrs. Iverson tells Bianca that she is pretty sure that Andrea's parents are unengaged and are not supporting her in her education. Mrs. Iverson says, "It's a shame, really. We see it time and again. Really bright kids with parents that just don't care about education."

Bianca decides to reach out to other teachers who have Andrea in their classes—they report a similar pattern. Bianca decides to reach out to the teachers of Andrea's younger siblings and finds out that they do not have the same issue with turning in their homework. In fact, neither of them had any missing assignments.

Perplexed, Bianca sets up an appointment to chat with Andrea. Andrea insists that she has simply "dropped the ball" and "will do better on her upcoming assignments." Bianca is unconvinced and discusses the issue with her supervisor. Her supervisor suggests a home visit. Bianca attempts to contact the parents but does not have any luck. She receives permission to drop by the home over the weekend along with her supervisor.

Bianca and her supervisor learn that Andrea's father and mother both work multiple part-time jobs to support their family, and neither of them get home until after the children are asleep. Andrea has taken on the role of caretaker for her two younger siblings, which includes assisting them on their studies and getting them dinner. Andrea simply does not have time to complete nightly homework on top of her other responsibilities.

Bianca knows that a justice-infused approach to this situation is one that advocates for equitable approaches that consider the impact of the economic conditions for the student. Bianca sets up a meeting with Mrs. Iverson, Andrea's other teachers, and her supervisors to brainstorm alternative approaches for Andrea's learning. However, she doesn't stop there—Bianca recognizes that this situation is likely happening to other students. Bianca wants to know, on an institutional level the following: What biases might be stopping teachers from trying to improve the situation for other students? How can these biases be addressed? What opportunities exist to create more equitable policies? Who needs to be at the table when brainstorming these solutions?

who is approaching the age of 18, having the opportunity to make his own decisions and not be denied the opportunity to attend an activity that may benefit him greatly. Using the NASW *Code of Ethics* as your guide, you would be able to challenge this decision in a constructive way and assert the client's right to self-determination and his right to nonoppressive service delivery from the agency.

ANTI-OPPRESSIVE PRACTICE, HUMAN RIGHTS, AND SOCIAL JUSTICE

As mentioned in previous chapters, AOP is a justice-infused framework for micro, mezzo, and macro practice (Baines & Benjamin, 2011). AOP is fundamental to human rights and social justice because anti-oppressive social work practice is meant to address social divisions and structural inequalities in the work done by clients and workers (Strier & Binyamin, 2014). AOP focuses upon a collaborative worker/client relationship, reducing inequalities in clients' lives, and reducing social hierarchies in how social workers and clients work together (Dominelli, 1996). Additionally, AOP works toward breaking down oppressive structures and practices by engaging in collaborative and client and community-centered practice at the community, institutional, and political levels. The rationale for AOP is that social work and social services need to promote nonhierarchical relationships between workers and clients and adopt structural and contextual views of clients' social problems (Baines & Benjamin, 2011). AOP recognizes inherent inequalities and the power differentials of marginalized people and groups of people.

AOP is similar to strengths-based approaches and cultural competency approaches. What sets it apart from other approaches is an analysis of power and identifying the processes by which power imbalances occur simultaneously at an individual, organizational, and systemic level, resulting in the exclusion of social groups (Wong & Yee, 2010). The power analysis recognizes that in all relationships power imbalances based on age, abilities, class, ethnicity, employment status, gender, geographic location, race, religion, sexual orientation, etc., exist and that the power imbalances are socially constructed (Wong & Yee, 2010).

Another distinguishing feature of AOP is a focus on social location. Social location is a way of expressing the core of a person's existence in the social and political world. Social locations are the groups people are a part of because of their place or position in history and society. Individuals all have a social location that is based on the intersection of all of their identities and group memberships (see Case 4.2). These identities include race, gender, ability, religion, sexual orientation, social class, age, actual geographic location, and more. Our identity, how we see the world, and how we are able to move through the world are greatly influenced by our group memberships. Specific roles, rules, power, and the existence or lack of privilege are a result of these memberships as well.

"Social location can be defined as the groups that people belong to because of their place or position in society and history. All people have a social location that is defined by their gender, race, social class, age, ability, religion, sexual orientation, geographic location, and so forth" (Wong & Yee, 2010, pp. 8–9). Those who are in the dominant group maintain privilege over marginalized groups. Each one of us has a social location that determines where we place on a continuum of privilege or marginalization in society. In our society, able-bodied persons,

CASE 4.2 — PUTTING ON A SHOW: APPLYING SOCIAL LOCATION, IDENTITY, BIAS, AND JUSTICE TO PRACTICE

Sara is a senior BSW student completing an internship at a local family service agency in a small city on the West Coast. The agency provides individual and family counseling services on a sliding fee scale. Mrs. J., a 28-year-old Latina female, has three children, Brenda, Tasha, and Darren. Mrs. J.'s children were removed due to substantiated charges of neglect. The children are aged 12, 6, and 3. The children stayed with Mrs. J.'s sister after they were removed from Mrs. J.'s care. Mrs. J. has been battling a substance use disorder, and she was unable to care for her children—their home was found to be squalid. After the removal of the children, Mrs. J. began her third attempt at completing a drug treatment program. She was successful and was reunified with the children 2 months prior.

Mrs. J. comes to weekly sessions and reports that she is doing well to maintain her sobriety. Sara spent a significant amount of time in her work discussing coping strategies for her stressors. Mrs. J. reports that the majority of her stresses include the demands of parenting three children with little support and financial stressors.

In a field seminar, one of Sara's peers, who is placed at a local middle school, shared a situation from her field placement that she was conflicted about. She stated that a student named "Jane" (not her real name) was expressing concerns about the fact that her mother had begun using marijuana at home. The personal use of marijuana is legal in the state, but it is not allowed under the conditions of the reunification agreement. This concerned "Jane" because she and her younger siblings just barely moved back in with their mom. "Jane" is very stressed that someone is going to find out and she and her siblings will be forced to move back in with her aunt.

Sara recognized the similarities in the story with her client Mrs. J. and knows that Brenda attends the same school that her peer is at for her field placement. It is clear that the young woman being described is her client's daughter.

1. Based on the information provided, what issues related to human rights and social, racial, economic, and environmental justice can you identify within this case?
2. Consider the case example in terms of social location. From the information provided, what are the different social identities that Mrs. J. may inhabit? How might these locations be influencing Mrs. J.'s construction of reality?
3. Similarly, think about Sara's social identities and social locations. How might they impact Sara's construction of reality?
4. What are some of the areas that Sara should focus her self-reflection on using a justice-infused lens?

males, Whites, employed persons, middle/upper income earners, heterosexuals, U.S. citizens, college-educated persons, English speakers, and Christians have dominant social locations of privilege. On the other hand, persons with disabilities; females; ethnic and racial minorities; gay, lesbian, bisexual, and transgender persons; noncollege-educated persons; non–English-speakers; immigrants; and non-Christians have nondominant social locations and belong to marginalized groups that are subject to the norms and values of the dominant group.

The concept of social identities is closely related to social location. Kirk and Okazawa-Rey (2010) define identity as how we define ourselves at any specific instance in time that is a process of growth, change, and renewal. Identity may seem fixed, but over the course of the life span, it is more fluid. An interplay of individual choices, particular life events, community recognition and expectations, societal categorization, classifications, and socialization all come into play in identity formation. Most definitions of identity point to the connections between us as individuals, how we are perceived by other people, and how we are classified by social institutions. "Classifying and labeling human beings, often according to real or assumed physical, biological, or genetic differences, is a way to distinguish who [is] included and who is excluded from a group, to ascribe particular characteristics" and to prescribe social locations (Kirk & Okazawa-Rey, 2010, p. 52). In sum, social location determines power and privilege, and social identity determines how one defines oneself.

At the micro level, AOP strives to change a client's perceptions about their social identity, social location, and power in the helping relationship. In essence, AOP work involves those who have privilege becoming allies of those who do not by sharing power and creating authentic collaboration (Wong & Yee, 2010). The following four self-reflection questions help incorporate AOP into micro social work practice with clients:

- In all interactions/situations, have I thought about power, privilege, and social location and how they impact my actions?
- Have I questioned/challenged dominant ways of thinking to transform power into equity?
- Have I ensured the actions I take are equitable, collaborative, and power sharing? How can I measure this?
- If yes, how can I promote these anti-oppressive actions at an institutional or systemic level? If no, what do I need to do differently? (Wong & Yee, 2010, p. 11)

These four questions can help you not take power imbalances for granted and as unquestioned norms. They will also prompt you to figure out ways you can incorporate AOP into your social work practice. Conducting power analysis in all situations and with all client interactions is the key component of effective AOP.

At the mezzo level, AOP strives to change the culture of human service organizations to reduce power imbalances, identify processes that create or promote power imbalances, and develop a collective mindset that consciously challenges and questions the status quo or the norms of the organization that foster inequalities. Change at the organizational/social service level is needed to effectively address social injustices and eliminate oppressive barriers caused by social location and power imbalances of marginalized groups. The institutions that foster the marginalization of oppressed groups must be changed if change is to occur. One way to begin to create organizational change is to

> ▶ **Reflection Questions**
>
> Charlotte is a BSW intern placed with a housing agency. Many of the clients in low-income housing face housing discrimination. Charlotte knows it is her duty to advocate for her clients both inside her agency and outside.
>
> 1. What are the potential justice-infused microlevel practice steps that Charlotte can take?
> 2. What are the mezzolevel justice-infused practice steps Charlotte can take?

conduct an anti-oppression assessment. Conducting an organizational assessment from the lens of anti-oppression will help identify organizational strengths as well as areas that need improvement (Ouvertes, 2013). Key areas to address in an anti-oppression assessment of an organization include:

- vision, mission, and purpose;
- identity, culture, and values;
- governance structure (board of directors, bylaws, and administrative structure);
- program evaluation and accountability;
- finance and fund development;
- hiring practices and staffing patterns (recruitment, retention, and promotion);
- human resources policies and procedures (training, working conditions, and complaints);
- physical environment (accessibility, location, and decorations);
- programs and services;
- work with community groups;
- internal communications; and
- external communications.

> ▶ **Reflection Questions**
>
> Consider some of the conflicts that Charlotte may encounter as she engages in the multilevel justice-infused practice you identified.
> 1. How might she work through those conflicts?
> 2. Is it Charlotte's role to bring justice-informed perspectives to her colleagues? Why or why not?

In each area of the organization, assess policies and procedures in terms of power balances and oppression. Identify areas that need to be changed, and create anti-oppression action steps to begin to implement the needed changes. For change to happen, it has to be an organization-wide effect with a collective will to make the organization less anti-oppressive. Often this requires a system-wide culture change in the organization's policies and procedures and in the mindset of the administrative, support staff, and frontline workers. Wong and Yee (2010, pp. 16–17) identified the following four recommendations for anti-oppression organizational change:

- Anti-oppression requires a change of culture reflected in the agency's work along with a focus on changes in the outcomes of child welfare.
- Anti-oppression should not be an add-on to the organization. It should be embedded in the values, mission, policies, processes, and practices in the organization at all levels.
- Anti-oppression is both a process and an outcome, where progress is measurable as demonstrated change within the organization's work.
- Agencies need to create a culture of openness and safety when implementing anti-oppression work.

The scenario in Case 4.3 demonstrates the AOP approach for caring for a child with special needs whose mother is terminally ill.

CASE 4.3 — WHAT WILL HAPPEN TO JUAN? APPLYING AN ANTI-OPPRESSIVE LENS TO SOCIAL WORK PRACTICE

Jose is a first-year MSW student completing his foundation field placement at the Hispanic Advocacy Center located in a predominately Spanish-speaking community. A community resident, Anna, contacted the center for help in dealing with child protective services. Child protective services had received a referral regarding Anna and her 11-year-old son, Juan. According to the referral information, the mother was in the last stages of terminal brain cancer and often confined to a hospital bed. The cancer had metastasized throughout her body and was not responding to treatment. Anna was becoming increasingly forgetful as a result of the repeated chemotherapy and radiation treatments, was physically weak, and was emotionally overwhelmed.

Juan had been born with fragile X syndrome and was diagnosed with mental retardation that presented intellectual as well as developmental challenges. He was recently withdrawn from school, as the family had initially planned to move to Oregon to live with Anna's sister. These plans fell through after Anna's sister found out that Anna was using marijuana to combat the side effects of her medical treatment. In addition, due to her forgetfulness, Anna often failed to give Juan his prescribed medications.

Anna and Juan were left with no money, little family support, and were living in a one-room apartment with a known drug dealer. The most recent report stated that Anna had left Juan with a friend from church with a small bag of clothes asking that he care for Juan until her condition improved. Both Anna and her friend were advised by Juan's case manager from the county's Mental Retardation Department to have Juan placed in a residential program.

Anna had been placed in a children's home as a child and remained there until she finished high school, craving contact with her extended family. After ending a physically abusive relationship with Juan's father, Anna raised Juan as a single mother. She was adamant that Juan not be placed in an institution. Fearing involvement of child protective services and the very real potential that Juan would be removed from her care, Anna dodged the caseworker's attempts at contact for several weeks. During this time, her physical condition continued to deteriorate, but she also began to gain the support of neighbors and community members who learned of her plight. An informal support network slowly embraced both Anna and Juan. Carol encouraged her to contact the Hispanic Advocacy Center for help, as it became clear that more formal plans would need to be made for Juan's ongoing care in the future.

Jose met with Anna, and together they agreed that she needed to meet with child protective services. Jose's supervisor suggested that they request a family group conference to plan for Juan's future that included other service providers in Anna's life as well as her friend and neighbors. Anna remained fearful of the intentions of the formal agencies, but strongly desired to be involved in planning for her son's future and agreed to the meeting with Jose's support. The visiting nurse, hospice social worker, and her attending physician advised against the meeting due to Anna's compromised condition, but after being assured that the meeting would be kept within a 2-hour limit, they reluctantly agreed.

(continued)

CASE 4.3 WHAT WILL HAPPEN TO JUAN? APPLYING AN ANTI-OPPRESSIVE LENS TO SOCIAL WORK PRACTICE (*CONTINUED*)

Going against protocol, the family group conference was held in the mother's apartment rather than on "neutral ground." The family group conference consisted of Anna, Jose's caseworker from the Mental Retardation Case Management Unit, Jose's school social worker, a priest from Anna's church, and the child protective services case worker. Also in attendance were Jose, Carol, and four other neighbors. Additionally, Jose arranged for an attorney from legal aid to be present.

Anna was placed on the couch by her hospice social worker and made as comfortable as possible. Her breathing was heavy, and the nurse prepared an oxygen mask. Prior to the family group conference, it was agreed that the purpose of the meeting would be to develop a plan to provide a safe and stable home for Juan for when his mother would no longer be able to do so herself. Almost immediately some of the service providers expressed their concern that the purpose was unrealistic and that child protective services would need to take custody of Juan in order for any plan to be successful. Anna was assured that while this was an option, she and her "family" could also plan around other options.

Wanting to save time, the nurse and hospice worker requested that the group forego the discussion about strengths and move directly into a discussion about the "grave" concerns facing both Anna and Juan. Jose, who was facilitating the meeting, asked Anna her preference, and the group followed the conference protocol and initiated a discussion about strengths. Throughout the discussion, the nurse and hospice worker continued to point at their watches, offering Anna medication and suggesting that she lie down. At the same time, Anna became more involved in the conversation, moving to a sitting position, and became increasingly engaged in the discussion. She expressed her surprise that in her "hopeless" situation, the group was able to identify over 30 strengths.

When the discussion turned to concerns, the service providers quickly interjected that the situation could be quickly resolved if Anna simply allowed child protective services to assume custody of Juan. Anna reminded the providers that according to the model, she would be given the opportunity to express her concerns first. Two main themes surfaced. Anna acknowledged that she was often unable to care for Juan and herself and identified that persons would need to be available to assist on a daily basis. Second, and just as important, an identified guardian had not been established for Juan, and clear steps would need to be taken to accomplish this task. The group was shocked at her honesty as well as the passion with which she expressed herself.

Although the first phase of the meeting lasted well over an hour and a half, Anna remained committed to the process over the objections of her nurse. After listening to the resources available through all of the formal systems, the services providers, with the exception of the hospice worker, the nurse, and the legal aid attorney, left the room while Anna and her friends along with Jose met together for another hour to address the concerns. After several interruptions regarding the length of the meeting, Anna asked her nurse and hospice worker to leave the room and wait in the hallway with the other service providers.

(continued)

| CASE 4.3 | **WHAT WILL HAPPEN TO JUAN? APPLYING AN ANTI-OPPRESSIVE LENS TO SOCIAL WORK PRACTICE (*CONTINUED*)** |

Unexpectedly, a detailed plan emerged, including an emergency contact list and a 24-hour schedule of support to maintain Anna in her home. It was agreed that Juan would remain in the family home as long as possible. When the need arose to move him, a family friend was identified as his permanent caretaker. Respite caregivers were also identified. The plan included detailed steps outlining how the legal transfer of custody would take place. In presenting their plan, it became apparent that Anna and her family had addressed almost all of the potential problematic issues that could arise in the future regarding Juan's care. At the end of the meeting, Anna addressed the group, thanking them for the opportunity to plan for her son's future. Anna explained the importance of being able to admit to herself that she was no longer able to care for Juan independently, a fact she refused to acknowledge when questioned in the past.

A month after Anna's death, Juan's mental retardation case manager contacted child protective services requesting that the agency assume custody of Juan. The case manager was referred to the family group conference plan, which was being implemented. Juan's well-being was assured by Carol and other members of the "family group" as previously arranged. Over the next several months, similar calls were received. Each concern was addressed by referring back to the plan that continued to work well for Juan.

1. What aspects of Jose's handling of Anna's case were consistent with an AOP approach?
2. What could have Jose done to strengthen his work with Anna in terms of AOP strategies?
3. What do you think would have happened to Anna and Juan if Jose and the Hispanic Advocacy Center had not been involved?
4. Compare the motivations and concerns of the nurse and hospice social worker with Jose's motivations and concerns? How are the similar? How do they differ?

POLICY ISSUE

A policy issue associated with the human rights and social, racial, economic, and environmental justice competency concerns recent changes to U.S. immigration policy. Early in 2018, the Trump administration implemented a new "zero-tolerance" policy to prosecute immigrants attempting entry into the United States. Part of this policy requires that children—including babies and toddlers—be separated from their parents; children are taken into temporary custody, while their parents are jailed or deported. In many cases, neither party is informed of the whereabouts of the other—they are simply torn apart and taken to undisclosed locations (Center for the Study of Social Policy, 2018, para. 1).

Between May 5 and June 9 in 2018 over 2,300 children were separated from their parents at the U.S.-Mexican border and placed in detention (Huffington Post, 2018). The children have been held in over 100 facilities scattered over 17 states. Children get their own case in immigration court and are entitled to a full hearing by an immigration judge, a process that can take months. Their parents are either prosecuted or deported separately. Often the parent was deported without their children. "This policy is utterly inhumane both for the immediate pain that it inflicts on the families and also for the long-term harm it will cause for the children. Research makes clear that the experiences of traumatic events—like being forcibly separated from your parent, thrown into a makeshift encampment, and given zero information about your situation or your family's whereabouts—can have lifelong negative consequences" (Center for the Study of Social Policy, 2018, para. 2).

> ▶ **Reflection Thinking Questions**
>
> 1. What NASW ethical principles and standards conflict with the "zero-tolerance" policy?
> 2. How does the "zero-tolerance" policy fit with your personal values regarding immigration?
> 3. As a social worker, what could you do to help change U.S. immigration policy?

The U.S. practice of separating families through detention and deportation is at odds with its obligations under the International Covenant on Civil and Political Rights (ICCPR), which recognizes "family as the natural and fundamental group unit of society" and assures protections of family rights and family unity, and its failure to consider the interests of the children of those facing deportation violates the right of the child to special protection, as guaranteed by the Convention on the Rights of the Child (CRC; Cordero et al., 2020).

A 2018 Department of Homeland Security (DHS) report on the "zero-tolerance" policy concluded:

- DHS was not fully prepared to implement the policy or deal with its after-effects.
- Customs and Border Protection (CBP) authorities broke the law and detained children for illegal amounts of time at facilities meant for short-term holding.
- A lack of communication between government agencies rendered officials unable to locate children's parents when they sought to reunite them.
- Parents were given misinformation about how (and if) they could reunite with their children.
- Policies at overwhelmed official ports of entry compelled many asylum seekers to attempt illegal border crossings. (Office of the Inspector General, 2018)

The Trump administration's zero-tolerance policy resulted in the United States breaking its own laws and in violating international human rights treaties. After a period of about 2 months President Trump signed an executive order to end the practice of separating immigrant children from their parents. His compromise was to detain entire families together. U.S. immigration policies and enforcement procedures continue to raise serious concerns about the violation of basic human rights of immigrants and those seeking asylum.

SUMMARY

As we already know, several of the issues facing people you work with are rooted in oppressive and far-reaching social, political, economic, and environmental conditions. Simultaneously, much of the assistance we as social workers are able to provide is done at an individual level. We must resist the urge to assume that the majority of problems are personal rather than a reflection of wider societal and structural problems. This chapter focused on different concepts related to injustices at multiple levels. First, conceptual and theoretical concepts around social justice were explored. This section focused on how social justice calls for the fair and unbiased treatment of all individuals, eradication of discriminatory practices and institutionalized oppression, and establishment of equality for members of historically marginalized and oppressed groups.

Competency 3 focuses on advancing human rights and social, racial, economic, and environmental justice. As a social worker, you are trained to keep the person-in-environment perspective as you engage with your clients. This uniquely positions you to maintain an anti-oppressive, justice-informed framework in your work. You must move beyond the understanding that discrimination is bad and move toward a full confrontation of your own power and privilege and how they impact the clients you wish to serve. You are also expected to recognize the impacts of oppression and economic disadvantages experienced by clients. Social justice and AOP require practitioner transparency, collaboration, and respectful curiosity and humility in work with clients. An understanding that social constructions are well suited for anti-oppressive and justice-informed practice due to their emphasis on contextual meanings is vital. It helps you to identify the ways in which individuals, families, and groups are judged on unbalanced standards. Advancing human rights and social justice is an ongoing, intentional process that is actively infused in every aspect of practice, not simply something that the social worker does on the side with their free time.

The final section of this chapter explores strategies for you to infuse an anti-oppressive and justice lens into your practice in the field. All of these strategies require intentional, critical self-reflection on the choices you make, the language you use, and the ways you, and others, are potentially abusing your power. Multiple theoretical frameworks and intervention models lend themselves to justice-informed practice, if you are intentional about applying them in such a way.

CASE SUMMARY: UNDOCUMENTED AND HOMELESS

Practice Setting Description

Jackie is a first-year MSW student completing an internship at an inner-city family service agency in the Southwest. The agency is located in a section of the city that has a high crime rate, gang activity, and failing schools. The area has a diverse population with a large number of immigrants from Central and South America and a substantial African American population. The agency provides individual and family counseling services on a sliding fee scale. The agency also runs a number of educational and treatment groups as well as a temporary shelter for women and their children. Jackie has been assigned to work with the women and their children in the shelter. Her primary tasks are to provide concrete services and supportive counseling to the shelter residents.

Background Information

Elicia and her daughter, Maria, are undocumented immigrants from Mexico. They have been in the United States for 5 years. Elicia and Maria fled to the area from another southwestern city to escape her abusive husband approximately 2 months ago. Elicia is 25 years old and Maria

(continued)

CASE SUMMARY: UNDOCUMENTED AND HOMELESS (*CONTINUED*)

8 years old. Elicia has a 2-year old daughter, Sarah, who was placed in foster care because of suspected abuse in the home. Sarah is in a foster home in a small rural community in the state hundreds of miles from Elicia's current residence. Since moving to the area Maria has not been attending school.

Elicia and Maria are currently residing in the agency's temporary shelter for families. They have been at the shelter for 2 weeks, and the agency has a 90-day limit. Prior to arriving at the shelter, Elicia and Maria were homeless and living on the streets.

Elicia is a high school drop-out and was a stay-at-home mother prior to leaving her husband and moving to a different part of the state. She chose to move there because she has two female cousins living in the area who are also undocumented immigrants. Elicia's native language is Spanish. She speaks some English but is not as comfortable speaking in English. Her English comprehension appears to be good. Maria speaks both English and Spanish well. When communicating with the staff, Maria acts as Elicia's interpreter since none of the staff at the shelter speak Spanish.

Maria appears to be behind academically. She struggles reading simple children's books written in English. It is unknown if her ability to read in Spanish is better than her English reading skills.

Other than her two cousins, Elicia has no other sources of support in the community. Her cousins have young families and limited resources but are well established and connected to a Latino community in the city and the local Catholic church. Her cousins refused to let Elicia and Maria live with them while she was trying to find her own place and a job. They stated that they did not have enough room and are concerned they would get in trouble with their landlord if it was found out that they were letting people stay with them. They sent her to the local church for help, and she was given the address for the agency's shelter by the priest.

Elicia has been looking for housing in the Latino community. The housing market is tight with limited options, and she has been unable to find anything that she could possibly afford. The only affordable housing she found was a room in a rundown motel that rents by the hour or by the month. It is in an area of town known for drug dealing and sex work.

Upon arriving in the community, Elicia found occasional work for a house cleaning company. The company hires undocumented workers, pays them very low cash wages, and threatens to turn them in to Immigration and Customs Enforcement (ICE) if they complain. The job bosses also exploit their female workers sexually, threatening to turn them in if they do not comply. Elicia was fearful about applying for other jobs because of her illegal status. She considered turning to sex work to be able to take care of her children, but her Catholic upbringing and thoughts of how doing so would shame her family have kept her from doing so. She is in constant fear of being detained, separated from her children, and having them placed in foster care. She is also afraid that she will end up homeless again and forced to live on the streets or return to her abusive husband.

Elicia is extremely reluctant to sign up for any federally funded services, even those that she and her children are entitled to receive. Upon the suggestion that she enroll for supplemental

(*continued*)

CASE SUMMARY UNDOCUMENTED AND HOMELESS (*CONTINUED*)

food through Supplemental Nutrition Assistance Program (SNAP), Elicia became nervous and refused, as she has heard that participation in SNAP services, and others like them would draw the attention of ICE, and she had heard stories on the news of individuals being deported after signing up for such programs.

Presenting Problems

Elicia and her children are facing multiple obstacles. They need to find permanent, affordable housing and a job that pays enough to cover her housing and living expenses. In addition, Maria needs to be enrolled in school. Elicia also wants to regain custody of her youngest daughter in foster care.

Additionally, Elicia is experiencing an immense amount of stress, anxiety, and possibly post-traumatic stress disorder (PTSD). She described an instance where she could not calm down her breathing, and she felt lightheaded. She is very fearful of men and tries to avoid all contact with men in the community. She reports difficulty sleeping at night and feeling exhausted most of the time.

She is concerned about Maria. She has started acting out at the shelter, getting into fights with the other children, disobeying her mother, and being disrespectful and defiant to the staff and other adults. Elicia and Maria fight frequently, and when Elicia tries to discipline Maria she throws a temper tantrum until Elicia gives up.

Elicia has many strengths. She had the strength to leave her abusive husband and move to a different city. She loves her daughters. She wants desperately to keep Maria with her and hopes to have Sarah returned to her custody. She is resilient and has managed to survive and keep her daughter safe despite not having a place to stay or a job and a limited support network. Additionally, Elicia is highly motivated to find her own accommodations and support her children.

DISCUSSION QUESTIONS

1. From the perspective of the Universal Declaration of Human Rights, what human rights violations has Elicia experienced?
2. What is Elicia's social location? How does her social location compare to Jackie's?
3. What can Jackie do to reduce the power differential between her and Elicia?
4. What form of discrimination has Elicia faced, and what possible effects have they had on her ability to find permanent housing and employment?
5. Using an AOP lens, identify how discrimination has impacted Elicia's mental health.

A robust set of instructor resources designed to supplement this text is located at http://connect.springerpub.com/content/book/978-0-8261-6683-8. Qualifying instructors may request access by emailing textbook@springerpub.com.

KEY REFERENCES

Only key references appear in the print edition. To access the full reference list, visit www.springerpub.com/courseconnect. See inside front cover and tear-out card for CourseConnect details.

Baines, D., & Benjamin, A. (Eds.). (2011). *Doing anti-oppressive practice: Social justice social work* (2nd ed). Fernwood Publishing.
Bonnycastle, C. R. (2011). Social justice along a continuum: A relational illustrative model. *Social Service Review, 85*(2), 267–295. https://doi.org/10.1086/660703
Council on Social Work Education. (2022). *Educational policy and accreditation standards.* https://www.cswe.org/getmedia/bb5d8afe-7680-42dc-a332-a6e6103f4998/2022-EPAS.pdf
Finn, J. L., & Jacobson, M. (2017). *What is social justice?* Oxford University Press. https://blog.oup.com/2017/03/what-is-social-justice/
Harrison, J., VanDeusen, K., & Way, I. (2016). Embedding social justice within micro social work curricula. *Smith College Studies in Social Work, 86*(3), 258273. https://doi.org/10.1080/00377317.2016.1191802
Lott, B., & Bullock, H. E. (2007). *Psychology and economic injustice: Personal, professional, and political intersections.* American Psychological Association.
McCormick, P. (2003). Whose justice? An examination of nine models of justice. *Social Thought, 22*(2/3), 7–25. https://doi.org/10.1080/15426432.2003.9960338
Rawls, J. (2001). *Justice as fairness: A restatement.* Balknap Press of Harvard University Press.
Reisch, M., & Garvin, C. D. (2016). *Social work and social justice: Concepts, challenges, and strategies.* Oxford University Press.
Strier, R. S., & Binyamin, S. (2014). Introducing anti-oppressive social work practices in public services: Rhetoric to practice. *British Journal of Social Work, 44*(8), 2095–2112. https://doi.org/10.1093/bjsw/bct049
Sue, D. W., & Sue, D. (2012). *Counseling the culturally diverse: Theory and practice.* Wiley.

5 Antiracism, Diversity, Equity, and Inclusion

Tara is a hospital social worker at a large urban children's hospital that is one of only two in the state. At the hospital, children and their families come from across the country for specialty care. As a result, Tara often works with people from a variety of cultural backgrounds. During her social work education, Tara studied human behavior in terms of social environment and diversity, so she felt that she had a good understanding about the importance of appreciating diversity and how culture influences an individual.

Tara is often interacting with individuals from diverse backgrounds. Thankfully, the hospital recognizes the diversity in the patients they serve, so they have set up a "lunch and learn" series on issues related to cultural competence. At these 30-minute sessions, hospital workers who are on their lunch break can meet together and learn about various diversity issues and topics. Tara appreciates the opportunity to learn more about the cultures of others so that she can better serve the patients and their families. Tara understands that she cannot know everything about every single culture, but rather operates from a position of cultural humility, honoring that the cultural experience of each person is unique to them. The individual is the expert of their own culture.

LEARNING OBJECTIVES

In this chapter, we will address antiracist practice and advancing antiracism, diversity, equity, and inclusion (ADEI) in practice. Social workers value diversity and promote equality regardless of difference. Differences can include a variety of areas such as age, class, color, culture, disability and ability, ethnicity, gender identity and expression, immigration status, marital status, political ideology, race, religion/spirituality, sex, sexual orientation, and tribal sovereign status. Social workers value all people and appreciate differences. Social workers go beyond valuing diversity and difference in practice by committing to antiracist and anti-oppressive practice of social work and to advancing ADEI through their practice at all levels. It is not enough to be nonracist; the field calls for social workers to actively fight against racism and in the pursuit of diversity, equity, and inclusion (Yearwood et al., 2021). Social workers are cognizant of their own personal culture and bias and are cautious to not allow their own experience of culture to supersede that of their clients. Self-awareness is necessary in order for social workers to be culturally competent professionals. By the end of this chapter you will:

- Understand the role of intersectionality as it relates to diversity and antiracism.
- Describe theories that inform antiracist practice.
- Define and provide examples of microaggressions.

- Describe levels of oppression and discrimination.
- Recognize and identify how personal biases could interfere with the helping process.
- Define intersectionality and describe how it relates to understanding the lived experiences of clients, including experiences of racism, oppression, and discrimination.
- Identify the 10 standards of culturally competent social work practice.
- Describe and appreciate the value of constituents as experts
- Describe cultural empathy and humility.

COMPETENCY 3: ENGAGE ANTIRACISM, DIVERSITY, EQUITY, AND INCLUSION IN PRACTICE

Social workers understand how racism and oppression shape human experiences and how these two constructs influence practice at the individual, family, group, organizational, and community levels and in policy and research. Social workers understand the pervasive impact of White supremacy and privilege and use their knowledge, awareness, and skills to engage in anti-racist practice. Social workers understand how diversity and intersectionality shape human experiences and identity development and affect equity and inclusion. The dimensions of diversity are understood as the intersectionality of factors including but not limited to age, caste, class, color, culture, disability and ability, ethnicity, gender, gender identity and expression, generational status, immigration status, legal status, marital status, political ideology, race, nationality, religion and spirituality, sex, sexual orientation, and tribal sovereign status. Social workers understand that this intersectionality means that a person's life experiences may include oppression, poverty, marginalization, and alienation as well as privilege and power. Social workers understand the societal and historical roots of social and racial injustices and the forms and mechanisms of oppression and discrimination. Social workers understand cultural humility and recognize the extent to which a culture's structures and values, including social, economic, political, racial, technological, and cultural exclusions, may create privilege and power resulting in systemic oppression. Social workers:

- demonstrate antiracist and anti-oppressive social work practice at the individual, family, group, organizational, community, research, and policy levels; and
- demonstrate cultural humility by applying critical reflection, self-awareness, and self-regulation to manage the influence of bias, power, privilege, and values in working with clients and constituencies, acknowledging them as experts of their own lived experiences.

NATIONAL ASSOCIATION OF SOCIAL WORKERS *CODE OF ETHICS*

Social workers are called upon to serve all populations while carrying out the professional mission to enhance human well-being. The ethical principles of service, social justice, and dignity and worth of the person clearly illustrate the value social workers place on advancing DEI and combatting racism. Social justice relates to the challenging of social injustice, which obviously includes justice related to equity, inclusion, the valuing and embracing of diversity, and fighting against racism. This value relates specifically to pursuing social change on behalf of individuals who are oppressed, and that oppression is so regularly based in difference, especially relating to cultural, racial, and ethnic diversity. Dignity and worth of the person relates to ADEI in that it calls upon social workers to recognize, honor, and value individual differences and cultural and ethnic diversity, while also working to resolve conflicts that exist between their clients' interests and the broader society's interest. These conflicts are so often rooted in oppression based on race, ethnicity, and other marginalized and historically included identities and social locations, because, as discussed in Chapter 4, society is designed to support and advance those with the most power. Service is related to ADEI in that it calls for social workers to elevate service to others above self-interest. Many social workers fulfill roles in which they are not held to the standards of advancing ADEI and practicing from an antiracist framework in order to fulfill their minimum job duties. They may not be evaluated by this standard for their annual evaluation at the agency in which they are employed. However, if we are to practice in line with the ethical principles of our profession, it is our duty to fulfill this expectation regardless of the job description. Specific standards that social workers must adhere to that relate to ADEI include cultural competence, which includes awareness and cultural humility, derogatory language, discrimination, social welfare, and social and political action. The National Association of Social Workers (NASW) *Code of Ethics* is available online at www.socialworkers.org/About/Ethics/Code-of-Ethics/Code-of-Ethics-English.

Social workers are mandated to challenge discrimination and other social injustices (NASW, 2021). Social justice requires equity of opportunity and resources for people to achieve their fullest potential. In order to promote social justice, social workers must be aware of social injustices that are occurring. Social workers must be aware of what is happening in their communities, country, and world. Once a social worker recognizes an injustice, they then need to seek out social change. Social workers should seek change at all levels of practice to ensure social justice for all. This explicitly ties to antiracist social work practice, which calls for social workers to move beyond competence and humility related to racism to becoming actively antiracist in their social work practice at the micro, mezzo, and macro levels.

At all times, social workers are also mandated to treat people in a caring and respectful manner regardless of their cultural and ethnic backgrounds (NASW, 2021). Social workers understand that diversity and cultural appreciation enhance the tapestry of society at all levels. Social workers are supportive of individual differences. Social workers see diversity and differences as something to be highlighted and celebrated while also striving to end discrimination, oppression, and social injustices.

Social workers are trained to understand culture and how it functions in society. Through human behavior in the social environment and diversity courses, social workers learn about diversity and oppression based on a myriad of difference. Social workers are called to appreciate culture, identifying strengths that exist in all cultures. Social workers are called to present with a level of cultural competence related to the clients they are serving. Beyond cultural competence, social workers should possess cultural humility in understanding that individuals present with a unique lived experience and their experience of their culture may be different. Social workers understand that oppression occurs based on the intersectionality of multiple identities and social locations.

Words have power. Social worker should not use language that is disrespectful to clients (NASW, 2021). Derogatory language can be explicit hate language but can also include a more covert bias or suggestive disrespect, including microaggressions discussed later in this chapter. Social workers should be considerate of words they choose to use and avoid using language that is disrespectful to any group of people.

Discrimination based on any type of difference is unethical (NASW, 2021). Social workers do not engage in discrimination. The great poet Maya Angelou is credited with saying "When you know better, do better." Social workers should know better and in turn do better with regard to promoting social justice. Discrimination sabotages social justice. Social workers do not accept the status quo of intentional or unintentional discrimination at any level. Social workers do not condone discrimination. Social workers speak up against any type of discrimination and do not collaborate with any form of discrimination either. This requires the social worker to be able to identify discrimination in its various forms, understanding the impact of discrimination on individuals and communities and their ability to access resources and experience equitable outcomes and address discrimination through a variety of interventions.

Caring for the welfare and well-being of all is a cornerstone foundation for the social work profession. Social workers are called to advocate for the human rights of all people and promote political, social, economic, and cultural values that promote the realization of social justice (NASW, 2021). Social workers do not operate from an ethnocentric lens, but should support the conditions that respect cultural and social diversity and antiracist perspectives. Social workers understand that culture influences all aspects of a person's life. Social workers do not diminish the culture of others, but rather celebrate those values and ensure that regardless of difference individuals are able to meet their own basic needs. As Fairfax et al. (2024, p. 265) state, "If students do not learn cultural histories and cultural empathy, their capacity to be impactful is truncated and diminished."

Social workers are also called upon to engage in social and political action whenever necessary in order to ensure that all people, regardless of difference, have equal access to their basic needs (NASW, 2021). This sets social work apart from other mental health professions. Social workers are called to be a voice for those who at times may not have been allowed a voice at the table. We must speak for others, especially those who are discriminated against or oppressed in any way. A way that social workers do this is to promote practices and policies that expand access to the metaphorical table for those that are most impacted by discriminatory actions and policies, actively infuse antiracism and anti-oppressive approaches, demonstrate respect for differences, safeguard human rights, and confirm equity and social justice for all people.

▶ **Reflection Questions**

1. Consider current events and identify two issues related to antiracism and/or equity that could benefit from social and political action from social workers.
2. Describe the issues and explain how you think social workers could best address them.

At all levels of practice social workers should strive to promote respect for all regardless of difference. In fact, social workers should work to promote the honoring of differences. By engaging in social and political action, social workers can inform policies to ensure that they are supportive of differences and not biased against particular groups (regardless of whether that bias is intended or unintended).

Social workers are called to end racism, discrimination, and prejudice that any person or group may experience based on any type of difference. Discrimination and other forms of oppression are toxic, and social workers seek to reduce them. Social workers personally and professionally challenge racism and discrimination, value diversity and difference, and promote policies, practices, and procedures that reduce oppression and inequities.

In the following section, theories that inform antiracist and anti-oppressive practice will be explored. Some of the theories were briefly explored in earlier chapters of the textbook with additional detail and connection to Competency 3: Engage Anti-Racism, Diversity, Equity, and Inclusion (ADEI) in Practice. Other theories are newly introduced.

CONFLICT THEORY

Conflict can be defined as a serious disagreement, dispute, or struggle. Some theorists suggest that conflicts are to obtain status, resources, or social change (Bartos & Wehr, 2002). Theories related to conflict set out with the goal to explain conflicts and provide an understanding of the conditions that create (or prolong) conflict. These theories also attempt to explain the process by which conflicts can be resolved or addressed by parties on both sides of the disagreement.

Karl Marx was an early conflict theorist who addressed conflict based on class struggle, and much of conflict theory is based on his initial works (Salem Press, 2014). Conflict theory is often used to describe social, economic, and political power struggles that occur within and between systems (Fogler, 2008). Several principles of conflict theory that Marx put forth was that conflict was inevitable, power differences exist in relationships, resources are scarce, and whoever is in power has control of the limited resources (Langer & Lietz, 2014).

Marx's work was based on other works that suggested that conflicts can be understood considering the thesis, antithesis, and synthesis. The thesis can be understood as the current situation or status quo. The antithesis is the opposition or opposing perspective to the thesis. This is the alternative view. Conflict occurs between the thesis and antithesis. As a result of this conflict, a synthesis is created. The synthesis is a new way or situation. Eventually the synthesis evolves into the thesis, and the process can resume with the new thesis and the new antithesis. Figure 5.1 illustrates this relationship. Let's consider an example to understand

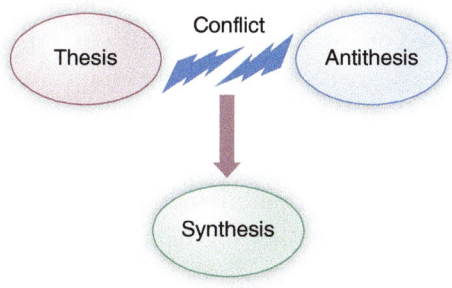

FIGURE 5.1 Conflict theory.

this concept related to diversity and difference. For many years in the United States only heterosexual couples had the opportunity to marry; this was the thesis. The antithesis to this position was that all people have the right to marry the person they love. Through years of conflict that included rallies, marches, and policy advocacy, a new synthesis of marriage equality was achieved nationally in 2015 in the United States.

The use of conflict theory to understand engaging ADEI in practice is useful because it wards against pathologizing oppressed groups; rather, it promotes "recognition of the historical, cultural, economic, and political context of their behavior" (Hutchinson, 2017, p. 37). Social workers strive to identify the influences on a person's experience in order to better be able to understand their current situation. When considering a person without paying attention to contextual influences, one risks misunderstanding the individual and their current state. Because of this, the application of this theory also rejects the notion of colorblindness as an antidote to racism, as it acknowledges that the White ruling class weaponizes racial prejudice as a way to maintain power and continue to accumulate resources. Ignoring the impact of race on lived experiences does nothing to put an end to the systemic weaponization of racism that influences the systems that impact overall well-being for individuals and communities.

CRITICAL RACE THEORY

Another vital theory for engaging ADEI in practice is critical race theory (CRT), which is rooted in conflict theory. CRT has its origins as a legal theory and has been adopted by various helping professions, including social work (Stovall, 2016). CRT views race and racism to be multifaceted, complex social constructs. CRT presents a counter-position to the dominant or majority view, focusing on the experience of racial minority groups, while demonstrating an inherent commitment to equality and social justice. This theory sets forth the premise that racism is so ingrained in culture that it can be difficult to recognize for those who are a part of the dominant group and familiar with the culture (Stefancic & Delgado, 2013). Some key points of CRT include the following (Simba, 2021):

- "Racism is an essential element of American culture" (Simba, 2021, para. 1). Racism is not an exception, but a constant presence in society's structures, customs, and daily interactions. People with racial privilege may be unaware of these effects.
- "White over Black involves not only material social relations but also has an immense ideological presence in society" (Simba, 2021, para. 1).
- Race and racism are social constructs. Race is not a biological reality, but a system created to categorize people based on physical features. This invents a system where individuals are limited in their free agency because they "are bound, in part, by their particular social class" (Simba, 2021, para. 1).
- "Law is an important glue that legitimizes the hierarchy of race, class, and gender inequality" (Simba, 2021, para. 1), meaning that the law has been used to maintain and perpetuate White supremacy and other acts of oppression.

CRT is fundamental to engaging ADEI in practice because it requires the social worker who applies it to confront how the law and other structures disadvantage people of color. CRT acknowledges that the concept of "colorblindness" ignores the privilege that White people have due to their race. Infusing CRT into practice lends itself to an antiracist and anti-oppressive approach because it requires the social worker to acknowledge that racism is deeply rooted in society, that racism limits opportunities for people of color, and that racism creates additional burdens that impact the overall health, safety, and well-being of people of color. It encourages social workers to consider how their own outcomes and those of their clients are impacted by race. It also requires that the social worker prioritize culturally aware treatment that requires them to learn from communities of color not only about their strengths and needs but also about their preferred approaches and interventions. Moving beyond the individual level, CRT helps social workers identify and fight against policies and practices that may be written in a colorblind way but in actuality perpetuate inequities among non-White racial groups.

INTERSECTIONALITY

Several theorists have contributed to the body of knowledge related to intersectionality, another concept that is at the core of CRT and highly relevant to engaging ADEI in practice. A contemporary theorist on this issue is Kimberlé Crenshaw. Crenshaw, a legal scholar, used the term "intersectionality" in an attempt to describe the cumulative experience based on difference. Intersectionality demonstrated how "single-axis thinking undermines legal thinking, disciplinary knowledge production, and struggles for social justice" (Cho et al., 2013, p. 787). When you think of an intersection, you may think of an area where multiple roads meet and cross, or intersect, each other. Intersectionality is a crossroads of human identity so to speak. Human beings are complex and multidimensional. It would be difficult and inaccurate to boil a person down to a single dimension. Figure 5.2 illustrates the intersectionality of four components of diversity—gender, race, class, and sexual orientation. When considering intersectionality, there can be a myriad of intersections related to any of the areas of difference we have previously noted. Through intersectionality, we are able to consider how the multiple levels of a person's cultural identity inform their experience.

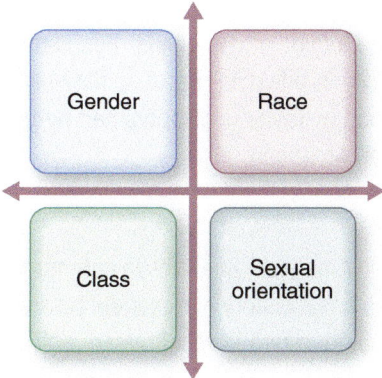

FIGURE 5.2 Intersectionality.

Intersectionality allows social workers to view the client in their entirety (Cox et al., 2016). If we only considered one level of this person's identity, we would lose the complexity that comes with being all of those things. Case 5.1 provides a brief introduction to three individuals. After reading their introductions, consider the various intersectionalities that are present for each.

The idea of intersectionality is based off the work of feminists of color. During the feminist movement during the mid-20th century, several authors put forth the view that the experience of women varied based on other areas of difference. They suggested that there were different experiences based on each level of difference, or intersectionality. For example, experiences based on gender identity were different. On the next level, among people who identified as the same gender, there would be differences based on race. For example, the experience of White females is different from that of Black females. Though both groups may experience oppression based on gender, Black females have the additional oppression based on race that White females do not. Furthermore, adding the intersectionality of sexual orientation could potentially add another layer of oppression. According to Bubar et al. (2016), "intersectionality is now considered to be one of the most significant contributions to feminist scholarship in the late 20th century" (p. 284).

CASE 5.1 LI AND TAYLOR: UNDERSTANDING THE ENTIRE PERSON USING INTERSECTIONALITY

Li

Li is a 36-year-old Asian American. Her parents were both born in Korea and immigrated to the United States when Li was 7 years old. Li's parents have worked quite hard to provide for her and her three younger siblings at the family restaurant. As Li's parents began aging, working 7 days a week in the restaurant started to take a toll on them. As the oldest child, Li felt obligated to step in at the restaurant to ease the burden on her parents. Li now works 7 days a week, but still finds herself struggling to make ends meet financially. Since taking on more responsibility at the restaurant, Li's relationship with her partner, Amy, has been struggling.

Taylor

Taylor is a 20-year-old college student who is gender nonconforming. Taylor's parents are not supportive of what they call Taylor's "lifestyle" because they believe it will not be well received in their devout religious community. Taylor is disappointed by this because church has always been enjoyable. Taylor is African American.

Teresa

Teresa is a 79-year-old Mexican American. She lives in community housing with her oldest son, Riccardo, and his family. Teresa has a history of major depressive disorder that has been worsening as her physical health has declined in recent years and after the death of her husband 2 years ago.

Intersectionality allows for the exploration of social discrimination processes with regard to various social identities, or categories of difference (Risberg & Pilhofer, 2018). Intersectionality can illustrate how some groups are more prone to social injustices due to the multiple dimensions of discrimination and oppression (Crenshaw, 2012). Using the concept of intersectionality provides a framework to deconstruct concepts of privilege and oppression based on differences (Bubar et al., 2016; Liu, 2018).

Privilege is a term used to describe the "sum of earned advantages of special group membership" (Marsiglia & Kulis, 2016, p. 23). Just as being a member of a specific group can place an individual in a position of oppression, some group memberships provide privilege simply by being a part of that group. Groups that maintain privilege are often considered the dominant group, whereas the group that is oppressed is often considered the minority group. The terms *dominant* and *minority* are not solely based on number; rather, it is a much more complex dynamic of social and political capital and power that results in some groups having power and other groups being oppressed. For example, though rates of males and females in the United States are nearly mathematically equal, gender equality does not exist. In the United States, as with most areas of the world, males are considered the dominant group and in turn possess privilege related to being assigned to that gender group.

> ▶ **Reflection Questions**
>
> 1. Reflect about your personal identity. How would you describe your personal intersectionality based on age, class, color, culture, disability and ability, ethnicity, gender identity and expression, immigration status, marital status, political ideology, race, religion/spirituality, sex, sexual orientation, and tribal sovereign status?
> 2. How does your intersectionality inform your worldview?
> 3. How might your worldview be different if the elements of your intersectionality were different (e.g., you identified as a different gender)?

> ▶ **Reflection Question**
>
> Describe how privilege and oppression can cross in regard to your personal intersectionality.

By viewing all of the dimensions of the person through the lens of intersectionality, we can see how at times individuals may experience oppression on multiple levels of their identify. Intersectionality provides a way to not only explore between-group differences but within-group differences as well. Systems of inequality are often interrelated (Marsiglia & Kulis, 2016). Intersectionality allows one to explore the multiple dimensions of inequality or oppression that a person may be experiencing based on their identity.

When thinking about the context of engaging ADEI in social work practice, utilizing the theory of intersectionality as a framework is invaluable in that it allows the social worker to recognize their clients' unique identities, experiences of privilege and oppression, and life experiences. Social workers must be able to attend to the individualized needs that each client system presents if they are to practice in a client-centered way. It is also important for the social worker to remember and consider that some identities change with time. Life changes can result in changes to identities and social statuses. The only constant is change, and we have to remember this as we engage ADEI in practice.

In addition to considering intersectionality, a culturagram may be a tool to assist workers helping diverse populations. A culturagram is much like an ecomap but focuses on cultural aspects of an individual or family system (Congress, 1994). Components of the culturagram include the following 10 areas (Congress & González, 2013). Figure 5.3 illustrates the components of a culturagram.

COMPA LOVE

Maglalang and Rao (2021) center ADEI theories written by Indigenous people and people of color that social workers can integrate into their practice. One of these theories is compa love, a theory originating from education scholars that emphasizes teachers' commitment to students' well-being and fosters a sense of shared humanity. It includes emotional support, addressing students' material needs, and using culturally relevant teaching methods. This moves away from traditional educational approaches in which teachers acknowledge student struggles but don't actively address them, potentially reinforcing existing

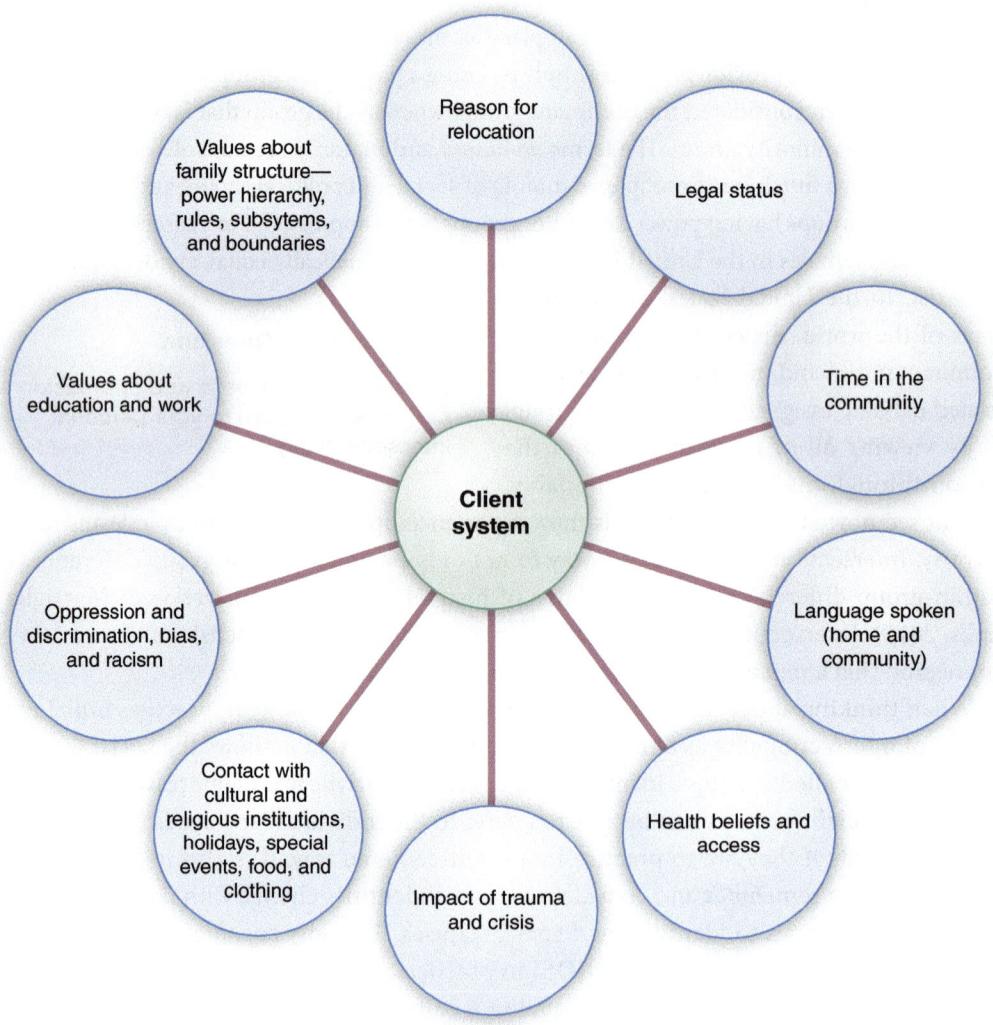

FIGURE 5.3 Culturagram.

inequalities; treat students as helpless and needing saving, ignoring their strengths and resources; hold high expectations but do not consider the challenges students face, potentially leading to punishment; and only fully support students who perform well, neglecting those who struggle (Hannegan-Martinez, 2019). Compa love seeks to create a safe space for students to share experiences and build empathy; connect students with resources to meet their basic needs; and use culturally relevant teaching methods that empower students and challenge the status quo. Social work education can benefit from compa love. While traditional approaches may acknowledge trauma, compa love goes further by emphasizing love and solidarity as core values. Social work and compa love have similar aims, including to build relationships, validate others' experiences, and create environments that foster critical thinking and social justice.

RACIAL TRIANGULATION THEORY

Maglalang and Rao (2021) also explore racial triangulation theory, which asserts that Asian Americans have been placed in the "model minority" role in the United States, which pits them against Black and African American individuals while still being disallowed full acceptance. This is achieved by presenting Asian Americans as a "successful" minority compared to Black Americans, using Asian American successes as evidence that other communities of color could also be successful in spite of racial discrimination. However, this stereotype ignores the diversity within Asian American groups and can be used to criticize other minorities. Additionally, Asian Americans are simultaneously viewed and treated as outsiders and even not truly American. Historical evidence of this kind of exclusion includes the internment of Japanese Americans during World War II. Racial triangulation theory can help social workers to engage ADEI in practice by helping them to better understand how race is used to divide groups, the challenges that Asian Americans face, and how diversity within groups highlights the necessity for culturally aware practice.

CULTURAL WEALTH

Cultural wealth is another theory that is in line with engaging ADEI in social work practice (Maglalang & Rao, 2021). Cultural wealth challenges the idea that people of color lack cultural capital (knowledge, skills) for success and argues that Black, Indigenous, and people of color (BIPOC) communities possess their own unique wealth of knowledge and tools to fight racism and oppression. The six forms of cultural wealth detailed include hope despite racism, skills to navigate racist systems, resources within ethnic communities, cultural language and knowledge, strength of family history and traditions, and strategies to challenge oppression. Cultural wealth theory is similar to the strengths-based approach, but cultural wealth goes further in that it acknowledges racism as a systemic barrier and emphasizes collective community resources. This can be useful for engaging ADEI in social work practice because it emphasizes strengths and assets within a culture and can inspire social workers to identify additional forms of wealth and avoid relying on dominant narratives that often emphasize deficits.

OPPRESSION THEORY

Theories of antiracist, anti-oppression, and culturally sensitive practice serve to provide social workers with a framework from which to view and better understand "ethnic barriers, conflicts and differences in societies so that they may practice in ways that respect people's individual and social identities and respond to oppression by dominant social groups" (Payne, 2016, p. 373). These theories underscore the importance of considering the whole person in light of their diversity and difference, as that is a formative piece to their identity.

Understanding oppression "contribute(s) an understanding of how low social power and lack of societal validation for certain individuals illuminates ways that populations can be marginalized, invalidated, and deemed invisible" (Chang-Muy & Congress, 2015, p. 100). Bulhan (1987) suggested a theory regarding oppression that explored constraints including social limitations on rights and other inequalities; personal feelings and perceptions, referred to as *strains;* and the presence of cultural norms. In order to understand the function of oppression in the lives of clients, Bulhan (1987) suggests exploring physical and economic space, roles and responsibilities, energy flow, access to information, and personal mobility.

FORMS AND MECHANISMS OF OPPRESSION AND DISCRIMINATION

Social workers must understand oppression and discrimination in order to be able to stand against it. Gil (2013) sets forth the following:

> "Oppression" refers to a mode of human relations involving domination and exploitation—economic, social, and psychological—among individuals, among social groups and classes within and beyond societies, and, globally, among entire societies. Injustice refers to coercively established and maintained inequalities, discrimination, and dehumanizing, development-inhibiting conditions of living (e.g., slavery, serfdom, and exploitative wage labor; unemployment, poverty, starvation, and homelessness; and inadequate health care and education) imposed by dominant social groups, classes, and people upon dominated and exploited groups, classes, and people. (p. 12)

Components, or important aspects, related to oppression are power and privilege (David & Derthick, 2017). Oppression exists as both an act and as a process. Explored in Chapter 4, common examples of oppression include racism, sexism, ageism, classism, ableism, and xenophobia. There are various forms of oppression. The forms of oppression we will be exploring are interpersonal, institutional, and internal.

Interpersonal oppression occurs between people at an interactional level. This type of oppression exists as attitudes and beliefs. This form of oppression can occur between people and may be overt or covert, intended or unintended. Hate language or slurs, jokes about groups of difference, bullying, and intimating are all examples of interpersonal oppression.

Institutional oppression occurs at the community or organization level and can pervade society. Some examples of institutional oppression would be oppressive laws, policies, and standards. At a macro level, societies can be oppressive or nonoppressive. Oppression of groups can at times be built into society's social structure (Beckett & Maynard, 2013). Nonoppressive societies are ones in which all people have equal rights and access to the resources that are necessary for them to meet their basic needs (Gil, 2013). These oppressive societies that have built-in mechanisms of oppression represent institutional oppression.

Another form of oppression is internalized oppression. Internalized oppression is a type of oppression that is self-imposed within a group that has been oppressed by others. David (2014) suggests that "because of its pervasiveness, oppression can also become internalized—the hidden injury of oppression that is often ignored or minimized" (p. 3). Internalized oppression often presents with shame or embarrassment. It is important for social workers to not view the oppressed as lesser due to the oppression. It is crucial not to consider the oppressed as "passive victims who do not even understand their own situation" (Beckett & Maynard, 2013, p. 124).

Discrimination is a prejudicial or unjust treatment of a person or group based on difference. There are a variety of types of discrimination including direct, indirect, associative, and perspective that are based on the Equality Act of 2010 (Gast et al., 2012). Direct discrimination refers to treating a person negatively due to a characteristic of difference. Indirect discrimination occurs via policies that can disadvantage members of a particular group. Associative discrimination is a type of discrimination in which a person is associated with a member of diverse group and is treated negatively due to that association. Perspective discrimination occurs when an individual is believed to possess characteristics of difference and treated negatively as a result of that perception.

Microaggressions

For this text, we will define microaggressions as "brief and commonplace daily verbal or/and environmental indignities whether intentional or unintentional that communicate hostile, derogatory, or negative racial slights and insults to the target person or group" (Sue et al., 2007, p. 273). Microaggressions can be blindly assuming characteristics of a culture and applying them to others, for example, believing that all Asian Americans have above-average intelligence or all African Americans are athletic. A lack of awareness does not excuse a microaggression.

▶ **Reflection Question**

Describe a microaggression that you have witnessed. How could a social worker address the microaggression you described?

Microaggressions also include the denial of personal bias (Fisher et al., 2017). As mentioned earlier in the chapter, sometimes people will claim they "don't see race" and therefore believe they hold no bias related to race. This minimizes the role of race on a person's experience and the existence of cultural diversity (Fisher et al., 2017). Social workers must combat such microaggressions by not allowing the histories of groups to be diminished or forgotten.

Microaggressions can also occur environmentally (Sue et al., 2015). Environmental microaggressions target groups and have the consequence of making members of that group "feel unwelcome, isolated, unsafe, and alienated" (Sue et al., 2015, p. 121). Case 5.2 illustrates some environmental microaggressions.

CASE 5.2 (NOT-SO-) WELCOME TO THE COMMUNITY: AN EXAMPLE OF ENVIRONMENTAL MICROAGGRESSION

Alice is a social worker at a community resource center in the heart of the Appalachian region. This area lacks much diversity; it is prudentially White and low to middle class. Much of the region lives in poverty. There is little racial or ethnic diversity. Many of the families in the region have been in the area for generations and do not often "venture out" to the nearby cities that are much more diverse.

Alice recently learned that a large Syrian refugee population is going to be settled in the community where her resource center is located. The contact at the refugee resettlement agency had reached out to Alice to ensure a smooth transition for the refugees. The resettlement agency was able to find several vacant properties in the area that they were able to secure for the refugees. While they would continue to assist the families, since their agency was based within the city (approximately 40 miles away), they were hopeful that Alice and her agency would be a local point of contact and support for the refugee families. Alice was excited to work with this population and assist them in their transition.

Move-in day finally came, and Alice her team of social workers from her agency were there to support the refugees and welcome them to the community. Unfortunately, not everyone in the community was as welcoming. Nearby neighbors sat on their porch and stared at the refugees as they were moving in. The neighbors stood with their arms crossed, staring and muttering about the group moving in, while shaking their heads with disapproval. Some people yelled slurs as they passed by. Alice was not expecting this reaction.

The first week was very difficult. When the refugees attempted to go to community establishments, they were treated poorly. For example, when a couple went to the local market, no staff would assist them even though it was obvious that they were having trouble navigating the store. At the local gas station, the normally chatty clerk would not make eye contact with the refugees and kept the conversation limited to the amount due. When walking in the community, long-term residents would switch sidewalks or hold their bags a little tighter when passing the new residents.

The community was not accepting of the new residents. Talk throughout the community continued about how they did not want "those kinds of people" in their town. At a town council meeting (which is normally near empty), dozens of community members packed the meeting room to express their concerns about the new residents. Alice, who often attends these meetings in order to be engaged in political action at the community level, was present. After hearing community member after community member spout off discriminatory, prejudiced comments, she decided she needed to speak up.

Alice waited in line for her chance to talk at the meeting. Though she was nervous, she knew that she needed to speak up for the refugees. Alice shared that she is a social worker and has been assisting the new residents. She urged the community to be more open to the refugees. She began describing her interactions with the refugees over the past week and how she has taken time to get to know them on a personal level. She encouraged other community members to do the same as well. She also encouraged the town council members to set up community

(continued)

| CASE 5.2 | **(NOT-SO-) WELCOME TO THE COMMUNITY: AN EXAMPLE OF ENVIRONMENTAL MICROAGGRESSION (*CONTINUED*)** |

dinners and other events to allow the long-term residents a chance to meet and interact with their new neighbors. The town council liked this idea and encouraged Alice to spearhead the event since she was both familiar with the local community and connected to the refugee population as well. Alice did not really expect to be in charge of this event, but she knew that it was important so she took on the task.

The next day at work, Alice and her team of social workers began discussing ideas for the event. The team agreed on the goal of bringing people together and giving them a chance to experience each other's cultures in a way that would allow them to appreciate their diversity. One of the workers suggested a community street fair, filled with food and music that incorporates both cultures. Alice reached out to her contact at the urban refugee resettlement agency and asked if they wanted to be involved at the event as well. They were excited to join the event.

The day of the street fair arrived. Alice and her team had worked hard getting the word out about the event and offering giveaways and other attractions in order to entice people to attend. The refugee resettlement agency pulled upon several urban resources to bring a Middle Eastern food truck to the event that was a big hit among the long-term residents. The event went well and had a great turnout. Alice knew that this was just the start and there was still much more work to be done in order to assist the community in fully welcoming their newest members, but for one night, the community was able to come together as one.

ENGAGING ANTIRACISM, DIVERSITY, EQUITY, AND INCLUSION IN SOCIAL WORK PRACTICE

The mission of the social work profession calls upon social workers to provide services to all, with particular attention to individuals who are vulnerable and oppressed while being sensitive to all forms of social injustice. As a result, many social service agencies provide services to diverse client groups with varied needs and goals. As social workers, we acknowledge that the intersectional dimensions of clients' identities have a significant impact on the ways in which they can move through the world and what they do and do not have access to. This includes elements of identity that are not visible and sometimes ignored or minimized (e.g., sexual orientation, class, disability status, religion, and others).

Social workers not only serve diverse populations but also recognize the importance of increasing diversity in the profession of social work and dismantling the White supremacist legacy social work has operated from historically (NASW, n.d.-a, n.d.-b). Recommendations put forth by NASW's (2022) *Undoing Racism Through Social Work* include ensuring a diverse workforce at every level, providing training focused on understanding and dismantling racism, providing all staff members supervision to support their work and address any issues, and fostering a healthy work environment. Additionally, the NASW seeks to ensure their leadership reflects the communities they serve and allocates budget funds to support antiracism efforts; acknowledge racism's history in social work and commit to learning from past mistakes to improve; promote antiracism through training, public education, and social justice efforts; fight racist policies and practices that uphold White supremacy; target poverty, wage gaps, and unconscious bias among social workers; challenge leaders who support racist structures and offer social work expertise to create antiracist policies; and oppose racist laws and advocate for legislation that addresses the negative impacts of racism on people's lives.

Self-Awareness

As discussed in Chapter 3, professional social workers must be reflective and possess self-awareness skills. Self-awareness refers to the social worker's ability to reflect upon and consider their own thoughts, beliefs, and reactions. Social workers utilize self-awareness to monitor their use of *self* in practice. Effective use of self requires social workers to consider how and why they are experiencing what they are as a result of their current situation and circumstances. Social workers can utilize supervision to assist them in finding meanings and connections that assist in an increased level of self-awareness. Social workers must possess self-awareness in order to be fully able to attend to the needs of clients and ensure that their own issues are not interfering in treatment. Though we fully understand and appreciate that social workers are human and as a result have their own experiences, professional social workers must be diligent to not allow their own issues interfere with the helping process and work of the client. If a social worker cannot contain themself or lacks self-awareness, they should seek support immediately, as the well-being of the clients is of the utmost paramount concern.

As we have noted, self-awareness is necessary for professional practice. Whether working with clients of similar cultures or not, it is necessary for social workers to be aware of different experiences of culture and challenges that could potentially occur as a result (Akhtar, 2013). Self-awareness leads to a social worker's ability to understand and engage in ADEI in practice. Social workers must first be self-reflective regarding their own cultural experience as well as their personal values and the biases that exist for them. Chang-Muy and Congress (2015) set forth the following questions that social workers can ask themselves regarding self-awareness related to cultural competence and sensitivity:

1. What awareness does the worker bring in relation to culturally based countertransference and societal projection?

2. What motivation and commitment does the worker have to explore these issues (e.g., same-ethnicity workers of different class backgrounds and/or acculturation levels)?

3. How will the worker manage their comfort and discomfort levels in practice (i.e., explore the triggers), particularly in relation to differences in affect conveyed in communication (i.e., differences in communication styles)? (p. 103)

▶ **Reflection Question**

Reflect upon your answers to the three questions posed here regarding diversity and self-awareness. How can you improve your self-awareness as it relates to engaging ADEI in social work practice?

In addition to considering these questions, social workers should critically think about their personal experiences with their own culture as well as the culture of others. Social workers should honestly reflect upon experiences and interactions that have been positive, negative, and indifferent. Then the social worker should consider mitigating circumstances to those situations and consider why and how they informed the experience on both sides of the interaction.

Self-reflection can also be very important in recognizing issues such as transference and counter-transference. Transference refers to when the client takes feelings from their past and applies them onto the social worker. At times, social workers may encounter a transference experience on behalf of the client. The feelings transferred can be positive or negative. It is important for the social worker to recognize transference when it arises in order to ensure that it does not interfere with the helping process. On the other hand, counter-transference is when a social worker applies feelings onto the client as a result of their interactions with others. Again, these feelings can be positive or negative. Regardless of the type of feelings, counter-transference must be recognized and the social worker should take immediate steps to address the issue, including supportive supervision. Case 5.3 illustrates scenarios of transference and counter-transference.

CASE 5.3 TRANSFERENCE AND COUNTER-TRANSFERENCE

Transference

Susan, a 24-year-old female, is seeking counseling services from a licensed clinical social worker, James, to address issues stemming from a conflicted romantic relationship. From their first meeting, James strives to build a rapport with Susan, engaging her in treatment and creating a safe place for her to explore her feelings. During the third session, Susan shared "I am so comfortable with you, I can tell you anything. I have never felt this way with a man before. I feel so connected to you. Do you feel it too?" James recognized that Susan may be experiencing some transference. Since Susan was currently in a relationship where her communication needs were not being met, she transferred those needs and desires onto her relationship with her social worker where she was being heard. James thought about how to respond for a second and then said, "I am glad that you feel comfortable, as that is important in the counseling process. I enjoy meeting with you as well, and I feel a connection through a social worker–client relationship." James understood that in transference responses, it was common for clients to treat the worker as an idealized figure. By responding the way he did, utilizing a self-involving disclosure, he was able to reflect Susan's sentiments and allow her to feel heard while setting a boundary regarding the nature of their relationship being solely a professional one.

Counter-Transference

Katie is a social worker at a long-term nursing and rehabilitation facility. Katie is tasked with meeting with all patients upon admission and completing an assessment and monitoring their progress and, when ready, prepare for discharge, ensuring the appropriate services, supplies, and supports are in place for transition to a lower level of care. One day, Katie walked into a patient room to meet with a new resident. She was taken aback at first when she saw the

(continued)

| CASE 5.3 | TRANSFERENCE AND COUNTER-TRANSFERENCE (*CONTINUED*) |

patient, an 88-year-old petite female who very much resembled Katie's own grandmother who had passed away a year ago. Katie, smiled, introduced herself, and began the assessment with the new resident. Throughout the assessment, Katie noticed she was having a hard time staying on task and focused. She found herself just staring at the patient and reflecting upon memories with her grandmother, with whom she had always been quite close. After the interaction was complete, Katie went back to the social work office to complete her documentation of her visit. When another social worker returned to the office, Katie shared her experience. Katie said, "I just had the weirdest intake. I met with a new resident who looks just like my grandma. It felt like I was sitting with my grandma again, it was so neat. I love this new patient." The other social worker recognized that Katie's recollection of the event may be reflective of a counter-transference response where Katie was placing her feelings of her grandmother onto the new patient. The social worker asked Katie about this, and the two discussed the potential for counter-transference and ways to ward against it. By the end of their conversation, Katie realized that maybe she was putting her own feelings onto the new resident and decided to reflect upon this interaction further and discuss this in her weekly supervision.

▶ **Reflection Questions**

1. Consider your professional goodness of fit. In what ways has your goodness of fit evolved during your social work education thus far?
2. After completing the values clarification exercise provided (Exhibit 5.1), how would you describe your professional goodness of fit?
3. What values that are important to you align with the social work profession?

Personal Values and Biases

Part of being a self-aware social worker is being aware of personal values and biases. It is important for social workers to routinely reflect upon their professional goodness of fit. Professional goodness of fit refers to the overlap between personal values and professional values. Figure 5.4 illustrates both good and poor fit between personal and professional values. Ideally, social workers find much overlap between their personal values and the values of the profession. As you may notice in Figure 5.4, the circles that represent good fit do not totally overlap; that is intentional. Social workers do not need to be cookie-cutter professionals that all think, act, and believe the same things. Just as social workers value diversity and difference in client systems, the profession of social work values diversity and difference in the practitioners. The diversity among social work professionals lends itself to the richness of our ever-evolving helping profession.

One tool that can be helpful to explore personal values is to complete a values clarification exercise. We have included a values exercise in Exhibit 5.1 to assist you in considering what you value personally. It is important to revisit your personal values periodically, as they may change over time. Our values inform our worldview, and so it is important to be aware of what matters to us. That is why it is so important to continuously engage in self-reflection as a professional social worker.

FIGURE 5.4 Professional goodness of fit.

Exhibit 5.1 Values Clarification Exercise

Directions: Read through the list of 48 values. Then rank the values from 1 to 48, with 1 representing the value that means the most to you and 48 representing the value that means the least to you. If there is a value you think is important to you that is not included on the list, please add your value and include it in your ranking order.

____ Fairness	____ Honesty	____ Solitude
____ Success	____ Love	____ Rest
____ Compassion	____ Friendship	____ Motivation
____ Reason	____ Nature	____ Kindness
____ Fun	____ Adventure	____ Fame
____ Security	____ Spirituality	____ Equity
____ Freedom	____ Integrity	____ Intimacy
____ Prestige	____ Safety	____ Community
____ Control	____ Money	____ Humor
____ Diversity	____ Character	____ Trust
____ Creativity	____ Communication	____ Autonomy
____ Dependability	____ Beauty	____ Change
____ Intelligence	____ Competence	____ Achievement
____ Stability	____ Challenge	____ Ethics
____ Connection	____ Power	____ Genuineness
____ Flexibility	____ Privacy	
____ Service		

Social workers must also be aware of personal biases that may exist. A bias is prejudice or partiality to a particular group. Social workers are human and as a result may have personal experiences or beliefs that represent potential biases. It is important for social workers to be aware of this, as they have the potential to interfere with the helping process and possibly harm the client. Even if a social worker possesses a bias of partiality, or what some might consider a "soft spot" for a particular group or population, that can be interfering and equally detrimental to treatment as a bias of prejudice.

In order to explore potential biases regarding the various dimensions of diversity, it is important for social workers to be open to exploring their own cultural formulation. It is important to consider how you learned about your own culture. Mahler (2013) suggests that culture is relational and something that we learn and interact with throughout our lives. As we discussed in relation to self-awareness, social workers should reflect upon relational interactions that have informed their development. Social workers should seek out cultural exposure and engagement with individuals who hold different beliefs and worldviews.

Social workers need to be able to support any individual who needs their assistance. Social workers are called upon to serve all people; thus social workers must be able to identify and challenge "personal prejudicial beliefs in a way that enables them to see each client as an individual and provide services to them without their personal values interfering" (Wahler, 2012, p. 1060). Self-awareness and critical reflection will provide an avenue to identify personal beliefs. Social workers should be honest with themselves regarding their self-appraisal of biases. Then social workers must seek to address such beliefs and attitudes. Challenging personal beliefs and attitudes can occur in a variety of ways, including exposure to new experiences through readings, discussions, and interactions.

Constituents as Experts

The helping process is designed for the social worker to assist the client in enhancing their personal well-being. Social workers should always be mindful of their role in the helping relationship. The job of a social worker is not *to do* or *do for* a client. Rather, social workers should strive to work with clients to address the mutually agreed-upon goals. As a profession we encourage and honor self-determination. Self-determination allows clients to make choices regarding their own lives. Self-determination is encouraged because clients understand their problems and needs better than anyone else. Social workers should be sensitive to what clients believe is best for themselves (Hepworth et al., 2017). As a result, they are the experts of their own experience. When considering diversity and difference, it is no different—clients are the experts of their own experiences as they relate to these aspects of their identity. Social workers should respect clients as the experts of their lives and approach clients with culturally humility.

Cultural Competence Standards

Social workers are ethically required to provide culturally competent practice to the clients they serve. Competence refers to having the knowledge and skills necessary to complete a prescribed task or activity. Social workers value competence. The professional value of competence asserts that social workers are continually learning and applying that information to their practice so that it is well informed. The professional value of competence refers to all areas of social work practice. Cultural competence refers more specifically to being well informed regarding culture, diversity, and difference. Ashford and Lecroy (2013) put forth that "the notion of cultural competence has been promoted for many years as a solution to the barriers to care and help encountered by ethnic, racial, and foreign-born groups in many of our service systems" (p. 15). Through cultural competence, social workers are aware of barriers that groups may experience in accessing, obtaining, or maintaining any needed social service supports. Social workers must advocate for solutions that provide opportunity for all.

A note of caution must be given to the idea of cultural competence. The word *competence* implies of set degree or level of knowing. Cultural competence, on the other hand, is not a position of "knowing it all" about culture. In fact, one can never really "know" everything there is to know about every culture (Walsh, 2013). Cultural competence encourages a level of understanding and recognizing that we do not know it all and appreciating between- and within-group differences that exist amidst all cultures.

Social workers must demonstrate culturally sensitive practice. The *Social Work Dictionary* defines culturally sensitive practice as "the process of professional intervention while being knowledgeable, perceptive, empathic, and skillful about the unique as well as common characteristics of clients who possess racial, ethnic, religious, gender, age, sexual orientation, or socioeconomic differences" (Barker, 2003, p. 105). In order to better understand what is encompassed in culturally competent practice, we will present 10 standards that have been developed by the NASW National Committee on Racial and Ethnic Diversity. The NASW cultural competence standards are available online at www.socialworkers.org/LinkClick.aspx?fileticket=PonPTDEBrn4%3D&portalid=0.

Ethics and Values

At the start of this chapter we explored the ethical standards and principles that were closely related to diversity and difference. The NASW *Code of Ethics* exists to safeguard the public and profession from unethical practice. Social workers must be familiar with all parts of the NASW *Code of Ethics*. In order to fulfill this standard, social workers must engage in ethical practice, practice cultural humility, promote social justice, and be able to professionally support vulnerable and oppressed groups during the helping process, considering barriers in place by the dominant culture (NASW, 2015).

Self-Awareness

Again, self-awareness is crucial for success as a social work professional. Just as social workers must understand the perspective of the client and the experiences that they have had, they must also be aware of their personal experiences and understand how they have influenced their worldview. Social workers must not only be culturally aware but also culturally sensitive (NASW, 2015). By exploring their personal cultural identity, social workers are better prepared to practice cultural humility.

Cross-Cultural Knowledge

Social workers understand that culture is multidimensional and essential to the human experience. They are trained to understand the influences of culture at micro, mezzo, and macro levels. Social workers are prepared to support systems across cultures. Social workers understand that culture is not static and, in turn, being a culturally competent social worker is an ongoing learning process (NASW, 2015).

Cross-Cultural Skills

Beyond cross-cultural knowledge, social workers possess cross-cultural skills. Social workers who demonstrate cross-cultural skills are able to communicate effectively in order to engage clients using tools such as warmth, authenticity, and genuineness (NASW, 2015). Social workers are required to ensure they are competent to meet the needs of their clients based on cultural differences.

Service Delivery

Social workers are not only concerned with their own cultural competence, but they are also concerned regarding the cultural competence of their organization (NASW, 2015). Social workers seek to remediate oppressive policies in order to ensure all persons have access to services. Social workers are uniquely prepared and qualified to monitor and evaluate agency systems, make appropriate recommendations based on the findings, and then implement and monitor said recommendations.

Empowerment and Advocacy

Social workers are agents of change. Social workers are leaders. Social workers are advocates. Social workers must use these roles in order to stand up against oppression and discrimination in any form (NASW, 2015). Advocacy can occur at various levels, including political advocacy at the community, state, and federal levels.

Diverse Workforce

Diversity should be represented in all aspects of the profession of social work. Social workers should strive to achieve a multicultural workforce and ensure policies are in place that promote equity. Within the workplace, social workers demonstrate the value of difference and encourage an open and welcoming environment (NASW, 2015).

Professional Education

Professional learning never ends for social workers. Ongoing training and education are necessary to be a competent social work professional (NASW, 2015). Social workers should ensure that they are adding to their cultural knowledge often. As we have stated, culture and experiences of culture are ever changing, so it is important for social workers to be current on best practices in order to provide high-quality services to client systems.

Language and Communication

Self-determination is valued by social workers. Social workers honor the rights of clients to make their own decisions. The right to self-determination continues regarding the right to choose the preferred language to communicate in. Legally, there are mandates that ensure individuals have access to supports such as a translator if necessary and deemed appropriate. To demonstrate this standard, social workers recognize the importance of language to a person's cultural identity and advocate for the rights of that person (NASW, 2015).

Leadership to Advance Cultural Competence

The final cultural competence standard set forth by NASW (2015) requires social workers to engage in the activity of leadership in order to promote practices and policies that are responsive to issues of diversity. Social workers use their power as a professional to advance cultural competence at all levels of practice. Leading social workers are at times in positions to have difficult conversations about difference but do not shy away from the mission to advance cultural competence.

Empowerment

Social workers strive to empower individuals, groups, and communities. Empowering systems gives them the tools and skills necessary to do something. Social workers may empower clients at the micro level by helping enhance self-efficacy or boosting self-confidence in clients. Empowerment may flourish out of a positive helping relationship. At the macro level, the social worker may assist in community organizing in order to give the community members a chance to advocate for themselves.

Empowerment theory is an advocacy-based approach used by social workers to promote social justice and bring about change at various levels while addressing differences in social power (Chang-Muy & Congress, 2015). Payne (2016) asserts that empowerment is a process. Throughout the process of empowerment, social workers assist clients in identifying and ameliorating circumstances, conditions, and situations.

As we discussed earlier, we should not view individuals who have experienced oppression as less in any way. Social workers should strive to empower clients to advocate on their own behalf whenever possible. Furthermore, social workers can empower clients to bring about social change based on their experiences. The social worker can assist the client while letting the client lead the movement. Social workers should be open to learning from clients regarding their experiences.

Empathy

Social workers utilize empathy throughout the helping process with clients to help them feel felt by the worker. In addition to emotional empathy, social workers can display cultural empathy. Cultural empathy has been defined as "a deepening of the human empathic response to permit a sense of mutuality and understanding, across the great differences in value and expectation, that cross-cultural interchange often involves" (Ridley & Lingle, 1996, p. 22). Helpers with high levels of empathy may be more aware of the needs of client systems from diverse backgrounds (Lindsey et al., 2015). Cultural empathy is important in helping professions to ensure client systems feel heard and valued (Trimble, 2010).

Humility

Humility refers to being humble. When a person is humble, they are not self-important. Cultural humility is a way of approaching diversity and difference in a humble way. Culturally humble practice seeks to understand the experiences of others (Charles et al., 2017). Cultural humility would be the opposite of ethnocentrism. Rosen et al. (2017) set forth that cultural humility is a "lifelong process with the attributes of openness, self-awareness, egolessness, self-reflection, and supportive interactions" (p. 291). Cultural humility is an ongoing process that

> encourages workers to take into account an individual's multiple identities and the ways in which their social experiences impact their worldview, particularly as it related to their expression of their culture. This perspective has the benefit of placing the worker in a learning mode as opposed to maintaining power, control and authority in the working relationship, especially over cultural experiences about which the client is far more knowledgeable. (Ortega & Faller, 2011, p. 33)

Culturally humble social workers seek to learn from clients about their cultural experiences, demonstrate standards of cultural competence, and value diversity and difference.

Rural Diversity

Often when one is considering diversity, they think of large metropolitan areas. It's also important to note that diversity exists within rural communities as well, and the experiences of diverse populations and rural communities can at times differ from same-group counterparts who live in urban areas. Often, rural communities are assumed to lack diversity (Daley, 2015). Though there may be dominant or majority groups in rural areas, often other groups are represented as well; furthermore, there is diversity between different rural areas (Ginsberg, 2005). Rural communities each possess their own patterns of communicating, making decisions, and relating to others (Johnson & Dunbar, 2005). Social workers must be mindful of the environment in which they are practicing to ensure that they are appreciating the nuances of the community, identifying strengths, and warding against potential barriers to services that may exist.

Rural social workers must be cognizant of the special needs of diverse populations in such settings. Oftentimes, rural social workers are faced with increased needs and decreased resources to meet those needs. With the lack of resources, it can at times be difficult to find services, providers, and resources to fit specific cultural needs. For example, in a rural area it may be difficult to find a translator who speaks a specific rare dialect. In some areas it can be difficult to find a translator for any language. All social workers must be aware of such barriers and identify ways to combat them. Utilizing the translator example provided later, the social worker may look into electronic or webpage translating services that are designed to support medical and social service workers (see Case 5.4).

Regarding rural diversity in small towns, there is often an array of diversity in regard to race, ethnicity, age, religion, and sexual orientation. At times, these differences are not "immediately apparent because the rural community does not always embrace difference" (Daley, 2015, p. 65). At times, minority groups are not actively engaged in the community due to this potential lack of acceptance. As a result, many groups at times remain hidden or closeted to avoid negative treatment (Daley, 2015).

CASE 5.4 DIVERSITY IN A RURAL AREA

Anna is a hospice social worker in a rural community. She has many years of experience working in this field of social work. Recently she was assigned a new client, Mrs. Jones. As she does with all of her clients, Anna called Mrs. Jones to schedule her first visit. When the day arrived for Anna to go out and meet Mrs. Jones and her family, Anna was surprised when she opened the door and saw Mrs. Jones in a hospital bed that had been set up in her living room surrounded by what seemed like a dozen people. Often when Anna made visits to her patients, there is family present, but she had never seen that many at one time. Mrs. Jones was alert and oriented and welcomed to Anna and her home. She began introducing Anna to all of her children, grandchildren, nieces, and nephews present.

During the intake assessment Anna learned that Mrs. Jones was from Haiti originally and came to the United States approximately 10 years ago to be closer to her children after her husband passed away.

(continued)

> **CASE 5.4** **DIVERSITY IN A RURAL AREA (*CONTINUED*)**
>
> During the intake, it was customary for Anna to do a biopsychosocial-spiritual assessment. During the assessment, Anna learned that Mrs. Jones practiced Haitian Vodou. Anna had never met anyone who practiced Vodou. And really everything she knew about Vodou had been what she saw on television or in the movies. All of her clients to this point had either been Christian or denied having any religious affiliation.
>
> When Anna went back to the office, she began researching information on Haitian Vodou. Even though she did not know about this specific religious practice, she did know that spiritual practices were often quite important in her line of work. She understood that spiritual practices often help the patient and their families deal with the death and dying experience.
>
> Anna began with a Google search, which led her to several resources. After nearly an hour of perusing the Web to learn about Vodou, Anna felt overwhelmed, so she stopped by her supervisor's office and shared with her about her new client.
>
> The supervisor encouraged Anna to remember that the client is the expert regarding their own practices and so it would make sense for Anna to just ask Mrs. Jones about what specific Vodou practices are important to her at this time in her life. Anna worried that if she had to ask Mrs. Jones, she would seem incompetent. But her supervisor reassured her, saying, "Anna, no one expects you to know it all. It's impossible for you to know about every practice everywhere in the world. You are doing the right thing by reaching out and trying to learn about this practice, but no book can teach you what Mrs. Jones wants in her life right now. You need to be open, curious, and culturally humble. I'm sure if you approach Mrs. Jones in a genuine and authentic way, she and her family would be happy to share more about their practice of Vodou with you."
>
> So during her next visit with Mrs. Jones and the several extended family members present, Anna did just that. She asked about Mrs. Jones's practices with Vodou and what would be important for her during the hospice experience.
>
> From this experience Anna learned that in order to provide culturally appropriate care, she is not expected to be an expert on every cultural practice that exists. Rather, she is called to practice cultural humility and honor the expertise of the clients regarding their own cultural experiences.

Social workers are called to promote policies and practices that safeguard the rights of all people and pursue social change in an effort to dismantle social injustice (NASW, 2021). *Undoing Racism Through Social Work* shares a vision for an antiracist future and includes recommendations to move our profession closer to this vision. In order to better understand how social workers can engage ADEI in practice, education, training, policy, research, and the workforce, those recommendations are shared in the following sections. You can find the full document here: www.socialworkers.org/LinkClick.aspx?fileticket=QsNmikJGKj0%3D&portalid=0.

Practice Recommendations

- Collect and publish data scorecards for best practice service delivery.
- Create standards, protocols, and strategic plans with an anti-oppressive lens.

- Prioritize growing and supporting a diverse workforce.
- Develop accountability mechanisms, including self-assessment tools.
- Provide training about White supremacy and how it affects all groups of people in society. (NASW, 2022, p. 34)

Education Recommendations

- Provide all social work students with a consistent antiracist orientation to the profession.
- Expand field placement and course options to include community activist organizations.
- Ensure faculty recruitment, retention, and development reflect DEI commitments. (NASW, 2022, p. 14)

Training Recommendations

- Model workplace inclusion in all social work employment settings.
- Require annual antiracist continuing education for all practitioners centered on harm reduction.
- Improve supervision quality through racial justice inquiry.
- Increase practitioner access to relevant antiracist, community-based research. (NASW, 2022, p. 17)

Policy Recommendations

- Prioritize social work public policy advocacy efforts for healthcare equity, economic security, public education, freedom and democracy, and criminal justice.
- Center community needs in all publicly funded social service program assessments.
- Educate the public on issues of inequity and discrimination through a social work lens. (NASW, 2022, p. 22)

Research Recommendations

- Conduct more social work research with community organizations as lead partners. Use community-based participatory research.
- Identify best practices for antiracist social work service delivery through antiracism practice implementation research.
- Translate more social work research for practice and policy application. (NASW, 2022, p. 26)

Workforce Recommendations

- Increase agency leadership support for growing a diverse workforce.
- Develop and promote antiracist organizational policies and accountability mechanisms to be shared publicly.

- Create alternative pathways to social work licensure.
- Ensure equitable career advancement, competitive wages and leadership opportunities. (NASW, 2022, p. 30)

POLICY ISSUE

Social workers know that policy impacts all areas of practice. In order to engage ADEI in practice, social workers must work to dismantle policies that are discriminatory or oppressive. The NASW *Code of Ethics* calls for social workers to work on behalf of oppressed populations (NASW, 2021). Social workers must advocate against policies that oppress individuals and groups.

One such oppressive policy would be "Don't Ask, Don't Tell," which was an official policy by the U.S. military since the mid-1990s. This policy discouraged military members from disclosing their sexual orientation in order to continue serving in the armed forces. This policy was repealed in 2011 by President Barack Obama, which allowed service members to openly share their sexual orientation without fear of retaliation or discharge. In 2016, policies were expanded to provide protections to transgender people serving in the military. Despite this gain, discrimination against LGBTQIA+ members of the military remains. There have been attempts to resume the "Don't Ask, Don't Tell" policy. If this policy were reenacted, it is unclear what would happen to service members who have openly shared their sexual orientation. Also, transgender individuals serving in the military have been targeted by discrimination. In 2017, President Trump instituted a policy that barred transgender individuals from serving in the military. In 2021, the Biden administration overturned the Trump administration's ban, and as of this textbook's publication, that ban is still overturned.

Discrimination against the LGBTQIA+ community is not limited to the military. LGBTQIA+ individuals report experiencing workplace discrimination and harassment, housing discrimination and harassment, mistreatment in healthcare and mental health care settings, and negative impacts to mental health due to the ongoing introduction of legislation designed to restrict the rights of LGBTQIA+ individuals (Medina & Mahowald, 2023).

In addition to fighting oppressive policies, social workers must also advocate for policies that provide protections to vulnerable and oppressed groups. In order to be an effective advocate for such groups, social workers must first recognize oppression and discrimination in all its forms against members of diverse groups. Social workers must attend to issues of racism, sexism, ageism, xenophobia, homophobia, and antisemitism. Social workers should champion policies that address these forms of oppression.

Religious discrimination and oppression, known as antisemitism, continues for many groups. In October 2018, a gunman entered a Jewish synagogue in urban Pittsburgh, Pennsylvania, and took the lives of 11 people. The gunman was heard yelling anti-Jewish sentiments, and even after the incident, when he was taken to the hospital for wounds he had received, his vile, hateful remarks continued. Unfortunately, this was not an isolated incident. In recent years, mass shootings have become nearly common occurrences in the United States. Vulnerable or oppressed groups are often targeted in such events. There has been a rise by 57% in antisemitic incidences in the past year alone, which is similar to an influx in all hate crimes across the United States (Gibbs et al., 2018).

Hate crimes are criminal acts against a victim who is an identified member of an oppressed group (Chakraborti & Garland, 2015). There are varying levels or degrees of hate crimes, though most often media attention focuses on murder (Lewis, 2014). It is important to understand that the term *hate crimes* also includes lesser, yet still deplorable acts against members of diverse groups.

In June 1998, James Byrd Jr., a Black man, was tortured and murdered in Jasper, Texas, by three White men, two of which had openly identified as White supremacists. Later that same year, in the rural town of Laramie, Colorado, in October 1998, Matthew Shephard was beaten, tortured, and left to die on a fence because he was an openly gay man. After his death, Matthew's parents established the Matthew Shepard Foundation. The Matthew Shepard and James Byrd Jr. Hate Crimes Prevention Act was signed into law by President Obama in 2009 (Sheerin, 2018). This foundation aided in expanding federal hate crime laws to include violence based on sexual orientation, gender, or disability (Chakraborti & Garland, 2015). Hate crime legislation was first signed by President Lyndon Johnson, with the initial law addressing race, color, religion, or national origin. Unfortunately, the latest report from the Southern Poverty Law Center (SPLC, 2023) has shown a 50% increase in White supremacist hate groups and a 33% rise in anti-LGBTQIA+ organizations over the last year. There is still much work to be done to push back on hate and extremism, and social workers should be on the front lines.

SOCIAL JUSTICE ISSUE

As we discussed at the start of this chapter, social workers value the principle of social justice. Related to advancing ADEI in practice, social workers are continuously striving to ameliorate conditions of racism, oppression, injustice, and inequality. Social workers must recognize that at present, many groups remain oppressed and marginalized. Some say we are in a postracial society. However, that discounts the experience of many groups who continue to face discrimination and prejudice based on an area of difference.

The Black Lives Matter movement exists in part to shine light upon the continued discrimination and oppression of African Americans in the United States. The Black Lives Matter movement uses marches and other means of protesting as well as online media platforms to spread their message and provide a forum for individuals to express their outrage (Edwards & Harris, 2016). What has evolved is a false dichotomy. Individuals feel there is a false choice to support the movement Black Lives Matter or the counter movement in support of law enforcement, Blue Lives Matter. When in actuality, all lives *do* matter. However, at present, all lives are not treated as such and that is why the Black Lives Matter movement is necessary. This movement raises awareness that the experience of Black people in the United States is different from that of those who identify as White. When dismissing the Black Lives Matter movement, people are dismissing the interactional and institutional discrimination and oppression that Black Americans have faced for decades. Some choose to believe that the civil rights movement of the mid-20th century had addressed all issues pertaining to racial equality in the United States. That is not true. Though there were great strides during the civil rights movements of the 1950s and 1960s, much more work remains to be done. Social workers can hold on to the eloquent words of Robert Frost, the American poet, who wrote,

"And miles to go before I sleep." We, as social workers, have miles to go before we sleep. We must not grow weary in our defense of social justice issues and must stand up against any efforts that diminish any group of people on the basis of any form of difference. Social workers are uniquely equipped with the knowledge and skills necessary to bring about change at all levels. We must never underestimate the power we hold as social workers. We are agents of change and must use this to live out the mission of our profession.

SUMMARY

In this chapter we discussed the importance of advancing ADEI in social work practice. Social workers value diversity and center ADEI in all forms of practice. Social workers also understand the intersectionality related to age, class, color, culture, disability and ability, ethnicity, gender identity and expression, immigration status, marital status, political ideology, race, religion/spirituality, sex, sexual orientation, and tribal sovereign status, which all impact an individual's life experiences and identity formation. We explored various forms and mechanisms of oppression and discrimination at various levels (micro, mezzo, and macro) as well as microaggressions. Theories were introduced to assist in ADEI-informed practice. Cultural competence standards set forth by NASW were shared as well as recommendations put forth to advance antiracist social work practice. To demonstrate cultural competence, social workers must continuously be mindful of culture and diversity. Social workers are reflective and self-aware of their own personal values and biases and how they influence their practice. Furthermore, social workers should embrace cultural empathy and cultural humility as they seek to empower the client systems they are working with throughout the helping process.

CASE SUMMARY | UNDOCUMENTED AND HOMELESS

Practice Setting Description

Jackie is a first-year master of social work (MSW) student completing an internship at an inner-city family service agency in the Southwest. The agency is located in a section of the city that has a high crime rate, gang activity, and failing schools. The area has a diverse population with a large number of immigrants from Central and South America and a substantial African American population. The agency provides individual and family counseling services on a sliding fee scale. The agency also runs a number of educational and treatment groups as well as a temporary shelter for women and their children. Jackie has been assigned to work with the women and their children in the shelter. Her primary tasks are to provide concrete services and supportive counseling to the shelter residents.

Background Information

Elicia and her daughter, Maria, are undocumented immigrants from Mexico. They have been in the United States for 5 years. Elicia and Maria fled to the area from another southwestern city to escape her abusive husband approximately 2 months ago. Elicia is 25 years old and Maria 8 years old. Elicia has a 2-year-old daughter, Sarah, who was placed in foster care because of suspected abuse in the home. Sarah is in a foster home in a small rural community in the state hundreds of miles from Elicia's current residence. Since moving to the area Maria has not been attending school.

(continued)

CASE SUMMARY UNDOCUMENTED AND HOMELESS (*CONTINUED*)

Elicia and Maria are currently residing in the agency's temporary shelter for families. They have been at the shelter for 2 weeks, and the agency has a 90-day limit. Prior to arriving at the shelter Elicia and Maria were homeless and living on the streets.

Elicia is a high school drop-out and was a stay-at-home mother prior to leaving her husband and moving to a different part of the state. She chose to move there because she has two female cousins living in the area who are also undocumented immigrants. Elicia's native language is Spanish. She speaks some English but is not as comfortable speaking in English. Her English comprehension appears to be good. Maria speaks both English and Spanish well. When communicating with the staff, Maria acts as Elicia's interpreter since none of the staff at the shelter speak Spanish.

Maria appears to be behind academically. She struggles reading simple children's books written in English. It is unknown if her ability to read in Spanish is better than her English reading skills.

Other than her two cousins, Elicia has no other sources of support in the community. Her cousins have young families and limited resources but are well established and connected to a Latino community in the city and the local Catholic church. Her cousins refused to let Elicia and Maria live with them while she was trying to find her own place and a job. They stated that they did not have enough room and are concerned they would get in trouble with their landlord if it was found out that they were letting people stay with them. They sent her to the local church for help, and she was given the address for the agency's shelter by the priest.

Elicia has been looking for housing in the Latino community. The housing market is tight with limited options, and she has been unable to find anything that she could possibly afford. The only affordable housing she found was a room in a rundown motel that rents by the hour or by the month. It is in an area of town known for drug dealing and sex work.

Upon arriving in the community Elicia found occasional work for a house cleaning company. The company hires undocumented workers, pays them very low cash wages, and threatens to turn them in to Immigration and Customs Enforcement (ICE) if they complain. The job bosses also exploit their female workers sexually, threatening to turn them in if they do not comply. Elicia was fearful about applying for other jobs because of her illegal status. She considered turning to sex work to be able to take care of her children, but her Catholic upbringing and thoughts of how doing so would shame her family have kept her from doing so. She is in constant fear of being detained, separated from her children, and having them placed in foster care. She is also afraid that she will end up homeless again and forced to live on the streets or return to her abusive husband.

Elicia is extremely reluctant to sign up for any federally funded services, even those that she and her children are entitled to receive. Upon the suggestion that she enroll for supplemental food through Supplemental Nutrition Assistance Program (SNAP), Elicia became nervous and refused, as she has heard that participation in SNAP services, and others like them, would draw the attention of ICE, and she had heard stories on the news of individuals being deported after signing up for such programs.

Presenting Problems

Elicia and her children are facing multiple obstacles. They need to find permanent, affordable housing and a job that pays enough to cover her housing and living expenses. In addition, Maria needs to be enrolled in school. Elicia also wants to regain custody of her youngest daughter in foster care.

(continued)

CASE SUMMARY: UNDOCUMENTED AND HOMELESS (*CONTINUED*)

Additionally, Elicia is experiencing an immense amount of stress, anxiety, and possibly post-traumatic stress disorder (PTSD). She described an instance where she could not calm down her breathing and she felt lightheaded. She is very fearful of men and tries to avoid all contact with men in the community. She reports difficulty sleeping at night and feeling exhausted most of the time.

She is concerned about Maria. She has started acting out at the shelter, getting into fights with the other children, disobeying her mother, and being disrespectful and defiant to the staff and other adults. Elicia and Maria fight frequently, and when Elicia tries to discipline Maria she throws a temper tantrum until Elicia gives up.

Elicia has many strengths. She had the strength to leave her abusive husband and move to a different city. She loves her daughters. She wants desperately to keep Maria with her and hopes to have Sarah returned to her custody. She is resilient and has managed to survive and keep her daughter safe despite not having a place to stay, a job and a limited support network. Additionally, Elicia is highly motivated to find her own accommodations and support her children.

DISCUSSION QUESTIONS

1. How can Jackie increase her cultural competence during her work with Elicia and Maria?
2. How can conflict theory inform Jackie's practice with Elicia and Maria?
3. What ADEI theory from this chapter do you feel would be most helpful to Jackie in her work with Elicia and Maria?
4. In what ways can Jackie utilize Elicia as a constituent expert? How would you present this to Elicia if you were the social worker?
5. Describe how Jackie can empower Elicia.
6. Describe Elicia's and Maria's individual intersectionalities.
7. Create a culturagram for Elicia and Maria.

A robust set of instructor resources designed to supplement this text is located at http://connect.springerpub.com/content/book/978-0-8261-6683-8. Qualifying instructors may request access by emailing textbook@springerpub.com.

KEY REFERENCES

Only key references appear in the print edition. To access the full reference list, visit www.springerpub.com/courseconnect. See inside front cover and tear-out card for CourseConnect details.

Bartos, O. J., & Wehr, P. E. (2002). *Using conflict theory*. Cambridge University Press.
Bubar, R., Cespedes, K., & Bundy-Fazioli, K. (2016). Intersectionality and social work: Omissions of race, class, and sexuality in graduate school education. *Journal of Social Work Education, 52*(3), 283–296. https://doi.org/10.1080/10437797.2016.1174636

Charles, J. L. K., Holley, L. C., & Kondrat, D. C. (2017). Addressing our own biases: Social work educators' experiences with students with mental illnesses. *Social Work Education, 36*(4), 414–429. https://doi.org/10.1080/02615479.2017.1297393

Cho, S., Crenshaw, K. W., & McCall, L. (2013). Toward a field of intersectionality studies: Theory, applications, and praxis. *Signs: Journal of Women in Culture & Society, 38*(4), 785–810. https://doi.org/10.1086/669608

Daley, M. R. (2015). *Rural social work in the 21st century*. Lyceum Books, Inc.

Fisher, A. K., Moore, D. J., Simmons, C., & Allen, S. C. (2017). Teaching social workers about microaggressions to enhance understanding of subtle racism. *Journal of Human Behavior in the Social Environment, 27*(4), 346–355. https://doi.org/10.1080/10911359.2017.1289877

Gil, D. G. (2013). *Confronting injustice and oppression: Concepts and strategies for social workers*. Columbia University Press.

Mahler, S. J. (2013). *Culture as comfort*. Pearson.

Maglalang, D. D., & Rao, S. (2021). "Theory's cool, but theory with no practice ain't shit. . .": Critical theories and frameworks to dismantle racism in social work education and practice. *Advances in Social Work, 21*(2–3), 672–689. https://doi.org/10.18060/24145

Marsiglia, F. F., & Kulis, S. (2016). *Diversity, oppression & change* (2nd ed.). Oxford University Press.

National Association of Social Workers. (2022). *Undoing racism through social work: Vol. 2*. NASW Press. https://www.socialworkers.org/LinkClick.aspx?fileticket=QsNmikJGKj0=&portalid=0

Ortega, R. M., & Faller, K. C. (2011). Training child welfare workers from an intersectional cultural humility perspective: A paradigm shift. *Child Welfare, 90*(5), 27–49. https://www.jstor.org/stable/48623301

Rosen, D., McCall, J., & Goodkind, S. (2017). Teaching critical self-reflection through the lens of cultural humility: An assignment in a social work diversity course. *Social Work Education, 36*(3), 289–298. https://doi.org/10.1080/02615479.2017.1287260

Walsh, J. (2013). *Theories for direct social work practice* (3rd ed.). Cengage.

6 Research-Informed Social Work Practice

Ky is a master of social work (MSW) student who is completing their practicum at a community mental health center. They transitioned from observing seasoned social workers and therapists to actively cofacilitating sessions alongside their MSW site supervisor. While initially nervous about working independently with clients, Ky's dedication to growth and learning led them to discuss their apprehensions openly during their weekly supervision sessions. Together with their MSW supervisor, Ky crafted a thoughtful plan to navigate this new territory.

During one supervision session, Ky and the MSW supervisor reviewed the intake paperwork of a 24-year-old woman diagnosed with depression who was going to be assigned to Ky. This collaborative review served to help Ky gain insight into the client's background and begin considering evidence-based treatment approaches. Drawing from their competence and the research supporting cognitive behavioral therapy (CBT) as an effective treatment for depressive symptoms, Ky and their supervisor agreed it was the most suitable intervention.

Ky's supervisor posed the question of how they would evaluate the intervention's effectiveness, Ky was momentarily stumped. Their supervisor reframed the question, encouraging Ky to reflect on how they would know whether their efforts were making a difference for the client. This shift in perspective underscored the importance of ongoing evaluation and critical reflection in social work practice, emphasizing the need for practitioners to actively gauge progress (or lack thereof) and adjust their approach as needed.

LEARNING OBJECTIVES

In this chapter, we explore how research is an integral component of professional social work practice. Often, social work students doubt their competence related to research much more than the other content areas of the social work curriculum. Research can seem intimidating, but we encourage you to view research as approachable. Research is infused in many aspects of the social work profession. Research drives the theories that inform our practice, the modalities we use to work with clients, and the methods we use to determine the degree to which our practice has been effective. The practice of social work is both an art and a science. Research supports the science component of practice. Research allows social workers to make important decisions at the micro, mezzo, and macro levels. It guides us in determining what is effective and what is not. It can also support us in identifying the best ways to support client systems. By the end of this chapter, you will be able to:

- Acknowledge the necessity for social workers to engage in research.
- Understand the importance of research-informed practice.

- Understand the importance of considering culturally-relevant research approaches.
- Identify social workers' ethical responsibilities related to evaluating practice effectiveness.
- Conduct informal evaluations of your practice effectiveness.
- Construct self-anchored rating scales and goal attainment scales.
- Use client logs and behavioral observation in measuring client system progress.

COMPETENCY 4: ENGAGE IN PRACTICE-INFORMED RESEARCH AND RESEARCH-INFORMED PRACTICE

Social workers use ethical, culturally informed, antiracist, and anti-oppressive approaches in conducting research and building knowledge. Social workers use research to inform their practice decision-making and articulate how their practice experience informs research and evaluation decisions. Social workers critically evaluate and critique current, empirically sound research to inform decisions pertaining to practice, policy, and programs. Social workers understand the inherent bias in research and evaluate design, analysis, and interpretation using an antiracist and anti-oppressive perspective. Social workers know how to access, critique, and synthesize the current literature to develop appropriate research questions and hypotheses. Social workers demonstrate knowledge and skills regarding qualitative and quantitative research methods and analysis, and they interpret data derived from these methods. Social workers demonstrate knowledge about methods to assess reliability and validity in social work research. Social workers can articulate and share research findings in ways that are usable to a variety of clients and constituencies. Social workers understand the value of evidence derived from interprofessional and diverse research methods, approaches, and sources.

Social workers:

- apply research findings to inform and improve practice, policy, and programs; and
- identify ethical, culturally informed, antiracist, and anti-oppressive strategies that address inherent biases for use in quantitative and qualitative research methods to advance the purposes of social work. (Council on Social Work Education [CSWE], 2022, p. 10)

COMPETENCY 9: EVALUATE PRACTICE WITH INDIVIDUALS, FAMILIES, GROUPS, ORGANIZATIONS, AND COMMUNITIES

Social workers understand that evaluation is an ongoing component of the dynamic and interactive process of social work practice with and on behalf of diverse individuals, families, groups, organizations, and communities. Social workers evaluate processes and outcomes to increase practice, policy, and service delivery effectiveness. Social workers apply antiracist and anti-oppressive perspectives in evaluating outcomes. Social workers understand theories of human behavior and person-in-environment, as well as interprofessional conceptual frameworks, and critically evaluate and apply this knowledge in evaluating outcomes. Social workers use qualitative and quantitative methods for evaluating outcomes and practice effectiveness.

Social workers:

- select and use culturally responsive methods for evaluation of outcomes; and
- critically analyze outcomes and apply evaluation findings to improve practice effectiveness with individuals, families, groups, organizations, and communities. (CSWE, 2022, pp. 12–13)

NATIONAL ASSOCIATION OF SOCIAL WORKERS *CODE OF ETHICS*

The National Association of Social Workers (NASW) *Code of Ethics* (2021) serves to orient social workers to engage in professional social worker practice that is ethical. The *Code of Ethics* serves to safeguard clients, communities, and the profession as a whole. It is imperative that social workers are familiar with all aspects of the *Code of Ethics* regarding what it puts forth for all types of social work practice. In the following sections, we will be looking specifically at how the *Code of Ethics* applies to research-informed practice. It is necessary that social workers only engage in research that is ethical. Throughout history, there have been egregious violations of human rights in the name of "research." These heinous acts have often targeted vulnerable and oppressed groups. An example of this would be the medical experiments conducted by Nazi doctors during World War II. During wartime, medical doctors used prisoners of concentration camps to conduct research. Some of their experiments were designed to provide insights into ways to support Nazi soldiers. One such way was to examine the use of anticoagulant medications in order to determine the best means to support a soldier who suffered an amputation. The experimenters would test their theories by amputating limbs from the war camp prisoners. This is just one example of the heinous experiments that were done in the name of science. As a result of these experiments, the Nuremberg trials began in the mid-1940s to address the blatant disregard for human rights. The Nuremberg Code, a document that addresses ethical research, was derived from these trials. This code established a set of standards and practices that were necessary when research involved human subjects.

Unfortunately, the development of this code did not stop unethical research on human participants. Another example of unethical research practices on human subjects is the infamous Tuskegee experiment that was conducted in the southern United States in the 20th century. During the Tuskegee experiment, researchers purposely injected low-income Black subjects with syphilis in the hopes of better understanding the disease and its treatment. This experiment continued for decades, long after a known cure for the disease (penicillin) was discovered. This experiment was deceptive and prevented participants from accessing the lifesaving medication that was known to be beneficial for this condition.

> ▶ **Reflection Questions**
>
> Why is it important to learn about past unethical research experiments? How can this inform present research endeavors?

As a result of these experiments, the Belmont Code was established to address ethical research practice. This code sets forth three core values, which include respect for the person, beneficence, and justice. These three values are well aligned with social work values. Respect for the person requires researchers to honor the autonomy of the person and protect those with diminished autonomy (Belmont Report, 1979).

Social workers value the dignity and worth of every individual. The profession calls upon social workers to treat all people with respect and to honor an individual's right to self-determination. Self-determination is the concept that individuals have the ability and agency to determine for themselves how they wish to live their life. The second value of beneficence refers to the necessity to have participants' welfare considered. In medicine, the phrase "do no harm" is often used to describe this principle. Within the confines of research, researchers should seek to minimize harm whenever possible. It is understood that some research may possess potential harm; it is the duty of the researcher to ensure that undue harm is not inflicted and that there are adequate and appropriate resources and supports to address any potential harm. The final value of the Belmont Report is justice. Justice in the Belmont Report encouraged equality.

Based on these advancements to protect human participants, institutional review boards (IRBs) have been established to ensure that research participants are protected from undue harm. Researchers who will be using human subjects must go through the IRB review process. This process involves sharing all materials involved with the research experience with this board. The purpose of the board is not to examine the efficacy of the research design, but solely to focus on protecting human subjects.

In all aspects of social work practice, social workers should be trustworthy and ethical; this includes when social workers are engaging in research. Regarding research, social workers must be aware of agency policies and procedures surrounding collecting and analyzing data. Furthermore, social workers must be aware of legal and ethical mandates related to research in their field of practice. As we have discussed, numerous ethical violations have been conducted in the name of research or science; social workers must not allow this to continue. Social workers must be able to recognize unethical research practices and stand against them.

Social workers should not only seek to understand professional knowledge but should also make efforts to contribute to the body of professional knowledge. Within the social work profession, practitioners and researchers had historically been siloed apart from one another. This is not conducive to good social work practice. It makes sense that research should inform practice and, conversely, practice should inform research. As a result of this, social workers have sought to encourage research-informed practice and practice-informed research. There is much to be gained from this integrated perspective of social work. Social workers should consciously attempt to be a part of this practice.

Social workers have ethical responsibilities to their profession. In order to maintain the integrity of the profession, social workers must consistently uphold the values of the profession in all areas of practice, including research. Research is an important component of your social work education. As one of the main content areas of the profession, research should not be viewed as an isolated endeavor. Rather, social workers must diligently seek out ways in which to infuse research in all other areas of practice. Research should also inform all parts of the social work helping process—engagement, assessment, intervention, and evaluation.

As discussed, social workers are strongly encouraged to share contributions of knowledge with the profession. There are many great social workers doing many great things with a variety of client systems in a variety of settings. Social workers should share what they have found to be effective with others in order to spread those good outcomes. The social work profession has a long history of sharing means and methods with others. Consider the early works of Mary Richmond and her casework manual. This book was a piece of disseminated research sharing what she had found to be effective in working with her clients. We must continue this in order to continually advance our profession.

We can share this knowledge in a variety of ways, including publications and presentations. Social workers should endeavor to disseminate their findings with other professionals to promote the ongoing integrity and evolution of the profession of social work. Without sharing our results, we are not fulfilling our ethical obligation to the social work profession.

The evaluation and research standard of the NASW *Code of Ethics* (2021) has more subpoints than any other standard in the *Code of Ethics*. You can review all of the subpoints of the *Code of Ethics* online (www.socialworkers.org/About/Ethics/Code-of-Ethics/Code-of-Ethics-English).

As you are aware, social workers are called upon to engage in various aspects of evaluation and research. This standard not only outlines the need for social workers to be engaged in research but also addresses the need to protect human rights during research. Social workers must obtain consent from research participants that is voluntary and informed. Social workers must be mindful of their position of power that could potentially be seen as coercive to some research participants. Furthermore, social workers often find themselves working with vulnerable and oppressed populations. It is important that the rights of these individuals are attended to during the consent and research process.

In addition to ensuring ethical consent procedures, social workers should also be sure that research participants understand their rights related to withdrawing from research as well. Participants who chose to begin participating in a research project have the right to discontinue their involvement at any time. Social workers must be sure to share with participants in the informed consent what will occur if participants withdraw from the study. For example, if the research is being done as an anonymous electronic survey, if a participant chooses to stop, there may not be a way to remove their previous answer selections from the data set.

Social workers should seek to minimize harm and not expose participants to any unnecessary harm or distress. This standard is clearly aligned with both the Nuremberg and Belmont codes we previously noted. Harm could be physical or emotional. For example, asking about sensitive topics, such as past traumatic experiences, could potentially bring up disturbing thoughts in the research participants. That is not to say that we should never ask about things that could bring up emotional discomfort. As social workers, we are often concerned with sensitive topics, and so it is important to know more about them. Before we ask about such things, we need to clearly outline that in the informed consent and provide adequate resources and supports to participants who experienced distress. For example, you could provide information for a crisis hotline or other community supports.

Social workers should be clear whether their research is anonymous or confidential. At times, these terms are incorrectly used interchangeably. *Anonymous participation* refers to collecting no identifiable information on the participants. On the other hand, *confidential participation* is when the identities of the participants are known to the researcher but not shared in the findings or with others outside the research team. Social workers have a duty to share with clients if their identity will be known during the research process. Social workers should inform clients how their data will be used.

POSITIVISM

The theory of positivism has had many contributors. However, a main contributor was Auguste Comte, who is considered to be one of the fathers of sociology. Positivism sets forth the need to be objective and fact based. It holds tightly to the scientific method, and there is an emphasis on empirical observation. It suggests that in order to truly know or understand something, it must be observable through one or more of the five senses (sight, touch, hearing, taste, and smell). Positivism asserts that knowledge about the world can be gained through observation, experimentation, and logical reasoning. It is rooted in the idea that our senses and our ability to measure and observe things are reliable sources of knowledge. Positivism encourages critical thinking, skepticism, and a reliance on evidence over mere speculation or intuition. Positivism requires us to hold a scientific mindset while we seek to uncover objective truths through systematic investigation using the scientific method. This form of thinking has deep roots in empiricism, which can be traced back to the time of Aristotle.

> ▶ **Reflection Question**
>
> What would be potential limitations to relying solely on the five senses?

From a positivism perspective, it is impossible to know anything if you cannot tangibly observe it. This can be troublesome for social scientists. For example, social workers are often concerned with feelings and emotions. However, some argue that these things cannot be empirically observed based on the truest standards of positivism. On the other hand, social work can benefit greatly from the theory of positivism regarding many quantitative designs, including various single-subject designs that are quite common in social work practice. Furthermore, Dybicz (2015) put forth that related to the person-in-environment model, "the strength of positivism in explaining cause-and-effect mechanisms contains the inherent shortcoming of emphasizing causal determinism when seeking to explain human behavior" (p. 237). As you can see, there are both benefits and limitations to utilizing this theory to inform social work practice and social work research. It is important for social work to hold to both the objective and the subjective—the tangible and the intangible—in order to fully understand the client system.

EMPIRICISM

As noted earlier, positivism is closely related to empiricism. Empirical evidence is evidence that is verifiable. By the nature of our profession, social workers serve as outside observers and are thus able to examine evidence and make observations. Many believe that social work is best served by a pursuit of "knowledge building, incorporating philosophy, theory, and methods that are congruent with empiricism" (Caputo et al., 2015, p. 645).

Empiricism emerged in response to skepticism, a philosophical challenge that traces its roots back to ancient Greek philosophy. In the 17th and 18th centuries, two prominent philosophical movements, empiricism and rationalism, arose to grapple with questions of knowledge and certainty. Rationalism suggested that reason was the primary avenue to reliable knowledge, while empiricism countered that sensory experience held greater credibility in understanding the world. Rationalism favored deductive reasoning methods, starting from general principles to reach specific conclusions, while empiricism leaned toward induction, drawing conclusions from specific observations.

However, relying solely on sensory information has its limitations, as our senses can sometimes deceive us. Philosopher John Locke addressed this by distinguishing between primary and secondary qualities. Primary qualities are inherent attributes of an object or experience, while secondary qualities are our perceptions or experiences of those attributes. Since secondary qualities are subjective, they can lead to varying interpretations. In the context of social work practice, it becomes crucial to reflect on the sources of our understanding. Are our insights based on the inherent qualities of a person or situation, or are they influenced by our subjective perceptions and personal experiences? By considering this, social workers can navigate the complexities of human experience with greater insight and awareness. As it is important to note, social workers are human. As a result, social workers have lived experience that will inform their perceptions; this is not necessarily a bad thing. At times, our personal experiences can inform the work we do in a very helpful way. The crucial consideration is that social workers are aware of their experiences, beliefs, and biases and make sure that they are engaging in self-awareness and self-reflection and not allowing these to interfere with their work.

SCIENTIFIC INQUIRY

A systematic, logical approach to understanding problems and providing answers is science. At some point in your schooling, you have most likely been introduced to the scientific method. The scientific method at its simplest starts with an observation that leads to a research question as well as a tentative hypothesis or educated guess. The scientific method is simply a standardized, step-based approach to collecting information to gain knowledge. The scientific method can be applied to more than just laboratory or clinical science. Social sciences, including social work, psychology, and sociology, utilize the scientific method to better understand people, experiences, and social phenomena.

Sometimes social work and other helping professions, including psychology and sociology, are referred to as the "soft sciences" because, due to the nature of what we are researching, we at times may have less strict measurement and intervention criteria as we would be able to have if we were working in a lab and able to control all conditions. With humans, we are unable to control some variables. Not being able to control all variables is part of the reason for referring to social work as a soft science. This term, which is slightly derogatory toward our profession, undermines the rigor and credibility that social workers strive to have in their research. Though it is true that social work research and science are different from laboratory research and science, they are not less credible. Good research is good research, just as poorly designed research is poorly designed research.

The scientific method has a long history within the social work profession. Social workers have long been aware of the necessity to explore their practice from the lens of science. Social workers must attempt to provide known and effective methods to address client needs whenever possible (see Case 6.1).

CASE 6.1   APPLYING POSITIVISM IN SOCIAL WORK PRACTICE RESEARCH

Bella is a social worker at a community food bank. The food bank operates much like a grocery store, where clients can come in and select the items that they wish to have. The agency strongly values the rights of the clients to determine what kinds of food they like and want rather than just giving a box of food to them. Bella loves that her agency values self-determination. She is interested in better understanding the needs of the clients serviced by her agency. Bella decided that she was going to use the theory of positivism to inform her quest for more knowledge about her clients. Bella understood that positivism is rooted in empirical evidence and scientific inquiry. She felt that this would be a good theoretical approach to guide her research, as it is often considered to be fact based and objective. Bella believed this would be an excellent source of data for her to share with the agency board of directors.

Bella believed that fresh foods (vegetables, fruits, dairy, and meat products) were more desirable than the typical nonperishable items typically available at the food bank. Bella decided to use a quantitative design where she would keep track of how many clients selected these items versus clients who did not select any of these items. Bella felt this was the best way to gain understanding about these items, as she can simply observe when these items are selected by clients. Furthermore, she worried that if she interviewed clients, their responses would be biased based on what they thought she wanted to hear.

As a result of Bella's positivist study, she was able to share with the board of directors that these perishable items were highly desired by clients. Based on these findings, the board decided to establish ongoing partnerships with other agencies in order to provide more of the desired perishable foods to the clients they serve.

ROLE OF RESEARCH IN SOCIAL WORK PRACTICE

We have discussed that social workers are called upon by the NASW *Code of Ethics* to engage in research in order to demonstrate commitment to the profession. Social workers must engage in research-informed practice and practice-informed research. We explore both of these concepts throughout this text. Social workers must integrate research information into their practice in order to be sure they are providing the best possible care for the clients they serve.

> ▶ **Reflection Question**
>
> Why do you think it is important for social workers to consider their practice a "practice of science?"

The profession of social work has a long history of providing a systematic approach to helping. A social work pioneer, Mary Richmond, in her early writings spoke to the need to support individuals on the basis of facts. As the profession evolved over time, we have seen an influx of research to influence our practice. Research has helped us better understand the individuals, families, communities, and organizations that we work with. Research has helped us better understand development and growth. Research has also helped us regarding how we can intervene and support these client systems.

As research has evolved across time to this point, research will continue to evolve. We continue to make advancements in what we know about client systems and how to best support them. Additionally, new conditions or concerns arise, and we must use research to determine the best means of support. We caution social work students to not consider their education done at the time of graduation. You must never stop learning. The knowledge of the profession is ongoing, and professional social workers must be continuous, lifelong learners.

RESEARCH-INFORMED PRACTICE

As we have discussed, social workers must rely on science to inform their practice. It is important that social workers speak out regarding research in order to be sure they are providing the best possible services to their clients. What we know is constantly evolving as we learn more and find better ways to address social problems. As social workers, we must be ready and willing to continually reflect back on and go to research to determine if there are new, better ways to address client conditions. Furthermore, social workers must identify when there are gaps in our research knowledge and assist to close the loop and provide feedback on their professional experiences related to such matters. Social work practitioners should be active contributors to the professional body of knowledge of the social work profession.

Some social workers cite barriers to incorporating research into their professional practice. Table 6.1 outlines several barriers that have been identified as potential barriers to research-informed practice (see Case 6.2).

TABLE 6.1 BARRIERS TO RESEARCH-INFORMED SOCIAL WORK PRACTICE

Barrier	Description
Busyness	Social workers are often busy. Increasingly, social workers are being called upon to do more with less. It may be difficult for social workers to find time to seek out relevant research that can inform their practice. Furthermore, some social workers may worry that if they are seen looking for research during their work day, others may think that they are not busy enough and in turn give them more duties or cases.
Lack of access	It can at times be difficult to locate reliable, valid research that is relevant to a specific area of practice. While in college, social work students often have access to library resources, including sophisticated search engines that are reliable in regard to finding pertinent research. Social workers must know where to look in order to find the appropriate information that is necessary to inform their practice. Thankfully, there are increasingly more and more avenues to find good-quality research through internet search engines designed to specifically disseminate information to professionals.
Difficulty in interpreting	For some, interpreting research can feel daunting. When social workers are insecure in their ability to read, interpret, and infer from the research they have found, it is difficult to integrate research into practice. Sometimes statistics can be quite complicated and overwhelming. For this reason, some avoid looking for scholarly research.

Source: From McLaughlin, H. (2012). *Understanding social work research* (2nd ed.). Sage.

> **CASE 6.2** **RESEARCH-INFORMED PRACTICE**
>
> Tony is a social worker at a behavioral health rehabilitation service provider. He has recently been assigned a case with a 3-year-old child who is diagnosed with autism. Tony's role is to serve as the behavior specialist consultant, and he needs to develop a treatment plan to address the needs of his client. Tony has worked with children diagnosed with autism previously. However, they were typically school-age children; he has no experience working with a child this young. Also, this child is currently nonverbal; all of Tony's other clients have been able to speak. Tony seeks out supervision from his supervisor to assist him in formulating a plan to work with this client. Tony and his supervisor discuss what practices are deemed evidence based for young children diagnosed with autism. Tony learns that applied behavioral analysis, which is grounded in behavioral theory, is a common approach to support such clients. Tony is familiar with behavioral theory and concepts related to applied behavior analysis from his schooling and ongoing training. Tony recognizes that it is important to brush up his skills, and so he seeks out a local training opportunity that will be happening next week. He also finds several journal articles related to using this modality with young children. Tony also makes it a point to schedule follow-up supervision with his supervisor weekly.

CRITIQUING EXISTING RESEARCH

It is not enough that social workers find research that relates to their area of practice; they must be sure that the research they are finding is valuable. Not all research is created equal, and social workers must recognize this before they begin fusing research into their practice. Before allowing research to inform one's professional practice, they should critically analyze and critique the source.

Unfortunately, bad research is out there. It is the duty and obligation of professional social workers to ensure that this research does not infiltrate their practice. One way that social workers can be sure they are not incorporating bad research into their practice is by applying critical thinking skills to the analysis of research. Critical thinking is a necessary piece of professional practice. To successfully integrate research into social work practice, it is necessary that social workers become critical thinkers and are able to critique existing research. It is important to not simply accept information without first considering several factors. First, where is this information coming from? It is important to consider who is authoring or supporting this research.

Another important consideration when critiquing existing research is to examine where the information was found. Information from peer-reviewed journals is typically held to a higher degree of scrutiny and thus can be relatively trustworthy. With that being said, not all journals are equal. It is important to consider the source.

Another place where social workers must use good critical judgment is when finding research online. The internet can provide exceptionally valuable research. Unfortunately, it can also provide useless research. It is important to critique where the information is found. We live in an age where information is more readily available than ever before. We are lucky that with a few clicks of the mouse, we are able to peruse a myriad of source material. Additionally, we are able to connect with other professionals more rapidly than ever before. These benefits are truly astounding and can assist us in enhancing our professional practice. However, we must be mindful that, as with most great advancements, there are potential drawbacks. Again, it is important for the social worker to consider who is putting this information forth and what their motivations may be to do so. Box 6.1 provides five points—accuracy, authority, objectivity, currency, and coverage—to consider when evaluating online sources. Furthermore, these guidelines to evaluating online material may be helpful to consider should you wish to present your own material online for others.

CULTURALLY RESPONSIVE RESEARCH

Globally, now, perhaps more than at any time previously, social workers find themselves practicing in a multicultural environment. Social workers seeking to provide culturally relevant care need to focus not simply on the awareness of various cultures but also on "an ability to negotiate and practice ethically and professionally within the demands of the culture of the

---

BOX 6.1

EVALUATING ONLINE SOURCES

When evaluating resources, consider the following five criteria:

1. *Accuracy*: It is important to consider if the information being presented is accurate. If there is a reference list, you can critically analyze the source material utilized. If there is no reference list of source material, you can verify the information on your own utilizing another source to check for accuracy.
2. *Authority*: Consider if the authors or contributors are listed on the site. If there are listed authors and contributors, you can look at their credentials to determine if they have the knowledge base to put forth the material you are reviewing. In addition to the person posting the information, you should notice if there are any organizational or institutional affiliations as well.
3. *Objectivity*: Objectivity refers to being based on facts, not opinions. In order to determine if the material is objective, you want to pay close attention to the language utilized in the material. Language can often provide clues as to whether the author is subjective (sharing opinion) or objective (presenting facts).
4. *Currency*: It is important to be mindful that the information you are gathering is currently relevant and not outdated. Looking for dates on a website can assist in determining when the material was posted or updated.
5. *Coverage*: It is important to consider if the source is comprehensive regarding its stated purpose.

Source: From Western Connecticut State University. (2023). *Research basics: Step-by-step guide on how to approach gathering resources for a research project.* https://libguides.wcsu.edu/c.php?g=119514&p=779931

people" (Forkuor et al., 2019, p. 865). It is of paramount importance that social workers not only consider the theories, frameworks, and perspectives they are familiar with but also consider cultural understanding and indigenous wisdom and knowledge relevant to the client at hand (Waqa et al., 2023). We must consider the full intersectionality of our clients' cultural identities in order to provide truly culturally responsive care (Chapple, 2019). When considering research, it is important to consider the methods used in the study and to not only critique their scientific rigor but also consider the extent to which they embraced culturally sensitive research practices. When conducting research in multicultural contexts, it's imperative to incorporate culturally responsive practices to ensure the validity, relevance, and ethical integrity of the study. Researchers should demonstrate cultural sensitivity by respecting and acknowledging the diverse backgrounds, values, and beliefs of the participants. Language accessibility is also a very important consideration. Researchers must make sure that research materials are available in languages or formats understood by the participants to promote inclusivity and enable full participation.

Community engagement also plays a vital role in culturally responsive research. Social work has a long history of engaging with communities, and this can be advantageous in the research process (Casado et al., 2012). Involving community members, leaders, or cultural brokers can ensure that the research aligns with community norms and preferences. Culturally adapting research methods and approaches, remaining flexible and open to diverse perspectives, and addressing ethical considerations specific to the cultural context are also essential. Equitable representation of diverse cultural groups within the research sample should be prioritized to avoid overgeneralization and capture the full spectrum of diversity within the population of interest. By integrating these considerations, researchers can foster meaningful engagement, respect diverse perspectives, and produce research that is both valid and culturally appropriate.

EVIDENCE-BASED PRACTICE

Evidence is a collection of facts that demonstrate a position to be true. Evidence-based practices (EBPs), which began flourishing in the late 20th century, are professional practices and strategies that have a basis in research, which indicates the method is successful to address a specific condition or with a particular population. EBPs are utilized by helping professions to provide the best practices.

EBP serves to ground the social work profession in empiricism (Okpych & Yu, 2014). There is a generally accepted process of EBP, which begins with identifying the need for information. That need for information must then be translated into a question. Evidence to answer this question is then sought. After finding evidence, it is then critically analyzed or critiqued to determine its validity. If the evidence is valid and applicable for the current need, it is then incorporated with the clinician's expertise. The clinician should also be mindful of the goodness of fit with the client system. If it is a good fit, the evidence is integrated into the social worker's practice with the client. The social worker monitors this implementation and seeks out additional evidence as necessary. Case 6.3 illustrates a social worker going through the process of EBP.

> **CASE 6.3   THE EVIDENCE-BASED PRACTICE PROCESS IN SOCIAL WORK**
>
> Melody is a social worker at a child welfare organization. She very much enjoys her job and supporting families. Melody was recently transferred to a new unit within the organization. As Melody was familiarizing herself with the new requirements of this position, she began to notice that many of the children on her new caseload have had multiple disrupted placements. Disrupted placement is when an out-of-home placement must be terminated and the child must be placed in a new home. Melody thought that this must be difficult for the children. Melody wondered what she could do to support placements in order to avoid multiple disruptive placements.
>
> Melody began searching scholarly material to find research on how to best support placements in order to avoid disruption. Melody found several articles and reports that address this issue. Among the practices that were found to be beneficial were those that provided additional support for foster families as well as respite care. Melody spoke with her supervisor about these recommendations to possibly improve placements. Both support and respite care were services that the organization already had available but were often underutilized. Melody and her supervisor discussed ways to share this information with families, including having the caseworkers speak with the family members about resources available to them. Melody began incorporating this into her practice. Over time, Melody noticed fewer and fewer disrupted placements.

EBP encourages social workers to be considerate of the importance of outcomes in practice, whether client situations are improving, staying the same, or worsening. As we have discussed related to assessment, good assessment is ongoing assessment. Social workers must be particularly thoughtful in recognizing changes in the client system when incorporating an EBP. Furthermore, social workers must be cautious in assuming causation between their EBP and client changes. This underscores the importance of a thorough assessment in order to determine if other changes are occurring that could account for the change in client presentation.

The process of EBP involves finding the "best available evidence to support clinical decision making that also considers a social worker's clinical judgment and professional ethics and the client's personal and cultural preferences" (Langer & Lietz, 2015, p. 13). Social workers must be aware that clients are not "passive recipients of social work practice," and therefore, EBP should be selected in consideration of the clients' rights to self-determination (McLaughlin, 2012). We must continuously be aware that clients come to us with their own unique histories and experiences, and we as professionals must meet the clients where they are. It is our job to begin where the client is.

MULTIPLE WAYS OF KNOWING

How do you know what you know? This may seem like quite a philosophical question, but it is an important one to consider. There are multiple ways of knowing, each coming with benefits and limitations. It is important that social workers be critical thinkers. In order to be a critical thinker, one must consider from where the information one is receiving originates. It is important for social workers to consider such things because social workers are often called upon to make many decisions every day that have implications for clients, communities, and the profession itself.

> ▶ **Reflection Questions**
>
> Consider how you know what you know. Think about current events in the country and abroad.
> 1. How do you get most of your information? How do you know this information is true?
> 2. Why is it necessary to critically analyze how you are getting information and whether or not it is coming from a trusted source?

Social workers must be aware that it is easy to make errors in logic. Common errors in reasoning include overgeneralization, selective observation, illogical reasoning, resistance to change, and adherence to authority (Engel & Schutt, 2014). Overgeneralization refers to the tendency of individuals to take what they know to be true in one case and apply it in all situations. This is a simplistic error that does not allow for individual experiences. As we know, most issues that social workers deal with are quite complex and multifaceted. Overgeneralizations do not take into account individual differences or experiences. Social workers must be cautious to avoid this error in logic. Selective observation occurs when an individual seeks out only information that confirms already held beliefs. For example, if a person believes that boys are more aggressive than girls, they may only notice situations in which boys are engaging in aggression, as that fits their predetermined belief. Illogical reasoning happens when an individual holds on to untrue assumptions or jumps to conclusions without support. Many times individuals always think a certain way about something, and as a result, they may be resistant to changing their beliefs. This is an error in logic, as the person is not open to new information. This error in logic is sometimes referred to as tradition. Social workers must recognize that at times people hold tightly on to traditionally held beliefs even when presented with evidence to the contrary. Adherence to authority refers to when a person believes something simply because they were told about it by a person in a (real or perceived) place of authority (see Case 6.4).

Social workers must also be on the lookout for pseudoscience. Pseudoscience is a belief or practice that claims to be scientific; however, it lacks any foundation in science. It sometimes looks like science, but upon closer inspection, one can identify flawed reasoning, anecdotal evidence, or unfounded claims. Believing pseudoscience can be an additional error in logic. In order for social workers to distinguish between true science and pseudoscience, they must have a basic understanding of good research methods in order to detect issues with a research design. Social workers must have a critical eye when evaluating research in order to determine if it is truly good science.

Practice wisdom is something that is valued in many professions, including social work. The capstone of the social work educational experience is a field experience where social work students are placed with competent social work professionals who guide students, many times with practice wisdom, toward becoming competent professionals themselves. Practice wisdom is complex and requires reflection and analysis that bring together various learning sources and contexts in order to encapsulate or understand better how things work

CASE 6.4	**WHY DO WE DO IT THIS WAY? THE IMPORTANCE OF RESEARCH-BASED SOCIAL WORK PRACTICE**

Tran is a new social worker who was recently hired at an outpatient facility that provides various services to veterans, including assistance in finding housing and employment in addition to providing onsite mental health and drug and alcohol counseling. Tran is very excited about her new position because she has always wanted to work with the military population. As a part of being a new hire, Tran is assigned to a mentor who is someone who has been with the agency and can show her the ropes. Tran will shadow her mentor for the first week at the agency. On the first day, Tran met her mentor, Kelly. Kelly has been with the agency for almost two decades.

Throughout the day, Tran was observing Kelly work with other colleagues as well as with clients. Tran kept notes on questions she had to ask Kelly about the way in which she was doing things so that she could better understand organizational expectations. Over lunch, Kelly asked Tran if she had any questions. Tran consulted her notebook and began to ask about the group session she observed Kelly facilitate that morning. She asked Kelly about how the group was run. Kelly shared that when she started at the agency all those years ago, that was the way the group was run and that is why she does it the way she does. This answer surprised Tran because she expected that the group was based on research or evidence related to the best practices with this population. As the training went on that week, Tran noticed more and more that things were just done the way they had always been done without a researched rationale as to why.

This concerned Tran. During her supervision, she directly asked her supervisor how clinical decisions such as what modalities to use in group or individual sessions are made. The supervisor shared with Tran that the agency follows a trauma-informed care model and relies heavily on cognitive behavioral approaches. Tran felt better after talking with her supervisor about how researched practices inform their organization. Tran was then able to seek out readings and source material regarding the specific perspectives that inform this agency. Throughout her first few months at the agency, Tran found that her weekly supervision was extremely helpful to review research related to the population and interventions. Her supervisor was also quite impressed with Tran's initiative to seek out research to inform and improve her practice.

(Shaw, 2016). Though practice wisdom is an integral part of our profession, we encourage social workers to not rely solely on practice wisdom. Practice wisdom based on best practices and sciences is best. As a result, social workers must be critical thinkers.

Various forms of research knowledge are available for social workers. Three types of research knowledge include descriptive, predictive, and prescriptive knowledge (Yegidis et al., 2018). Descriptive knowledge, as its name implies, seeks to describe how things are. This type of knowledge may describe things currently and as they change over time. Predictive knowledge attempts to predict what will happen in the future. This type of knowledge is possible when we have enough descriptive knowledge in order to be able to make reasonable inferences about future occurrences. Prescriptive knowledge provides insights into the intervention to address a current condition. Yegidis et al. (2018) set forth that "in EBP, social workers use prescriptive knowledge, along with their experience, client preferences, and so forth, to decide what intervention should be used to address an existing problem or to prevent one that they predict will occur" (p. 14).

TRANSLATING FINDINGS INTO PRACTICE

Research findings are only beneficial if they can be used and applied to practice. As we discussed at the start of this chapter, it is unreasonable to separate research and practice from one another. Research must be integrated into practice in order to be of any value or use. When thinking about integrating research findings into professional practice, social workers should thoroughly learn about the proposed methods. Furthermore, social workers must be critical thinkers in order to determine if these new methods would be a good fit for their client population. Social workers must be considerate of cultural limitations regarding some findings. For example, some EBPs have only been researched on specific populations (age, gender, race/ethnicity, etc.). Also, it is necessary that social workers implement EBP and other findings in their practice only if they have been sufficiently trained and are competent in the EBP. If a social worker is not trained in a specific EBP, it would be unethical to administer it. Social workers should also be mindful of their limits of competence and seek out ongoing learning opportunities to enhance their practice skills related to innovative methods.

EVALUATING MICROPRACTICE EFFECTIVENESS: INFORMAL APPROACHES

This section focuses on the practice effectiveness component of the evaluating practice competency. It addresses methods or approaches to determine the effectiveness of your social work practice with individuals, families, and groups. It is about evaluating micro social work practice using informal approaches. Chapter 14 reviews more formal methods of evaluating micro social work practice.

Supervision and Self-Reflection

One approach to evaluating the effectiveness of your social work practice with clients is through supervision. Social work supervision entails three components: administration, education, and support. It is the educational component that can be used to evaluate your practice effectiveness.

An important part of the supervisory process is the willingness to share and be vulnerable. Sometimes we may not want to share certain things because they make us feel at risk. Vulnerability refers to a state of being open or exposed to criticism or judgment. It can be scary, especially within the context of your supervisory relationship. Despite that, being vulnerable is necessary if you are engaged in a process of self-reflection and discussion of your social work practice and practice effectiveness with your supervisor.

Effective use of supervision to assess your social work practice effectiveness is dependent on the establishment of a trusting worker/supervisor relationship. A key to developing a strong positive worker/supervisor relationship is establishing some level of trust. The social worker must be able to trust the supervisor. Relationships cannot be built in the absence of trust. A certain degree of trust must be established between workers and supervisors for the workers to engage in the process of self-evaluation and the evaluation of their practice effectiveness.

Trust is essential for relationships to develop and grow between social workers and their supervisors. A strong relationship requires the absence of fear and suspicion and the presence of feelings of acceptance, support, and affirmation. Building trust with supervisors is an interactional process. Trust cannot be built in the absence of interpersonal interactions between the worker and the supervisor. It is built upon a sequence of trusting and trustworthy interactions. The worker must act in a trusting manner, and the supervisor must respond with trustworthy actions.

The bond of trust is built over time through a series of trusting actions (risks) and trustworthy responses (confirmations). Although it takes time for trust to be established, it can be destroyed through a single worker risk and supervisor disconfirmation (nontrustworthy) response (Fong & Cox, 1983).

The critical element in developing trust is risk. The supervisor is an active partner in the search for understanding and insights. This cannot happen if the worker is unable to take a risk by being open and honest about their social work practice with clients. Social workers have to be willing to share their thoughts, insights, feelings, and questions about their practice to be able to use the supervisory relationship to access their practice effectiveness. The primary task for the supervisor is to facilitate risk taking. The worker's task is to be self-reflective and to be willing to share information about their successes, mistakes, and ongoing challenges to assess client progress and possibly needed adjustments in their work together.

Ongoing Client Feedback

The social work value of competency discussed earlier implies that ethical social work practice involves an ongoing assessment of practice effectiveness throughout the helping relationship. This type of informal practice evaluation is based on the subjective responses of the clients. It is a joint and collaborative effort. Both the worker and the client have roles in this type of practice evaluation.

Ongoing informal evaluation is a relatively easy way for social workers to evaluate the effectiveness of their work with clients. In keeping with the principles of collaboration and empowerment in which the client is the expert about their progress, subjective assessments play a prominent role in strengths-based social work practice and other practice models. Clients' subjective assessments of their situations are the primary basis for evaluating the effectiveness of the helping process. The critical factor is whether the issues or concerns for which they are seeking help have, in their view, improved. It also helps the social worker and client identify what is working and what is not.

> ▶ **Reflection Questions**
>
> 1. What do you think is helpful to build trust with your supervisor?
> 2. What do you think is helpful to build trust with your clients?

Informal evaluation is an ongoing process. The client and worker begin by exploring the client's person-in-environment system and life experiences in order to identify concerns and factors that potentially affect them. During this and later stages, the social worker makes sure that their interpretations of the client's experiences are consistent with the client's perceptions. This approach to practice emphasizes listening to the client's story and understanding the client's perceptions of experiences. The worker needs to continually evaluate the extent to which their understanding of the client's experiences is consistent with the client's understanding.

As work continues, informal evaluation techniques identical to the process described earlier play a role. The social worker has to make a conscious effort to ensure that there is agreement about the identified goals and specifics of the helping contract. The worker and client need to evaluate the client's commitment to the plan. Is it genuine? How strong is it? What can the social worker do to help the client maintain or strengthen their commitment to change?

The key to ongoing assessment of client progress and practice effectiveness is persistently and relentlessly following through on the intervention plan. It is checking in with your client between meetings. It is regularly monitoring progress and exploring why progress is or is not being made. In addition to providing feedback, seeking ongoing client feedback helps create expectations for success and for making the identified changes. It communicates that you care and that you are committed to helping your clients overcome the challenges they are facing. The following section describes some measurement tools that can be used in your practice to informally evaluate client progress and practice effectiveness.

Measurement Tools

There are a number of measurement methods that involve clients, that are easy to construct and implement, and that are appropriate for social work practice evaluations. The following are more frequently used measurement tools:

- client logs
- behavioral observations
- rating scales
- goal attainment scales

Client Logs

Having clients prepare narrative accounts of their activities, thoughts, and feelings is an effective method of monitoring progress. Client logs or journals help clarify the nature of client problems and the circumstances that contribute to the problem situation. Clients often find that keeping a log helps them increase their understanding and awareness of the factors that contribute to the identified problem situation. A client log is a tool for clients to self-report on their behaviors, feelings, and thoughts. Client logs allow a client to systematically take notes on the occurrence of a target problem and the events surrounding each occurrence. Client logs are a good strategy to collect data between sessions instead of simply asking the client to recall all events since the last meeting.

Client logs also serve as a source of baseline data on the frequency of the target problem. Baseline data obtained from logs serve as clinical measurements of client thoughts, feelings, and behaviors Using logs throughout treatment can also serve as a method to monitor progress.

Client logs are easy to construct. Most are divided into columns, with the types of information the client should record listed at the top of each column. The client log serves as a template for clients to input information related to their behaviors, thoughts, and feelings. The columns should record the incident or behavior, when it occurred, and how the client responded to it (Bloom et al., 2009). Information on circumstances just prior to and just after the problem event may also be included in client logs.

Two decisions need to be made regarding the completion of logs. The first is when to record the information, and the second is what to record. Clients can record at preset time periods or immediately following the occurrence of the target event. Recording at preset time periods works if you have narrowed down the occurrence of a target event to a specific period, that is, if you know in advance approximately when the target problem is likely to occur. For example, a family might complain about sibling fights after school and during dinner. The client log then might cover the time period of 3:00 p.m. to 7:00 p.m. in the evening. The client keeping the log would record all the sibling fights that occurred during this period.

The second option is to use open time categories. This method is sometimes referred to as critical incident recording (Bloom et al., 2009). With this type of log, the client decides whether to record an event. The client decides if the event is related to the problem or target and then records it as soon as possible after it occurs. This method works best when you need information about events that are likely to be spread out over the entire day.

In addition to specifying when the recording will take place, you also need to clarify in advance what will be recorded. By design, client logs give the client control over the content. Clients choose which of the many thoughts, feelings, and behaviors they experience daily to include and exclude. They employ a great deal of subjective judgment in completing logs. Information recorded on the log should be limited to what the client believes is important (Bloom et al., 2009). Thus, you and the client need to be clear about what constitutes a critical incident. Discuss with the client the types of events that would be appropriate for inclusion in the log. In the beginning, encourage clients to be inclusive rather than exclusive in their recordings. Review the first logs together with an eye toward the appropriateness of the entries as well as events that the client did not record but should have. Exhibit 6.1 shows a sample client log.

Exhibit 6.1 Sample Client Log

Date and Time	Event (Thoughts, Feelings, or Behavior)	Circumstances Before Event	Circumstances After Event	Reflection on Event

Behavioral Observations

Behavioral observations are direct observations made by others of the client behavior. This is not a self-report method, as it requires someone outside of that individual to record this information. The frequency and duration of specific client behaviors can be observed and recorded (Bloom et al., 2009). Behavioral observation can provide detailed information on the occurrence of client behaviors and the context of those behaviors. It represents one of the most reliable and valid methods of measuring client change.

Typically, the first step in using behavioral observation is to operationally define the target behavior. An example would be specifying the types of disruptive behavior a child displays in the classroom, such as getting out of their seat or talking with classmates while the teacher is talking. The target problem must be clearly defined in behavioral terms and must be observable. Observation cannot be used to measure target problems that focus on feelings or thoughts. Observation typically measures the frequency, duration, and context of behaviors.

The second step is to select the observer or observers. Often, the observers are significant others, family members, or other professionals who have access to the client's person-in-environment interactions. For example, a young child having a problem controlling their temper can be observed at home by a parent and at school by a teacher or teacher's aide.

The third step is to train the observers. Observers must know in advance exactly what behavior to look for and how to recognize the behavior when it occurs. In addition, they have to be trained to conduct the observations. You must decide whether to record all instances of the behavior or a sample. Continuous recording involves recording every occurrence of a target behavior every time it occurs (Bloom et al., 2009). A simple form can be created that includes at a minimum the date, time, location, and brief description of the behavior. The continuous recording approach requires the observer to be willing and available, and it works best when the target behavior does not occur with great frequency. Often, these conditions cannot be satisfied, and a sampling strategy is used.

Time sampling is appropriate when events occur continuously or frequently. Time sampling in behavior observation involves systematically recording behavior at predetermined intervals rather than continuously monitoring it. This method allows observers to gain insights into patterns of behavior over time without the need for constant observation. By sampling behavior at specific time points, one can efficiently gather data while still capturing a representative snapshot of the individual's behavior.

Overall, direct observation is an excellent method for assessing client outcomes. It is one of the most effective tools we have for measuring behavior. When it is used with two or more observers, it can provide reliable and valid outcome data. It also has the potential to provide valuable clinical information on the context within which target problems occur. Direct observation should be seriously considered when a target problem is behavioral in nature, the situation allows for direct observation, and implementing direct observation is feasible. Exhibit 6.2 is a sample behavioral observation form.

Rating Scales

Rating scales are tools that can be created by the social workers and client to measure any problem or concern present for the client. The major advantage of an individualized rating scale is that it measures the specific problem or concern that you and your client have identified as the focus of intervention. Thus, a rating scale is directly linked to the feeling, thought, or event that is being addressed in the helping process.

Another advantage of individualized rating scales is that they are based on the client's unique experiences and perceptions. The anchor points of the scale are defined by the client. The low, middle, and high points of the scale are labeled with short, succinct terms. The labels (anchors) describe what the numbers represent (e.g., behaviors, thoughts, and feelings that the client would experience at various points along the scale). Having the client define the anchor points gives the measure great relevance for the client. It becomes a unique measure of the client's feelings, thoughts, or behaviors and represents their perceptions and experiences.

Individualized rating scales usually have 5 to 10 points. Research suggests avoiding a scale that has too many options. Scales that have more than 10 points are difficult for clients to score and are therefore not recommended (Bloom et al., 2009). For example, if a self-esteem scale had 1 to 100 points, it would be very difficult to determine the difference between ratings of 70 and 75. An example of an individualized rating scale is shown in Exhibit 6.3.

Individualized rating scales are easy to construct. Identify with the client the behavior, thought, or feeling that is targeted for change. A wide range of characteristics of the target can be rated (Bloom et al., 2009). It is important for the target to be clearly defined and that the rating scale is only measuring one specific problem or concern. If you wish to explore various considerations, then it is beneficial to have multiple rating scales to avoid complication and confusion. Bloom et al. (2009) warn against using different dimensions at each end of the scale, such as happy at one end and sad at the other. People often experience contradictory feelings and can feel happy and sad at the same time. It is preferable to develop two measures, a sadness scale and a happiness scale, rather than one scale on which both dimensions are rated. They also recommend that the target and its measurement be worded positively,

---

Exhibit 6.2 Sample Behavioral Observation

Client's Name _____ Recorder's Name _____

Target Behavior _____

Location _____

Date & Time _____ Description of Behavior and Context_____
_____

Exhibit 6.3 Sample Individualized Rating Scale

Comfort in social situations

1	2	3	4	5	6	7
Terrified, overwhelmed, completely unable to engage in conversation with strangers		Somewhat anxious, yet able to respond when spoken to			Relaxed, confident, able to initiate conversations with strangers	

something the client wants to achieve, not just something eliminating a negative (Bloom et al., 2009). For example, if the problem is feelings of sadness, the goal might be to increase feelings of happiness, and the rating scale would measure the level of happiness.

The next step is to decide on the number of scale points and develop anchor descriptions for the two end points and possibly the middle point. Scales with seven or nine points are popular because they have a clear midpoint. The numbers on the scale represent gradations for the target problem from low to high. The higher the score, the more frequent, serious, important, or problematic the target issue. The end points of the scale are defined by the client, as are the descriptions or examples of the low, middle, and high numbers. These anchor descriptions define the meaning of the numbers on the rating scale. Begin by asking the client to describe what it would be like at one end of the scale for the given target problem. Repeat the process for the other end of the scale and for the midpoint. Anchors should describe the behaviors, thoughts, or feelings the client would experience along the continuum of the scale (Bloom et al., 2009).

After you and your client construct the scale, make sure that the anchors fit the client's perception of the situation and that both of you are clear about what constitutes a low or high score. This is best accomplished by practicing using the scale and asking the client to retrospectively complete a rating for different points in their life. This will increase the client's comfort in using the scale and provides an opportunity to determine whether the anchor points provide adequate differentiation of the target problem.

An important point to keep in mind in constructing individualized rating scales is that they must be truly *individualized*. The anchors reflect images and pictures of what the situation is like for the client. Your job is to help the client put those images into words. Make sure the words are the client's, not yours or someone else's. The strength of individualized rating scales is that they are client defined and derived directly from the identified target problem.

An alternative to individually constructed anchors is general anchor descriptions. Rating scales with general anchors can be used for different client situations. For example, a general rating scale that measures feelings of connectedness could be used to measure a client's relationship with each member of their family. The disadvantage of general anchors is that they are more ambiguous and less precise than individually tailored anchors. Exhibit 6.4 shows two general rating scales.

Individualized and general rating scales are excellent tools for measuring client progress and change on identified target problems. They have a high level of face validity because

---

Exhibit 6.4 Sample General Rating Scales

Amount of anxiety

1	2	3	4	5	6	7
Little or no anxiety		Moderate anxiety			Extreme anxiety	

Frequency of feeling lonely

1	2	3	4	5	6	7
Never		Sometimes			All the time	

they are derived directly from client problems or concerns. Despite their advantages, it is important to note that the validity and reliability of individualized rating scales cannot be readily established. Rating scales do, however, have a high level of clinical applicability and are excellent tools for measuring client target problems and assessing progress.

Goal Attainment Scales

Goal attainment scaling (GAS) was developed in the field of mental health during the 1960s (Royse et al., 2016). It has been used in a large number of settings and with a wide range of client populations. GAS is similar to individualized rating scales in that the client develops and defines the scale anchors or descriptors. The two methods differ, however, in that goal attainment scales are based directly on the client's goals rather than on behaviors, thoughts, or feelings. A strength of GAS is that it can be used to monitor your client's perception of progress toward the identified treatment goals (Jordan & Franklin, 2015). Thus, GAS is effective in assessing client progress toward goals.

To use GAS, you and your client need to have specified change goals. The number of goals measured should correspond to the number of goals being addressed in the helping relationship. The number of goals being addressed at any given time should be limited.

In conjunction with the client, list each goal on a 5-point scale ranging from 0 to 4. The scale categories are: (4) Optimal progress, (3) Major progress, (2) Moderate progress, (1) Some progress, and (0) No progress.

Work with the client to develop anchors for each scale point. The anchors should represent potential outcomes related to each category and should be as specific as possible. Avoid vague, general outcome statements. Table 6.2 shows a sample goal attainment scale that was

TABLE 6.2 SAMPLE GOAL ATTAINMENT SCALE		
Level	**Goal 1** **Increase Ability to Deal With Panic Attacks**	**Goal 2** **Make Plans for Son's Future**
No progress (0)	Unable to calm myself down, unable to catch breath, heart racing, extreme anxiety	Unable to discuss with son his future needs and plans
Some progress (1)	Limited ability to calm myself down, some difficulty breathing, pacing the floor, moderate anxiety	Discussed son's future with other members of the family
Moderate progress (2)	Able to calm down using breathing/relaxation techniques, maintain composure, low anxiety	Discussed with son his future needs
Major progress (3)	Able to verbalize feelings, remain calm in stressful situations, almost no anxiety	Discussed with son his future needs and involved family and outside agencies in assessing son's needs
Optimal progress (4)	Able to deal with stressful situations without experiencing panic attacks, very low anxiety, calm and relaxed	Working with son, family, and outside agencies and services to prepare son to care for himself in the future

developed with an 80-year-old woman who was caring for her 55-year-old mentally retarded son. The social worker was helping the women address her anxiety and concern about her son's future.

GAS is a client-focused method of measuring progress. It is a direct extension of the goal-oriented approach to practice and is easily incorporated into generalist social work practice with a diverse range of client populations. GAS also empowers clients by placing responsibility for defining and monitoring progress with them. The client is viewed as the expert on what constitutes progress and on determining the extent to which progress is being made. In these respects, GAS is useful as a clinical measurement tool for engaging clients in the helping process.

SOCIAL JUSTICE CONSIDERATIONS

Social workers understand that social justice considerations are present across all areas and levels of practice. Related to research, social workers must practice with integrity and ensure that human participants are treated in an ethical and respectful manner. The mission of the social work profession calls for social workers to support vulnerable and oppressed populations. As mentioned earlier in this chapter, these are the same groups who have often been historically targeted by unethical research Social workers should ensure that research practices related to all populations are ethical and humane, with particular attention to these vulnerable and oppressed groups. Research that targets vulnerable populations should be particularly cautious to ensure adequate safeguards are in place to guarantee ethical conditions.

Social workers must address a myriad of social justice issues including such things as "health disparities, mass incarceration, the interrelationship between substance use and incarceration, unemployment and education, and racial and ethnic inequalities in the juvenile and criminal justice systems" while "relying on social innovation to increase health and well-being among vulnerable populations" (Maschi & Leibowitz, 2017, p. 4). Furthermore, Maschi and Leibowitz (2017) underscore that social workers must be "data driven and apply the empirical literature and the evidence from scientific research to address the most pressing social problems" (p. 4). In order to be data driven, research must be conducted with these vulnerable populations and shared with the profession. Let us explore social justice issues that would arise in terms of racial and ethnic inequalities in the juvenile and criminal justice systems (see Case 6.5).

This population is vulnerable on the basis of their complex intersectionality. First, they are juveniles (under the age of 18). Though ages of consent vary from state to state, in general 18 years old is deemed the age at which a person can provide full informed consent for a research study. In this case, the youth would need to complete an assent form, and parents or guardians would need to be contacted in order to gain written informed consent.

As the youth are in the criminal justice system, if they are in custody, they would be considered prisoners, or individuals who are incarcerated. This population has special protections in addition to those for other human participants (Christopher et al., 2017). There

> **CASE 6.5** **PRACTICE-INFORMED RESEARCH WITHIN A JUVENILE DETENTION CENTER**
>
> Angela is a social worker at a juvenile detention center in an urban community. The facility has 100 beds, and it is always at capacity. Angela is one of two mental health social workers. Her role in the facility is to provide mental health counseling individually and in groups. At any given time, Angela has approximately half of the population on her caseload to support. She loves her job and is continually looking for ways to improve her clinical skills so that she can provide better services to the youth she works with.
>
> Angela often runs an anger management group with the youth, many of whom can benefit from learning how to better cope with intense emotions in an acceptable manner. Angela had been to a social work conference recently where she was learning about new strategies to address anger issues utilizing mindfulness and breathing exercises. She thought that it was a very interesting presentation and wants to incorporate it into her next group. Angela wants to be able to measure if this new intervention will be more successful than her previous intervention. Angela talks to her supervisor about having the youth complete an anger rating scale at the start of the anger management group and then repeat the measure at the end of the group. Angela was excited about this idea.
>
> During supervision, Angela shared her idea with her supervisor, Penelope. Penelope listened intently to Angela, noticing her excitement regarding her idea for practice-informed research. After Angela finished explaining her idea, she asked Penelope what she thought. Penelope smiled and acknowledged that Angela was very passionate about her job and this new idea. However, she recognized a few concerns regarding this proposed research plan. Penelope shared with Angela that she was concerned regarding the lack of informed consent. Angela brought up that her anger management group is a voluntary group and wondered if that would be enough to proceed. Penelope shared that in order to conduct research, specific steps must be followed to protect the participants. Penelope then pulled out her copy of the NASW *Code of Ethics* to share with Angela. Angela was almost offended, thinking that Penelope was suggesting that what she was doing was unethical. Penelope quickly assured Angela that she recognized that Angela was not intentionally being unethical; however, there are specific ethical guidelines for conducting research that she had missed in the creation of her plan. Together, Angela and Penelope reviewed the applicable portions of the *Code of Ethics* and decided to come up with a plan to be able to introduce these new techniques and measure their effectiveness in a way that was fully aligned with the *Code of Ethics*.

are only four categories of research that can be conducted on incarcerated individuals, which include

> minimal-risk studies on possible causes, effects, and processes of incarceration and of criminal behavior; minimal-risk studies of prisons as institutional structures or of prisoners as incarcerated persons; research on conditions particularly affecting prisoners as a class; and research on practices that are intended and deemed likely to improve the health or well-being of participants. (Christopher et al., 2017, p. 21)

Due to the inherent power imbalance in such a situation, social workers must be extra cognizant in order to avoid coercion. Coercion can occur, even if it was not intended. Intentions are important, but intentions of good will are simply not enough to safeguard vulnerable populations. Social workers must consider how the participant will perceive the experience as well in order to ensure that best efforts are made to protect participants.

A final area of intersectionality would relate to their racial or ethnic minority status. In the United States, there is disproportionate incarceration rates for people of color. African American and Hispanic American males are incarcerated at much higher rates than any other group. The presence of systemic inequities within the criminal justice system may be the cause of these disproportionate rates. If we do not account for these systemic factors, it could lead to incomplete or misleading interpretations of the data, perpetuating injustices and hindering efforts for meaningful reform. Ethically, research involving vulnerable populations requires careful consideration of fairness, justice, and respect for human dignity. Not considering the sample risks violating these principles and worsening the marginalization. Ignoring the overrepresentation of people of color in the sample may perpetuate systemic injustices and impede efforts to address the root causes of inequality within the criminal justice system. Addressing these concerns is paramount for conducting rigorous, ethical research that accurately reflects the realities of incarceration and promotes social justice.

SUMMARY

Throughout this chapter, we introduced the importance of research for social workers. We particularly focused on the importance of research-informed practice. Social workers must be able to integrate science into their professional practice in order to ensure best outcomes for client systems. It is necessary for social workers to be critical thinkers regarding the information they are receiving, recognizing that there are multiple ways of knowing. When considering how to critically analyze information, social workers seek to understand the strengths and limitations related to various types of knowing. Professional social workers recognize that research-informed practice is necessary to support clients and the profession as a whole. Throughout this chapter, we talked about how research can inform all aspects of social work practice at all levels: micro, mezzo, and macro. We have reviewed the importance of using evidence to inform practice and utilize EBPs whenever possible to ensure the best outcome for clients.

CASE SUMMARY   UNDOCUMENTED AND HOMELESS

Practice Setting Description

Jackie is a first-year MSW student completing an internship at an inner-city family service agency in the Southwest. The agency is in a section of the city that has a high crime rate, gang activity, and failing schools. The area has a diverse population with many immigrants from Central and South America and a substantial African American population. The agency provides individual and family counseling services on a sliding fee scale. The agency also runs several educational

(continued)

CASE SUMMARY UNDOCUMENTED AND HOMELESS (*CONTINUED*)

and treatment groups as well as a temporary shelter for women and their children. Jackie has been assigned to work with the women and their children in the shelter. Her primary tasks are to provide concrete services and supportive counseling to the shelter residents.

Background Information

Elicia and her daughter, Maria, are undocumented immigrants from Mexico. They have been in the United States for 5 years. Elicia and Maria fled to the area from another southwestern city to escape her abusive husband approximately 2 months ago. Elicia is 25 years old and Maria 8 years old. Elicia has a 2-year-old daughter, Sarah, who was placed in foster care because of suspected abuse in the home. Sarah is in a foster home in a small rural community in the state hundreds of miles from Elicia's current residence. Since moving to the area, Maria has not been attending school.

Elicia and Maria are currently residing in the agency's temporary shelter for families. They have been at the shelter for 2 weeks, and the agency has a 90-day limit. Prior to arriving at the shelter, Elicia and Maria were homeless and living on the streets.

Elicia is a high school drop-out and was a stay-at-home mother prior to leaving her husband and moving to a different part of the state. She chose to move there because she has two female cousins living in the area who are also undocumented immigrants. Elicia's native language is Spanish. She speaks some English but is not as comfortable speaking in English. Her English comprehension appears to be good. Maria speaks both English and Spanish well. When communicating with the staff, Maria acts as Elicia's interpreter since none of the staff at the shelter speak Spanish.

Maria appears to be behind academically. She struggles reading simple children's books written in English. It is unknown if her ability to read in Spanish is better than her English reading skills.

Other than her two cousins, Elicia has no other sources of support in the community. Her cousins have young families and limited resources but are well established and connected to a Latino community in the city and the local Catholic church. Her cousins refused to let Elicia and Maria live with them while she was trying to find her own place and a job. They stated that they did not have enough room and are concerned they would get in trouble with their landlord if it was found out that they were letting people stay with them. They sent her to the local church for help, and she was given the address for the agency's shelter by the priest.

Elicia has been looking for housing in the Latino community. The housing market is tight with limited options, and she has been unable to find anything that she could possibly afford. The only affordable housing she found was a room in a rundown motel that rents by the hour or by the month. It is in an area of town known for drug dealing and sex work.

On arrival in the community, Elicia found occasional work for a house cleaning company. The company hires undocumented workers, pays them very low cash wages, and threatens to turn them in to Immigration and Customs Enforcement (ICE) if they complain. The job bosses also exploit their female workers sexually, threatening to turn them in if they do not comply. Elicia was fearful about applying for other jobs because of her illegal status. She considered turning to sex work to be able to take care of her children, but her Catholic upbringing and thoughts of how

(continued)

CASE SUMMARY UNDOCUMENTED AND HOMELESS (*CONTINUED*)

doing so would shame her family have kept her from doing so. She is in constant fear of being detained, separated from Maria, and having her placed in foster care. She is also afraid that she will end up homeless again and forced to live on the streets or return to her abusive husband.

Elicia is extremely reluctant to sign up for any federally funded services, even those that she and her child are entitled to receive. On the suggestion that she enroll for supplemental food through Supplemental Nutrition Assistance Program (SNAP), Elicia became nervous and refused, as she has heard that participation in SNAP services, and others like them, would draw the attention of ICE, and she had heard stories on the news of individuals being deported after signing up for such programs.

Presenting Problems

Elicia and her child are facing multiple obstacles. They need to find permanent, affordable housing and a job that pays enough to cover her housing and living expenses. In addition, Maria needs to be enrolled in school.

Additionally, Elicia is experiencing an immense amount of stress, anxiety, and possibly post-traumatic stress disorder (PTSD). She described an instance where she could not calm down her breathing and she felt lightheaded. She is very fearful of men and tries to avoid all contact with men in the community. She reports difficulty sleeping at night and feeling exhausted most of the time.

She is concerned about Maria. She has started acting out at the shelter, getting into fights with the other children, disobeying her mother, and being disrespectful and defiant to the staff and other adults. Elicia and Maria fight frequently, and when Elicia tries to discipline Maria, she throws a temper tantrum until Elicia gives up.

Elicia has many strengths. She had the strength to leave her abusive husband and move to a different city. She loves her daughter and wants desperately to keep Maria with her. She is resilient and has managed to survive and keep her daughter safe despite not having a place to stay, a job, and a limited support network. Elicia feels safe in the shelter, but she is very fearful of being caught as an illegal immigrant and is generally mistrustful of helping professionals and persons of authority.

DISCUSSION QUESTIONS

1. If you were working with Elicia and Maria, what research would you need to locate and review to inform your practice? How would you go about finding this research? How would you ensure this research is culturally responsive to their needs?

2. As the social worker working with Elicia and Maria, how would research inform your practice? Provide two specific examples.

3. Identify a micro practice issue that you would address with Elicia and/or Maria. How would you informally evaluate your practice effectiveness for one of your identified issues? What client measure would you use?

4. Identify a second micro practice that you would address in your work with Elicia and/or Maria. How would you formally evaluate your practice effectiveness? What standardized measure would you use? What single-system design would you choose? What type of baseline would be appropriate and why?

A robust set of instructor resources designed to supplement this text is located at http://connect.springerpub.com/content/book/978-0-8261-6683-8. Qualifying instructors may request access by emailing textbook@springerpub.com.

KEY REFERENCES

Only key references appear in the print edition. To access the full reference list, visit www.springerpub.com/courseconnect. See inside front cover and tear-out card for CourseConnect details.

Bloom, M., Fischer, J., & Orme, J. (2009). *Evaluating practice: Guidelines for the accountable professional* (6th ed.). Pearson.

Corcoran, K., & Fischer, J. (2013). *Measures for clinical practice: A sourcebook* (Vols. 1 and 2, 5th ed.). Oxford University Press.

Engel, R. J., & Schutt, R. K. (2014). *Fundamentals of social work research* (2nd ed.). Sage.

National Association of Social Workers. (2021). *Code of ethics.* https://www.socialworkers.org/About/Ethics/Code-of-Ethics/Code-of-Ethics-English

Royse, D., Thyer, B. A., & Padgett, D. K. (2016). *Program evaluation: An introduction to an evidence-based approach* (6th ed.). Cengage.

7 Policy-Informed Practice

Stephen Kauffman and Heather Witt

Devon, a second-year master of social work (MSW) student, realized that the opiate addiction problem in his community was serious when his younger brother, Felix, overdosed. Felix survived, but only due to an extremely fortunate set of circumstances. But 93 others (by Devon's count) had not been so lucky over the past year. Something had to be done, and now.

The problem was how to build support for two very effective harm reduction strategies: greater naltrexone availability and funding a new methadone maintenance center. But his community and state were quite conservative, and drugs were viewed as evil. As were people who (many believed) supported drug use. So Devon began to build awareness around the problem and to attempt to gain supporters at the state capitol. Because he was in school and had virtually no economic resources to draw upon, he needed to develop a plan to achieve his goals. But what should he do first? Whom should he turn to for support?

Devon did, however, know that he needed to start with research about the problem. He worked with a number of community groups in the area. Among these groups, he found past users, some providers, and first responders who were in agreement with his efforts. Further, many family members were willing to provide information to him. On the other hand, some groups of traditional substance abuse treatment were wary. Devon wondered about that wariness—why? It would appear that services for some would be a plus for all. But overall, Devon gathered some impressive statistical information on the community issue. Now, what to do with it—where to go?

LEARNING OBJECTIVES

This chapter focuses on Competency 5: Policy Practice, with the primary emphasis on policy formation, structural aspects of social welfare policy, and the ways social workers may participate in the policy process. The chapter begins with a review of the National Association of Social Workers (NASW) ethical principle and standards that address policy and social justice. This is followed by a definition of policy and a definition of policy practice. Then the chapter will discuss the major characteristics and components of social welfare policy. We will examine the policy process and the associated primary tasks. The chapter will also look closely at ways that social workers may participate in policy through various forms of policy practice. In particular, we will examine problem identification and characterization, political mobilization and political advocacy, policy implementation, and then policy analysis. At each of these stages, a close analysis of how the social worker can participate and affect policy will be examined. By the end of this chapter, you will be able to:

- Define policy, social welfare, and social welfare policy.
- Understand the centrality of policy in the NASW *Code of Ethics*.
- Understand the role of policy in addressing social welfare and social justice needs.
- Articulate major structural components of social policies and services.
- Describe the role of practice and the practitioner in policy development.
- Understand how to actively engage in policy practice to affect change.
- Know how to evaluate policies.
- Apply critical thinking to analyze, formulate, and advocate for policies that advance human rights and social, racial, economic, and environmental justice.

COMPETENCY 5: ENGAGE IN POLICY PRACTICE

Social workers identify social policy at the local, state, federal, and global level that affects well-being, human rights and justice, service delivery, and access to social services. Social workers recognize the historical, social, racial, cultural, economic, organizational, environmental, and global influences that affect social policy. Social workers understand and critique the history and current structures of social policies and services and the role of policy in service delivery through rights-based, anti-oppressive, and antiracist lenses. Social workers influence policy formulation, analysis, implementation, and evaluation within their practice settings with individuals, families, groups, organizations, and communities. Social workers actively engage in and advocate for antiracist and anti-oppressive policy practice to effect change in those settings. Social workers:

- use social justice, antiracist, and anti-oppressive lenses to assess how social welfare policies affect the delivery of and access to social services; and
- apply critical thinking to analyze, formulate, and advocate for policies that advance human rights and social, racial, economic, and environmental justice.

NATIONAL ASSOCIATION OF SOCIAL WORKERS *CODE OF ETHICS*

The NASW *Code of Ethics* is a policy document that addresses concerns over social policy throughout. And the importance of policy is clear from the preamble onward. Indeed, the very first sentence in the preamble lays out the basic guiding statement: "The primary mission of the social work profession is to enhance human well-being and help meet the basic human needs of all people, with particular attention to the needs and empowerment of people who are vulnerable, oppressed, and living in poverty" (NASW, 2021, p. 1). As you will see in the following narrative, the *Code of Ethics* is itself a policy document!

And from it, the profession draws its interpretation of what social welfare policies should do and why.

The ethical principles that guide our understanding of policy are clearly articulated in the *Code of Ethics*. While all the principles have applicability in terms of policy, two are very clear. The first is about helping people in need and to address social problems. The second is about challenging social injustice (NASW, 2021). The specific language of these two principles can be found online.

Furthermore, these two principles are expanded in several places in the *Code of Ethics* through the standards. As with the principles, virtually all have applicability, but perhaps the most direct statements are found under Social Workers' Ethical Responsibilities to the Broader Society. Here, the standards are very clear. Social workers should promote the general welfare of society, they should facilitate public participation in the policy process, and they should engage in social and political action (NASW, 2021).

SOCIAL WELFARE POLICIES: WHAT THEY ARE AND WHY WE CARE

Macrolevel practice, including policy practice, is often the kind of social work practice that social work students associate with social justice and anti-oppressive practice. While many social workers practice in micro and mezzo spaces, policy practice provides social workers the opportunity to enact the change that they see needs to happen within oppressive systems. These systems and institutions maintain and advance the very oppressive social conditions we seek to dismantle through our work. Social workers use policy practice and advocacy to solve or reduce the impact of social problems.

Definition of Policies: What Are Policies?

The formal definition of a policy is conceptually straightforward, although there is no absolute, perfect universal definition. In the simplest terms, a policy is really nothing more than a rule or plan of action. But from here on, things get interesting! Why? Every group, from a family to organizations representing everyone on the planet, wants or needs to regulate or change the behaviors of its members. This can be done in several ways. Sometimes, there are formal rules or methods, and sometimes there are just unspoken expectations. Sometimes there are agreed-upon ways that the rules or methods are made, but sometimes the expectations "just sort of show up." Sometimes, these rules address earth-changing issues like global climate change or the rights of refugees. Sometimes the rules affect just persons residing in the United States, such as who may receive heating or housing assistance, or perhaps who and how a person may become a resident of the United States. Or sometimes the rules might address whether a state provides healthcare to persons above 180% of the poverty line or the cost a person must bear to go to college. And other times, the rules might simply determine the acceptability of the name of the fashion designer on our sneakers, or the kind of music we listen to, or even where we sit in a classroom.

What Are Social Welfare Policies?

Policies, as you might conceive, affect many areas of our lives. We have policies that affect how fast we can drive on roads (think about speed limits), or what kinds of products are acceptable to sell in stores (when was the last time you saw plutonium at the grocery?), or how many ships our navy should have, or what our field placement considers appropriate dress (as presented in the employee handbook, if your agency has one). While a good argument can be made that all of these are incredibly important, social work tends to be more concerned with the policies affecting some life domains more than others. Many of these policies address human need and are what are called *social welfare policies*. Most directly, social welfare policies are policies that target human need or quality-of-life concerns.

But the kinds of problems or issues that such policies may include is an open question. Some narrow perspectives suggest that it only includes policies designed to help the disadvantaged (Merriam-Webster, 2018), while others suggest more expansive domains, such as social services in general (Dictionary.com, 2018). And some are thought of even more broadly.

The difference in how inclusive we interpret social welfare policies to be is based on how one defines social welfare and how extensive, how broadly, or even how important one sees the role of social welfare activities in the society in question. In the broadest sense, any organized activity seeking to meet a human need or improve quality of life is "social welfare." This may include the domains identified by Maslow in his famous hierarchy of needs (Maslow, 1954). These include physiological needs, safety needs, belonging, esteem, self-actualization, and, added in later years (Maslow, 1971), self-transcendence. Another, more recent perspective looks at the problem from the aspect of well-being, with dimensions including objective well-being (health) and subjective well-being (happiness; Harvard University, T.H. Chan School of Public Health, 2017). Such a perspective has enabled the construction and application of a *World Happiness Report* (Helliwell et al., 2024), as well as the measurement of national happiness. Using this approach, in 2024, Finland, Denmark, Iceland, and Sweden were ranked as the world's happiest countries. The United States ranked 23 and is dropping in the measures!

> ▶ **Reflection Questions**
>
> 1. Why do you think the United States rates 23rd in world happiness and not higher?
> 2. How do you define happiness? Are there any policies you can think of that would directly influence your level of happiness?

Interestingly, it may not be a coincidence that all of the countries with the highest rankings have the most expansive systems of social welfare policies. Is there a connection? What do you think?

Every society must create and support the systems necessary to meet human need and the quality of life that are associated with each of these domains. And this creation and support almost always take place through the use of policies and norms. Indeed, history is rife with societies that fail in one or more of these domains, and as a result, decay and sometimes failure would affect the society.

There are a couple of interesting historical examples that might show how important these become. The ancient Chinese empires often talked about the "mandate of heaven," meaning that a leader (an emperor usually) could only lead if the "mandate of heaven" applied. Evidence that the mandate was in danger or was lost came about as famine, wars, or other social strife affected society. Many societies have collapsed because they could no longer feed their people. Not to project too far without supportive evidence, but one wonders what the effects of climate change will do to social order in a few decades!

> **Reflection Questions**
>
> 1. What does the word *welfare* mean to you?
> 2. How do you think most Americans define the word *welfare*?

Thus, for our purposes of definition, policies that affect all these domains might be considered social welfare policies. But there are distinctions—relative priorities are often assigned to that domain in different societies, resulting in some policies clearly considered social welfare policies, while other policies may not be considered such. But what might determine the distinction? Here is a hint. Consider the word *welfare*.

There are actually conceptual categories that are used to clarify how we think about the centrality of social welfare in terms of society. As discussed earlier, social welfare policies may or may not be at the core of what the society sees as important. So ask yourself: Should social welfare include all (or perhaps most) of the social functions within its domain, or is it a bit of an afterthought? How you answer that question will classify your distinction as either an institutional perspective or a residual perspective.

How a society classifies its thinking about the difference has some pretty significant consequences. For one thing, it has critical effects on how social policies are structured. For example, do policies address everyone or just some people? The *residual* perspective is the name we give to policies that target just some recipients—for example, food stamps (Supplemental Nutrition Assistance Program [SNAP] or Electronic Benefits Transfer [EBT]), welfare cash assistance (Temporary Assistance to Needy Families [TANF]), and Medicaid are provided to only a part of the population—generally those who are most vulnerable to poverty. Indeed, most American social welfare policies are targeted in such a way. It is useful to examine the assumptions people make to support the residual perspective (see Table 7.1).

On the other hand, some societies believe that meeting human needs is one of the central and most important roles for government. Such societies implement what is called the *institutional* approach. In these societies, the assumption is that personal efforts and the market are unable to address need because of cost, market limitation (such as consistent unemployment), and historical factors like racism or sexism. Almost all of the so-called "developed" nations of the world except the United States maintain such a position. In consequence, a preventative mindset and sense of social care are dominant. Again, Table 7.1 shows the assumptions underlying the institutional perspective.

Rush and Keenan (2014) argue that challenges lie in the context of different welfare regimes that prioritize social justice (e.g., Scandinavia) or market values (e.g., Anglo-Saxon countries). Social workers struggle to balance anti-oppressive practice (AOP) values with the economic realities of approaches, but also need to recognize that AOP in social work can only be achieved by interfacing with these systems.

TABLE 7.1 TYPES OF SOCIAL WELFARE POLICIES

Characteristics	Institutional Approach	Residual Approach	
Role of social welfare	Central function of government—replaces or highly regulates market to ensure needs are met	Secondary function of government—limited replacement of market functions (to address temporary market failures or support those unable to function in marketplace)	
Assumption of need	Everyone	Only those unable to function in market	
Service mindset	Proactive and preventative	Reactive	
Service eligibility	Universal (eligibility open to all)	Selective (eligibility based on assessment of need)	
Methods for determining eligibility	Citizenship or presence	Means-testing (income and assets)	Demographics (family composition, disability, employment status)
Justifications	• Some needs are ubiquitous • Costs of meeting needs are high for everyone • Concern about stigmatization of recipients	• Needs are best filled by market • Focus on the truly needy ensures adequate resources for those in need • Keeps taxes low	
Consequences of choice	• Everyone has care • Tax rates tend to be higher • Generally strong political support • No stigma on recipients	• Some "fall through" cracks and get no/little care • Tax rates tend to be lower • Political support varies • May be anger/stigma directed at recipients • Encourages cheating	
Examples	• Universal health insurance (UK, France, Norway, etc.) • Family support cash benefits (France and Sweden)	• TANF • Medicaid (medical assistance for low-income Americans)	

TANF, Temporary Assistance for Needy Families.

What Are the Important Components of Social Welfare Policies?

Whether a society follows a residual or institutional approach to social welfare, there are important questions or components associated with any social welfare policies. This means what does the policy actually do and how does it do it. To a degree, these can be thought of as the "who, what, how, and why" of social welfare policies. And how these questions are answered in a given society is often linked to that initial difference between the residual and the institutional approaches.

Eligibility: Selective Versus Universal Programs

Take the question of "who is eligible?" for example. This question affects every single policy, and often a clue for how it may be answered is found by knowing how central social welfare is to a society. In other words, who is allowed to receive the benefit? There are a range of possible answers, although what is commonly found in societies with a residual approach are programs where eligibility is narrowly targeted; that is, some people are eligible, but not others. These types of social welfare policies are called *selective* because the recipients are, well, selected based on some criteria. Most often, this selection is based on a combination of a person's demographic characteristics (such as gender, disability, employment, and/or family composition) and their economic status (usually their income and assets). Importantly, this can mean that every single person who seeks the benefit must be closely reviewed to see if they meet all of the eligibility criteria. How this is done differs from country to country, and even policy to policy. But the demographic criteria are usually examined by either self-report or some referral based on some previous examination. On the other hand, the name given to the examination of their economic status is *means-testing*. This requires a close review of the person's ability to support themselves—their "means." It may involve everything from looking at a person's bank accounts, credit scores, and tax returns all the way to a visit and review of where the person lives and what they own.

Justifications have been made to support selective eligibility. As shown in Table 7.1, these justifications range from value assumptions held by the society as a whole, to beliefs about human psychology, all the way to the cost of the policy. But overwhelmingly, the strongest assumptions are that selective policies will ensure sufficient resources are available to those most in need, with greater efficiency and lower cost (and therefore lower taxes) and better controls over cheating.

Some societies, however, including mainly those who most generally follow the institutional approach, acknowledge other factors largely ignored by selective applications to justify a different level of eligibility. These types of policies are said to have universal eligibility. First among these is that some types of need, like the need for healthcare, are experienced by everyone, and the costs of addressing those needs are high enough that even higher-income persons have difficulty affording care. Second, greater efficiencies are found by including everyone, as there are always problems when making distinctions between people as to benefit or no benefit. For example, the line drawn between those who may receive the benefit and those who do not may result in a number of persons deemed ineligible who only earn a few dollars more than those who get the benefit. As a consequence, the ineligible may feel angry, frustrated, or cheated. And further, they may feel resentment toward those persons who received the benefit even though they are in essentially the same situation. Or those potentially ineligible may feel inclined to lie or cheat in order to pass the means test. Finally, many in the society as a whole may attach stigma to those who receive the benefit.

Thus, the alternative to selectivity is to provide the benefits to everyone in the society. These types of policies have been called universal, because eligibility is open to everyone (sometimes only to citizens, but sometimes anyone who is in the country has at least some access). Worldwide, the most common example is healthcare, where again as seen in many developed countries, the benefit is available to everyone in the society—not just to those who can pay or those who are poor enough for assistance (see Case 7.1).

> **CASE 7.1** **YOU'RE COVERED OVER HERE: AN EXAMPLE OF UNIVERSAL HEALTHCARE**
>
> Recently, William returned from a trip to Sweden. While he was there, his aunt, who lived there and who he was visiting, had a very serious illness. For part of the illness, she lapsed into a coma for about 6 days. William was prepared to stay as long as necessary to care for his aunt. But on the third day after she came out of the coma, a social worker visited and explained what would happen during the course of his aunt's treatment and recovery. Putting William's mind at ease, the social worker told William that with Sweden's social insurance system, his aunt would receive care in the hospital for as long as medically necessary. Then, she would receive care in a nursing facility with full vocational and occupational rehabilitation for as long as needed. And when she returned home, she would have a home health aide for as much of the day as needed. She also would receive her needed medications and a cash support stipend for as long as needed.
>
> All of this sounded wonderful to William, but he knew his aunt was far from wealthy. He asked what the cost would be and how much he might need to contribute. The social worker simply smiled.

Benefits: Hard Versus Soft Benefits

Another distinction in social welfare policies is what people get—what comprises the benefits. If you think about all of the different types of things that you need to live, you can guess that benefits can be many different things. Indeed, the range of items or services that could go on this list is as long as the range of items or services that are needed for a person's quality of life or happiness. That said, the list is typically much narrower, and there are distinctions. Table 7.2 describes each and shows the strengths and weaknesses of each general type, which typically form the common justifications for or against their use.

> ▶ **Reflection Question**
>
> Which of these two approaches, institutional or residual, is most in line with anti-oppressive social work practice and why?

Overall, the issue of any given benefit selection comes down to a debate about a number of factors. Among these are degree of recipient control, degree of external (public) control, administrative cost and complexity, and the influence of external interests. Looking at the question by type of participant, while there are plenty of discrete exceptions, recipients prefer maximum control and choice, while the public prefers some degree of control to ensure the benefit is used as a benefit. What is interesting, however, is the role that some external interests (including social workers) beyond policy makers and recipients may play in the selection and support for given choices. Take the SNAP or EBT, once known as food stamps, for example. There is huge support for this program from America's agricultural and commercial sectors due to the amount of money it pours into commercial activity. Even when there are calls to cut benefits for the poor, SNAP is often reasonably free from such cuts for this reason.

TABLE 7.2 TYPES OF SOCIAL SERVICE BENEFITS IN THE UNITED STATES

Type of Benefits	Strengths, Advantages	Weaknesses, Disadvantages	Common Examples
Hard Benefits			
Cash (or checks)	• Allows recipient to determine use • Administrative costs are low	• Recipient must apply • Concern about improper use/diversion • No/little external control over recipient	• TANF • Social Security old age pensions • Unemployment Insurance
Vouchers (including targeted EBT transfers)—generally allows choice of vendor but within a category	• May be moderate choice by recipient over selected vendor • Less concern about improper use than cash • Some external control over recipient	• Recipient must apply • May be limited number of qualified vendors • Administrative costs moderate to high	• Food stamps • WIC vouchers • Vouchers for school choice
Commodity distributions (food, clothes, etc.)	• High external control over recipient • Ensures commodity gets "in hands" of recipient	• Recipient must apply • Recipient has little/no choice over quality, quantity, or type • Administrative costs moderate to high	• Bread, cheese commodities • Heating assistance
Soft Benefits			
Tax deductions	• High external control over recipient • Encourages desirable behaviors	• Applies only if tax return filed • Applies only if tax paid • Requires high degree of knowledge by recipient • Administrative costs moderate to high	• Bread, cheese commodities • Child care deduction • Deduction for college loan interest

(continued)

TABLE 7.2 TYPES OF SOCIAL SERVICE BENEFITS IN THE UNITED STATES (*CONTINUED*)

Type of Benefits	Strengths, Advantages	Weaknesses, Disadvantages	Common Examples
Soft Benefits (Continued)			
Tax credits/deductions	• High external control over recipient • Encourages desirable behaviors	• Applies only if tax return filed • Requires high degree of knowledge by recipient • Administrative costs moderate to high	• Earned income tax credit
Services	• High external control over recipient • Use of services provides interface with experts/professionals	• Recipient may have little choice over provider or service • May be wait-lists for service	• Most counseling programs • Most educational programs
Rights	• Generally widest impact • Makes powerful statements	• Hard to measure • Often debates over meaning	• Civil rights laws • Right to know acts

EBT, electronic benefits transfer; TANF, Temporary Assistance for Needy Families; WIC, Special Supplemental Nutrition Program for Women, Infants, and Children.

Why Should We Care: The Social Work Role in Policy and Policy Practice

Why any person should care about the social welfare policies in the society they live in should be coming clearer. Every society must concern itself with meeting needs. Social welfare policies are one of the most important tools a society has for addressing needs and quality of life. Imagine for a moment living in a society that did not care for, or had no systems to care for, the elderly, the sick or disabled, the hungry, or youth seeking an education? Or living in a society that did not have adequate clean water or had bad air quality? Or living in a society that allowed just a few people—perhaps those of only a certain skin color, age, or ethnicity to own everything and make all decisions affecting a person's occupation? These are the kinds of questions a person, family, community, nation, or even the collective population of the planet must be to able answer, and that will tell us why we should care about our policies.

But what about a social worker in particular? Why is it important to our profession? The simplest answers here are probably the most correct ones. On the one hand, as several previous chapters have articulated, our profession is deeply rooted in values and ethics. At the core, the answer is both straightforward and profound. As articulated in both the NASW *Code of Ethics* and the Council on Social Work Education (CSWE) Educational Policy and Accreditation Standards (EPAS), work on and for social welfare policies plays a central role in our profession.

There are many different ways our profession can implement these positions, many of which will be described later in the chapter.

POLICY FORMATION: WHY DO WE CHOOSE THE SOCIAL WELFARE POLICIES WE DO?

As you might suspect from what has already been stated, there are any number of different problem areas that could be targets for social welfare policies. There are also a number of different ways policies could be focused to address need. But importantly, all social policies are constructs of the entity (nation, state, organization) that creates them. Other countries may have very different policies—or even no policy at all—that affect the same problem or need. Consider the problem of healthcare. Some countries, like France, Norway, or Sweden have a system by which all healthcare is provided by government employees and all services are paid by tax revenues. The United States has a very different model, where healthcare services are overwhelmingly done by independent, private individuals. But even different states in the United States have different policies that address the need. You may have heard of the "Medicaid Expansion" that came as a part of the Affordable Care Act (ACA). Some states have chosen to participate, while others have not.

The big question is *why*? Why do some countries or states have social welfare policies to address healthcare needs, while others do not? Why do some countries like the United States have a patchwork approach, while others fully centralize it? Why do some countries pay virtually all healthcare costs through tax revenues, while others, like the United States, have much of the cost borne by individuals and businesses? And why might some countries have little or no healthcare social welfare policies? There is no simple answer. But there are important clues drawn from economics, political science, sociology, and other academic disciplines. This section will hopefully illuminate the "why" problem.

There are at least three important sets of factors (or concepts) that might be called *policy foundational concepts* that affect your answers. Policy foundation concepts change, grow, and are altered over time. What is "true" about a society now may in fact be false in the past or future. For example, the United States did not "believe in" or provide much social welfare from the federal government prior to the 1930s. After the 1930s, however, federal efforts became the norm. Additionally, *policy foundational concepts* influence, and are strongly influenced by, each other. For example, there is much evidence to suggest that a person's beliefs about money and social responsibility change as income and wealth levels change. These concepts include resources, values and ideology, and social relationships (including social structure and power relationships), and altogether they influence policy in many ways.

Resources refer to the things a society needs to address its problems. This includes money, people, technology, and natural resources. The United States spends a significant amount on social welfare programs, but these programs are still necessary. *Values and ideology* encompass the beliefs that guide a society's policies. There are three instrumental values: freedom, equality, and justice. *Freedom* really has two different major meanings. When we think of freedom, we think of freedom to do something, as well as the freedom from some form of oppression or constraint. Within these two interpretations are vast ranges of possibilities and worlds of nuance. But in practice, this has generally meant that people may make economic and political choices (freedom "to") with minimal external political coercion (freedom "from"), although it is not too difficult to find lots of exceptions to this perspective. This leads us the next value, because as we know, freedom is not currently accessible to all. Formally, *equality* generally means equal treatment, the domains where this applies and how we apply it can vary widely—at least politically. But the various implications of different interpretations of equality can result in widely incompatible results. One such complication is found between the ideal of equal treatment or opportunity versus the ideal of equal results. Most Americans support the idea of equal treatment, while somewhat less agree with the idea of equal opportunity, and there is even less support for the idea of equal outcomes. These differences have played out over the last century in the quest, through policy, to promote civil rights. *Justice* refers to the idea that people should be treated fairly. These values can sometimes conflict with each other, and they can play out in different policy decisions. Generally, most Americans believe in and support the concept of fair treatment. Consider for a moment how we compensate people for their work efforts. Our economic system tends to value (perhaps overvalue?) and therefore reward people who have rare skills or talents, as well as those who spend long periods of time in educational efforts and/or work hard. Yet the model isn't perfect. There are plenty of examples of people who study for years or work endless hours who in fact struggle to get by. Is that fair? Is that just?

> ▶ **Reflection Question**
>
> What social problems concern you most due to their possible impact in your life? Why?

To that list, we also want to add a term with particular meaning for social workers and much of the work we do—*social justice*. Social justice is essentially fairness/fair treatment applied to the societal domain. One definition puts it this way:

> Social justice encompasses economic justice. Social justice is the virtue which guides us in creating those organized human interactions we call institutions. In turn, social institutions, when justly organized, provide us with access to what is good for the person, both individually and in our associations with others. Social justice also imposes on each of us a personal responsibility to collaborate with others, at whatever level of the "Common Good" in which we participate, to design and continually perfect our institutions as tools for personal and social development. (Center for Economic and Social Justice, 2019)

One of the most interesting aspects of this definition, but unfortunately one we do not have the time to explore, is the concept of the "common good." Does such a thing exist? And what does it look like? Finding a fully agreed-upon answer to those questions would go far toward eliminating conflict in our society. Unfortunately, we do not have a common definition.

> ▶ **Reflection Questions**
>
> 1. Does something called "the common good" exist? Why or why not?
> 2. If so, what does it mean?

But we do have some understanding (although not universally shared) of what social justice might mean in the policy domain. This vision also often incorporates the idea of economic justice as well. Again, drawing on the work of the Center for Economic and Social Justice (2019), economic justice means:

> Economic justice, which touches the individual person as well as the social order, encompasses the moral principles which guide us in designing our economic institutions. These institutions determine how each person earns a living, enters into contracts, exchanges goods and services with others and otherwise produces an independent material foundation for his or her economic sustenance. The ultimate purpose of economic justice is to free each person to engage creatively in the unlimited work beyond economics, that of the mind and the spirit.

The point in this definition, as with social justice, is that participation in a society ought to ensure a fair balance between what a person contributes to their society, and what a person gets back. In so many areas of our collective life, the returns for our efforts are not anywhere near commensurate with what we put into it. Consider the problem of wealth. From 1963 to 2022, the difference in percentage of income earned by the lowest and highest 10% of income earners grew dramatically. In 1963, the difference in average income between the two groups was about 700%. In 2013, it had grown to about 1,200% (Urban Institute, 2024). In 2022, the wealthiest had 71 times more wealth than the middle class, up from 36 times more in 1963. In 1963, families near the bottom of the wealth distribution (those at the 10th percentile) went from having no wealth on average to having about $450 in 2022, while families at the top of the distribution experienced a 650% increase to almost $2 million in wealth (Urban Institute, 2024). This is a transfer of wealth from the lower socioeconomic classes to the highest socioeconomic classes.

Why do such differences exist? Well, while a number of important factors are at play, among them are the relative growth in wages at the top and bottom of the distribution, the loss of protections by labor unions, and tax law changes that have all benefited people at the top of the distribution. But factors outside of economics are also critically important. Race (Conley, 2010; Oliver & Shapiro, 2006), gender (Correll et al., 2007; Fortin, 2005; Matsumoto, 2001; Nakdimen, 1984; Weichselbaumer, 2004; Young, 2009), age (c.f. Petit, 2007), and similar demographic factors have impacts. Such factors exist. Now, the question is, are these differences acceptable? Are they just? Anti-oppressive social work practice contends that it is neither acceptable nor just and that social workers have a responsibility to change this.

One area where the problem of social justice serves as a case in point that clearly shows the issues of distributive and compensatory justice is the problem of environmental justice. This concept, little understood before the 1980s, is focused on how the consequences and benefits of environmental actions have been unequally shared across society. Often, the benefits—such as profit—from manufacturing, development, mining, or waste disposal accrue to a small number of people (or even sometimes society at large), while the consequences—such as a polluted environment—fall heavily on a different group. This different group commonly includes the poor, communities of color, children, and/or indigenous peoples (c.f. Bullard, 1990; Chavis, 1994; Gray et al., 2013; Hicken et al., 2012; Hornberg & Pauli, 2007; Nesmith & Smyth, 2015; United States Environmental Protection Agency, 2016). And the negative consequences can include very serious physical health impacts, as well as decreased property values and a variety of mental health issues. And to make the problem even worse, this unequal distribution of costs and benefits often includes barriers to meaningful participation by such groups about environmental actions (Nesmith & Smyth, 2015; United States Environmental Protection Agency, 2016), a vital component of AOP. Social work has come to the realization of this important domain rather late, even as issues of lead poisoning and occupational health issues were among the earliest concerns of our settlement house ancestors, and the connection between health, poverty, and environment are being better understood all of the time.

Children of color and low-income children exposed to environmental risks have a greater likelihood of fetal death; birth defects; being small for gestational age; preterm birth; clinically overt cognitive, neurologic, and behavioral abnormalities; subtle neuropsychological deficits; cancer; asthma and other respiratory diseases; obesity; and acute poisoning. And many chemical exposures can negatively impact brain development and cognitive function, and can lead to antisocial behavior, violence, and substance abuse, all of which result in burdensome costs to individuals, families, and society. Again, these burdens are unequally distributed and negatively impact those with the least power in society.

And it is quite likely that some of our greatest challenges in the next few decades are associated here. Children exposed to traumatic events such as natural disasters, exacerbated by climate change, can suffer from posttraumatic stress disorder. The number and type of problems associated with climate change are only now beginning to be seen. Evidence for all of these environmentally linked issues, and their effects on both humans in general, and disenfranchised populations in particular, grow literally by the hour. Basic consequences such as how to feed, clothe, house, and provide clean water to these increasing populations are already acute. And when you add the issues of environmental impacts, especially differentiated by such constructs as race, class, gender, and others (to be discussed later), the problems quickly inflate. Two examples of such impacts—one global and one local—highlight these concerns.

Globally, climate change may well be the critical issue humans confront during the next several decades. Climate affects everything from temperature, weather, and coastlines to what crops can be grown, what species live or die, and where it is or is not comfortable to live. For all of the history of the planet until at least the agricultural age, climate was exclusively driven by natural processes. Changes occasionally happened quickly (such as when volcanoes erupted or meteors struck the Earth), but generally change was slow, taking centuries or millennia. But with the increasing human population, the actions of production/consumption and waste creation have become critical factors. In particular, the burning of fossil fuels, the use of refrigerants, the production of methane, and the transitioning of forests to other uses have caused the planet to warm. This temperature increase (likely between 2°C and 7°C) makes some areas of the Earth warmer (such as arctic areas and the oceans) and provides extra energy for weather. Anticipated and actual effects of this heat and energy include rising sea levels (as glaciers and sea ice melt), warmer oceans (with changes to ocean life), stronger and more frequent storms, and changes in weather leading to changes in agricultural zones. Recent research suggests that how we treat the planet, even in the past, has huge impacts.

> ▶ **Reflection Questions**
> 1. Have you seen evidence of climate change in your life? In your clients' lives?
> 2. What do those changes mean for you and your clients?

While these issues will affect all of us, communities of color and low-income populations will suffer the greatest effects. Although humans are reasonably good at adapting to environmental changes—even climate changes (Jacobs, 2019) across the planet—the poor and disenfranchised around the world will find it difficult or impossible to adapt. Migrant farmworkers, for example, will find it difficult to work in oppressive heat and therefore find it difficult to feed their families. Pacific Islanders will become migratory as islands sink (Thompson, 2019). Poor individuals and communities across the planet will face the greatest degree of hardship in assessments in Liberia (Front Page Africa, 2019). Fishing stocks and costs will be harmful to fisherman across the world (Daileda, 2019). And these poor countries are leading the call for action (Beam, 2019).

Social Structure and Power

Now, suppose there was some social problem that, although expensive, we could afford to resolve and that virtually everyone agrees should be provided. Under these conditions, there is a fair chance the policy would exist. But in many cases, the policy still remains unenacted. Why? What is stopping the society from having the policy? The answer in many situations is because of the last set of policy foundational concepts—what we call the social or power structure of a society. In other words, who in a society has the power to ensure a need is addressed through a policy. The point is that in some societies, some policies have greater opposition than others. But like beliefs, social and political structures must be examined through a complex and broad set of concepts that come from sociology, political science, economics, and others. All these concepts, however, "boil down" to a couple of straightforward observations that feed off of each other.

First, all societies have an unequal distribution of power and resources. Different groups and individuals have different levels of wealth, power, rights, and control over their lives. Depending on the society, this may be due to relatively desirable differential awards (think here of justice), or it might be due to a range of other things such as religious beliefs, past political values and choices, beliefs about occupational status, economic theory, beliefs about the relative value of personal characteristics (like gender, age, race, or ethnicity), how wealth and power are transferred from one generation to the next, or even just luck. Often, these differences are labeled as differences of class. The two major ways a status or class is gained are ascription, whereby an individual receives the status involuntarily (at birth or later in life), or by achievement and some degree of individual effort (Parsons, 1951, 1991).

But a person's status/position may be helped through policy. The truth of the matter is that all policies have winners and losers. A law raising or lowering tax rates or inheritance taxes or outlawing certain kinds of discrimination are examples. All of these will enhance or detract from an individual's status and power. For our purposes here, status refers to a person's position in society, and power refers to the capacity to influence decisions. Making this last statement a bit more ominous, however, is that power can be leveraged. This means the more resources and power a person or group has, the more influence they have over the policy-making process and over policies selected. But the final important observation will hopefully drive this home. Once an individual or group starts winning, the more likely they are to continue to win, meaning that as you amass power and influence, it is possible to use these things to achieve even more!

As important as it is to examine these last statements and their influence in the United States, time does not allow a deeper discussion here. Instead, we will look at who the winners and losers are in the United States, particularly why we have major differences in power and what this means for policy and quality of life.

WHAT IS POLICY PRACTICE?

In reality, almost everything we as social workers do has a connection to policy practice, although we may not see the connections. Formally, "policy practice encompasses the professional efforts to influence the development, enactment, implementation, modification, or assessment of social policies, primarily to ensure social justice and equal access to basic social goods" (Barker, 2003, p. 330). From a slightly different perspective, what this means is we take our social work skills, theories, and beliefs and apply them to the policy domain. It may involve what we normally consider to be macro-practice, with a focus on such activities as advocacy, policy analysis, lobbying, community work, and administrative practice. But it also involves "bringing the macro to the micro"—bringing important policy change tools into our daily direct contact with and for clients. To explain this process, we will begin by presenting a path for the flow of policy implementation from the first indication that a need exists through the selection of a policy response to the direct practice resulting from that policy and beyond. This flow is what is known as "the policy process." Over the years, many different models of the policy process have been constructed, but the model we will use is shown in Table 7.3. Somewhat different social work skill sets are applicable at each step of the process, although some overlap exists. These too are shown in Table 7.3. We will examine these steps and some useful policy practice skills.

> ▶ **Reflection Questions**
> 1. What micropractice skills do you think might have applicability in policy work?
> 2. Why do you think these skills might apply?

Stages of the Policy Process and the Associated Primary Tasks

As is shown in Table 7.3, our model of the policy process comprises four stages, each of which has associated primary tasks. As you examine the table, please understand that this model is not the only such model and that different models may organize the stages somewhat differently. Furthermore, while the stages are generally sequential and chronologically

7: Policy-Informed Practice

TABLE 7.3 POLICY PROCESS AND SOCIAL WORKER POLICY PRACTICE ACTIVITIES

Policy Stage	Primary Task	Social Worker Roles/ Activities
Problem identification and characterization	• Social problem identified from direct practice experience • Social problem defined and characterized (includes how problem is constructed and measurement of size and scope) ↓	• Research—monitor client's experience, identify patterns, collect data. • Ensures that impacted individuals and communities are involved at the earliest possible stages
Political mobilization and political advocacy	• Develop support for policy response. • Selection of policy-making domain and policy alternatives • Advocate for policy and apply pressure on policy makers. • Advocate for adequate budget. ↓	• Social problem identified from direct practice experience • Social problem defined and characterized (includes how problem is constructed and measurement of size and scope)
Policy implementation	• Develop regulations from enacted policy. • Organizational capacity developed ↓	
Evaluation and policy improvement	• Review and critique policy and implementation.	

connected, the model is dynamic, with purposes and activities at one stage informing and influencing other stages of the model. Similarly, skills examined throughout this entire book are applicable at many places in the policy practice model, and the needed skills at any one stage are also needed at other stages. Thus, like many models, this should serve as a starting point for understanding and conducting policy practice—not as a complete and perfect model.

In our model, the four stages are (a) problem identification and characterization, where the primary tasks are identification of the problem, definition of the problem, and establishing the scope of the problem (including measuring and mapping the problem); (b) political mobilization and political advocacy, where the primary tasks are related to building support for a policy; (c) policy implementation, where the primary tasks are to ensure the best and most successful policy implementation; and (d) evaluation and policy improvement, where the primary tasks are to review and critique policy and implementation. Rush and Keenan (2014) argue that AOP in social work practice combines social policy advocacy, research with user participation, and direct practice with clients. They emphasize the importance of user voices in research and social work practice. To mitigate power imbalances, an anti-oppressive (AO) approach to this requires the social worker to include the impacted individuals and communities at the earliest possible stage to critically evaluate their work, with assistance from others, for bias, inaccuracies, and unintentional perpetuation of oppressive approaches.

POLICY STAGES: PROBLEM IDENTIFICATION AND CHARACTERIZATION

Problem Identification

No issue was ever addressed by a policy or even by direct practice that was not first identified as a problem. In our practice, the closeness we maintain with client systems places us in a unique position to see emerging situations in our clients' lives early and/or throughout the treatment process. This requires ongoing observation of the domains of our clients' lives. Social work can and does play a critical role in this stage and in "transforming private troubles, such as unemployment, domestic violence, homelessness, and mass incarceration, into public issues" (Reisch, 2017, p. 4). This means we must observe, document, and articulate what we see.

Interestingly, some professional fields maintain this observational perspective as a matter of standard practice and have even developed institutions to support it. For example, in the medical and public health world, there is a system known as *surveillance* designed to catch emerging health issues while they are still small and manageable. This system is so well developed that it includes virtually every hospital and physician on the planet, and organizations such as the large and well funded World Health Organization (WHO) and Centers for Disease Control and Prevention (CDC) in the United States have created a system that ideally catches emerging problems anywhere on the planet. How is it done? Well, according to the CDC, the system is designed with several goals in mind. The system is designed to be inclusive, to provide timely information, to provide an accurate representation of the problem, to be sensitive to problem characteristics, and to be specific to the disease in question (CDC, 2018). Consider the COVID-19 pandemic or the annual flu shot campaign. Both of these are the result of knowledge developed through surveillance.

Even now, there are a number of emerging policy areas where social workers will serve on the frontline of problem identification. For example, as the effects of climate change come more to the fore, the ways it affects clients become more and more evident. The number and type of problems associated with climate change are beginning to be seen in the very communities we work with. In part, this is because it creates a shock to our systems and is creating disequilibrium throughout our world, but such trauma may look different in different localities (see Case 7.2). For example, food production shocks are becoming more common, and new diseases and forms of trauma and differential effects on different client groups and communities are likely to come to the fore. You, as a social worker, can identify and publicize the need for responses where you find them.

Thus, at this early stage, no particularly unique set of policy skills is required other than vigilance and the ability to self-reflect about your potential for bias in relation to the problem characterization process. These are vital tasks. Think about it. Who first identified the needs of persons with the HIV/AIDS virus? Or large numbers of persons overdosing from opiates? Or changes in the characteristics of the homeless population in the 2010s? We cannot guarantee that in all of these cases it was a social worker, but it may well have been!

Problem Characterization

As this stage continues, better evidence needs to be developed about the problem. Who is affected? How many persons? What are the parameters of the problem in question? And how shall we define it and talk about it?

> **▶ Reflection Questions**
> 1. What comprises "good evidence" when thinking about a problem?
> 2. What methods do you think can be used to gather information that will carry the greatest weight in an argument?

The answers to the questions are important, as social problems do not appear as fully formed, discrete, easily understood issues. Indeed, the way we understand a social problem is the result of persons like yourself who examine, define, and characterize the issue. From a purely intellectual perspective, this in some ways is one of the most interesting but perhaps difficult aspects of the policy process. There are two somewhat different processes here—problem social construction and definition and problem measurement (application of how the problem is constructed to measurement of size and scope). Social workers have clear policy practice opportunities during this phase.

Social Constructions and Definition

To attempt to better understand these two processes, let's first think about the construction and definition. Consider the following questions. First, if you were to ask any 100 Americans, "What is the problem with immigration?" you likely would get a variety of answers. Among some of the answers might be: (a) there are too many immigrants of all types coming into the United States; (b) there are too many low-skilled immigrants coming into the United States; (c) there are too many Muslim (or non-European, or Asian, or . . .) immigrants coming into the United States; (d) there are not enough legal immigrants coming into the United States to meet the needs of business; and (e) our immigration laws are discriminatory to persons of color.

CASE 7.2 | TIRED AND SCARED: PROBLEM CHARACTERIZATION

Salya enjoyed working with refugees. Overwhelmingly in the 4 years she had worked at the facility, she had found the clients kind but scared. All had been traumatized and had spent significant time getting here. But what she was hearing on the news, and even from some of her coworkers, was frightening. She had never met a refugee who was anything other than honestly in need and never showed any criminal intent.

Knowing how the problem was being talked about in the media, she decided to do research on her own. As her clients overwhelmingly spoke Spanish and the few that did not spoke a local language that she knew, she began to conduct interviews with the clients. She wanted the "real" stories from the clients, and as such she decided to use primarily open-ended, qualitative surveys. She did have some questions about the proper methodological approach, because she wanted the data to be as robust as possible. So she contacted a former professor from her MSW program. But beyond those issues, she found the clients willing to tell their story. And what she heard, particularly from young women, was frightening. And she could not help growing more and more angry with her coworkers and the folks telling these stories.

The answers to these questions show the range of positions the questions evoke. Why? What is important about the differences? The answer is that each response leads to a different understanding of what the problem means to the person responding. And depending on how they answered, the possible solution to the problem at hand is constrained. Virtually everyone agrees that the United States is a nation of immigrants; the vast majority are either an immigrant or in a family whose line includes immigrants. Even today, the numbers are large. According to the U.S. Census Bureau (2024), from 2018 to 2022, over 13% of the U.S. population was foreign born. In terms of what are called legal immigrants, in 2022, about 1 million foreign nationals were either granted lawful permanent residence, were admitted on a temporary basis, applied for asylum or refugee status, or were naturalized (Department of Homeland Security [DHS], 2024).

> ▶ **Reflection Questions**
>
> 1. What does AOP have to do with social construction?
> 2. How might someone utilizing an AO approach conceptualize immigration?

But despite the numbers and the history, immigration is not without controversy. A large number of Americans want to limit immigrants (Fussell, 2014) for a variety of reasons, from general fear of outsiders (Critchley, 2007), to national security, to the effects on low-income workers and salaries (Boreas, 2003) and the general risk they bring to society (Tan, 2015). At the same time, many people believe that immigrants bring benefits to a society (Faver, 2004).

A similar example in recent years is how our understanding about "the problem of drugs" has changed. In the lifetime of many of the people reading this chapter, marijuana has gone from an evil substance subverting the youth of America and causing depraved behavior, to a somewhat more benign substance but that might serve as a "gateway" to the use of other drugs, to a drug that as of 2024, is fully legal in 24 states and at least partially legal for medical purposes in 46 states. That is a dramatic change! And to some degree, many people would no longer include marijuana in a conversation talking about the problem of drugs.

At the same time, opiates are now the central part of a discussion about the problem of drugs. A few current statistics show how opiates have become the core of the discussion: more than 130 persons die from overdose every day in the United States (U.S. Department of Health and Human Services, 2023); "the economic burden" of prescription opioids alone in the United States is $78.5 billion a year (Florence et al., 2016); opioid overdoses increased 30% in 18 months from 2016 through 2017 in many areas in the United States (Vivolo-Kantor et al., 2017); and drug overdose is the leading cause of death of persons under 50 in the United States, with recent deaths rising fastest among Black and Indigenous communities (Vital Strategies, 2023).

Why the problem of drugs has changed so dramatically is one of the clearest examples of changes in what is seen as important and how the problem definition has evolved. Importantly, the definition is associated with what is called the social construction of the problem. The idea of social construction is, at the same time, fairly easy and immensely complex to understand. Formally, it is the process by which humans attach meaning to things or events. The point to these different perspectives is that the way the problems are conceptualized leads to important distinctions in our understanding of the causes, or how serious it is, or what we believe the solutions could be. And this points to an important "truth" about a problem—that definitions of the problem are not fixed, permanent concepts with clear boundaries. Instead, they are socially constructed. As one writer states, "a social construct is something that exists not in objective reality, but as a result of human interaction. It exists because humans agree that it exists" (Bainbridge, 2018).

Everything in our lives is affected by the same general phenomena. We value, fear, or seek some items, people, or experiences, while we dislike, undervalue, or avoid almost identical phenomena. And the only difference is what meanings we attach to and how we think about the thing. In other words, the meanings we attach are the critical difference!

Now, how is this useful? We can participate in this process. Our understanding of the problem—what we see and what our clients tell us—can be useful in shaping the discussion around a problem.

Research Skills

The major skill set associated with problem characterization is research skills. They are the tools we use to "capture" and frame a problem. And such data are useful in shaping and understanding the size and scope of a given problem. All social work practitioners, even those who do not engage in research as a part of their job description, need to develop various skills in research. And one policy practice domain where this comes to the fore is in our efforts to understand a problem. Several types of research skills are useful here.

Tools for Assessing Need

At this phase, understanding the scope of the problem is critical. There are any number of excellent "how to" guides that will help you in this process. But for our purposes, we will focus on the kinds of information that will be useful to know. What you want to focus on are a series of questions that, if answered, will help to better understand the problem. The following questions serve as useful starting points:

- What is the etiology of the condition? In other words, how and/or where did it begin? So, data about the history would be useful.
- Where and when was it first seen?
- Who first identified it?
- What are its causes? Are there identifiable possible antecedents?
- What are the characteristics of those who can be defined as having the condition?
- How many people are affected?
- How quickly is the problem expanding?
- How severely are people affected?
- In what ways are people affected?
- Can they be located geographically? Consider looking at comparative geographic areas as a way of showing severity or change.
- How widely is the condition recognized?
- Are there unique, identifiable characteristics?

As with any research, how you collect the data matters. But a variety of methods may be appropriate. Likewise, both qualitative data (narrative, nonstatistical information) and quantitative statistical data may be useful. Qualitative data, in the form of first-person accounts, are excellent ways to tell the clients' stories, while statistical data show the extent of the experiences. This is also the phase in which it is important to ensure those most impacted by the social issue are brought into the discussion, if this has not already occurred. From an AO perspective, who better to assist in the development and implementation of programs and practices that shift societal dynamics to decrease and eliminate oppression than those most likely to be impacted by the programs and practices? Those most likely to experience oppression due to the social issue? To assist in the answering of the questions listed earlier?

A further and highly valuable approach at this stage of the process is mapping, as mapping the physical extent of an emerging problem is of great value as we try and understand the scope of the problem. One recent example where mapping has been used to examine an emerging problem is mapping areas of vulnerability to climate change. For example, many areas in North Carolina were identified as highly at risk from hurricane damage (Mock, 2018), and by such knowledge, prevention and remediation were made more possible. Several excellent such tools are now available—even down to the street level—including the Environmental Protection Agency's (EPA's) Environmental Justice Screening and Mapping Tool or through sources at Climate Central (n.d.).

Political Mobilization and Political Advocacy

Once the problem has been identified and characterized, the concern turns to building support for the policy response, as well as using appropriate forms of pressure on policy makers to ensure that action is taken. This phase, in many ways, is the one that not only requires the greatest creativity from the social worker but also best fits the entire range of social worker skills. And there have been some major successes over the years. These include women's suffrage, the civil rights movement, the gay rights movement, and resistance against apartheid (Schwartz & Sanchez, 2016). But here is the critical point. Not one of these changes took place because of social workers alone. In every case, it took broad pressure from across the societies in question. And this "broad pressure" is the fruit of mobilization!

By necessity, political mobilization involves organizing and advocacy. Policy makers and the public need to be made aware of what the problem is, who is affected and how, what options are available, and which is the preferred option and why. There are several themes that affect these needs. But before examining the specific themes, the issue of power will be examined.

Why power? What is power in this context? Here, we are largely talking about power as social or political power, and in the political world, power is just about the whole ball game. Politics and social change depend on its application. And unfortunately, many of the things we as humans care about—friendship, love, personal growth—matter much less than the medium of power. So let's begin with an understanding of what power is and what power does.

As a starting point, power is not easy to define, despite (or perhaps because of) the fact that power is one of the most-studied phenomena in the social sciences. For our purposes, power means the ability to exert social and political influence. The sources of power are many and varied. Among some of the identified aspects are personal charisma, authority, position, status, expertise (knowledge and skills), wealth, numbers of followers, technology, and more (Fiske & Berdahl, 2007; Weber, 1978 ; c.f. French & Raven, 1959). But regardless of the source or basis of power used, the point is that power is the one critical tool that forms the core of virtually all effective organizational activities and that must be developed and used for effective policy work.

How? Well, digging a bit deeper, Fiske and Berdahl (2007), in an attempt to understand the phenomenon, suggest that three categories of definitions apply here. They are power as influence, power as potential influence, and power as outcome. Thinking about our purposes of creating or changing policy, there is value in all three categories. Power as influence refers to the direct application to achieve a result. A vote in a referendum is an example or, conversely, a large cash contribution to a candidate given along with an expressed desire about how to vote on a piece of legislation. Power as potential influence has many contemporary examples. Until very recently, all a politician needed to hear was the expressed desire about how to vote on a piece of firearm legislation from the National Rifle Association (NRA), and the candidate would know that if they voted differently, large numbers of persons would work against their reelection.

Finally, power as outcome means empowerment. This is a goal of almost all advocacy efforts to at least some degree. One other definitional aspect of power should be acknowledged. Power can be implied and quiet, or it can be coercive and overt. As social workers, we generally prefer the more quiet and implied forms. But history has shown that sometimes the application of power can be loud and messy. So how loud and messy should the effort to influence be? Is there a role for conflict, and if so, is there a role for violence? Well virtually everyone would say that violence is out of the question.

> **Reflection Questions**
>
> 1. Is violence ever acceptable on behalf of social change? Why or why not?
> 2. What indicates to you that a need to change approaches is needed to bring about a policy change?

But the broader answer is that applying power should be as loud as it needs to be to get people involved, to continue to stay involved, and to have policy makers act. This suggests at least some need for balance. You need to activate and motivate enough of the public (or the right people) but not alienate people because of your tactics. In Martin Luther King Jr.'s famous *Letter from Birmingham Jail* (King, 1963), Dr. King talks about the flow of effort that leads to the direct actions employed. In this case, the direct actions occurred because nothing else worked. In his words:

> As the weeks and months unfolded, we realized that we were the victims of a broken promise. The signs remained. As in so many experiences of the past, we were confronted with blasted hopes, and the dark shadow of a deep disappointment settled upon us. So we had no alternative except that of preparing for direct action, whereby we would present our very bodies as a means of laying our case before the conscience of the local and national community. We were not unmindful of the difficulties involved. So we decided to go through a process of self-purification.

We started having workshops on nonviolence and repeatedly asked ourselves the questions, "Are you able to accept blows without retaliating?" and "Are you able to endure the ordeals of jail?" We decided to set our direct-action program around the Easter season, realizing that, with exception of Christmas, this was the largest shopping period of the year. Knowing that a strong economic withdrawal program would be the by-product of direct action, we felt that this was the best time to bring pressure on the merchants for the needed change.

And overall, in many cases, some types of direct action are needed to bring focus and attention to the problem. A large variety of such actions are possible. They range from the generally quiet activities of letter writing, emails, calls, or text campaigns to policy makers, to direct in-person meetings with policy makers, to much larger and more powerful events, such as lawsuits, protests, and boycotts. Often, as is the case as described by Dr. King, there will be a "ratcheting up" of efforts.

What are some of the effective methods that can be used in the process of mobilization? As indicated, here we will address a few important aspects of the process of mobilization—lobbying, campaign funding, and public mobilization. But before examining a few domains in depth, it is worthwhile to consider a much longer list of ways that social workers may influence the policy maker. Among the methods that are available are networking with other organizations, providing training to key people, commenting on draft policy documents, organizing policy seminars, publications on policy issues, providing services, articles in the media, pilots of alternative policy approaches, insider lobbying, websites; newsletters to policy makers, and work on projects commissioned by policy makers (Kornsweig et al., 2006).

Lobbying

One form of attempt to change policy that is ubiquitous in our political system is what is called "lobbying." Formally, it is defined as "any attempt by individuals or private interest groups to influence the decisions of government; in its original meaning it referred to efforts to influence the votes of legislators, generally in the lobby outside the legislative chamber" (Encyclopaedia Britannica, 2024). Although the actual etymology of the term is somewhat lost in history, it does appear to have a connection with the presence of persons attempting to influence legislation in areas such as lobbying.

What is important, however, is that it is generally accepted in our political world. Indeed, our Constitution protects persons' right to free speech, right to peaceable assembly, and right to petition lawmakers. And with these rights, there is a long history of persons and interest groups attempting to change or bend legislation and other policies in ways that help them. What is more problematic is what kinds of lobbying work, what kinds of lobbying are legal, and what kinds of lobbying are otherwise illegal or unethical?

Effective Forms of Lobbying

There are a great variety of ways to lobby, each with strengths and limitations. For example, lobbying can be thought of as inside (direct) lobbying or outside (indirect) lobbying. Inside lobbying largely comprises direct contact with policy makers, while outside lobbying is more typically mobilizing the public to bring numbers or attention to an issue (Kollman, 1998). Inside lobbying may include one-on-one meetings with policy makers or their staff. But it also includes the general or policy-specific meetings that policy makers often hold with constituents.

Now, when many of us think of lobbying, we have a narrow and sometimes negative view of the activity. Often, it is associated with professional lobbyists, and the scope of such lobbying activity across America is huge. Indeed, the numbers of lobbyists and lobbying organizations are great (in Washington, DC, there is an area called K Street, where hundreds of lobbyists are located), and both the states and the federal government have laws that govern how lobbyists may operate. To give an idea of how large the industry is, between 1998 and 2018, 18 organizations (corporations and trade organizations) spent over $200 million each on lobbying, and one entity, the U.S. Chamber of Commerce, spent over $1.5 billion (Center for Responsive Politics, 2019a).

Importantly, this number of lobbying organizations, while overwhelmingly from the business world, is not exclusively so. The profession of social work has professional lobbying organizations, and many of the advocacy and issue groups associated with the profession and allies do likewise (c.f. AARP, Boys & Girls Clubs, National Education Association [NEA], etc.). Indeed, most social workers, either through an advocacy organization or on their own, will have at least some opportunity to participate in lobbying in one form or another. Following are some of the types of lobbying we are likely to experience and use. A nonexhaustive list of methods (Kornsweig et al., 2006) may include:

- working with policy makers ("insider advocacy" [many lobbyists develop direct relationships with policy makers through volunteering and participation in advisory groups]);
- consultations (often based on direct outreach from policy makers);
- face-to-face meetings with policy makers;
- presentations to policy makers;
- presentations at conferences, seminars, public meetings, etc.;
- international conferences;
- creating written materials about problems and possible solutions, such as through policy briefs (discussed later); and
- legal challenges (many times, citizens and groups may bring lawsuits to ensure governments act as needed).

If you have the opportunity to meet with policy makers and/or their staff to directly lobby, a few general guidelines will help to maximize the effectiveness of the effort. First of all, you are more likely to talk to a staff person than to the actual policy maker. That's okay. You are not being ignored (in most cases!), but rather you are attempting to talk to a person (the policy maker) with many demands on their time. And generally, the staff person is good at reporting to the policy maker what their constituents are saying. Indeed, the same applies to calling a policy maker and talking by phone. The staff member will pass the information on. Now, would we rather talk to the actual policy maker? Sure. But in our system, that opportunity often comes with strings attached (see "Campaign Funding" section).

Importantly, the policy maker usually sets the rules about who they will talk to, what they will and will not talk about, and for how long and under what conditions. As you may recall, in the last few years, many public meetings with lawmakers became quite heated over the ACA (Obamacare). Congress itself has established some basic ethical standards for constituent meetings (United States House of Representatives, n.d.), but many congresspersons have established their own rules. Often, being a constituent in a group of constituents is high priority (Bowman, 2014). Furthermore, being a contributor to a politician is a serious plus (see "Campaign Funding" section), with one study finding it 231% more likely a politician will meet with you if you contributed to their campaign (Kalla & Broockman, 2015).

However, regardless of which type of lobbying you choose, there are a few general rules and skill sets you want to consider. First, do your research. You need to know the subject, but also the individuals you will be interacting with. Often, you will not be seeing the actual politician, but one of the staff. Knowing their names is a plus (National Association of Social Workers Massachusetts Chapter, n.d.). In your remarks, be brief, direct, and clear. You may be as passionate as you feel, even angry, but not vulgar. And never, ever, ever be threatening or violent. And acknowledge and thank the politician (National Association of Social Workers Massachusetts Chapter, n.d.).

Campaign Funding

One of the most commonly used ways to try and influence politicians is to give money tto help fund their campaigns. Why? In our democratic republican form of government, we elect politicians to represent us. And not surprisingly, politicians want our support as they run for election. At its base, running for office is very inexpensive—only a few dollars to file papers, and voila, a person becomes a candidate.

On the other hand, *successfully* running for office can be incredibly expensive. Candidates need to mobilize the public, hire staff, do research, establish plans, and engage the media. To do these things, money is necessary. How much? Well, the numbers are a bit frightening. The estimated cost of the 2022 midterm elections was almost $9 billion (OpenSecrets, 2023), which was the most in history for a midterm. Similarly, the 2020 election (president and Congress combined) cost $14.4 billion (Ingraham, 2017). And in the 2018 election the average senator seeking reelection spent $13,460,873 (Center for Responsive Politics, 2019b). In practical terms, this means that the typical successful senator over their 6-year term has to raise over $43,000 every single week they are in office! That's a lot of money!

So giving money to politicians is desirable. But there are important caveats. First, it is illegal everywhere to "buy" a vote. You cannot make a deal with a politician that says "I will give you $1,000 if you vote for/against this bill." And the reverse is also true: a politician cannot promise to vote a certain way based only on a contribution. Similarly, there are currently a number of restrictions on how much money a person can give to any specific politician during a calendar year or election. Generally, most individual donors are limited to a few thousand dollars per cycle (see the Federal Election Commission at www.fec.gov for the limits). But there are also a number of ways people attempt to get around these restrictions. For example, the individual limits are easily multiplied by the number of persons in a family (so if a limit is $2,800, but there are six people in a family, then the contribution is as much as $16,800).

More importantly, restrictions are lessened by giving money to political parties rather than individuals or by creating special types of organizations that are exempt from many regulations. Among these are what are known as political action committees (PACs), which can bundle monies from many sources, or certain types of 501(c) organizations, whose primary function is issue advocacy (as opposed to political advocacy), or 527 organizations (called super PACs) who intend to publicly educate on issues. Again, these organizations have a number of exemptions related to contribution limits and/or donor disclosure.

Furthermore, as the result of some important Supreme Court decisions, the ability of the government to regulate political spending has been diminished. In 2010, the court decided in *Citizens United v. FEC* that corporations could spend money for political advocacy on the basis of their free speech rights. A second case, *SpeechNOW.org v. FEC* (2010), took this a step further and basically removed all contribution limits from certain kinds of nonprofit organizations as long as the spending organization did not coordinate with a candidate.

But the biggest issue, and thus one to remember, is rarely will "the little person" have enough funds to compete on this field. Think of it this way. If Bill Gates and you both call you senator and leave a message, who is the senator more likely to call back? Probably not you. But that is perhaps not as bad as it sounds. First, in recent years it has become clear how important small campaign contributions can be. The 2016 and 2020 campaigns of politicians like Bernie Sanders, Kamala Harris, and others have demonstrated that enough small donations can quickly grow large sums.

Furthermore, we need instead to utilize other tools to influence politicians. Thus, the expanded forms of mobilization are critical.

Educating, Mobilizing, and Organizing the Public

While both lobbying of policy makers and contributing money to campaigns are necessary, unfortunately, limits on time and cash resources restrict how much effect these methods have among practicing social workers. In part, we can address these restrictions by joining advocacy organizations. By doing so, we bring the power of numbers to our efforts. Numbers are often (though unfortunately not always) the key to almost any effective application of power. But whether it is through participation in such an organization or on our own, one very critical tool we have at our disposal is a more general mobilization of the public. As that theme is more fully covered in chapters on mezzo social work practice with organizations and communities, only a few words on the subject are presented here. (*Note*: For a resource guide that covers all aspects of organizing, please look at the *Community Toolbox* from University of Kansas [n.d.], which gives a virtual step-by-step description of the organizing process.)

Here, instead, we will focus on one set of skills that has wide utility in policy work: educating policy makers and the public. Three types of written educational materials are particularly valuable, as they can be developed and applied by individual social workers, as well as the use of social media. In other words, joining a group is not necessary to develop and apply these materials.

The reality and importance of this activity are weighty. In our complex and highly stimulating world, both policy makers and the general public typically have limited information about any given problem or possible solutions. Like any human knowledge area, these limitations are influenced by things like personal interest and time. No one can know everything. Interestingly, sometimes the knowledge limitations of policy makers are associated with the very positions the policy makers hold. For example, one common observation about Congress is that differences in policy knowledge exist by body (c.f. Edwards & Lippucci, 1998; O'Connor et al., 2004). Senators tend to be "policy generalists," meaning that because they serve entire states, they need to know at least a little bit about a lot of policy areas, but not necessarily a lot about any specific policy problem. On the other hand, members of the House of Representatives tend to be "policy specialists" and perhaps quite knowledgeable about the areas important to their district but perhaps ignorant of less relevant issues.

But regardless of the level of knowledge about any given problem, you bring important perspectives and evidence that should be presented. So you, the individual social worker or as a member of an advocacy organization, can help to address these problems. The "inside" perspective of a one-on-one conversation with the policy maker (or, more likely, the staff of a policy maker) is only one way to educate and inform. Other ways are equally important. These may include testifying before policy makers in a hearing of one form or another and writing policy briefs.

Giving Testimony

Social workers are often asked to present testimony in what are called "hearings." These times are great opportunities to carry your "on the ground" expertise and to present valuable alternatives. Unfortunately, these won't always be pleasant activities—sometimes the events are used to kill policies that are desirable from our perspective (National Association of Social Workers Massachusetts Chapter, n.d.) or to give the illusion of community input, but our voices and the information we provide can be invaluable.

The opportunities come as policy makers seek testimony from persons like yourself in any one of several types of hearings. These may include legislative hearings that seek information about policies, oversight hearings that review existing programs and agencies, investigative hearings that look into allegations of wrong-doing by persons in the government, and confirmation hearings that address appointees to government positions (Heitshusen, 2018). If it is an area you know something about, you may ask or be asked to provide testimony, and this could be either written and in person, or both (Heitshusen, 2017).

What you say is up to you. You may bring statistics, anecdotes from the field, or stories heard from clients. As a social worker, you are (hopefully) well trained in public communication. But always be brief, to the point, and factual—and know the committee members. There will be some participants who are friendly to you and others who are not.

Unfortunately, not all hearings are the same. The hearing may be an event for "show" with little chance it will influence policy. Or you might find yourself presenting your testimony to an empty room (congresspersons are not obligated to attend), or you might find you are facing one or more hostile politicians who ask questions that are more like diatribes with little opportunity for you to respond. But always be polite, even as you are assertive, if your goal is to have the opportunity to complete your testimony. Congresspersons have been known to respond quite testily even if they agree with you if you "impugn" a member. Overall, this is a fabulous opportunity to get information to the people who make the decisions.

Policy Briefs

While the testimony is quick and ephemeral, putting the material "on paper" allows the wider distribution of information. Indeed, it is a nearly critical aspect of almost all mobilization efforts. In particular, the form called the "policy brief" is very useful. It is a presentation of written facts associated with a policy or problem. While there is no one format universally defined as the policy brief, there are some characteristics associated with most forms. A good brief will be, well, brief. But in general, the information should include a strong title, problem/policy background and significance, your position and desired steps or outcomes, and reputable references (Domingo, 2015). A number of excellent examples and step-by-step models are found at Slideshare.

Here is one format that is "tried and true," although the content in a policy brief is, to a degree, up to you and what it is that you hope the audience will take from it. Generally, but not always, a good policy brief will include the following: A description of the problem you are hoping to resolve. This should include a definition, a few powerful statistics, and perhaps a very quick history of previous attempts to resolve the problem. Or if the brief is attempting to inform the reader about failings in existing policy, you will want to describe the policy currently in place and the reasons the policy is not adequate. It should include a description of the goals of the policy response and a description of the necessary components of the policy response. At a minimum, this could include such things as who needs the potential benefit and what the potential benefit should be and a statement of what you are asking the reader to do. This could include contacts, names of organizations that advocate for the policy, and governmental committees or individuals that need to hear from the reader, and information about who is responsible for this brief.

These briefs may then be distributed in person, through email, or through social media. As a final thought, in the experience of the author, you will find that the audiences who read these briefs vary widely. As such, you might consider two or three different formats, each written slightly differently to address the needs and concerns of a given group.

Letters to the Editor

If the goal of your written work is to reach a wide audience, few methods and formats are as effective as the letter to the editor. Of course, we assume this means in newspapers, but similar components and formats apply to any number of online opportunities, such as blogs or other social media posts. As with the policy brief, a number of appropriate structures exist, but the general content areas are similar with just a couple of differences. The major differences relate to the difference in audience. Newspapers and social media posts are usually seen primarily by people with some commonality; for instance, they live in the same town or have the same interests. Therefore, when you write such a letter, make sure you have written it in such a way to address that commonality. As the Maryland State Education Association (n.d.) states, "Newspaper readers care about how an issue will impact them or their families locally. Including brief information on the economic or other impacts of an issue in the community will draw readers' interest."

Social Media

Our informational universe has been transformed by technology and its democratization. Cell phones and the internet, without much exaggeration, place the entire knowledge base of humanity at our fingertips. Further, the ease and availability of digital cameras and easy-to-use editing software and "cloud" storage have made video production and distribution a common activity.

For social workers, this educational medium is almost too good to ignore. How widely does this format reach? It is reported that YouTube has almost 2.5 billion people using the platform monthly (Global Media Insight, 2024). Many of these videos are created by users

> **Reflection Questions**
> 1. What "catches your attention" when you are reviewing the news or a website?
> 2. What kinds of information might you include to maximize interest in a letter to the editor?

like yourselves, and in just a few hours, you can create a video with the potential for a worldwide distribution and impact. Of course, just creating and posting is no guarantee that people will watch and will act on what they see.

Fortunately, a number of YouTube videos can help you develop an effective presence. But like the policy brief and the letters to the editor, direct, uncluttered information is best. There is, however, one technique that seems to be very important with effective videos—start with a story. In our work life, we undoubtedly hear interesting, insightful, and powerful stories all the time. As long as you are respectful of the ethical aspects of a client's life and maintain confidentiality and anonymity, feel free to use these stories. They will help to get the message across.

POLICY IMPLEMENTATION

One of the real shocks to many people who interact with the policy world is that even when a policy is enacted at the federal, state, or local level, a whole process of implementation begins. Generally stated, policy implementation runs the gamut of activities that occur from the time a given law becomes law, through the regulatory process, and on through the final activities that take place between the social worker and client. And such a process can enhance, but also undermine, the actual law. Importantly, policy itself often lays out little more than statements of intention, a budget, and directed bureaucratic control through an agency or department. With those limited components, a system "kicks in" to write the rules or regulations associated with the policy. It is at this point that the phrase "the devil is in the details" makes sense. Choices about these details can affect the whole domain of policy issues about the who, what, where, and how of the policy. Two domains in particular are important here—regulations (often called rule making) and organizational or administrative practice.

Regulatory Actions

Many of the choices affecting policy come out in the regulatory process. The process may be long and complex, but it is governed by laws that set the parameters of the regulatory flow, with virtually every unit of federal and state departments and agencies having unique procedures that govern how this works. But there are some general principles that we will examine next. Further, for more detail on many of the unique elements of the process, a useful overview has been published by the United States Office of the Federal Register (n.d.) that goes into greater specificity. The general steps include the following:

1. Initiating events—some specific action initiates the regulatory process, such as passage of a law or a court decision.
2. Determining whether a rule is needed—the lead agency makes a determination if a rule should be put in place.

3. Preparing the proposed rule—the lead agency is required to draft a proposed regulation.
4. OMB review of proposed rule—the Office of Management and Budget (OMB) examines the proposed rule to see if it aligns with all relevant federal laws.
5. Publishing the proposed rule—the lead agency is required to notify the public that a proposed rule is being examined.
6. Public comments—the public is given a 30-, 60-, or 90-day period to make comments about the proposed regulation
7. Preparing the final rule, interim final rule, or direct final rule—This occurs after the comment period ends.
8. OMB review of final rule, interim final rule, or direct final rule.
9. Publihsing the final rule, interim final rule, or direct final rule.

Within this process, there are several important points of access and opportunities for social workers to participate. These points are largely related to the opportunities to comment on the proposed rules. What is of particular importance is knowledge about the opportunities, as well as procedures that must be used for the comments. In reality, both can be overwhelming. And this is one of the times when connection to an advocacy group is critical. Most of the advocacy organizations social workers work with have established methods to keep track of relevant regulations under development and review. Thus, connection with these organizations will provide access to strong supportive action.

Organizational Practice

But even the regulatory decision process is not the end of the implementation stage. For the services and actions determined by the regulation still need to be provided! This moves us into the realm of organizational practice. While organizational theory and practice are generally outside of the frame of this chapter, it is critical to understand how organizations work, as virtually all policies are implemented—not to mention created —by organizations. They provide the primary medium for our work, and it is no exaggeration to say that all we do with and for clients takes place through our, and their, connection to organizations whether they be government departments, county services offices, or small, local agencies.

One way this can be understood is by examining what is sometimes classified as organizational or administrative practice. Birkenmaier and Berg-Warner (2007) provide a useful listing of the knowledge and skills associated with this practice. This listing includes budgeting and financial management; working with boards of directors; resource development; program evaluation; organizational design, development, assessment, and diagnosis; computer information systems and technology; leadership and personnel management; networking; fundraising; and media and marketing (Birkenmaier & Berg-Weger, 2007). Chapters 12 and 13 discuss organizations in much greater detail. But the point cannot be downplayed here. Organizations are where the action takes place! And as such, participation in policy means working to maximize the chances that organizations will be successful.

Policy Evaluation

The last area of policy practice we will examine is the area commonly known as policy evaluation or policy analysis. Formally defined, "Policy evaluation applies evaluation principles and methods to examine the content, implementation or impact of a policy. Evaluation is the activity through which we develop an understanding of the merit, worth, and utility of a policy" (CDC, 2011, p. 1). Policy analysis provides the opportunity to examine and provide informed critical analysis of existing policies. And as such, this form of analysis may have value at any point in the policy process, but it is listed here because it implies the policy has been enacted. And with that in mind, one of the most useful aspects of the policy analysis is that it can be used to provide feedback to change and improve policy if needed.

Indeed, policy analysis can serve a variety of purposes, and a wide variety of approaches and methods can be used. In part, this is due to the fact that policies are complex, and in part this is because a wide variety of different questions can be asked about a policy. In addition, policy analysis does not belong to any unique academic discipline, and as such, the various paradigms of the different disciplines may affect the project.

With those provisos in mind, there are a number of general types of issues to consider in a policy analysis. These include the purpose of the analysis (why it is being done), what the policy does (the policy description), and how the analysis is done. Exhibit 7.1 goes over several types of policy analysis and the questions the analysis seeks to answer. But before we discuss the questions and methods of the various forms of policy analysis, we will look at the various purposes for conducting policy analysis.

The WHO (2013) provides a list of possible purposes that forms a reasonable baseline. According to their guiding document, evaluation may focus on an "activity, project, programme, strategy, policy, topic, theme, sector, or operational area institutional performance." They should consider the following:

- Focus on expected and achieved accomplishments, examining the results chain, processes, contextual factors and causality, in order to understand achievements or the lack thereof.
- Determine the relevance, impact, effectiveness, efficiency, and sustainability of the interventions and contributions of the organization.
- Provide evidence-based information that is credible, reliable and useful, enabling the timely incorporation of findings, recommendations and lessons learnt into the decision-making processes of the organization.
- Be an integral part of each stage of the programming cycle and not only an end-of-programme activity. (p. 1)

As a social worker, you are in a wonderful place to examine the implementation of policy. Now, it is understood that you might not have the time and resources to conduct major evaluations of major policies. But even small pieces can make for major contributions.

So what makes for a "good" evaluation? Well, again, that in part depends on the discipline and purpose of the evaluation. A slightly more "political" interpretation of what comprises a

Exhibit 7.1 Types of Policy Analysis

Descriptive analysis: Generally, this type attempts to understand the "what" of a policy, rather than "why." It includes the following questions:

- What is the target problem; how large is the problem; how is the problem defined?
- Who receives the benefit or sanction?
- What do beneficiaries receive? How do beneficiaries receive the benefit?
- How is it paid for?
- Does the policy reduce the size of the target problem? What remains to be done?

Historical analysis: This type attempts to understand how a policy "came to be." There are a number of questions that might be included, such as:

- When was the target problem first identified and by whom? By whom and how was the problem defined?
- What policy alternatives existed?
- What groups or individuals supported and opposed the policy response?
- What was the evolution of the policy selected? What was the "legislative" chronology?
- What does the final policy include or not include?

Values analysis: This type attempts to understand the "why" of a policy. There are several different models, but generally they are all guided by some similar questions, which include:

- What social values does the policy hope to affect or support?
- What social values affected the definition and policy alternatives and final selection?
- Has the policy actually achieved the desired value outcomes? Why or why not?

Power analysis: Closely related to the values analysis, this approach seeks to analyze the power relationships that affected the policy. There are two (of many) types shown here:

- Marxist analysis—This seeks to examine how the policy supports economic structures in society.
- Feminist analysis—This seeks to examine how a policy reinforces power relationships (such as patriarchy) in a society.

Economic analysis: These approaches attempt to analyze the economic characteristics of a policy. There are several types, but questions often include:

- What are the economic costs and benefits of the policy?
- Are there unanticipated consequences to the policy?
- Has the economic benefit exceeded the costs?

---

good evaluation comes from the CDC (2011, p. 1), who suggests that a good evaluation must meet the standards of "utility, feasibility, propriety and accuracy." Similarly, the CDC offers a useful way of comparing program evaluation to policy evaluation. They suggest the major differences are the level of analysis required (e.g., system or community level for policy evaluation; program level for program evaluation); the degree of control and clear "boundaries" may be more challenging with policy evaluation; the ability to identify an equivalent comparison community may be more challenging with policy evaluation; the scale and scope of data collection may be greater with policy evaluation; policy evaluation may require increased emphasis on the use of surveillance and administrative data; and the type and number of stakeholders involved may differ.

Types of Policy Analysis

With the previous discussion in mind, there are several different types of policy analysis. Exhibit 7.1 demonstrates some of the various types, which again, are based on the kinds of questions the analysis seeks to answer.

Descriptive Analysis

The most ubiquitous type, and in fact one that often is a component of many types or may stand alone, is what may be called a descriptive analysis. The specific questions that comprise a descriptive analysis differ, but usually are guided by the kinds of questions presented by Terrell (2012). Specifically, these include the following: social allocations—who gets the benefit?; social provision—what is the benefit?; delivery—how are the benefits distributed?; and finance—how is the benefit paid for?

Again, these questions apply to almost all kinds of policy analysis. It is critical to understand what a policy does before more substantive analyses that address more complicated questions.

Historical Analysis

In a similar vein, the second type of analysis, the historical analysis, may also be a component of other analyses as well as a stand-alone approach, and it seeks to examine and describe the historical issues or legislative history associated with a given policy. Such an analysis may examine many different components of the history. For example, what interest groups or individuals supported and opposed the enactment of a piece of legislation? Or, if the policy was associated with a court decision or an executive order, what were the precipitating actions that led to the actions?

Values, Power, and Economic Analysis

Several types of analysis begin to look at deeper questions about the policy. The first of these are what might be called a values analysis. This type of analysis examines the values and beliefs that inform the policy. Values, as discussed earlier in this chapter, serve several functions in policy. Among such functions, they can serve as goals for a policy or as guides for processes of policy implementation. Analyses that examine values seek to "uncover" the informing values or to assess how well the policy helps the society to achieve its values.

A good model of the application of this approach is found in Terrell's (2012) *Dimensions of Social Welfare Policy*. This model focuses on the dominant values of our political system—equality, equity, freedom, and adequacy.

Closely related are evaluations that seek to examine what the relationship of the policy is to such things as power in a society. There are many permutations of this approach. For example, Marxist analyses attempt to determine how policies serve to maintain power relationships between various class groups. Feminist models likewise examine the relationship between dominant/subordinate groups. Such evaluations have been useful in the past in helping to clarify methods of oppression and how social structures are maintained to support such systems. An AO framework for policy advocacy ensures that values often ignored are included in policy practice, including policy analysis. These can include social equality, collectivity, interdependency, and spirituality. AO approaches to policy analysis acknowledge that neutrality in policy around topics such as race and gender are assumed, and yet, White men tend to dominate the creation of policy, and communities that already experience oppression are most likely to have that oppression perpetuated through new policy creation. McPhail (2003) created additional questions using a feminist framework, yet these questions can apply to communities that have been excluded and oppressed beyond gender. Those adapted questions can be found in Box 7.1.

Finally, economic analyses are used as tools to examine the relative costs and benefits of both past and prospective policy choices. One of the most interesting aspects of these types of evaluations is how they have attempted to quantify noneconomic factors in policy assessments.

SUMMARY

The chapter explained what policy is and what policy practice is and also explained major characteristics, components, and approaches to social welfare policy. This included an examination of residual and intuitional approaches and how those apply to AO social work practice. We explored the policy process and the associated primary tasks, including policy foundational concepts and the related concepts of resources, values and ideology, and social relationships. Social justice, social structure, and power were explored in the context of social welfare policy. Additionally, while this chapter does not address community organizing per se, there are a number of critical overlaps. Similarly, there are a number of wonderful models for community organizing that the social worker must be familiar with to be effective. First, and perhaps most important, are the common purposes of both organizing and political mobilization and advocacy. Both domains are concerned with consolidating and/or creating power. In some cases, this is the process of empowerment, and in other cases, this means using power to leverage.

In this chapter, we examined how social workers may participate in policy through what is called policy practice. Throughout the policy process, there are opportunities for social workers to engage in policy. Among these are assisting to identify and characterize emerging problems when first encountering them. Then, the social worker can help to publicize and educate the policy-making and general communities about the problems and mobilize these

BOX 7.1

ANTI-OPPRESSIVE POLICY ANALYSIS QUESTIONS

- How well does the policy reflect anti-oppressive values?
- Does this policy further social justice?
- How well does the policy account for intersectionality?
- Does the policy advance racial and gender equality?
- Is the language in this policy inclusive?

groups to address the issue. At the stage of policy implementation, the social worker can participate in the regulatory process and help make the regulations through joining the commenting period. Further, engaging in organizational practice to provide the service as effectively as possible is necessary. And at the last stage of the policy process, the social worker can participate in policy analysis and evaluation. Information here can be used to feed back into the policy process and hopefully facilitate change as needed. AOP in social work requires that we pay special attention to the inclusion of community members impacted by the policy at all stages of the process.

CASE SUMMARY UNDOCUMENTED AND HOMELESS

Practice Setting Description

Jackie is a first-year MSW student completing an internship at an inner-city family service agency in the Southwest. The agency is in a section of the city that has a high crime rate, gang activity, and failing schools. The area has a diverse population with many immigrants from Central and South America and a substantial African American population. The agency provides individual and family counseling services on a sliding fee scale. The agency also runs several educational and treatment groups as well as a temporary shelter for women and their children. Jackie has been assigned to work with the women and their children in the shelter. Her primary tasks are to provide concrete services and supportive counselling to the shelter residents.

Background Information

Elicia T and her daughter, Maria, are undocumented immigrants from Mexico. They have been in the United States for 5 years. Elicia and Maria fled to the area from another southwestern city to escape her abusive husband approximately 2 months ago. Elicia is 25 years old and Maria 8 years old. Elicia has a 2-year-old daughter, Sarah, who was placed in foster care because of suspected abuse in the home. Sarah is in a foster home in a small rural community in the state hundreds of miles from Elicia's current residence. Since moving to the area, Maria has not been attending school.

Elicia and Maria are currently residing in the agency's temporary shelter for families. They have been at the shelter for 2 weeks, and the agency has a 90-day limit. Prior to arriving at the shelter, Elicia and Maria were homeless and living on the streets.

Elicia is a high school drop-out and was a stay-at-home mother prior to leaving her husband and moving to a different part of the state. She chose to move there because she has two female cousins living in the area who are also undocumented immigrants. Elicia's native language is Spanish. She speaks some English but is not as comfortable speaking in English. Her English comprehension appears to be good. Maria speaks both English and Spanish well. When communicating with the staff, Maria acts as Elicia's interpreter since none of the staff at the shelter speak Spanish.

Maria appears to be behind academically. She struggles reading simple children's books written in English. It is unknown if her ability to read in Spanish is better than her English reading skills.

(continued)

CASE SUMMARY UNDOCUMENTED AND HOMELESS (*CONTINUED*)

Other than her two cousins, Elicia has no other sources of support in the community. Her cousins have young families and limited resources but are well established and connected to a Latino community in the city and the local Catholic church. Her cousins refused to let Elicia and Maria live with them while she was trying to find her own place and a job. They stated that they did not have enough room and are concerned they would get in trouble with their landlord if it was found out that they were letting people stay with them. They sent her to the local church for help, and she was given the address for the agency's shelter by the priest.

Elicia has been looking for housing in the Latino community. The housing market is tight with limited options, and she has been unable to find anything that she could possibly afford. The only affordable housing she found was a room in a rundown motel that rents by the hour or by the month. It is in an area of town known for drug dealing and sex work.

On arrival in the community, Elicia found occasional work for a house cleaning company. The company hires undocumented workers, pays them very low cash wages, and threatens to turn them in to Immigration and Customs Enforcement (ICE) if they complain. The job bosses also exploit their female workers sexually, threatening to turn them in if they do not comply. Elicia was fearful about applying for other jobs because of her illegal status. She considered turning to sex work to be able to take care of her children, but her Catholic upbringing and thoughts of how this would shame her family have kept her from doing so. She is in constant fear of being detained, separated from Maria, and having her placed in foster care. She is also afraid that she will end up homeless again and forced to live on the streets or return to her abusive husband.

Elicia is extremely reluctant to sign up for any federally funded services, even those that she and her child are entitled to receive. On the suggestion that she enroll for supplemental food through SNAP, Elicia became nervous and refused as she has heard that participation in SNAP services, and others like them, would draw the attention of ICE, and she had heard stories on the news of individuals being deported after signing up for such programs.

Presenting Problems

Elicia and her child are facing multiple obstacles. They need to find permanent, affordable housing and a job that pays enough to cover her housing and living expenses. In addition, Maria needs to be enrolled in school.

Additionally, Elicia is experiencing an immense amount of stress, anxiety, and possibly posttraumatic stress disorder (PTSD). She described an instance where she could not calm down her breathing and she felt lightheaded. She is very fearful of men and tries to avoid all contact with men in the community. She reports difficulty sleeping at night and feeling exhausted most of the time.

She is concerned about Maria. She has started acting out at the shelter, getting into fights with the other children, disobeying her mother, and being disrespectful and defiant to the staff and other adults. Elicia and Maria fight frequently, and when Elicia tries to discipline Maria, she throws a temper tantrum until Elicia gives up.

(continued)

CASE SUMMARY UNDOCUMENTED AND HOMELESS (*CONTINUED*)

Elicia has many strengths. She had the strength to leave her abusive husband and move to a different city. She loves her daughter and wants desperately to keep Maria with her. She is resilient and has managed to survive and keep her daughter safe despite not having a place to stay, a job, and a limited support network. Elicia feels safe in the shelter, but she is very fearful of being caught as an illegal immigrant and is generally mistrustful of helping professionals and persons of authority.

DISCUSSION QUESTIONS

1. What kinds of information about the client population would be useful to Jackie as she attempts to develop appropriate services for women like Elicia and girls like Maria?

2. What assumptions do you think affect the current social construction of the immigrant in America? How accurate do you think these assumptions are in the present case?

3. Looking at the policies that affect the services Elicia and Maria are eligible for in the case, what do you see that might be challenged and changed through legal action (the courts)? What policies do you think could only be changed by legislation?

4. How might Jackie publicize the situation of the clients in the community as a way of mobilizing support for some important policy changes?

A robust set of instructor resources designed to supplement this text is located at http://connect.springerpub.com/content/book/978-0-8261-6683-8. Qualifying instructors may request access by emailing textbook@springerpub.com.

KEY REFERENCES

Only key references appear in the print edition. To access the full reference list, visit www.springerpub.com/courseconnect. See inside front cover and tear-out card for CourseConnect details.

Centers for Disease Control and Prevention. (2011). *Brief 1: Overview of policy evaluation*. https://mandeguidelines.iom.int/sites/g/files/tmzbdl2306/files/2023-03/Brief%201-a.pdf

Conley, D. (2010). *Being black, living in the red: Race, wealth, and social policy in America*. University of California Press.

Critchley, S. (2007). *Infinitely demanding: Ethics of commitment, politics of resistance*. Verso.

Domingo, A. (2015). *Introduction to technical writing: The policy brief*. https://www.slideshare.net/slideshow/introduction-to-technical-writing-the-policy-brief/52274157

Florence, C. S., Zhou, C., Luo, F., & Xu, L. (2016). The economic burden of prescription opioid overdose, abuse, and dependence in the United States, 2013. *Medical Care, 54*(10), 901–906. https://doi.org/10.1097/MLR.0000000000000625

Fussell, E. (2014). Warmth of the welcome: Attitudes toward immigrants and immigration policy in the United States. *Annual Review of Sociology, 40*(1), 479–498. https://doi.org/10.1146/annurev-soc-071913-043325

Hicken, M. T., Gee, G. C., Morenoff, J., Connell, C. M., Snow, R. C., & Hu, H. (2012). A novel look at racial health disparities: The interaction between social disadvantage and environmental health. *American Journal of Public Health*, *102*(12), 2344–2351. https://doi.org/10.2105%2FAJPH.2012.300774

Kalla, J. L., & Broockman, D. E. (2016). Campaign contributions facilitate access to congressional officials: A randomized field experiment. *American Journal of Political Science*, *60*(3), 545–558. https://doi.org/10.1111/ajps.12180

National Education Association. (2019). *Writing effective letters to the editor*. http://www.nea.org/home/19683.htm

Nesmith, A., &. Smyth, N. (2015). Environmental justice and social work education. *Social Work Education*, *34*(5), 484–501. https://doi.org/10.1080/02615479.2015.1063600

Reisch, M. (2017). Why macro practice matters. *Human Service Organizations: Management, Leadership & Governance*, *41*(1), 6–9. https://doi.org/10.1080/23303131.2016.1179537

Schwartz, M., & Sanchez, E. (2016). *Social movements that have changed the world*. Global Citizen. https://www.globalcitizen.org/en/content/movements-social-change-apartheid-civil-rights-suf/

Tan, K. (2015). *Reconfiguring citizenship and national identity in the North American literary imagination*. Wayne Street University Press.

Terrell, P. (2012). *Dimensions of social welfare policy* (8th ed.). Allyn & Bacon.

Urban Institute. (2024). *Nine charts about wealth inequality in America (Updated)*. http://apps.urban.org/features/wealth-inequality-charts/

Young, L. (2009). The motherhood penalty: Working moms face pay gap vs. childless peers. *Bloomberg Businessweek*. The Wall Street Journal.

8 Engagement and Social Work Practice

Nicole is a master of social work (MSW) at a large children's hospital. She works in the emergency department. Nicole is often required to consult on cases for a variety of reasons. Sometimes, Nicole is paged to a room without knowing why she was paged. Today she was paged by the charge nurse to assist a family in identifying community resources. When Nicole entered the room, she saw the patient, Katie, a 6-year-old, in the bed and her parents, Joe and Lois, by her side.

In order for Nicole to do her job effectively, she must engage with the clients quickly. As a hospital social worker, she must often build rapport quickly to work on the issues at hand. Nicole is also mindful that she must not only engage with the child but the parents as well. Engagement will vary for both, as strategies to engage with children are different from strategies to engage with adults.

When she walks into the room, she warmly greets Katie with a smile and a hello and then extends her hand to introduce herself to Joe and Lois. Nicole explains to the family that she is a social worker and she has been called in to assist the family in locating some resources. She shares that she is willing to help but asks if it would be okay for her to ask a few questions in order to be able to help them better. The family is agreeable, and Nicole can begin gathering information to start the helping process.

LEARNING OBJECTIVES

This chapter focuses on theories and skills related to Council on Social Work Education (CSWE, 2022) Competency 6, which asserts that social workers must be aware of how engagement influences the helping relationship throughout the helping process from the beginning to the end. Engagement is not simply a stage in the helping process that can be accomplished and then forgotten. Rather, good engagement is an ongoing process that evolves throughout the helping process, regardless of the level of practice. *To engage with* means to interact, participate, or become involved with. Social workers engage within their practice often in order to promote change. This competency requires social workers to recognize and be able to utilize theories that are related to human behavior and the social environment. Furthermore, social workers should be mindful of how their use of self can influence their ability to engage with clients at all levels of practice. Last, this competency asserts that social workers find worth and engage in collaboration and interprofessional relationships. Engagement across professions on behalf of client populations is often critical and necessary for client success. By the end of this chapter, you will be able to:

- Identify and describe the National Association of Social Workers (NASW) principles and standards that relate to engagement.
- Describe how policy can influence engagement.

- Identify commonalities and differences related to engagement with differing client systems.
- Describe the stages of the helping process.
- Identify strategies that promote engagement and build relationships.
- Identify benefits and challenges to collaboration.

COMPETENCY 6: ENGAGE WITH INDIVIDUALS, FAMILIES, GROUPS, ORGANIZATIONS, AND COMMUNITIES

Social workers understand that engagement is an ongoing component of the dynamic and interactive process of social work practice with and on behalf of individuals, families, groups, organizations, and communities. Social workers value the importance of human relationships. Social workers understand theories of human behavior and person-in-environment and critically evaluate and apply this knowledge to facilitate engagement with clients and constituencies, including individuals, families, groups, organizations, and communities. Social workers are self-reflective and understand how bias, power, and privilege, as well as their personal values and personal experiences may affect their ability to engage effectively with diverse clients and constituencies. Social workers use the principles of interprofessional collaboration to facilitate engagement with clients, constituencies, and other professionals as appropriate.

Social workers:

- apply knowledge of human behavior and person-in-environment, as well as interprofessional conceptual frameworks, to engage with clients and constituencies; and
- use empathy, reflection, and interpersonal skills to engage in culturally responsive practice with clients and constituencies. (CSWE, 2022, p. 11)

NATIONAL ASSOCIATION OF SOCIAL WORKERS *CODE OF ETHICS*

There are two ethical principles within the NASW *Code of Ethics* (2021) that closely relate to the concept of engagement. The principles of *importance of human relationships* and *dignity and worth of the individual* both illustrate the importance and necessity of engagement throughout the helping process (NASW, 2021). There are several ethical standards that relate to engagement including commitment to clients, informed consent, conflict of interests, privacy, and confidentiality. The *Code of Ethics* is available online on the NASW website.

The practice of social work is not something that a social worker does *to* or *for* another; rather, it is a collaborative process where the worker engages *with* the client to bring about change. In order to be able to effectively work with clients, social workers must be mindful of their ability to utilize engagement as a means to support the helping relationship.

Every single person has an inherent dignity and worth, and as a result, social workers treat every person as such. Social workers are called upon to treat all people with respect and dignity. When truly engaging with another, the social worker must first recognize the client's strengths, including their dignity and worth, in order to observe more clearly any concerns or problems.

In the context of anti-oppressive practice, social workers must consider various factors during the engagement phase. As emphasized throughout this text, it is crucial for social workers to reflect on their own experiences, privilege, power, and biases. It is important to recognize how these elements may influence professional interactions. According to Gerassi and Nichols (2021):

> A key principle of anti-oppressive practice (AOP) is for social workers to work towards acknowledging their own roles in perpetuating oppression and homogenizing experiences in client groups. AOP demands specific worker actions towards equalizing the power and position, particularly of client groups who enter spaces with various degrees of power. Social workers using this framework actively prepare to address sexism, racism, heterosexism and other *-isms* that manifest individually, in groups, and across all cultural, legislative, and political practices. (p. 31)

Additionally, social workers need to be mindful of and actively work toward mitigating the hierarchical relationship inherent in the social worker–client relationship. While acknowledging that completely dismantling this hierarchy may be unattainable, it is necessary to recognize its existence. For instance, social workers often have the authority to make decisions that can significantly impact the lives of clients. For example, social workers determine eligibility for services, develop treatment plans, or recommend interventions. While client input is typically sought out and is valued during these activities, the final decision ultimately rests with the social worker, giving them considerable power over the direction and outcome of the client's experience during the helping process. This emphasizes the intrinsic power imbalance.

One strategy to address this issue is through fostering transparent and collaborative communication with clients whenever possible. By involving clients in decision-making processes and respecting their autonomy and right to self-determination, social workers can try to mitigate the impact of this power imbalance. Although complete elimination may not be possible, conscientious awareness of this disparity is crucial throughout the helping process and a key element of ethical practice. Social workers are often called upon to work toward social change. Thyberg (2023) asserts, "due to its legacy of advocacy and social action, social work has the potential to be one of the professions that leads this social movement that seeks to undo the environment of anti-Black racism and systemic oppression that haunts the United States" (p. 407).

Social workers are tasked with holding the needs of their clients as an utmost priority. Within the practice of social work, the work is not and should not be about social workers. Rather, the focus should always be on clients and what would best serve their needs at the present time. In order to demonstrate this commitment to the well-being of clients, social workers can be engaged and present with clients throughout all interactions. Engagement is not a task that can be completed in the first session; rather, successful engagement is an ongoing process that requires reflection and commitment on behalf of the social worker. In this ongoing process with clients, social workers are tasked with the responsibility of sustaining engagement from the initial interaction to the eventual termination of services. This requires a continuous commitment to engaging throughout services. Should any disruptions or concerns occur within this engagement (or rapport) between the social worker and the client, the social worker should promptly address and repair it in collaboration with the client. Additionally, it is important for social workers to initiate conversations with clients to check in regarding their perceptions related to engagement and the overall progress of the helping process. By fostering an open dialogue, social workers can cultivate a supportive and empowering environment that encourages meaningful growth and change.

In order to ensure that the helping relationship is a true relationship between the social worker and the client, there must be informed consent. It is the responsibility of the social worker to ensure that the client is made aware of the purpose of their services, risks, limits, costs, and alternatives prior to starting (NASW, 2021). The social worker is tasked with sharing this information with the client in a clear and understandable way. Ensuring informed consent occurs early on during the process of engagement ensures that the client is aware of their rights.

In order to ensure ethical practice, social workers should attempt to avoid dual relationships when possible. Dual relationships occur when the social worker and client have another relationship outside of the helping relationship. For example, a dual relationship would be if a social worker hired a client to do maintenance on their home. First, the social worker and client have a helping relationship; second, the social worker and client also have a business relationship in the form of the social worker hiring the client. Dual relationships often cause boundary confusion and could harm the client. The social worker is charged with establishing and maintaining boundaries. When engaging with clients, the social worker should be friendly; however, it is beyond the scope of ethical practice for social workers to become friends with their clients. Due to the work that we do as social workers, it is understandable that we as social workers must be mindful of boundaries throughout care. Also, when there is boundary confusion on the part of the client—maybe the client invites you to an event—it is the responsibility of the social worker to clarify their role and the purpose of their interactions. In situations such as this, when the social worker has well-established engagement with the client, conversations such as these often go easier.

Clients have a right to privacy and confidentiality. There are laws that have been established with the purpose of keeping personal information about clients private. Not only do social workers need to safeguard the information they have about their clients, but they should also be respectful of the clients' rights to privacy. In addition to their primary responsibilities, social workers must navigate the complexities of integrating technology into their practice ethically. This includes grappling with potential dilemmas concerning privacy and confidentiality when using technology as a part of a social work practice (telehealth, email, messaging, etc.). Social workers must have a comprehensive understanding of these issues, recognizing the boundaries and constraints imposed by technology on safeguarding client information. This understanding is necessary because social workers are ethically required to share such information with clients during the informed consent process at the start of services. It is important to include this information in the consent process, as it empowers clients to make informed decisions about their engagement with technology-related services while fostering a sense of trust and transparency in the helping relationship. Additionally, social workers must remain aware of any emerging ethical concerns or evolving laws or regulations related to the use of technology. This awareness serves to safeguard the integrity and ethical standards of their practice in an increasingly digital world.

THEORIES RELATED TO ENGAGEMENT

A variety of theories can inform the dynamic process of engagement. Theories can provide a framework for understanding how to engage with client systems and can also provide insights into the benefits and potential barriers related to engagement. As with all aspects of social work practice, it is important to have a theoretical orientation and basis for your work with clients. The following theories can serve to provide you with a foundation to engage with clients.

Psychodynamic Theories

It is essential to consider theories of human behavior in order to effectively engage with client systems. The human experience is complex. As a result, it is necessary to draw upon a theoretical understanding of human behavior in order to assist you in your social work practice. Related to engagement, we consider attachment theory and personality theory.

Attachment Theory

Attachment is essential to the human experience. Humans are a social species. Unlike some species, humans must connect with others in order to continue to survive. Attachment refers to the connection that we have with other people; more specifically, we can explore the level of attachment or quality of the connection with others.

Many theories address attachments as they relate to the overall healthy development of young children. Brisch (2012) reports that attachment theory focuses on "the fundamental early influences on the emotional development of the child and attempts to explain the development of and changes in strong emotional attachments between individuals throughout the life cycle" (p. 14). Attachments serve to provide young children with a framework for understanding how the environment around them functions. As early as infancy, through dyadic relationships, children are able to produce "some sort of pattern out of chaos" (Winnicott, 1988).

The quality of the attachment need not be perfect, but rather a "good enough" child rearing is sufficient to aid in healthy psychological development (Winnicott, 1988). The child does not need a perfect attachment, but rather a usually reliable and ready caregiver who is generally responsive to the needs of the child is a sufficient connection. From these early attachments, children can begin to explore their worlds. Bowlby (1988) asserts that a secure base is necessary for children so that they can fully experience their world, all the while knowing on their return to their caregiver:

> He will be welcomed when he gets there, nourished physically and emotionally, comforted when distressed, reassured if frightened. In essence this role is one of being available, ready to respond when called upon to encourage and perhaps assist, but to intervene actively when necessary. (p. 11)

Bowlby (1988) suggests that "attachment behavior is any form of behavior in a person attaining or maintaining proximity to some other clearly identified individual who is conceived as better able to cope with the world" (pp. 26–27). Attachment behaviors are present not only in children but in adolescents and adults of both genders as well (Bowlby, 1988). Bowlby asserts that attachment behaviors are evident "throughout the life cycle," especially during difficult times (p. 27).

The need for attachment is essential to the human experience; Bowlby (1988) puts forth "since it is seen in virtually all human beings (though in varying patterns), it is regarded as an integral part of human nature and one we share (to a varying extent) with members of other species" (p. 27). These healthy and appropriate attachments are necessary in life to safeguard the individual against negative experiences and risk factors that they may experience during their lifetime. There is significant research that demonstrates the positive impact caring attachments early in life have across the life span.

Though the early roots of attachment theory focused on the relationship between mother and child, there is a great deal of evidence that other attachments such as fathers, grandparent-caregivers, and other stable adult models are just as beneficial to developing a healthy attachment style. Uri Bronfenbrenner, a psychologist and key leader in the development of the national Head Start program, once stated that all children need just one person who is insanely in love with them. It is through this one quality attachment, this secure base, that individuals are given the resources and esteem to grow and flourish into thriving, productive, and well-adjusted resilient beings. The presence of another individual serves an instinctual human need to seek protection (Bowlby, 1988). The presence of simply one secure attachment can serve as a significant protective factor (Brisch, 2012).

Connections and attachments can be present at varying levels. Individuals can feel connected to another individual at the micro level, or connected as a family at the mezzo level, or even still connected to a community or culture at the macro level. When we consider the ecological perspective and the interconnection of relationships, it is important to consider attachments as central to understanding the various levels (micro, mezzo, and macro) and interactions between levels. Understanding attachment is central to better understanding the network of relationships that permeate individuals' lives, from one-on-one connections to the family and beyond, to communities and societies. At the core of human interaction at various levels of the environment is the fundamental human need for attachment. Attachment shapes an individual's sense of security, identity, and belonging.

Attachment theory informs engagement with client systems by providing the social worker with information to better understand where the client may be starting from. Within social work practice, it is commonly stated that we must "start where the client is," and to be able to do that, we need a theoretical foundation to understand influences that may have shaped the individual into who they are at present. As with any theoretical model, we must be careful to avoid overgeneralizations; however, the tenets of the theory allow us to formulate a case assessment and consider appropriate engagement styles.

Humanistic Theory

Humanistic theory centers around the person with whom you are engaging. Social work practice calls upon us to meet clients where they are in order to help them reach where they want to be. Social work has a long history of practice based on individualized humanistic principles including a nonjudgmental approach and an emphasis on strengths rather than on dysfunction (Misca & Unwin, 2016). A humanistic approach considers the "full range of human experiences and values human dignity" (Lonn & Dantzler, 2017, p. 65).

Maslow's Theory of Motivation

Maslow (1962) created a theory of motivation that was informed by a hierarchy of needs. Maslow set forth that for one to be able to meet goals and fulfill personal needs, a systematic (hierarchical) approach was necessary (see Figure 8.1). Maslow ranked needs from the most basic to higher levels. In order for a person to be able to achieve success at a higher-level need, all of the previous (lower-level) needs had to be addressed first. For example, before someone could reach the highest level (self-actualization) where they could engage in such tasks as being creative and solving problems, that person must first achieve the basic levels of feeling safe and having physiological needs for food and water met. At each level of need, individuals are motivated to have their needs meet; then once their need is met at that level, they can be motivated by the higher-level need (Fisher, 2009).

During engagement, social workers should consider the client's current level of motivation and where they are regarding the hierarchy of needs. Considering where the client is can also serve as a means to address current strengths, in the form of currently accomplished or met needs, as well as areas for attention, in the form of the unmet needs.

FIGURE 8.1 Maslow's hierarchy of needs.

Personality Theory and Client-Centered Therapy

Personality theory provides a humanistic approach to understanding the person. Carl Rogers believed that in order to thrive within their environments, people needed genuineness, acceptance, and empathy. Furthermore, he believed that people possessed the inner resources necessary to confront any challenges or problems that they were facing. Trust was also crucial to his theory:

> Trust in the subjective experience and the belief in the essential trustworthiness of human nature went hand in hand. He discovered in the early years of his clinical practice that when he was able to commit himself to a deep understanding of his client's subjective world and was perceived as doing so by the client, then almost invariably the client would begin to behave in ways which were positive and forward moving. (Thorne et al., 2013, p. 26)

Genuineness refers to being authentic. When people are authentic, they are acting as their real self, not pretending or projecting to be viewed as anything other than who they are. Genuineness relates to being present, honest, and kind. Genuine interactions foster an environment where clients feel valued, heard, and respected. Being genuine or authentic allows social workers to connect with clients on a deeper level, enhancing the effectiveness of interventions and support. By being genuine, social workers can model honesty and integrity, which can empower clients to engage more openly in the therapeutic process. Ultimately, authenticity is fundamental to building meaningful and sustainable relationships that promote positive outcomes for clients.

Acceptance, also known as unconditional positive regard, is the action of agreement with a client without confrontation. Based on previous experiences, individuals have often learned socially that their worth is conditional. The concept of unconditional positive regard is counter to learned conditions of acceptance. Rather, regardless of performance or behavior, the person is accepted as is, simply for just being themselves.

Empathy, or the process of feeling with, is something that is often emphasized within social work practice. At the roots of empathy is compassion. Compassion is a fellow feeling or shared feeling. Empathy allows the social worker to demonstrate to the client a fellow feeling or understanding of what the client is expressing.

Self-concept is a central aspect of personality theory. Self-concept refers to the collective set of organized thoughts one has regarding their self. Related to this are self-esteem, self-image, and the ideal self. All of these are aspects of the person's internal representation of themselves.

Utilizing personality theory, or a Rogerian approach, can enhance engagement. This approach is aligned with the social work value of self-determination and client involvement. Understanding the person's inherent strengths, being genuine, providing unconditional positive regard, and expressing empathy are all strategies that can encourage a client to engage with you, which will strengthen the professional relationship. Research is clear that a strong relationship between the social worker and client is a positive indicator for success in treatment. Case 8.1 illustrates the use of this approach while engaging with a client.

> **CASE 8.1** **BACK IN SERVICES AGAIN: UTILIZING THE PERSONALITY THEORY APPROACH IN SOCIAL WORK PRACTICE**
>
> Holly is a social worker at a local shelter for individuals facing housing insecurity. She assists the residents in addressing their needs related to locating stable employment, housing, or other resources. Holly tries to meet with the residents at least a couple of times a week, as they are often working on multiple goals at a time.
>
> Macy had been at the shelter about 4 months ago. She had worked with Holly to find a full-time job and locate an apartment she could afford. Together they were able to locate resources to modestly furnish the apartment. Holly also helped Macy in linking to financial resources for energy assistance to help with the utility bills.
>
> Today as Holly was looking over the roster of residents to plan her meetings for the day, she saw Macy's name was on the list of new admissions. Holly stopped what she was doing to find Macy. When Holly walked up to Macy, Macy said, "I know. I know. I know you must be so disappointed in me. I messed up. I lost my place. I'm sorry. Don't be mad." Holly smiled softly and said, "Macy, I am not upset at all. Actually, I am happy that you were able to return to this facility so that we can assist you." Macy asked, "Are you sure you are not mad?" "I'm sure," Holly said. "We all need some help from time to time. You were able to do this before, and I am sure we can learn from what happened to better help you this time."
>
> Later in supervision, Holly was discussing her interaction with her supervisor. Holly shared that she chose to use this approach while working with Macy because, "If I would have said I was disappointed she was back, that would not have helped the situation. Macy has a history of being emotionally neglected and told that she was never good enough. Why would I want to add to the idea that she messed up again? Instead, I am going to focus on her strengths and help her meet her goals."

SOCIAL CONSTRUCTIVISM AND CONFLICT THEORIES

Social constructivism refers to the idea that all reality (in social affairs) has been agreed on or constructed socially between people because it is beneficial to have a shared view to promote social order (Payne, 2016). In order to effectively engage with client systems, social workers must be aware of these social constructs. Furthermore, social workers must be aware that social construction changes over time and should be mindful about how that can impact client systems.

Conflict theories attempt to provide a framework for understanding the struggle among various groups. There are specific theories that relate to specific characteristics (race, class, and gender). Regardless of characteristic, conflict theory suggests an inequality and the battle to obtain equality despite the characteristic of difference. Conflict theories often present a challenge to the status quo.

Feminist Standpoint Theory

Feminism refers to a wide range of beliefs that reflect the idea that inequality based on gender is oppressive and should be challenged and corrected. Often, feminism is used synonymously with women's rights; though that is in part what feminism is, it diminishes feminism to reduce it to simply that. At times, the concept of feminism is met with hostility or suspicion and often brings to mind negative views of women. There are many varieties of feminism.

> ▶ **Reflection Questions**
> 1. How do you believe feminism is perceived by society?
> 2. How can this perception hinder or promote the quest for gender equality?

Feminist social work emerged in the 20th century through challenging several areas, including clinical mental health frameworks, gender role divisions, and gender power differences (Eyal-Lubling & Krumer-Nevo, 2016). The social work profession has a long history of feminism, though at many times it was not labeled as such (Anyikwa et al., 2015). Standpoint feminism emphasizes giving a voice to and listening to women. This theory understands and values that women have cognitive styles that could promote equality and ameliorate oppression (Hartsock, 1983).

Related to engagement, social workers can utilize feminist standpoint theory as a reminder to consider the position of clients on the basis of their gender and in turn their perspective as it is influenced by culture and environmental factors. Social workers should be ever mindful that each person's experience is unique to that person, and it should not be generalized on the basis of any single characteristic. However, it is important to be considerate of views (current and historical) that may be influencing the client's perception of the current state.

Oppression Theory

Oppression is the "act or process of placing restrictions on an individual, group, or institution" (Hutchison, 2017, p. 323). Oppression can be intended or unintended. There are various common mechanisms of oppression. Mechanisms of oppression include but are not limited to such things as stereotyping, blaming the victim, othering, microaggressions, and violence. Mechanisms of oppression are used by the dominant group to maintain a position above the oppressed group.

Oppression theory, sometimes referred to as anti-oppressive theory, seeks to provide a framework for understanding the impact of oppression and can provide great insights to social work professionals as we are called to champion for oppressed groups. Related to engagement, social workers can use oppression theory to understand how members of historically oppressed groups may face barriers to engagement in the helping process. Social workers can be ready to address such barriers and advocate for anti-oppressive policies to promote engagement among such groups.

Trauma Theory

The concept of trauma and trauma-informed practice has been burgeoning in the literature in recent decades. In order to understand trauma theory, it is important to have an understanding of what trauma is and how it often presents. Trauma is an experience that overwhelms a person's ability to cope. Due to this definition of trauma, what is deemed to be traumatic is subjective and varies from person to person. What may be traumatic to one individual may not necessarily elicit the same response in another individual. There are a variety of risk and protective factors that interplay in determining whether an individual is able to cope with an experience (see Table 8.1). Common traumatic experiences include single instances or ongoing exposures. Traumatic events could include such things as verbal, physical, or sexual abuse; neglect; war; natural disasters (hurricanes, tornados, and earthquakes); mass shootings; crime (rape, burglary, and assault); and transportation accidents (car, train, and plane). In addition to individual experiences of trauma, it is noteworthy to recognize the role of collective trauma that some groups experience. It is important to avoid overgeneralizations when considering the impact of collective trauma, but it is important to recognize its existence. When approaching collective trauma, the use of an AOP can be helpful to support your clients. "Researchers, professionals and activists are starting to combine anti-oppressive theory and practice with understandings of collective trauma" (Sunderland et al., 2023, p. 2432).

Regardless of whether the experience occurs once or over a period of time, the impact of the trauma is not varied. Trauma can impact an individual's emotions, behaviors, cognitions, and physiology. Just as responses to events are individualized, so are the impacts of trauma. Table 8.2 illustrates some examples of the ways that trauma can present

TABLE 8.1 RISK AND PROTECTIVE FACTORS FOR COPING WITH TRAUMA

Risk Factors	Protective Factors
Low self-esteem Drug or alcohol use Poverty Homelessness Neighborhood crime Lack of positive role models Racism, discrimination, and oppression Poor mental, physical, spiritual, and emotional health Low literacy Family violence	Positive attitudes, values, or beliefs Good mental, physical, spiritual, and emotional health Positive self-esteem Success at school Parental supervision Strong social supports Community engagement Problem-solving skills Positive adult role models, coaches, and mentors Positive peer group/friends Stable housing

TABLE 8.2 COGNITIVE, BEHAVIORAL, EMOTIONAL, AND PHYSIOLOGICAL SYMPTOMS OF TRAUMA

Cognitive	Behavioral	Emotional	Physiological
Fear of going crazy Distractibility Preoccupation Denial of the importance Problems setting priorities Difficulty problem-solving Time distortions Orientation toward the past Confusion	Hyperactivity Out-of-control behavior Sleep problems Social withdrawal Need to talk compulsively about the event Relationship problems Flashbacks Memory problems	Anger, frustration Phobias Fear of recurrence Anxiety Oversensitivity Depression Grief Worry about physical health Shame/guilt Resentment	Pounding heart Sweating Nausea Headaches Muffled hearing Fatigue More prone to illness Hyperarousal Startle response

within individuals. Trauma can change a person's worldview and how they perceive their environment. For example, someone who has been the victim of a crime may, as a result, see the world as an unsafe or dangerous place.

One of the largest studies of the impact of trauma was the Adverse Childhood Experience (ACE) study. Throughout this large, longitudinal study, it was determined that adverse experiences in childhood have an impact on both physical and emotional health throughout the life span (Felitti et al., 1998). Adverse childhood experiences include the following events (prior to 18 years of age): physical abuse by a parent, emotional abuse by a parent, sexual abuse by anyone, growing up with an alcohol and/or drug abuser in the household, experiencing the incarceration of a household member, living with a family member experiencing mental illness, domestic violence, loss of a parent, emotional neglect, and physical neglect. This study provided a better understanding of the prevalence of trauma. With a better understanding of how prevalent the experience of trauma is, the need for trauma-informed approaches to helping was seen as more important.

> **Reflection Question**
>
> Why do you think that adverse childhood experiences have such a detrimental impact on long-term functioning?

Trauma theory and trauma-informed care have been strongly informed by the work of Judith Herman. Herman (1998) suggests that trauma disconnects and disempowers individuals; in order to address trauma, it must occur via connection or in a relationship and cannot occur in isolation. Trauma theory holds fast to a recovery model that promotes personal resilience and encourages healing through safety, stabilization, and reconnection (Herman, 1997).

Social workers who engage in trauma-informed practice "rely on their knowledge about trauma to respond to clients in ways that convey respect and compassion, honor self-determination, and enable the rebuilding of healthy interpersonal skills and coping strategies" (Levenson, 2017, p. 105). The CSWE (2012) asserts that it is imperative for social work students to be prepared to provide trauma-informed care with all client systems. Related to engagement, social workers must be mindful that trauma can impact a client system's ability or willingness to engage. To that end, when using trauma theory to inform the practice of engagement, social workers should promote a trusting relationship "focusing on pacing, empathetic responding, mirroring, attending, and awareness of nonverbal behavior" (CSWE, 2018, p. 111). The CSWE (2018) set forth trauma-informed engagement behaviors for social workers to support clients who have experienced trauma (see Box 8.1).

PERSON-IN-ENVIRONMENT PERSPECTIVE

Imagine that you are holding a single puzzle piece in your hand. Using that puzzle piece, can you describe the full picture of the puzzle? Of course it is impossible to describe the big picture because you are only looking at one small piece of the puzzle. The puzzle metaphor serves to underscore the importance of seeing as many pieces of the puzzle as possible in

> **BOX 8.1**
>
> **TRAUMA-INFORMED ENGAGEMENT BEHAVIORS**
>
> - The trauma-informed social worker consistently demonstrates attention to nonverbal behaviors and cues, emotional dysregulation, and wariness of institutions that impede the establishment of a therapeutic alliance.
> - The trauma-informed practitioner uses a range of interventions to address underlying motivations that influence help-seeking and help-rejecting behaviors in a variety of contexts (e.g., from micro to macro) that affect engagement.
> - The trauma-informed practitioner identifies, understands, respects, and addresses the range of coping strategies trauma survivors, both mandated and voluntary, may demonstrate that create barriers to engagement.
> - The trauma-informed social worker uses supervision and mentorship to reflect on effective use of self and affective self-regulation while navigating the engagement process, including issues such as the worker's own history of trauma, secondary traumatization, potential triggers (for both client and practitioner), and the worker's responses to those triggers.
> - The trauma-informed social worker implements trauma-informed principles of engagement with services at the individual, organizational, and societal levels that are responsive to those underrepresented and oppressed in society.
>
> *Source:* From Council on Social Work Education. (2018). *Specialized practice curricular guide for trauma-informed social work practice.* https://www.cswe.org/products/specialized-practice-curricular-guide-for-trauma-informed-social-work-practice/

order to have the clearest, most accurate image of the entire picture. When engaging with clients, it is important not to reduce them to a single piece, but rather embrace all of the pieces of the environment that surrounds them.

The person-in-environment perspective is informed by systems and ecological theories and is a fundamental perspective for the social work profession. It is a multidisciplinary theoretical framework that can be used with client systems at all levels of practice. When we consider a person's environment, we consider not only the physical environment but also relationships; involvement with systems, both formally and informally; and resources that may or may not be available to the person.

This perspective asserts that people are complex beings and, furthermore, the environments within which these people exist are equally complex. As a result, it is important that the social worker looks at all of the complex dimensions of people and the environments, or systems, within which they find themselves belonging. Complex personal dimensions may include biological, psychological, social, or spiritual determinants, whereas complex environment dimensions may exist within families, groups, communities, organizations, culture, the physical environment, social movements, or social institutions (Hutchison, 2017).

Using this perspective, nearly all concerns or problems identified by the client can have "intervention implications that may include helping the client create an environment that is more 'conducive' to their particular needs" (Walsh, 2013, p. 26). A central aspect to contemplate within the person-in-environment framework is how well the individual aligns with their surroundings across different levels—micro, mezzo, and macro. In examining the person-in-environment perspective, it is clear that it involves a dynamic interplay where individuals interact with and are influenced by their surroundings at multiple levels. Understanding the goodness of fit between individuals and their environments across these various levels is essential for promoting well-being, resilience, and social justice. By recognizing and addressing mismatches or barriers within these systems, social workers can work toward creating more supportive and empowering environments. If there is a discrepancy between the current environment at any level and a client need, that can be an area for a social worker to focus attention to identify appropriate resources to ameliorate the discrepancy and increase the goodness of fit. For example, if a client is homeless due to a lack of affordable housing options in the community, that could be an example of a poor goodness of fit between the person and their environment.

This perspective is closely related to early social work practice in the United States. For example, the work of Mary Richmond in New York City used what could be considered a person-in-environment perspective, though that label did not exist at that time. If we consider the work of Richmond and others, they sought to bring about change within the person by addressing the environments in which they lived.

ENGAGEMENT WITH DIFFERENT CLIENT SYSTEMS

Regardless of the level of practice, engagement is a necessary and ongoing process. Social workers must be able to engage with client systems at the micro, mezzo, and macro levels of practice. Engagement sets the foundation for other stages of the helping process, including assessment and intervention. Just as a house with a shaky foundation is not secure and in risk of collapsing, success within the social work helping process is reliant on a good foundation built with quality engagement. Furthermore, engagement should be holistic, in that it is multilayered and multileveled (Adam & Pyles, 2016). The multilayered aspect of engagement refers to elements of the biopsychosocial-spiritual assessment that social workers are trained in. The multileveled aspect of engagement refers to the levels of social work practice with individuals (micro), families and groups (mezzo), or communities and organizations (macro).

> ▶ **Reflection Question**
>
> How can you tell if someone is being authentic? Give specific examples.

Commonalities

Regardless of the population or level of practice, quality engagement begins with the social worker. The social worker is tasked with creating an environment or atmosphere that fosters authenticity and a space for genuine connection. In order to create such a place, the social worker must first be reflective and self-aware.

The social worker should not attempt to enact a persona; rather, the social worker should work on embracing their own style of practice. When engaging with clients, social workers should strive to be present and with clients, meet clients where they are, and be clear about their role and function as the worker in their interaction. Authenticity is an important element of engagement. To be authentic is to be what one has said they will be—to be real. Social workers place a special value on the principle of integrity. In a way, authenticity is a form of integrity, in that social workers hold themselves out in a way that is honest and forthcoming.

In addition to personal awareness, it is important that the social worker be well versed in interviewing skills. A good interview is not scripted or robotic; rather, it is a dynamic, evolving process that seeks to gather information necessary for the social worker to begin working with the client. We discuss some of these skills later in this chapter. However, though the skills we discuss are ways to improve the helping relationship and gather information, we encourage you to consider ways in which you already engage with others to connect. Most people who enter the social work profession consider themselves to be what is often referred to as a "people person," or as very social. Some of those skills that are used in everyday life can be transferable to engagement.

Differences

An effective social worker starts where the client is and goes from there. Engagement with clients is no exception. The social worker should begin where the client is to start the process of engaging. Where the client "is" may depend on many factors including but not limited to age, cognitive level, and culture. How a social worker would engage with a 5-year-old versus a 65-year-old would most likely look different due to the difference in age. Differing engagement based on the population you are working with is appropriate.

BUILDING RELATIONSHIPS

Social workers build relationships and connections. As discussed earlier, social workers value the importance of human relationships. Taking that one step further, social workers value strong relationships. Through engagement, social workers can strive to create strong relationships with clients. Through strong engagement, or rapport, social work practice can occur. Much of the research available on the therapeutic process suggests that the number one predictor of success in treatment is the worker–client relationship. The quality of that relationship has been shown to be more indicative of success than the length of treatment or even treatment modality. Later in this chapter, we discuss ways to assess the helping relationship. First, let us explore ways to establish strong relationships.

Affective Reactions

There is an adage that goes "It is not what you said, but how you said it." Affective reactions are included in the "how you said it" part of that expression. Nonverbal communication is powerful. Research suggests that nonverbal communication is more important than verbal communication. In addition to things such as body positioning and posture, what our face is doing is important nonverbal communication.

Social workers should not be robots; we should be able to express ourselves using our face. Responding to a client using facial expressions can be quite a helpful way to further the conversation with a minimal prompt. Despite the importance of being able to show expression, the social worker must be in control of the reactions given to the client at all times. The social worker must be able to express or show a reaction that is beneficial in the helping process for the client. The term *poker face* is used to describe, when playing a game of poker, a facial expression that does not reveal the cards in one's hand. Consider having a "social work poker face" in that you do not reveal any reaction that comes to mind, but rather you present a controlled response that is helpful for the client. Case 8.2 illustrates the importance of appropriately managing facial expressions when working with a client. As with much of social work practice, there is a blend of art and science. Related to facial expressions and affective responses, we encourage you to be mindful of how you demonstrate expressions and to perhaps use a mirror or videotape yourself to have the opportunity to see what your face is saying when you are listening.

CASE 8.2   WHAT YOU SAY WITHOUT SAYING ANYTHING OUT LOUD

Maggie is a social worker at a community mental health setting. Her role is to conduct intake assessments with all new patients in order to determine the appropriate level of care. Due to the nature of her role, it is important for her to quickly engage with clients, as she only has an hour and a half to complete a full biopsychosocial assessment and make treatment recommendations based on that information.

In a session with a new patient, Maggie asks about the patient's trauma history. The patient was hesitant at first, but Maggie was able to engage with the client, and the client opened up. The client shared an extensive history of physical and sexual abuse that began during childhood and lasted over a decade. Maggie felt bad for the client when listening to the recount of abuse. Without realizing it, Maggie's face was frowning and appeared quite sad. She wasn't aware of this until the client pointed out Maggie's facial expression and sharply said, "I don't need your pity. That is not why I am here."

Maggie was initially taken aback by the client's response and quickly shook her head and said, "Oh no, it's not that, I mean, I don't pity you, it's just, I feel bad that you had to experience that." As soon as Maggie said it, she realized that it did sound like she was pitying the client.

Later, in supervision, Maggie was able to process the situation and how her facial expressions were not helpful to the client in this case. She had always thought that wearing her heart on her sleeve was a way to increase engagement. Maggie is now considering how she could better manage her affective responses to meet the needs of the patients she works with.

Self-Reflection and Biases

Self-reflection is an invaluable tool for professional social workers. Social workers should continuously use self-reflection to enhance self-awareness related to practice. It is especially important for social workers to be aware of personal biases that may exist. It is necessary to be aware of these biases in order to ensure that they do not interfere with one's work with clients. Again, the work that social workers do is not about the worker; rather, it is about meeting clients where they are, supporting them, working with them, and assisting them in improving their well-being.

Though social workers must be able to work with anyone, it is necessary to understand and recognize that not all types of social work are for all people. It is important that social workers embrace the notion of being able to work with anyone. In some situations or settings, especially in rural areas, there may only be one social worker available, so the worker must be able to engage with anyone in order to meet the needs of clients. Social workers cannot discriminate care based on any biases. On the other hand, if a social worker finds that a particular area of practice is too personal for them, then it is mindful to avoid employment in such an area. For example, someone who grew up in a home with domestic violence may find it challenging or even triggering to work in a domestic violence shelter. Though the social worker recognizes potential limitations in their ability to be effective in such a setting, the social worker is aware that in their chosen area of practice, they may work with clients who have experienced domestic violence. The social worker will be required to provide the same level of care and support, regardless of personal experiences or biases.

Trust Building

Trust building is an important step to building strong relationships. Trust is also a cornerstone in the helping relationship. It is the responsibility of the social worker to build and maintain trust with the client. This should begin during the initial session during the process of informed consent. The social worker should always be honest, open, and forthcoming with all policies, expectations, and rights and responsibilities of both the worker and the client. During this initial discussion, the social worker should explicitly discuss privacy and confidentiality with the client. This includes clearly outlining limits to confidentiality, such as a threat to harm oneself or another person or child abuse.

When establishing trust with a client, the social worker should always act with integrity. The social worker should keep all appointments and be on time for those appointments. Being on time for and maintaining appointments is a way to demonstrate that you value clients and their time. This also demonstrates integrity, which will assist in building trust. As with any relationship, when trust is lost, it is harder to gain it back. As a result, social workers should make great efforts to avoid diminishing the trust of their clients. However, there may be some legal or ethical limitations to the trusting relationship that you have with your clients.

THE HELPING RELATIONSHIP INVENTORY

At the heart of social work practice is the relationship between the worker and the client system. As discussed previously, much research has been done across helping professions that indicates the quality of the helping relationship is a greater predictor in client success. Knowing how important the therapeutic relationship is, it is necessary to examine and reflect upon the quality of the helping relationship in order to be a competent social worker.

> ▶ **Reflection Question**
>
> Why do you think that the quality of the helping relationship is the number one predictor of success?

In addition to self-reflection and supervision, social workers can utilize resources available to them to examine the quality of the helping relationships they currently have. One such tool is the Helping Relationship Inventory. This inventory was developed in order to assist helpers in examining the quality of their helping relationships with clients. This measure, developed by Poulin and Young (1997), was created in order to be specifically applicable to social workers across areas of practice, whereas many other helping relationship inventories are focused solely on clinical (therapeutic) practice. The inventory has two components: a structural component (see Box 8.2) and an interpersonal component (see Box 8.3). Each component can be reversed to a client version by replacing the word *social worker* with *client*. The measure has been found to be effective and useful across domains of practice. It also provides an easily accessible way to assess and improve the helping relationship (Young & Poulin, 1998).

BOX 8.2

HELPING RELATIONSHIP INVENTORY: STRUCTURAL COMPONENT

1. How much have you and your social worker discussed how you are going to approach your work together?
2. How clear are you about what is expected in your work together?
3. How clear are you about what is expected of your social worker and your work together?
4. How much input have you had in determining how the two of you will work together?
5. How much have you and your social worker discussed the specific problem(s) with which you want help?
6. How much input have you had in determining the specific problems you are addressing and your work together?
7. How clear are you about the specific problems that you and your social worker are addressing?
8. To what extent have you and your social worker discussed the specific goals you hope to accomplish in your work together?
9. How much input have you had in determining the goals you are working on?
10. How clear are you about the goals you hope to accomplish?

(continued)

BOX 8.2 (CONTINUED)

11. To what extent have you and your social worker discussed the specific actions you will take to add your difficulties?
12. To what extent have you and your social worker discussed the specific actions your social worker will take to address your difficulties?
13. How much input have you had in determining the actions you are taking to address your difficulties?
14. How clear are you about the actions you are expected to take?
15. How clear are you about the actions your social worker is taking?
16. How much have you and your social worker discussed how your progress is going to be assessed?
17. How much input do you have in determining how you and your social worker will assess your progress?
18. How clear are you about how you and your social worker are assessing your progress?
19. To what extent have you and your social worker discussed your progress?

BOX 8.3

HELPING RELATIONSHIP INVENTORY: INTERPERSONAL COMPONENT

1. Do you and your social worker work well together?
2. Do you feel your social worker pays attention to you?
3. Does your social worker explain to you their understanding of your difficulties?
4. Is your social worker's understanding of your difficulties similar to your own?
5. Does your social worker acknowledge your efforts to cope with your difficulties in addition to talking about your difficulties?
6. Does your social worker give you the impression that they enjoy meeting and talking with you?
7. Does talking with your social worker help you get more organized about resolving your difficulties?
8. Does talking with your social worker have a calming or soothing effect on you?
9. Is your social worker able to handle the emotional aspects of your difficulties?
10. Does talking to your social worker give you hope?
11. Does your social worker help you think more clearly about your difficulties?
12. Does talking with your social worker help you believe more in yourself in general?
13. Do you feel you and your social worker see things in similar ways?
14. Does your social worker help you to think more clearly about yourself?
15. Do you and your social worker talk about things you care about?
16. Do you feel that you and your social worker are alike in some ways?

THE HELPING PROCESS

As social workers, we are called upon to help a variety of people in a variety of settings. Regardless of population or setting, the helping process often stays the same. The process of helping begins with engaging with the client. From the engagement, we are able to begin the assessment. Based on the assessment, we are able to determine how best to intervene. Following the intervention, we evaluate if the change efforts have been successful. To conclude the helping process, the final stage is termination. This five-step process should guide your social work practice.

Engage

Throughout this chapter, we have been exploring engagement in order to connect with clients. Initially, it is important to engage and build rapport. Rapport is the close relationship where the individuals understand one another and are able to communicate with each other. Rapport is helpful when trying to engage with clients.

Elaboration Skills

While engaging with clients, there will be times that we need to encourage the client to continue communicating with us. The ways in which we encourage the client to continue talking are called elaboration skills and are sometimes called furthering skills. The goal of these skills is to promote ongoing dialogue. Elaboration skills can be verbal or nonverbal. An example of a verbal elaboration skill would be statements that encourage the client to share more. In a similar way, nonverbal elaboration skills also set out to further the client's communication; however, they utilize nonverbal behaviors, not words. Table 8.3 provides several examples of verbal and nonverbal elaboration skills.

Empathy Skills

Think about a time that you were talking to someone and you really felt heard. There is a good chance that the person was demonstrating empathy skills. When social workers use empathy skills, they are allowing the client to feel heard or understood. There are several empathy skills that social workers can employ including using active listening skills and validating. Active listening skills refer to being truly engaged in the receiving portion of communication. An active listener demonstrates nonverbal behaviors that demonstrate they are listening such as eye contact, open body position, leaning in, or perhaps even nodding along at times. An active listener is listening with the purpose to understand. When validating another person, you are recognizing and understanding their perspective. Validation can help someone feel understood.

TABLE 8.3 VERBAL AND NONVERBAL ELABORATION SKILLS

Verbal Elaboration Skills	Nonverbal Elaboration Skills
"Tell me more." "Go on." "Can you say more about that?" "Mm-hmm." "I see."	Nodding Eye contact Leaning in Facial expressions

Assess

Assessment is the process by which we collect data and, based on our clinical experiences, theoretical knowledge, and these data, make recommendations. Good assessment is ongoing assessment. Often agencies have a template for completing an assessment that must be finished within the first session or two. However, despite being done with formalized assessments, we encourage you to engage in ongoing assessment in order to monitor for new needs or other relevant information that may come to light at a later time. Assessments should also be comprehensive. Often social workers rely on biopsychosocial-spiritual assessments to guide their practice. These assessments seek to gain information about various aspects of the person's life regarding biological, psychological, social, and spiritual determinants of behavior.

Contracting Skills

A contract is the formal agreement between the social worker and client related to treatment recommendations that were developed based on the assessment. Ideally, the contract is mutually constructed between the social worker and client. Utilizing engagement skills, the social worker should engage the client in the contracting process in order to establish mutually agreed-on goals and SMART (**S**pecific, **M**easureable, **A**chievable, **R**elevant, **T**ime-bound) objectives. When clients are a part of the contracting process, particularly the development of treatment goals, there is often a sense of increased buy-in, which can lead to better results than if goals are just prescribed to clients without their input or insights.

Intervene

Social workers intervene by engaging in an intervention that is designed to address the issues identified in the assessment phase. Throughout the intervention, social workers are continually engaging with clients. Often the interventions selected are evidence-based practice, meaning they are the researched best approach for a specific situation or issue.

Intervention Skills

Though intervention skills will vary from intervention to intervention, there are a few general skills that are common across interventions. One common intervention skill that social workers must possess is the ability to clearly communicate throughout the intervention process. The social worker should explain in a clear way the expectations of the intervention to the client. These expectations include but are not limited to how long the client can expect the intervention to last as well as client requirements or responsibilities during this phase. Another common skill is ongoing assessment during the intervention implementation. The social worker should be monitoring changes that are both observed and reported during this phase of treatment.

Evaluate

Evaluation is the process by which social workers determine whether or not the intervention has been successful. Evaluations can occur throughout the intervention or at the end of the intervention. Evaluations sometimes use formal methods such as scales or assessments. Sometimes evaluations are more informal, based on observations and client self-reports.

Evaluation Skills

Social workers are required to be research-informed professionals. When social workers engage in evaluating their practice, they are undertaking practice-based research. When evaluating, skills that the social worker should possess are good critical thinking skills and organization.

Good critical thinking skills are necessary for social workers engaging in evaluation because the social worker needs to decide how and when to evaluate based on the work they are doing. Further, the social worker must also be able to critically weigh or assess the data that are received during the evaluation process in order to make clinical determinations. Organization is important for research-informed social workers because they need to know when to evaluate and at times keep track of data over a period of time.

Terminate

At the end of the social work helping process is the phase of termination. Planning for termination should begin from the first session. Termination planning should also include discharge plans including possible alternative services and resources and a plan for follow-up. Termination can be a time filled with a variety of emotions for both the client and the social worker. Ideally, termination is planned and prepared for; however, under some circumstances, termination occurs abruptly. Early planning for termination is particularly helpful in cases in which an abrupt termination occurs.

Ending Skills

As throughout the helping process, the social worker should remain engaged with the client throughout the termination or ending phase. Engagement can help to diminish negative or worried feelings the client may be experiencing in response to termination.

During the termination phase, the social worker and client are in essence ending their contract together. The social worker should be sure to share gains with the client regarding progress made during their time working together. The social worker should also be clear about continued areas of focus and how those can and will be addressed in the discharge plan.

INTERPROFESSIONAL

Just as no person is an island, no social worker is an island. In turn, no social worker is a lone helper. Since there are often a variety of helpers in the lives of the clients we serve, it is necessary for social workers to be skilled at working interprofessionally both within an agency and outside of it. There are a variety of ways that social workers can work interprofessionally including collaboration, building professional relationships, and working on a team.

Collaboration

Social workers must ensure that clients receive continuity of care. Continuity of care refers to the seamless or consistent integration of care across providers, time, and/or setting and requires collaboration among professionals. Collaboration is the professional action of working together on a common task or project. For the purposes of this text, we define collaboration as the professional action of working with other professionals in order to provide continuity of care on behalf of a client. Good, clear, consistent collaboration is necessary for competent social work practice. Social workers are well positioned to participate in collaboration. According to Parris (2012):

> The multidisciplinary nature of modern social work involves joint working and information-sharing between professionals and agencies, and it is vital that this is done effectively in the interests of service users, so that the appropriate actions are taken and services put in place. Failure to communicate effectively between agencies can lead to profound and sometimes tragic consequences. . . . Effective multi-agency communication is important in working with all service users because social workers intervene at times of crisis or difficulty in people's lives and their input can have far-reaching consequences. (p. 107)

Social workers have an ethical responsibility to engage in interprofessional collaboration on behalf of clients. The NASW *Code of Ethics* (2021) puts forth:

> Social workers who are members of an interdisciplinary team should participate in and contribute to decisions that affect the well-being of clients by drawing on the perspectives, values, and experiences of the social work profession. Professional and ethical obligations of the interdisciplinary team as a whole and of its individual members should be clearly established. (2.03 Interdisciplinary Collaboration, para. a)

Collaboration Challenges

Though collaboration is necessary within social work practice for the benefit of our clients, at times, challenges related to collaboration can arise. Some challenges related to collaboration include lack of engagement with other professionals, lack of emphasis on continuity of care, and legal considerations.

Just as social workers must engage with clients, social workers must also engage with other professionals in order to collaborate. At times, engaging with other professionals can be difficult. When engaging in interdisciplinary collaboration or collaboration with individuals from a variety of professions or disciplines (e.g., teacher, nurse, psychiatrist, pediatrician, school counselor, and case manager), each professional may be approaching the case from a different perspective based on their professional orientation. Just as social workers must be aware of their role and function when engaging with a client, it is helpful for the social workers to be clear regarding the roles and functions of the other professionals with which they are engaging in order to benefit the most from the collaborative process. Social workers should strive to engage and collaborate with all appropriate service providers to ensure continuity of care for the client. In order to successfully do this, the social worker must be clear regarding the reason for and need to collaborate with the other professionals. At times, a lack of emphasis on continuity of care exists. Within some areas of practice, collaboration is a nonreimbursable task and, as a result, sometimes a forgotten task.

> **Reflection Question**
>
> As a social worker, how would you promote interdisciplinary collaboration with other professionals?

We caution against this. Collaboration that is helpful to the client should always be a priority to maintain, even amid discouraging situations. Related to this, the social worker may need to be proactive and seek out collaborative relationships. In order to seek out or engage in collaborative relationships, the social worker should be mindful of legal considerations. One legal consideration is having clients sign a document allowing you permission to contact other professionals and share information related to their treatment. Clients have the right to refuse to sign releases of information, in which case, collaboration cannot exist. However, if collaboration would be beneficial for the client, the social worker should share the potential benefits and risks with the clients before honoring the client's right to self-determine whether or not to sign the release of information. Though the social worker may feel collaboration would be helpful, without a signed release of information, any communication with another professional would be a breach of privacy and confidentiality, which has serious implications and ramifications for the professional.

Building Professional Relationships

Valuing the importance of human relationships for social workers also extends to the value placed on other professionals. Professional relationships and collaborations are an integral part of the helping process in order to ensure continuity of care and promote the best outcomes possible for clients, all the while trying to avoid duplication of services.

Roles and Responsibilities

Just as it is necessary for social workers to be clear on their role with clients early on in the engagement process, it is equally necessary for social workers and other professionals to be clear on each other's roles as well. Social workers can wear a variety of hats. Due to this, it is important not to assume that by simply identifying yourself as a social worker, another professional will accurately understand your role. It is necessary to consider that social workers may have a variety of different roles, including but not limited to counselor, mediator, broker, case manager, researcher, supervisor, organizer, and educator. Depending on the role in which the social worker is acting, it is important to be clear with other professionals what your functions are in regard to the scope of practice with the shared client. Furthermore, collaborating professionals should be clear on responsibilities related to various tasks, assessments, and interventions regarding mutual cases.

Working on a Team

Working on a team can be very rewarding but can also have some challenges. When you are working as a part of a team, you have the benefit of a variety of perspectives and experiences that can inform the discussion. Team brainstorming can lead to creative ideas that someone may not have thought of on their own. Also, when working on a team, there can be a sharing of tasks, and there is less likely to be a duplication of services for the consumers, as all of the providers are working together and on the same page. Challenges that may arise when working on a team include a conflict of personalities or perspectives. Sometimes team members do not agree. As social workers, we must find a way to have conversations and reach an end agreement that is best for the client.

> ▶ **Reflection Questions**
>
> Describe your experiences working on a team.
> 1. What elements of being on a team have been positive?
> 2. What elements of being on a team have been difficult?

POLICY ISSUES

Policy issues influence all social workers in all areas of practice and can play a significant role in the engagement process. In order to be able to engage with clients, you must first have access to clients. Policies can serve to attract or deter potential clients from seeking support from a social worker.

Policies can serve to promote engagement. For example, policies that have been established to ensure that individuals have equal access to resources, services, and opportunities can enhance the likelihood of an individual reaching out for services. One such policy would be the Patient Protection and Affordable Care Act of 2010, which provides access to mental health and drug- and alcohol-related services to more people than ever before through insurance coverage. Due to this act, individuals who had been previously uninsured or underinsured were given access to services and resources to meet their needs.

On the other hand, some policies can hinder engagement with certain groups. For example, current U.S. policies are viewed by many to be unwelcoming to individuals who are considered refugees or have an undocumented status. An individual who has an undocumented status may be hesitant to engage with a social worker out of fear that their immigration status may be uncovered and that they may be reported. The NASW has set forth that social workers are called to serve all individuals, regardless of their immigration status. However, despite this decree on behalf of the social work profession, many legal and government departments will refuse services or report individuals based on this. Social workers must be mindful of such policy issues that could serve as a barrier to engagement with clients and reflect upon ways to meet clients where they are in order to engage and provide resources, services, and supports (see Case 8.3).

> ▶ **Reflection Questions**
>
> 1. As a social worker, do you need to know if your client has documentation? Why or why not?
> 2. Would your answer change based on your social work role? If so, describe.

CASE 8.3 AFRAID TO ASK FOR HELP: UNDOCUMENTED CLIENTS IN THE SOCIAL WORK PRACTICE

Rose is a social worker at a small nonprofit charity-based organization that is connected to several local churches in the community. The organization is Christian based but nondenominational. At the agency, donated clothes are sold at an extreme discount or even given away to people who demonstrate financial need. The agency also has access to its own food pantry and a small furniture store to provide housewares and home goods to individuals with financial need. They also have an allotted monthly allowance to be able to assist individuals in paying bills that may be too large or in danger of having a utility shut off. Rose's job is to meet with individuals coming in who are requesting assistance of some kind whether it be for clothes, food, furniture, or help with bills. Sometimes people have appointments to meet with Rose. However, the agency has a policy that no one is turned away; so if someone shows up, it is Rose's responsibility to see them and assess their need.

During these meetings, Rose asks demographic data information on finances and spending habits. Rose knows that sometimes people feel uncomfortable coming in and asking for help. In order to help people, Rose strives to engage with people early on so that the interview process can go smoothly. Rose makes sure that when she leaves her office, she is smiling and polite to all customers, as any one of them may be there for an interview. Rose found that by being friendly, it often helps people feel more comfortable speaking with her. During meetings, Rose tries to display empathy, she monitors her affective responses, and she uses elaboration skills in order to keep the interview running smoothly. Rose knows that if she does not get people to engage with her, it may be difficult to determine their full level of need and in turn provide them with the services to meet their needs.

Carla recently traveled to America in order to escape the horrific violence in her home country in South America. Carla came to the United States with very little, only what she could carry for both herself and her 7-year-old daughter, Anna, who accompanied her on her journey. After months traveling to the United States, Carla and Anna were able to connect with cousins who had been in the United States for some time. Soon after settling in the same community as her cousins, Carla was able to find housing. However, since Carla has yet to find a steady, good-paying job, she and her daughter have been sleeping on the floor of the apartment. Carla remains private, but through discussion with the priest at her Catholic church, she learned about a local agency that could assist her in getting some furniture for the home. She was told she could just show up at the agency and they would give her furniture, "no questions asked."

At the agency, Rose was having a busy day with back-to-back appointments. After what she thought was her last appointment of the day when she stepped out of her office, she saw a woman and her daughter sitting in her waiting area. Though Rose was tired, she took a deep breath, smiled, and greeted the pair in the waiting area. She smiled, reached out her hand, and said, "Hello, I am Rose. I am a social worker. Can I help you?" Carla softly said, "I am here for furniture." Rose said, "Okay, great, please come in my office so we can get started on the paperwork." Carla's face looked confused and worried all at once. She said, "No. No, paperwork, I just need furniture. I was told 'no questions asked.' I just need furniture." Carla was worried

(continued)

CASE 8.3	**AFRICAN TO ASK FOR HELP: UNDOCUMENTED CLIENTS IN THE SOCIAL WORK PRACTICE (*CONTINUED*)**

> that if she needed to complete paperwork, the social worker would find out that she and her daughter are undocumented, and she is in fear of deportation. Rose could tell that Carla was concerned about completing paperwork, but she needs to have documentation for all of the goods she gives away. Rose thought for a moment. She did not know what the big deal was; it was just a couple of forms that people fill out every day. But Rose could tell that something was bothering Carla, so she did not want to push it because she wanted to find a way to help.
>
> Rose considered her role and the purpose of meeting with Carla. Rose knew that the NASW promotes supporting clients regardless of their documentation status. Rose also knew that the paperwork she completed at her agency was used to tally the types of services provided. Thinking about all of this, Rose considered what she could do to promote engagement with Carla, who was visibly nervous. Then, Rose remembered that during her initial training at the agency she was told that clients who are reluctant to share personally identifiable data (such as name, address, or phone number) were allowed to not disclose such information. In the training, they emphasized that due to the nature of this agency, paperwork could include an alias or even initials. Rose asked Carla if she would like to use an alias on the paperwork. Rose shared with Carla that the purpose of this paperwork is to demonstrate that the agency is helping community members and that she could use an alias if that would help her feel more comfortable. Carla seemed to be more at ease after moving past the personally identifiable information. In fact, by the end of the intake session, Carla was smiling and nodding along with Rose as she continued the interview.

In order to fully meet clients where they are, social workers must consider and be respectful of diversity and difference. The NASW *Code of Ethics* (2021) asserts that social workers must be culturally aware and recognize that the process of engaging and engagement ought to be based on culture.

Social workers must appreciate differences in diversity and be mindful of how the engagement process may need to be modified in order to be culturally sensitive. For example, though the social worker may be comfortable and used to greeting clients with a handshake and lengthy eye contact, the social worker should appreciate that in some cultures, that would be a very offensive or off-putting introduction. We encourage cultural humility regarding identifying what works best to engage with each client. Though there are some generalizations related to interaction based on culture, social workers should not assume that their clients ascribe to those beliefs. Utilizing a culturally humble approach to engagement may be as simple as asking clients how they would like to be referred to by you.

SOCIAL JUSTICE ISSUES

Social workers are required by the NASW *Code of Ethics* to challenge social injustice and to fight on behalf of poor, vulnerable, and oppressed populations. Social workers are called to be a voice for those who need their assistance the most. There can be struggles when engaging with the groups mentioned previously. For example, when a social worker is engaging with an individual without economic means or resources, the social worker must be aware of how this will influence their time together. If the client does not have the money or means to have access to food, shelter, or other basic needs, it could be quite difficult to conduct therapy. According to Maslow's hierarchy of needs (see Figure 8.1), individuals must first have their basic needs met and feel safe before conquering tasks related to esteem, belonging, or self-actualization. Many schools across the United States now offer breakfast for students and have antibullying policies in place. These two examples would show how schools are attempting to address the two most basic needs of the students: first, the physiological need for food to ward against hunger, and second, the safety needed to decrease bullying. By addressing these two needs, students can be in a better state to be able to learn. In the same way, we as social workers must be mindful of the lower-level needs in the hierarchy that may be barriers to our work with clients and resources, which we can identify to support our clients. Through good engagement, we can assess each level of need and discuss ways to ameliorate each area as well.

We must be considerate of vulnerable populations when considering engagement. Earlier in this chapter when we discussed policy issues, we explored policies that may hinder populations from seeking out services or being resistant to engaging with a social worker. In addition to the example provided earlier, other vulnerable populations may include children, older adults, and prisoners. Social workers who are serving children need to be mindful of the age of consent laws in their jurisdiction. However, regardless of the age of consent, social workers should make every effort possible to discuss with the child in an age-appropriate manner the role and purpose of the services being provided. Including the child in as many aspects of the informed consent process as possible is an important consideration.

When considering engagement with elderly populations, the social worker should be cognizant of issues related to consent, ensuring that the individual can adequately hear what the social worker is explaining as well as read the print on the initial paperwork. Also, social workers, as with any population, should be sure to explain the purpose of their services clearly in an understandable way. Furthermore, social workers should be considerate of potential limits in the availability or use of technology by some seniors. The NASW *Code of Ethics* (2021) sets forth that social workers must be aware of limits related to technology that clients may present with to ensure this will not be a barrier to their care. Engaging older adults by utilizing their strengths has been found to promote the outcome of client empowerment (Vishal, 2018). Social workers are well positioned to utilize the strengths perspective with all clients, including older adults.

Last, when considering engagement with individuals who find themselves incarcerated, it is important to be mindful of potential issues related to informed consent, perceived coercion, and privacy. When engaging with someone who is incarcerated, it is understandable that they may be hesitant to fully open up and engage. With populations such as this, the social worker should be aware how the setting in which the interactions are occurring may be tempering the information gathered. For example, it is not uncommon for a prisoner to remain guarded during a session as a result of the prison setting. When considering engagement, the social worker should strive to provide as safe an environment as possible in which the individual feels like they have the ability to genuinely engage.

SUMMARY

Throughout this chapter, we explored the process of engagement. Engagement is a dynamic and ongoing process between the social worker and the client systems. Engagement is the necessary foundation upon which later processes such as intervention and assessment are built. We explored how attachment theory, personality theory, feminist standpoint theory, trauma theory, humanistic theory, and the person-in-environment perspective can all be utilized to inform engagement with client systems. We reviewed the phases of the helping process while underscoring the importance of the helping relationship in predicting client success. The Helping Relationship Inventory was provided as a tool to assist social workers in monitoring the quality of their helping relationships with clients. Last, we explored the benefits and challenges related to interprofessional collaboration and working on a team, which are necessary aspects of competent social work practice.

CASE SUMMARY: UNDOCUMENTED AND HOMELESS

Practice Setting Description

Jackie is a first-year master of social work (MSW) student completing an internship at an inner-city family service agency in the Southwest. The agency is in a section of the city that has a high crime rate, gang activity, and failing schools. The area has a diverse population with many immigrants from Central and South America and a substantial African American population. The agency provides individual and family counseling services on a sliding fee scale. The agency also runs several educational and treatment groups as well as a temporary shelter for women and their children. Jackie has been assigned to work with the women and their children in the shelter. Her primary tasks are to provide concrete services and supportive counseling to the shelter residents.

Background Information

Elicia and her daughter, Maria, are undocumented immigrants from Mexico. They have been in the United States for 5 years. Elicia and Maria fled to the area from another southwestern city to escape her abusive husband approximately 2 months ago. Elicia is 25 years old and Maria 8 years old. Elicia has a 2-year-old daughter, Sarah, who was placed in foster care because of suspected abuse in the home. Sarah is in a foster home in a small rural community in the state hundreds of miles from Elicia's current residence. Since moving to the area, Maria has not been attending school.

Elicia and Maria are currently residing in the agency's temporary shelter for families. They have been at the shelter for 2 weeks, and the agency has a 90-day limit. Prior to arriving at the shelter, Elicia and Maria were homeless and living on the streets.

Elicia is a high school drop-out and was a stay-at-home mother prior to leaving her husband and moving to a different part of the state. She chose to move there because she has two female cousins living in the area who are also undocumented immigrants. Elicia's native language is Spanish. She speaks some English but is not as comfortable speaking in English. Her English comprehension appears to be good. Maria speaks both English and Spanish well. When communicating with the staff, Maria acts as Elicia's interpreter since none of the staff at the shelter speak Spanish.

(continued)

| CASE SUMMARY | UNDOCUMENTED AND HOMELESS (*CONTINUED*) |

Maria appears to be behind academically. She struggles reading simple children's books written in English. It is unknown if her ability to read in Spanish is better than her English reading skills.

Other than her two cousins, Elicia has no other sources of support in the community. Her cousins have young families and limited resources but are well established and connected to a Latino community in the city and the local Catholic church. Her cousins refused to let Elicia and Maria live with them while she was trying to find her own place and a job. They stated that they did not have enough room and are concerned they would get in trouble with their landlord if it was found out that they were letting people stay with them. They sent her to the local church for help, and she was given the address for the agency's shelter by the priest.

Elicia has been looking for housing in the Latino community. The housing market is tight with limited options, and she has been unable to find anything that she could possibly afford. The only affordable housing she found was a room in a rundown motel that rents by the hour or by the month. It is in an area of town known for drug dealing and sex work.

On arrival in the community, Elicia found occasional work for a house cleaning company. The company hires undocumented workers, pays them very low cash wages, and threatens to turn them in to Immigration and Customs Enforcement (ICE) if they complain. The job bosses also exploit their female workers sexually, threatening to turn them in if they do not comply. Elicia was fearful about applying for other jobs because of her illegal status. She considered turning to sex work to be able to take care of her children, but her Catholic upbringing and thoughts of how this would shame her family have kept her from doing so. She is in constant fear of being detained, separated from Maria, and having her placed in foster care. She is also afraid that she will end up homeless again and forced to live on the streets or return to her abusive husband.

Elicia is extremely reluctant to sign up for any federally funded services, even those that she and her child are entitled to receive. On the suggestion that she enroll for supplemental food through the Supplemental Nutrition Assistance Program (SNAP), Elicia became nervous and refused, as she has heard that participation in SNAP services, and others like them, would draw the attention of ICE, and she had heard stories on the news of individuals being deported after signing up for such programs.

Presenting Problems

Elicia and her child are facing multiple obstacles. They need to find permanent, affordable housing and a job that pays enough to cover her housing and living expenses. In addition, Maria needs to be enrolled in school.

Additionally, Elicia is experiencing an immense amount of stress, anxiety, and possibly post-traumatic stress disorder (PTSD). She described an instance where she could not calm down her breathing and she felt lightheaded. She is very fearful of men and tries to avoid all contact with men in the community. She reports difficulty sleeping at night and feeling exhausted most of the time.

(*continued*)

| CASE SUMMARY | UNDOCUMENTED AND HOMELESS (*CONTINUED*) |

She is concerned about Maria. She has started acting out at the shelter, getting into fights with the other children, disobeying her mother, and being disrespectful and defiant to the staff and other adults. Elicia and Maria fight frequently, and when Elicia tries to discipline Maria, she throws a temper tantrum until Elicia gives up.

Elicia has many strengths. She had the strength to leave her abusive husband and move to a different city. She loves her daughter and wants desperately to keep Maria with her. She is resilient and has managed to survive and keep her daughter safe despite not having a place to stay, a job, and a limited support network. Elicia feels safe in the shelter, but she is very fearful of being caught as an illegal immigrant and is generally mistrustful of helping professionals and persons of authority.

DISCUSSION QUESTIONS

1. What barriers may Jackie encounter when attempting to engage with Elicia and Maria? How can Jackie address these barriers?
2. How can Jackie utilize her understanding of trauma-informed practices to assist her in engaging with Elicia and Maria?
3. Considering the theories presented in this chapter, select two and describe how Jackie could use those theories to inform her engagement with Elicia and Maria.
4. How could interprofessional collaboration aid Jackie in helping Elicia and Maria?

A robust set of instructor resources designed to supplement this text is located at http://connect.springerpub.com/content/book/978-0-8261-6683-8. Qualifying instructors may request access by emailing textbook@springerpub.com.

KEY REFERENCE

Only key references appear in the print edition. To access the full reference list, visit www.springerpub.com/courseconnect. See inside front cover and tear-out card for CourseConnect details.

National Association of Social Workers. (2021). *Code of ethics*. https://www.socialworkers.org/About/Ethics/Code-of-Ethics/Code-of-Ethics-English

9 Generalist Practice With Individuals: Assessment and Intervention

Jordan is a recent graduate in social work and has just completed their orientation at a facility that provided support to individuals experiencing mental health and substance use issues. Excited and eager to put their knowledge into practice, Jordan is about to embark on their journey of working with clients in one-on-one sessions on a weekly basis.

Jordan's first client is Mark, a 35-year-old individual struggling with depression and alcohol use disorder. Mark has been attending therapy sessions sporadically but has expressed a desire to commit to regular sessions to address his challenges more effectively. He works as a delivery driver and has been experiencing increased stress and anxiety, which have led to worsening depressive symptoms and increased alcohol consumption.

In their first session with Mark, Jordan establishes a warm and supportive rapport, creating a safe space for Mark to open up about his experiences and concerns. They conduct a thorough assessment of Mark's mental health and substance use history, exploring his triggers, coping mechanisms, and goals for therapy. Together, they collaboratively develop a treatment plan that includes strategies for managing depression, reducing alcohol intake, and improving coping skills.

Over the course of several weeks, Jordan and Mark continue to meet regularly for one-on-one sessions. Jordan utilizes evidence-based interventions such as cognitive behavioral therapy (CBT) to help Mark challenge negative thought patterns and develop healthier coping strategies. They also provide psychoeducation on the effects of alcohol on mental health and support Mark in exploring alternative ways to manage stress and emotions.

As therapy progresses, Jordan observes positive changes in Mark's mood and behavior. Mark reports feeling more hopeful and motivated to make positive changes in his life. However, there are also challenges along the way, including occasional relapses in alcohol use and setbacks in mood. Jordan remains supportive and nonjudgmental, encouraging Mark to focus on his progress and learn from setbacks rather than becoming discouraged.

Jordan's journey as a new social worker in mental health and substance use services is marked by both successes and challenges. Through their dedication, empathy, and evidence-based practice, they make a meaningful difference in the lives of clients like Mark, empowering them to navigate their struggles and work toward recovery and well-being. As they continue to grow and learn in their role, Jordan remains committed to making a positive impact on the lives of individuals they serve.

LEARNING OBJECTIVES

In this chapter, we explore the practice of social work with individuals, particularly assessment and intervention with individual clients. Social workers often support individuals through the various stages of the helping process. Assessment is a stage within this process.

However, good assessment is ongoing assessment, not limited to an intake that gets recorded and stuffed in a client chart. Assessment begins with the first encounter with clients and continues through termination. As social workers, when we are assessing clients, we are gathering and examining information from a myriad of sources. Assessments should be thorough and comprehensive. Assessments should aim to get a complete snapshot of clients, their history, and their current functioning. We will also focus on intervention with individuals, another stage in the helping process. During the intervention phase of treatment, we often are working on bringing about some sort of change with our clients. The type of intervention selected is dependent on practice setting, expertise, and client presentation. As with most aspects of social work practice, selecting an intervention depends on the role and goal of the social worker. If we are in the role of broker, our selected intervention may be quite different from that of an advocate or even a mediator who are all working with the same client. As social workers, we must be able to recognize where our clients are regarding the change process. Some clients seek out the support of a social worker to assist them with a change for which they have already identified a desire to address. On other occasions, clients may be mandated to treatment or reluctant to pursue change for a variety of reasons. In such cases, it is the duty of the social worker to recognize this and address it with the client directly. By the end of this chapter, you will be able to:

- Review theories that inform assessment.
- Recognize the stages of human development proposed by Erikson and how they inform assessment.
- Identify the various stages related to the stages of change model.
- Describe generalist practice and identify various generalist practice techniques.
- Explain various clinical practice models that are commonly used in intervention with individuals.

COMPETENCY 7: ASSESSMENT WITH INDIVIDUALS, FAMILIES, GROUPS, ORGANIZATIONS, AND COMMUNITIES

Social workers understand that assessment is an ongoing component of the dynamic and interactive process of social work practice. Social workers understand theories of human behavior and person-in-environment, as well as interprofessional conceptual frameworks, and they critically evaluate and apply this knowledge in culturally responsive assessment with clients and constituencies, including individuals, families, groups, organizations, and communities. Assessment involves a collaborative process of defining presenting challenges and identifying strengths with individuals, families, groups, organizations, and communities to develop a mutually agreed-upon plan. Social workers recognize the implications of the larger practice context in the assessment process and use interprofessional collaboration in this process. Social workers are self-reflective and understand how bias, power, privilege, and their personal values and experiences may affect their assessment and decision-making.

Social workers:

- apply theories of human behavior and person-in-environment, as well as other culturally responsive and interprofessional conceptual frameworks, when assessing clients and constituencies; and
- demonstrate respect for client self-determination during the assessment process by collaborating with clients and constituencies in developing a mutually agreed-upon plan. (Council on Social Work Education [CSWE], 2022, pp. 11–12)

COMPETENCY 8: INTERVENE WITH INDIVIDUALS, FAMILIES, GROUPS, ORGANIZATIONS, AND COMMUNITIES

Social workers understand that intervention is an ongoing component of the dynamic and interactive process of social work practice. Social workers understand theories of human behavior, person-in-environment, and other interprofessional conceptual frameworks, and they critically evaluate and apply this knowledge in selecting culturally responsive interventions with clients and constituencies, including individuals, families, groups, organizations, and communities. Social workers understand methods of identifying, analyzing, and implementing evidence-informed interventions and participate in interprofessional collaboration to achieve client and constituency goals. Social workers facilitate effective transitions and endings.

Social workers:

- engage with clients and constituencies to critically choose and implement culturally responsive, evidence-informed interventions to achieve client and constituency goals; and
- incorporate culturally responsive methods to negotiate, mediate, and advocate with and on behalf of clients and constituencies. (CSWE, 2022, p. 12)

NATIONAL ASSOCIATION OF SOCIAL WORKERS *CODE OF ETHICS*

The National Association of Social Workders (NASW) *Code of Ethics* serves as a guide throughout the helping process, including during and throughout the assessment and intervention phases. Assessments can be complex yet must be ethical in all aspects. The ethical principles that relate to assessment include importance of human relationships as well as competence. The related ethical standards are privacy and confidentiality, clients who lack decision-making capacity, and referral for services.

When social workers are engaging in interventions with client systems, they must be mindful of the NASW *Code of Ethics* (2021) and how that mandates their professional and ethical duties to clients. Social workers must ensure that they are providing an unwavering commitment to what is best for the client. Recognizing the importance of the work that they do with clients, social workers also recognize that at times, difficulties can arise during the intervention stage of treatment. For example, maybe the client needs another level of care and a referral or termination in services is warranted. In such a case, social workers must follow the guidelines set forth within the *Code of Ethics* in order to ensure that the client is taken care of during this transition.

Social workers value human relationships. We understand that people do not exist in isolation. Humans exist within the context of their relationships with others. The work that social workers do with clients is important work. Social workers must be mindful of the importance of this therapeutic relationship and at all times do their best to support the client, demonstrating commitment above all else. Social workers must also abide by the *Code of Ethics* regarding all aspects of intervention. When we are intervening with client systems, we must be mindful of the relationships that exist. Both informal and formal relationships are important to note when intervening with families and groups. It is particularly important to monitor the nature and quality of all relationships as you proceed through the helping process.

Especially as it relates to assessment and intervention, human relationships are vital. The quality of the therapeutic relationship is a strong predictor of treatment success. The quality of the therapeutic relationship between social workers and clients is dependent on many factors. The relationship can begin, being enhanced early in the treatment process, by establishing rapport and enhancing engagement. Social workers should strive to help clients feel heard. Social workers should be present for clients and attend to their needs. Our profession values a commitment to our clients. When clients feel this commitment to them, that can enhance the therapeutic relationship.

All people have value. Throughout the helping process, we must never forget that. Social workers must be mindful to respect the dignity of all people during the intervention phase; we must tirelessly work to reduce stigma related to seeking help. Unfortunately, many who need the help of social workers do not seek it out because of the stigma that still exists around treatments (such as mental health treatment) in the United States.

Throughout the helping process, social workers must be mindful to never make clients feel less inferior or inadequate. Even amid adversity and challenge, clients have dignity. Social workers must treat all clients in a humane and dignified manner. This relates back to the importance of the therapeutic relationship and how social workers can help clients feel a part of the service. We should never attempt to do for clients; rather, we should make every effort to work with clients to increase their self-determination, empowerment, and overall self-efficacy.

Social workers must demonstrate a continuous commitment to their clients. Demonstrating their commitment to clients, social workers should strive to avoid interruptions of services; however, there may be times when interruptions of services are unavoidable. During such a time, social workers should make reasonable efforts to provide service continuity (NASW, 2021). Reasonable effort means different things based on the area of practice and type of social work that is being performed. The spirit of the standard is that in the event of an interruption of service, the client is taken care of. Interruptions can include things such as staff unavailability, relocations, or illness.

At times, a referral becomes clinically necessary. Sometimes a referral is necessary if a client needs specialized treatment or expertise that the social worker does not have. In such a case, the ethical principle of competence would come into play. It is important that social workers recognize limitations to their professional competence and make referrals when necessary. If it is necessary to make a referral to another provider, social workers must make every attempt to provide continuity of care. Continuity of care refers to the process of collaborating with the new provider so that the transition can be as smooth as possible for the client.

Just as referrals for services may be necessary, at times clients may need to be transferred. A transfer of care may be warranted in situations when a conflict of interest arises or when a worker is leaving their current position. Like the previous standard, it is important for social workers to ensure continuity of care and do whatever is possible to support the client during the transfer.

Throughout the helping process, social workers should be mindful to consider if the client continues to need services. Should a client no longer need services or the services no longer fit the client's needs, the social worker should take the steps necessary to terminate the helping relationship. Social workers should not continue helping relationships that are not in the best interests of the client. When a termination must occur, for whatever reason, social workers should not abandon clients. When appropriate, social workers should provide continuity of care to other service providers. Should the client not need another service provider, the social worker may provide the client with resources or share who to contact should the client need future assistance. Termination is something that should be planned for and addressed in session. Planning for termination should begin early in treatment and should evolve as necessary. By addressing termination during treatment, it is preparing clients for the final phase of the helping process.

ASSESSMENT

Assessment is an important stage in the helping process, extending beyond the intake session. Assessment begins during the initial encounter with a client and persists until the termination phase. As social workers, assessment practices entail gathering and analyzing information from diverse sources. These assessments should be thorough and comprehensive, aiming to provide a holistic snapshot of the client. A thorough assessment encompasses client history and current functioning.

Having a solid understanding of human development theories is important for social workers, particularly in relation to assessment. These theories provide social workers with a framework for understanding typical developmental patterns and obstacles individuals may confront at various life stages. With this knowledge, social workers can effectively assess clients' developmental progress, pinpoint any deviations or delays, and then intervene accordingly. Human development theories enable social workers to identify both risk factors that may impede development and protective factors that foster resilience. With this theoretical understanding, social workers can conduct assessments that take into account a client's environmental, familial, and socioeconomic contexts, identifying areas of concern and strengths alike. Understanding the relationship between theory and practice allows for social workers to be better able to conduct thorough, culturally competent assessments and tailor interventions that support a client's growth and well-being throughout their lives.

HUMAN DEVELOPMENT THEORIES

To be effective in social work practice with individuals, one must have a strong knowledge base of theories to understand the human condition and experiences. Humans are constantly developing. From infancy through late adulthood, there are a variety of physical and psychological stages and milestones. During typical development, humans progress through these stages and milestones in a predictable pattern. However, at times, stages and milestones may be delayed or unattended to due to a variety of causes. Theories of human development assist social workers in better understanding the progression of stages and milestones that are a part of maturation.

Social workers recognize that there are various forms of development: physical, psychological, social, and cognitive. Physical development refers to such things as biological milestones and growth. Physical development can also refer to things such as gross motor skills like sitting up, walking, or running. Fine motor skills, including the ability to write and manipulate objects, are also a part of physical development. Psychological development includes the transition from egocentric to being able to take on the perspectives of others and even moral development. Social development includes interacting with friends and family and play. The legendary children's show host Mister Rogers is credited with saying that "play is the work of childhood." As children engage in play with others, they are developing socially and move through the stages of play from parallel play on to cooperative or even reciprocal play. Last, cognitive development includes the ability to think and reason, beginning with concrete, tangible thoughts onto more complex, abstract reasoning. Social workers understand that despite these orderly progressions of typical development, not all individuals will progress through each type of development the same way. Some may have an advanced physical development and a delayed cognitive development. Others may have extremely advanced cognitive development and delayed social development. This is why social workers must assess each individual in every area of human development. Social workers must assess where the person is in their development and how this influences participation in the person's environments.

Psychosocial Theories

Psychosocial theories set out to address psychological stages and milestones throughout the life span. These theories attempt to explore how social interactions influence psychological growth and development at various ages or stages. Much of this work is based on the initial works of Sigmund Freud, who is often considered the father of modern psychology. Freud initially put forth his stages of psychosexual development as an attempt to explain how children progress through orderly stages, facing a crisis or task at each stage (see Table 9.1). As you will read, many of the stage theorists we introduce have built their work upon Freud's initial proposals. These theories focus on the process of psychological aging that occurs while individuals physically age. Psychological aging refers to developments regarding personality, mental reasoning, and functioning, as well as the creation of a sense of self, or personal identity (Morgan & Kunkel, 2016).

TABLE 9.1 FREUD'S STAGES OF PSYCHOSEXUAL DEVELOPMENT

Stage	Approximate Age Range
Oral	Birth to 1 year
Anal	1–3 years
Phallic	3–6 years
Latency	6 years to puberty
Genital	Puberty to adulthood

Theories of Motivation

Maslow's theory of motivation can inform assessment by determining client levels of motivation in treatment. Social workers should assess client motivation to change. Maslow provides a foundation for considering client assessment regarding their needs, including their physiological needs, safety, love and belonging, esteem, and self-actualization, as explored in Chapter 8 (see Figure 8.1). It is important to assess client needs and functioning across each area of need. Considering Maslow's work, it is critically necessary to understand where there are areas of need so that they can be attended to before the client is able to address higher levels of need. For example, if a client is facing housing insecurity or does not have adequate food to eat, their basic needs are not being met, and it will be difficult (physically, mentally, and emotionally) to sit with a social worker to explore and process feelings (see Case 9.1).

CASE 9.1 APPLYING MASLOW'S HIERARCHY OF NEEDS TO A CASE

Sally, a 26-year-old single mother of two young children, found herself in a dire situation after leaving an abusive relationship. Seeking refuge, she sought shelter in a facility for survivors of domestic violence. Struggling to make ends meet, Sally was faced with the challenge of providing for her family amidst financial insecurity exacerbated by the loss of her job as a cashier due to the economy. Physically safe but emotionally scarred, Sally grappled with feelings of isolation and worthlessness; she desperately wanted the support and connection she once had with friends and family. Her self-esteem was shattered by the trauma of the abuse she endured, and Sally felt lost and uncertain about her future.

On her second day at the shelter, Sally had a meeting with the agency social worker, Georgia. Georgia was a social worker who understood Maslow's hierarchy of needs and was committed to empowering Sally on her journey toward self-actualization. Through a combination of practical assistance, safety planning, supportive counseling, empowerment, and goal-setting, the social worker and Sally worked together to navigate the challenges of rebuilding her life and pursuing her dreams. With each intervention, Sally found strength she never knew she had, gradually reclaiming her sense of agency, dignity, and purpose. By the end of their journey together, Sally emerged not only as a survivor but as a resilient, empowered individual, ready to embrace the possibilities of a brighter future for herself and her children.

Psychosocial Development Theory

Erik Erikson set forth a theory for understanding the human experience, utilizing stages from infancy to late adulthood, and "at each stage, the rational mind deals with a maturational crisis presented by the social circumstances of our life" (Payne, 2016, p. 107). Each of the stages is outlined in Table 9.2. In each stage, the individual is faced with a crisis that must be addressed. Should the individual come through the crisis in a positive manner, the individual will gain a core strength that aids in ongoing development. Erikson's theories can be quite useful during the helping process, as each stage has

> a specific kind of existential search or quest for "something missing." In this regard, clients come to therapy because they feel uncomfortable about something in their lives and have a vague sense that something is missing or is not right. They want to feel better about themselves and be "all right" in the world. They are often unaware that this sense of something missing or wanting to feel better is often the same thing. The search for something missing is experienced differently at the different life cycle stages, and thus the nature of the search is stage-related and developmental. The resolution of the search at one stage of therapy often leads to the development of another search, which implies that the therapy process comprises a series of searches as clients progress through their therapy. (Knight, 2017, p. 1048)

Through a comprehensive biopsychosocial-spiritual assessment process that explores all aspects of human development, social workers can work with clients to explore areas of concern that may be related to a conflict or crisis at a particular stage of development. Social workers must be good critical thinkers and use their professional judgment in order to assist clients in identifying previous conflicts with current concerns. Social workers who are aware of these eight stages can be mindful during the assessment process to address potential issues that may have arose throughout development and then be in a better place to move forward in the helping process.

TABLE 9.2 STAGES OF PSYCHOSOCIAL DEVELOPMENT IN THE INDIVIDUAL FROM INFANCY TO ADULTHOOD

Age	Crisis or Conflict
Infancy	Trust vs. mistrust
Toddlerhood	Autonomy vs. shame and doubt
Early childhood	Initiative vs. guilt
Middle childhood	Industry vs. inferiority
Adolescence	Identity vs. role confusion
Early adulthood	Intimacy vs. isolation
Middle adulthood	Generativity vs. stagnation
Late adulthood	Integrity vs. despair

Trust Versus Mistrust

During infancy, human babies are totally dependent on others to have their needs met. When infants have a need, whether it be to eat or have a diaper change, they vocalize their needs through their cry. Infants who have their needs consistently attended to are able to develop a sense of trust in others, knowing that their needs will be met. On the other hand, infants who do not consistently have their needs met begin to establish mistrust. This mistrust couples with a feeling that others may be unpredictable, undependable, or even dangerous. In extreme cases, when infants find that their cries are not responded to, they may even stop crying. In cases when children have stopped crying to have their needs met, there can be various concerns related to development. At times, parental concerns from physical or mental illnesses, including postpartum depression, can be common barriers to providing consistent care during infancy. Case 9.2 illustrates such an example.

When this stage is successfully addressed and the child develops trust in the world, the strength of hope is instilled with the child. Hope is often thought of as a feeling; rather, some theorists have suggested that hope is not an emotion, but a way of thinking (Snyder, 2002). Hope is defined as a motivational state based on a sense of successful goals, pathways, and

CASE 9.2 OVERWHELMED: CLIENTS WITH POSTPARTUM DEPRESSION IN SOCIAL WORK PRACTICE

Ava recently gave birth to her first child, a son, Tyler. Ava is a single mother and has limited supports. Her mother and grandmother have both offered to help, but Ava does not want to inconvenience anyone and does not want to seem like she cannot take care of the baby on her own. Ever since coming home from the hospital after the birth, Ava has not felt like herself. She has felt really overwhelmed, tired, and sad. She often finds herself crying in her bed with little energy to get up. She has no appetite and does not even want to eat. She has Tyler in a bassinet in her bedroom, but sometimes she is just too exhausted to pick him up when he starts to cry. Ava feels like something is not right, but she is not sure what it is. Ava feels like maybe she is just a bad mother and does not have what it takes to be there for Tyler. At her checkup with her obstetrician, Ava started to cry and shared some of how she has been feeling. The doctor was very understanding and reassuring with Ava. He said that it sounds like she may be experiencing postpartum depression. The doctor also shared how it is really important for Ava to reach out to supports so that Tyler has his needs attended to regularly in a consistent and timely manner. The doctor shared how detrimental it can be for the baby to have inconsistent care during infancy and how that can have long-standing negative impacts on the child's physical and psychological growth. After this appointment, Ava realized that she did need help, not just for herself but for Tyler too, as his needs should be addressed consistently.

Ava began seeing a social worker and taking an antidepressant medication prescribed by her doctor. She also had her mother and grandmother over much more to help her with the day-to-day household tasks and caring for Tyler. Ava began to recognize that as she was starting to feel better and with the help of her family, Tyler was becoming more engaging and was able to be comforted more easily. She realized that it was less important to appear to be able to do it all on her own and more important to give Tyler the consistent support he needs to develop into a healthy and happy baby.

agency (Snyder, 2002). Hope is important for future personal psychological success. Hopelessness is a strong predictor of low levels of resilience across the adult life span (Gooding et al., 2011). Brown (2010) suggests, "in order to learn hopefulness children need relationships that are characterized by boundaries, consistency, and support" (p. 66).

When conducting an assessment, it is important for social workers to ask questions about early childhood experiences. Most comprehensive biopsychosocial-spiritual assessments include questions about early development, including information about the pregnancy. Though social workers are not medical professionals, it is important to gather such information because social workers understand that physical development can impact psychological and social development throughout the life span. Also, competent social work professionals understand that, at times, medical conditions can cause psychological and/or social impairments. In such cases, social workers should refer the client for a medical examination to rule out any underlying medical conditions that may be the source of impairment.

Social workers who have an understanding of human growth and development throughout the life span can assist clients in identifying possible areas of concern that the client may be unaware of. Case 9.3 illustrates such an example. It is important to be

CASE 9.3 RELATIONSHIP PROBLEMS: APPLYING ERIKSON'S THEORY OF DEVELOPMENT IN SOCIAL WORK PRACTICE

Shelly recently ended a 1-year relationship and is seeking the support of a social worker to help her deal with feelings related to the breakup. During the first session, the social worker, Gina, began engaging with Shelly and building a rapport. Gina began conducting a biopsychosocial-spiritual assessment with Shelly. Though Shelly stated she was interested in having a long-term relationship and getting married one day, but she also shared that she is hesitant to engage in relationships because she knows they usually do not work out. Throughout the interview, Shelly makes several references to a history of poor relationships she has had and shares that she has a hard time opening up and feeling close to others. When asking about her early childhood, Gina learned that Shelly spent her first 2 years of life in the child welfare system due to neglectful living conditions in her family of origin.

Gina asked Shelly about her early experiences, which included multiple foster care placements and inadequate care on the part of her parents. Shelly shared that she has not really thought much about it because she was so young, she does not remember any of it. As the assessment continued, Gina was able to identify several examples where Shelly has been closed off to others and at times distrustful of people, which has hindered her ability to be fully engaged in relationships with family, friends, and romantic partners. Gina recognized that Shelly may be having relationship difficulties due to an early imprinting of mistrust since her needs were not met consistently during her infancy.

Gina shared information with Shelly about early development, including the tasks of development suggested by Erikson. At first, Shelly felt overwhelmed and worried that she missed this milestone and now there was no hope for her. Gina reassured Shelly that this was something that they could work on together in treatment. Gina and Shelly discussed how they could develop treatment goals in order to increase trust in others and mend Shelly's current worldview.

cautious, however, when considering the etiology of concerns. Theories can be extremely beneficial in providing a framework for understanding a myriad of phenomena related to human growth and behavior. However, theories cannot provide evidence of direct causation in all cases. For instance, an individual may have experienced inconsistent caregiving during their infancy; this does not mean that person will have a pathological distrust of all others and will be unable to have long-term relationships. Social workers should be ever mindful not to overly pathologize individuals. Theories, such as Erikson's stages of development, provide an opportunity to better understand how development occurs and in turn explain some behaviors that may occur as a result of various influences throughout the life span.

Autonomy Versus Shame and Doubt

As toddlers, children are beginning to explore their world in new ways. As children become more ambulatory, they can experience their world through their senses and have a greater sense of independence than they did as toddlers. A critical task for children during this stage is often toilet training. During this stage, when children are validated for their experiences interacting with their environment, they can develop a sense of autonomy. Autonomy refers to an independence or free will of one's own actions. At this stage of a child's life, they are learning if it is okay to be themselves and explore their world. Children who successfully master this stage will freely explore their world as they continue to learn and grow. To be autonomous, it is important for young children to have the opportunity to be in control of their body and make choices. Conversely, children who are not allowed to explore their environment or are harshly criticized for their explorations will develop shame and doubt. This shame and doubt will begin to permeate throughout their experiences, and they will not freely explore their environment.

Children who can successfully gain autonomy develop the strength of will. Will relates to a personal drive or determination. Children with strong will do not give up easily, even in the face of adversity or challenge. This strong will can be closely linked to the concept of grit. Tough (2012) puts forth that grit is "a passionate commitment to a single mission and an unswerving dedication to achieve that mission" (p. 74).

Initiative Versus Guilt

In early childhood, children become much more active. Children who are promoted to play, act, imagine, and engage with their world can become creative and develop a sense of initiative. On the other hand, children who are not encouraged to do such things often develop a sense of guilt. They may feel that they are wrong and do not explore their world. When children are able to achieve initiative at this stage, they inherit the strength of purpose. Purpose relates closely with having intention or drive for a particular task.

When conducting an assessment, social workers should inquire about schooling experiences. Formalized schooling is a large part of childhood. Children spend a significant amount of time in school from the age of 6 to 18. Understanding how this experience was perceived by the client is important. It is essential to ask about what was positive as well as what was disliked about these experiences. School serves as a critical environment that children engage in on a regular basis. During the school year, many children spend just as much, if not more, time in school with their teachers and friends than at home. These relationships can have an extreme impact on the development of a child.

Industry Versus Inferiority

As childhood progress, children often enroll into formalized schooling. As a part of this process, children begin to create work products frequently. When a child receives praise or feels proud of their productive work, they can develop a sense of competence. When this occurs, the child experiences industry. However, if a child feels inadequate, they may develop a sense of inferiority, feeling less than or incapable.

When this stage is successfully addressed and industry is achieved, children develop the strength of competence. Competence refers to one's capacity to do something effectively and efficiently to the best of one's ability. Children with the strength of competence believe in their own ability to complete a task. This coupled with the previous strengths of will and purpose allows for youth to become quite productive.

Identity Versus Role Confusion

During adolescence, young people are seeking out an identity and trying to answer the questions, "Who am I?" and "Who do I want to be?" This stage of life is a transition between childhood and adulthood. When youth feel they are able to belong and develop a personal image of their self, they develop identity. When youth feel unable to develop their own identity or lack peer relationships or future plans for their self, they may develop a sense of confusion related to their role in this world. Case 9.4 illustrates a common search for personal identity that adolescents experience.

CASE 9.4 WHO AM I? DEVELOPING A SENSE OF IDENTITY IN ADOLESCENCE

Brian is a high school sophomore. Growing up, he had always enjoyed playing sports. He tried out for the high school basketball team, but unfortunately he did not make the team. Brian was crushed. He always thought of himself as a "jock," but now that he did not make the team, he did not know who he was. Making matters worse, his two best friends did make the team. Within a few weeks, Brian found he was not spending much time with his best friends because they were busy every day after school with practices and conditioning. Brian found himself alone and with nothing to do. Brian started coming home from school and going straight to his room and going to sleep.

Brian's parents recognized that he was not acting himself and talked to him about what was going on. Brian did not want to talk to his parents about what was going on because he did not think that they would understand. He felt all alone and lost. His parents suggested he invite his friends over to hang out. This was proof to Brian that his parents just did not get it because he felt like he did not have any friends right now.

The next week at school, there was a club fair. Brian was not interested in joining any clubs because he was only ever interested in basketball. But as he walked through the hall, he

(continued)

CASE 9.4	**WHO AM I? DEVELOPING A SENSE OF IDENTITY IN ADOLESCENCE (*CONTINUED*)**

> noticed a group of people laughing and having fun together. He wondered what was going on over there. As he slowed down, someone at the table said hi to him and asked him how he was. Brian stopped to exchange introductions. The club representative, Len, asked Brian if he was interested in theater. Brian smirked and said, "Nah." Len said they have something for everyone: "not everyone goes on stage; there are actually a lot of guys who build and move the sets around." Brian was not sure if he wanted to be in the theater club, but he did like how everyone was getting along and he wanted to be a part of something. Within a few weeks, Brian found he really enjoyed being a part of the stage crew for the theater department. He was meeting lots of new people and making new friendships.
>
> As the school year progressed, Brian realized that though basketball had been an important part of his life and something that he still enjoyed, there were many parts to himself that he could explore. Brian was becoming more engaged with others and more confident in his own skin again. Brian felt like he belonged to a group and liked who he was becoming.

At this stage, youth sometimes experience an identity crisis in the midst of trying to find themselves. It is not uncommon for youth to try out a variety of social identities when attempting to find which one best fits them. When adolescents are able to successfully develop a sense of identity and avoid identity confusion, they are able to develop the strength of fidelity. Fidelity refers to the ability of the adolescent to be true to their own self, the identity that they have developed.

Intimacy Versus Isolation

In early adulthood, the primary task is to seek out close intimate relationships with others. Intimacy refers to a deep closeness. Sometimes this occurs via romantic relationships but can also exist through friendships. When young adults feel that they can care about and share experiences with others, they develop a sense of intimacy and in turn strong relationships. When a person does not experience the closeness of others, they can feel uncared for and alone, which leads to isolation. When individuals can achieve intimacy, they also achieve the strength of love.

When assessing intimacy, social workers should be mindful to explore various types of relationships. There may be a tendency to overly focus on romantic relationships, but it is also important to consider other close relationships during the assessment process. Social workers value human relationships and understand how important they are for individuals. Understanding this, social workers seek to assess all relationships present in a client's life. Social workers also seek to enhance client awareness of personal relationships. It is important for social workers to explicitly identify personal supports present for clients.

> ▶ **Reflection Question**
>
> Considering the stages of development covered so far, self-reflect on your lived experience. How does this information apply to you?

Generativity Versus Stagnation

At times, clients may have difficulty identifying informal supports or relationships. Tools such as genograms, which we discuss later in this chapter, can be beneficial in assisting clients in identifying personal supports during the assessment process.

Generativity Versus Stagnation

The task of middle adulthood is making life count. When adults experience a sense that they are productive and contributing to future generations, they can develop generativity. When adults do not feel productive or involved in contributing to the future, they may experience stagnation. Stagnation refers to experiencing no movement or growth. When an adult can achieve generativity, they are able to obtain the strength of care. Care refers to the concern or interest shown in something. Care at this stage relates to the care of others and future generations.

Integrity Versus Despair

During late adulthood, the final task of development is to reflect upon life and determine if it has been a good life. When people look back on their life with fond feelings, they experience integrity. However, when one has many regrets or bitterness, this can lead to despair. At this point in the life span, "dying is the final developmental stage, with its own central crisis, potential, and pitfalls. Successful handling of the crisis leads to the development of a special potential or virtues" (Zalenski & Raspa, 2016, p. 804). Death is a natural part of the life cycle; however, in some cultures, death is avoided or minimized and as a result not considered until it is imminent. Reflecting upon one's life when death is near can be either rewarding and fulfilling or filled with despair and regrets. At times, individuals experience the phenomenon of death anxiety. Schwarz (2017) puts forth that death anxiety is the anxiety that arises as individuals age and reflect upon their life and ultimate death, which can be compounded by the loss of other loved ones, particularly for individuals who are alone.

When this stage can be successfully addressed through the attainment of integrity, the strength of wisdom is achieved. Wisdom relates to having awareness, judgment, and insights. Wisdom is closely related to a sense of inner peace and acceptance (see Case 9.5).

Stage Theory

John Piaget was a cognitive theorist who developed a stage theory to better understand how children are able to think, reason, and in turn learn. Piaget set out to further the understanding of cognitive development in children. Cognition refers to the ability to acquire or learn new information. Piaget believed that the cognition, or mental processes, of a child evolved in an orderly logical progression. Table 9.3 outlines the four stages of cognitive development that Piaget identified: sensorimotor, preoperational, concrete operational, and formal operational. Throughout these stages, Piaget put forth that individuals developed via their thought processes and how they were able to understand and interact with the environment around them (Misca & Unwin, 2016). Piaget's stages demonstrate that children begin learning through very tactile experiences, and as they grow and develop, they are able to think in more complex ways.

CASE 9.5   WANTING TO SHARE WISDOM: PSYCHOSOCIAL DEVELOPMENT IN LATE ADULTHOOD

Lily is an 84-year-old female who lives alone in an assisted living facility. She has been in this facility for the past 2 years, ever since her husband of 50 years passed away. Lily and her husband had five children, but as the children grew up, they each moved away and now live out of town. Lily's children try to visit a couple of times a year and call every now and then. Lily feels lonely. She has fond memories of her childhood and young adult life. She was lucky to meet her husband at a young age and live what she calls a "fairy tale" with him. Lily and her husband had a great relationship and were together all the time. Since his passing, Lily does not do any of the things she used to enjoy doing like shopping, playing bingo, or going to church. Lily spends most of her time sitting in her living room watching TV. The staff at the facility have noticed that Lily is becoming increasingly isolated and not engaging in the group activities that happen regularly at the facility. The facility social worker, Ashley, was notified about Lily and decided to set up a visit to talk with her.

When Ashley arrived at Lily's room, Lily was eager to invite her in and had a plate of cookies ready for the social worker to enjoy. Ashley sat with Lily in the living room, and Lily was glad to speak with her. Ashley realized early on that Lily was lonely. She had a lifetime of memories but no one with whom to share her stories and reflect back on her memories. Ashley asked Lily if she would like to meet more regularly to chat. Lily said she would very much like that. Ashley began to meet with Lily once or twice a week. Lily would share stories from throughout her life with Ashley and was able to identify that she was sad that she did not have the chance to share her stories with anyone before meeting with Ashley.

Ashley understood the importance for older adults to be able to share their personal experiences with others. It is important for them to reflect on their lives and to share their cumulative wisdom with others. By meeting with Ashley, Lily was able to share her experiences and feel a sense of pride in the life that she lived.

TABLE 9.3 PIAGET'S THEORY OF COGNITIVE DEVELOPMENT

Sensorimotor	Birth to age 2	Children experience the world through their senses (touch, taste, see, hear, and smell).
Preoperational	2–6 years	Children begin to use words and images to represent items in their world.
Concrete operational	7–11 years	Children are able to begin thinking logically about concrete events.
Formal operational	12+ years	Children are able to begin thinking abstractly about events and scenarios.

Piaget believed that all information received by people would be categorized into schemas. Schemas are mental representations or structures. The information would either be assimilated or accommodated based on previous experiences. Assimilation involves incorporating new information with existing schema. Accommodation involves creating a new schema or modifying an existing schema. Case 9.6 provides an example of assimilation and accommodation.

> **CASE 9.6 SORTING NEW INFORMATION: ASSIMILATION AND ACCOMMODATION IN SOCIAL WORK PRACTICE**
>
> **Assimilation**
>
> Riley is a 6-year-old girl about to start kindergarten. She had attended preschool for 2 years, so when her parents shared with her that she would be going to kindergarten and likened it to preschool, Riley had a preexisting schema to incorporate this information. Because Riley has experienced preschool, she has an existing idea of what to expect from kindergarten. Though there will be some differences, overall this information was able to be assimilated into the existing schema.
>
> **Accommodation**
>
> Benet is a 3-year-old boy. At home, Benet lives with his parents and two cats. One day while out for a walk with his parents, they pass a dog park. Benet sees the furry, four-legged animals. He points and says "kitty cats." His mother smiled and said, "No, those are dogs." Benet had never seen a dog before. Prior to this experience, all furry, four-legged creatures with tails were cats. This is new information that does not fit into the existing schema of cat, so Benet must accommodate this information by creating a new schema for the category of dogs.

PSYCHODYNAMIC THEORIES

Psychodynamic theories are approaches that are derived from the work of Freud that attempt to understand human development through exploring the role of the ego, drives, and structures of the personality. To understand these approaches, it is necessary to be familiar with the levels of consciousness that Freud proposed: conscious, preconscious, and unconscious. The conscious mind is that which you are readily aware of at any given moment. Right now, you may be conscious of what you are reading or how you are feeling. The preconscious refers to that which can be called into the unconscious quite easily. For example, if you were asked to recall the name of your favorite elementary school teacher, you are most likely able to readily remember the teacher's name and maybe even some other fond memories of that classroom experience even though you had not been thinking about it prior to being asked about it. The unconscious mind refers to thoughts that we are generally unaware of that may be suppressed as a defense mechanism.

Another Freudian concept that is important to understand is how Freud viewed the structures of the mind: id, ego, and superego. These structures are not actual parts of the brain like the limbic system or prefrontal cortex; rather, these are conceptual structures to help understand personality and internal drives that influence personality and behavior. The id represents the instinctual drives that are present at birth. The primary concern of the id is having wants and needs met. The id is sometimes referred to as the pleasure seeker. The ego is the representation of the self that is most in touch with reality. The superego is the ideal self that is interested in following the rules and being moral. The ego must mediate between the id and superego.

Ego Psychology

Ego psychology derives closely from Freud's work on the structures of personality. Heinz Hartmann, the founder of ego psychology, believed that conflicts were part of the human condition, and it is the role of the ego to mediate conflicts. It is noteworthy, though, that he believed that there were conflict-free times as well. Hartmann set forth that the ego and id were continuously interacting with the environment and influencing each other.

Hartmann explored not only pathological development but also typical development. He set forth the notion of an "average acceptable environment" that was necessary for children to grow within. This environment includes parental involvement and interactions between the parent and child. Hartmann's work was influential, as it set out

> focusing on healthy and adaptive development. In contrast to others before him who saw ego development as dominated by conflict, Hartmann saw it as a progression. The ego develops along parallel tracks. One is in conflict, the other in conflict-free capacities within the id and ego. These capacities include perception, memory, motor coordination, language, gifts, and talents. As long as there is a predictable environment, these conflict-free capacities develop into ego functions, which function independently from id drives. (Danzer, 2012, p. 10)

When social workers are conducting assessments, it is important to be mindful not only of conflicts but also of the typical progression of client development free from conflict. This approach is much aligned with the strengths-based approach of social work assessment, which we discuss later in this chapter.

Object Relations Theory

Melanie Klein established object relations theory based on the previous works of Freud. This theory explores the relationships between infants and their primary caregivers. The caregivers are considered the objects. This theory explores the relationship between the infant and the object, or caregivers. It is then, based on this relationship, that the child develops and creates a sense of self with their world. The term *object* was used to refer to others, emphasizing how people may perceive others not as they truly are, but based on their own imagination (Frankland, 2010).

Klein was a pioneer in analyzing children, whereas previous psychoanalytic theorists, like Freud, had focused their work on adults. Klein suggested that children fluctuated between periods of pleasure, when their needs are being met, and pain, when needs are unmet. As children grow, they can eventually understand that there is a combination of both pleasure and pain, which is defined as "ambivalence." Ambivalence relates to understanding that there is both good and bad, positives and negatives, in an object or situation. Through reality testing, children can grow from a primitive state to this depressive position that supports ambivalence (Polat, 2017).

Another key concept that Klein set forth was that of the depressive position. This is a stage where children recognize the existence of ambivalence in many aspects of life. The depressive position holds that there is uncertainty, contradiction, and at times inconsistency within the world. Klein notes that not all children will come to the place of the depressive position and may never fully accept this state of ambiguity. When children do not reach the depressive position, she set forth that they were stuck in a stage where they cannot tolerate these ambivalences, which she called the paranoid-schizoid position. Within this position, individuals fluctuate between positive and negative without holding a position or space in the middle. Whereas an individual with a depressive position can understand that a person can have positive qualities that they love and some negative qualities that may, at times, be annoying, they can still love the person. An individual with a paranoid-schizoid position, on the other hand, cannot embrace the juxtaposition of the two opposing qualities and either loves or hates the person.

When considering Klein's theory and assessment, social workers can explore how individuals interact and view their relationships with others. In fact, there may be patterns of interactions that social workers can assess for during this process. Clients who come forth with a limited ability to tolerate the ambiguity of others may need the assistance of the social worker to help them more accurately identify the positives and negatives that exist within most people. Social workers understand that very little can be described by all-or-nothing thinking. Rather, social workers appreciate that instead of black or white, there is much gray. Social workers can assess if clients possess all-or-nothing thought patterns and if these interfere with their functioning.

Self-Psychology

Heinz Kohut was a theorist who was highly influenced by the work of Sigmund Freud. Kohut recognized the necessary importance of empathy related to human development. He set forth concepts such as mirroring and healthy narcissism. Previously narcissism had been viewed as pathological. Kohut set forth that healthy narcissism is a healthy sense of self, even a component of self-efficacy. Self-efficacy is the belief in one's own ability to complete a task or mission.

Social workers should assess clients for healthy narcissism, or their sense of self. Social workers should consider if the clients view themselves as inflated, deflated, or relatively accurate. In cases of an inflated sense of self, some may recognize this as more closely fitting with traditional views on narcissism. An inflated sense of self can, at times, be damaging or problematic for clients and their relationships with others. On the other hand, a deflated sense of self may be evidenced by poor self-esteem or self-concept. This view of oneself can be equally damaging and problematic for clients and should be assessed by the social worker.

Furthermore, considering self-psychology can also be a beneficial approach for social workers, as many individuals from time to time may experience copious amounts of stress or some other trial or tribulation. As put forth by Cooper and Randall (2012), "every one of us, even the most self-secure, even those with highly empathic self-objects in our past, can lose our self-cohesion and begin to fragment to some degree when burdens and injuries become too heavy" (p. 7). Self-psychology provides a framework for addressing such concerns.

INTERVENTION

Once the social worker has compiled the necessary information for a thorough client assessment, they transition into the intervention phase of the helping process. It's crucial that the intervention decisions are guided by the assessment process itself. Social workers rely on the insights from the assessment, as well as ongoing information gathering, to formulate informed treatment recommendations and decisions. This process is informed by the theories examined previously in this chapter, ensuring that intervention strategies are tailored to effectively address the diverse needs of clients throughout their life span. By integrating theory-driven approaches into our interventions, we strive to provide the most comprehensive and impactful support possible.

STAGES OF CHANGE

Intervention is all about change. To fully understand intervention, it is necessary to be familiar with the stages of change model presented by Prochaska and Clemente (Figure 9.1). This model was initially developed to address stages of change related to health behaviors; it is a good framework for understanding most types of change social workers will undertake with clients. This model has also been found to be highly useful in both clinical and nonclinical settings (Abel & O'Brien, 2014). Their model for understanding change has six stages: precontemplation, contemplation, preparation, action, maintenance, and relapse. We explore each stage and discuss how each could influence your intervention with a client.

The initial stage of this model is the precontemplation stage of change. At this stage, there are no active thoughts regarding the need or desire to change. If clients have sought out social work services on their own, they have often considered or contemplated change.

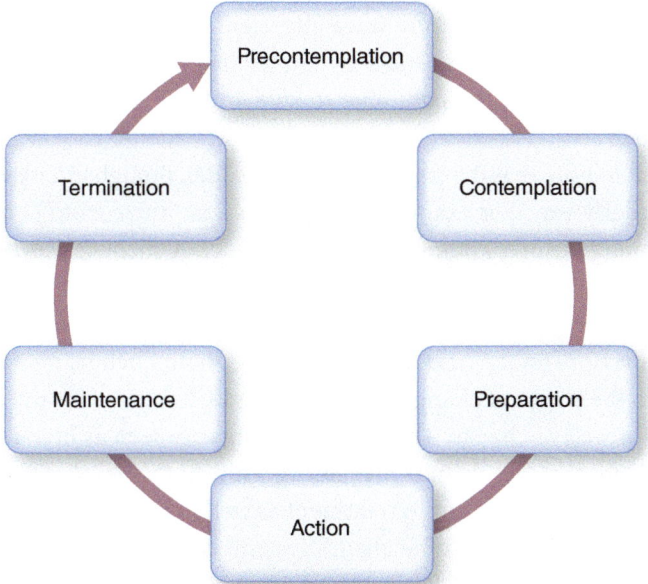

FIGURE 9.1 Stages of change model in social work practice.

Source: Adapted from Prochaska, J.O., & DiClemente, C.C. (1983). Stages and processes of self-change of smoking: Toward an integrative model of change. *Journal of Consulting and Clinical Psychology, 51*(3), 390–395.

Contemplation is the second stage in this model. You may be wondering how a person could be meeting with a social worker if they have not even considered change. Well, this could happen in several ways. For example, a client may have sought out the support of a social worker for another issue and upon meeting and assessing, the social worker noticed an area to address. Another example would be if the person did not initially seek out the social worker, but rather the social worker sought out the client. This often happens in hospital settings when the medical staff page the social worker for a consultation. It could also happen when a child welfare agency receives a report and as a result must initiate services with a family. If a client is in the precontemplation stage, the goal of the intervention is to bring the condition or problem into the client's awareness.

Once the client is aware of the issue that would benefit from change and is considering change, the client would be in the stage of contemplation. In this stage, the client is aware of the need for a change but is not actively changing or preparing to change. At this time, the intervention would focus on addressing the idea of change. At this stage, there are several variables, including the person's beliefs about the problem, their insight into how the problem is impacting them and others, and the amount of energy the person has available to address the issue (Cooper, 2012).

Following contemplation, the next stage is preparation. At this stage, the client has recognized the desire to change and is taking steps to prepare to make changes. The actual change efforts have not yet begun. Rather, the planning for them is underway. This stage can be likened to buying exercise equipment to later work out and get in shape. Buying the equipment itself does not change the individual's health status, but it is a way to prepare to address personal fitness. In the realm of social work interventions, preparations can be quite varied. Case 9.7 illustrates a social worker assisting a client through the various stages of change.

The next stage in the model is the action stage. It is at this point that the actual change efforts begin to occur. During the action stage, the client initiates behaviors that are designed to bring about change. The following stage is maintenance, where the action stage is sustained long-term. For some clients who are able to sustain their change, termination is the final stage of the model.

It is important to note that the stages of change model, though circular, is not always completed in this orderly way. For example, a client can just move from contemplation directly into action, skipping the preparation stage of the model. A client can move through this cycle numerous times while working on the same issue or condition. It is noteworthy that each time a stage in the circle is revisited, there is now a history of experiences that can serve to inform client behaviors on the next attempt to bring about change.

In addition to the stages of change, Prochaska and Clemente also put forth the process of change as well as levels of change. The levels of change are seen as hierarchical. At the lowest level is the symptom that the client is presenting with. At this level of change, it is important to consider what brought the client to treatment as well as how these symptoms are being impacted by other goings-on within the client's system. At the level of maladaptive cognitions, clients may have problematic thoughts related to their problem, need for change, or another aspect of their life. Interpersonal conflicts can sometimes occur as a result of the problem of concern. If that is what has brought the client to treatment, this and the lower levels of change

CASE 9.7 INTERVENING AT THE VARIOUS STAGES OF CHANGE IN SOCIAL WORK PRACTICE

Stephanie is a hospital social worker. She is often called in on consult by the medical staff in order to support the emotional, behavioral, and social needs of patients. Stephanie was called in for a consult when an adolescent female presented to the emergency department with alcohol intoxication. Before entering the room, Stephanie reviewed the patient's electronic medical records in order to have a better understanding of what she was walking in on.

Upon arriving at the patient's room, Stephanie knocked on the door and introduced herself lightly; identifying herself as the social worker, she asked the patient, Michelle, if she would be willing to talk to her. Michelle agreed. Stephanie asked Michelle about what brought her into the hospital today. Michelle shared that she did not understand what the big deal was, as in her words, "I had some drinks with my friends, this whole thing is being blown out of proportion." Stephanie asked Michelle if it would be okay to talk about her use of alcohol. Michelle reluctantly agreed, adding that they can talk about it but reassuring Stephanie that she does not have a problem. Stephanie began to ask Michelle about her typical alcohol use and ways that it impacts her life. Though having multiple hospitalizations for alcohol intoxication, being in danger, failing her current grade, and having conflict with her family, Michelle denies having a problem and due to this denial is not even considering the need or possibility for change.

Stephanie recognizes that Michelle is in the precontemplation stage of change. Based on this recognition, she realizes that in order to have an effective intervention with Michelle, she will need to help her begin considering the possibility of change.

Later in her shift, Stephanie received another page. This time Stephanie was paged for a consult to support a 38-year-old male who was in the hospital for a medical procedure but while there shared with the staff that he has been depressed. Again before going into the room, Stephanie reviewed the patient's chart to prepare for their meeting.

Again, Stephanie knocked on the door and introduced herself warmly. She was welcomed in by the patient, Charlie. Stephanie asked Charlie if it would be okay to talk about how he has been feeling lately. Charlie agreed. Charlie shared that he has long been considering getting help for his depression, and he had even made an appointment once or twice but never followed through and attended.

Stephanie recognized that Charlie had contemplated making a change in the past and had even attempted to engage in the preparation stage of change by making an appointment for himself. However, the breakdown occurred in the action stage exchange. Based on this information, Stephanie knows where to begin her intervention with Charlie.

---

would all need to be addressed. For example, if clients who have been dealing with addiction are seeking out services because their employer has required them to do so, that would be an example of an interpersonal conflict. The next level is that of family–systems conflicts. This is similar to the previous level; however, in the previous level, conflicts were with friends and colleagues, whereas at this level, conflicts are with family members. At the highest level of change are intrapersonal conflicts, which are conflicts that exist within the person.

GENERALIST PRACTICE INTERVENTIONS

Generalist practice requires that social workers have a skill set that can be generalized across settings and populations to provide support. Social workers who have a generalist background are well versed in a variety of ways to help or intervene with client systems. In this chapter, we introduce a variety of approaches that can be utilized to support clients. Generalist practice models provide a guide for social workers to support clients at various levels (micro, mezzo, and macro) in various practice settings. This model is often a problem-solving approach that seeks to assess and then intervene to reduce client problems. Generalist practitioners are often trained in the areas of casework (or management), one-on-one work, and group work. We explore these three areas now.

> ▶ **Reflection Question**
>
> Why do you think it is beneficial for social workers to have generalist skills?

Case Management

Social work has a long tradition in casework, which is now often referred to as case management. Case management involves identifying client needs and linking the client to appropriate services that can address those needs. A case manager does not address each of the client needs directly, but rather acts as a broker to coordinate services. Case managers remain open and supportive of the client as a formal service provider. Case managers are tasked with ensuring continuity of care and do a great deal of collaboration with other formal service providers present in the client's life.

Social work case managers support clients in a variety of ways including such things as education and advocacy. The case manager does not simply prescribe services for the client, but rather works together with the client to identify appropriate needs that are areas to target. Over time, there has been a shift from considering the work of case management to that of case coordination (Blundo & Simon, 2016). In some areas, this language has already transitioned to be more inclusive of the process and less hierarchical. Whether called case management or case coordination, the involvement of social workers to ensure appropriate interventions for clients is an important role.

Supportive Counseling

Supportive counseling refers to the intervention that is often used in a variety of social work practice settings. Supportive counseling is not the same as talk therapy. Supportive counseling often involves comfort and guidance. In this intervention, clients are able to express their thoughts and feelings with a social worker. This may seem similar to therapy, but in supportive counseling, the social worker is not seeking to address specific psychological causes of distress. If an issue related to a specific psychological stressor arises, the social worker refers the client to another professional, such as a clinical social worker who specializes in such therapeutic treatment. Supportive counseling is common in settings such as child welfare organizations, community organizations, hospitals, and schools. This can occur in individual or family sessions. Supportive counseling, as its name implies, offers support to the client. The therapist will often listen and provide feedback. Authenticity and empathy are extremely important in this intervention.

CLINICAL PRACTICE MODELS

Clinical practice models can be used in an array of social work practice settings. Clinical practice models provide an approach to treatment. Each model, which is based on a theoretical orientation, provides a direction to take in supportive counseling. Social workers provide the majority of mental health services in the United States (Dziegielewski, 2014). Knowing this, it is important for social workers to be familiar with various clinical practice models.

Ecological Perspective

The ecological perspective seeks to assist social workers in understanding the complex dynamics of the person-in-environment experience. As social workers, we study human behavior in the social environment because we understand the importance of recognizing interactions that influence people. When we are considering the social environment, we are not only examining the physical environment but also considering conditions and relationships. Social environments are multifaceted. Understanding the way in which clients exist within the contexts of their social environments is a necessary function of our profession.

The ecosystem perspective of intervention seeks to bring attention to the principles of the ecological and systems theories. This theory focuses on various principles including the interconnection of systems, the importance of goodness of fit, boundaries, and patterns of relationships. Social workers find that "consistent with ecological and system theories, the intervention seeks to enhance the functioning of a system by improving the goodness of fit between the client and the systems with which she interacts" (Langer & Leitz, 2015, p. 42).

Life Model

The life model also has a long tradition in the profession of social work. From the earliest days of social work in the United States, during the time of the Settlement House movement, the life model is evident. The term was officially coined during the mid-20th century based on the idea of social work practice resembling life itself. Gitterman and Germain (2008) put forth that "such a life-modeled practice fits the social work profession's purpose of releasing the potential for growth and satisfying social functioning of individuals, families, and groups, while increasing the responsiveness of their environment to people's needs, rights, and aspirations" (p. 71). As you can see, within the life model it is critically important to consider the client's social environment holistically. By focusing on the transactions between clients and their environments, the social worker can identify means of coping that clients already possess. By exploring these existing coping mechanisms, social workers can encourage and enhance clients' overall functioning.

This model requires that social workers learn from clients and join them in the process of life. Life can be difficult and, at times, messy. As professionals, we must recognize this reality. As a profession, we often say that we must meet clients where they are. In order to do so fully, we must recognize where the client is within their life. Throughout life, people grow, develop, and change. We must recognize where the client has been and where they are now. Equally important, we must understand where it is that the client seeks to go. One way that the social worker can gain these insights is through listening to the client tell their life story. The client's life story is the personal narrative of their experiences.

The life model is characterized by the 10 features outlined in Table 9.4. The model has four phases: preparatory, initial, ongoing, and ending. During the preparatory phase of the life model intervention, the social worker must be prepared to be empathetic to the client and their life story. We have discussed in previous chapters the importance of empathy within social work practice. Without empathy, clients may not open up and share their experiences with the worker. If clients do not feel that they can be open and honest, this will detrimentally hinder the intervention.

During the initial phase of this model, the social worker seeks to create a supportive relationship with the client. This relationship creates an accepting environment in which clients

TABLE 9.4 LIFE MODEL FEATURES IN SOCIAL WORK PRACTICE

Professional function	The role of the social worker in this model is to ameliorate client stressors and improve coping strategies. Social workers seek to match client needs with available resources.
Ethical practice	Social workers view ethical principles within a hierarchy to determine priority. From the highest to the lowest priority: protection of life, equality and inequality, autonomy and freedom, least harm, quality of life, privacy and confidentiality, truthfulness, and full disclosure.
Diversity-sensitive	Social workers respect all clients and engage in culturally competent practice. Furthermore, social workers honor individual differences.
Empowerment	Empowerment and addressing social justice issues are central to this model.
Integrated methods	Numerous modalities and methods are utilized in this approach to address change.
Partnership	The relationship between the social worker and client is viewed as a partnership rather than a hierarchical relationship.
Mutual agreement	Shared definitions are a critical piece of this model. These shared definitions must be mutually agreed on.
Strengths	This approach is inherently strengths based.
Significance of culture and environment	Social workers appreciate the role of culture and environment on the individual.
Evaluation	Various methods exist that can assist in determining if the approach was successful.

Source: From Gitterman, A., & Germain, C. B. (2008). *The life model of social work practice: Advances in theory and practice* (3rd ed.). Columbia University Press.

can share their experiences and social workers can use empathy and curiosity to elicit more information from clients. In this phase, there is an emphasis on defining stressors and degree of choice. At this stage, the social worker and client must clearly identify all stressors that are of concern. As with many social work interventions, it is very important that the client and social worker are on the same page in terms of the identified problems. Problems should not just be stated; when problems are defined as clearly as possible, it will ensure that both have a mutual understanding are on the same page.

The degree of choice refers to the client's choice of services. As we have discussed at the start of this chapter, at times, clients seek out social work support for concerns, whereas at other times, social workers are made available to clients due to a referral of some sort. When clients have not sought out the service for themselves but are rather offered or, in some cases, mandated social work support, there may be a reluctance to participate. Social workers should acknowledge this and address any feelings the client may have regarding this from an empathetic stance.

Other tasks that occur during this stage include obtaining the client's informed consent for treatment as well as reviewing agency policies and procedures. The social worker and client also work together to develop goals for treatment. It is important that goal setting is a mutual process. The social worker and client also discuss expectations for their work together.

The next phase of treatment is the ongoing phase. Within this phase, the social worker is intervening, utilizing a variety of modalities. Social workers seek to clarify client responses and encourage further exploration. Social workers identify client strengths that can be used to address areas of concern. Supporting clients as they move through the problem-solving process is another way in which social workers support clients during this phase of treatment.

The final phase of this model is the ending phase. The social worker must plan for this stage with the client in order to avoid negative feelings related to the termination of services. The social worker reflects with the client upon their work together and assists the client in identifying areas of growth and progress gained throughout the process.

Strengths Perspective

The strengths perspective seeks to identify the strengths present within our clients. As social workers, we believe in the inherent worth of all people. The strengths perspective seeks to have us identify these strengths. Strengths may be internal or external. Examples of internal strengths include things such as "a sense of humor, insight, and flexibility that help people cope with challenges they face," whereas external strengths include things such as "resources outside of the person . . . extended family, connection to a faith community, [and] services available in a client's local geographic area" (Langer & Leitz, 2015, p. 61).

During the assessment process, social workers should begin identifying client strengths. These identified strengths can inform the intervention process and support the ongoing work between the client and social worker. At times, it may be difficult for clients to identify their own personal strengths. In such cases, it is the role of the social worker to identify the strengths. Case 9.8 illustrates a social worker utilizing the strengths perspective to assist a client.

▶ **Reflection Question**

As a social worker, how would you help clients identify personal strengths?

> **CASE 9.8** **FINDING STRENGTHS: UTILIZING THE STRENGTHS PERSPECTIVE IN SOCIAL WORK PRACTICE**
>
> Megan is a social worker who is a case manager at a drug rehabilitation center. A part of Megan's job is to meet with the patients at the facility and work with them to find education or job opportunities. This requires Megan spending time getting to know the patients and their interests. It is also important for Megan to pay attention to what the patient strengths are and try to find a good match between their strengths and the skills and requirements needed for various educational and job opportunities.
>
> Today Megan met with Jack, a patient who has been at the facility for approximately 3 months and is looking to be discharged soon and is in need of employment. During their meeting, Megan asked Jack what he thought his strengths were. Jack did not know how to answer the question. Megan rephrased the question and asked him again to tell her about the things he was good at; again, Jack did not have a response. Nevertheless, Megan persisted asking in another way. Finally, Jack said, "I'm not good at anything, I've never had a real job. I don't know what I would even be able to do." Megan asked Jack what he did to make money before coming into rehab. Jack shared that he had always made ends meet by hustling on the streets. Then, Megan said, "Well, there you have it; that is one of your strengths." Jack was surprised, so he said to Meghan, "What do you mean? There is no way that I can go back to hustling on the streets and stay clean." Megan agreed, but she helped Jack to see that some of the skills he used in order to hustle would help him in the job market. She pointed out to Jack that he dealt with many people; this translates into good people skills. Those people skills would be helpful in a customer service position. She pointed out to Jack that he often had to manage his money and keep track of money in and money out. Those are great financial skills. Megan and Jack went on to identify other strengths that he had based on his previous experiences that would be helpful in future endeavors. By the end of the session, Jack was proud of his strengths and had a new confidence about himself.

Some critique this perspective, noting that it is conceptually vague and overly emphasizes the strengths of the clients and in turn diminishes the problems the client is presenting with (Simmons et al., 2016). Simmons et al. (2016) go on to state that due to the lack of clarity, "a strength may be defined entirely different in every intervention stage" (p. 149). Social workers should recognize these critiques but not allow them to hinder efforts to identify strengths. Yes, it is important to recognize and address problems. However, social workers must not become consumed by a deficit-based approach. Rather, we must seek to identify strengths to inform our interventions and empower the client systems we work with.

A key concept related to the strengths perspective is the concept of resilience. Resilience is often considered the ability to bounce back from difficulty. Graham (2013) defines resilience as "the capacity to respond to pressures and tragedies quickly, adaptively, and effectively" (p. xxv). According to Rutter (2006), resilience is an "interactive concept" that must be considered in relation to both risk and protective factors (p. 3). Resilience is often influenced by factors that are external from the individual (Luthar et al., 2000). Within a social work framework, influences at the micro, mezzo, and macro levels affect the development of resilience. Luthar et al. (2000) set forth that attributes of the individual, the family system, and the wider social environment influence resilience. Factors influencing resilience include such things as support systems, coping skills, and resources available.

Many researchers have identified protective factors as well as risk factors in an attempt to classify the influences on resilience at the micro and mezzo levels. Protective factors refer to a set of characteristics that are often shared by individuals who are considered to be resilient (Earvolino-Ramirez, 2007). Protective factors can include but are not limited to such things as healthy relationships, quality educational opportunities, healthy self-esteem, and a good sense of humor. Studies from different countries demonstrate that some factors are universally experienced as protective (Gunnestad & Thwala, 2011). Canavan (2008) asserts that protective factors serve to diminish the likelihood of impaired development as the result of experiencing one or multiple risk factors. Within the literature, protective factors include such things as:

Good natured, easy temperament, positive relationships, communicates effectively, sense of personal worthiness, sense of control over fate, effective in work, play, love, positive social orientation, assertive, asks for help, above average social intelligence, informal social support network, ability to have close relationships, healthy expectations and needs, use of talents to personal advantage, delays gratification, internal locus of control, flexible, believes in her or his self-efficacy, desires to improve, interpersonal sensitivity, problem-solving ability, decision-making ability, future oriented, trusts in others, hope for the future, sense of humor, productive critical thinking skills, manages range of emotions, adaptive distancing, high expectations. (Earvolino-Ramirez, 2007, p. 75)

Narrative Therapy

Every person has a story. As social workers, we are invested in hearing those stories and honoring them. Narrative therapy is a technique where the client's story is the focus of the intervention. The premise of this technique is that individuals are constantly engaged in constructing their personal narrative or life story (Walsh, 2013). The self-narratives that are constructed in narrative therapy provide a sense of identity for the client (Allen, 2011). This relatively newer technique was developed by Michael White and David Epston. White and Epston (1990) put forth the following:

In striving to make sense of their lives, persons face the task of arranging their experiences of events in sequences across time in such a way as to arrive at a coherent account of themselves and the world around them. (p. 10)

During the fluid process of human development, stories may change. These stories are extremely powerful, as they not only account for our experiences but can shape our experiences as well. These stories can be a focus in treatment. This technique has been found effective with individuals as well as with couples (White, 2009).

Within narrative therapy, there is an emphasis on understanding personal meaning. Much research and theory have been dedicated to the necessity of meaning-making in human life. Frankl (2006) sets forth that "man's search for meaning is the primary motivation in his life . . . it must and can be fulfilled by him alone" (p. 99). Frankl (2006) also asserts that nothing exists that "would so effectively help one to survive even the worst conditions as the knowledge that there is meaning in one's life . . . he who has a why to live for can bear almost any how" (p. 104).

Hauser and Allen (2006) set forth that "personal meaning and meaning making can foster unexpected pathways from adolescent misfortune to young adult competence in friendships, marriage, and parenting" (p. 574). Research suggests that making positive meaning from negative life events can assist the individual in reframing the adversity and in turn buffering the impact of the adversity on the mind and the person's overall well-being (Lightsey, 2006). Some view meaning-making as a necessary human experience (Brown, 2015).

Within narrative therapy, the personal story is deconstructed by the social worker and the client. Deconstructed refers to the critical analysis that occurs by the social worker and client when exploring the personal narrative. Assumptions are addressed and challenged when appropriate. Another aspect of narrative therapy includes reconstruction. During the stage of reconstruction, the client creates a new, more functional, personal narrative. The social worker is often very active in assisting the client in identifying options for this new narrative. However, as with most elements of social work practice, the construction of a new narrative relies on the self-determination of the client. The final stage of narrative therapy is connecting. During this stage, the client integrates the new personal narrative into their life and engages with others. This is also a stage of celebrating the new narrative (see Case 9.9).

CASE 9.9 FINDING THE STORY: THE IMPORTANCE OF THE PERSONAL NARRATIVE IN SOCIAL WORK PRACTICE

Paige is a social worker who works at a counseling center. In her role, she provides individual counseling services. She just began meeting weekly with a client, Denise. Denise sought out services to deal with her low self-esteem. Paige and Denise have been exploring the personal story Denise has about herself. Denise has been able to identify that she long had a personal narrative that she is a screwup and no one will ever love her.

Together Paige and Denise work to re-create her personal narrative. Paige asks Denise what she would rather her story be. Denise recognizes that she wants to feel good about herself and acknowledges she has talents and close friends who do love her.

Over time, Paige and Denise work together to solidify this personal narrative. Eventually comes the time to celebrate Denise's new personal narrative. Denise feels like a new person and wants to celebrate her vibrant self with her friends. Denise feels more comfortable being herself and living her new narrative.

Task-Centered Practice

Task-centered practice is a problem-solving approach that can be utilized as a social work intervention with clients. This is a highly adaptable model that can be used in a variety of practice settings. It is a short-term model that emphasizes taking action to address the problem rather than ruminating on the problem (Langer & Leitz, 2015). This approach emphasizes completing specific tasks to address the problem. The problems are the wants and needs of the clients. Within this approach, problems are viewed as an inevitable piece of the human experience. In practice, the problem selected to be addressed during the intervention is called the target problem. It is important to note that a client may present with numerous problems, and it may not be within the scope of your practice to be able to address all problems. Or it may not be feasible to address all the problems at once. In such a case, it is important to work with the client to prioritize problems so that the most urgent problem can be addressed first. Again, considering client self-determination is important. Once a target problem has been identified, target tasks, or the tasks necessary to ameliorate or lessen the problem, are identified. There are three phases of treatment in the task-centered approach, which are illustrated in Table 9.5.

Solution-Focused Brief Therapy

Solution-focused brief therapy was designed based on both the task-centered approach and the strengths perspective. In this short-term intervention, the focus is on solutions. This approach is very much future-oriented. The social worker builds rapport through joining with the client. The social worker assists the client in seeking change, starting where the client is. A key component of this approach is the notion that "people possess all of the skills and strengths necessary to solve their problems" (Langer & Leitz, 2015, p. 212). The social worker must at times assist the client in recognizing these skills and strengths. Although in other models there is an emphasis on the social worker teaching new skills, this approach relies on what the client already has available to them.

TABLE 9.5 PHASES IN THE TASK-CENTERED MODEL	
Initial phases	The social worker engages with the client in order to establish rapport. The social worker then begins the assessment in order to identify problems and their contexts. Target problems are discussed in specific detail. Once the target problem has been clearly specified, the social worker and client develop a contract including goals with specific steps to address the target problem.
Intervention	During this stage, the client is completing the goals outlined in the contract to reduce the target problem. The social worker and client often work together in order to identify various possibilities to meet the specified goals. During meetings together, the social worker and client review progress toward achieving goals. If goals have not yet been achieved, the social worker and client discuss the reasons for this and make changes as necessary.
Termination	This is the final stage of the task-centered model. Termination is the overarching goal of this brief treatment approach and as a result should be discussed early in treatment. The social worker and client reflect upon accomplishments and plan for ongoing maintenance.

Source: From Langer, C. L., & Lietz, C. A. (2015). *Applying theory to generalist social work practice.* Wiley.

In order to set appropriate goals for this approach, the miracle question is a technique that is often utilized. The miracle question requires clients to consider their future without their current problem. Through this question, social workers can gain insights into how clients envision their future through a hopeful perspective. This can provide the social worker with ideas regarding possible skills and resources that can be useful in this approach. Another important technique is the scaling question. This question asks the client to rate, often on a scale of 1 to 10, how present the problem is in their lives: 1 represents no problem, whereas 10 represents the problem is fully present. This question can be helpful in evaluating progress throughout your work with the client.

Social Learning Theory

Albert Bandura sought out to better understand how individuals learned. He conducted the famous Bobo doll experiment. In this experiment, Bandura had a Bobo doll, a clown-like punching toy. It was in a room with other toys. Children were invited into the room to play. Children were then shown a video of adults playing roughly, punching and knocking down the toy. After watching this video, the children emulated the behaviors of the adult models that they had seen in the videos. As a result of this experiment, Bandura put forth that children learn through the observation of models. Furthermore, he asserted the experience of vicarious learning. Vicarious learning refers to the ability to learn solely through the observation of others.

Social learning theory can inform social work intervention, as it also directs social workers to use models for clients to learn new behaviors. This can be particularly helpful for individuals with social skill deficits. The use of modeling to teach appropriate social skills is a common intervention that utilizes vicarious learning. This approach is grounded in both behavioral theory and cognitive theory.

When considering learning, it is important to understand reinforcement and punishment, which are important aspects of behavioral theory (Figure 9.2). Social workers often rely on intervention strategies that address these two behavior change principles. Reinforcement is used when we want to have a behavior increase. However, on the other hand, punishment is used when we want to have a behavior decrease. We can use the terms *positive* and *negative* to

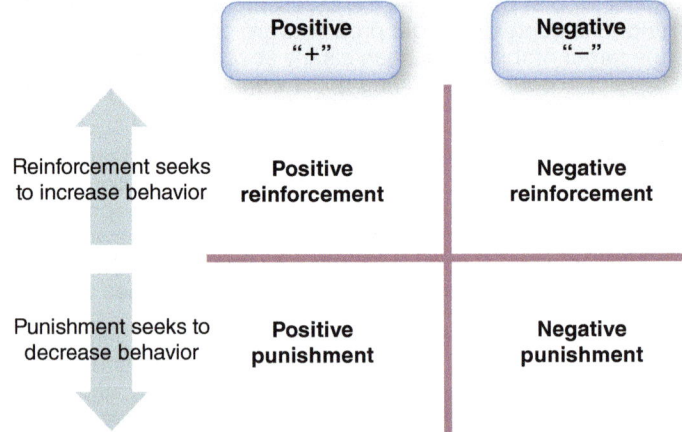

FIGURE 9.2 Reinforcement and punishment in cognitive behavioral therapy.

describe types of reinforcement and punishment. These terms can sometimes become confusing. We are not using them to describe good or bad; rather, we are using them to describe the addition or removal of some stimuli. Positive reinforcement occurs when a stimulus is added in the hopes of increasing a behavior. An example of a positive reinforcement would be praising a child who used appropriate social skills. The praise was added in the hopes of reinforcing the appropriate social skill behaviors. Negative reinforcement occurs when a stimulus is removed in the hopes of increasing a behavior. Positive punishment occurs when a stimulus is added with the intention of decreasing a behavior. An example of positive punishment would be if a child talks back to their parent, the child must then write an apology note. Negative punishment occurs when a stimulus is removed with the intention of decreasing a behavior. An example of negative punishment is when a child is throwing a tantrum and the parents send the child to their room. In this case, the parents want the tantrum behavior to decrease. In an attempt to reduce the tantrums, the parents have the child removed from the current environment and placed in their room.

Cognitive Behavioral Therapy

CBT is an evidence-based practice with roots in both cognitive and behavioral theories that was developed by Aaron Beck. This is often used in talk therapy interventions. It is popular due to its transferability across settings, populations, and problems. CBT is rooted in the premise that our thoughts, feelings, and behaviors are interconnected (see Figure 9.3). CBT asserts that individuals have control over what thoughts they choose to believe and which, in turn, can shape their outlooks. González-Prendes and Brisebois (2012) find that the intervention of CBT is congruent with social work values:

> CBT does this by promoting self-respect through the development of unconditional self-acceptance; adopting a strength perspective that recognizes clients' abilities to change and the expertise that they have about themselves; promoting a collaborative therapeutic relationship that respects and seeks out clients' input and participation in every step of the process; empowering clients to become active agents in the resolution of their problems; and acknowledging the impact of one's social context on core beliefs and schemas, as well as the oppressive nature of internalized biases and stigmas. (p. 29)

With such good alignment, social workers should, at the very least, be aware of CBT and, when appropriate, consider this intervention with clients. Skill training is a key piece to the

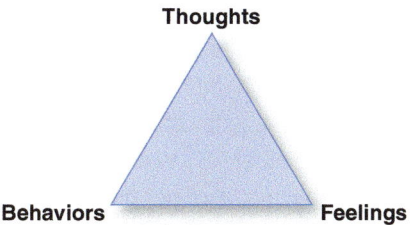

FIGURE 9.3 The cognitive behavioral therapy triangle.

CBT intervention (Fisher & O'Donohue, 2012). In skill training, it is the obligation of the social worker to provide the client with the skills necessary to combat the problem at hand. Case 9.10 illustrates the use of CBT as an intervention.

> ### CASE 9.10 CONNECTING THOUGHTS, BEHAVIORS, AND FEELINGS IN SOCIAL WORK PRACTICE
>
> Giada is a school social worker. She is working with a high school freshman, Karley, who has been experiencing school anxiety. After a thorough assessment, Giada finds that the best method of intervention is CBT. She believes that the student will strongly benefit from recognizing the relationship among thoughts, behaviors, and feelings. In a session, Giada shared with Karley the CBT triangle. She explained the triangle by saying, "Our thoughts, feelings, and behaviors are all interrelated. If we can change our thoughts, we can change what we feel, and in turn change how we behave, or react. Let me give you an example. Imagine you see a couple of friends down the hall and you see them talking to each other. You cannot hear what they are saying, but you see them laugh. What might you think?" Karley thought for a moment, "Well, maybe they are talking about me." Giada then asked, "How would you feel if you thought your friends were talking about you?" "I would be upset," Karley responded quickly. "Okay, if you were upset with your friends, how might you behave or react to them?" Giada asked. Karley thought, "Well, I probably would not even want to talk to them, so I would turn around and walk the other way." Giada then said, "Okay, let's try something different. What if instead of thinking your friends were talking about you, you thought to yourself that they must be laughing because they told a funny joke?" Karley responded, "Well, I would probably be curious about what they are talking about." "And how might that change how you behave?" Giada asked. Karley was quick to say, "I would probably walk up to them and ask what they are talking about."
>
> After discussing the hypothetical situation, Giada felt that Karley had a good understanding of the interrelationship among thoughts, behaviors, and feelings. Giada then began to work with Karley to apply the CBT triangle to her current problem. Giada asked, "So, Karley, what are the thoughts that you usually have about school that upset you?" Karley thought. "Well, I worry about all of the work I am going to have to do throughout the day and worry I might forget something for class, and I worry that I might get bullied. I just worry that it is going to be an awful day." Giada asked, "And how does that make you feel?" "Anxious, worried, upset!" Karley was quick to respond. "And how do you behave as a result?" Giada asked. "Sometimes I avoid school, other times, when I am here I am quieter than usual because I am wrapped up in my thoughts in my head." Giada then encouraged Karley to think about things that could be different if she would change her thoughts. Karley was able to recognize that if she changed her thought to "today is going to be a good day at school," she would probably feel neutral, or maybe even excited. She also realized that if she felt excited to be at school, she would probably want to go to school and be more engaged while there.
>
> Giada was excited to see Karley's insight into the situation. The intervention was not over; they would still have work to do. However, today they made a good first step in addressing the problem at hand. Giada plans to utilize other CBT tools and techniques such as the thought record to help Karley continue to see the impact of her thoughts and encourage her to challenge negative automatic thoughts.

Motivational Interviewing

Motivational interviewing (MI) is a short-term, evidence-based practice. It seeks to build motivation and focus on change-oriented talk to promote change (Dix, 2016). This is a non-confrontational approach to bringing about change with clients. According to Miller and Rollnick (2013):

> Motivational interviewing is a collaborative, goal-oriented style of communication with particular attention to the language of change. It is designed to strengthen personal motivation for and commitment to a specific goal by eliciting and exploring the person's own reasons for change within an atmosphere of acceptance and compassion. (p. 29)

MI is practical in its focus. The strategies are more persuasive than coercive and more supportive than argumentative. The five general principles of MI are:

1. Express empathy through reflective listening.
2. Develop discrepancy between clients' goals or values and their current behavior.
3. Avoid argument and direct confrontation.
4. Adjust to client resistance rather than opposing it directly.
5. Support self-efficacy and optimism. (Miller & Rollnick, 2013, p. 51)

Empathy "is a specifiable and learnable skill for *understanding* another's meaning through the use of reflective listening" (Miller & Rollnick, 1991, p. 20). An empathic style:

- communicates respect for and acceptance of clients and their feelings;
- encourages a nonjudgmental, collaborative relationship;
- allows you to be a supportive and knowledgeable consultant;
- sincerely compliments rather than denigrates;
- listens rather than tells;
- gently persuades, with the understanding that the decision to change is the client's; and
- provides support throughout the recovery process. (Substance Abuse and Mental Health Services Administration [SAMHSA], 1999)

Empathic MI seeks to create a safe and open environment to examine issues and elicit personal reasons for change. A fundamental component of MI is understanding each client's unique perspective, feelings, and values while conveying acceptance, but not necessarily approval or agreement.

Motivation for change is enhanced when clients perceive discrepancies between their current situation and their hopes for the future. The work involves helping clients see how their current behavior differs from their desired behavior. Separate the behavior from the person and help your client explore how important personal goals (e.g., good health, marital happiness, financial success) are being undermined by current behaviors. If the client shows concern about the effects of personal behavior, highlight this concern to heighten the client's perception and acknowledgment of discrepancy (SAMHSA, 1999).

Avoid arguments about your clients' behavior. You may occasionally be tempted to argue with a client. However, trying to convince a client that a problem exists or that change is needed could precipitate even more resistance. When it is the client, not you, who voices arguments for change, progress can be made. The goal is to "walk" with clients (i.e., accompany clients through treatment), not "drag" them along (i.e., direct clients' treatment; SAMHSA, 1999). Accusing clients of being in denial or resistant is more likely to increase their resistance than to instill motivation for change.

Common to MI are scaling questions, including utilizing a readiness ruler. The readiness ruler utilizes a 0-to-10 scale that seeks to have clients rate their motivation to change. When using the ruler in practice, if the patient would select a 6, as the social worker, you would probe the client to determine why they selected a 6 versus a lower or higher number. The rationale for their selection can be helpful in providing you insights into the client's current state. In addition, MI entails asking open-ended questions, listening reflectively, summarizing, affirming, and eliciting self-motivational statements. The goal is to help motivate client change. It is not to create change, but help clients self-identify the need and desire for change.

Rational Emotive Behavioral Therapy

Rational emotive behavioral therapy (REBT), previously referred to as rational therapy, is a short-term intervention approach that emphasizes challenging irrational thoughts by replacing them with more rational or productive thoughts. This intervention was developed by Albert Ellis. This approach draws on a variety of theories including humanistic, cognitive, and behavioral.

The intervention of REBT is viewed to be one of the main pillars of CBT (David et al., 2018). Though there are many similarities between REBT and CBT, there are some distinct differences. REBT places emphasis on unconditional self-acceptance. Clients are encouraged to accept themselves rather than rate themselves in any way. Another distinction is that REBT asserts that some negative emotions are helpful or appropriate. For example, grief would be viewed as an appropriate negative emotion.

There are six principles of REBT. The first principle is that all people have both rational and irrational thoughts. This is human nature. The second principle is that experiences may increase irrational thinking. These experiences may include elements related to family and culture. The third principle is that people think, feel, and behave at the same time, and these functions are interrelated. The fourth principle is that the social worker must at times be critical and provide confrontation to the client in order to address concerns. The fifth principle is that a variety of strategies can be used to promote rational thinking. The final principle is that irrational beliefs cause emotional problems.

Empowerment Therapy

Empowerment therapy is a clinical approach that is closely aligned with social work values. Social workers often seek to empower client systems. Within this approach, social workers engage with clients to increase empowerment. According to Langer and Leitz (2015):

> Empowerment is both a concept and a practice model. Social workers empower individuals to create change on their own behalf, taking personal responsibility for change,

by identifying personal strengths, recognizing and removing structural barriers, or through various other methods, such as advocacy. (p. 168)

When considering the empowerment approach, it is important to consider self-efficacy. Self-efficacy is the belief in one's self to be able to succeed or accomplish a task. Self-efficacy can increase as a result of increased empowerment. Specific techniques to empower a client include honoring the client's position so that the client feels heard, believed, and valued. It is then important for the social worker and client to identify strengths. It is important to then consider power dynamics, including unequal distributions of power that are present in the client's system. The social worker then provides skills, tools, and resources to the client. It is important that this stage occurs through mutual participation. The social worker does not simply pass down this information, but facilitates this learning with the client. During the final phase, the client is able to use the new skills, tools, and resources.

Conflict Theory

As we discussed in Chapter 3, conflict theory seeks to understand the tensions between groups. Key points related to conflict theory are the competition for resources and an unequal treatment or lack of opportunities for one group in comparison to another. Several intervention approaches are derived from this theory.

Feminist Therapy

Feminist therapy involves "a collaborative relationship between social worker and client [which] is critical as there should be a focus on breaking down power differentials and imbalances and fostering positive, healthy relationships" (Teater, 2014, p. 96). Furthermore, goals of feminist therapy often involve addressing symptoms of presenting problems, self-esteem and body image, relationships, diversity, and social action (Teater, 2014).

This approach developed to provide a feminist-informed approach to therapy. Also, it provides a means by which to explore problems from a feminist perspective. This approach acknowledges socialization based on gender as well as issues related to gender inequality or discrimination that may impact the client. This approach can integrate a variety of techniques and clinical practice approaches.

It is important to note that feminist therapy is not only an intervention for women. Men can benefit from feminist therapy as well, as they often "experience negative consequences due to societal expectations of their gender role" (Teater, 2014, p. 96). This approach can also assist men in addressing issues related to gender stereotyping. It can also be helpful to address issues related to intimacy and vulnerability.

Anti-Oppressive Practice

Anti-oppressive practice is a social work intervention approach that seeks to address and end oppressive practices. This intervention approach is closely connected to the social work value of social justice. The approach seeks to reduce inequalities and enhance opportunities. Social workers who engage in anti-oppressive practice can utilize this approach at all levels of practice. Anti-oppressive practice, much like feminist therapy, utilizes a variety of other techniques and intervention strategies to bring about change while considering the role of oppression on the client. Focus within anti-oppressive practice could be related to systemic issues of oppression or issues related to internalized oppression. Individuals and groups who have experienced oppression often feel devalued or marginalized. These concerns often need to be attended to within anti-oppressive practice.

TRANSITIONS AND ENDINGS

There will come a time when our work with a client will transition or end. We, as social workers, must be prepared for this. More importantly, we must make every effort to ensure our clients are prepared for this as well. Change, including transitions and endings, can be difficult. As a result, it is important for social workers to discuss plans for this early on and often with clients. Planning for termination is often called discharge planning. Discharge planning should begin early in treatment, even during the initial meeting whenever possible. Discharge planning will require individualized planning (just like treatment planning). Sometimes discharge planning involves referrals to lower levels of care. In such an event, when other formalized services are still required by the client, the social worker should make every effort to provide continuity of care so that the transition can be as seamless as possible and as supportive as possible of the client.

For many clients who are working with a social worker, it is important to have a positive ending. Unfortunately, they may have had disruptions and negative endings and transitions in the past. It is important that, as the social worker, you provide a positive experience related to an ending.

> ▶ **Reflection Questions**
>
> Consider a transition or ending that you have experienced.
> 1. What things influenced how you felt about the transition or ending?
> 2. What can you take from your experience and apply to future transitions and endings?

POLICY ISSUES

Social workers must be mindful of policy issues in all areas of practice. At the level of assessment, social workers should be aware of potential policy issues that may arise based on the information gained during the assessment process. Social workers hold tightly to the value of self-determination. However, there are times when a social worker must limit a client's right to self-determination in order to protect the client or others from harm.

One such example may be if a client is expressing suicidal ideation with an intent to hurt themself. If a client is a threat to self, social workers must ensure client safety by seeking a higher level of care. After conducting a suicide assessment, if the client is deemed to be a threat to self, the social worker should follow organization and state policies. In the United States, there are policies established by each state regarding specific criteria for voluntary and involuntary mental health commitments. Voluntary commitments refer to when a client is willing to sign themself into the psychiatric facility. Involuntary commitments refer to when a client is refusing to agree to treatment in a psychiatric facility, but due to the imminent danger they pose, a delegate can determine that the client must be committed regardless of their wish not to be.

In addition to policies that relate to commitment for clients likely to commit suicide, many states have policies in place regarding requirements of social workers and other helping professionals to receive continuing education on suicide assessment. In 2012, the state of Washington passed the Matt Adler Suicide Assessment, Treatment, and Management Act (House Bill 2366), the first statewide law to require ongoing suicide training. The bill is named after Matt Adler, who completed suicide in 2011. Matt, a lawyer, was experiencing a great deal of stress in his life. He sought out a counselor; however, when he told the professional that he was thinking about suicide, the professional did not take him seriously and refused to provide further treatment (Volk, 2014). His wife, Jenn, has championed for legislation to address suicide assessment. Since 2012, several other states have adopted policies regarding suicide assessment, many named after Matt Adler, including Pennsylvania, Indiana, Kentucky, California, New Hampshire, Nevada, Tennessee, and West Virginia (Graves et al., 2018).

Sometimes clients can present as a harm to others. When a client expresses a direct threat to harm another person or group of people, social workers and other helping professionals have an obligation or duty to warn the identified victim. Policies surrounding a helping professional's duty to warn are often influenced by the Tarasoff ruling. Tarasoff policies are named after Tatiana "Tanya" Tarasoff, a college student in California who was murdered in 1969 by a fellow student, who had previously stated his desire to kill her in a counseling session (Rothstein, 2014). When assessing the dangerousness of a client and the likelihood of imminent risk to others, social workers must consider a variety of factors including such things as age, gender, intellectual ability, family and community experiences, peer culture, coping patterns, and history of violent acts (Kagle & Kopels, 1994).

From the Tarasoff ruling, social workers and other mental health helping professionals have the obligation to address threats. Tarasoff imposed the following legal duty:

> Warn a person who was the potential targeted victim of a violent act by their patient. The duty to warn ruling triggers action on the part of the health care provider when a patient reveals an intent to inflict physical or bodily harm on an identified victim(s). Once triggered, providers can institute any one or more of the following actions to fulfill the duty: warning the intended target of the threat, alerting law enforcement, or initiating the process of having the patient confined voluntarily or involuntary. (Henderson, 2015, p. 193)

A policy issue related to intervention that requires social work attention relates to insurance coverage and access to services for clients. Unfortunately, at times, decisions related to length of stay in treatment are not made by the frontline clinicians working with the client directly; rather, they are often made by insurance companies and managed care organizations. As a result of this, social workers must be prepared to advocate for clients to receive the level and amount of care that is clinically appropriate for them. Social workers can advocate for specific clients during collaborative contacts with their insurance but also on a larger scale. Social workers are policy advocates. They should be sure to use their policy skills to promote change at the state and federal levels related to insurance coverage language.

SOCIAL JUSTICE ISSUES

When considering social justice issues that relate to assessment, social workers must consider issues related to drug and alcohol use by clients. Since the war on drugs was initiated by President Richard Nixon, there have been massive incarcerations for low-level drug crimes but little progress in reducing the drug epidemic in the United States. It is important to recognize that although drugs are used across racial and ethnic divides, the war on drugs has disproportionately criminalized minority groups (Bowen & Redmond, 2016).

Due to the pervasive nature of drug abuse, it is likely that regardless of the type of practice, social workers will encounter someone directly impacted by drug abuse. Social workers must be aware of current drug trends in their regions and how they can impact their clients. Currently, the opioid epidemic is crippling much of the United States. Though issues related to opioid use are global, the United States has the highest rates of opioid overdoses internationally (Vakharia, 2014). When considering the opioid epidemic, social workers can utilize a systems perspective, as it

> provides an ideal frame through which to view the current opioid overdose crisis because it can help students to view this seemingly individual-level phenomenon as one that is actually dynamically impacting (and impacted by) interpersonal and family systems, health care delivery systems, human service agencies, the criminal justice system, the pharmaceutical industry, local/national drug policy, and local/national public health policy. (Vakharia, 2014, p. 695)

Training to utilize the lifesaving opioid Narcan can be a simple way to address the opioid epidemic while maintaining the dignity and worth of all people, even those currently struggling with addiction. Social workers must champion for policies and procedures that promote the value of life for all people.

SUMMARY

Throughout this chapter, we explored the role of the social worker during the assessment and intervention stages of the helping process. Social workers must employ comprehensive assessment practices to best serve their clients, utilizing ongoing assessment throughout the helping process to adapt to new information. Collaboration between social workers and clients is integral to the assessment process. Effective social work professionals draw on various theoretical approaches and frameworks identified during assessment to tailor interventions to meet client needs. Additionally, we explored the role of social workers during the intervention stages, emphasizing the importance of recognizing clients' stage of change and employing appropriate intervention strategies. The generalist perspective model, along with case management, supportive counseling, and group work, were explored as valuable intervention techniques. Lastly, attention was given to the significance of transitions and endings in the helping relationship, underscoring the importance of preparing and supporting clients throughout all phases of treatment.

CASE SUMMARY UNDOCUMENTED AND HOMELESS

Practice Setting Description

Jackie is a first-year master of social work (MSW) student completing an internship at an inner-city family service agency in the Southwest. The agency is in a section of the city that has a high crime rate, gang activity, and failing schools. The area has a diverse population with many immigrants from Central and South America and a substantial African American population. The agency provides individual and family counseling services on a sliding fee scale. The agency also runs several educational and treatment groups as well as a temporary shelter for women and their children. Jackie has been assigned to work with the women and their children in the shelter. Her primary tasks are to provide concrete services and supportive counseling to the shelter residents.

Background Information

Elicia and her daughter, Maria, are undocumented immigrants from Mexico. They have been in the United States for 5 years. Elicia and Maria fled to the area from another southwestern city to escape her abusive husband approximately 2 months ago. Elicia is 25 years old, and Maria 8 years old. Elicia has a 2-year-old daughter, Sarah, who was placed in foster care because of suspected abuse in the home. Sarah is in a foster home in a small rural community in the state hundreds of miles from Elicia's current residence. Since moving to the area, Maria has not been attending school.

Elicia and Maria are currently residing in the agency's temporary shelter for families. They have been at the shelter for 2 weeks, and the agency has a 90-day limit. Prior to arriving at the shelter, Elicia and Maria were homeless and living on the streets.

Elicia is a high school drop-out and was a stay-at-home mother prior to leaving her husband and moving to a different part of the state. She chose to move there because she has two female cousins living in the area who are also undocumented immigrants. Elicia's native language is Spanish. She speaks some English but is not as comfortable speaking in English. Her English comprehension appears to be good. Maria speaks both English and Spanish well. When communicating with the staff, Maria acts as Elicia's interpreter since none of the staff at the shelter speak Spanish.

Maria appears to be behind academically. She struggles reading simple children's books written in English. It is unknown if her ability to read in Spanish is better than her English reading skills.

Other than her two cousins, Elicia has no other sources of support in the community. Her cousins have young families and limited resources but are well established and connected to a Latino community in the city and the local Catholic church. Her cousins refused to let Elicia and Maria live with them while she was trying to find her own place and a job. They stated that they did not have enough room and are concerned they would get in trouble with their landlord if it was found out that they were letting people stay with them. They sent her to the local church for help, and she was given the address for the agency's shelter by the priest.

Elicia has been looking for housing in the Latino community. The housing market is tight with limited options, and she has been unable to find anything that she could possibly afford. The only affordable housing she found was a room in a rundown motel that rents by the hour or by the month. It is in an area of town known for drug dealing and sex work.

(continued)

CASE SUMMARY UNDOCUMENTED AND HOMELESS (*CONTINUED*)

On arrival in the community, Elicia found occasional work for a house cleaning company. The company hires undocumented workers, pays them very low cash wages, and threatens to turn them in to Immigration and Customs Enforcement (ICE) if they complain. The job bosses also exploit their female workers sexually, threatening to turn them in if they do not comply. Elicia was fearful about applying for other jobs because of her illegal status. She considered turning to sex work to be able to take care of her children, but her Catholic upbringing and thoughts of how this would shame her family have kept her from doing so. She is in constant fear of being detained, separated from Maria, and having her placed in foster care. She is also afraid that she will end up homeless again and forced to live on the streets or return to her abusive husband.

Elicia is extremely reluctant to sign up for any federally funded services, even those that she and her child are entitled to receive. On the suggestion that she enroll for supplemental food through the Supplemental Nutrition Assistance Program (SNAP), Elicia became nervous and refused, as she has heard that participation in SNAP services, and others like them, would draw the attention of ICE, and she had heard stories on the news of individuals being deported after signing up for such programs.

Presenting Problems

Elicia and her child are facing multiple obstacles. They need to find permanent, affordable housing and a job that pays enough to cover her housing and living expenses. In addition, Maria needs to be enrolled in school.

Additionally, Elicia is experiencing an immense amount of stress, anxiety, and possibly post-traumatic stress disorder (PTSD). She described an instance where she could not calm down her breathing and she felt lightheaded. She is very fearful of men and tries to avoid all contact with men in the community. She reports difficulty sleeping at night and feeling exhausted most of the time.

She is concerned about Maria. She has started acting out at the shelter, getting into fights with the other children, disobeying her mother, and being disrespectful and defiant to the staff and other adults. Elicia and Maria fight frequently, and when Elicia tries to discipline Maria, she throws a temper tantrum until Elicia gives up.

Elicia has many strengths. She had the strength to leave her abusive husband and move to a different city. She loves her daughter and wants desperately to keep Maria with her. She is resilient and has managed to survive and keep her daughter safe despite not having a place to stay, a job, and a limited support network. Elicia feels safe in the shelter, but she is very fearful of being caught as an illegal immigrant and is generally mistrustful of helping professionals and persons of authority.

DISCUSSION QUESTIONS

1. Consider Erikson's stages of psychosocial development. At what stages are Elicia and Maria currently? How do their current stage and experiences at past stages influence your approach as a social worker?

2. Consider the stages of change. How would you determine Elicia's and Maria's stages of change?

3. As the social worker, which of the several models that were presented in this chapter would you select for your work with Elicia and Maria? Justify your selection.

4. How would you prepare Elicia and Maria for termination of services?

 A robust set of instructor resources designed to supplement this text is located at http://connect.springerpub.com/content/book/978-0-8261-6683-8. Qualifying instructors may request access by emailing textbook@springerpub.com.

KEY REFERENCES

Only key references appear in the print edition. To access the full reference list, visit www.springerpub.com/courseconnect. See inside front cover and tear-out card for CourseConnect details.

Knight, Z. G. (2017). A proposed model of psychodynamic psychotherapy linked to Erik Erikson's eight stages of psychosocial development. *Clinical Psychology & Psychotherapy*, 24(5), 1047–1058. https://doi.org/10.1002/cpp.2066

Langer, C. L., & Lietz, C. A. (2015). *Applying theory to generalist social work practice*. Wiley.

National Association of Social Workers. (2021). *Code of ethics*. https://www.socialworkers.org/About/Ethics/Code-of-Ethics/Code-of-Ethics-English

Payne, M. (2016). *Modern social work theory* (4th ed.). Oxford University Press.

Teater, B. (2014). *An introduction to applying social work theories and methods* (2nd ed.). McGraw-Hill Education.

10 Generalist Practice With Families: Assessment and Intervention

Maria is a social worker who provides family counseling at the local health center, where she provides support to families in need. The Johnson family was recently referred to her. In their first meeting, Maria introduced herself to the family: parents Carlos and Elena and their children, Maddison and Miguel. By conducting a thorough initial assessment, Maria uncovered some of the challenges the Johnsons faced upon migrating to the United States in search of better opportunities. The family encountered systemic hurdles, including limited access to education and employment.

Maria's approach to assessment was holistic, focusing not only on identifying problems but also on recognizing the family's inherent strengths. She noted the Johnsons' resilience and their willingness to participate in services. Drawing from a strengths-based perspective, Maria collaborated with the family to establish SMART (**S**pecific, **M**easureable, **A**chievable, **R**elevant, **T**ime-bound) goals.

The intervention plan included individual sessions, family therapy, and community outreach. Recognizing the importance of addressing basic, immediate needs, Maria leveraged her connections with local organizations to ensure the Johnson family received essential resources. This included access to food assistance and legal aid. Maria fostered a safe space for open communication, creating an opportunity for the family to come together and discuss concerns and hopes for their future.

LEARNING OBJECTIVES

Social workers possess a unique set of skills and perspectives that make them well equipped to support families through various challenges and transitions. Armed with a comprehensive understanding of the interconnected dynamics within familial systems, social workers can employ a systems perspective lens to navigate the complexities of family life. By using this holistic approach, social workers can effectively identify underlying issues, concerns, and strengths within the family unit. This allows them to be better able to tailor interventions and support strategies that can address the unique needs of each family member while also considering the collective well-being of the family as a whole.

Working within the framework of a family system requires that the social worker not only employ techniques and strategies typically utilized in individual counseling but also manage group dynamics within the familial context. This involves fostering open communication, promoting healthy boundaries, and facilitating constructive problem-solving among family members.

Social workers can play a pivotal role in empowering families to harness their inherent strengths and resources to overcome challenges and achieve their goals. By fostering a collaborative and empowering environment, they help families cultivate resilience and develop sustainable coping mechanisms to navigate life's ups and downs. By the end of this chapter, you will be able to:

- Review theories that inform practice with families.
- Understand how an ecomap can be used to assess client systems.
- Understand how a genogram can be used to assess client family systems.
- Describe how the strengths-based perspective supports social work practice.

COMPETENCY 7: ASSESSMENT WITH INDIVIDUALS, FAMILIES, GROUPS, ORGANIZATIONS, AND COMMUNITIES

Social workers understand that assessment is an ongoing component of the dynamic and interactive process of social work practice. Social workers understand theories of human behavior and person-in-environment, as well as interprofessional conceptual frameworks, and they critically evaluate and apply this knowledge in culturally responsive assessment with clients and constituencies, including individuals, families, groups, organizations, and communities. Assessment involves a collaborative process of defining presenting challenges and identifying strengths with individuals, families, groups, organizations, and communities to develop a mutually agreed-upon plan. Social workers recognize the implications of the larger practice context in the assessment process and use interprofessional collaboration in this process. Social workers are self-reflective and understand how bias, power, privilege, and their personal values and experiences may affect their assessment and decision-making.

Social workers:

- apply theories of human behavior and person-in-environment, as well as other culturally responsive and interprofessional conceptual frameworks, when assessing clients and constituencies; and
- demonstrate respect for client self-determination during the assessment process by collaborating with clients and constituencies in developing a mutually agreed-upon plan. (Council on Social Work Education [CSWE], 2022, pp. 11–12)

COMPETENCY 8: INTERVENE WITH INDIVIDUALS, FAMILIES, GROUPS, ORGANIZATIONS, AND COMMUNITIES

Social workers understand that intervention is an ongoing component of the dynamic and interactive process of social work practice. Social workers understand theories of human behavior, person-in-environment, and other interprofessional conceptual frameworks, and they critically evaluate and apply this knowledge in selecting culturally responsive interventions with clients and constituencies, including individuals, families, groups, organizations, and communities. Social workers understand methods of identifying, analyzing, and implementing evidence-informed interventions and participate in interprofessional collaboration to achieve client and constituency goals. Social workers facilitate effective transitions and endings.

Social workers:

- engage with clients and constituencies to critically choose and implement culturally responsive, evidence-informed interventions to achieve client and constituency goals; and
- incorporate culturally responsive methods to negotiate, mediate, and advocate with and on behalf of clients and constituencies. (CSWE, 2022, p. 12)

NATIONAL ASSOCIATION OF SOCIAL WORKERS *CODE OF ETHICS*

Social work practice with families requires a variety of ethical considerations. These considerations serve to guide the professional conduct of social workers and safeguard the well-being of the individuals and families they serve.

One fundamental ethical principle is confidentiality, which requires social workers to uphold the privacy of family members and maintain the confidentiality of sensitive information shared during sessions. Balancing this commitment to confidentiality with the necessity of sharing information with relevant parties, such as other professionals involved in the family's care, requires careful judgment to ensure that the family's autonomy and dignity are respected while promoting their best interests. When working with families, social workers must be clear during the informed consent process how confidentiality will work in their sessions together.

Closely related to confidentiality is privacy. Social workers honor the privacy of their clients and practice precautions to ensure client privacy and confidentiality are maintained. Social workers cannot share client information without the written permission of the client. Social workers cannot seek information about a client without written permission as well.

Another ethical consideration is the principle of self-determination, which emphasizes the right of individuals and families to make informed decisions about their lives and receive support that aligns with their values and preferences. Social workers strive to promote client involvement in all aspects of treatment. However, at times, social workers must limit or restrict clients' right to self-determination when clients put themselves or others at risk. Social workers should actively involve families in the decision-making process, providing them with accurate information, exploring alternative options, and respecting their right to choose their preferred course of action. This requires a collaborative and empowering approach that honors the agency of each family member while recognizing the interconnectedness of their decisions and actions within the family system. Social workers can serve as a mediator when individuals in the family are not in consensus regarding their goals or desired outcomes. It is important that the social worker holds space for all members of the family and avoids negative triangulation (taking sides).

Cultural competence is also vital in social work practice with families. It requires an understanding and appreciation of the diverse cultural backgrounds, beliefs, and practices that shape individuals' and families' experiences. Social workers must actively engage in ongoing learning and reflection to enhance their cultural competence and ensure that their interventions are respectful, inclusive, and responsive to the unique needs and perspectives of the families they serve. This may involve collaborating with cultural brokers, seeking consultation

> **Reflection Questions**
>
> 1. What are some of your personal beliefs and biases about family?
> 2. How can you manage these to not let them negatively impact your work with clients?

from experts, or engaging in community-based initiatives to promote cultural humility and sensitivity. Social workers should be aware of their own cultural experiences and beliefs and biases related to families. It is important that social workers remember that families can look very different, and each family has their own sets of rules, roles, and beliefs. Social workers must navigate the complex dynamics of power and privilege inherent in family systems, recognizing their own positionality and privilege relative to the families they work with. This requires a commitment to social justice and equity, advocating for the rights and interests of marginalized and oppressed families, and challenging systemic barriers that perpetuate inequality and injustice. Social workers must also be vigilant to avoid imposing their own values, beliefs, or biases on families, fostering an environment of openness, respect, and empathy that encourages honest dialogue and mutual understanding. If a social worker finds themselves working with a family that has a different value system than they personally do, they must be aware not to force their own beliefs onto the client.

PRACTICE WITH FAMILIES

Working with families can be a rich and rewarding experience for social workers. Working with families can also be challenging. A social worker must make special considerations when working with a family and recognize and respect the complex dynamics often present in families. Every family is different, and social workers must take heed to ensure that they are not projecting their own family beliefs onto the client. Unlike working with individuals, social workers supporting families must navigate complex family dynamics, including communication patterns, power structures, and intergenerational conflicts. Understanding these dynamics is essential for effective intervention and fostering positive change within the family unit.

Additionally, when working with a family, the social worker will be working with multiple individuals and holding space for them at one time in a session. It can be a delicate balancing act to maintain a safe and supportive environment where all family members feel free to discuss their concerns and aspirations with one another. Family therapy, though similar to group therapy, is different in the sense that in family therapy, the focus is often on addressing systemic issues that impact the family's functioning. When working with individuals, the focus is primarily on the client's perspective and needs. However, in family work, social workers must consider the perspectives and needs of multiple family members. Each family member may have different experiences, priorities, and goals, requiring the social worker to engage in multifaceted assessment and intervention strategies. Family work requires facilitating communication and collaboration among family members. This approach fosters mutual understanding, strengthens family bonds, and can often empower families to work together toward positive outcomes.

Social workers supporting families often adopt a systems perspective, recognizing that individual behaviors and challenges are influenced by larger systemic factors such as socioeconomic status, cultural norms, and community resources. This view allows social workers to identify systemic barriers impacting the family's well-being and advocate for systemic changes (internally and externally) to promote positive outcomes. Social workers may employ a range of interventions, including (but not limited to) family therapy, psychoeducation, resource linkage, and advocacy, to address the diverse needs of families.

SYSTEMS THEORY

A system is a set of things that work together. Systems theory seeks to understand the interactions of people and the systems in their lives. Systems often exist in order to achieve a mutual purpose; common systems that social workers engage with are families, communities, and organizations (Langer & Lietz, 2015). When considering systems theory, there are several key concepts to understanding the relationship of systems.

Homeostasis is a systems concept that refers to the desire to avoid change. Humans desire homeostasis. Homeostasis is a state of normal order or being. Homeostasis is not equivalent to optimal functioning, but rather the typical or common state of functioning that a system is accustomed to. Inputs and outputs influence the system and impact homeostasis. Inputs and outputs occur via a feedback loop where energy is brought in and taken away from the system. Equifinality is a systems concept that suggests that there are multiple ways to achieve or reach a desired outcome. Multifinality asserts that multiple outcomes can be reached via the same paths.

Systems theory can be useful for social workers who are engaging in assessment. If you consider this theory while examining the interrelated workings of various parts during the assessment, you can explore not only how each part is functioning independently but also how they are functioning or working together. This is a practical approach to assessment. Though independently one aspect of an individual's life may not be of concern, when you consider it in combination with or in relation to the other parts present, there may indeed be room for growth and remediation.

FAMILY SYSTEMS THEORY

Families are a special type of system or group. The work of Bowen on family systems was based on the work of systems theorists (Langer & Lietz, 2015). Families have long been studied by social workers and other helping professionals. Understanding the family unit is important. Social workers recognize that all human relationships, including families, are important. Regardless of family composition (nuclear, blended, multigenerational, etc.), it is important to appreciate that every family is unique. In order to best understand the family of a client, it is best to ask the client to describe their family. Assumptions based on personal experiences of families should be avoided, as they may bias your work with client systems.

Bowen set forth a specific family theory to assist helping professionals in better understanding family systems. Bowen's work observing and working with families allowed him to set forth that families had predictable patterns of interactions. This organized, predictable pattern of interaction is a family's homeostasis. His view of families was that they are an "emotional unit that governs the biology and behavior of each member. Everyone plays a part when symptoms occur for any family member. Any symptom is a function of common factors" (Harrison, 2018, p. 167). Bowen also set forth other concepts such as differentiation of self and triangles that assist in assessing and understanding families better.

Differentiation of self refers to the need or desires of each person to be an individual as well as a part of the family group. Differentiation explores how close and separate members of a family system are to one another. Humans experience two drives, or needs, for closeness and connection and another for individualization, and the concept of differentiation from one's family illustrates these two drives (Frederick et al., 2016). Differentiation and the development of one's self outside of the family are healthy pieces of development; however, differentiation may occur abruptly or not at all, which can lead to areas of concern. In order to assess the degree to which people have differentiation themselves, the Differentiation of Self Scale provides a metric that ranges from 0 to 100, where higher scores represent a higher level of "solid self" and low scores represent a "pseudo self" (MacKay, 2017). This scale can be a helpful assessment tool for social workers when assessing individuals and families.

Just as a triangle has three sides, triangles within families are dynamic relationships among three persons where there is tension. At times there are "insiders" and at other times there are "outsiders" when considering triangulation within family systems. Sometimes these present via alliances, which are overt relationships within the family, or as collations, which are covert relationships within the family. Case 10.1 illustrates a family triangle that is problematic and impeding optimal functioning in a multigenerational family system. Triangles and triangulation are not unique to family systems but can occur in a variety of other group contexts as well, as it is often common for individuals who are experiencing conflict to seek out the support of a third party (Crabtree-Nelson & Kohli, 2017).

CASE 10.1 ADDRESSING FAMILY TRIANGLES IN SOCIAL WORK PRACTICE

Quinn is a social worker who works as an in-home family therapist. Quinn received a referral for a new client, Amy, a 10-year-old female who lives with her mother, Sheri, and grandmother, Elizabeth. Amy has been acting out at school and is in danger of expulsion. At home, she fights with her mother verbally and has threatened to hit her. Quinn sets up a time to visit the home and meet with Sheri while Amy is at school.

At the house during the intake, Quinn meets both Sheri and Elizabeth. Quinn notices that Sheri seems quite distraught with Amy's current behaviors and at her wit's end, not sure what to do next. She also notices that Elizabeth seems to minimize Amy's behaviors and at times even blames Sheri for inconsistent parenting that causes the problems in the home. Quinn completed all of the required paperwork and reviewed policies and procedures for the services she would be able to provide, including confidentiality and informed consent. Quinn set up her next appointment with the family for the following day in the evening when she could meet Amy.

When Quinn got back to the office after the first visit, she completed all of her paperwork and created the following genogram based on the information she had collected thus far. She gathered some materials that she would take out to the home during her next visit with the family as well.

(continued)

10: Generalist Practice With Families: Assessment and Intervention

CASE 10.1 ADDRESSING FAMILY TRIANGLES IN SOCIAL WORK PRACTICE (*CONTINUED*)

The next day, Quinn returned to the family home for her first visit with Amy. Amy was reluctant to meet with Quinn. Sheri told Amy that Quinn was there to help the family and to help Amy stay in her school, which is something she wants. Amy was still hesitant to engage with Quinn. Then her grandmother jumped in and said, "Come on baby, come and sit with me, we can talk to this nice lady." Quinn noticed that Amy responded much more favorably to her grandmother, even cuddling up next to her on the couch. Grandma then continued, "Go ahead, tell her about what a good softball player you are. You are my shining star." Amy's face lit up. Quinn could obviously see that Amy and her grandmother had an especially close relationship.

As the session progressed, Quinn noticed how though Amy and her grandmother were quite close, Sheri seemed to not be close with either of them. It appeared she was left out of many of the special things that Amy and her grandmother shared. Actually, though Sheri would try to engage with them, either Elizabeth or Amy would often dismiss Sheri and return to only interacting with each other.

As Quinn continued to assess while working with the family, she began to notice patterns of interaction and was better able to understand the triangulation occurring in the home between Amy and her grandmother that left Sheri, as the mother, out of the loop. Because she felt like an outsider, Sheri was often in conflict with her mother and with her daughter. Quinn was able to depict the family's pattern of interaction using the following triangle. During a session with Sheri and Elizabeth, Quinn shared about how the concept of triangulation can impact families and provided examples of how it can hinder family functioning. Quinn asked the family to depict how they felt their family functioned in relationship to triangulation. Sheri was able to express to her mother how she often feels like an outsider and how that is difficult for her. Elizabeth was receptive to what Sheri was saying. Quinn was able to then teach Sheri and Elizabeth some strategies that could assist them in coparenting Amy and ways to avoid the conflicts of triangulation in the future.

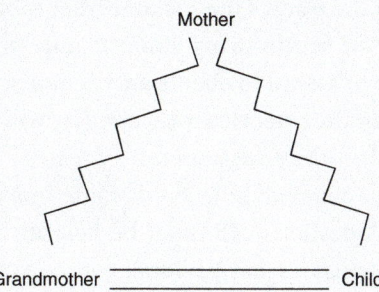

FAMILY ASSESSMENT

The assessment process is a key phase in the helping relationship. Assessment involves gathering information necessary to provide services to the client. As a result, assessment serves as a foundation for the future step of intervening with client systems. Formal assessments typically begin during the initial meeting with clients and occur concurrently while engaging with clients. Most formal assessments are completed in the first few initial meetings. It is important to address assessment early in the helping process since it does serve to inform future work with clients.

It is important to distinguish between assessment and diagnosis. These terms are different, though at times, some attempt to use them interchangeably. Diagnosis is the process of identifying the appropriate condition that represents the presenting symptoms and concerns. Many social workers do in fact participate in the diagnosis process. Social workers, more than all other types of helping professionals combined, provide the majority of mental health services in the United States (Dziegielewski, 2015). In order to provide mental health services, a *Diagnostic and Statistical Manual of Mental Disorders* (5th ed.; *DSM-5-TR*; American Psychiatric Association, 2022) diagnosis is often required in order to meet eligibility requirements or to seek reimbursement for services from insurance companies. In order to provide an accurate and appropriate diagnosis, social workers must conduct a thorough and comprehensive assessment. So, in fact, all social workers who diagnose do conduct assessments. However, not all social workers who complete assessments diagnose clients.

Social workers should be mindful of the scope of information needed and should limit their assessment to such material. Just because you can ask a question does not mean you should. Social workers should avoid being overly instructive solely for the sake of curiosity or interest. Rather, social workers should only seek out information that informs the helping relationship and assist the client in addressing treatment goals.

The assessment process depends on the type of services the social worker is providing. Furthermore, organizational policies will often guide the assessment process. In addition to those factors, the expectations of the clients should also be considered when conducting an assessment. Additionally, other priorities to include in the assessment process are such things as identifying the client perception of the problem/concern, any legal mandates that may direct treatment, and specific health and safety concerns (Hepworth et al., 2017).

Use of Self

All professions have tools of the trade. One social worker tool is the self. Social workers must be able to effectively use their self to bring about change throughout the helping process. Social workers must be able to attend to clients and demonstrate good verbal and nonverbal communication skills during the interview process that will promote the client sharing the information needed to conduct the assessment.

The social worker must be aware of how to ask sometimes difficult or personal questions. Preparing a client for such questions can often be helpful. Simply acknowledging that the questions you are able to ask may seem personal can be enough to provide ease in such a situation. Also, asking the client if you may ask about such things promotes the client's role in the assessment process and honors their right to determine what information they would like to share with you.

Affective Reactions

When conducting an assessment, paying attention to affective responses can be useful. Social workers should be aware of not only what the client is saying but also how they are saying it, as well as what they are not saying. That may sound like a lot to pay attention to during the assessment, and it is, but as a developing social worker, you will have the opportunity to practice these skills in order to be able to be fully attuned to clients.

At times, clients will be sharing information verbally and their affect will be incongruent with what they have said. For example, if a client says that they are "fine" but you see that they are teary-eyed and has a flat affect, this would be an example of incongruence. Social workers can use a clarification response to address such incongruence to seek further clarification. The social worker may say, "You say that you are fine, but I noticed that you are teary-eyed. Can you tell me more about that?" It may be that the person is indeed fine and just suffering from allergies that have their eyes watering. Or it may be a sign of something else. Social workers are not tasked to be mind readers and are encouraged to seek clarification from clients when it is needed.

Value Conflicts

Values are important within professional social work practice. Social workers must be aware of personal and professional values and recognize when value conflicts arise. During the assessment process, social workers seek to better understand the values of the client. It is important to recognize what is important for the client. As we have stated, it is critical that social workers start where the client is, and with assessment, it is no different. In order to be able to start where the client is, social workers must know what clients value. Social workers should directly ask clients what they value and what is important for them. Social workers recognize that successful treatment may look different for different clients and respect the rights of clients to determine their own definition of success whenever possible.

Once social workers are aware of what the client values, then they are better positioned to identify potential value conflicts when they arise. Social workers can use the skill of confrontation to address any potential value conflicts that they have identified with clients. Sometimes clients do not recognize when there is a conflict between their stated values and current actions, so a social worker illuminating this can be a useful tool in the helping process. A sample confrontation response related to a value conflict could be, "You have shared that it is important for you to earn your GED. However, you haven't been attending the necessary classes that are required to take the exam." You will notice in the sample response there are two parts. First, the social worker states the value the client shared. In the second part of the statement, the social worker identifies the contradictory actions that are in conflict with the value in the first part of the response.

Person-in-Environment Perspective in Assessment

As we have discussed throughout this text, people are complex. It is impossible to understand people fully without considering the full context of their lives, including the environments in which they exist. The person-in-environment perspective explores all systems or environments in which a person exists. Social workers should also explore the physical environment in which a person resides.

When assessing the person and their environments, the social worker must first be aware of all of the environments within which the person exists. This requires a good, comprehensive, ongoing assessment. Social workers must be thorough during the assessment process and ask follow-up questions for clarification whenever necessary. Social workers must use good interviewing skills as well as good nonverbal communication strategies to engage clients so that they can share the information that is necessary for social workers to conduct a thorough assessment.

Strengths-Based Assessment

Social workers are trained to identify strengths. Social workers understand that though problems and concerns may exist, so do strengths. Sometimes clients are able to identify their own strengths; other times, the social worker must assist clients in viewing their own strengths. At times, society operates from more of a deficit-based perspective. In order to receive many social services, individuals must be able to identify problems, issues, or needs. Rarely are people called to identify personal strengths. Since this is not the customary approach or orientation of all social services, social workers must be sure to assist clients in recognizing and honoring personal strengths, as this can be a source of empowerment. Danzer (2012) sets forth that the goal of strengths-based social work practice is to help clients "explore and re-claim their natural talents and abilities, cultural, creative, and spiritual practices," adding that these internal resources have allowed clients to "survive a lifetime of stress and oppression and can be mobilized to facilitate positive coping in the present" (p. 10).

During the assessment process, social workers should directly address and assess client strengths. Sometimes social workers must reframe client conditions as strengths; for example, if a client believes that they are unable to do so. Social workers should recognize that it can at times be very difficult for clients to engage in treatment, so by the very nature that they are working with you, the clients have demonstrated a commitment to addressing the concern that brought them to you. Case 10.2 illustrates a strengths-based approach to client assessment.

Strengths Perspective Principles

A strengths-based approach may seem to be an obvious hallmark of the social work profession, as social workers often explore strengths, resources, and talents available at micro, mezzo, and macro levels of the client's environment. In order to better understand the strengths-based perspective as it relates to assessment, it is helpful to consider the six strengths perspective principles. These principles set forth by Saleebey (2013) assist social workers in incorporating strengths-based approaches in all areas of the helping process. Box 10.1 lists the six principles.

CASE 10.2 THE SOCIAL WORKER'S ROLE IN HELPING CLIENTS FIND THEIR STRENGTHS

Nadine is seeking the support of a clinical social worker to address her current stress levels. Nadine is married to John. Nadine and John met while both were attending Narcotics Anonymous (NA) meetings. They found that they were able to be supportive to each other as they were both in the early stages of recovery. John had a history of using cocaine, and Nadine a history of using opioids.

Two years ago, Nadine and John experienced a second-trimester miscarriage. Nadine recalls that was a very difficult time for her because not only did she suffer the miscarriage but only 1 month earlier her father had passed away suddenly. As a result of all of the stress, Nadine relapsed after 15 months clean. Nadine blamed herself for the miscarriage, thinking that her past drug use may have been the reason she lost the baby. After going to treatment for her drug use again, Nadine has been clean for about 11 months.

Two months ago, Nadine and John had a son, Leo. Leo was born 6 weeks early, so he had to spend time in the neonatal intensive care unit (NICU) at the hospital. Nadine did not want to leave Leo's side, so she stayed in the hospital room with him during his stay. Again, Nadine began blaming herself for the baby being born early. Though she did not use during her pregnancy, she feared that her past use was at fault. Nadine felt immense guilt.

Since Leo's release from the hospital, Nadine has been staying home with him while John has returned to work. John works as a truck driver and has not been home much since Leo's birth because he is trying to earn as much overtime as possible to pay for the medical bills from the birth and NICU stay.

Nadine's mother, Bev, has offered to help Nadine and John out financially, but John is reluctant to accept the help. John says, "family shouldn't borrow money from family." Nadine's younger sister, Susan, has offered to help by babysitting, but Nadine worries at the thought of leaving Leo. Also, Nadine does not really have anywhere to go if she did leave the house. Part of her recovery was to change the people she used to hang out with and the places she used to go in order to avoid a relapse. Nadine knows she is safest when she is home with baby Leo.

Nadine had been close to her mother-in-law, but since she passed away the previous year, she has not had much contact with her father-in-law or John's older brother or sister. Nadine feels overwhelmed managing her household and new baby all by herself. At the same time, she is having a hard time accepting support from others. Nadine thinks that a social worker may be able to help give her some perspective. She had always enjoyed working with the counselors at the drug and alcohol facility, so she thought she would look into talking to someone.

During the initial meeting with Nadine, the social worker asked about her strengths. Nadine was not sure how to answer that question. She had never really thought about that before. Nadine still viewed herself as an addict and did not really have anything positive to say about herself. The social worker talked with Nadine and began offering possible strengths, such as she is a good mother, as evidenced by how she makes sure Leo is always fed and changed when he cries. After hearing it from the social worker, Nadine nodded in agreement. The social worker added, "I think it is a strength that you knew you needed someone to talk to and reached out to make your appointment here today." Nadine had not thought of it that way, "I guess I do have some strengths." After the start from the social worker, Nadine was able to identify other strengths, including her supportive family and commitment to her recovery.

> **BOX 10.1**
>
> **STRENGTHS-PERSPECTIVE PRINCIPLES IN SOCIAL WORK PRACTICE**
>
> *Principle 1:* Every individual, group, family, and community has strengths.
>
> *Principle 2:* Trauma, abuse, illness, and struggle may be injurious, but they may also be sources of challenge and opportunity.
>
> *Principle 3:* Assume that you do not know the upper limits of the capacity to grow and change, and take individual, group, and community aspirations seriously.
>
> *Principle 4:* We best serve clients by collaborating with them.
>
> *Principle 5:* Every environment is full of resources.
>
> *Principle 6:* Caring, caretaking, and context are important.
>
> *Source:* Data from Saleebey, D. (2013). *The strengths-perspective in social work practice* (6th ed.). Pearson.

> ▶ **Reflection Question**
>
> Why do you think it is important for social workers to use a strengths-based perspective in their practice?

At the heart of these principles is the inherent belief that strengths exist within every individual, every group, every family, and every community. Despite what may appear as adversity, resilience exists. Further, the capacity for resilience is limitless, and social workers must allow clients to identify their own hopes, goals, and desires for their future during the helping process.

Strengths and Obstacles Worksheet

At times, it can be helpful to have a resource or tool to support you in identifying strengths across various domains. One such tool is the strengths and obstacles worksheet that is illustrated in Exhibit 10.1. When possible, the client should complete this worksheet and it should be reviewed by the social worker. This worksheet can serve to inform the assessment process by attempting to provide a comprehensive look at what may hinder or promote client success and progress during the helping process.

Ecomaps

Ecomaps are visual representations of the systems present in a client's environment. Ecomaps assist in gathering information and assessing the relationship between clients and other systems present in their lives. Social workers can use an ecomap to measure progress or change over time with clients when conducting ongoing assessment.

Ecomaps should be individualized to address the unique experiences of the client. Based on this, ecomaps may need to contain various domains that are pertinent to the life of the client. For example, if a client is in college, higher education would be included on the ecomap, whereas if a client has no involvement or engagement with formalized education systems, then education would not need to be listed as a domain. Domains that are often included on ecomaps include family, community, employer, education and training, friends, formal services, providers, and social welfare. Ecomaps are often depicted using

Exhibit 10.1 Individual and Family Strengths and Obstacles Worksheet

Client: _____ **Worker:** _____ **Date:** _____

Instructions: Briefly describe to the best of your knowledge as many items on the worksheet as possible. Base your assessment on information you have obtained directly from your client and that obtained indirectly through your observations, case records, contacts with collaterals, and any other sources of information. The first page focuses on a description of the client's concerns/problem situation. The remaining pages comprise an assessment of personal, family, and environmental factors. For each relevant factor, describe potential obstacles, strengths, and their impact on the problem situation.

Concerns/Problem Situation

Briefly summarize client concerns and/or problems that the client wants to address.

List concerns or problems in order of priority from the highest to the lowest.

Individual Factors			
Subsystem	**Obstacles**	**Strengths**	**Impact Problem**
Motivation and commitment			
Coping and resourcefulness			
Values and beliefs			
Developmental life stage			
Mental health status			
Health status			
Employment/economic status			
Interpersonal relationships			
Family Factors			
Subsystem	**Obstacles**	**Strengths**	**Impact Problem**
Family structure			
Power and authority			
Family life cycle stage			
Family values and beliefs			
Family rules and myths			
Emotional climate			
Communication patterns			
Boundaries			

(continued)

Exhibit 10.1 Individual and Family Strengths and Obstacles Worksheet (*continued*)

Environmental Factors			
Subsystem	**Obstacles**	**Strengths**	**Impact Problem**
Work/school			
Clubs, churches, and associations			
Community/neighborhood			
Service organizations			
Other factors and considerations			

Source: From Poulin, J., Matis, S., & Witt, H. (2024). *The social work field placement: A competency-based approach* (2nd ed.). Springer Publishing Company.

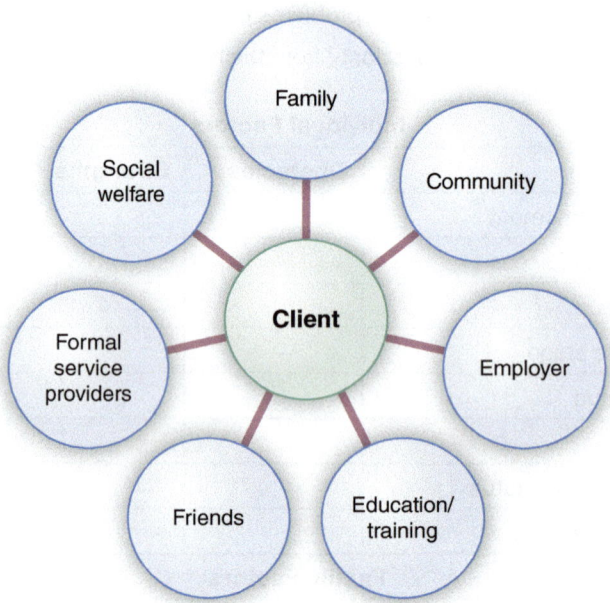

FIGURE 10.1 Sample ecomap domains present in the client's environment.

circles. At the center of the ecomap is the client. Radiating around the client are circles that include the various applicable domains (see Figure 10.1 for a sample image of an ecomap).

When conducting assessments, social workers should be comprehensive in exploring the various domains that are influencing the client. We suggested several domains to explore when creating an ecomap. First, when considering the domain of family, social workers should consider immediate and extended familial relationships. Families are complex systems; social workers are aware of this and must assess them as such. Social workers should not make assumptions about relationships, but rather gather information throughout the assessment process. Regardless of the nature of the relationships, whether it be positive, neutral, or negative, social workers can use this information to inform their work with clients, and it provides insights into the clients' current environments.

> ▶ **Reflection Question**
>
> Consider your life and the environments in which you engage. Create an ecomap that represents you currently.

When considering community, social workers should explore various communities and cultural experiences that the client engages in. Community can include the physical community in which clients reside but may also include ethnic, racial, religious, or social communities. For example, belonging to a religious organization or church community should be depicted on a client ecomap. Other types of community may include groups where a client feels a sense of belonging.

Domains related to employment, education, and training are also important to explore when constructing an ecomap. Even if a client is currently unemployed but hoping to obtain employment, this domain can be depicted on the ecomap, noting the current strain. In the event that the domain is not applicable, meaning it is not present or sought after in the client's life, it is not necessary to include that domain on the ecomap.

As we have discussed, relationships are important. Social workers should consider friendships and other informal supports available to clients. Informal supports may include friends, neighbors, work colleagues, or school peers. In addition to informal supports, social workers should assess for formal service providers such as social workers, medical professionals, caseworkers, or other professionals who are providing a service of some sort in the life of the client. Closely related to formal providers is the domain of social welfare. Sometimes there are professionals related to social welfare present in the client's life. Other social welfare considerations may include medical assistance or supplemental nutrition assistance programs.

Ecomaps not only include the domains applicable to the client but also represent the type or quality of relationship present between the client and each domain. Ecomaps can visually depict relationships that are positive, neutral, negative, and even cut off. As with any type of map, it is important to include a key with your ecomap to represent interactions. This is important, as there are various methods to illustrate the quality of relationships. This ensures that the ecomap is as clear as possible in order to avoid misinterpretation. Figure 10.2 illustrates common symbols to denote the type or quality of relationship present between clients and their various domains.

When considering a family systems intervention, social workers should consider how systems are influencing the family. It is important to consider how systems influence the family as a whole and how they influence members of the family individually as well. Completing an ecomap with each member of the family can be a strategy to identify such systems. Creating a family ecomap follows the same process as you would when creating an individual ecomap.

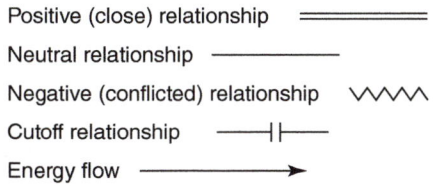

FIGURE 10.2 Ecomap interactional symbols.

However, instead of having the individual client at the center, you would include the identified family members. Figure 10.3 shows a sample family ecomap. When constructing a family ecomap, you can indicate both relationships between outside systems and individuals within the family and the relationship between outside systems and the family as a whole system.

Genograms

A genogram is a visual representation of a client's family system. In some ways, genograms are like a family tree, but they are able to represent so much more. Genograms are great assessment tools that assist in building rapport and joining with clients. Genograms are also a practical tool that can be used to keep track of family systems and patterns of interactions. There is the old adage that a picture is worth a thousand words. A genogram is a picture that represents family systems that, at times, can be quite complex. See Case 10.3 for a discussion of multiple families within one family.

Within a genogram, people are represented by shapes. Typically squares represent males and circles represent females. When considering individuals who identify as a gender other than that assigned to them at birth, you can represent that within the genogram by having their identified gender as the outer shape. For individuals who identify as nonbinary, a diamond can be used. To represent the identified client, you will double their symbol (e.g., include a square with a square around it). When creating a genogram,

> ▶ **Reflection Question**
>
> Consider your family. Create a genogram to represent you.

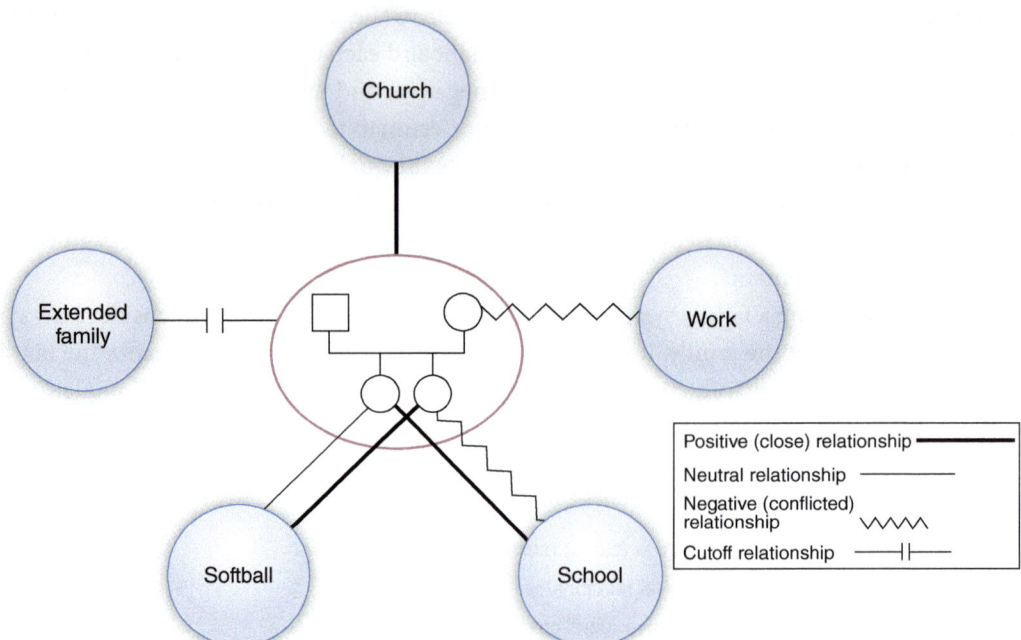

FIGURE 10.3 Family ecomap: Diagram illustrating the relationship between the family and outside systems.

CASE 10.3 MULTIPLE FAMILIES IN ONE FAMILY

Katie is a 16-year-old female who resides with her father Howard, paternal grandmother Gloria, her older sister Kelly, and Kelly's paramour Greg. Also residing in the home with Katie is her 3-month-old daughter Ashley. Howard separated from Katie's mother, Mary Ann, when Katie was only 4 years old. During that same year, Katie's paternal grandfather passed away and a paternal aunt with whom Katie was close moved to another state. Howard recognizes that at that time, Katie became much more introverted and, as he describes, "clingy."

Throughout her youth, Katie has participated in community activities such as softball and soccer. She reports having very few close friends even though she was actively involved in social activities. The family denies any current affiliation with a religious organization or church, though on several occasions Katie has attended teen nights at a local Baptist church, which she reports enjoying.

Two years ago, Katie met Roger at school. Shortly after the couple began dating, Katie became pregnant. Katie decided she wanted to keep the baby and raise it on her own with Roger's help. Roger has a history of mental health issues and aggressive behaviors. Roger has abused Katie in several domestic violence instances, including hitting Katie with a fan on her stomach, which induced labor. Since baby Ashley's birth, Roger has continued his domestic violence tendencies and has sprained Katie's wrist during an argument.

Howard is seeking help for his daughter. Katie agrees that she needs help managing her depression and admits having someone to talk to would be helpful. During the first meeting, the social worker began the assessment process.

Consider that you are the social worker in this case:

- How can you implement the strengths perspective principles in your work with this client system?
- What systems would you include in the ecomap for this client system?
- Create a genogram for this family.

---

relationships are evidenced by horizontal lines, and children are evidenced by vertical lines that are drawn off relationship lines. Figure 10.4 illustrates common genogram symbols.

When constructing a genogram, there are general rules that should be followed. For example, when drawing a relationship, men are typically on the left and women are typically on the right. Children should be ordered from oldest to youngest from left to right. Similarly, relationships should be shown from first to the most recent, again from left to right. Deceased family members should be included in genograms. To indicate that a person is deceased, an "X" can be drawn over their shape. Clients are identified on the genogram by doubling their gender symbol. After adding all of the individuals to a genogram, use a circle to identify who resides in the home together. See Figure 10.5 for an example of a genogram and Box 10.2 for a report of what the genogram depicts.

304 Generalist Social Work Practice

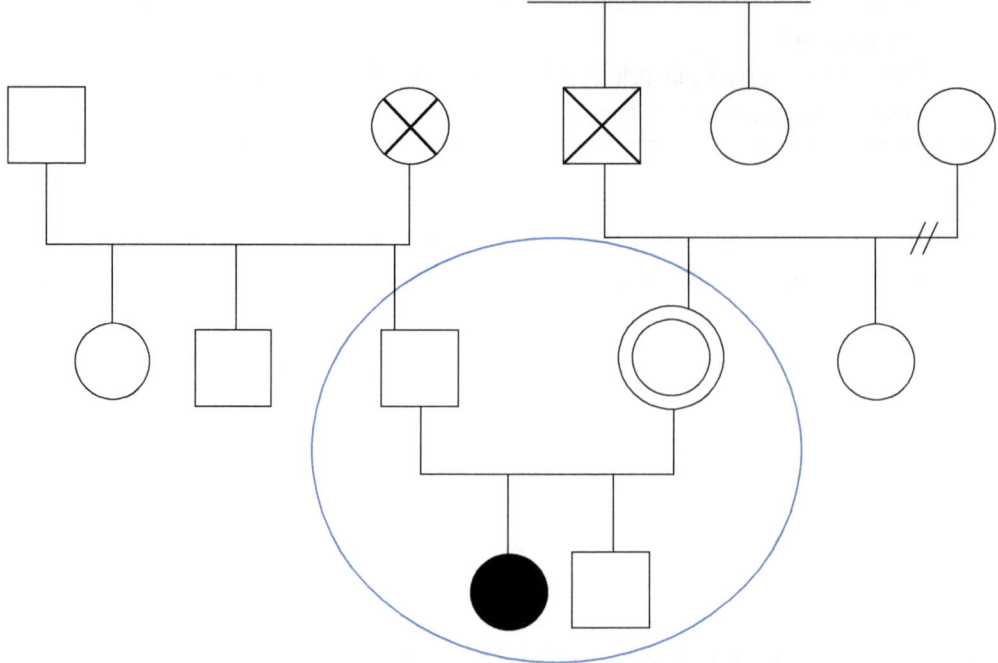

FIGURE 10.4 Common genogram symbols.

FIGURE 10.5 Sample genogram of a client's family system.

BOX 10.2

THE STORY FIGURE 10.5 TELLS

Before reading on, review the genogram in Figure 10.5. What can you learn about this family from the genogram provided? The following is some information about the family based on that genogram:

- The identified client is a female.
- The client lives with her husband and son.
- The client had a miscarriage prior to having her son.
- The client's parents are divorced.
- The client's father was remarried.
- The client's father is deceased.
- The client has a younger sister.
- The client has a sister-in-law and brother-in-law (both are older than her husband).
- The client's mother-in-law is deceased.

FAMILY INTERVENTIONS

Social workers recognize that working with families is important. Working with families can be challenging, but it can also be quite rewarding. There are several different clinical approaches to supporting families that we will cover. Regardless of the approach, social workers must recognize that families are complex groups. Social workers must also understand that all families have strengths. The strengths perspective can, and should, be applied to family systems. While working with families, social workers should consider who within the family system should be participating in treatment. Furthermore, it is important to recognize that it may not always be appropriate to have all members of the family present at all times. For example, there may be times when it would be inappropriate to have the children present during some conversations between the parents and the social worker. Social workers must utilize their professional judgment in regard to such decisions.

Family Systems Therapy

Family systems therapy is an intervention approach that involves the whole family to address problems within the family system. This approach was developed by psychiatrist Murray Bowen and is sometimes called Bowenian therapy. This approach relies on the premise of interconnection from systems theory. Based on this, the approach puts forth that a change in one family member will impact everyone in the family (see Table 10.1).

Functional Family Therapy

Functional family therapy (FFT) is a short-term treatment model designed to support families with children who are identified as at-risk. FFT combined both systems theory and cognitive behavioral theory to create this intervention approach (Robbins et al., 2016).

TABLE 10.1 KEY FAMILY SYSTEMS CONCEPTS

Family as a system	Central to family systems therapy is the concept of the family as a dynamic and interconnected system. Rather than focusing solely on individual members, this approach views the family as a complex network of relationships, roles, and interactions that influence each member's thoughts, feelings, and behaviors.
Interconnectedness and interdependence	Family systems therapy emphasizes the interconnectedness and interdependence of family members. Actions and behaviors of one member can impact and be influenced by other members, creating patterns of interaction that shape the overall functioning of the family system.
Differentiation of self	Differentiation refers to the ability of individuals to maintain a sense of self while remaining emotionally connected to others. Family systems therapy seeks to help individuals and families develop greater differentiation, allowing them to navigate relationships and manage emotions more effectively.
Triangles and triangulation	Triangles represent the basic building blocks of family systems, involving three individuals or relationships. Triangulation occurs when tension or conflict between two individuals is relieved by involving a third person or issue. Family systems therapy aims to help families recognize and address triangulation patterns to promote healthier communication and boundaries.
Emotional fusion	Emotional fusion refers to a lack of emotional differentiation within a family, where boundaries between individual emotions become blurred. Family systems therapy seeks to help individuals achieve a balance between emotional connection and autonomy.
Emotional cutoff	Emotional cutoff occurs when individuals distance themselves from their families of origin to manage intense emotions or conflicts.
Multigenerational transmission process	This concept explores how patterns of behavior, communication, and emotional functioning are transmitted across generations within a family. Family systems therapy examines how past experiences and family dynamics influence current functioning and interpersonal relationships.
Therapist neutrality	Family systems therapists strive to maintain neutrality and objectivity while remaining aware of their own emotions, biases, and reactions.

FFT is a manualized evidence-based practice. There are five phases of FFT: engagement, motivation, relational assessment, behavior change, and generalization (Robbins et al., 2016). During the engagement phase, the social worker is tasked with engaging the family to the extent that they will continue treatment. According to Hartnett et al. (2017), "the goal of the engagement and motivation phase of treatment is the reduction of negativity and blame between family members and the development of a more family-focused view of their presenting problems" (p. 83). During the motivation stage, the social worker seeks to support the family in developing a congruent motivation for change. At times, things such as blame, alliances, and conflicts need to be addressed. The third stage of FFT is relational assessment, which involves exploring the functional behaviors and interactions among the family. It is important to recognize that all behavior fulfills some function. Though the person engaging in the behavior is not aware of the functions of the behavior at present, the social worker can assist in bringing such things to light. The next stage of the intervention involves the social worker teaching skills and strategies to address the identified problem(s). The goal is to diminish dysfunctional behaviors and interactions within the family system. During the final stage, generalization occurs when the family is able to take what they have learned in therapy and apply it outside of the therapeutic environment.

Multisystemic Therapy

Multisystemic therapy (MST) is an evidence-based practice that has been shown to be effective at addressing severe behavioral and antisocial problems and reducing out-of-home placements for youth. MST seeks to support caregivers and increase their abilities to parent, as the "ultimate goal is to create a context that supports adaptive, rather than deviant, youth and parent behavior" (Henggeler & Schaeffer, 2016, p. 515).

MST is a brief intervention designed to support youth with severe psychosocial or behavioral issues. This is a home- and community-based treatment program. As the name implies, the MST intervention seeks to engage all of the systems involved in the youth's life to provide support. Various systems that could be involved in treatment include mental health providers, child welfare, juvenile justice or probation, and school. A critical target of MST is to empower caregivers in order to bring about change within the family system (Fox et al., 2017).

In this specific intervention, the caregiver is viewed as the "main facilitator of change" (Fox et al., 2017, p. 244). The social worker is tasked with supporting families and empowering the caregivers of the identified child. This intervention seeks to address and improve family functioning in order to then have an impact on the other systems in the life of the child. Nine MST treatment principles guide this intervention (Table 10.2).

Brief Structural Family Therapy

Brief structural family therapy was developed by Salvador Minuchin. This form of family therapy occurs in the home and community setting. Services are often delivered by a team of two clinicians (one at the master's level and the other at the bachelor's level). The team works intensively with the family to bring about change within the structure. Originally developed as an alternative to traditional talk therapies, structural family therapy seeks to address family systems and subsystems to improve functioning (McAdams et al., 2016).

This intervention approach requires that the social worker assist the family in addressing issues related to family structure. This may include family roles, rules, boundaries, and subsystems. Roles refer to the assigned positions that each person in the family fulfills. There are a variety of family roles that are appropriate; for example, the role of caretaker for a parent. However, there may be dysfunctional roles, such as the scapegoat, which can disrupt family functioning. Rules are another important focus of structural family therapy. All family systems have rules. Some rules are explicit, whereas others are not overtly stated but are still just as powerful. Boundaries reflect the parameters of the relationships within the family system. Healthy boundaries are clear. However, at times, boundaries may be unclear or diffused. When there are unclear boundaries, this can negatively impact the family structure.

TABLE 10.2 MST PRINCIPLES IN SOCIAL WORK PRACTICE	
Finding the fit	The social worker must conduct a complete assessment in order to fully understand how the problems fit within the family system.
Focusing on positives and strengths	The social worker utilizes a strengths-based approach throughout treatment.
Increasing responsibility	A goal of MST treatment is to increase responsibility for the identified child as well as other members of the family, including caregivers.
Present-focused, action-oriented, and well-defined	The social worker is primarily concerned with the present functioning of the family. The social worker and family together strive to identify specific action steps to address treatment goals.
Targeting sequences	Treatment addresses all systems of the child's life including home, school, and community.
Developmentally appropriate	This treatment is client specific. There is no MST manual or scripting. This flexibility allows for the services to be tailored to the specific developmental needs of the clients.
Continuous effort	This is an intensive service that requires the child and family to do a significant amount of work. Families must be engaged and working on treatment for this model to succeed.
Evaluation and accountability	Progress (or lack thereof) is measured frequently to determine how treatment is going. If treatment is not progressing, the social worker explores how they can make changes to improve outcomes. Families cannot fail at MST; rather, social workers have not tailored the treatment to reach the family.
Generalization	The intervention of MST is driven by the caregiver with the assistance of the social worker. As a result, the caregiver has realized their ability to address family needs, which can be used in future situations.

MST, multisystemic therapy.

Source: From Henggeler, S. W., & Schaeffer, C. M. (2016). Multisystemic therapy: Clinical overview, outcomes, and implementation research. *Family Process, 55*(3), 514–528. https://doi.org/10.1111/famp.12232

Subsystems within this approach refer to the mini-systems present within the family system. For example, mother and father make up the parent subsystem. Subsystems can be positive and healthy. Some subsystems are not helpful and may create issues related to triangulation.

POLICY ISSUES

Policy issues play a significant role in shaping social work practice with families, influencing the availability of resources, the provision of services, and the overall well-being of families. Policies governing child welfare services, including foster care, adoption, and family preservation, impact how social workers engage with families experiencing child maltreatment or in need of support to maintain family stability. Policies related to the funding and availability of family support services, such as parenting education, childcare assistance, and financial assistance programs, affect the accessibility of resources for families facing various challenges.

Education policies, such as early childhood education programs, school-based interventions, and special education services, influence the educational opportunities and outcomes for children and families, particularly those facing socioeconomic challenges or disabilities.

Policies related to family leave, flexible work arrangements, and workplace supports impact the ability of parents to balance work and family responsibilities, affecting family well-being and child development outcomes. Policies addressing family violence, including domestic violence prevention programs, victim support services, and legal protections for survivors, impact how social workers respond to and support families experiencing violence and abuse within the home. These policy issues intersect with social work practice at various levels, from direct service provision to advocacy efforts aimed at promoting systemic change and addressing inequities within the broader social welfare system. Social workers play a crucial role in advocating for policies that support families' well-being, address systemic barriers to access and opportunity, and promote social justice and equity for all families.

SOCIAL JUSTICE ISSUES

Immigration policies profoundly impact immigrant families, shaping their access to social services, legal protections, and pathways to citizenship, while also intersecting with broader social justice and social work issues. Deportation enforcement policies, in particular, pose significant challenges for immigrant families, often leading to family separation, economic instability, and psychological distress. Social workers frequently encounter families affected by deportation enforcement, providing crucial support and advocacy to mitigate its harmful effects.

Family reunification processes play a pivotal role in shaping immigrant families' experiences and well-being. Lengthy visa backlogs, restrictive eligibility criteria, and bureaucratic hurdles can hinder family reunification efforts, keeping families separated for extended periods and worsening emotional strain and financial hardship. Social workers should advocate for policies that prioritize family unity and streamline the reunification process, recognizing its importance for family stability and cohesion.

Refugee resettlement programs also intersect with social justice and social work issues, as they address the needs of individuals and families fleeing persecution, violence, and instability in their home countries. These programs provide critical support to refugees as they rebuild their lives in a new country, including access to housing, healthcare, education, and employment opportunities. However, limited resources, inadequate support services, and systemic barriers can impede refugees' successful integration and adaptation, worsening their vulnerability and marginalization. Social workers can advocate for comprehensive and culturally responsive services for refugees, addressing their unique needs and facilitating their transition to self-sufficiency and community inclusion.

SUMMARY

Throughout this chapter we explored various ethical considerations, theories, and challenges related to social work practice with families. We explored how despite family work being challenging at times, it is also profoundly rewarding. Witnessing families overcome adversity, strengthen their relationships, and achieve their goals through the support and guidance of social workers can be incredibly gratifying. Building trusting relationships with families, empowering them to harness their strengths and resources, and witnessing their resilience in the face of adversity are powerful reminders of the impact of social work on individuals, families, and communities. When social workers have the opportunity to contribute to positive systemic change and advocate for policies and practices that promote social justice and equity, it adds another layer of fulfillment to social work practice with families. By addressing root causes of social problems, challenging oppressive systems, and promoting inclusive and equitable practices, social workers play a vital role in creating a more just and compassionate society where all families can thrive.

CASE SUMMARY: UNDOCUMENTED AND HOMELESS

Practice Setting Description

Jackie is a first-year master of social work (MSW) student completing an internship at an inner-city family service agency in the Southwest. The agency is in a section of the city that has a high crime rate, gang activity, and failing schools. The area has a diverse population with many immigrants from Central and South America and a substantial African American population. The agency provides individual and family counseling services on a sliding fee scale. The agency also runs several educational and treatment groups as well as a temporary shelter for women and their children. Jackie has been assigned to work with the women and their children in the shelter. Her primary tasks are to provide concrete services and supportive counseling to the shelter residents.

Background Information

Elicia and her daughter, Maria, are undocumented immigrants from Mexico. They have been in the United States for 5 years. Elicia and Maria fled to the area from another southwestern city to escape her abusive husband approximately 2 months ago. Elicia is 25 years old, and Maria 8 years old. Elicia has a 2-year-old daughter, Sarah, who was placed in foster care because of suspected abuse in the home. Sarah is in a foster home in a small rural community in the state hundreds of miles from Elicia's current residence. Since moving to the area, Maria has not been attending school.

Elicia and Maria are currently residing in the agency's temporary shelter for families. They have been at the shelter for two weeks, and the agency has a 90-day limit. Prior to arriving at the shelter, Elicia and Maria were homeless and living on the streets.

Elicia is a high school drop-out and was a stay-at-home mother prior to leaving her husband and moving to a different part of the state. She chose to move there because she has two female cousins living in the area who are also undocumented immigrants. Elicia's native language is Spanish. She speaks some English but is not as comfortable speaking in English. Her English comprehension appears to be good. Maria speaks both English and Spanish well. When communicating with the staff, Maria acts as Elicia's interpreter since none of the staff at the shelter speak Spanish.

Maria appears to be behind academically. She struggles reading simple children's books written in English. It is unknown if her ability to read in Spanish is better than her English reading skills.

Other than her two cousins, Elicia has no other sources of support in the community. Her cousins have young families and limited resources but are well established and connected to a Latino community in the city and the local Catholic church. Her cousins refused to let Elicia and

(continued)

CASE SUMMARY — UNDOCUMENTED AND HOMELESS (*CONTINUED*)

Maria live with them while she was trying to find her own place and a job. They stated that they did not have enough room and are concerned they would get in trouble with their landlord if it was found out that they were letting people stay with them. They sent her to the local church for help, and she was given the address for the agency's shelter by the priest.

Elicia has been looking for housing in the Latino community. The housing market is tight with limited options, and she has been unable to find anything that she could possibly afford. The only affordable housing she found was a room in a rundown motel that rents by the hour or by the month. It is in an area of town known for drug dealing and sex work.

On arrival in the community, Elicia found occasional work for a house cleaning company. The company hires undocumented workers, pays them very low cash wages, and threatens to turn them in to Immigration and Customs Enforcement (ICE) if they complain. The job bosses also exploit their female workers sexually, threatening to turn them in if they do not comply. Elicia was fearful about applying for other jobs because of her illegal status. She considered turning to sex work to be able to take care of her child, but her Catholic upbringing and thoughts of how this would shame her family have kept her from doing so. She is in constant fear of being detained, separated from Maria, and having her placed in foster care. She is also afraid that she will end up homeless again and forced to live on the streets or return to her abusive husband.

Elicia is extremely reluctant to sign up for any federally funded services, even those that she and her child are entitled to receive. On the suggestion that she enroll for supplemental food through the Supplemental Nutrition Assistance Program (SNAP), Elicia became nervous and refused, as she has heard that participation in SNAP services, and others like them, would draw the attention of ICE, and she had heard stories on the news of individuals being deported after signing up for such programs.

Presenting Problems

Elicia and her child are facing multiple obstacles. They need to find permanent, affordable housing and a job that pays enough to cover her housing and living expenses. In addition, Maria needs to be enrolled in school.

Additionally, Elicia is experiencing an immense amount of stress, anxiety, and possibly post-traumatic stress disorder (PTSD). She described an instance where she could not calm down her breathing and she felt lightheaded. She is very fearful of men and tries to avoid all contact with men in the community. She reports difficulty sleeping at night and feeling exhausted most of the time.

She is concerned about Maria. She has started acting out at the shelter, getting into fights with the other children, disobeying her mother, and being disrespectful and defiant to the staff and other adults. Elicia and Maria fight frequently, and when Elicia tries to discipline Maria, she throws a temper tantrum until Elicia gives up.

Elicia has many strengths. She had the strength to leave her abusive husband and move to a different city. She loves her daughter and wants desperately to keep Maria with her. She is resilient and has managed to survive and keep her daughter safe despite not having a place to stay, a job, and a limited support network. Elicia feels safe in the shelter, but she is very fearful of being caught as an illegal immigrant and is generally mistrustful of helping professionals and persons of authority.

DISCUSSION QUESTIONS

1. Utilizing a family systems theory approach to assessing Elicia and Maria, how does the concept of "differentiation of self" relate to this case and your work with both of them, individually and together?
2. Create an ecomap that represents the systems currently involved in Elicia's and Maria's lives.
3. Create a genogram for Elicia and Maria.

A robust set of instructor resources designed to supplement this text is located at http://connect.springerpub.com/content/book/978-0-8261-6683-8. Qualifying instructors may request access by emailing textbook@springerpub.com.

KEY REFERENCES

Only key references appear in the print edition. To access the full reference list, visit www.springerpub.com/courseconnect. See inside front cover and tear-out card for CourseConnect details.

Henggeler, S. W., & Schaeffer, C. M. (2016). Multisystemic therapy: Clinical overview, outcomes, and implementation research. *Family Process*, *55*(3), 514–528. https://doi.org/10.1111/famp.12232

Langer, C. L., & Lietz, C. A. (2015). *Applying theory to generalist social work practice*. Wiley.

11 Generalist Practice With Groups: Assessment and Intervention

Janet is a social worker at a children's partial hospitalization program. Janet's duties include monitoring the classroom behavior of her clients, conducting individual therapeutic sessions, and facilitating group sessions. Janet must determine the appropriate interventions for her clients in the classroom as well as an individual sessions and in groups. Janet is well aware of the importance of selecting evidence-based practices that drive intervention decisions. Furthermore, Janet takes into consideration the individualized needs of each client when selecting intervention strategies.

Janet has recently noticed a pattern emerging in the classroom. The children are having trouble staying on task during class. She has conducted an assessment that has given her insights into the motives of their behaviors. It seemed the children were inadvertently being rewarded for going off-task. Whenever they strayed from their work, a staff member would swoop in, offering individual attention in the form of gentle reprimands or attempts to redirect their focus. While the staff's intentions were well meaning, the unintended consequence was that the children were unknowingly being positively reinforced for the very behavior Janet was trying to extinguish.

Equipped with this newfound knowledge, Janet approached the staff team. She explained her observations and proposed an intervention: the plan involved redirecting the staff's well-intentioned attention. Instead of focusing on the off-task behavior, they would support the children with praise and positive reinforcement whenever they remained focused and engaged in their work. Janet believed that by shifting the focus of the rewards, they could create a classroom environment that incentivized the behavior they desired. It was Janet's hope that by implementing this intervention, she and the team will be able to change the negative problem behavior in the classroom.

LEARNING OBJECTIVES

This chapter explores social work practice with groups. This chapter addresses Competency 7: Assess Individuals, Families, Groups, Organizations, and Communities, and Competency 8: Intervene With Individuals, Families, Groups, Organizations, and Communities. It covers theory, development, assessment and intervention, and advocacy-based group work. By the end of this chapter, you will be able to:

- Review historical foundations of social work with groups.
- Review theories that inform social work practice with groups.
- Recognize the stages of group development proposed by Tuckman.

- Understand how to assess group client systems.
- Understand interventions with group client systems.
- Understand advocacy-based group work.

COMPETENCY 7: ASSESS INDIVIDUALS, FAMILIES, GROUPS, ORGANIZATIONS, AND COMMUNITIES

Social workers understand that assessment is an ongoing component of the dynamic and interactive process of social work practice. Social workers understand theories of human behavior and person-in-environment, as well as interprofessional conceptual frameworks, and they critically evaluate and apply this knowledge in culturally responsive assessment with clients and constituencies, including individuals, families, groups, organizations, and communities. Assessment involves a collaborative process of defining presenting challenges and identifying strengths with individuals, families, groups, organizations, and communities to develop a mutually agreed-upon plan. Social workers recognize the implications of the larger practice context in the assessment process and use interprofessional collaboration in this process. Social workers are self-reflective and understand how bias, power, privilege, and their personal values and experiences may affect their assessment and decision-making.

Social workers:
- apply theories of human behavior and person-in-environment, as well as other culturally responsive and interprofessional conceptual frameworks, when assessing clients and constituencies; and
- demonstrate respect for client self-determination during the assessment process by collaborating with clients and constituencies in developing a mutually agreed-upon plan.

COMPETENCY 8: INTERVENE WITH INDIVIDUALS, FAMILIES, GROUPS, ORGANIZATIONS, AND COMMUNITIES

Social workers understand that intervention is an ongoing component of the dynamic and interactive process of social work practice. Social workers understand theories of human behavior, person-in-environment, and other interprofessional conceptual frameworks, and they critically evaluate and apply this knowledge in selecting culturally responsive interventions with clients and constituencies, including individuals, families, groups, organizations, and communities. Social workers understand methods of identifying, analyzing, and implementing evidence-informed interventions and participate in interprofessional collaboration to achieve client and constituency goals. Social workers facilitate effective transitions and endings.

Social workers:
- engage with clients and constituencies to critically choose and implement culturally responsive, evidence-informed interventions to achieve client and constituency goals; and
- incorporate culturally responsive methods to negotiate, mediate, and advocate with and on behalf of clients and constituencies.

NATIONAL ASSOCIATION OF SOCIAL WORKERS *CODE OF ETHICS*

The National Association of Social Workers (NASW) *Code of Ethics* serves as a guide throughout the helping process, including during and throughout the assessment and evaluation process. Similar to the previous chapter on practice with individuals and families, the ethical principles that relate to assessment include the importance of human relationships as well as competence. The related ethical standards are privacy and confidentiality, clients who lack decision-making capacity, and referral for services. The NASW *Code of Ethics* is available online. Some of the many ethical principles that relate to social work practice with groups include the importance of human relationships, competence, and dignity and worth of the person. Some standards that are related to social work practice with groups include standards related to interruption of services, referral for services, client transfer, and termination of services.

Social workers consider the importance of human relationships when assessing clients, understanding their social networks (formal and informal). Competence is crucial. Social workers should only use assessment tools they are trained for and seek additional training if needed. Client self-determination is respected but may be limited if they pose a risk to themselves or others. Client privacy and confidentiality are maintained. Social workers cannot share or obtain client information without their consent. Social workers assess if clients have decision-making capacity and follow legal guidelines in such situations. Social workers value the therapeutic relationship and strive to build rapport with clients, making them feel heard and supported. The dignity of all people is respected. Social workers work to reduce stigma related to seeking help. Clients are treated with respect and encouraged to increase their self-determination and empowerment. Social workers should avoid service interruptions whenever possible, but if unavoidable, continuity of care is prioritized. Referrals are made when a client needs specialized expertise beyond the social worker's competence. Continuity of care is ensured during the transition. Similar to referrals, transfers may be necessary due to conflicts of interest or a worker leaving their position. Continuity of care is again a priority. Social workers assess if clients continue to need services and terminate the helping relationship when it is no longer in the client's best interest. Termination should be planned for and addressed throughout the intervention process to prepare clients for this final stage.

Social work practice with groups presents some unique ethical considerations on top of the general ethical principles that apply to social work practice with individuals. Here are some key areas to consider:

- *Balancing individual and group needs*: Social workers must navigate the potential conflict between meeting the needs of individual group members and ensuring the overall well-being and progress of the group.
- *Confidentiality and privacy*: Balancing confidentiality for individual members' shared experiences within the group and the need for open communication and trust among members. Of course, social work group facilitators cannot guarantee this because there are exceptions (e.g., threat of harm). It's crucial to discuss these limitations with the group.

- *Power dynamics and group cohesion*: Social workers need to be aware of power imbalances within the group and how they can be addressed to ensure all members feel safe to participate. This includes their own potential influence on the group dynamic.
- *Mitigating risk*: Social workers need to be mindful of potential risks that can arise in groups, such as contagion of negative emotions, scapegoating, or manipulation by certain members. Strategies to mitigate these risks should be in place.
- *Member recruitment and screening*: The social worker should consider the compatibility of potential members with the group's purpose and ensure the group environment is safe for all participants.
- *Worker self-awareness*: The social worker's own biases and experiences can influence group dynamics. They need to be self-aware and manage these factors to facilitate a healthy group environment.

SOCIAL WORK PRACTICE WITH GROUPS

The core purpose of group social work practice is to enhance social functioning, connections, support, coping skills, and personal fulfillment of members (Giacomucci, 2021). Group work can also provide psychoeducation and stimulate community action. The key principles for group work of any kind include inclusion and respect, mutual aid (group members supporting each other), group cohesion, conflict resolution, interpersonal communication, and group development.

In group work, the group works together to benefit itself through members offering support to each other. This type of practice requires treating the group as a whole, not individuals. Do not be mistaken—this should not be misconstrued as the social worker needing to provide no effort. However, with a collaborative approach, outcomes can include increasing self-esteem and problem-solving abilities and reducing social isolation. Group interventions can be used for a countless number of presenting issues. Social work and group practice are closely aligned because social work emphasizes the importance of social connections and context. Social work practice with groups can be designed for various needs, populations, settings, and goals and can be open- or closed-ended, time-limited or ongoing, task-centered or growth-oriented (Giacomucci, 2021).

Group work is increasingly sought after in social work practice and psychotherapy. However, despite its demand, group work is being sidelined within the social work profession. Some reasons for this sidelining include a shift toward a medicalized approach that focuses on individual treatment within psychotherapy, neglecting the social aspects addressed by group work; the emphasis on individualism in social work aligns more with individual therapy than with group work, which fosters both individuality and group connection; and the fact that social work education often omits specialized group work training, creating a shortage of qualified practitioners (Giacomucci, 2021).

There is a difference between group work and group therapy, although social work practice with groups includes both. Anti-oppressive group practice infuses principles of social justice and centers on dismantling systems of oppression. Focus can include addressing how societal power structures and discrimination impact mental health and empowering individuals from oppressed communities to heal and find support within a safe space that acknowledges their unique experiences. Social justice, empowerment, intersectionality, and cultural humility, all discussed in previous chapters, remain at the heart of anti-oppressive practice (AOP) with groups. Social work practice with groups allows members to share experiences with others who understand the specific challenges of facing oppression, which can foster a sense of belonging and reduce feelings of isolation. Additionally, group work can explore healthy ways to navigate microaggressions, discrimination, and internalized oppression. Members may find support and motivation within the group to advocate for social change within their communities.

THEORIES RELATED TO SOCIAL WORK PRACTICE WITH GROUPS

Systems Theory

Systems theory in social work has been discussed in earlier chapters, but a refresher is provided here before applying it specifically to group work. Systems theory looks at people within the context of their social environment. This environment is seen as an ecosystem with many parts, including family, school, work, and community. Social workers consider how these parts interact and influence the individual's well-being. By understanding these interactions, social workers can develop better interventions for individuals, families, communities, and, of course, groups. The theory emphasizes that individual behavior is a result of complex feedback loops between the person and their environment. Social workers can use this approach to identify problems and create solutions that address the whole system, not just the individual. This can involve connecting clients with social services, advocating for changes in social programs, or helping families improve communication. Overall, systems theory provides a holistic framework for social workers to understand and help people in need.

Group systems theory is an umbrella term for various models that use systems concepts to understand group dynamics and improve group work (Connor & Caple, 2005). It emphasizes holism, focusing on the whole group rather than just individual members. Questions like "How well is the group working?" encourage this perspective. Interdependence is another core concept. All group members and the group itself are interconnected and affect each other. A balanced and equal environment is preferred. Complementary perspectives are valued. Differences in viewpoints provide valuable information for the group. Structure includes elements like facilitation style, group norms, and activities. Boundaries define the group and manage information flow between the group and its environment. Control and power structure deal with decision-making and how the group operates. Less controlling facilitation tends to have better outcomes.

Systems theory suggests groups go through stages of development, starting from forming a group, then experiencing conflict, establishing norms, performing the group's task, and finally adjourning. There are different models for group development stages, some sequential and some cyclical. Tuckman's five-stage model is the most widely accepted and is described later in this chapter. Systems theory emphasizes that groups are dynamic and can be unstable, especially early on. This instability can lead to growth and change. Perturbation refers to the introduction of new information that challenges the group. It can lead to chaos, a state of disorder that can be an opportunity for growth if managed well. Junction points are the moment of greatest instability where the group needs to decide how to adapt. It can lead to positive change (evolution) or collapse. Self-organizing systems naturally adapt and change to survive in their environment. Groups function similarly, with a balance between stability and change.

Psychodynamic Theory

The psychodynamic perspective is an approach to "the study of group behavior that focuses on the relationship between the emotional nonconscious processes and the conscious rational processes of interpersonal interaction" (McLeod & Kettner-Polley, 2005, p. 63). Psychodynamic theory can be useful in considering the complicated interactions that occur within group practice, as it emphasizes unconscious thoughts, feelings, and experiences that influence our behavior in groups. This includes defense mechanisms, transference (projecting past experiences onto others), and countertransference (worker's feelings toward the group). Understanding these dynamics assists the social worker in building trust and navigating group interactions. Psychodynamic theory can be used throughout the social group work process: assessing individual needs and group dynamics, guiding interventions like discussions or role-playing to raise awareness of unconscious processes, and even managing the ending stage (termination) by helping members process feelings of loss. Some of the goals of utilizing this theory are increased self-awareness, improved relationships within the group; externally, enhanced group functioning and fostering personal growth are some of the advantages. Critiques include that there is difficulty in accessing the unconscious, there can be resistance from members to exploring these aspects, and the time-consuming nature of the approach. Additionally, historically, this approach has been critiqued as individualizing problems rather than considering and addressing the larger social systems contributing to the issue, therefore contributing to oppression of marginalized and excluded communities.

Cognitive Theory

Cognitive theories are characterized by their focus on the idea that how and what people think lead to specific emotions and that negative thoughts and beliefs contribute to problematic emotions and behaviors, while others contribute to beneficial emotions and adaptive behavior (DiGiuseppe et al., 2016). The goal of cognitive theory is to identify negative thought patterns, restructure thinking, and try new behaviors. Group discussions and interactions can help individuals recognize unhelpful thinking patterns they might not have been aware of before. Hearing others share similar struggles can normalize experiences and encourage self-reflection. Through discussions and feedback from the group, individuals can learn to challenge and reframe negative thoughts into more realistic and positive ones. This shift in thinking can lead to improved emotional responses and behaviors. Group therapy can provide a supportive environment to practice new behaviors based on cognitive restructuring. Individuals can experiment with healthier coping mechanisms, communication styles, or problem-solving approaches, receiving encouragement and feedback from the group.

Humanism

Humanism focuses on how healthy people grow and thrive, emphasizing our natural desire to reach our full potential and be creative. This framework underscores individuals' ability to change and overcome limitations, rejecting the idea that biology dictates our behavior. This theory emphasizes a holistic view of each unique individual and assumes that people have free will and are motivated to achieve their potential (McLeod, 2023). Humanism approaches in group settings prioritize understanding each member's unique experiences and challenges rather than solely focusing on symptoms or diagnoses. The goal is for the group to become a safe space for individuals to share their struggles and perspectives openly and authentically. The social worker attempts to create a warm and accepting environment where all members feel valued and respected, regardless of their background or issues, in order to foster trust and psychological safety, encouraging members to participate actively and support each other. The social worker guides the group process to create opportunities for members to explore their potential, develop their self-awareness, and identify their personal goals. By interacting with others in the group, members can learn new coping mechanisms, communication skills, and healthy ways of relating to others.

Mutual Aid

The framework of mutual aid is simple: the acknowledgment that group members learn from one another and that social workers benefit and learn from their involvement in the group as well. As Steinberg (2014) points out, mutual aid is about people helping one another. Mutual aid is a powerful approach for social group work in mental health, and it aligns with the recovery model's focus on self-management and empowerment. Mutual aid emphasizes collaboration and sharing knowledge among members and the facilitator, and there is a focus on building on existing strengths and developing new skills. Mutual aid aligns with AOP by valuing the lived experiences and expertise of all group members. Hyde (2012, p. 44) points out that using this approach, personal narratives are often used to "raise consciousness, find common ground, unite group members, and reduce feelings of isolation." Cohen and Graybeal (2007) stated that mutual aid can help people gain a sense of control over their lives. They stated that one of the objectives of a mutual aid group is to encourage the resourcefulness and creativity of the group and diminish the necessity for intervention. Also in line with AOP, the mutual aid approach requires the group worker to share power with group members so that the helping process is collaborative. This is closely related to empowerment theories, explained later. Gitterman and Shulman (2005) identified some mutual aid processes in group social work, including sharing resources, discussing ideas, discussing topics that are too sensitive to discuss elsewhere, sharing similar life experiences, offering support, holding each other accountable, working together on individual members' problems, and preparing one another for individual experiences outside of the group.

Empowerment

Empowerment theories, discussed in previous chapters, create a framework for group practice that fosters individual and collective growth, promotes self-determination, and equips

> **▶ Reflection Questions**
>
> 1. Think back to Janet's experience at the beginning of the chapter. Which perspective(s) do you feel informed her approach to the issue that arose in her classroom?
> 2. Which perspective do you envision adhering to when facilitating groups and why?

people with the tools and confidence to navigate life's challenges. Empowerment approaches to group practice in social work are complementary, as they focus on strengths; strive to increase self-awareness; promote self-determination; can be a source of collective power; can help identify and challenge systems of oppression that may be limiting individuals' potential; can develop skills like communication, problem-solving, and assertiveness; and can reduce feelings of isolation and empower individuals to feel part of a supportive community.

TYPES OF GROUPS

There are many different types of groups. Some are explained based on approach, and others are based on the goal of the group. These categories can overlap, and groups can utilize elements from many different approaches depending on the needs and goals of the group. Some examples:

- *Cognitive behavioral therapy (CBT) groups*: These groups apply CBT principles to help members identify and challenge negative thinking patterns that contribute to their difficulties. They learn coping skills and strategies to manage emotions and behaviors more effectively.
- *Interpersonal process groups*: These groups focus on how individuals interact with others within the group setting. Members explore their communication styles and relationship patterns and how these may be impacting their lives.
- *Treatment groups*: These focus on addressing specific mental health concerns like anxiety, depression, substance abuse, or trauma. These groups are run by social workers and other mental health professionals that facilitate discussions and activities aimed at symptom reduction, skill development, and emotional support.
- *Psychoeducational groups*: These focus on educating clients about their disorders and ways of coping; often based on the principles of CBT.
- *Skills development groups*: These groups focus on improving social skills in people, often focused on individuals with mental disorders or developmental disabilities.
- *Support groups*: These groups provide a wide range of benefits for people with a variety of mental health conditions as well as their loved ones.
- *Experiential groups*: These groups emphasize the importance of the here-and-now experience. They use techniques like movement, art therapy, or role-playing to help members gain insight into their emotions and behavior patterns.

GROUP DEVELOPMENT

As groups develop, the interactions change. Many ideas exist on how groups function over time. A key concept across these theories is that groups act like social systems (Toseland et al., 2004). When people in a group interact, they create a social system with unique dynamics. These dynamics are the forces that develop as members bounce ideas off each other and are influenced by both the immediate group interactions and the broader social experiences they bring to the table. Researchers have created various models to explain these changes using stages. Two popular examples are Tuckman's (1965) model (explained in the following section) with forming, storming, norming, and performing stages, and Garland et al.'s (1976) model with preaffiliation, power and control, intimacy, differentiation, and separation stages.

Tuckman's Five Stages of Group Development

Tuckman's five stages of group development model identifies five stages that groups go through: forming, storming, norming, performing, and adjourning (see Figure 11.1). As the group matures and gets better at working together, relationships become stronger and leadership becomes more collaborative or shared.

The first stage of group development is called *forming*. In this stage:

- People are still feeling each other out. They act cautiously and rely on the leader for instructions. Their main concern is fitting in and feeling secure within the group.
- They're getting acquainted. Members are figuring out what the group is about, how they'll work together, and who they have things in common with.
- Avoiding conflict is key. They stick to safe topics and avoid anything potentially controversial.

FIGURE 11.1 Five stages of group development.

Source: From Tuckman, B. W. (1965). Developmental sequence in small groups. *Psychological Bulletin, 63*(6), 384–399. https://doi.org/10.1037%2Fh0022100

- Moving on requires taking a leap. To progress, members need to be comfortable discussing more challenging topics and potentially facing some disagreements.

Stage two is called *storming*:

- This stage is filled with competition and disagreements as members figure out how to work together. They have to adjust their ideas and personalities to fit the group dynamic, which can lead to clashes.
- Fear and uncertainty take hold. People might become quiet or try to take control due to anxieties about being exposed or failing.
- Conflicts arise over leadership, rules, rewards and how success is measured.
- Members' behavior can be unpredictable as they navigate these competing interests and potential hostility.
- To progress, the group needs to move from trying to prove themselves to each other and instead focus on solving problems together. The key seems to be good listening skills.

Stage three is called *norming*:

- In this stage, teamwork takes center stage. People acknowledge each other's contributions, build a strong sense of community, and work together to solve problems. They're open to changing their minds based on new information and actively ask questions. Leadership is shared, and any initial in-groups or cliques disappear. Trust and a sense of belonging grow as members get to know each other better.
- People feel good about being part of the team and relieved to have resolved earlier conflicts. They openly share ideas and feelings, give and receive feedback, and explore solutions together. This fosters a lot of creativity.
- Members might become resistant to any changes because they're worried about the group eventually breaking up.

Stage four is *performing*:

- If they make it to this stage, it might be considered the "dream" stage. Not all groups reach this level, but for those that do, it's a mutually beneficial experience. Members can work together seamlessly in any combination—independently, in smaller groups, or as a whole team. They are flexible and adjust their roles and leadership based on what's needed at the moment.
- This stage is marked by teamwork, both in solving problems and supporting each other. Everyone feels confident and doesn't need constant approval from the group. They're all in it together—focused on the task and each other's well-being.
- The group tackles challenges head-on, aiming for the best possible solutions. They're open to trying new things and achieving great things together. The main focus is getting the job done efficiently through effective problem-solving and collaboration.

Stage five, the final stage, is *adjourning*:

- The wrap-up stage, where the group's work comes to an end and people move on. Ideally, there's a planned conclusion that acknowledges everyone's contributions and allows an opportunity for everyone to say their goodbyes.

- Saying goodbye can be tough. Ending a group can be bittersweet, causing some anxiety as people give up control of the project and their involvement with the team. It's a loss.
- The best approach here is to help the group members finish their tasks effectively and gracefully disband.

The Social Justice Model

Ratts et al. (2010) created the dimensions of social justice model as a framework for social workers and other group facilitators to consider social justice at each developmental stage of the group. This model is in line with AOP with groups in that it centers on social justice principles and provides a structure from which the social worker can operate. Ratt et al.'s model conceptualizes social justice as both a process and a goal and consists of five stages: naiveté, multicultural integration, liberatory critical consciousness, empowerment, and social justice advocacy.

- *Naiveté*: At this stage, the group is seen through a culturally universal perspective, ignoring the influence of cultural factors like race, ethnicity, and gender on group dynamics. In this stage, the facilitator has the most power and group input is limited.
- *Multicultural integration*: At this stage, the group moves to a focus in which members' discussions move from individual experiences to a broader understanding of each other's backgrounds. This culturally specific approach considers members' social identities (race, ethnicity, etc.) to explain group dynamics. Group members and the leader are seen as unique individuals with different backgrounds and experiences. Problems are viewed through the lens of cultural misunderstandings or diverse worldviews, and the facilitator helps members appreciate these differences and build connections. Power is distributed among members, not solely held by the facilitator.
- *Liberatory critical consciousness*: At this stage, group members explore how their personal experiences are shaped by broader social, political, and economic factors. Freire (1993) conceptualizes this as critical consciousness, or *conscientizaco*. Understanding these connections leads to a critical awareness of how societal structures contribute to problems they face. This awakening empowers group members to see their situations beyond personal failings. Problems in the group and interactions are viewed as products of social inequities and oppression, not individual shortcomings. Group activities help members analyze power structures and identify systems of oppression. This critical awareness fosters a desire to take action and challenge the oppressive structures.
- *Empowerment*: At this stage, the group equips members with tools to advocate for themselves and navigate their social environment. Simply knowing about social inequalities isn't enough. Empowerment goes further to create lasting change. Group activities help members find their voice, identify and build on strengths, and develop self-advocacy skills. The goal is to empower members to become self-sufficient and confident individuals.

- *Social justice advocacy*: At this stage, the group goes beyond traditional group work. Both members and leaders may take action outside the group setting to advocate for a cause or issue related to the group's experiences. Advocacy efforts aim to address the social structures that create the problems group members face, not just individual issues within the group. This dimension emphasizes using the group experience as a springboard for collective action to create positive change in the larger social environment.

Based on these concepts, Brubaker et al. (2010) created a list of six questions for the social worker to ask of the group and themselves (p. 128):

- What did I learn from the group today?
- What did I teach others in the group today?
- How are we oppressed by society and others?
- How do we oppress each other?
- How do we allow ourselves to be oppressed?
- How did the group help me reinforce or liberate the oppression I experience?

GROUP STRUCTURE

There are a number of variables to consider when forming a group structure. Some considerations (Rose, 2004) include:

- *Group size*: Ideal size depends on the purpose of the group and need for individualization. Outpatient groups are typically three to eight members, while institutional groups can be larger and meet more frequently.
- *Timeframe of the group*: The specific number depends on the group's goals and complexity of problems, with research supporting short-term groups for some issues and long-term and open-ended groups for chronic conditions (Gitterman & Shulman, 2005). Outpatient groups usually have 6 to 18 weekly sessions, while inpatient groups meet daily for 3 to 6 weeks (Rose, 2004).
- *Number of group facilitators*: One experienced group social worker is typically sufficient for most groups. However, two social workers may be helpful for large groups, new therapists, or groups with a lot of tension. Morgaine and Capous-Desyllas (2023) point out that a facilitation team can disrupt privilege based on categories of difference.
- *Group membership*: Group membership will influence group characteristic. There are many factors in group composition (gender, age, race, ethnicity, etc.). For some groups, a homogenous group may be preferred, such as gender-specific groups. This is especially true for groups that are focused on issues relating to oppression and racial identity (Brown & Mistry, 2005). Groups may also be intentionally or unintentionally heterogeneous.

Factors relating to AOP in group work include (Morgaine & Capous-Desyllas, 2023):

- Easily accessible location.
- Collaboration with group members on the plan, including negotiations.

- Balancing members of differing identities to avoid feelings of isolation.
- Group norms/rules should be based in anti-oppression (AO) and empowerment principles.
- Social workers facilitating groups should be trained and willing to address discrimination, microaggressions, and other oppressive behaviors, whether they are intentional or unintentional, obvious or subtle.

GROUP DYNAMICS

Group dynamics change over the life of the group, which is why an understanding of group development (explained earlier in this chapter) is important. According to Toseland et al. (2004) and Toseland and Rivas (2001), there are five specific group dynamic areas.

Communication Processes and Interaction Patterns

Communication can be verbal, nonverbal, or virtual. Misunderstandings can occur due to unclear messages or cultural differences. Effective communication requires feedback to check for understanding. Toseland and Rivas (2001) specify that effective feedback reflects back the communication as it was received, should be reflected back immediately upon receipt, and should be reflected back in a way that makes it clear that it is for clarification purposes. The goal is that group interaction patterns allow all members to participate and contribute. The social worker facilitator can influence interaction patterns by acknowledging contributions, directing attention, or changing seating arrangements. Subgroups naturally form in groups, but they can become problematic if they become more important than the whole group. An important goal of group work is to help members accept and interact with people who are different from them.

> ▶ **Reflection Question**
>
> Does treating each group member the same reflect an AO approach in group practice? Why or why not?

Interpersonal Attraction and Cohesion

Why do certain group members like each other? This is explained by interpersonal attraction, which can be influenced by factors like proximity (sitting close together), similarity (shared interests), and positive behavior (complimenting others). Cohesion is the overall feeling of togetherness in a group. It's influenced by interpersonal attraction, but also by other factors like feeling like the group meets your needs and compares favorably to other groups. Groups with high cohesion have members who are more likely to achieve goals, feel satisfied with the group, and show up to meetings. However, groups with too much cohesion can become too dependent on each other or become resistant to new ideas.

Social Integration and Influence

Social integration refers to how well members fit together in a group. It's influenced by norms (rules about behavior), roles (expected functions of members), and status (importance of

> **Reflection Question**
>
> Is a truly AO approach possible in heterogeneous groups where members hold disparate levels of privilege in society (e.g., wealth differences, racial privilege)? Why or why not?

members). Strong social integration helps groups function smoothly and achieve goals. Norms can be explicit, meaning they are openly stated, or implicit, understood but not stated. Roles can be task-oriented, such as keeping the group on focus or social-emotional (for example, encouraging others). Status hierarchies can affect how much people conform to group norms. Groups can exert social influence on members, pressuring them to conform. However, minority viewpoints can also influence the majority if they are presented well. In line with AOP, the social worker must pay attention to norm development in heterogeneous groups, especially when there are members of oppressed groups. Being the sole member of an oppressed group can make it more challenging to relate to others, they may feel their experiences are devalued, and the group may be less beneficial for them (Fenster, 1996; Han & Vasquez, 1995).

Power and Control

AOP requires that social workers acknowledge power and control in practice. However, in group work, designated leaders have power. There are two types of power: attributed (based on perception of effectiveness as a leader) and actual (based on resources to change conditions for the group). Leaders have different sources of power, like expertise, connection, reward, or even coercive power. A leader's power is especially strong early on in a group but continues throughout. Cultural sensitivity is a necessity for group leaders, particularly when working with culturally diverse groups because people from different cultures may have different expectations and experiences with power dynamics. Leaders should understand their own cultural background and how it shapes their view of power. If a leader isn't sensitive to cultural differences in power dynamics, it can result in an oppressive environment for individuals from marginalized groups. Some power is needed to keep groups functioning well and members motivated. Leaders can use power to address issues like social loafing (reduced effort in groups). As groups progress, leaders should share power with members. There are different leadership styles. Authoritarian styles are less effective than democratic or transformational styles. Transformational leaders inspire members, empower them, and set high expectations. The most effective leaders create safe and welcoming group environments.

Culture

Group culture is a set of shared values, beliefs, and ways of doing things that develop over time through group interaction. It emerges from the backgrounds and preferences of individual members. Group culture has different depths: surface level (symbols and rituals), midlevel (interaction styles), and deep level (core values). Culture is also influenced by the larger society and sponsoring organizations. Culturally diverse groups present a unique challenge because members come from diverse backgrounds with different values. A leader who is insensitive to these differences can negatively affect group dynamics. Homogeneous groups develop a culture faster, while heterogeneous groups offer opportunities for learning and growth but require careful facilitation to avoid oppression. A strong group culture can make members feel like they belong, but those who don't feel included may become isolated or receive less benefit. Leaders can help by providing individual attention and promoting values that embrace differences and AOP principles.

ASSESSMENT PROCESS IN GROUP WORK

The assessment phase, when keeping in line with AOP, requires that social workers approach assessment as an opportunity for learning through shared information. Assessment in group work is an opportunity for group members to share their stories and explain their goals and concerns. Group members and the social worker work together to build an understanding of each group member's unique situation and work as partners in the assessment process. Social workers recognize that group members are participating in a deeply vulnerable process as they share the information required for the assessment process. Centering the social work value of clients as the experts of their own experiences and lives helps us as social workers to place ourselves in a learning position as opposed to an expert position. Utilizing the theories listed earlier in this chapter, which highlight the necessity for unconditional positive regard and the promotion of self-determination, reminds us of the importance of specific skills that should be used throughout the assessment process.

PERSON-IN-ENVIRONMENT PERSPECTIVE IN ASSESSMENT

As we have discussed throughout this text, people are complex. It is impossible to understand a person fully without considering the complete context of their lives, including the environments in which they exist. The person-in-environment perspective explores all systems or environments in which a person exists. Social workers should also consider the physical environment in which a person resides (Akesson et al., 2017).

When assessing the person and their environments, the social worker must first be aware of all of the environments within which the person exists. This requires a good, comprehensive, ongoing assessment. Social workers must be thorough during the assessment process and ask follow-up questions for clarification whenever necessary. Social workers must use good interviewing skills as well as good nonverbal communication strategies to engage the client so that they can share the information that is necessary for the social worker to conduct a thorough assessment.

Strengths Perspective Principles

A strengths-based approach may seem to be an obvious hallmark of the social work profession, as social workers often explore strengths, resources, and talents available at the micro, mezzo, and macro levels of the client's environment. In order to better under the strengths-based perspective as it relates to assessment, it is helpful to consider the six strengths perspective principles. These principles set forth by Saleeby (2013) assist social workers in incorporating strengths-based approaches in all areas of the helping process. Box 10.1 from the previous chapter lists the six principles.

At the heart of these principles is the inherent belief that strengths exist within every individual, every group, every family, and every community. Despite what may appear as adversity, resilience exists. Further, the capacity for resilience is limitless, and social workers must allow clients to identify their own hopes, goals, and desires for their future during the helping process.

STRENGTHS-BASED ASSESSMENT: GROUPS

It is necessary to be clear that all groups are inherently unique as they are composed of unique individuals. Based on this, every group will have their own strengths and obstacles. As a social worker, it may be helpful to reflect on the group as a whole as well as the members of the group to assist in assessing the group. Assessment at the group level is much like micro and family assessment. Social workers approach group assessment from the same strengths-based perspective and apply the same six strengths perspective principles to this process. At times, social workers assess the group as a whole, whereas at other times social workers assess the individual members of the group.

Assessing the Group as a Whole

Sometimes during the assessment process, social workers must assess groups as a whole. One such way to assess groups as a whole is to assess at what stage the group is functioning. There are various stages of group functioning detailed earlier in this chapter. It can be helpful to assess what stage the group is functioning at to ensure that the group is developing through the stages appropriately and at the desired rate based on the anticipated length of the group. This can be useful for a variety of different reasons, including practical concerns. For example, if a social worker is running a 6-week-long group and at week 3 assesses that the group is still in the forming stages, the social worker recognizes that the group is delayed in formation and as a result of limited time may not be able to complete the other stages in the remaining 3 weeks. The social worker can then encourage the group to move on to the next stage in group development based on how they approach and attend to the group in the next session.

Assessing Individual Group Members

Sometimes it is necessary for social workers to assess individual members of a group. When doing this, often the assessment may look like a typical micro assessment. However, sometimes the social worker may be assessing an individual in relationship to the group. In such cases, the social worker would be exploring the individual's relationship with other members of the group or the individual's participation in the group process.

It is important for social workers to recognize that power exists within all groups. Social workers must assess in an ongoing manner the power dynamics of a group. It is important to be mindful of the group purpose and be sure that individual members or alliances within the group are not disrupting the purpose or process of the group. When it is interfering with the group, the social worker should take action to ameliorate such conditions and assist the group in getting back on track.

> ▶ **Reflection Questions**
>
> 1. Reflect upon your experiences working in groups. How were you assessed (as an individual or as a group)?
> 2. Did the way you were assessed accurately reflect the group? If so, how; if not, why not?

Strengths-Based Group Assessment

Strengths-based group assessment recognizes and honors that strengths exist in the group as a collective and within each member of the group. When operating from a strengths-based perspective when assessing groups, it is important for social workers to be aware that self-determination still exists. Groups have the right to self-determine. The way in which they decide what determination to reach is, in fact, an example of such that. As we have stated, all groups are unique, and as a result, social workers must allow space for groups to come together and work on, and at times through, issues. This can be a difficult task for social workers, but they must lean in to the group work process.

Assessment in Group Therapy

There are various assessment tools clinical social workers can use to examine how group therapy is going. These tools help the clinical social worker understand how well the group is functioning and how members interact with each other. Analyzing group therapy involves looking at the overall process, how members interact, and how individuals behave within the group setting. Therapists often use questionnaires and rating scales. Commonly used items include the Group Questionnaire, Group Climate Questionnaire, Group Cohesiveness Scale, Group Work Engagement Measure, Therapeutic Factors Scale, Group Session Rating Scale, Individual Group Member Interpersonal Process Scale, Interpersonal Relation Checklist, Group Emotionality Rating System, Hill Interaction Matrix, Member–Leader scoring system, Hostility/Support Scale, and System for the Multiple Level Observation of Groups (Ezhumalai et al., 2018). These tools assess different aspects of group therapy, such as:

> ▶ **Reflection Question**
>
> Think back to Janet's experience at the beginning of the chapter. Which kind of assessment approach did she utilize?

- *Group climate*: How comfortable and safe the group feels for members.
- *Group cohesiveness*: How well the group members connect and feel like a team.
- *Engagement*: How involved members are in the group process.
- *Therapeutic factors*: Whether elements like empathy and trust are present in the group.
- *Session quality*: How productive and helpful each session is.
- *Individual behavior*: How each member interacts with others and the clinical social worker.

- *Emotions*: The overall emotional tone of the group.
- *Roles and norms*: How members behave within the group and what's considered acceptable.

GROUP INTERVENTIONS

As discussed earlier, social workers often work with groups across types of practice. Social work with groups involves individuals joining together to work on a particular goal. There are numerous types of groups (therapeutic, education, etc.). Regardless of group type, it is important for social workers to be able to support groups as a whole while simultaneously supporting the individual members of the group. The social worker must be mindful of group objectives, membership, decision-making, atmosphere, and action (Dominelli, 2012). Group objectives refer to what needs to be considered during the group planning process. It is important for the social worker to properly plan out the structure of the group prior to implementation. It is often helpful for the social worker to consider the type of group and what the purpose of the group is. Social workers should clearly identify what the group is designed to achieve. Another factor to contemplate during the planning process relates to membership. The social worker should determine the ideal size of the group. It is important to know who will (and will not) be granted access to the group. These are important considerations prior to starting the recruitment process. Also, the social worker must consider whether the group will have open or closed membership. Group decision-making is a dynamic process. Social workers should be aware of the ways in which groups make decisions and how groupthink can influence group members. Furthermore, social workers should determine if there will be leadership roles within the groups and, if so, how those roles will be assigned. The atmosphere of the group is another component of group work that social workers must attend to. Social workers seek to help clients feel comfortable—that goal is the same within the group setting. Furthermore, because of the nature of group work, the social worker should be mindful as to how to intervene should conflict arise. The final consideration is action. Group action refers to tasks and activities of the group. It is important to determine how group success will be measured. Within the field of social work, success can mean a variety of different things depending on the practice setting. A deep dive on different interventions is beyond the scope of this chapter, but an overview of different interventions utilized in different types of groups is included.

Psychoeducational Groups

With psychoeducational groups, the aim is to educate and teach participants new skills or knowledge on a specific topic (Roffman, 2004). There are two main phases in planning a psychoeducational group: conceptual (setting goals) and operational (planning activities). When setting goals, the social worker should consider the target population, purpose (e.g., education, prevention), and desired outcomes (e.g., changing behavior). The chosen theory (e.g., cognitive behavioral) should inform the group activities and how the social work facilitator interacts with participants. Common group activities include didactic presentations (teaching), experiential exercises (applying knowledge), and processing discussions (reflecting on learnings). Social workers should assess participants' progress and adapt the group as needed. As previously mentioned in the chapter, different theoretical perspectives can inform psychoeducational groups. These include the stages of change model (discussed in earlier chapters), in which people progress through stages (precontemplation, contemplation, preparation, action, maintenance) when changing behaviors, and interventions should match the participant's current stage. Behavioral approaches focus on teaching new behaviors by using techniques like positive reinforcement. Cognitive approaches aim to identify and change unhelpful thinking patterns. Humanistic approaches emphasize empathy and creating a safe space for participants to explore their experiences and grow. Ideas and behaviors are more likely to be adopted if seen as beneficial, compatible with existing beliefs, and communicated by trusted people.

Prevention Groups

Prevention groups apply prevention concepts to a wide range of issues (Nash & Snyder, 2004). For social workers, preventing problems relating to mental health and psychosocial functioning is a natural fit. Social work has been utilizing a public health framework for prevention that emphasizes understanding the causes of problems, identifying risk and protective factors, and translating this knowledge into interventions. Social work groups can target a variety of problems in diverse populations. They can focus on building knowledge and skills, providing support, and developing social networks. Effective prevention groups are based on research about risk and protective factors. Interventions aim to interrupt risk processes or promote protective processes.

Social work groups can be used for universal prevention (entire populations), selective prevention (high-risk individuals), or indicated prevention (symptomatic individuals). Selective prevention groups target individuals who are at heightened risk of developing a problem. They aim to interrupt an emerging risk process. Social work groups are well suited for selective prevention because they can provide opportunities for shared experience, social learning, skill practice, and support. Culturally competent practice is essential for effective prevention groups and in line with AOP. This includes using culturally relevant language and collaborating with community members.

Social and recreational groups can be a powerful tool for preventing mental health and social problems, particularly for adolescents. For interventions, social workers can utilize existing social and recreational groups (sports teams, clubs, etc.) to prevent problems. Participation in these groups can foster essential skills and social connections that act as buffers against mental health problems. Especially for youth, participation in these kinds of groups decreases opportunities for engaging in risky behaviors. Groups can provide a chance to develop a bond with a caring adult, another protective factor. Social workers can connect people to these groups, address barriers to participation, and advocate for more such programs. However, for individuals to benefit, the groups should align with their interests.

Mental and Physical Health Groups

Group work in healthcare settings, particularly for mental health and social problems, offers various benefits, including addressing social problems and providing peer support, education, and skill development for managing illnesses and mental health conditions (Getzel, 2004). Group work is used in various healthcare settings for conditions like chronic mental illness, substance abuse, cancer, sickle cell disease, and AIDS/HIV. It can address issues like coping with illness, emotional distress, social isolation, and self-care. There are different approaches to group work, such as cognitive behavioral groups that focus on changing negative thought patterns, psychoeducational groups that provide information about illnesses, and support groups that offer emotional support and social connection. The future of group work in healthcare involves using a unified approach that considers both medical and psychiatric aspects of illness. It also requires social workers to stay updated on medical advancements and their impact on patients. Group work is likely to play a significant role in supporting people with chronic illnesses, those facing complex medical technologies, and aging populations.

Interactional Group Psychotherapy

The goal of group psychotherapy is to improve participants' abilities to understand their mental state, facilitating interactions between peers and their social worker in a safe environment (Arias-Pujol & Anguera, 2017; Fisher, 2004). This approach assumes that interpersonal relationships are key to a person's development and mental health and that mental health problems arise from unhealthy interaction patterns. Therefore, the therapy focuses on how people interact in the "here and now" of the group session. By examining these interactions, clients gain insights and learn new ways to behave. Some techniques used in this type of group focused on substance use (Fisher, 2004) include:

- *Confrontation*: Providing honest feedback with empathy and concern
- *Managing anxiety*: Balancing challenge with support to promote growth
- *Here-and-now focus*: Examining interactions within the group
- *Addressing group obstacles*: Ensuring safety, honesty, and openness
- *Accountability*: Addressing denial and maintaining humility

Social Skills Training Groups

Social skills training is a behavioral approach that focuses on improving social skills in a specific area. Using a social skills training approach in a group includes assessing skill deficits; teaching coping behaviors through instruction, modeling, practice, and feedback; using psychoeducation and self-reward systems; and peer-to-peer modeling and practice (Fisher, 2004). Groups can use role-playing to practice new behaviors, brainstorm problem-solving strategies, and use self-reward systems to reinforce positive behaviors.

Group Cognitive Behavioral Therapy

Some groups utilize cognitive behavioral therapy (CBT) to address negative thought patterns and improve behaviors and emotions. These groups offer a supportive environment to learn coping skills with others facing similar challenges. These groups typically have 5 to 10 members and meet weekly for 1.5 to 2 hours. Sessions involve a variety of activities that focus on different techniques, including (Saxena, 2022):

- *Cognitive restructuring*: Identifying and replacing negative thoughts with healthier ones
- *Normalization*: Realizing others share similar experiences
- *Collaborative relationships*: Supporting each other's progress
- *In vivo exposure*: Facing fears in a safe group setting
- *Positive reinforcement and vicarious learning*: Encouragement and observing others succeed

Rational Emotive Behavior Therapy

Rational emotive behavior therapy is a type of CBT therapy focused on helping people identify and change irrational beliefs. This approach aims to improve emotional and mental health by teaching people to respond rationally to situations, and it can be used in group settings. This approach utilizes the ABC model, which explains how **A**ctivating events, **B**eliefs about those events, and **C**onsequences of those beliefs impact us. Group members identify irrational beliefs and substitute them with rational beliefs and coping statements (Erford, 2018). Some techniques used include:

- *Disputation*: Challenging irrational beliefs to help the individual see them from a different perspective
- *Targeting emotional responses*: Develops healthier emotional responses alongside changing beliefs

GROUP SKILLS

To facilitate groups utilizing an empowerment approach, the social worker focuses on collaborating with group members, providing skilled guidance and avoiding imposing solutions, and empowering members to take ownership of the process (Fleming & Ward, n.d.). This is important because self-directed group work empowers members and helps them achieve social change, it challenges social injustices and transforms power dynamics, and it allows people to experience new ways of being involved in their communities. This approach is in line with AOP, as it avoids negative labels, respects group member rights, and uses a power analysis. The social worker acts as a facilitator; focuses on external goals identified by the group; asks "why" to understand the root causes of problems; views people as capable of finding solutions, not problems; and encourages critical thinking and social awareness. One model that has been identified as in line with this approach is the self-directed model, which has five stages (Mullender et al., 2013):

1. *Taking stock*: Planning and establishing core principles
2. *Taking off*: Collaborative group planning
3. *Preparing to take action*: Identifying and analyzing problems
4. *Taking action*: Implementing solutions
5. *Taking over*: Group members take full ownership

> **Reflection Questions**
> 1. Which techniques listed do you feel would be easiest for you to utilize?
> 2. Which would be more difficult? How can you build strength in that technique?

This model aims for continual improvement and social change through collective action, not individual therapy.

Coholic and MacEwan (2022) also identified seven key group facilitation skills. They are attending, focusing group communication, guiding group interactions, working with group processes, summarizing and analyzing information, modeling and role-playing, and confronting and resolving conflict.

- *Attending*: This includes using verbal and nonverbal cues to show warmth, authenticity, and respect. It also involves making eye contact and acknowledging people's feelings.
- *Focusing group communication*: This involves helping the group stay on topic and ensuring that everyone who wants to participate gets a chance to do so.
- *Guiding group interactions*: This involves directing conversations to achieve a goal and addressing issues that may be affecting group cohesion.
- *Working with group processes*: This involves paying attention to both the content of the discussion and the underlying patterns of behavior within the group.
- *Summarizing and analyzing information*: This involves identifying the main points of a discussion and helping the group to problem-solve.
- *Modeling and role-playing*: This involves demonstrating appropriate behaviors and using role-playing to help members practice new skills.
- *Confronting and resolving conflicts*: This involves helping the group to address disagreements and tensions in a constructive way.

SOCIAL ACTION GROUPS

Social action is a confrontational approach that aims to empower people to change the system through collective action (Staples, 2004). Social action groups pinpoint an issue and collaborate to create solutions and work to reach collective goals. Members in social action groups identify issues, analyze causes, create and implement action plans, and assess progress (Arches, 2012). It involves tactics like persuasion, pressure, and adversarial contest. Some basic assumptions of social action groups (Staples, 2004) include a focus on disadvantaged communities and an aim to change relations of power.

Small groups play a large role in social action. These groups provide a platform for participation, discussion, and leadership development. Examples of small groups include (Staples, 2004):

- *Organizing committees*: An organizing committee is a group of 12 to 15 well-respected people who lead the creation of a new social action organization or revitalize an existing one. This committee helps with tasks like choosing the organization's first issue, creating a plan, and recruiting new members. These committees are important for both new and established organizations.
- *House meetings*: House meetings are small gatherings of 5 to 15 people held in familiar locations to either recruit new members or discuss complex issues. They are designed

to be comfortable and informal to encourage participation. These meetings can be a valuable tool for new organizations and can be used to develop leadership skills among members.

- *Issue committees*: Issue committees are small groups within social action organizations that focus on specific issues. These committees conduct research, develop plans, and choose tactics for campaigns on those issues. They play an important role in helping the organization decide which issues to take on and how to approach them. Issue committees allow members to share experiences and develop a collective understanding of the problem and provide a safe space for members to challenge their own beliefs about their power and ability to affect change, and working in a committee allows for a division of labor based on members' interests and skills. Issue committees are a good place for discussions about strategy and tactics.
- *Lobbying committees*: Lobbying committees are groups that focus on influencing legislation by contacting legislators. Lobbying is effective because legislators are interested in what their constituents think.
- *Negotiating teams*: Negotiating teams are used in social action situations where bargaining is necessary. Steps before negotiating include forming the team, setting a time limit, and establishing how the team will communicate with the larger organization they represent.

People play many different roles in social action groups. Members can be involved to varying degrees, from simply following instructions to actively participating in decisions. Social action groups try to recruit new members through various methods and strive to be inclusive. Leaders can be formal or informal and can focus on tasks or group processes. Shared leadership models are considered to be the best because they allow for more expertise and can prevent power from becoming concentrated in the hands of a few. Organizers are responsible for motivating people to get involved in the group. They help develop goals, strategies, and structures for the group. Organizers should not take over the decision-making for the group, but instead facilitate participation by members and leaders.

POLICY ISSUES

Policy can impact social work practice with group therapy in several ways, both positively and negatively. Policies that promote mental health services and expand insurance coverage for therapy, such as the Affordable Care Act, can make group therapy more accessible to individuals who might not otherwise be able to afford it. Government grants or programs, like the Substance Use Prevention, Treatment, and Recovery Services Block Grant, can specifically target group therapy for certain populations or issues, increasing the availability of these groups. Policies that emphasize preventive mental health care can lead to a rise in support groups aimed at promoting mental well-being and reducing the need for intensive therapy. A main issue related to policy is that, due to inequitable access to mental health care, already oppressed and marginalized groups have limited or no access to resources, including group therapy. For those that actually do have coverage, insurance policies with limited coverage for mental health services or limitations on group therapy specifically can make it difficult for people to participate. Additionally, excessive regulations or paperwork requirements for group therapists could create barriers to setting up and running therapy groups. Privacy policies around health information might make it challenging for group therapy to function effectively, as some level of disclosure is often necessary. Policies that prioritize evidence-based practices in mental health care could put pressure on group therapy to demonstrate its effectiveness through research, which can be challenging due to the dynamic nature of group work. Finally, policies targeting specific populations might limit the diversity of experiences within a group, which can be a valuable aspect of group therapy.

SOCIAL JUSTICE ISSUES

Social work has a rich tradition of social justice–oriented group work focused on social change. Social work emphasizes group dynamics in social movements, similar to therapy groups. Social action is a political act that challenges social work's traditional neutrality, which many social workers are uncomfortable with. However, social action allows individuals to participate in meaningful change. Contrary to what many think, social action can be positive and creative, and it can encompass a diversity of strategies (Dudziak & Profitt, 2012). By reframing power as a tool for positive change, social workers can motivate other social workers and the community members they serve to become change agents. Social action can be combined with education and involve creative expression. Through social movements, social work can help people achieve liberation from oppression by addressing systemic issues. An example of what this can look like can be found in Brubaker et al.'s (2010) chapter "Justice Making in Groups for Homeless Adults: The Emancipatory Communitarian Way," in which the need for group services for adults experiencing homelessness that prioritizes both healing and support along with community action to challenge myths related to homelessness.

> ▶ **Reflection Questions**
>
> 1. Identify a current social justice issue impacting your community. How does it relate to social justice?
> 2. Are there any local social action groups working on this issue? If not, what might a social action group do to support individuals that are impacted by this social justice issue?

SUMMARY

Throughout this chapter we explored the topic of social work practice with groups. Social workers must understand theories related to group practice and how those theories may or may not employ AOP principles. Social workers should understand the different kinds of groups and how they vary based on approach, purpose, and/or goals. Additionally, social workers must understand group development in order to assess groups and infuse social justice principles to advance AOP. Social workers working with groups must employ comprehensive assessment practices in order to ensure that they are best serving their client groups and the community at large. Good assessment is ongoing assessment and can be a tool used throughout the helping process as new information arises, greater details are learned, or new goals emerge from the group. Social workers and group members collaborate at every stage in order to avoid oppressive practices and pathologizing of group members. Social workers understand a variety of theoretical approaches, orientations, and frameworks in order to assist them in better meeting group needs and achieving mutually agreed-upon goals. Social workers also recognize the power of practice with groups, specifically, to enhance individual belonging and advance change efforts for group members' identified concerns as they relate to social justice.

CASE SUMMARY: UNDOCUMENTED AND HOMELESS

Practice Setting Description

Jackie is a first-year master of social work (MSW) student completing an internship at an inner-city family service agency in the Southwest. The agency is in a section of the city that has a high crime rate, gang activity, and failing schools. The area has a diverse population with many immigrants from Central and South America and a substantial African American population. The agency provides individual and family counseling services on a sliding fee scale. The agency also runs several educational and treatment groups as well as a temporary shelter for women and their children. Jackie has been assigned to work with the women and their children in the shelter. Her primary tasks are to provide concrete services and supportive counselling to the shelter residents.

Background Information

Elicia and her daughter, Maria, are undocumented immigrants from Mexico. They have been in the United States for 5 years. Elicia and Maria fled to the area from another southwestern city to escape her abusive husband approximately 2 months ago. Elicia is 25 years old, and Maria 8 years old. Elicia has a 2-year-old daughter, Sarah, who was placed in foster care because of suspected abuse in the home. Sarah is in a foster home in a small rural community in the state hundreds of miles from Elicia's current residence. Since moving to the area, Maria has not been attending school.

Elicia and Maria are currently residing in the agency's temporary shelter for families. They have been at the shelter for 2 weeks, and the agency has a 90-day limit. Prior to arriving at the shelter, Elicia and Maria were homeless and living on the streets.

Elicia is a high school drop-out and was a stay-at-home mother prior to leaving her husband and moving to a different part of the state. She chose to move there because she has two female cousins living in the area who are also undocumented immigrants. Elicia's native language is Spanish. She speaks some English but is not as comfortable speaking in English. Her English comprehension appears to be good. Maria speaks both English and Spanish well. When communicating with the staff, Maria acts as Elicia's interpreter since none of the staff at the shelter speak Spanish.

Maria appears to be behind academically. She struggles reading simple children's books written in English. It is unknown if her ability to read in Spanish is better than her English reading skills.

Other than her two cousins, Elicia has no other sources of support in the community. Her cousins have young families and limited resources but are well established and connected to a Latino community in the city and the local Catholic church. Her cousins refused to let Elicia and Maria live with them while she was trying to find her own place and a job. They stated that they did not have enough room and are concerned they would get in trouble with their landlord if it

(continued)

CASE SUMMARY UNDOCUMENTED AND HOMELESS (*CONTINUED*)

was found out that they were letting people stay with them. They sent her to the local church for help, and she was given the address for the agency's shelter by the priest.

Elicia has been looking for housing in the Latino community. The housing market is tight with limited options, and she has been unable to find anything that she could possibly afford. The only affordable housing she found was a room in a rundown motel that rents by the hour or by the month. It is in an area of town known for drug dealing and sex work.

On arrival in the community, Elicia found occasional work for a house cleaning company. The company hires undocumented workers, pays them very low cash wages, and threatens to turn them in to Immigration and Customs Enforcement (ICE) if they complain. The job bosses also exploit their female workers sexually, threatening to turn them in if they do not comply. Elicia was fearful about applying for other jobs because of her illegal status. She considered turning to sex work to be able to take care of her child, but her Catholic upbringing and thoughts of how this would shame her family have kept her from doing so. She is in constant fear of being detained, separated from Maria, and having her placed in foster care. She is also afraid that she will end up homeless again and forced to live on the streets or return to her abusive husband.

Elicia is extremely reluctant to sign up for any federally funded services, even those that she and her child are entitled to receive. On the suggestion that she enroll for supplemental food through the Supplemental Nutrition Assistance Program (SNAP), Elicia became nervous and refused, as she has heard that participation in SNAP services, and others like them, would draw the attention of ICE, and she had heard stories on the news of individuals being deported after signing up for such programs.

Presenting Problems

Elicia and her child are facing multiple obstacles. They need to find permanent, affordable housing and a job that pays enough to cover her housing and living expenses. In addition, Maria needs to be enrolled in school.

Additionally, Elicia is experiencing an immense amount of stress, anxiety, and possibly post-traumatic stress disorder (PTSD). She described an instance where she could not calm down her breathing and she felt lightheaded. She is very fearful of men and tries to avoid all contact with men in the community. She reports difficulty sleeping at night and feeling exhausted most of the time.

She is concerned about Maria. She has started acting out at the shelter, getting into fights with the other children, disobeying her mother, and being disrespectful and defiant to the staff and other adults. Elicia and Maria fight frequently, and when Elicia tries to discipline Maria, she throws a temper tantrum until Elicia gives up.

Elicia has many strengths. She had the strength to leave her abusive husband and move to a different city. She loves her daughter and wants desperately to keep Maria with her. She is resilient and has managed to survive and keep her daughter safe despite not having a place to stay, a job, and a limited support network. Elicia feels safe in the shelter, but she is very fearful of being caught as an illegal immigrant and is generally mistrustful of helping professionals and persons of authority.

DISCUSSION QUESTIONS

1. Consider what type of group might benefit Elicia? What type of group might benefit Maria?

2. If Elicia was part of a social action group, what social justice issue might be identified by group members to focus on?

3. What approaches may make sense for the group to consider when thinking about actions to take relating to the social justice issue identified earlier?

A robust set of instructor resources designed to supplement this text is located at http://connect.springerpub.com/content/book/978-0-8261-6683-8. Qualifying instructors may request access by emailing textbook@springerpub.com.

KEY REFERENCES

Only key references appear in the print edition. To access the full reference list, visit www.springerpub.com/courseconnect. See inside front cover and tear-out card for CourseConnect details.

Akesson, B., Burns, V., & Hordyk, S.-R. (2017). The place of place in social work: Rethinking the person-in-environment model in social work education and practice. *Journal of Social Work Education*, *53*(3), 372–383. http://dx.doi.org/10.2139/ssrn.2486156

Dominelli, L. (2012). Group work: A critical addition to the social work repertoire. In C. Glisson, K. M. Sowers, & C. N. Dulmus (Eds.), *Social work practice with groups, communities, and organizations: Evidence-based assessments and interventions* (pp. 41–58). Wiley.

Freire, P. (1993). *Education for critical consciousness*. Continuum.

Mullender, A., Ward, D., & Fleming, J. (2013). *Empowerment in action: Self-directed groupwork*. Palgrave Macmillan.

Saleeby, D. (2013). *The strengths-perspective in social work practice* (6th ed.). Pearson.

Tuckman, B. W. (1965). Developmental sequence in small groups. *Psychological Bulletin*, *63*(6), 384–399. https://doi.org/10.1037/h0022100

12
Generalist Practice With Organizations: Assessment and Intervention

Stephen Kauffman and John Poulin

John's generalist master of social work (MSW) field placement is with a large nonprofit agency providing residential placement and foster care services to abused and neglected children and their families. The agency has a professional staff of about 200 social workers providing a wide range of services. During his first month, John worked closely with his field instructor to learn the agency's operating procedures and began his work with his caseload of foster children, biological parents, and foster families. He liked his field instructor, his team, and the work.

Over the next few months, John noticed some concerning organizational issues. The first was that staff morale was very low. Most of the social workers were unhappy, and many were looking for other jobs. The staff were distrustful of the administration, and several of the social workers advised John to never admit any mistake and to be very careful in what he said to supervisors and administrators. John also began to realize that many of the social workers made disparaging comments and jokes about their clients. They seemed to view them as failures incapable of change and with almost no compassion or empathy.

As members of the staff left, the caseloads of the remaining staff were increased. Staff morale continued to plummet. By the end of his first semester, there were several unfilled positions, and the workers' caseloads continued to increase. John found the atmosphere in the office depressing. There was very little interaction among the staff, with most working behind closed doors. The staff were angry at the administration. The administration distrusted the staff, and neither the staff nor the administrators appeared to care about the clients.

LEARNING OBJECTIVES

The chapter addresses Council on Social Work Education (CSWE) Competency 7: Access, and Competency 8: Intervene With Individuals, Families, Groups, Organizations, and Communities. The focus in this chapter is on assessment and intervention with organizations incorporating an anti-oppressive practice (AOP) perspective. By the end of this chapter, you will be able to:

- Identify the ethical principles and standards related to organizational assessment and intervention.
- Describe three organizational theories and how they relate to AOP concepts and practice principles.
- Design an organizational assessment.
- Identify generalist social work practice interventions with organizations.

- Develop goals and measurable objectives.
- Create a program logic model.
- Prepare a grant proposal.
- Research external program funding opportunities.

COMPETENCY 7: ASSESS INDIVIDUALS, FAMILIES, GROUPS, ORGANIZATIONS, AND COMMUNITIES

Social workers understand that assessment is an ongoing component of the dynamic and interactive process of social work practice. Social workers understand theories of human behavior and person-in-environment, as well as interprofessional conceptual frameworks, and they critically evaluate and apply this knowledge in culturally responsive assessment with clients and constituencies, including individuals, families, groups, organizations, and communities. Assessment involves a collaborative process of defining the challenges present and identifying strengths with individuals, families, groups, organizations, and communities to develop a mutually agreed-upon plan. Social workers recognize the implications of the larger practice context in the assessment process and use interprofessional collaboration in this process. Social workers are self-reflective and understand how bias, power, privilege, and their personal values and experiences may affect their assessment and decision-making.

Social workers:

- apply theories of human behavior and person-in-environment, as well as other culturally responsive and interprofessional conceptual frameworks, when assessing clients and constituencies; and
- demonstrate respect for client self-determination during the assessment process by collaborating with clients and constituencies in developing a mutually agreed-upon plan.

COMPETENCY 8: INTERVENE WITH INDIVIDUALS, FAMILIES, GROUPS, ORGANIZATIONS, AND COMMUNITIES

Social workers understand that intervention is an ongoing component of the dynamic and interactive process of social work practice. Social workers understand theories of human behavior, person-in-environment, and other interprofessional conceptual frameworks, and they critically evaluate and apply this knowledge in selecting culturally responsive interventions with clients and constituencies, including individuals, families, groups, organizations, and communities. Social workers understand methods of identifying, analyzing, and implementing evidence-informed interventions and participate in interprofessional collaboration to achieve client and constituency goals. Social workers facilitate effective transitions and endings.

Social workers:

- engage with clients and constituencies to critically choose and implement culturally responsive, evidence-informed interventions to achieve client and constituency goals; and

- incorporate culturally responsive methods to negotiate, mediate, and advocate with and on behalf of clients and constituencies.

NATIONAL ASSOCIATION OF SOCIAL WORKERS *CODE OF ETHICS*

The National Association of Social Workers (NASW) *Code of Ethics* (2021) has four ethical standards that are related to organizational assessment. Three ethical standards are in the ethical responsibilities to the practice setting domain. The first is about advocating for adequate resources to meet client needs. The second is about ensuring adequate resources to provide staff supervision, and the third is about ensuring a work environment that encourages compliance with the NASW *Code of Ethics* (2021). Compliance with these ethical standards requires some sort of organizational assessment to determine if the organization is meeting the resource needs of clients, providing adequate resources for staff supervision, and creating an organizational environment that is consistent with and encourages compliance with the *Code of Ethics*.

A fourth ethical standard related to organizational assessment is about improving agency policies and procedures to improve client services. Again, accomplishing this requires some kind of organizational assessment to identify policies and procedures that need to be improved.

The *Code of Ethics* value of service is related to intervening with organizations. Its associated ethical principle is that social workers' primary goal is to help people in need and to address social problems. The social justice value is also related to intervening with organizations. Its associated ethical principle is that social workers challenge social injustice. Organizational interventions in social work are designed to help those in need and to address social problems as well as social justice issues.

> ▶ **Reflection Questions**
>
> Based on the chapter's opening case example:
> 1. What ethical standards potentially apply to the functioning of the agency?
> 2. As a social work intern, what could John have done to address possible ethical violations?

ORGANIZATIONAL THEORIES

This section focuses on a review of three theories of organizations that are consistent with AOP generalist social work practice. The three theories adhere to the idea that an organization is a tool for achieving a definable goal or set of goals. The theories reviewed in this chapter are rational decision-making theory, organizational development theory, and change theory.

Rational Decision-Making Theory

Herbert Simon recognized that administration is largely a process of human decision-making with the publication of *Administrative Behavior: A Study of Decision-Making Processes in Administrative Organizations* in 1947. Administration is the behavioral and cognitive process of making rational choices or decisions. Rational decision-making is a multistep process, from problem identification through solution, for making logically sound decisions among alternatives. The steps in the decision-making process include:

1. formulating a goal(s)
2. identifying the criteria for making the decision
3. identifying alternatives
4. performing an analysis
5. making a final decision

Rational decision-making favors objective data and a formal process of analysis over subjectivity and intuition. The model of rational decision-making assumes that decision-makers have full or perfect information about alternatives; it also assumes they have the time, cognitive ability, and resources to evaluate each choice against the others. This model assumes that people will make choices that will maximize benefits for themselves and minimize any cost and that measurable criteria exist for which data can be collected and analyzed. The rational decision-making model does not consider factors that cannot be quantified, such as ethical concerns or the value of altruism. It leaves out consideration of personal feelings, loyalties, or sense of obligation.

Critics of rational choice theory—or the rational model of decision-making—claim that this model makes unrealistic and oversimplified assumptions. The model assumes that people have full (or perfect) information. This is rarely the case. Often the information is not available, the person might not be able to access it, or it might take too much time or too many resources to acquire. Additionally, individual rationality is limited by a person's ability to conduct analysis and think through competing alternatives. The more complex a decision, the greater the limits are to making completely rational choices (Course Sidekick, 2019).

In response to the limitations of rational decision-making theory, Simon proposed the idea of bounded rationality (1957). Bounded rationality recognizes that individuals' rationality is limited by the information they have, the cognitive limitations of their minds, and the finite amount of time they have to make a decision. While acknowledging that decision-making is a rational process, it recognizes that people act based on limited information. Because decision-makers usually lack full information, they instead apply their rationality to a set of choices that are bounded by the more satisfying (rather than maximizing or optimizing) choices in complex situations.

Collaborative decision-making is an alternative to a hierarchical approach to decision-making and consistent with the AOP practice principle of collaboration. It applies a group decision-making model to the rational decision-making process. Collaborative decision-making is an inclusionary process that promotes lateral communication and shared decision-making. Its strength is that it fosters a greater buy-in to the decisions and increased stakeholder participation in the decision process. Collaboration can offer members full responsibility for achieving change. By enhancing members' roles in governance and decision-making, buy-in to implementation and the outcomes will be strengthened.

Collaborative decision-making is a process with six guiding principles. The guiding principles are as follows: people need a reason to participate; involve all those with a significant interest; educate all the participants; participation is voluntary; everyone has an opportunity to participate in the design of the collaborative process; and the process is flexible, egalitarian, respectful, time-limited, accountable, and achievable (Global Development Research Center, 2019).

When implementing a collaborative decision-making approach, organizations need to determine the method that will be used. The two most common are the consensus and democratic approaches. The consensus approach involves the entire group in the decision-making process. The goal of consensus decision-making is to find common ground, exploring issues and opinions from everyone's perspective. Discussions leading to consensus aim to bring the group to mutual agreement by addressing all concerns. Consensus does not require unanimity. Rather, everyone must agree they can "live with" the decision.

Organizational assessments based on decision-making theory, the concept of bounded rationality, and collaborative decision-making are consistent with the AOP generalist social work practice. These types of organizational assessments can profoundly impact the availability and quality of service delivery to clients. They can also significantly affect the organizational climate, work environment, and morale of the agency's direct service workers as well as its supervisors and managers.

Organizational Development Theory

Lewin is generally considered the founder of organizational development theory in the 1940s and 1950s. Organizational development focuses on expanding the knowledge and effectiveness of people to accomplish more successful organizational change and performance. It is a comprehensive strategy for organizational improvement, particularly through a more effective and collaborative management culture.

The objectives of organizational development are:

- Increase the level of trust and support among organizational members.
- Increase the incidence of confrontation of organizational problems, both within groups and among groups, in contrast to "sweeping problems under the rug."
- Create an environment in which designation of assigned roles is augmented based on knowledge and skills.
- Increase the openness of communication laterally, vertically, and diagonally.
- Increase the level of personal enthusiasm and satisfaction in the organization.
- Find synergistic solutions to problems with greater frequency. Synergistic solutions are creative solutions in which 2 + 2 equals more than 4 and through which all parties gain more through cooperation than through conflict.
- Increase the level of self and group responsibility in planning and implementation. (French & Bell, 1999)

Lewin identified three key areas of organizational functioning: organizational climate, organizational culture, and organizational strategies. The organizational climate is the mood or unique "personality" of an organization. The administrators' and managers' attitudes and beliefs about organizational practices help create organizational climate and influence members' collective behavior. Climate features and characteristics may be associated with employee satisfaction, stress, service quality and outcomes, and successful implementation of new programs. Climate features and characteristics include leadership, openness of communication, participatory management, role clarity, conflict resolution, leader support, and leader control.

The organizational culture is the deeply seated norms, values, and behaviors that members share. The elements of an organization's culture include assumptions, values, behavioral norms, behavioral patterns, and organizational artifacts. These elements help shape the organization's behavior and the decision-making process. Organizational strategies, on the other hand, are the actions taken to create organizational change and improvement. Change strategies usually involve four action steps. The first is diagnosis. Diagnosis is done to identify problem areas and underlying causes. An organizational development approach to diagnosis seeks to identify problems by examining the organization's mission, goals, policies, structures, and technologies; climate and culture; environmental factors; desired outcomes; and readiness to act (French & Bell, 1999).

The second action step is planning. Organizations need to formulate change plans and strategies. The planning step involves identifying options and assessing feasibility. At this stage, the preferred strategy or strategies are identified, as are the goals and objectives of the planned intervention strategy. The third action step is intervention. This results in the identified plan being put into action to address the identified need and diagnosed problem(s). The final and fourth action step is evaluation. This involves assessing the planned change efforts by tracking the organization's progress in implementing the change and by documenting its impact on the organization.

Organizational development theory identifies three major components of organizations that greatly impact an organization's ability to achieve its goals and objectives. Organizational climate, culture, and the strategies employed to improve an organization's performance impact the delivery of services to clients as well as the job satisfaction, commitment, and motivation of the professional staff and administrators. Thus, organizational development theory has great relevance for organizational assessments that are consistent with the practice principles of AOP generalist social work.

Change Theory

Lewin's change theory (1947) is useful in creating organizational change. Social service organizations, both not-for-profit and government agencies, like any other organization, are resistant to change. They develop set ways of doing things, and creating change, even if it is beneficial, is challenging. To overcome resistance, people need to let go of old habits and structures. This is a difficult assignment because change leads to a disruption of a stable situation. People like to keep the old situation as it is because it is safe and predictable. People are only capable of accepting change when they know what this change will bring them. Lewin's change model conceptualizes change in a three-step process. The steps in this model are the unfreeze stage, the change stage, and the refreeze stage.

Unfreezing

This is the preparing for change stage. It is preparing the organization and its members for change. It involves breaking down the old way of doing things and changing peoples' mindset about how the organization functions. The key is showing people that the current way cannot continue and that change will lead to improved outcomes for clients and/or the organization. Unfreezing means getting people to open up to new ways of reaching their objectives. Basically, the current practices and processes must be reassessed before organizational change can take place. During the unfreezing stage, you need to determine what needs to be changed. Several different methods can be used to identify areas that need to be changed. Possible methods include outcome studies, consumer surveys, employee surveys, and focus groups. The greater the level of participation in identifying the change targets, the greater the likelihood that the change goals will be achieved (Schein, 1996). It is also important to create a clear message about why change must occur. The "why" needs to be tied to the organization's vision and mission. Finally, during the unfreezing stage, it is important to address doubts and concerns. Being open to employee concerns and addressing them from the perspective of the need to change will help overcome stakeholder concerns (Schein, 1996).

Change

This is the implementation stage. Once the organization members have accepted that change is needed, then change can start. It is important that the change is implemented within a short time. The longer the change process takes, the more likely employees will relapse into old habits and behaviors (Schein, 1996). By acting quickly and implementing the change within a short time, the stakeholders will accept the importance of the change effort more quickly. After the uncertainty created in the unfreeze stage, the change stage is where the uncertainty is replaced with new ways to do things. People start to believe and act in ways that support the new direction. Time and communication are the two keys to the changes occurring successfully. People need time to understand the changes, and they also need to feel highly connected to the organization throughout the transition period. During the change stage, it is important to communicate often to prepare people for the change and to dispel rumors that can undermine the change process. It is also important to empower action and provide lots of opportunities for employee involvement.

Refreeze

The refreeze stage is where the changes become internalized and incorporated into the overall functioning of the organization. It is about solidifying the change. Employees need to feel comfortable and confident with the new ways of working. The refreezing stage is important. Without it, employees are not sure how things should be done, so nothing ever gets done to full capacity. It then becomes a short-term change, and people revert to the old ways of doing things. During the refreezing stage, the goal is to anchor the changes into the culture of the organization as well as identify what supports the change and what barriers need to be overcome to support long-term change (Schein, 1996).

> ▶ **Reflection Questions**
> 1. Which of the three theories reviewed is most consistent with your values and beliefs about organizations? Why?
> 2. Which theory in your opinion best supports AOP generalist practice with organizations? Why?

Change theory is compatible with AOP generalist social work practice. It emphasizes and incorporates the AOP practice principles of collaboration and empowerment. It also utilizes self-reflection during the unfreezing stage where the aspects of the organization that need to be changed are identified.

ANTI-OPPRESSIVE GENERALIST PRACTICE WITH ORGANIZATIONS

AOP generalist practice with organizations incorporates the four phases of the helping process—engagement, assessment, intervention, and evaluation. The aim of AOP generalist practice with organizations typically focuses on improving organizational functioning, program development and/or service delivery. AOP generalist social workers approach their work with organizations from a social justice perspective and seek to address inequality, oppression, discrimination, and power and privilege.

Engagement

The engagement phase consists of the preengagement stage, establishing a helping relationship and maintaining the helping relationship. The first order of business is self-reflection. How do your values align with the mission of the organization? What organizational issues need to be addressed? What are your feelings about the organizational issues? Who are the stakeholders affected by the organizational issues? Who benefits from the status quo? Who is negatively impacted? Are there social justice concerns? How are power and privilege manifested in the organization? Engaging in critical self-reflection is a vital first step in preparing for an organizational assessment.

Establishing a helping relationship is the second stage of the engagement process. In AOP generalist practice with organizations, this entails identifying the stakeholders involved in the organizational assessment. The stakeholders are those that will use the information obtained from the assessment process as well as those impacted by the organizational change. Potential stakeholders include organizational administrators, board members, task force members, managers, supervisors, professional staff, support staff, and service users. As with social work practice with individuals, families, and groups, establishing a helping relationship with organizational stakeholders is built upon trust. Trust is established through shared positive experiences. It is a process and often challenging. Change can be threating to some stakeholders and welcomed by others. Engaging all the stakeholders in an organizational assessment to address some issue, in our opinion, is the most difficult aspect of conducting an organizational assessment.

Assessment

The assessment phase is where the actual assessment is conducted. The initial assessment stage entails several steps. Completing each step collaboratively helps build trust and establish a positive helping relationship. The first task is to collectively identify the organizational issue or issues to be examined. Obtaining agreement on the focus of the assessment is critical. If the various stakeholders disagree upon need, then resistance is likely to hinder the process. Once the overall focus of the assessment is established, the next task is to develop the assessment plan. Again, this should be a collaborative process. This entails identifying the variables or components of the organization that will be assessed; the data sources; and how the data will be collected, analyzed, and disseminated.

An often-overlooked component of an organizational assessment is including a component for establishing an ongoing assessment process. Stabilizing and maintaining organizational change are difficult. AOP generalist practice with organizations emphasizes social justice and the welfare of clients. Ongoing organizational assessment and follow-up are needed to ensure that the organizational changes are having the desired effect and that the change has not regressed back to the former practices.

There are several possible reasons to conduct an organizational assessment. An organizational assessment can be useful in identifying an organization's strengths and weaknesses. They are often used to:

- provide stakeholders with information about the organization's performance and generate information that will be useful in planning and decision-making;
- identify resources (human and otherwise) that the organization can use to effectively improve its performance;
- identify needs that should be addressed through specific actions; and
- respond to a need or desire to change an organization's performance.

Organizational assessments can also be used to help make strategic decisions. Should the organization grow or change its mission? An organizational assessment can also be helpful in making program decisions. Should you expand your programs? Should you offer new services? Organizational assessments can also help with funding decisions as well as staffing considerations.

The key to a good assessment is knowing what represents optimal functioning of the organization. Yet at the same time, there is no "one best way" to construct an organization to meet all desired ends. Organizations may be structured in any one of several ways, each of which may be effective at achieving the goals of the organization under some conditions but at the same time may be problematic under other conditions. Various groups, or "constituencies," make up an organization. These may include line staff, supervisors, support staff, administration, clients, and external collaborators. Each typically has their own set of needs and perceptions about the organization, and thus each will have something valuable to contribute to the assessment (Kauffman, 2010).

Social service organizations, like all organizations, have the dimensions or components. These dimensions can be classified into two broad groups: internal and environmental characteristics. From each of these groupings is found many elements that either strengthen and support the organization or act as stressors or obstacles to optimal functioning. The characteristics within each group contribute to organizational functioning and are important components of an organizational assessment.

Internal Organizational Characteristics

Beyond the issues of identity, many elements are associated with the internal characteristics of the organization that could be included in an assessment. These characteristics can be placed into three groupings: foundation policies, internal structure, and internal processes. Elements from each grouping must be examined for their possible usefulness as strengths to the organization or serving as an obstacle or stressor to the organization (Kauffman & Barnett, 2019).

Foundation Policies

Foundation policies refer to the documents and guidelines (generally written) that give meaning and guidance to the agency. Organizations exist for a purpose, and these policies express both this purpose and a description of the overarching structure and processes of the organization. At the same time, simply because something is written does not mean it is followed, and it may be that this disconnect between what is written and what is real may cause some of the organization's difficulties. The most important types of foundation policies are the constitution and bylaws, vision, mission, goals, and strategic plans.

Organizational Mission and Vision

Organizations are guided by a set of principles outlined in their mission. Mission statements specify the fundamental purpose of the organization. The mission statement documents the needs that the organization seeks to address (purpose), specifies how the organization addresses those needs (business), and states the principles or beliefs (values) of the organization. According to Kettner et al. (2017), the mission statement "should focus on what lies ahead for its clients and/or consumers if the agency is successful in addressing their problems and meeting their needs" (p. 110).

Organizations also have vision statements. Vision statements are statements of the future. They are statements about what the organization hopes to become. The values and philosophy of the organization determine the priorities of the mission and the design and implementation of programs and activities. The organization's mission and vision statements set the stage to identify programs and activities.

An assessment of an organization's mission and vision would involve examination of the statements themselves to determine clarity of content as well as the extent to which the mission and vision statements are consistent with the organization's programs and services. Are the mission and vision statements guiding the organization's programs and services, initiatives, and the operation of the organization? To what extent are the mission and vision statements guiding the direction and functioning of the agency?

Organizational Goals and Objectives

Much of what has been stated about microsystem client goals and the goal setting process applies to organizations as well. Organizational goals are the statements of the desired qualities in human and social conditions. Goals suggest intended outcomes, provide organizational direction, and provide standards or criteria for evaluation and legitimacy (Coley & Scheinberg, 2017). Goals are broad, nonmeasurable statements that describe a "desired state."

Goals are often confused with objectives, but these are not interchangeable concepts. While goals provide the direction for the organization's focus, objectives establish precise expectations of what the organization is attempting to achieve, including a time frame (Kettner et al., 2017). Objectives are how the goals are achieved. While goals are broad statements of what we would like to see, objectives should be specific, measurable, achievable, realistic, and time-bound.

In assessing an organization's goals and objectives, first determine if the goals are written in terms of a broad desired end state. Are the goals broad statements about what the organization hopes to achieve? Are the goals nonmeasurable statements of a desired positive outcome? On the other hand, are the organization's objectives specific and measurable? Do they describe in very concrete terms exactly what will be accomplished? Are they measurable and achievable? Are the organization's objectives time-limited and related to a single result? Box 12.1 includes examples of two organizational goals and their associated objectives.

Internal Structure

The structure of an organization varies dramatically by the purposes of the organization, but there are some commonalities that crosscut most types. Simply stated, these are the administration, frontline workers, and a large variety of support staff. The central questions that an assessment should focus on here relate to the qualifications and skills of each of the positions in these structural components, as well as how staff are supported and/or how the work responsibilities create burdens for the staff (Kauffman, 2010).

BOX 12.1

SAMPLE ORGANIZATIONAL GOALS AND OBJECTIVES

Goal 1: Seven Arrows Center will provide a variety of effective, evidence-based substance abuse treatment services, both inpatient and outpatient, to all persons in need in the North Hills region.

Objective 1.1: To provide inpatient, residential treatment services to a minimum of 250 clients per year.

Objective 1.2: To provide methadone maintenance services for a maximum of 500 clients per year.

Objective 1.3: To provide outpatient counseling services for a maximum of 1,000 clients per year.

Goal 2: Seven Arrows Center will achieve the highest standards of quality through support of staff, nondiscriminatory practices, and community involvement.

Objective 2.1: Seven Arrows Center will provide a minimum of 100 hours of advanced training to each staff member each year.

Objective 2.2: Staff satisfaction will be maximized by establishing a benefits package, customized for each employee, that will include health and dental care, retirement plans, and rotating sabbaticals for all full-time employees.

Objective 2.3: To establish a community advisory board to assist the agency in developing policies that help the agency better meet community needs.

Thus, most social workers are in administrative, middle-line, or frontline positions. These are the workers who are most concerned with the primary tasks of the organization, whatever they may be. Generally, administrators are concerned with the overall functioning of the organization. This often includes policy development, planning, personnel, resource development and acquisition, and compliance with external (and legal) requirements, as well as leadership and setting the tone of the organization. In other words, the administration sets the informal climate of the organization. A climate where workers feel supported can go a long way in overcoming the stress that is created by clients or the environment in which the organization rests. On the other hand, a climate that feels oppressive and uncaring may make even pleasant work tasks feel stressful.

Supervisors (the middle line), on the other hand, serve as intermediaries between the administration and the frontline worker. Their task in the human service organization is to translate policies from the administration to the frontline, communicate information both up and down the chain of command, oversee job function, and provide guidance to the frontline worker. The quality by which these functions are carried out may be a source of either serious problems for the organization or its greatest successes. The assumption is that the supervisor understands both the needs and problems of the frontline worker, while also understanding the work requirements of the administration.

Finally, the frontline represents the employee who is most responsible for carrying out the primary tasks of the organization. In social service agency settings, this usually applies to working with people in some form. The tasks of the frontline staff are vastly different depending on the agency's function, so it is somewhat difficult to provide any generalities. It is, however, critical to consider frontline workers' training, education, preparedness, and support. The quality of their work is a function of their ability, resources, and workload.

Internal Processes

How the staff and structure operate represents the final element of the internal organizational considerations. These are what are called the processes, and how they function often proves to be the most problematic concerns for an organization. Among these, the most well-known are power (and its manifestations as authority and leadership) and information (and its manifestation as communication).

Every organization demonstrates some degree of applied power. It is this applied power that ensures that the right work is done in the right amount at the right time. This form of power is what people refer to as authority, or the degree and type of control exerted within the organization.

How this authority is applied, in what settings, and to what degree need to be considered. Authority that is used correctly and judiciously will be positive for the organization, while incorrectly applied authority may damage or hurt the organization. Most particularly, authority is necessary to motivate staff to move the organization in the desired direction. This is a function of leadership. Staff may work to achieve organizational goals without some form of external authority, but the odds of success are greatly improved in the presence of an effective leader. Organizational assessments very often find that the problems that exist in the social service agency are closely connected to the quality of the leadership provided and how well the leader manages the agency. Thus, a good assessment will spend time examining the quality of leadership.

Along with authority, a second internal process is information and how this information is communicated. An organization cannot function without the free flow of information both up and down the structure. Several obstacles can affect the flow of communication, and as with leadership, a major focus of an organizational assessment should be on communication.

Organizational Environmental Considerations

From the standpoint of assessment, there are several direct variables that might be included. For example, a major potential barrier to any organization is access to resources. Resources for different organizations may mean different things—people, technology, and information are examples. But few, if any, social service organizations can continue to exist for very long without one critically important resource—money.

The methods and degree of success by which the agency can fund its services affect almost all aspects of the agency, from the quality of services provided to the level of employee satisfaction. The key questions relating to resources are simple enough: Is funding adequate? Has there been a change in the funding source? Is the method effective? In any case, funding shortages, or even the possibility of changes in funding, can be enough to cause significant fear and disruption to the agency.

Technology has changed, and continues to change, at impressive rates. In brief, technology is how the organization does what it does. It may be counseling, or methadone maintenance, or community organization, or use of computers. The big issue associated with technology that any assessment should consider is its effectiveness.

Organizational Assessment Variables

Burke and Litwin (1992) developed a performance and change model that identifies the primary variables that need to be considered to understand an organization's functioning. The model is shown in Figure 12.1.

The Burke–Litwin model is a helpful tool in structuring an organizational assessment. One of its strengths is that it shows the interrelationships among the various organizational variables. Table 12.1 lists the model's 12 organizational variables and some sample assessment questions for each variable.

Intervention

AOP generalist social work practice interventions with organizations aim to improve organizational functioning and service delivery for oppressed and discriminated populations. Table 12.2 lists social work practice interventions related to organizations.

As shown in Table 12.2, typical client systems at the organizational level are organizational leaders, task forces, committees, and advisory boards. The system level is the organization, and the client systems that the social worker engages are the decision-makers and decision-making structures of the organization. The worker usually participates in formally organized work groups, such as agency task forces or committees, often to develop new

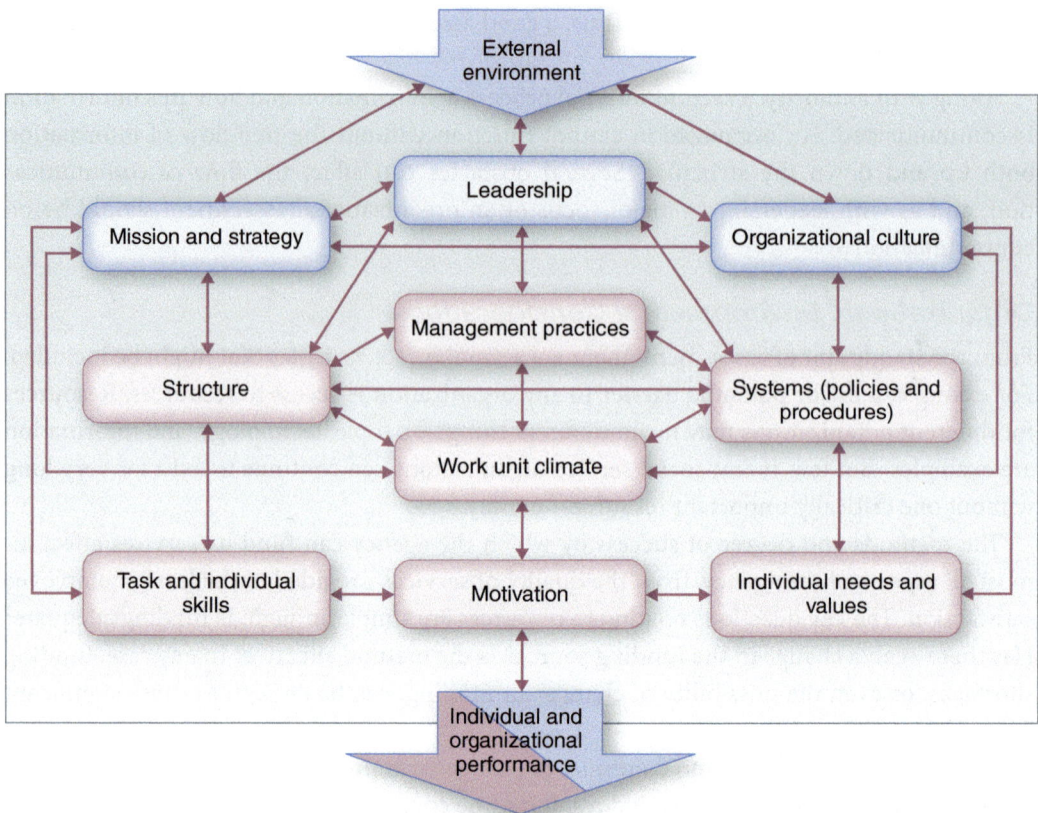

FIGURE 12.1 Organizational assessment variables.

services or improve existing services. The client system might also be the organization's decision-makers, that is, administrators and supervisors. Thus, an AOP social worker seeking to change an organization may view the decision-makers or the decision-making structures as the client system to improve how decisions are made or how the organization communicates about decisions, activities, or services. Addressing these client systems is often of the greatest importance because organizations are often where individual clients turn to for help. An organization that does not function well may not serve its clients or even the very staff that work within those organizations. Thus, at the organizational level, the purpose of AOP generalist social work practice is to improve the functioning of the organization, improve services and service delivery, or develop new services through program development and/or grant writing. Organizational interventions from an AOP perspective focus on social justice and the AOP concepts of discrimination and oppression, power and privilege, collaboration, empowerment, and minimal intervention.

After the organizational or community assessment is completed, the AOP generalist social worker proceeds to the intervention phase of the helping process. The stages of the intervention phase are plan, develop, implementation, adjust and revise, and termination. The AOP model of generalist practice calls for simultaneously implementing the evaluation phase of the helping process. During the intervention phase there is an ongoing process evaluation of the intervention. This ongoing process evaluation informs the adjust and revise stage of the intervention process.

TABLE 12.1 ORGANIZATIONAL VARIABLES AND SAMPLE QUESTIONS

Dimensions of Model	Key Questions
1. External environment	• What are the key external drivers? • How are these likely to impact the organization? • Does the organization recognize these?
2. Mission and strategy	• What does top management see as the organization's mission and strategy? • Is there a clear vision and mission statement? • What are employees' perceptions of these?
3. Leadership	• Who provides overall direction for the organization? • Who are the role models? • What is the style of leadership? • What are the perspectives of employees?
4. Organizational culture	• What are the overt and covert rules, values, customs, and principles that guide organizational behavior?
5. Structure	• How are functions and people arranged in specific areas and levels of responsibility? • What are the key decision-making, communication, and control relationships?
6. Systems	• What are the organization's policies and procedures, including systems for reward and performance appraisal, management information, human resources, and resource planning?
7. Management practices	• How do managers use human and material resources to carry out the organization's strategy? • What is their style of management, and how do they relate to subordinates?
8. Work unit climate	• What are the collective impressions, expectations, and feelings of staff? • What is the nature of relationship with work unit colleagues and those in other work units?
9. Task and individual skills	• What are the task requirements and individual skills/abilities/knowledge needed for task effectiveness? • How appropriate is the organization's "job–person" match?
10. Individual needs and values	• What do staff members value in their work? • What are the psychological factors that would enrich their jobs and increase job satisfaction?
11. Motivation	• Do staff feel motivated to take the action necessary to achieve the organization's strategy? • Of factors 1 through 10, which seem to impact motivation the most?
12. Individual and organizational performance	• What is the level of performance in terms of productivity, customer satisfaction, quality, and so on? • Which factors are critical for motivation and therefore performance?

TABLE 12.2 GENERALIST INTERVENTIONS WITH ORGANIZATIONS

System Level	Client System	Interventions
Organization	Administrators Task forces Committees Advisory boards	Education and training Planning and program development

Develop the Intervention Plan

Setting Goals and Objectives

Goals serve a variety of critical purposes in the overall intervention. As well as serving as positive outcomes to the intervention activity, they help provide meaning and definition to the agency and giving direction and helping to keep everyone focused. Goals may also serve as an internal source of motivation and commitment. Commonly, goals are viewed as the desired end states of the activity or intervention. As such, it is essential that the goal is linked to a problem or, more specifically, to the "resolution" of the problem. Note the examples in Table 12.3.

But importantly, there is an issue that requires our attention here. Very often, end states have different "dimensions" or qualities, and as such it may be a bit difficult for us to really be certain that we have achieved that end state. For example, common organizational problems like "staff morale," "high-quality services," or even "client satisfaction" may each have two, three, or even more aspects, each of which must be addressed if we are to be certain that we have achieved the goal.

So, if goals have multiple dimensions, and each of these dimensions may serve as an indicator of goal attainment, how do we organize the information for planning purposes? The answer is to break the goals down into three stages: *goals*, *objectives*, and *tasks* (or action steps or activities), with each stage presenting an increasingly specific level of information. The goals, again, are the first level and are the desired end states, again often with different dimensions. The objective, or the next level, now becomes an indicator of goal attainment, and it contains a single dimension of the goal. Indeed, for complex goals, we may choose to select two, three, or even more indicators, each of which focuses on one of the dimensions of the goal. The final level, the task or activity, speaks to the specific responsibilities of the staff or client in carrying out the intervention. More on tasks/action steps is provided later as we conceptualize the interventions a bit more thoroughly.

Notice the difference between the measurability and specificity of the goals in Table 12.3 (examples of agency goals) and the objectives in Table 12.4 (examples of measurable agency objectives).

The objectives are the indicators of goal attainment, and these indicators are the measurable dimensions of the problem (and goal) at hand. Unlike goals, therefore, objectives must be highly specific in every way. Any ambiguity may potentially misconstrue the meaning of

TABLE 12.3 EXAMPLES OF AGENCY GOALS	
Problem	**Goal Response**
Low staff morale	Goal 1: The agency will achieve a high level of employee morale.
Financial difficulties	Goal 2: The agency will achieve complete financial solvency.
Poor client satisfaction	Goal 3: The agency will achieve a high level of customer satisfaction
Communication problems	Goal 4: The agency will achieve a high level of quality of communication, both inside and outside of the organization.

TABLE 12.4 EXAMPLES OF MEASURABLE AGENCY OBJECTIVES

Problem	Goal and Objective Response
Low staff morale	**Goal 1:** The agency will achieve a high level of employee morale.
Objective 1.1	The agency will improve staff retention, as measured by employees with more than 2 years of service, by 50% by March 2025.
Objective 1.2	Employee satisfaction with employment, as measured by quarterly satisfaction surveys, will increase by 80% from current levels by March 2025.
Objective 1.3	The rate of employees daily absenteeism will fall by 75% from current levels by March 2025.
Financial difficulties	**Goal 2:** The agency will achieve complete financial solvency.
Objective 2.1	The number of authorized client admissions will increase by 30% from current levels by March 2025.
Objective 2.2	The time between submission and payment of staff travel reimbursements for all employees will reduce from 90 days to 14 days by December 2025.
Objective 2.3	The number of successful grant applications written by the agency will increase by 100% from current levels by March 2025.
Poor client satisfaction	**Goal 3:** The agency will achieve a high level of customer satisfaction.
Objective 3.1	The agency will improve client retention, as measured by clients completing treatment, by 50% by March 2025.
Objective 3.2	The agency will improve client treatment compliance, as measured by the percentage of clients who meet monthly task assignments, by 75% by December 2025.
Objective 3.3	The rate of clients' daily absenteeism will fall by 75% from current levels by March 2025.
Communication problems	**Goal 4:** The agency will achieve a high level of quality of communication, both inside and outside of the organization.
Objective 4.1	The number of missed meetings by staff due to failure to inform will fall by 75% from current levels by March 2025.
Objective 4.2	Worker level of reported satisfaction with communication, as measured by quarterly satisfaction surveys, will increase by 80% from current levels by March 2025.
Objective 4.3	The number of conflicts between workers with communication identified as the cause will fall by 75% from current levels by March 2025.

the objective. But by enhancing the measurability of the objective, demonstration of objective attainment becomes easier.

Surprisingly, there is no mystery in writing good objectives; a few guidelines will greatly assist you in creating sharp and useful objectives. Indeed, the acronym SMART will help. SMART stands for statements that are:

- **S**pecific
- **M**easurable

- **A**ttainable
- **R**elevant
- **T**ime-bound

The characteristics of each of these terms have been nicely described (Cothran et al., 2019):

- *Specific* means that the statement has fully addressed four questions:
  - Who is to be involved?
  - What is to be accomplished?
  - Where is it to be done?
  - When is it to be done?
- *Measurable* means that the statement has fully addressed three questions:
  - How much?
  - How will you know when it is accomplished?
  - How many?
- *Attainable* means that the statement has a real chance of success.
- *Relevant* means the statement is consistent with the mission of the organization.
- *Time-bound* means the statement has a beginning and an ending point.

Interventions

One type of organizational intervention that is widely used is structured trainings, often through workshops. Trainings may be designed to be short and narrowly targeted events, or they may be designed to take place over a longer period and address a large variety of issues. Among the kinds of issues that many social workers confront and for which trainings may be useful include improving productivity and the use of technology.

Trainings to Enhance Productivity and Technology

One common issue that social workers confront is how to improve a group's productivity. Productivity refers to the output of work relative to the effort involved. Often, it is the case that a group may have to "do more with less." Indeed, organizations may be otherwise effective, but service demands exceed the resources necessary to address those demands. In these situations, the organization may be improved by enhancing or correcting the procedures already in place (Brody, 2014). In other words, work to improve the productivity of the group by focusing on the strengths of the group. Rarely are organizations so lost that everything must be changed. Commonly, it only requires some element of reform or enhancement.

Technology, for example, is a common tool for enhancing productivity. The NASW *Code of Ethics* (2021) provides some guidance in the use of technology in the provision of social work services. The guidelines cover the competent use of technology, and the second is about complying with the laws governing the use of technology. The specific language of these ethical standards can be found online at www.socialworkers.org/About/Ethics/Code-of-Ethics/Code-of-Ethics-English.

In recent years, a variety of technological applications have become available that have aided everything from communication, to diagnosis, to service provision. Consider for a moment the difficulties associated with agency paperwork. With the development and application of some simple programs and perhaps an intranet, many routine tasks such as case notes, internal communication, and even diagnosis may be improved. A generalist social worker can convene or coordinate work groups to help choose and then train group members to use the proper technology.

The problem of group communication processes also serves as a case in point. It is not that difficult to greatly enhance communication through very simple processes. These may include selecting a better method of communication through matching the needs and purposes of the communication with the technique (Brody, 2014). Meetings, important as they are, do not need to be held if information can be more effectively passed on through individual contacts or electronic means.

Technology resources such as videoconferencing, online scheduling, and cloud document management can increase collaboration and productivity in organizations. These resources make more time available to staff, while reducing some complexity for administrators and clients. Again, the generalist social worker can convene or coordinate work groups to help select the appropriate solution and then train group members in how to use it.

Trainings to Improve Group Skills

Trainings may also be used to enhance other needed skills. Many of us, for example, have benefited from trainings to address issues as broad as diversity and culture or as narrow as the application of a particular counseling technique. The question to address in planning for this intervention is whether the need may be corrected in a single event, or if the need is for a multievent, long-term set of trainings. The social worker can facilitate the training and/or coordinate the planning for the training.

Case 12.1 illustrates the beginning steps in developing a staff workshop. This example highlights the importance of getting input from members of the target group before implementing a training program. The probation officers' perceptions of what they were interested in were very different from their director's perceptions. The workshop turned out to be a success and was well received by the probation officers, even though it was not exactly what the director originally envisioned. If the training team had proceeded without any input from the participants, it would most likely have been less well received. The workshop would have been a trying experience for both the training team and the participants.

Trainings to Enhance Leadership

Social workers are called upon to be leaders in the fight against social injustice. Leadership development is a critical component that may require focus in training activities. Many people mistakenly consider leadership to be of concern only to managers or administrators. But in reality, everyone can benefit from enhanced leadership skills. It is very difficult for any mezzo-level group to function well without effective leadership.

While leadership has been widely studied, recent studies have resulted in a number of important breakthroughs in understanding the concept. Organizational performance in the human services is enhanced by utilizing a transformational leadership style accompanied by participatory decision-making (Fuller et al., 1999; Gellis, 2001). Transformational leaders

CASE 12.1 — EARLY STEPS IN STAFF WORKSHOP DEVELOPMENT

Christiana, Laurie, and Pat all were graduate social work students doing their second-year field placements at Social Work Consultation Services (SWCS). SWCS provided generalist social work learning experiences for student interns and social work and capacity-building services for residents and organizations of an economically disadvantaged community. The director of adult probation in the county contacted SWCS about conducting a staff development workshop for her probation officers. Christiana, Laurie, and Pat took on the project under the supervision of a school faculty member.

The training team scheduled a meeting with the director of adult probation to get a better understanding of the agency's needs and her expectations about the purpose and objectives of the workshop. The director felt that her staff could benefit from a workshop on relationship-building skills and on how to engage reluctant, resistant, or hostile clients in a collaborative working relationship. She felt that many of the probation officers were showing signs of burnout and a lot of frustration with their clients and the legal system. Many seemed to have given up trying to make a difference in their clients' lives and were not making any efforts to connect with them. The team left the meeting with a clear understanding of what the director wanted. They felt it was something that they would be able to put together and deliver effectively.

With the approval of the director, the training team scheduled a preworkshop meeting with the probation officers who would be attending the workshop. The purpose of the meeting was to get an understanding of their training needs and interests. The meeting did not go as expected. The probation officers had absolutely no interest in learning "soft" relationship skills and were totally against the idea of having to attend a workshop on how to connect with reluctant or hostile clients. They felt that such training would be a total waste of time. They used the meeting to vent their feelings about the system and working with clients who lied and were manipulative.

The team struggled to find some common ground between the director's and staff's perceived needs. Because the probation officers were so clear about the frustrations of their job, Pat asked if they would be interested in a workshop that focused on coping strategies and burnout prevention. This, too, was rejected as a waste of time. Most of the group members claimed not to have any problems in that area and said they could take care of themselves just fine.

Having struck out making suggestions to this group, Christiana asked them what would be helpful. After quite a bit of back-and-forth discussion among the probation officers, it was decided that a workshop on the link between mental health and substance abuse would be helpful. All their clients were substance abusers, and the workers felt that for many, mental health issues compounded their difficulties with substance abuse and the law. The team agreed to the proposed focus, pending approval by the probation officers' director.

---

are proactive, positive, and are able to motivate and influence others. Participatory leadership styles allow employees to engage in the problem-solving process. All members of the organization are viewed as having individual skills, abilities, and talents that can enhance the functioning of the organization or the community.

Emotional intelligence (the ability to accurately interpret emotional states and needs) is also a critical element of leadership (Ovans, 2015). Consisting of such attributes as self-awareness, self-regulation, empathy, and solid social skills (Goleman, 1998; Goleman & Boyatzis, 2017), the idea is that a leader who understands people will help improve many workplace conditions. Emotional intelligence can be improved through training.

Trainings to Address Organizational and Group Trauma

In recent years, the concept of "trauma" has taken root as an effective way to understand the causes and consequences of problems within group, organizational, and community systems. The problem of how to address trauma in groups can be addressed through trainings developing knowledge and skills as related to trauma. Why? Trauma implies disruption, and how well the system can cope with disruption should be of major concern to any system. For example, trauma affects communication, power and empowerment, emotions, conflict, and cognitions, and these are closely linked to trust and the capacity to form and support human bonds and relationships. As such, trauma may create disruption in a variety of ways. Clients may come to the agency with personal trauma. Workers can experience this as vicarious trauma by working closely with such clients. But further, the organizations may in fact be producing trauma themselves! Because of ongoing issues of underresourcing or poor (or traumatized) leadership or stressful environments, the organization may become maladapted. Indeed, many social service organizations are functioning as trauma-organized systems (Bloom & Sreedhar, 2008). Consequences include authoritarian and punitive administrators, and workers become more aggressive and exhibit passive-aggressive behaviors. The entire organizational environment may become progressively more unjust (Bloom & Sreedhar, 2008).

Community Education

The value of education and training does not stop with small groups and organizations. Often, larger mezzo groups, such as communities can benefit from education and training activities. In recent years, for example, social workers have created or participated in community education programs to address issues as disparate as sexually transmitted disease (STD) prevention, violence reduction, health education, cultural sensitivity, and environmental concerns.

Developing the appropriate education program is often complex. A number of issues as diverse as how to choose the best model all the way to how to effectively communicate in a small group has to be taken into consideration. Further, social media provides useful tools for both identifying and contacting potential target groups, as well as actually distributing informational content.

Ideally, community education seeks to empower and build internal capacity among the members or residents. As with organizational training and education, it is important for the members of the target community to be involved in the definition of the problems and the structuring of interventions. Education and training at the community level tend to focus on increasing community awareness and understanding of social issues and community problems. Social workers make formal presentations at community meetings, serve as panelists at public forums, and conduct community workshops and seminars. The two examples in Case 12.2 illustrate how social workers may use education and training as a mezzo-level practice intervention.

CASE 12.2 | EDUCATION AND TRAINING INTERVENTIONS FOR SOCIAL WORKERS

Marcus

Marcus is the social worker with the Chester Community Improvement Project, a grant-funded agency that provides community residents with information to assist them in home ownership. The project seeks to address the needs of families through its rehabilitation project, new housing construction project, mortgage counseling, and job training for youth. Marcus designed a series of workshops for residents to educate them about financial literacy, saving for the first home, and understanding mortgages. Marcus discussed the current condition of the local neighborhood and cited statistics showing that the neighborhood could be stabilized by increasing home ownership among the residents.

Sharon

Sharon is a second-year student placed with the local charter school. The past year the school was in jeopardy of not making the annual yearly progress benchmarks. Significant numbers of students scored below grade level in reading and math.

In consultation with parents, students, and staff, Sharon and a staff member from the school developed a homework after-school project for parents. The program is designed to tutor parents in upper-level math and science so that they will be able to provide assistance to their children. In addition to the classes, Sharon has developed a monthly newsletter to communicate to parents about school events and provide tips on subjects such as time management and reducing stress.

Planning and Program Development

Generalist social workers may also find planning and program development as a necessary organizational intervention. Many of the problems identified by the target system may best be addressed by creating new programs and services. Sometimes, an organization may choose to provide a new service. Planning, like education and training, has many dimensions and considerations. But there are two broad types: strategic planning and planning for program development.

Strategic Planning

Strategic planning focuses on giving the client system longer-term direction and identifies the steps to achieve the identified outcomes. Both organizations and communities may benefit from the development of strategic plans. Such plans can help identify concerns, assess and identify group values, create and operationalize goals, articulate specific steps, and help to characterize challenges and opportunities. Further, external funding may be enhanced through strategic planning. Often, funders require strategic plans. The funder may see the plans as evidence that the group has adequately examined the need for certain programs, as well as the strengths and weaknesses of the system. Showing alignment between a strategic plan and a grant proposal will greatly improve the system being funded.

While what specifically goes into a strategic plan should be dictated by the group's needs, it usually describes the goals, needs, problems, and tasks for the group over the intermediate- to longer-term future. While it makes total sense that having a plan is a critical element for an organization or community, it is often the case that plans are old, out of date, and no longer relevant to the realities in which a group may find itself. A generalist social worker can help in the development or updating of a strategic plan.

In some ways, the strategic plan should be a priority concern for an organization or community. As such, it can become not just a guide, but a real review of what is relevant or what is not. Brody (2014) presents a series of steps and questions that can guide the strategic planning process. These include the following:

1. Carefully examine the purposes for the plan.
2. Determine the level of commitment of major constituencies.
3. Establish a committee to oversee the effort.
4. Assess the problems, opportunities, and strengths of the organization.
5. Analyze and/or re-create the organizational vision.
6. Examine and revise and/or draft a mission statement.
7. Prioritize the challenges to the organization.
8. Develop mid- and long-term goals.
9. Submit a draft of the plan for multiple reviews by different constituencies.
10. Implement the plan.
11. Update annually. (p. 35)

SWOT Analysis

One model to assist in this process is called a SWOT analysis, which stands for **S**trengths, **W**eaknesses, **O**pportunities, and **T**hreats. The results of the data analysis are organized into a four-component framework, which is divided into two internal analysis components (strengths and weaknesses) and two external components (opportunities and threats). Strengths and opportunities are helpful to the organization, whereas weaknesses and threats are those things that may be harmful to the organization. This perspective is shown in Table 12.5.

Program Funding

Program development is not only a strategic activity but also a necessary activity at the level of the program. The "program" is one of the central organizing units of social work practice. A program is defined as a coordinated service or set of services, often with its own set of resources, workers, and administrators. It is here that planning often connects with the issue of resources for the system. Resources and money are often the source of a group's problems. At the very least, creating new programs often requires newly developed funds. As such, identifying and/or developing resources is often an essential concern of the social worker.

TABLE 12.5 SWOT ANALYSIS

Strengths	Weaknesses
• What do we do best? • What unique knowledge, talent, or resources do we have? • What advantages do we have? • What do other people say we do well? • What resources do we have available? • What is our greatest achievement?	• What could we improve? • What knowledge, talent, skills and/or resources are we lacking? • What disadvantages do we have? • What do other people say we don't do well? • In what areas do we need more training? • What complaints have we had about our service?
Opportunities	**Threats**
• How can we turn our strengths into opportunities? • How can we turn our weaknesses into opportunities? • Is there a need in our agency that no one is meeting? • What could we do today that isn't being done? • How is our field changing? How can we take advantage of those changes? • Who could we support? How could we support them?	• What obstacles do we face? • Could any of our weaknesses prevent our unit from meeting our goals? • Who and/or what might cause us problems in the future? How? • Are there any standards, policies, and/or legislation changing that might negatively impact us? • Are we competing with others to provide service? • Are there changes in our field or in technology that could threaten our success?

SWOT, strengths, weaknesses, opportunities, and threats.

Source: From Louisiana State Civil Service. (n.d.). *SWOT analysis: Questions for conducting an analysis with your team.* http://www.civilservice.louisiana.gov/files/divisions/Training/Job%20Aid/Supervisor%20Toolbox/Questions%20for%20Professional%20SWOT.pdf.

There are many ways a program may enhance its resources. A description of each type of funding is provided in Table 12.6, with a short description of the considerations needed for each.

Grant Writing

While having knowledge about all these areas is often necessary, the one resource development skill set that all generalist social workers should develop is grant writing. Many organizations supplement or expand their resources through grant writing; it is easy to see why. Americans have a long history of giving, and between federal, state, and local governmental sources and the vast number of grant-making foundations, there are literally thousands of sources with billions of dollars. Indeed, in 2016, statistics show that Americans' total charitable contributions exceeded $390 billion (IUPUI Lilly Family School of Philanthropy, 2017). Although most of this funding (71%) came from individuals, 68 foundations donated more than $75 million each in 2013 (Philanthropy Roundtable, 2018), and many dozens more gave $1 million or more. Berlin (2017) reports that in 2016, the U.S. government allocated approximately $666 billion in federal grants to support state and local programs.

The process of writing a grant can range from an endeavor that is very short and simple—typically for small, community grants—to complex and exhaustive. But in general, the

TABLE 12.6 METHODS OF PROGRAM FUNDING IN SOCIAL WORK PRACTICE

Funding Method	Description	Issues
Fee for service	Client pays for service provided	Requires enough clients who have disposable income to support agency. Client numbers change, making planning difficult.
Third-party payments, insurance reimbursements	Payments made by insurer for services	Limited types of services covered. Requires certification/licensure. Services may require preauthorization by insurance company.
Loans—commercial source	Loans provided at market rates	Market rates fluctuate—rates based on agency credit rating.
Loans—government or noncommercial source	Loans provided at nonmarket rates, often by government agencies	Eligibility often linked to specific policy/problem areas.
Contract with governmental source	Governmental source (federal, state, and county) preselects types of services/clients, and chooses and contracts with agency to provide services	Dependent on political and legislative action. Agency must meet eligibility criteria. Contracts are competitive. Time-limited. Applies only to limited types of services or clients.
Grants—governmental source	Agency writes grant proposal for funds to underwrite program. Government source evaluates and chooses among submitting agencies.	Dependent on political and legislative action. Requires grant-writing expertise. Long application period with no guarantee of funding. Time-limited funding. Many limits on use of funds.
Grants—foundation source	Agency writes grant proposal for funds to underwrite program. Foundation source evaluates and chooses among submitting agencies.	Dependent on foundation attention to problem area. Requires grant-writing expertise. Long application period with no guarantee of funding. Time-limited funding. Most funding sources are small. Many limits on use of funds.
Grants—general source (United Way, Walmart)	Agency writes grant proposal for funds to underwrite program. Foundation source evaluates and chooses among submitting agencies.	Dependent on foundation attention to problem area. Requires grant-writing expertise. Long application period with no guarantee of funding. Time-limited funding. Many limits on use of funds.
Direct solicitation fundraising	Bake sales, direct mail requests, employee contributions	Unless the organization is well known or "in the public spotlight," contributions tend to be small. Usually very undependable.

process of applying for and organizing most grant proposals is more or less done the same way. The general steps are: (a) develop a clear project or problem; (b) select the grant source; and (c) write the proposal. Each of these steps is described in detail.

Step 1: Develop a Clear Project or Problem

This part of the process is not really very different from planning for any intervention, with perhaps two important differences. First, in many cases, the focus of the project now may expand beyond the needs of a specific agency to possibly include other system client needs as well. Often effective interventions will be strongest if many "partners" are a part of the process. While you might consider seeking funding for what is known as "capacity building," enhancement of skills, or agency infrastructure, you might also consider writing a grant to address an unmet client need through partnerships with other organizations as well. In doing so, the funding may be of value in addressing the organization needs at the same time as it is helping the clients.

A second difference that may apply here is that most successful grants depend on a grounding in the literature. An empirical basis for any project, as drawn from the literature of social work, sociology, psychology, or similar fields, will have a much greater chance of success than one that is based on anecdotes or practice wisdom alone. Funders, especially for larger grants, want to provide money to projects that are likely to succeed. And the empirical basis may provide the evidence needed to support that sense.

Overall, you can think about the types of project or problems as one of several types. You will want to identify the type that is closest to your intent. Doing so will make searching for grants a bit easier and will improve the chances of being funded. The various types of projects and problems include the following:

- *Research or planning projects/problems:* Funds provide money for projects designed to help the agency examine a problem and/or plan for new services.
- *Demonstration projects:* Projects designed to implement new or untested services.
- *Operating expenses and services support:* Projects designed to raise funds for existing services.
- *Endowment development:* Projects designed to help build the endowment and long-term assets of the agency.
- *Construction projects:* Projects designed to help the agency build a new physical plant or renovate the physical plant.
- *Capacity building:* Projects designed to enhance the skills or knowledge of the staff or to improve the agency's infrastructure.

While grants are available for all of these types of projects, some are more available than others. Typically, funding will be somewhat more available for research or planning, demonstration projects, or capacity building than for construction or endowment development. Operating expenses and service support, commonly an ongoing need in any organization, are fairly easy to find funding for, but rarely in large amounts or in the amounts necessary to do anything more than partially support a major project. To put this another way, funding is an ongoing activity, and grant writing, while of unquestionable value, is also an ongoing process.

Step 2: Select the Grant Source

To begin, you must find out who (what organization) is providing funding. This is, at least "on paper," fairly easy, as organizations that give away money must notify the public that funds are available, although finding the right source might be more difficult. The notifications you will be seeking are variously known as a request for proposal (RFP), notice of funding availability (NOFA), funding opportunity announcements (FOAs), or super NOFAs (groups of NOFAs). Table 12.7 shows the content RFPs typically describe.

Make sure you review these sections carefully. Many grant sources receive hundreds of applications, so you must prepare the right proposal for the right source. Although individuals may provide grant funds, most conceptualizations of grant funding sources focus on government (federal, state, and local) or a foundation. There are advantages and disadvantages to the different grant sources. Government sources are often considered to be more prestigious and high-dollar, but very competitive, restrictive, and extremely complex to write. Foundations, on the other hand, are more varied. With literally thousands of different sources, it is possible to find everything from large, high-dollar, complex grants to small and essentially noncompetitive microgrants.

Where does one find an RFP or learn about grant sources? The *Catalog of Domestic Federal Assistance*, pubished by the federal government, was the standard until the opportunities provided by the internet. Now, almost every government agency provides information about sources at their websites. And even easier source is www.grants.gov, which collects information across agencies.

For foundations, comprehensive information is harder to find simply because of the number of foundations that exist. Yet again, several websites exist that can help, although they are often fee or subscription based. Table 12.8 presents some useful sites for government and foundational supports.

TABLE 12.7 COMPONENTS OF RFPs IN SOCIAL WORK PRACTICE

Section	Information Provided
Information about funder	Name of program Name of organization and auspice
Funding amounts and time frames	Minimum, maximum, and average grant size Duration of grant (typically 1–3 years, sometimes renewable) Expected match amount
Selection criteria—what may be funded	This could involve • Discipline(s) • Problem area(s) • Client characteristics • Geography • Intervention approach, methods, or activities
Selection criteria—what may not be funded	Commonly seen • Limitations on overhead (indirect costs), administration, travel, etc. • Construction, lobbying, endowments
Application process	Due dates Contact information Where to get application forms (if necessary) Grant/technical assistance advisor

RFP, request for proposal.

TABLE 12.8 GRANT SEARCH ENGINE WEBSITES

Website	Agency/Foundation
www.grants.gov	Grants Learning Center is your gateway to the federal grants world. Grants Learning Center is where you can learn more about the federal grants life cycle, policies on grants management, and profiles on grant making.
www.foundation center.org	The Foundation Center is the leading source of information about philanthropy worldwide. Maintains a comprehensive database about U.S. and global grants.
www.grantspace.org	A database maintained by the Foundation Center, GrantSpace provides easy-to-use, self-service tools and resources to help nonprofits worldwide become more viable grant applicants and build strong, sustainable organizations.
https://grantwatch.com	Website for international, Canada, and U.S. federal, state, local, foundation, and corporation grants.

Step 3: Write the Proposal

Writing the proposal may seem complex, but in many ways it really only involves drawing together information that may already exist, although it must be put together in a clear, concise, and logical way. While every proposal *must* be specific to the RFP and *must* follow all of the directions perfectly, it is also the case that the components of most proposals are similar. These components are shown in Table 12.9 (Coley & Scheinberg, 2008, p. 4).

TABLE 12.9 COMMON GRANT PROPOSAL SECTIONS

Grant Section	Information Provided
Title or cover page	Often supplied by funder; includes contact information for submitting organization
Abstract	Short overview of proposal; typically 100–150 words
Introduction/ summary	One- to three-page summary of the project; introduces the project and the agency to the funder and includes the mission and vision of the agency
Needs statement (problem statement)	The statement of need describes what the problem/issue is that the grant wants to address. Typically, it includes a problem definition, statistics describing the community setting, the size of the problem, and some evidence about the seriousness of the problem (such as a comparison statistic of your target group to other groups).
Project description	Identifies the project goals and objectives and provides details about the implementation plan, including the timeline to complete project activities. This section often includes a scope of work grid of the project delivery plan.
Evaluation plan	Explains the measurement procedures that will be used to determine if the goals and objectives have been met
Budget request	Itemizes the expenditures of the project and includes a rationale or budget justification for the expenses
Applicant capability	Demonstrates the applicant's past performance and ability to accomplish the proposed project; often includes an organizational chart
Organizational sustainability	Indicates the plan to continue the project beyond the requested funding period

(continued)

TABLE 12.9 COMMON GRANT PROPOSAL SECTIONS (*CONTINUED*)	
Grant Section	**Information Provided**
Letters of support	Letters reflecting support for the proposed project from program recipients, community leaders, partnering agencies, coalitions, religious organizations, universities, or political leaders
Memorandum of understanding	A written agreement from each of the partners or coapplicant agencies on how they will cooperate to implement the grant
Appendix materials	These may include an audited financial statement, insurance documentation, or any other documentation required by the funder.

Each of these sections should be logically connected to the others. This means that every section of the proposal builds on what has gone before and prepares for what comes after. While this might seem evident and obvious, the lack of logical connection is a common flaw. One way to avoid this is to remember that the strongest proposals will have a clear relationship between indicators of need, your outcome objectives, and the degree of change in outcomes you seek to demonstrate in your evaluation. Do not identify and measure a need one way, while focusing your objectives and evaluation criteria somewhere else.

One tool that is commonly used as part of the grant development process is a logic model. The logic model serves several useful purposes, both to the organization that is submitting it and for the funders, who are increasingly requiring these with grant submissions. A logic model presents a picture of how your effort or initiative is supposed to work. It explains why your strategy is a good solution to the problem at hand. Effective logic models make an explicit, often visual, statement of the activities that will bring about change and the results you expect to see for the community and its people. A logic model keeps participants in the effort moving in the same direction by providing a common language and point of reference; see Figure 12.2 (University of Kansas Center for Health and Development, 2017).

While there are several useful resources as to what is included in a logic model and everything else related to grant development, you should follow the explicit directions given by a potential funder. A logic model typically provides a table that describes:

- *Purpose*, or mission: What motivates the need for change? This can also be expressed as the problems or opportunities that the program is addressing.
- *Context*, or conditions: What is the climate in which change will take place? How will new policies and programs be aligned with existing ones? What trends compete with the proposed program?
- *Inputs*, or resources or infrastructure: What raw materials will be used to conduct the effort or initiative? Inputs can also include constraints on the program, such as regulations or funding gaps, which are barriers to your objectives.
- *Activities*, or interventions: What will the initiative do with its resources to direct the course of change? Your intervention, and thus your logic model, should be guided by a clear analysis of risk and protective factors.
- *Outputs*: What evidence is there that the activities were performed as planned? Indicators might include the number of mentors trained and youth referred and the frequency, type, duration, and intensity of mentoring contacts.

FIGURE 12.2 Logic model for the grant development process.

Source: From Milstein, B., & Chapel, T. (n.d.). *Developing a logic model or theory of change*. https://ctb.ku.edu/en/table-of-contents/overview/models-for-community-health-and-development/logic-model-development/main.

Tasks and Responsibilities

The intervention plan lays out the tasks/action steps and responsibilities for all parties in the change process. Essentially, this is an action plan and a contract that provides a great amount of detail for the successful implementation of the intervention. In other words, it again presents the tasks/action steps for the project.

Tasks/action steps, as initially discussed, come from your goals and objectives, but they are also closely connected to the intervention. They are, very simply, the specific activities that each person involved in the intervention must carry out if the intervention is to be successful. They are statements of the "who, what, when, and where" of the plan. Questions such as what needs to be done, who will do what, and when it needs to be completed should be addressed.

Generally, the more detail and specificity within the plan, the more successful it will be. The specifics, however, are again linked to the objectives and the interventions. The following are some examples of organization and community interventions. Exhibit 12.1 shows an example of an intervention planning form. The intervention planning form is used in conjunction with the goal planning form.

Another component of the intervention plan is how it will be evaluated. Each of the objectives identified needs to be evaluated or measured. The program goals are not evaluated; the more specific objectives are. Thus, for each objective, identify the measure that will be used, the data source for the measure, a time frame, a baseline, and the benchmark for the objective.

Exhibit 12.1 Organization Intervention Planning Form

Goal 1: _____

Objective 1.1 _____

Task/Action	Responsibility	Completion Date	Comments	Completed?

Evaluation

The evaluation of an organizational intervention is the same as with other client systems. It consists of an ongoing process evaluation. The process evaluation provides information on the implementation of the intervention. Potential sources of data for the process evaluation include clients, line staff, administrators, supervisors, and documents. Is the intervention being implemented as designed? Are there any issues affecting the intervention? What adjustments need to be made? Chapter 14 provides a detailed discussion of process evaluations.

Adjust and Revise

This stage of the helping process entails making any adjustments to the intervention identified in the ongoing process evaluation. The goal in AOP generalist social work is to provide empowering services to those who have experienced oppression and discrimination. Most social work interventions are agency based. Organizations need to function in ways consistent with the concepts and principles of AOP practice. Therefore, organizational processes and interventions must be willing to change if they are not providing AOP-compatible services.

Termination

The final stage of an organizational intervention is a planned termination. Termination is closely associated with the program's outcome evaluation. The outcome evaluation provides data on the success of the program in terms of achieving its goals and objectives. The outcome evaluation can be qualitative, quantitative, or a combination of both. Chapter 14 provides detailed information on program outcome evaluations.

Termination with organizational interventions is usually planned or occurs naturally. Educational training usually has a fixed number of sessions. The termination process typically entails reviewing with the participants what work and did not work with the training and other forms of feedback. Program development interventions also typically have fixed end points. The grant is completed and submitted. If it is successful, then the organization moves into the program implementation phase. If not successful, the participants involved in developing the proposal review the feedback to decide whether to proceed with another grant application or not.

SUMMARY

This chapter focused on the social work competency related to the organizational assessments and interventions. Conducting AOP organizational assessments is guided by the ethical responsibilities to the clients and the practice setting. Organizational assessments determine if the organization is meeting the resource needs of clients, providing adequate resources for staff supervision, and creating an organizational environment that is consistent with and encourages compliance with the *Code of Ethics* and the AOP concepts and principles.

We also reviewed three organizational theories that help inform AOP organizational assessments. The theories reviewed were rational decision-making theory, organizational development theory, and change theory. Organizational assessment methods were then reviewed. This included a discussion of internal and external organizational considerations and a review of common organizational assessment tools.

AOP generalist social work utilizes organizational interventions to address social, economic, and environmental justice issues. Two broad categories of organizational interventions were reviewed: education and training and program development. The purposes of these organizational interventions are to improve the functioning of organizations, to improve the delivery of existing services, and to develop new services.

CASE SUMMARY   UNDOCUMENTED AND HOMELESS

Practice Setting Description

Jackie is a first-year MSW student completing an internship at an inner-city family service agency in the Southwest. The agency is in a section of the city that has a high crime rate, gang activity, and failing schools. The area has a diverse population with many immigrants from Central and South America and a substantial African American population. The agency provides individual and family counseling services on a sliding fee scale. The agency also runs several educational and treatment groups as well as a temporary shelter for women and their children. Jackie has been assigned to work with the women and their children in the shelter. Her primary tasks are to provide concrete services and supportive counseling to the shelter residents.

Background Information

Elicia and her daughter, Maria, are undocumented immigrants from Mexico. They have been in the United States for 5 years. Elicia and Maria fled to the area from another southwestern city to escape her abusive husband approximately 2 months ago. Elicia is 25 years old, and Maria 8 years old. Elicia has a 2-year-old daughter, Sarah, who was placed in foster care because of

(continued)

CASE SUMMARY: UNDOCUMENTED AND HOMELESS (*CONTINUED*)

suspected abuse in the home. Sarah is in a foster home in a small rural community in the state hundreds of miles from Elicia's current residence. Since moving to the area, Maria has not been attending school.

Elicia and Maria are currently residing in the agency's temporary shelter for families. They have been at the shelter for 2 weeks, and the agency has a 90-day limit. Prior to arriving at the shelter, Elicia and Maria were homeless and living on the streets.

Elicia is a high school drop-out and was a stay-at-home mother prior to leaving her husband and moving to a different part of the state. She chose to move there because she has two female cousins living in the area who are also undocumented immigrants. Elicia's native language is Spanish. She speaks some English but is not as comfortable speaking in English. Her English comprehension appears to be good. Maria speaks both English and Spanish well. When communicating with the staff, Maria acts as Elicia's interpreter since none of the staff at the shelter speak Spanish.

Maria appears to be behind academically. She struggles reading simple children's books written in English. It is unknown if her ability to read in Spanish is better than her English reading skills.

Other than her two cousins, Elicia has no other sources of support in the community. Her cousins have young families and limited resources but are well established and connected to a Latino community in the city and the local Catholic church. Her cousins refused to let Elicia and Maria live with them while she was trying to find her own place and a job. They stated that they did not have enough room and are concerned they would get in trouble with their landlord if it was found out that they were letting people stay with them. They sent her to the local church for help, and she was given the address for the agency's shelter by the priest.

Elicia has been looking for housing in the Latino community. The housing market is tight with limited options, and she has been unable to find anything that she could possibly afford. The only affordable housing she found was a room in a rundown motel that rents by the hour or by the month. It is in an area of town known for drug dealing and sex work.

On arrival in the community, Elicia found occasional work for a house cleaning company. The company hires undocumented workers, pays them very low cash wages, and threatens to turn them in to Immigration and Customs Enforcement (ICE) if they complain. The job bosses also exploit their female workers sexually, threatening to turn them in if they do not comply. Elicia was fearful about applying for other jobs because of her illegal status. She considered turning to sex work to be able to take care of her child, but her Catholic upbringing and thoughts of how this would shame her family have kept her from doing so. She is in constant fear of being detained, separated from Maria, and having her placed in foster care. She is also afraid that she will end up homeless again and forced to live on the streets or return to her abusive husband.

Elicia is extremely reluctant to sign up for any federally funded services, even those that she and her child are entitled to receive. On the suggestion that she enroll for supplemental food through the Supplemental Nutrition Assistance Program (SNAP), Elicia became nervous and refused, as she has heard that participation in SNAP services, and others like them, would draw the attention of ICE, and she had heard stories on the news of individuals being deported after signing up for such programs.

(continued)

CASE SUMMARY: UNDOCUMENTED AND HOMELESS (*CONTINUED*)

Presenting Problems

Elicia and her child are facing multiple obstacles. They need to find permanent, affordable housing and a job that pays enough to cover her housing and living expenses. In addition, Maria needs to be enrolled in school.

Additionally, Elicia is experiencing an immense amount of stress, anxiety, and possibly post-traumatic stress disorder (PTSD). She described an instance where she could not calm down her breathing and she felt lightheaded. She is very fearful of men and tries to avoid all contact with men in the community. She reports difficulty sleeping at night and feeling exhausted most of the time.

She is concerned about Maria. She has started acting out at the shelter, getting into fights with the other children, disobeying her mother, and being disrespectful and defiant to the staff and other adults. Elicia and Maria fight frequently, and when Elicia tries to discipline Maria, she throws a temper tantrum until Elicia gives up.

Elicia has many strengths. She had the strength to leave her abusive husband and move to a different city. She loves her daughter and wants desperately to keep Maria with her. She is resilient and has managed to survive and keep her daughter safe despite not having a place to stay, a job, and a limited support network. Elicia feels safe in the shelter, but she is very fearful of being caught as an illegal immigrant and is generally mistrustful of helping professionals and persons of authority.

DISCUSSION QUESTIONS

1. Identify an organizational (agency) issue that is impacting Elicia and her daughter. How does the organizational issue intersect with AOP concepts and practice principles?

2. Identify an AOP organizational (agency) intervention that would help Elicia and/or her daughter deal with their current situation. Discuss why you think your new intervention would be helpful.

3. For the preceding intervention, create a logic model. What components of your logic model were challenging to complete? Why?

4. Identify a potential funding source for your intervention. What are the funding requirements of your identified source?

A robust set of instructor resources designed to supplement this text is located at http://connect.springerpub.com/content/book/978-0-8261-6683-8. Qualifying instructors may request access by emailing textbook@springerpub.com.

KEY REFERENCES

Only key references appear in the print edition. To access the full reference list, visit www.springerpub.com/courseconnect. See inside front cover and tear-out card for CourseConnect details.

Bloom, S. L., & Sreedhar, S. Y. (2008). The sanctuary model of trauma-informed organizational change. *Reclaiming Children and Youth from Trauma to Trust, 17*(3), 48–53.

Brody, R. (2014). *Effectively managing human service organizations* (4th ed.). Sage.

Coley, S. M., & Scheinberg, C. A. (2017). *Proposal writing: Effective grantsmanship for funding* (5th ed.). Sage.

Cothran, H., Wysocki, A., Farnsworth, D., & Clark, J. L. (2019). *Developing smart goal for your organization.* Food and Resource Economics Department, UF/IFAS Extension. https://edis.ifas.ufl.edu/pdffiles/FE/FE57700.pdf

Course Sidekick. (2019). *Rational and non-rational decision making.* https://courses.lumenlearning.com/boundless-management/chapter/rational-and-nonrational-decision-making

French, W. L., & Bell, C. H. (1999). *Organization development: Behavioral science interventions for organization improvement* (6th ed.). Pearson.

Gellis, Z. D. (2001). Social work perceptions of transformational and transactional leadership in health care. *Social Work Research, 25*(1), 17–25. https://doi.org/10.1093/swr/25.1.17

IUPUI Lilly Family School of Philanthropy. (2017). *Giving USA.* https://givingusa.org/giving-usa-2017-total-charitable-donations-rise-to-new-high-of-390-05-billion

Kettner, P. M., Moroney, R. M., & Rettman, S. (2017). *Designing and managing programs: An effectiveness-based approach* (5th ed.). Sage.

13 Generalist Practice With Communities: Assessment and Intervention

Marina Barnett and John Poulin

James is a first-year master of social work (MSW) student placed in a community-based program that provides consultation services to grassroots human service programs in an economically disadvantaged community with numerous social problems. The agency's mission is to increase the number of services available to community residents as well as to strengthen the capacities of the local service organizations. A second community-based agency operates an after-school program that serves low-income families, many of whom also need social work and case management services. A large proportion of the children in the after-school program are struggling in school because of issues and challenges that are occurring in their homes and with their families. The two agencies have agreed to explore the possibility of developing a new service that provides case management and counseling services to the children's families. James has been tasked with helping develop the new family service.

James is excited about his field assignment and the opportunity to help families overcome the challenges of poverty and to help low-income children to become more successful in school. James knows that his first step is to learn all he can about the community and the experiences of the low-income residents who will use the new program. He also has many unanswered questions that he will need to address: How will he partner with the community members? What professional and community groups need to be involved in the planning process? What are the families' needs? What kinds of services and assistance will best address those needs? How will they fund the new program? How best to prepare a grant proposal?

LEARNING OBJECTIVES

This chapter addresses Competency 7: Assess Individuals, Families, Groups, Organizations, and Communities, and Competency 8: Intervene With Individuals, Families, Groups, Organizations, and Communities. It covers community assessment and intervention. By the end of this chapter, you will be able to:

- Understand the purposes of anti-oppressive practice (AOP) generalist social work practice with communities.
- Identify the ethical principles and standards related to community assessment.
- Describe three theories related to assessing communities.
- Design a community assessment.
- Identify generalist social work practice interventions with communities.

- Identify the ethical principles and standards related to community intervention.
- Describe three types of community interventions.

COMPETENCY 7: ASSESSMENT WITH INDIVIDUALS, FAMILIES, GROUPS, ORGANIZATIONS, AND COMMUNITIES

Social workers understand that assessment is an ongoing component of the dynamic and interactive process of social work practice. Social workers understand theories of human behavior and person-in-environment, as well as interprofessional conceptual frameworks, and they critically evaluate and apply this knowledge in culturally responsive assessment with clients and constituencies, including individuals, families, groups, organizations, and communities. Assessment involves a collaborative process of defining presenting challenges and identifying strengths with individuals, families, groups, organizations, and communities to develop a mutually agreed-upon plan. Social workers recognize the implications of the larger practice context in the assessment process and use interprofessional collaboration in this process. Social workers are self-reflective and understand how bias, power, privilege, and their personal values and experiences may affect their assessment and decision-making.

Social workers:

- apply theories of human behavior and person-in-environment, as well as other culturally responsive and interprofessional conceptual frameworks, when assessing clients and constituencies; and
- demonstrate respect for client self-determination during the assessment process by collaborating with clients and constituencies in developing a mutually agreed-upon plan. (Council on Social Work Education [CSWE], 2022, pp. 11–12)

COMPETENCY 8: INTERVENE WITH INDIVIDUALS, FAMILIES, GROUPS, ORGANIZATIONS, AND COMMUNITIES

Social workers understand that intervention is an ongoing component of the dynamic and interactive process of social work practice. Social workers understand theories of human behavior, person-in-environment, and other interprofessional conceptual frameworks, and they critically evaluate and apply this knowledge in selecting culturally responsive interventions with clients and constituencies, including individuals, families, groups, organizations, and communities. Social workers understand methods of identifying, analyzing, and implementing evidence-informed interventions and participate in interprofessional collaboration to achieve client and constituency goals. Social workers facilitate effective transitions and endings.

Social workers:

- engage with clients and constituencies to critically choose and implement culturally responsive, evidence-informed interventions to achieve client and constituency goals; and
- incorporate culturally responsive methods to negotiate, mediate, and advocate with and on behalf of clients and constituencies. (CSWE, 2022, p. 12)

NATIONAL ASSOCIATION OF SOCIAL WORKERS *CODE OF ETHICS*

The National Association of Social Workers (NASW) *Code of Ethics* (2021) has two ethical standards under the ethical responsibilities to the broader society, which are relevant to assessing communities. The first ethical standard is about advocating for improved living conditions, and the second is about facilitating public participation in the development of social policies and institutions. Compliance with both ethical standards requires some type of community assessment to identify community needs and resources.

The NASW *Code of Ethics* (2021) value of service is related to intervening with communities. Its associated ethical principle is that social workers' primary goal is to help people in need and to address social problems. The social justice value is also related to intervening with communities. Its associated ethical principle is that social workers challenge social injustice. Community interventions in social work are designed to help those in need and to address social problems as well as social justice issues.

Three ethical standards under the ethical responsibilities to the broader society are relevant to the community interventions (NASW, 2021). The first is about promoting the general welfare of communities. The second ethical standard is about informed participation, and the third is about social and political action.

COMMUNITY THEORIES

Community Development Theory

Community development theory has taken a number of forms. Schiele (2005) defines community development collective problem-solving, self-help, and empowerment. Paiva (1977) identified four major concepts of community development: structural change, socioeconomic integration, institutional development, and institutional renewal. What the various definitions have in common is a focus on the capacity building and empowerment of the local community in order to bring socioeconomic, political, and environmental changes to the community.

The goal and substance of social development are the welfare of the people, as determined by the people themselves, and the consequent creation or alteration of institutions (including people's values, individual behavior, and motivation) so as to create a capacity for meeting human needs at all levels (especially those at the lower levels) and for improving the quality of human relationships and relationships between people and societal institutions (Paiva, 1977).

Tan's influential 2009 paper on community development theory and practice incorporated Perkins's (1982) three Rs of community development: relocation, redistribution, and reconciliation. Relocation refers to the physical relocation of the social worker or another change agent into the community they seek to serve. Relocation highlights the collaborative and empowering aspects of community development theory. In this model the social worker is a community partner and not an outside expert.

Relocation allows for the social worker to develop shared experiences with their clients. It allows for a more authentic ability to build rapport with clients and, especially in diverse and oppressed communities, can serve as a tremendous and powerful catalyst in establishing trust (Tan, 2009, pp. 9–10).

In addition to physically relocating to the community, relocation in community development theory also refers to the relocation of power back to the community. This entails collaboration with community members, a belief in people's abilities to solve their own community's problems, and the development of indigenous leadership.

Redistribution refers to the acquisition or redistribution of resources. "Redistribution, from a framework of Community Development, requires first the identification of issues of injustice and gaps in resources and then the collective advocacy of the community to secure those resources" (Tan, 2009, p. 11). Oppressed communities, by definition, lack resources. Community development theory emphasizes the importance of increasing available resources to strengthen and improve community well-being.

Reconciliation in community development is the process of acknowledging roles of the oppressed and oppressors in the hopes of creating a new or changed relationship. The emphasis is on the oppressor's awareness of their role in the oppression. Thus, an important tenet of community development theory and community development practice is the reconciliation between the social worker and the community members. "Reconciliation calls into account the past or present hurt and oppression individual clients or entire communities bring into the helping relationship" (Tan, 2009, p. 12).

Some of the core principles of community development theory include the following:

- *Community participation*: All members of the community can make valued contributions and are invited to participate in the change process.
- *Community ownership*: Community members have ownership and control of the decision-making process and the community change efforts.
- *Empowerment*: Power is vested in the community and its members. Change occurs through empowering individuals and communities.
- *Indigenous leadership*: Sustained community change can only occur when the knowledge, skills, and expertise of the community members are strengthened and leadership is in the hands of community members.
- *Social action*: Factors that negatively impact the community are analyzed and addressed through collective action.
- *Structural change*: Structural change is critical to community development. Without it, there can be no significant impact on the community and people's well-being.

A community development theory places the social worker firmly in the role of facilitator, not expert. The social worker's job is to help the development of community leadership and mobilization and development of community change strategies. It is about helping organize self-help rather than providing expertise and leading change efforts.

Conflict Theory

Conflict is a relationship where two or more parties want the same resources, power, status, or control and both parties act on their desire (Hardcastle et al., 2011). Conflict theory has its roots in classical Marxism and Marx's theory of dialectical materialism, which provides a basis for understanding and distinguishing power differentials in relationships (Langer & Lietz, 2015). Marx identified four principles or assumptions of conflict theory. They are as follows:

1. Conflict is inevitable.
2. There is an unequal distribution of power in relationships.
3. There is an ongoing struggle for scarce resources.
4. Whoever has the most power controls the distribution of resources. (Langer & Lietz, 2015, p. 102)

Dahrendorf (1959) viewed social systems as dynamic systems in a constant state of change resulting in ongoing conflict. Dahrendorf, as well as Marx, believed that social systems systematically generate conflict and that conflict is a pervasive feature of society. He also postulated that conflict is dialectical in that the resolution of one conflict creates a new set of opposed interests, which creates further conflict (Hardcastle et al., 2011). In short, unequal distribution of scarce resources and power among dominant and subordinate groups creates conflict.

Conflict theory helps explain how power structures and power disparities impact people's lives. Power is unequally divided in every society. Structural inequalities contribute to and maintain various forms of oppression and social, economic, and environmental injustices. Dominant groups maintain social order through manipulation and control. But social change can be achieved through conflict—that is, interrupting periods of stability. In this theory, life is characterized by conflict (either open or through exploitation) instead of consensus. By addressing these asymmetric power relationships and the distribution of resources, social workers can help disadvantaged and oppressed communities improve the well-being of individuals, families, and communities. Conflict theory helps AOP generalist social workers empower communities and community members to create change. Rather than helping people adjust to the "status quo," social work practice from a conflict theory perspective seeks transformative change through a redistribution of power and resources.

> **Reflection Questions**
>
> 1. What are the similarities between community development theory and conflict theory?
> 2. How are they different?
> 3. Which of the two theories is most compatible with your values and beliefs?
> 4. How comfortable are you incorporating conflict theory into your AOP generalist practice?

In terms of community assessment, conflict theory highlights the need to assess community power structures, decision-making processes, and the allocation and distribution of resources to the community. Social workers conducting community assessments can also use conflict theory to help assess a community's willingness and readiness to engage in the struggle to increase power and obtain needed resources through personal and social change.

Structural Functionalism

Structural functionalism theory sees society as a complex system whose parts work together to promote solidarity and stability. Two theorists, Herbert Spencer and Robert Merton, were major contributors to this perspective. Important concepts in functionalism include social structure, social functions, manifest functions, and latent functions.

Social Structure

Society is viewed as having interrelated parts or structures designed to meet the biological and social needs of the individuals in that society. These structures are relatively stable patterns of social behavior. They give shape to our lives. Social structures are the social patterns through which a society is organized and can be horizontal or vertical. Horizontal social structure refers to the social relationships and the social and physical characteristics of communities to which individuals belong, while vertical social structure refers to ways in which a society or group ranks people in a hierarchy.

Social structures at the macro level are the major social institutions and patterns of institutionalized relationships. The major social institutions include family, religion, education, media, law, politics, and economy. These are understood as distinct institutions that are interrelated and interdependent and together help compose the overarching social structure of a society.

At the mezzo level, social structure refers to the experiences of groups and the interactions among groups. It is the social networks that have been organized by the social institutions and institutionalized social relationships. The social networks act as structuring forces by shaping the opportunities that may or may not be available and by fostering particular behavioral and interactional norms that determine social relationships. For example, sexism fosters discrimination against women, which results in male-dominated social networks and interaction patterns.

At the micro level, social structure refers to everyday interactions among people in the forms of norms and customs. Micro-social structures are what we expect from others, how we expect to be seen by them, and how we interact together. It is the way we interact with others based on institutionalized norms and customs of behavior.

Social Functions

Structural functionalism theory postulates that all social structures have social functions. Social functions serve as the purposes of social structures. For example, education serves several important social functions in society, such as socialization, learning, and social status. Social functions can also be divided into manifest and latent functions.

Manifest and Latent Functions

Manifest functions are those that are intended and recognized. Latent functions are unrecognized and unintended. A manifest function of college education, for example, includes gaining knowledge, preparing for a career, and finding a good job that utilizes that education. These are the intended purposes of the social process of education. Latent functions of education could be questioning your values and beliefs, meeting people from diverse backgrounds, and finding new and unexpected interests and activities. Latent functions can be beneficial, neutral, or harmful. Social processes that have undesirable consequences for the operation of society are called dysfunctions. In education, examples of dysfunction include getting bad grades, truancy, dropping out, not graduating, and not finding suitable employment.

A major criticism of structural functionalism theory is that it supports the status quo. Structural functionalism does not account for the possibilities of social change. It is an equilibrium model based on assumptions of consensus. Conflict situations have been neglected. Social institutions, because they are functional, cannot be changed or abolished without endangering the social system. Social change is not addressed by structural functionalism theory.

Structural functionalism theory can contribute to designing a community assessment. One of its contributions would be in the social structures in the community and their interrelationships. The structures and their relationships impact the functioning of the community. Assessing their manifest and latent functioning can help identify areas of dysfunction that can lead to recommendations for improved functioning and change. Thus, while structural functionalism is not consistent with the practice principles of AOP generalist practice, it can be used to help identify targets for social change.

Critical Race Theory

Critical race theory (CRT) was briefly described in Chapter 1. As noted, CRT is a critical perspective for AOP generalist social work practice. It provides a framework examining how racism and oppression impact disadvantaged communities and their residents. CRT helps community members understand how power, privilege and discrimination have impacted the wellness of their communities. While CRT focuses on racism, it supports the social justice perspective of AOP generalist social work with communities. It provides a framework for identifying and assessing implicit and explicit racism in community power structures and government organizations. CRT places race and racism at the center of localized patterns of community disempowerment and inequality.

ANTI-OPPRESSIVE GENERALIST PRACTICE WITH COMMUNITIES

As with the other four system levels of generalist social work practice, AOP generalist practice with communities incorporates the four phases of the helping process—engagement, assessment, intervention, and evaluation. The aim of AOP generalist practice with communities typically focuses on community development; community empowerment; and addressing the effects of oppression, discrimination, and power imbalances in the community. Thus, AOP generalist social workers approach their work with communities from a social justice perspective and seek to address inequality, oppression, and discrimination by challenging oppressive structures and practices.

Engagement

The engagement phase for AOP generalist practice with communities includes the same stages as the other client systems—what is different are the questions asked and the stakeholders. As with all froms of AOP practice, the first order of business is self-reflection. How do your values align with the values of the community? What community issues need to be addressed? Who are the stakeholders affected by the community issues? Who benefits from the status quo? Who is negatively impacted? Are there social justice concerns? How are power and privilege manifested in the community? Engaging in critical self-reflection is a vital first step in preparing for AOP community practice.

Establishing a helping relationship is the second stage of the engagement process. In AOP generalist practice with community, this entails identifying the stakeholders involved in the community assessment. The stakeholders are those that will use the information obtained from the assessment process as well as those impacted by the community intervention. Potential stakeholders include community members, grassroots community leaders, community task forces, community service organizational leaders, and local government officials. As with social work practice with individuals, families, groups, and organizations, establishing a helping relationship with community stakeholders is built upon trust. Trust is established through shared positive experiences. It is a process and often challenging. This is especially true if you are working with community members and grassroots community leaders. As a social worker, you most likely will be viewed as part of the oppressive power structure. Many disadvantaged community members have experienced disappointment and disempowerment in their experiences with helping professionals. Case 13.1 illustrates some of the challenges of community engagement.

CASE 13.1 COME ONLY IF YOU INTEND TO STAY

Chester is a small city located in an affluent county in Pennsylvania. It was once a thriving city but has fallen upon hard times with the closure of a shipbuilding yard and other light industry jobs. Currently, it is the poorest city in Pennsylvania and has the highest unemployment rate, highest levels of poverty, lowest educational levels, and failing schools. It is by any measure a disadvantaged community with a predominantly African American population. Most social services are located outside of the city and not readily accessible to many of the community residents. There are a number small grassroots community organizations, most of which are faith based.

A relatively small private university with bachelor of social work (BSW) and MSW social work programs is in Chester. The university had a strained relationship with the community. Most community members felt unwelcomed and were not allowed to use university facilities or to even be on campus. The social work faculty valued community service and were frustrated that very few of the student field placements were in Chester, which had the greatest need. The obstacle was that accreditation requirements mandated that field placement students be supervised by professional social workers. Few of the grassroots community organizations had BSW or MSW social workers on their staff.

The social work faculty concluded that one possible way to support the local community by increasing social work services was to create a community-based pro bono field agency primarily staffed by social work interns. Social work faculty and part-time field instructors hired by the school would provide the mandated MSW supervision. The concept was to partner with community-based organizations to provide needed human resources to help them deliver services to community residents as well to provide capacity-building support to the organizations.

(continued)

CASE 13.1 COME ONLY IF YOU INTEND TO STAY (*CONTINUED*)

The first step in engaging with the community was to meet with community leaders and those running the grassroots organizations to explore community interest and possible partnerships. To their surprise, most were indifferent to the idea. They seemed to be taking a polite wait-and-see approach. Nevertheless, the social work faculty held a community meeting inviting community members and recognized community leaders. The community feedback was almost all negative. Community members talked about how the university used to be more open and welcoming to the community, with a lot of community activities taking place on campus such as dances and the use of the facilities for high school sports. Resentment was expressed that it is now walled off and the university students are told never to cross over to the other side of the highway that separates the university from most of the city. Leaders talked about faculty from the university using the community for research projects and giving nothing in return to the community residents. They also expressed resentment toward social service agencies from outside of the city imposing rules and regulations that made it difficult for low-income community members to access services. And they talked about the multitude of needs facing the community and their impression that the county power structure was indifferent at best.

By the end of the meeting the social work faculty were told "yes we need help, and your proposed idea might work if you include us in the process." One community member summed up the feeling of the group: "Don't come unless you plan to stay. Don't come if we are not partners." They were willing to take baby steps, and the faculty had to prove their trustworthiness.

Assessment

One approach Trina could pursue in Case 13.2 would be to use a community development and/or conflict theory approach in conducting the needs assessment. Both theoretical approaches focus on building relationships with community members in assessing needs. With these perspectives, both of which are consistent with AOP practice principles, the community is viewed as capable of identifying and addressing its own issues. As a social worker, you are a partner in the assessment process. You provide technical assistance and support to the community members and constituent groups. The following section describes the steps in conducting an AOP community needs assessment (Barnett, 2010).

Community needs assessments help to empower community residents to create services and programs that respond to their challenges, concerns, and opportunities. It is a systematic way to identify the resources and needs of residents by gathering data, soliciting the perspectives of residents and leaders, and surveying service providers and other community resources (Samuels et al., 1995, p. 8).

The social worker and the community partners develop a community profile that incorporates the use of quantitative statistics, demographic indicators, focus groups, and key

CASE 13.2 IT'S NOT JUST ME—IT'S A COMMUNITY PROBLEM: CONDUCTING A NEEDS ASSESSMENT IN SOCIAL WORK PRACTICE

Trina is a first-year MSW student placed in an inner-city school district as a school social worker intern. She has been working with Adia, a fifth-grade girl who has been skipping school. Sessions with Adia reveal that she does not like coming to school because she is being teased by other students in the class. Trina schedules a home visit with Adia's parents to discuss the truancy issue. Adia's parents both work at the local university. Adia's mother is an administrative assistant, and her father is a security guard.

"I don't know what to do with that girl," Adia's mother states dispiritedly. "I take her to school every day and drop her off myself. She won't stay. Those kids down there are so mean to her. We've tried to help her lose weight. Her doctor says that she is 25 pounds overweight now, and it seems to be getting worse. She has gained 10 pounds in the past 3 months since this mess all started." "We try to keep the junk out of the house," said Adia's father, "but she sneaks it. And that cafeteria is the worst! Hot dogs, hamburgers, pizza, hot wings! Soda machines in the cafeteria and candy galore in the school store. The homemade lunches we send with her every day can't compete with that. Not to mention that they just got rid of another gym period at the school in order to give more time to preparing for the achievement tests. We can't keep up."

Trina asks the parents if they are members of the home and school associations. Both parents indicate that their schedules are hectic and that they do not have time to attend the meetings. Trina lets them know that there is a meeting scheduled every third Wednesday at 7:30 p.m. The meetings only last an hour, and Trina encourages them to come to the meeting to discuss their concerns about the nutrition and exercise program at the school. Adia's mother attends the meeting and brings up the issues. At the meeting, she meets several parents who have the same concerns. They form a committee to investigate the issue further.

The next day, Trina receives a call from Adia's mother. Several of the parents are getting together to discuss a strategy for addressing obesity among their children, and she invites Trina to attend. Trina asks if it is okay to invite her supervisor and the school nurse to the meeting. At the meeting, the school nurse indicates that their last round of health screenings indicated that as many as 20% of the youth in the district are overweight.

Trina is excited about the possibility of helping the parents with their concerns about the health of their children. Her field instructor discusses the possibilities and decides to suggest conducting a community needs assessment on the extent of obesity in the community to determine if obesity is a community-wide issue and the possible social and structural factors contributing to the problem. Trina also suspects that the needs assessment will find that the obesity problem will be concentrated among the lower-income African American population in the community.

---

informant interviews that provide information on political and sociocultural factors. Needs assessments can be used to:

1. Determine if an intervention exists in a community.
2. Determine if there are enough clients with a particular problem to justify creating a new program.

3. Determine if existing interventions are known or recognized by potential clients.
4. Determine what barriers prevent clients from accessing existing services.
5. Document the existence of an ongoing or exacerbating social problem. (Royse et al., 2005, p. 53)

Conducting an Anti-Oppressive Practice Community Needs Assessment

The following describes the steps to conduct an AOP community needs assessment. While the various tasks are listed as separate steps, the process is not linear. Some tasks often take place simultaneously, and the process is often circular, much in the same way as the helping process. The various tasks involved in conducting a community needs assessment were initially developed by the Philadelphia Health Management Corporation (1997). They have been modified here to ensure a community needs assessment is consistent with AOP practice principles. The process presented here is from the perspective of a community-based social worker tasked with helping a community group conduct a needs assessment.

Critical Self-Reflection

A fundamental principle of AOP generalist social work practice is critical self-reflection. This is especially true in community practice with disadvantaged participants living in communities characterized by oppression, discrimination, inequality, and multiple intersectionality. Self-reflection entails examining your values, beliefs, power, and privilege in relation to the experiences of the community members. How are your experiences and beliefs different from the community members you will be working with and those that will be part of the community needs assessment? How will you be perceived by community members? If your roles were reversed, how would you react to having a professional social worker ask you questions about your life and experiences? How can you build trust given your power and privilege?

When working with a community group, we recommend that you engage the group in the process of self-reflection as well. Having the group members examine and reflect on their assumptions, values, and beliefs is important for group functioning. An open dialogue about their feelings and reactions to working with a noncommunity member coming from a different background and possibly representing what they believe, at some level, to represent an oppressive system needs to take place. As in any community, there will be differences among the group members in terms of their beliefs and values, experiences with oppression and discrimination, and their intersectionality. Do not assume that the members are a homogeneous group. This conversation will help improve the effectiveness of the group in accomplishing the tasks and improve communication between you and the group members as well as between the group members.

Acknowledge and Confront Oppression

As part of your conversation with the group members, an important component of AOP community practice is to engage the group in an open discussion about their experiences with oppression and discrimination. Often coming from a position of privilege and power, this is a difficult task. Your critical self-reflection will help you prepare for this conversation. Part of the difficulty is that you won't know how the group members will respond. Will it bring up negative emotions or anger? Will you bear the brunt of their anger? This is a sensitive conversation. You will need to be comfortable with it and encourage an open dialogue. Your job is to listen and encourage their exploration of oppression on the personal, interpersonal, institutional, and structural levels.

The aim of AOP generalist social work practice is to challenge and dismantle oppressive structures and practices. For this to happen, the community members will need to understand how systems and structures have contributed to their experiences of oppression and discrimination. It will be important to understand how social, political, cultural, and institutional factors have contributed to the needs of the community. This understanding will help shape the community needs assessment, interpretation of the findings, and possible solutions to the identified needs.

Define the Purpose

In collaboration with the community members, it is important to determine how the needs assessment will be used and the purpose for conducting the community needs assessment. Needs assessments can have many purposes. They can be used to provide information to mobilize for social action, identify potential partners, provide data for funding projects, identify gaps in services, document community needs, build community "buy-in", identify community leaders, and/or identify community resources. The key to conducting an assessment from an AOP perspective is empowerment. The purpose of the needs assessment is defined by the community members, not by the social worker.

As part of this conversation, it is important the various roles and responsibilities are clarified. It is your responsibility to specify how you will work together on the project. Your role is to support and facilitate the process. The community members are the decision-makers and own the project. Do not assume the expert role. It is a collaborative process, and collaboration is a core practice principle of AOP generalist social work practice. Some community members may expect the social work professional to lead the process and be the expert. In your conversation, acknowledge that you have some expertise but that the community members know their community better than anyone. They have firsthand knowledge about the issues facing their community, and they have a sense of the pulse of the community as well as the history and cultural traditions of the community. Often community residents are aware of issues or concerns that may not be known to the professional community.

Define the Community

Communities encompass various geographic localities, interests, and a diversity of people. It is necessary to define the boundaries of the community in which you are working. Examples of community definitions may include physical boundaries (e.g., counties, ZIP codes, neighborhoods where the agency provides services) or may include a specific population (e.g., immigrants from Vietnam, Spanish-speaking residents). It is important to involve the community members in defining the community.

The community members with whom you are working may have different definitions of community based on their interests and who they represent in the community group.

This can be a major hurdle in conducting the community assessment. Defining the community to be assessed is a collaborative process. As the social work professional, you can help facilitate the process to achieve some sort of compromise that is acceptable to the group. Make sure all voices are heard and that adjustments are made. If a small group of members dictate to the rest of the group, there will be resentment and resistance.

Define the Goals and Objectives

Now that the community group has clarified the purpose of the community needs assessment and defined the community, the group now needs to develop the overall goals of the community assessment as well as specific measurable objects. This step will inform the design of the community needs assessment. The purpose statement identifies in the broadest sense why the needs assessment is being conducted. The project goals specify what the community group hopes to achieve with the needs assessment. Project objectives are specific, measurable outcomes that a project aims to achieve within a defined timeframe. They essentially break down the project goals into more specific and measurable terms.

Defining the project goals and objectives may seem antithetical to AOP generalist social work practice where the emphasis is on social justice and the elimination of oppression and discrimination. In some ways, it is. However, it depends on the purpose of the needs assessment. If the purpose is to mobilize the community or promote self-help initiatives, then formulating measurable objectives is probably not needed. A more informal approach would be appropriate. If, however, the purpose is to document community needs to obtain funding or to advocate for social change, the credibility of the findings with funding sources or with noncommunity members will increase if the needs assessment utilizes accepted research protocols. Again, this is not your decision. You can suggest and advise, but it is ultimately up to the community members and the purpose of the needs assessment.

Identify and Collect Existing Data

Prior to collecting new data for the community needs assessment, we recommend researching existing data. Again, this should be a collaborative and empowering process. Your role is not to do all the research, but to help the community members with the process. In documenting the needs of a community, multiple sources of information and a variety of research methodologies are available. A mixed-methods approach to analyzing needs will allow for a balanced presentation of the information that not only describes phenomena in a community but also may provide information on the history of the phenomena and potential explanations for causes or contributing factors. You can find information about a social problem in a variety of places. A good place to start is with your clients and professionals in the field who may know something about the existence of the problem that you are trying to address. You will also need to obtain data from the research literature as well as from existing sources of secondary data.

Effective needs assessments must be grounded in the research literature. In conducting analyses of the literature, we want to consider the following questions: What do we know about the causes and consequences of the problem? What are the magnitude and scope of the problem? What has worked? What has not worked? How does the target community or population vary from those reported in the literature?

Answers to these and other questions place your needs assessment within a context and provide a basis for comparing the significance of the problem being studied and the relevance of the proposed solution with the problem in general and in other communities.

The use of multiple population-based and resource-based pieces of information is needed to provide a demographic profile of the community. Population-based information includes the use of census data, public health vital statistics data, and community surveys conducted by either professionals or community residents. These data are generally available from government agencies at the federal, state, and local levels. Census data are available online and can be analyzed by state, county, municipality, and census tract. A wealth of population and neighborhood data are contained within the census data. In addition to federal data, "every state maintains a wealth of useful data for planners and evaluators" (Royse et al., 2005, p. 59). Most states have databases of crime and arrest statistics, health indicators, teen pregnancy rates, educational statistics, and many other kinds of information that can be helpful in conducting needs assessments. Other types of government data from over 70 federal government agencies can be accessed on the internet.

Resource data are government reports that are available on a specific topic. Data from published reports and from private foundations can also be used to document needs. Secondary data sources are excellent resources for needs assessments. These reports are available from service providers or private vendors, are relatively cheap to access, and provide a wealth of quantitative and qualitative data on many social and community problems.

There are several internet sites where you can access demographic data and reports. *Research Navigator Guide: The Helping Professions* is an excellent reference for social workers (Kjosness et al., 2004). You might also check with the reference librarian at your university. Often academic departments have designated library liaisons that create specialized reference listings of resources on the internet that are discipline specific. The categories are usually listed on the library's website. Websites such as PolicyMap.com utilize the census to compile all of the relevant data in a complete report. PolicyMap also offers easy-to-use online mapping with data on demographics, real estate, health, jobs, and more in communities across the United States.

Conducting an assessment of the population and resource data will provide you with information regarding age, race, ethnicity, educational attainment, population size, marital status, morbidity and mortality, income inequality and socioeconomic status, wages, population mobility, employment trends, and community and academic definitions of social problems and previous attempts to address them.

Analyze the Existing Data

Once the available data have been collected, the group can now prepare a profile of the community that describes the population (socioeconomic, demographic, health, crime, etc.). The aim here is to provide an overall summary of the community. Your summary will describe who lives in the community, what it looks like, and what some of the social, health, and/or economic issues impacting the community are. These types of data are most useful if they are compared to other communities or groups. For example, reporting that 67% of the households in the community are living below the poverty line is a descriptive fact. It is useful to know that there is a high level of poverty in the community. However, knowing that 67% are in poverty compared to 13% for the other districts in the city provides additional information on the severity of the problem and places the need in a wider context. If possible, it is always better to conduct your secondary analysis with a comparison group.

The quantitative analysis of the existing data tells us what the conditions are, but not necessarily what caused the conditions or why they continue to exist. The analysis may also not give us an accurate picture of the composition of the community. In many communities, disenfranchised populations do not necessarily show up in census data. Many minorities go undercounted and unnoticed. Accurate measures of, say, the number of gay or lesbian Spanish-speaking residents in a community are not likely to be documented in a report or on the Web. This information can often only be discovered through discussion with community members. At this phase of the project, it is necessary to determine what information you still need to collect in order complete your community profile. The team then decides how to collect the needed data to fill in any gaps in the description of the community. The process continues until the community group is satisfied with their community profile.

The collection and analysis of the secondary data should be collaborative. The community members should have ownership of the data and be empowered to interpret the findings from their perspective. The group members can decide what to do with the findings from the secondary analysis. First and foremost, it provides direction for the community needs assessment. However, the findings could be disseminated to the community to build support for the needs assessment or inform community members about issues identified in the data. The finding could also be publicized through the traditional media and on social media to help build public support for the community needs. In accordance with AOP practice principles, the members of the community group are empowered to make the decisions on the dissemination process.

Data Collection

Based on the project's goals and objective as well as the findings from the community profile, the community group, with input from the social work professional, is ready to determine what data will be collected and how they will be collected. The data needed for the needs assessment are driven by the project's objectives. The community group reviews each objective and determines what the best source of data is to provide information related to the objective. They then collectively decide how the data will be collected. This is done for each objective. For example, one objective may identify factors contributing to a high rate of school truancy. One possible source of information could be high school students. Another possible source of data could be parents of high school students. The next step, as mentioned, is then determining how the data will be collected. One possible way would be to conduct focus groups with the students and/or parents. Another possible way could be conducting in-depth interviews of the selected data source. The following briefly describes data collection methods that are frequently used in community needs assessments.

Observation, surveys, and focus groups provide three options. *Observation data* focus on documenting behavior as it occurs. The observation may be conducted independently from the group being observed or as a participant. Observation includes going out into the community, walking the streets, interacting with community members, or attending meetings. This allows you to get to know the people and the environment.

Survey data use questionnaires and/or interview schedules. Both tools are excellent ways of "checking the pulse of the community and getting specific and current information from a cross section of residents in a timely manner" (Andranovich & Howell, 1995, p. 1). When developing a community survey, it is important to consult with community partners to understand the purpose for conducting the survey. Reaffirm the need or problem that they seek to address. What information do they want to know in the end? How will the information be used? Who are the best people to interview? How can interviewing these people help the community to achieve its goals? What is your time frame for completing the analysis? The three most common types of community assessment surveys are key informant surveys, community surveys, and client satisfaction surveys. The following briefly describes data collection methods that are frequently used in community needs assessments.

Key informant surveys obtain data from those who are informed about a given problem because of training or work experience—usually because they are involved in some sort of service with that population (Royse et al., 2005). Typically, they are the community residents, block captains, organizational leaders, local politicians, ward leaders, local business owners, law enforcement officers, school officials, and human services professionals who work with the client population whose need is being assessed.

"Snowball" sampling techniques are often used to generate a list of key informants. One begins with a few key informants and asks them to identify other persons knowledgeable about the problem or population being studied. Depending on the size of the key informant list, the key informants can be interviewed by telephone, in person, or by a mailed questionnaire. The interview or questionnaire obtains their perceptions of the community issue being studied as well as information about possible solutions. Survey research methods are used to construct the questionnaire and to conduct the data analysis. Key informant surveys are a relatively inexpensive and convenient way to obtain subjective (expert opinion) needs assessment data.

Community surveys of households or community residents is another approach for assessing needs. Typically, these types of surveys are more expensive and require a high level of survey research expertise to carry out. Community surveys can provide information on residents' perceptions of their needs and community conditions as well as empirical data that can be extrapolated to the community or population being investigated. The benefit of a well-executed community survey is that the findings are representative and can be generalized with a specified degree of confidence to the community or population being studied. The downside is cost and difficulties in carrying them out.

Client satisfaction surveys are similar to community surveys except that current or past recipients of a service or program are queried instead of community residents in general. Obtaining a sample of former or current clients tends to be easier than community surveys because the study population is known, defined, and more limited. Client satisfaction studies can provide useful information for needs assessments. Clients are in a unique position to provide feedback on how well the service or program is meeting their needs, additional unmet needs, and the operation of the service or program.

Focus groups are another approach to documenting needs using key informants, community members, or clients. The social worker facilitating the focus group uses open-ended questioning and elaboration skills to obtain in-depth information on the topic under investigation. Focus group participants are selected based on their knowledge of the problem as well as how representative they are of the population group.

Analyze Data

The analysis of the community needs assessment data is determined by the type of data collected. It could be a quantitative analysis, a qualitative analysis, or a combination of both. Often the professional social worker will have the skills needed to conduct the data analysis. It is important that whoever conducts the data analysis actively involve the community group in reviewing the preliminary findings and that they pose questions for further analysis.

This stage involves the use of critical analysis skills to compare problems and needs that have been identified to existing resources. Here it is necessary to determine whether you have the resources available in the community to address the social problem. Part of this process is identifying gaps in services to meet the needs of the community members.

Social workers engage community members in a discussion to decide which problems they would like to address first. This is not an easy process. We all have our own conceptions about which problem we think is the most important. Addressing the problems is a collaborative process that will involve all of the community partners. The challenge is to encourage buy-in and to keep partners engaged throughout.

The community group is responsible for approving the final results of the data analysis. The group needs ownership of the project findings. Having the social worker or data analyst conduct the analysis and present the findings to the group in a vacuum is inconsistent with the AOP practice principles. This is easy to do, especially when the social work professional is working with community members unfamiliar with research protocols and quantitative or qualitative research methods. Guard against falling into the "it is easier if I just do it myself" trap. In the long run, it will work against the long-term AOP goals of social change. Community ownership is vital.

Preparing a Needs Assessment Report and Dissemination

The needs assessment report consists of two major components. The first is a detailed description of the project. This component should include the purpose of the project, a clear definition of the community being assessed, a list of the project participants and community partners, the project goals and objectives, the sources of data, data collection methods and data analyses used, the assessment findings, limitations, and project recommendations. The full report describes in detail the issues and problems the community faces. It should provide enough detail on the methods used that the quality of the data can be assessed by outside evaluators or funding sources. The findings should be supported by evidence gathered from your community assessment, including your own experience, quantitative data/statistics, and qualitative data from persons or organizations that are knowledgeable about the community. The statement should be clearly related to the goals articulated by the community, clear and concise, and stated in terms of those who will benefit in the community rather than the needs or problems faced by your organization.

The second component of the needs assessment report is an executive summary. This is a brief report on the major findings and recommendations. It provides a brief but comprehensive overview of the community needs assessment. The executive summary is a useful document for disseminating the project findings and recommendations to build community and organizational support for the changes needed to address the identified issues or problems. The community group plays a key role in disseminating the findings and recommendations to mobilize support for community change. Case 13.3 is an example of a community assessment.

CASE 13.3 COMMUNITY RESOURCE DATABASE

The Community Education Foundation (CEF) is a nonprofit organization located in a low-income, predominately African American community. The community by every indicator is disadvantaged with numerous deficits and very few strengths. CEF's mission is to strengthen the educational resources of the community and to promote improved academic performance of the children attending the public schools in the district. In pursuit of its mission, CEF organized and facilitates a large coalition of the social service providers in the community and surrounding, more affluent communities. The coalition is composed of nonprofit human service organizations, city and county government agencies, faith-based community organizations, and neighborhood groups. CEF works with the coalition members to obtain funding for service programs and to support the development and implementation of educational enrichment programs for elementary, middle school, and high school students.

At a monthly meeting of the coalition, an unmet community need was identified. The issue was that there was no up-date directory of the various services available to community residents. Individual organizations and their staff members have their own resource list, but there was not a central listing and certainly no comprehensive and up-to-date directory of community resources and services. The coalition decided to form a small work group to explore possible solutions to address this need.

The work group met several times to brainstorm possible ways to create a community resource directory. Two obstacles were identified. The first was that identifying available community resources and obtaining up-to-date information would require a considerable amount of human resources to complete the tasks. None of the coalition members had the financial resources to fund the project. An alternative source of person power to collect the necessary data was needed. The second obstacle was keeping the resource directory up-to-date. Traditional paper-bound directories are out of date by the time they are published. The solution appeared to be creating an electronic database that could be easily updated. Again, funding the creation of the database and maintaining were major obstacles. The work group members decided to find a community partner willing to take on the project. One member recommended that they

(continued)

CASE 13.3 COMMUNITY RESOURCE DATABASE (*CONTINUED*)

contact the local social work school to see if they would be able to use social work students to collect the data and possibly create a searchable community resource database.

A workgroup representative met with the dean of the school and was referred to the faculty member overseeing the school's new pro bono community field agency. The proposed project was a perfect fit for the new community field agency that was looking for community partners for capacity-building projects. A social work faculty member and four MSW student interns took on the project of researching community resources and creating a searchable web-based database that could be accessed via the internet by community residents and community service providers. The field agency director also agreed to take on the maintenance of the database long-term, updating it on an annual basis.

The social work team met monthly with the community work group to collaboratively develop the project. The community coalition had ownership of the project, and the school team supported the project by providing expertise and the person power to accomplish it. In collaboration with the work group members, the information on the database entries was identified and a data collection instrument was created. The work group developed a multi dimensional plan to identify all the community resources. The social work team formed two work groups. One group began the data collection process with the known organizations. The other group began the process of identifying additional resources. With the help of the community work group, they divided the city into neighborhoods and began the process of canvasing each neighborhood. The community coalition hired a computer science student part-time to create a web-based database. The social work team was responsible for data entry. When the database became operational, the community work group presented it to the community coalition. The coalition members then began the process of informing community members and community services organizations about the existence of the database and how to access it.

We believe that this case study is an excellent example of an AOP community assessment. The project originated in the community by community members. The community members were empowered throughout the process. They were the decision-makers. The social work team worked collaboratively, providing support and expertise for the community needs assessment. Finally, the aim of the project was to improve access to needed services for oppressed and disadvantaged community members. Consistent with AOP practice principles, the project had a social justice mission that sought to improve community organizations and structures.

Community-Based Participatory Research

Community-based participatory research (CBPR) is an approach to conducting community needs assessments that is based on conflict theory. It is an empowering approach to assessing community needs and change in oppressive community structures. CBPR has increasingly been used for eliminating racial and ethnic health disparities through engaging community members as partners in research design, collaborative discourse about knowledge, and intervention development and health policy making (Belone et al., 2016). CBPR emphasizes joining with the community as full and equal partners in all phases of the research process.

CBPR recognizes the importance of involving members of a study population as active and equal participants in all phases of the community needs assessment, if the process is to be a means of facilitating change. CBPR is used to assess social, structural, and physical environmental inequities through the active involvement of community members, organizational representatives, and researchers in all aspects of the research process (Holkup et al., 2004).

Implementing a community needs assessment following the CBPR model is similar to the steps followed in a traditional needs assessment where the researcher is the expert. The difference, however, is in the process and the roles community members play in the needs assessment. Throughout the process, community members are equal partners in (a) identifying the research question or target problem to be assessed, (b) identifying the community stakeholders and participants, (c) designing the needs assessment and data collection methods, (d) implementing the data collection process, (e) analyzing the data, (f) interpreting the results, and (g) disseminating the results.

Asset Assessment

Asset assessment is the process of determining the amount of social capital within the community. The solutions to community challenges are seen as residing within the community residents themselves. Community assets, as defined by Kretzmann and colleagues (2005), refer to those strengths that exist in a community. These strengths include individual, economic, institutional, and organizational resources that are available to community residents. Additionally, a strengths-based assessment reveals the existing opportunities for residents to both access needed resources and contribute their individual "gifts" toward the betterment of the communities in which they live. Components of an asset assessment may include the following:

- *Local residents*: their skills, experiences, passions, capacities, and willingness to contribute to the project, with special attention paid to residents who are sometimes "marginalized"
- *Local voluntary associations, clubs, and networks*: for example, all of the athletic, cultural, social, faith-based, and other groups powered by volunteer members who might contribute to the project
- *Local institutions*: for example, public institutions such as schools, libraries, parks, police stations, and so on, along with local businesses and nonprofits who might contribute to the project
- *Physical assets*: for example, the land, the buildings, the infrastructure, transportation, and so on who might contribute to the project
- *Economic assets*: for example, what people produce and consume, businesses, informal economic exchanges, barter relationships, and so on

An excellent resource for organizers seeking to understand asset-based community development is the Asset-Based Community Development (ABCD) Institute at DePaul University. The three basic steps of ABCD are (a) discovering the strengths in our communities, (b) connecting with each other and our community, and (c) coming together to build on our knowledge and skills. The ABCD website provides a detailed description of the steps, tools and instruments for conducting assessments, and case examples of the use of ABCD.

Asset Mapping

A useful community assessment tool is the development of an asset map. Asset maps are visual representations of a community's resources. Organizers use capacity assessment instruments to determine the strengths and skills of individual residents (individual capacity assessment) and opportunities and resources available to residents through the provision of social service programs offered by agencies or organizations (organizational capacity assessment). Once information is collected regarding community resources, community social workers use geographic information system (GIS) mapping to represent the special relationships of the existing resources and the community residents. Simple asset maps can be created by conducting a community resource assessment and plotting the addresses of the resources found on a map. The community resource assessment allows the social worker to identify potential assets and resources that are available to the client.

Some resources can be found by conducting a simple internet search. Many resources in low-income communities may still not be documented. In order to uncover hidden assets, walk the neighborhood in which your agency resides. Often, services exist in faith-based organizations, hospitals, within fraternal and sorority organizations, or even in recreation centers. Social workers can provide a helpful resource to their agencies and their clients by collecting this information and geographically plotting it on a map. These asset maps allow clients to see where resources exist and how far they are from their homes, as well as identify gaps or underresourced areas.

Programs that use GIS software are available at ESRI.com. Mapping for 200 addresses or fewer can be plotted using free programs such as Batchgeo.com. Both of these programs interface with Excel spreadsheets. Be sure to read licensing agreements to determine charges for your organization or personal use. A helpful guide to community asset mapping can be found online.

Community Members' Capacity Assessment

This type of assessment is designed to measure the skills of individual residents in the community and to determine what resources they have available to address a particular social problem. Community members respond to questions that assess their vocational, interpersonal, and associational capacities. The goal is to ascertain not only the individual's personal assets but also the amount of interaction that person has in the community. Often community members belong to or have connections with organizations or associations that can be helpful in addressing a problem. The inventory also asks residents to identify skills they would like to learn or that they could teach.

Community Organizational Capacity Assessment

This type of assessment involves bringing together the various organizations, agencies, and associations in a given area to determine who can provide what services to your client population or who can contribute to the elimination of the identified social problem. Organizations are asked to provide a description of the services they provide, the population they serve, and their level of community involvement.

Resource Mapping

One of the functions of social work is that we often act as resource managers. In order for us to provide adequate services to our clients, we must be knowledgeable about what resources, assets, or opportunities exist in our community. Resource mapping requires us to leave our offices to look around the community to see what is out there and available to our clients. There are various sources of resource data. These include personal observation, existing resource manuals, and the internet. Useful tools for identifying resources include the Individual Capacity Assessment and the Organizational Assessment. A more detailed explanation of these tools follows in the next section on asset assessment.

Resource mapping is a visual representation of the data that allows you to see where the resources in a community are in relation to your client population. Data can be mapped using a variety of tools that are available either through purchase or by using free resources on the internet. Programs like Microsoft's MapPoint are relatively inexpensive and are fairly easy to learn. It is necessary to develop a database of information to categorize your resource findings prior to mapping.

Intervention

AOP generalist social work practice interventions with communities aim to challenge and dismantle oppressive structures and practices negatively impacting disadvantaged communities and community members. The focus is on social justice, the elimination of discrimination and oppression, and the empowerment of community members to strengthen and revitalize the social, psychological, and economic well-being of disadvantaged communities.

Models of Community Practice

Rothman (1995) identified three models of community organization and macropractice. Originally developed in 1970, Rothman's three models of community practice have probably been one of the most influential conceptualizations of community social work practice. The three approaches are:

- locality development
- social planning
- social action

The locality development model is referred to as a bottom-up approach because it is a self-help, participatory model of change. It is based on the premise that for change to occur, it is necessary to include the broadest possible participation of community citizens in the planning implementation and evaluation process (see Case 13.4). It places a great deal of emphasis on self-determination and the democratic process. Professionals cannot change the community for the people; they must do that themselves. The overall goal of locality development is to enhance the relationship between the community power structure and its citizens. This approach assumes that all parties have, or can come to have, common interests, and any differences are reconcilable through rational discussion and interaction (Hyman, 1990). Considerable attention is given to group dynamics; participation in the planning, implementation, and evaluation process; democratic procedures; self-help; the development of community leaders; and education. This model places great emphasis on consensus and cooperation.

CASE 13.4 EXAMPLE OF A LOCALITY DEVELOPMENT MODEL: THE PRESTON ARTISTIC HISTORY

Preston, Pennsylvania, has a long history of participation in the arts, and although neither its size nor its wealth would suggest it, many famous musicians and artists lived or worked in Preston throughout the 20th century. Famous artists such as Bill Haley, John Coltrane, and many others had connections to or lived in Preston in earlier times. Many visual artists and dancers also lived and performed in Preston in the years immediately preceding and closely following World War II.

Sadly, however, major economic changes affected the city from the 1960s onward. Indeed, Preston lost its tax base and virtually all of its manufacturing jobs, as well as a vibrant commercial community. These events, as well as a period of political corruption, decimated the artistic community. All of the organizations and institutions that supported the arts (except for two small community groups) were forced to close. And to make matters even worse, the arts and music programs in the local school district were dramatically cut back and even eliminated for many grades.

By the early 1990s, no art galleries existed in Preston and no clubs of any type supported music, (again) except for a small school program and small programs offered by the YWCA and one other group. At the same time, a core of artists and musicians continued to exist in the city. And thanks to one very dedicated city resident who was able to form a 501c(3) nonprofit organization, a small art gallery was established in 1993 for the first time since the 1960s. The agency, called the Irving Fine Arts Center, grew quite fast under the direction of its founder, Elise Irving. Within just a few years, the agency had established a number of programs, including a gallery, several children's art programs, a visiting artist in residence program, a Friday night local music series, and an annual children's art show at the local university social work program.

Assessment

Over time, however, the director and the organization began to experience tensions. The director had a staff of three to five all-volunteer employees. Materials for the children's programs were chronically short, and after three very successful years, funding to support the visiting artist program ran short. One of the visiting artists, a long-time friend of the director, left in the middle of the season, with no reason given. Further, the volunteers seemed to be staying for shorter times.

To make matters more complicated still, many of the funding sources used to establish the programs were no longer available, either for reasons of state art program cutbacks or changes in foundation priorities. Some additional grants were available, but accessing them in the time available required information that the art center did not have. This information included a full description of the numbers served through the various programs, ages and other characteristics of their students, and benefits that the programs were providing for their students and the larger community.

Intervention

Due to the relationship that already existed between the art center and the local university social work program, the art center director contacted the dean and asked for help. As luck

(continued)

CASE 13.4 EXAMPLE OF A LOCALITY DEVELOPMENT MODEL: THE PRESTON ARTISTIC HISTORY (*CONTINUED*)

would have it, the social work program had recently redesigned a course in social work practice with organizations and communities, and the primary assignment for that course was working with an organization. The course instructor asked the class to complete the following tasks: (a) to conduct a thorough collaborative assessment of the strengths and challenges facing the organization, (b) to collaboratively develop goals and objectives for the organization, and (c) to develop an intervention plan. Due to the semester time frame, the actual intervention and its assessment would have to be implemented by others, but this did not appear to be a problem for any of those involved.

The assessment the students developed and carried out was quite extensive. Using a combination of focus groups and surveys to examine the perspectives of the various constituencies (staff/volunteers, students, advisory board, and community residents) and an examination of the records the organization maintained, the assessment determined that the primary strengths of the organization were Elise (her energy and love of the project), community need and interest, and the relationship with the social work program. Challenges, on the other hand, included Elise (excessive micromanagement and fear of delegation of tasks), finances and lack of a financial/strategic plan, and no system for tracking services and clients.

The students then followed up this assessment with goal-planning conversations with Elsie and members of the advisory board. They came up with two goals for the organization as objectives and the intervention plan. The two goals and objectives were:

Goal I: Strengthen the long- and short-term financial health of the Irving Fine Arts Center.
Objective 1.1: Develop a comprehensive, 5-year strategic plan by July 2025.
Objective 1.2: Identify and apply for a minimum of five grant proposals each year between 2025 and 2030.
Objective 1.3: Establish a fundraising committee, composed of members of the advisory board and community volunteers, who will develop and implement fundraising activities on an ongoing basis.
Goal II: Establish a flexible and user-friendly data management system for the Irving Fine Arts Center.
Objective 2.1: Develop and implement a computer information management system for data tracking by December 2025.
Objective 2.2: Identify and develop goals, objectives, and an evaluation plan for each program of the Irving Fine Arts Center by November 2025.
Objective 2.3: Select and train an evaluation committee, composed of members of the advisory board and community volunteers, who will oversee evaluation activities on an ongoing basis.

Beyond these goals and objectives, the action steps and responsibilities in the intervention plan were laid out in a way that *reduced* the workload on Ms. Irving. Her micromanagement

(*continued*)

> **CASE 13.4** **EXAMPLE OF A LOCALITY DEVELOPMENT MODEL: THE PRESTON ARTISTIC HISTORY (*CONTINUED*)**
>
> style, it seemed to all, was more of a response to a small organization that grew faster than the number of employees, rather than any intrinsic issues with the director. As such, it was hoped that time, along with the removal of many fundraising duties from Ms. Irving, would correct the problem of micromanagement.
>
> Further, several students and faculty of the social work program took it upon themselves *after* the end of the semester to work as volunteers to assist with some of the objectives. Two of the students, for example, wrote the software program for the data management objective and then taught volunteers how to use it. In addition, one of the members of the faculty developed evaluation tools and then analyzed data as it was needed. These results were used for assistance in writing several grants over the next 2 years.
>
> Finally, programs were developed over time that enlisted social work students to provide case management services to families and individuals associated with the programs.
>
> ## Evaluation
>
> While the center continues to face many problems, and Preston itself is undergoing changes that have unclear results, it appears that the center is making progress in overcoming its difficulties. Several grant proposals have been successfully funded, volunteers are staying longer, and Ms. Irving now has a funded, part-time assistant. In addition, two venues for music performance have opened in the city, and two charter schools have implemented arts programs. There is hope that all of these efforts will reawaken the artistic spirit that once permeated the community, but only time will tell.

Social planning is referred to as a top-down model of community change. It emphasizes the technical aspects of solving problems. Professionals who have specialized expertise guide and control the change process through the use of technical skills such as sophisticated data collection and analysis. The model provides little opportunity for citizen input into the planning process. Although not consistent with AOP principles, the social planning model is a form of generalist social work practice.

Rothman's social action model assumes one segment of the community is being overlooked or bypassed. The focus of this model is on organizing those segments of the community to stand up for their rights and demand that their needs and concerns be addressed. This model emphasizes social justice and advocacy to bring about change in communities or community practices and to redistribute power, resources, and decision-making processes in the community. This model brings issues of social justice, equity, oppression, and discrimination to the forefront of the community's consciousness.

Community Development

Rothman's models of community organizing significantly impacted the field of community social work. Current community practice, referred to as community development, incorporates all aspects of his three models. Community development involves the participation of community members in developing a capacity and consensus in identifying and solving their own problems (Fellin, 2001). Social work interventions are often aimed at improving community conditions and empowering residents to seek community change. Community development also has a social action component, which includes activities aimed at challenging inequalities, confronting decision-makers, and empowering people to change unjust conditions (Rubin & Rubin, 2008; Zastrow, 2009; Zastrow & Kirst-Ashman, 2009). Recognizing that power/disempowerment is often at the core of many social problems, social action focuses on social, political, and economic justice for the disadvantaged and disenfranchised (Weil & Gamble, 1995; Zastrow, 2009; Zastrow & Kirst-Ashman, 2009).

Community development strategies seek to improve community conditions, empower residents, develop resources, and mobilize citizen groups. To achieve these purposes, the generalist social worker organizes constituent groups, builds community coalitions, conducts community needs assessments, lobbies political and government leaders, and advocates on behalf of constituent groups. Community development activities may also involve economic development projects, installation of public facilities, establishment of community centers, recruitment of new businesses, code enforcement, and developing homeowner assistance programs.

To achieve the varying ends of community development, almost every social work practice skill is necessary. Social workers involved in organizing constituent groups often take responsibility for convening and facilitating meetings. They do the planning and the legwork to get participants to attend. This requires skill in managing groups and conducting meetings. An empowering approach to the process focuses on having community residents assume control and leadership of the development effort. The social worker helps get the process going, but the ultimate responsibility for the effort rests with participants and indigenous leadership. Case 13.5 illustrates an empowering approach.

CASE 13.5 SENIORS UNITE

Cheryl is a first-year MSW student with a field placement at the school's community-based pro bono field agency. She is assigned to the senior services team with three other interns. The agency developed a collaborative partnership with the city's public housing authority. The student team is assigned to provide case management and counseling services to the 150 elderly residents living in the Towers.

The Towers is very run-down and understaffed. It has a manager, janitorial workers, and food service staff. There are no other staff to help meet the needs of the low-income African American elderly residents. The social work interns are the only professional resource on site to service the Tower residents. The residents have very little income or social support. Many are physically disabled or experiencing multiple health problems. All have experienced a lifetime of discrimination and oppression. They are among the poorest of the poor in a low-income, disadvantaged community.

(continued)

CASE 13.5 SENIORS UNITE (*CONTINUED*)

The social work team was welcomed with open arms by the residents. They were thankful for any kind of support. Very quickly each student had a full caseload of residents that they met with weekly. During group supervision with their faculty mentor/supervisor, Cheryl began to notice common concerns among her clients and those of her fellow team members. Time and time again, the issue of getting healthcare services for a Tower resident was very difficult, if not impossible. Many of the residents' health issues were not addressed unless they went to the emergency room of the local hospital. During group supervision, Cheryl shared her concern. Everyone agreed that it was a major unmet need for the seniors living in the Towers. Their faculty supervisor suggested that the team brainstorm possible strategies to address the problem.

Cheryl and her fellow interns met at the Towers to discuss possible strategies. After discussing it, they agreed to talk to their clients experiencing health issues to get their ideas on how to proceed. The following week they met again to share their findings. Cheryl reported that a couple of her clients suggested holding an open meeting for the Tower residents to get feedback. The other team members reported similar sentiments for a few clients, but most were resigned to having nothing happen except making the building manager angry. This was an issue since he had absolute power over their lives. He had the power to evict at his discretion. Nevertheless, the team decided to organize an open meeting to discuss residents' concerns. The team decided to try and get at least five of their clients to attend.

Twenty-two residents attended the meeting. They were invited to share any concerns they had about living in the Towers. It was a lively meeting with a number of issues or concerns raised. However, most were fearful about being evicted by the building manager if they complained. The social work team made a list of resident concerns and summarized it for the group. Access to healthcare headed the list. Cheryl then facilitated a discussion of next steps to see what the residents wanted and were comfortable doing. The group decided that Mrs. Harrison, a resident well respected among her peers, and Cheryl would request a meeting with the building manager to discuss healthcare concerns. The building manager refused to meet, saying he was too busy and that the Towers was an independent living facility. If the residents needed heathcare, it was up to them to get it. He also said that if residents cannot live independently, then they should live elsewhere.

The social work team organized a second open meeting with the residents. About 30 residents attended the meeting. Mrs. Harrison informed the group of the building manager's response to their request to meet. Mrs. Harrison led the group in a discussion of what could be done. After much heated debate, it was decided that the group members would circulate a petition among the residents to request an open meeting with the housing authority administration. The social work team agreed to prepare a brief petition, and the group members took on the task of getting the signatures. Cheryl suggested that if they were unsuccessful in getting a meeting with the housing authority, the group could see if they could interest the local newspaper to run a story. The group members suggested that a reporter be invited to the meeting with the housing authority if it took place.

(continued)

> **CASE 13.5** **SENIORS UNITE (*CONTINUED*)**
>
> The petition obtained 100 signatures. The petition and a request to meet were sent to the housing authority. The request also mentioned that a news reporter would be invited by the residents to also attend the meeting. Much to the surprise of everyone, the housing authority agreed to meet with the Tower residents. Mrs Harrison was chosen as the group's spokesperson, and the group members began compiling resident stories to share with the housing authority.
>
> The meeting was held with about 50 Tower residents attending. A reporter from the newspaper also attended along with the social work team and their faculty supervisor. Mrs. Harrison presented their concerns about the lack of any healthcare professional being available onsite and the difficulty many residents have in accessing healthcare offsite. The housing authority CEO acknowledged the residents' concerns and agreed that access to healthcare should be a priority for a senior living facility. He promised that the housing authority would pursue possible solutions within their budget constraints.
>
> The housing authority arranged to have a team of nursing students and a nursing faculty member visit the Towers monthly to have wellness checks and evaluate resident health issues. They also contracted with the local hospital to have a geriatric physician make house calls to the residents referred by the nursing team. The social work team also began advocating with the country's handicapped transportation service to improve availability for Tower residents. All were positive steps in addressing the seniors' heathcare concerns.
>
> In processing the interns' community intervention during supervision, their supervisor believed that the students' social action community intervention was in part successful because of political concerns of the housing authority. The housing authority had some new low-income projects in the works, and their supervisor suspected that they were very interested in avoiding any negative press. Nevertheless, the social work interns used social action successfully to improve the living conditions of the elderly residents of the Towers. We feel that this case example is a good illustration of an AOP community intervention.

Coalition Building

Both as an independent activity and as a component of community development, coalition building occurs when representatives of diverse community groups join forces to influence external institutions on one or more issues affecting their constituencies (Mizrahi & Rosenthal, 2001). The process may be intended as short- or long-term, but the idea is that there is strength in numbers; often the problems to be addressed are larger and more intractable than a single individual or group can effectively address—in other words, a "common goal" exists (University of Kansas Center for Health and Development, 2017). A coalition, then, has as its goal to build a power base sufficient to influence decision-making and the allocation of resources (Weil & Gamble, 1995).

Unfortunately, coalitions are difficult to create and hold together. Often, there is inherent tension between the coalition members' interest in maintaining the autonomy and power of their constituent groups and the need to share power and resources to make the coalition successful. Additionally, several barriers often exist to a successful coalition. These may include issues of turf ownership, history, attempted dominance by one group or professionals over the larger public, inadequate leadership, or real or perceived costs (University of Kansas Center for Health and Development, 2017). With such difficulties, all of a social worker's micro and mezzo skills may be needed. Social workers need well-developed mediation and negotiation skills to effectively build coalitions, as well as skills in interorganizational relations and planning (Gamble & Weil, 2010).

Evaluation

The evaluation of a community intervention is the same as with other client systems. It consists of an ongoing process evaluation. The process evaluation provides information on the implementation of the intervention. Potential sources of data for a community intervention process evaluation include community members, community leaders or key informants, members of community task forces and local government officials.

The key questions are: What worked and did not work? What still needs to be done? How can the process be improved? Typically, these types of evaluations entail surveys of the various stakeholders or focus groups with the stakeholders. Ideally, for AOP generalist practice, the community stakeholders are in charge of the who, what, and how the process evaluation is conducted and are the decision-makers in interpreting and disseminating the findings.

Adjust and Revise

A critical step in an ongoing process evaluation is making needed adjustments throughout the intervention. This the adjust and revise stage. Again, in AOP community practice, the community stakeholders are the decision-makers in terms of any revisions or adjustments to the intervention. As noted earlier, Chapter 14 provides a detailed discussion of process evaluations.

Termination

The final stage of a community intervention is a planned termination. Termination is closely associated with the intervention's outcome evaluation. The outcome evaluation provides data on the success of the program in terms of achieving its goals and objectives. The outcome evaluation can be qualitative, quantitative, or a combination of both. As noted earlier, Chapter 14 provides detailed information on program outcome evaluations.

Termination of specific community interventions that have limited and specific goals is usually planned. However, the goals of AOP community generalist practice typically involve challenging and dismantling oppressive structures and practice that contribute to the oppression and discrimination experienced by the community and its members. These are long-term goals that require a sustained effort. Thus, interventions designed to achieve specific objectives may include an outcome evaluation as part of the termination process, but the overall goals of AOP community work will, most likely, be ongoing and not include a planned termination.

SUMMARY

This chapter focused on the social work competency related to the community assessment and intervention. Conducting community assessments is associated with the ethical responsibilities to the broader society. Social workers have an ethical responsibility to promote the welfare of communities and to facilitate informed participation in shaping social policies and institutions.

The chapter then reviewed three community theories that can be used in a community assessment. The two theories derived from a social constructivism perspective were community development theory and conflict theory. The third community theory reviewed was structural functionalism, which falls under the systems perspective. The three theories can be used to help inform the design and implementation of a community assessment. The discussion of community theories was followed by a review of community assessment methods and tools.

Social work values and ethics utilize community interventions to address social, economic, and environmental justice issues. Community interventions aim to improve community conditions, empower residents, develop community resources, increase citizen awareness of community issues, and mobilize citizens to work for change. AOP social workers engage in a partnership to work collaboratively with community members to address oppression and discrimination in the structures and practices impacting the community and its members. The chapter reviewed AOP community practice and its four phases—engagement, assessment, intervention, and evaluation. Several assessment methods and intervention strategies were reviewed.

CASE SUMMARY: UNDOCUMENTED AND HOMELESS

Practice Setting Description

Jackie is a first-year MSW student completing an internship at an inner-city family service agency in the Southwest. The agency is in a section of the city that has a high crime rate, gang activity, and failing schools. The area has a diverse population with many immigrants from Central and South America and a substantial African American population. The agency provides individual and family counseling services on a sliding fee scale. The agency also runs several educational and treatment groups as well as a temporary shelter for women and their children. Jackie has been assigned to work with the women and their children in the shelter. Her primary tasks are to provide concrete services and supportive counselling to the shelter residents.

Background Information

Elicia and her daughter, Maria, are undocumented immigrants from Mexico. They have been in the United States for 5 years. Elicia and Maria fled to the area from another southwestern city to escape her abusive husband approximately 2 months ago. Elicia is 25 years old, and Maria 8 years old. Elicia has a 2-year-old daughter, Sarah, who was placed in foster care because of

(continued)

CASE SUMMARY: UNDOCUMENTED AND HOMELESS (*CONTINUED*)

suspected abuse in the home. Sarah is in a foster home in a small rural community in the state hundreds of miles from Elicia's current residence. Since moving to the area, Maria has not been attending school.

Elicia and Maria are currently residing in the agency's temporary shelter for families. They have been at the shelter for 2 weeks, and the agency has a 90-day limit. Prior to arriving at the shelter, Elicia and Maria were homeless and living on the streets.

Elicia is a high school drop-out and was a stay-at-home mother prior to leaving her husband and moving to a different part of the state. She chose to move there because she has two female cousins living in the area who are also undocumented immigrants. Elicia's native language is Spanish. She speaks some English but is not as comfortable speaking in English. Her English comprehension appears to be good. Maria speaks both English and Spanish well. When communicating with the staff, Maria acts as Elicia's interpreter since none of the staff at the shelter speak Spanish.

Maria appears to be behind academically. She struggles reading simple children's books written in English. It is unknown if her ability to read in Spanish is better than her English reading skills.

Other than her two cousins, Elicia has no other sources of support in the community. Her cousins have young families and limited resources but are well established and connected to a Latino community in the city and the local Catholic church. Her cousins refused to let Elicia and Maria live with them while she was trying to find her own place and a job. They stated that they did not have enough room and are concerned they would get in trouble with their landlord if it was found out that they were letting people stay with them. They sent her to the local church for help, and she was given the address for the agency's shelter by the priest.

Elicia has been looking for housing in the Latino community. The housing market is tight with limited options, and she has been unable to find anything that she could possibly afford. The only affordable housing she found was a room in a rundown motel that rents by the hour or by the month. It is in an area of town known for drug dealing and sex work.

On arrival in the community, Elicia found occasional work for a house cleaning company. The company hires undocumented workers, pays them very low cash wages, and threatens to turn them in to Immigration and Customs Enforcement (ICE) if they complain. The job bosses also exploit their female workers sexually, threatening to turn them in if they do not comply. Elicia was fearful about applying for other jobs because of her illegal status. She considered turning to sex work to be able to take care of her child, but her Catholic upbringing and thoughts of how this would shame her family have kept her from doing so. She is in constant fear of being detained, separated from Maria, and having her placed in foster care. She is also afraid that she will end up homeless again and forced to live on the streets or return to her abusive husband.

Elicia is extremely reluctant to sign up for any federally funded services, even those that she and her child are entitled to receive. On the suggestion that she enroll for supplemental food through the Supplemental Nutrition Assistance Program (SNAP), Elicia became nervous and refused, as she has heard that participation in SNAP services, and others like them, would draw the attention of ICE, and she had heard stories on the news of individuals being deported after signing up for such programs.

(*continued*)

CASE SUMMARY: UNDOCUMENTED AND HOMELESS (*CONTINUED*)

Presenting Problems

Elicia and her child are facing multiple obstacles. They need to find permanent, affordable housing and a job that pays enough to cover her housing and living expenses. In addition, Maria needs to be enrolled in school.

Additionally, Elicia is experiencing an immense amount of stress, anxiety, and possibly post-traumatic stress disorder (PTSD). She described an instance where she could not calm down her breathing and she felt lightheaded. She is very fearful of men and tries to avoid all contact with men in the community. She reports difficulty sleeping at night and feeling exhausted most of the time.

She is concerned about Maria. She has started acting out at the shelter, getting into fights with the other children, disobeying her mother, and being disrespectful and defiant to the staff and other adults. Elicia and Maria fight frequently, and when Elicia tries to discipline Maria, she throws a temper tantrum until Elicia gives up.

Elicia has many strengths. She had the strength to leave her abusive husband and move to a different city. She loves her daughter and wants desperately to keep Maria with her. She is resilient and has managed to survive and keep her daughter safe despite not having a place to stay, a job, and a limited support network. Elicia feels safe in the shelter, but she is very fearful of being caught as an illegal immigrant and is generally mistrustful of helping professionals and persons of authority.

DISCUSSION QUESTIONS

1. Identify two community issues that are impacting Elicia and her daughter. What theory or theories would you use to conduct an AOP community assessment of the identified issues?
2. How would you approach doing your community assessment?
3. What stakeholders would you collaborate with in designing and implementing your AOP community assessment?
4. What interventions would you recommend for addressing the identified community issues?

A robust set of instructor resources designed to supplement this text is located at http://connect.springerpub.com/content/book/978-0-8261-6683-8. Qualifying instructors may request access by emailing textbook@springerpub.com.

KEY REFERENCES

Only key references appear in the print edition. To access the full reference list, visit www.springerpub.com/courseconnect. See inside front cover and tear-out card for CourseConnect details.

Belone, L., Lucero, J. E., Duran, B., Tafoya, G., Baker, E. A., Chan, D., Chang, C., Greene-Moton, E., Kelley, M. A., & Wallerstein, N. (2016). Community-based participatory research conceptual model: Community partner consultation and face validity. *Qualitative Health Research*, *26*(1), 117–135. https://doi.org/10.1177/1049732314557084

Gamble, D., & Weil, M. (2010). *Community practice skills: Local to global perspectives*. Columbia University Press.

Hardcastle, D. A., Powers, P. R., & Wenocur, S. (2011). *Community practice: Theories and skills for social workers* (3rd ed.). Oxford University Press.

Hyman, D. (1990). Six models of community intervention: A dialectical synthesis of social theory and social action. *Sociological Practice*, *8*(1), 32–47. http://digitalcommons.wayne.edu/socprac/vol8/iss1/5

Kretzmann, J., McKnight, J., Dobrowolski, S., & Puntenney, D. (2005). *Discovering community power: A guide to mobilizing local assets and your organization's capacity*. https://resources.depaul.edu/abcd-institute/publications/publications-by-topic/Documents/kelloggabcd.pdf

Langer, C. L., & Lietz, C. A. (2015). *Applying theory to generalist social work practice*. John Wiley & Sons, Inc.

Royse, D., Thyer, B., Padgett, D., & Logan, T. (2005). *Program evaluation: An introduction* (4th ed.). Brooks Cole.

Rubin, H., & Rubin, I. (2008). *Community organizing and development* (4th ed.). Pearson/Allyn & Bacon.

Samuels, B., Ahsan, N., & Garcia, J. (1995). *Know your community: A step-by-step guide to community needs and resources assessment* (2nd ed.). Family Resource Coalition. http://eric.ed.gov/ERICDocs/data/ericdocs2sql/content_storage_01/0000019b/80/15/c3/fc.pdf

Tan, A. (2009, October). *Community development theory and practice: Bridging the divide between "micro" and "macro" practice*. Paper presented at the North American Association of Christian Social Workers.

University of Kansas Center for Health and Development. (2017). *Other models for promoting community health and development. The community toolbox*. https://ctb.ku.edu/en/table-of-contents/overview/models-for-community-health-and-development/logic-model-development/main

14 Evaluation in Generalist Social Work Practice

Carolyn is a school social worker at an elementary school complex. She meets with students individually and in groups. At times, teachers and other school personnel will seek out Carolyn's clinical expertise to determine how to address larger, school-wide concerns. Recently, the principal asked Carolyn to meet with her and several other employees to address recent concerns related to bullying that have arisen at school. During the meeting, all present were designated as the antibullying task force for the school and were charged with the duty of developing an antibullying policy and curriculum for the school to adopt and implement at the start of the next term.

During the initial task force meeting, each participant agreed to research antibullying programs and bring back their findings to the next meeting. At the second meeting, all of the participants shared what they had found. One member shared that she found out about an antibullying program that a neighboring school district is currently using. He reported that this program has been really successful in addressing bullying for that school based on conversations with teachers their. Carolyn asked how success was measured with this program, and the member was not able to answer that.

Another task force member shared an antibullying program that had been used in the past. She shared, "It has worked before, so it will work again." Again, Carolyn asked various follow-up questions, but the member was not able to answer her inquiries. A third member shared that if the team wanted to develop a successful antibullying program, they should adopt a "zero-tolerance" policy because that is what would make the most sense in order to reduce the problem of bullying. It did make logical sense, but Carolyn remembered her research courses and learning about ways of knowing. She recalled that, at times, logical does not mean that it is supported by research.

After all of the other team members had shared their ideas, Carolyn provided her insights based on her research from professional publications. Carolyn shared that the professional organization that she is a member of routinely shares information on best practices related to school social work practice, and recently an issue was devoted to addressing bullying in the school setting. Carolyn shared this research with the group and presented her pitch to utilize an evidence-based model that had been empirically evaluated and shown to be effective.

LEARNING OBJECTIVES

This chapter addresses Competency 9: Evaluate Practice With Individuals, Families, Groups, Organizations, and Communities. It focuses on evaluating social work practice at the micro and the mezzo level. By the end of this chapter, you will be able to:

- Understand the purpose of anti-oppressive practice (AOP) social work research.
- Describe the differences between basic research and action research.

- Distinguish between qualitative and quantitative research methods.
- Identify social workers' ethical responsibilities related to evaluating program outcomes.
- Use a logic model to organize a program evaluation.
- Design a practice effectiveness evaluation.
- Design a program outcome evaluation.

COMPETENCY 9: EVALUATE PRACTICE WITH INDIVIDUALS, FAMILIES, GROUPS, ORGANIZATIONS, AND COMMUNITIES

Social workers understand that evaluation is an ongoing component of the dynamic and interactive process of social work practice with and on behalf of diverse individuals, families, groups, organizations, and communities. Social workers evaluate processes and outcomes to increase practice, policy, and service delivery effectiveness. Social workers apply antiracist and anti-oppressive perspectives in evaluating outcomes. Social workers understand theories of human behavior and person-in-environment, as well as interprofessional conceptual frameworks, and critically evaluate and apply this knowledge in evaluating outcomes. Social workers use qualitative and quantitative methods for evaluating outcomes and practice effectiveness.

Social workers:

- select and use culturally responsive methods for evaluation of outcomes; and
- critically analyze outcomes and apply evaluation findings to improve practice effectiveness with individuals, families, groups, organizations, and communities. (Council on Social Work Education [CSWE], 2022, pp. 12–13)

NATIONAL ASSOCIATION OF SOCIAL WORKERS *CODE OF ETHICS*

The National Association of Social Workers (NASW) *Code of Ethics* (2021) value of competence is related to evaluating the practice effectiveness component of the CSWE evaluating practice competency. To be a competent social work practitioner and to be committed to enhancing one's professional expertise requires an ongoing evaluation of one's practice effectiveness. Not knowing if your social work practice is doing what you hope to achieve in your work with clients is unethical. Social work ethics require that we evaluate our practice effectiveness to help ensure that our clients are receiving the help they need and the best services possible. Additionally, social work ethics require competence and the ongoing development of our professional expertise. Developing competence and expertise requires ongoing evaluation of our social work practice effectiveness.

The NASW *Code of Ethics* standard on evaluation and research directly addresses the evaluating outcomes component of the CSWE evaluating practice competency. This ethical standard has 17 subsections related to evaluating organizational and community interventions and outcomes. The subsections of the standard can be reviewed online.

In sum, social workers have an ethical responsibility to evaluate program implementation and outcomes using appropriate research practices that protect human subjects. Social workers also have an ethical responsibility to avoid conflicts of interest in conducting evaluations of social work programs and interventions and to disseminate accurate evaluation findings.

> **Reflection Questions**
>
> Based on the opening chapter case vignette:
> 1. What ethical principles and standards apply to Carolyn's evaluation plan?
> 2. Why do they apply, and what will Carolyn need to do to be compliant with the ethical principles?

APPLIED RESEARCH

Applied research in social work typically focuses on finding solutions to organizational, community, and service delivery problems. Applied research addresses practical issues encountered in the provision of social work services to clients and constituents (Poulin et al., 2022). Basic research, on the other hand, tends to focus on generalizations and theory development. Basic social science research seeks understanding of social phenomena. Thus, the major difference between applied and basic research is in their purposes. The purpose of applied research is to solve problems, while the purpose of basic research is to generate new knowledge or add to the existing body of knowledge.

Action Research and Anti-Oppressive Practice Social Work Research

Action research is a type of applied research. It focuses on experiences, thoughts, opinions, and suggestions of those most impacted by social problems or conditions. It aims to address social problems with participation from the people who are part of the system being examined (Coghlan, 2011). The primary purpose of action research is to improve or change what it seeks to study. When conducting this type of research, you stand with and alongside the participants of your study (Berg, 2007), engaging in collaborative and transparent relationships to create a space for open and honest dialogues (Reason & Bradbury, 2008). Important themes in action research are the importance of practice effectiveness, client life experiences, the web of relationships, community building, and social change (Rutman et al., 2005).

AOP social work research is a form of action research that focuses on social and structural inequalities, oppression, and discrimination by including underrepresented populations in all aspects of the inquiry process with the aim of social and structural change (Boog, 2003).

Strier (2006) provides a comprehensive definition of anti-oppressive social work research. The following summarizes the nine key components of this definition:

- *Goal*: The systemic study of oppression and the development of knowledge that supports people's actions to achieve freedom from oppression
- *Population*: The most oppressed populations that are largely excluded from the main spheres of public and economic life and disconnected from social services

- *Methodologies*: A mixed-method approach that address the complex, multifaceted character of oppression, with its objective, structural aspects as well as its subjective, phenomenological dimensions
- *Research environment*: An environment that is responsive to the long-term traumatic nature of oppression; the research environment should establish a safe space for reflection and self-inquiry and should provide ongoing therapeutic support through the different stages of the research.
- *Role of participants*: The study participants are actively involved in all aspects of the research process.
- *Researcher–participant relations*: An egalitarian power relationship between researchers and participants
- *Ownership of knowledge*: Research knowledge is the property of the oppressed.
- *Knowledge–action relationship*: The generation of actionable knowledge that is used to counter oppression
- *Boundaries of research*: The research that extends the scope from the study of oppression to the dissemination of knowledge and the creation of opportunities for social change. (Strier, 2006)

PRACTICE-INFORMED RESEARCH AND EVALUATION

Practice-informed research seeks to allow practice knowledge and experience to influence research conducted during the practice of social work. Practice-informed research occurs when social workers collect and analyze data during their practice with clients and use those findings to make practice decisions or use practice experience to inform research endeavors. The notion of conducting research or evaluation may seem daunting to some social workers. We encourage you to approach this task with an open mind. Many of the skills necessary to be an effective social worker are the same skills necessary to conduct effective practice-informed research. In practice, social workers identify problems and needs with clients. They then gather information during the assessment, select an intervention, and monitor the intervention to determine effectiveness. There are a variety of ways to conduct research. It is beyond the scope of this book to explore all types of research designs. Instead, we will focus on quantitative and qualitative applied program and practice evaluation research.

Quantitative Research

Quantitative research is a category of research where the data are statistically analyzed or quantified in some way. In its simplest form, quantitative research is often distinguished from qualitative research in that quantitative research emphasizes numeric data, whereas qualitative research emphasizes data that are words and phrases. Both quantitative and qualitative designs are important components in social work research. The CSWE (2022) puts forth that social workers must be able to understand both quantitative and qualitative methods so that they can determine if their practice is effective and to monitor outcomes.

Quantitative research is a deductive approach to finding answers. A deductive approach means that you start with a premise or idea and then, through a systematic process, lead to a conclusion. Quantitative research often begins with identifying a problem and then developing a research question. After a review of the current literature, a hypothesis is formed. Based on the research question, a design is selected and then data collection begins. After all of the data have been collected, the data are then analyzed using statistical means. The results are then interpreted and shared with others.

Qualitative Research

Qualitative research "seeks to explore and address concerns or topics that bridge knowledge, meaning, tangible experience, emotions and reflexive understanding to the applied practice of social work" (Carey, 2012, p. 8). Research that is qualitative in nature and that is consistent with social work values can serve to advance the profession's mission, as it allows us to explore and gain a better understanding into the experiences of vulnerable populations (Reamer, 2012). While quantitative research looks at quantifiable data to analyze it statistically, qualitative research looks at words in an attempt to identify codes or themes. Qualitative research designs are often much more flexible than quantitative designs by comparison (Maxwell, 2013).

▶ **Reflection Questions**

1. What do you like about quantitative research? Why?
2. What do you like about qualitative research? Why?
3. Which type of research are you most comfortable doing?

Qualitative research is often critiqued in relation to positivism. At times, qualitative research has been viewed as "less scientific" than quantitative research. This is not the case. Both qualitative and quantitative methods, though different, are valuable and useful (see Case 14.1). When considering the strengths and limitations with each type of research, the researcher must consider the purpose of the research in order to determine which method would be the better fit. According to Ruch et al. (2016):

> Qualitative research has always had to struggle to justify its existence and its distinctive characteristics, one of which is the focus on relationships in the research process. Consequently, discussions regarding how relationships are understood in qualitative research have largely been determined by the dominant discourse of objectivity associated with positivism, which configures the researcher and research subject as separate, rational individuals. From this positivist standpoint, subjectivity and any notion of relationship are problematic. The overriding endeavor is to minimize their significance—their interference in the research process—by rendering objective, as far as possible, any hint of subjectivity or relationality. In this context, reflexivity, another distinctive feature of qualitative research, is simply a means to an end, that is, the means by which subjectivity can be rendered objective, rather than being understood as important in its own right as a different source of knowing. (p. 29)

> **CASE 14.1** **QUANTITATIVE OR QUALITATIVE RESEARCH DESIGNS**
>
> George works for an agency that provides supports for families with children who have disabilities. One of the agency's programs is respite care. Respite care provides families with a trained sitter so that they can leave the home to run errands or other tasks while the caregiver is home with the child. George feels like the respite program is a great benefit for families but noticed that it is not utilized often. George wants to determine why this is so. George has come up with two different ideas for gaining insights into this issue.
>
> The first plan involves a quantitative design where George will review charts and determine the number of respite days used in the past 3 months. He will then begin sending families information about this program. After the intervention of sending information to families, George will begin tracking the number of respite days used. After 3 months, George will compare the number of days used before and after his intervention.
>
> The second plan involves a qualitative design. George will send out flyers asking interested families to participate in a phone interview regarding how they feel about the respite program. If families call in, George has a list of three general questions to ask but is also open to letting clients lead the direction of the conversation around the topic of respite care.
>
> George is unsure which design would be best for the agency and the respite care program and met with his supervisor to share his ideas. Throughout the supervision process, both George and his supervisor agreed that they could learn beneficial information from both designs and discussed ways to integrate both to create a mixed-method design.

EVALUATING PRACTICE EFFECTIVENESS

This section focuses on the practice effectiveness component of the evaluating practice competency. It addresses methods or approaches to determine the effectiveness of your social work practice with individuals, families, and groups. It is about evaluating micro social work practice with individuals, families, and small groups.

Social workers should continually be seeking to improve their practice. As a profession, we value continued and ongoing education because we recognize that what we know is ever evolving. In addition to being concerned about improving our own practice, we should strive to improve the practice of our fellow social workers. One way that we can contribute to improving the practice of social workers is by sharing what we have found to be effective. This is often a common occurrence on an informal level in many social work organizations. We encourage social workers to be mindful about this process and go beyond informal sharing of "what works" and to formally share personal findings of ways to enhance, enrich, or improve professional practice. This section begins with a discussion of measurement guidelines and standardized measures. Designing single-system evaluations and analyzing single-systems data are then reviewed.

Measurement Guidelines

Social workers engaged in practice evaluation need to follow established research guidelines regarding measurement (Poulin, 2010). Berlin and Marsh (1993) suggest that the data collection effort will be enhanced if you:

- specify the client's problems and goals clearly;
- use multiple measures for each objective;
- collect information that is relevant rather than convenient;
- collect information early in the course of the work with the client;
- use good and accurate measures;
- organize the data; and
- obtain the client's cooperation and consent. (p. 93)

Clearly Specify Problems and Goals

This guideline is fundamental to the measurement process. As noted earlier, client problems and expected outcomes must be specific and stated in clear, unambiguous terms. Measurable objectives related to each goal must be developed. Collecting client data is impossible without specific and observable indicators attached to each objective (Poulin, 2010).

Use Multiple Measures

The use of more than one measure to assess a single phenomenon is a basic research strategy referred to as triangulation (Royse et al., 2016). The assumption behind this strategy is that all measures are to some extent flawed or imperfect. Because any one measure may not be accurate, it is necessary to use more than one measure to assess client progress. The logical assumption is that if two or more imperfect measures indicate change, there is more reason to be confident that change has occurred than if only one imperfect measure is used. Relying on a single measure of client progress is risky. The problems addressed by generalist social workers and their clients are too complex to be assessed with a single imperfect measure.

The inaccuracy of measurement strategies should not discourage you from using quantitative measures in your practice. Crude indicators of progress are preferable to no indicators. What is important is to be aware of the limitations of measurement tools. The data alone will not provide you and your clients with definitive answers. The data will, however, provide you and your clients with helpful information that can be incorporated into your work together. Analyzing the data with your clients will facilitate the helping process and provide a basis for ongoing assessment of your work together (Poulin, 2010).

Collect Relevant Information

Berlin and Marsh warn that "one of the most frequent mistakes that clinicians make is to track something that is not very important" (1993, p. 94). Typically, the client's problem is reconceptualized to fit an existing measure or instrument. The convenience factor is high, but the relevance factor is low. If you cannot specify the expected changes, the problem may not have been conceptualized accurately or the terms may not be specific enough. Relevant measures should flow directly from clearly conceptualized problems and objectives.

Collect Information Early

There are several reasons to begin the process of collecting data early in the helping process. The first reason is that measuring the target problem or objective prior to implementing the intervention provides baseline data, which are a basis for future comparisons. Change must be evaluated comparatively. Without some sort of comparison, it is impossible to assess the extent to which the desired changes have occurred. Collecting assessment data early in the helping process will allow you to periodically evaluate the effectiveness of the work throughout the helping relationship (Poulin, 2010).

A second reason to begin collecting data early in the helping process is to communicate to clients that you are interested in understanding their situation and that you are committed to helping them successfully address their concerns or problems. Measurement is an active and concrete process. Developing measures communicates that you take clients' concerns seriously and that their concerns are important enough to warrant the effort required to develop measures and collect data.

A third reason to start the measurement process early is that it engages the client in a collaborative activity. You and the client define the target problem, develop the objectives, and develop the measurement plan. You and your client may even develop many of the measures used. The client becomes an active participant in the process. This communicates expectations about how you will work together as well as the idea that the client is the expert on their situation (Poulin, 2010).

Use Good and Accurate Measures

Every effort should be made to use the best measures available. According to Berlin and Marsh (1993), four criteria are useful in judging the adequacy of different measures: relevance, sensitivity to change, reliability, and validity.

Relevance refers to the extent the measure is directly related to the targeted outcomes. Is there a good fit between the measure and the expected changes? The relevance of any measure is a function of the identified target problem or the specific change objectives. Make sure the measure you choose matches what the client hopes to change.

Sensitivity to change is the second criterion of a good measure. Not all measures are capable of capturing change. Some are more sensitive than others. It may be possible to use measures that have shown change in previous evaluations and have thus been proved useful. A measure's track record of detecting change is one of the best indicators of its sensitivity to change (Bloom et al., 2009). Often, however, information on a measure's sensitivity is not available; thus, it is not always possible to know in advance whether a measure will be sensitive to change. Berlin and Marsh (1993) suggest that global measures are usually less sensitive to change than measures directly related to specific behaviors targeted for change. Measures of behaviors that occur more frequently are likely to be more sensitive than measures of behaviors that occur less frequently. High-frequency behaviors are more responsive to small changes, while low-frequency behaviors may only respond to major changes (Bloom et al., 2009).

Reliability refers to the consistency of measurements. When measuring client change, you want to be reasonably confident that the differences among the first measurement and subsequent ones relate to changes in the client and not to problems with the measure. An instrument that can do this is said to be reliable. "Every type of measure involves some kind of error, and the measure is reliable to the extent that the error is minimal" (Berlin & Marsh, 1993, p. 97). The two most common ways of testing the reliability of a measure are to assess its internal consistency and its test–retest characteristics. Internal consistency reliability is the extent to which the individual items that make up a scale or index are correlated with one another. Test–retest reliability refers to the extent to which the same result is obtained when the same measure is administered to the same client at two different points in time. Both types of reliability are important. However, in evaluating client change, test–retest reliability is critical. To the extent possible, use at least one measure that has been tested for reliability and has a reliability coefficient of .80 or higher (Poulin, 2010).

Validity refers to the extent to which an instrument measures what it is supposed to measure and not anything else (Royse et al., 2016). For example, if you are assessing a client's self-confidence, the instrument should measure self-confidence, not a related concept such as self-esteem. Because concepts in social work tend to be complex, no measure will be entirely valid—only more or less so (Royse et al., 2016).

There are various ways to determine the validity of an instrument. The least rigorous kind of validity is face validity. Does the instrument appear to measure the concept? A measure is said to have face validity if knowledgeable persons agree that it measures what it is intended to measure (Poulin, 2010).

Another type of validity is content validity. This method also relies on expert opinion. In this case, experts are asked to review it to see if the entire range of the concept is represented in the sample of items selected for the scale (Royse et al., 2016). For example, a scale designed to measure stress should have items that represent the different components of stress, such as feeling tense, feeling pressured, having difficulty sleeping, and being short-tempered.

Neither content nor face validity empirically demonstrates a scale's validity. This can be done in a number of ways.

A scale's concurrent validity is demonstrated by comparing its results with another scale that has previously been determined (proven) to have validity when administered to the same group of subjects (Royse et al., 2016). If the two scales are highly correlated, at .80 or above, the new scale has demonstrated concurrent validity.

Construct validity refers to the extent to which an instrument actually measures the concept in question. Construct validity is established by demonstrating convergent validity and discriminant validity. A measure is said to have convergent validity if it is correlated in a predicted manner with other measures with which it theoretically should correlate (Bloom et al., 2009). For example, a measure of the strength of a helping relationship should correlate positively with measures of trust and openness. Those who are more trusting and open are more likely to develop strong helping relationships with their social workers than those who are less trusting and open.

A measure's discriminant validity is demonstrated by a lack of correlation with measures with which it theoretically should not be correlated. This indicates that the measure can discriminate between concepts. For example, there is no theoretical basis for predicting how certain client problems will correlate with the development of a helping relationship with the social worker. Clients with high self-esteem are as likely to develop a strong helping relationship as those with low self-esteem. Similarly, a client's level of depression is not associated with the strength of the helping relationship (Poulin, 2010).

Construct validity is demonstrated when a measure is correlated with other measures that it theoretically should be related to (convergent validity) and not correlated with measures with which it theoretically should not be correlated (discriminant validity). When selecting measures to evaluate client change, look for some evidence of the validity of the measure. At the very least, the measure should have face validity. Empirical verification of the measure's validity is preferable.

Organize the Data

For data to be useful, they have to be organized in some systematic way. It is difficult to interpret or draw meaning from unorganized raw data. Data need to be presented in a way that makes sense to both you and your client. Typically, data obtained to evaluate client change can be easily computed and presented in simple graphs.

The basic graphic presentation of change data is a line graph on which the client's scores are plotted over time. A visual inspection of the data points provides feedback on client progress. Time is plotted on the horizontal (x) axis, and scores measuring the target problem on the vertical (y) axis. The time dimension reflects the number of times the measure of the target problem is completed and the time period between measurements. The time unit selected depends on the nature of the target problem. Typically, measures of the target problem are completed on a daily or weekly basis. Figure 14.1 is a sample line graph on which a client's level of self-esteem is plotted over an 11-week period.

An important component of the helping process is reviewing the data on the graphic displays with clients. In collaborative social work, the clients are actively involved in inspecting the organized data and interpreting the patterns and results. Most clients are interested in examining graphs of their progress and in providing interpretations of what is happening. Involving clients in this process

▶ **Reflection Question**

Why do social workers need to understand research measurement guidelines?

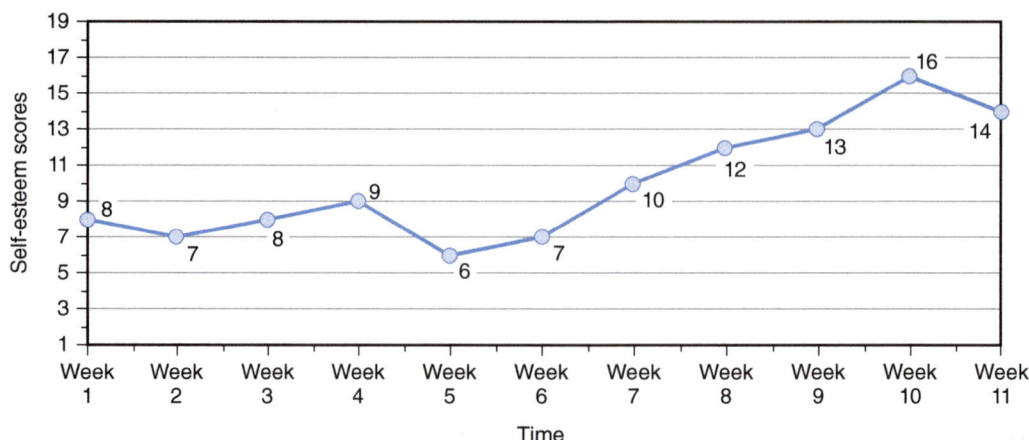

FIGURE 14.1 Client's weekly self-esteem scores.

can be a powerful tool. It keeps your work focused on the change objectives, and it provides an opportunity for you and the client to review progress, tasks, and effort as well as the appropriateness of goals and objectives. If strides are being made, it can motivate further efforts. If progress is not forthcoming, you and the client can assess the situation and adjust as needed.

Obtain Client Cooperation and Consent

Naturally, the process of selecting and incorporating measurement strategies into social work practice requires the full cooperation of clients. Most models of social work practice are based on the assumption that clients are full partners in the helping process. Measuring client progress without their full cooperation is a waste of time. Clients need to have ownership of the measures and be willing to engage in a process of self-assessment and change. Their commitment to the data collection and evaluation process reflects their commitment to achieving the changes they are seeking.

Standardized Measures

Standardized measures are instruments developed following empirical scale construction techniques with uniform administration and scoring procedures (Jordan & Franklin, 2015). Their reliability is known, and their validity has usually been empirically tested.

Standardized measures are available for a wide range of client behaviors, including marital satisfaction, self-esteem, anxiety, and family relations. Some standardized measures assess global behaviors, such as generalized contentment, while others assess specific behaviors and problems, such as fear, depression, or sexual satisfaction. Standardized measures are available in rapid assessment formats with up to 25 scale items, as well as in lengthy, comprehensive formats with hundreds of scale items. Rapid assessment instruments are easy to use and to incorporate into a generalist social work practice.

"Standardized measures represent the most useful quantitative clinical measurement tools that are available to practitioners" (Jordan & Franklin, 2015, p. 53). There are numerous sources of standardized measures. *Measures for Clinical Practice* by Corcoran and Fischer (2013) is an excellent two-volume collection of rapid assessment instruments. Volume 1 contains measures for use with couples, families, and children, and Volume 2 contains instruments for individual adults. The two-volume set contains more than 300 different brief assessment instruments, with supporting information on each instrument's purpose, scoring, reliability, and validity. Another great source of rapid assessment instruments is *Measures of Personality and Social Psychological Attitudes* by Robinson et al. (1991). In this book, measures are organized by clinical topic (e.g., self-esteem, depression, and anxiety).

A useful list of commercially available measures can be found in *Clinical Assessment for Social Workers* by Jordan and Franklin (2015). The Walmyr Publishing Company is also an excellent source for commercially available measurement instruments designed specifically for use in social work practice. Walmyr sells a number of individual and family adjustment scales as well as comprehensive multidimensional assessment instruments.

Standardized measures, especially the rapid assessment variety, are well suited for use in social work practice. If you can locate one that closely corresponds to identified client problems or concerns, standardized measures offer several advantages. They have known psychometric properties, that is, their reliability and validity have been established. They are also efficient, do not require extensive training, and are easy to administer and score (Corcoran & Fischer, 2013).

Designing the Evaluation

Having established measurable goals and selected measurement strategies, the next step is to determine how you are going to implement the evaluation process. The term *evaluation design* is often used to describe how practitioners plan to evaluate progress and case outcomes (Bloom et al., 2009). One of the most widely used ways to evaluate practice effectiveness in social work is the single-system design (Miley et al., 2013). Single-system designs are used in formal case-level evaluations. They involve the study of one client involving repeated measurements over time in order to measure change (Bloom et al., 2009).

Single-system designs hold great promise for social workers. The requirements for using them fit well with social work practice. Single-system designs require clear specification of the target problem, development of measurable goals, selection and implementation of an intervention, and continued monitoring of the client's progress on the identified target problem. All these requirements are consistent with the requirements of sound social work practice.

Bloom et al. (2009) provide a comprehensive and detailed description of numerous types of single-system designs. However, the designs that are likely to be used as part of a social worker's ongoing practice are more limited. The single-system design selected depends primarily on what questions you are attempting to answer (Berlin & Marsh, 1993). Two questions appropriate for social work practice evaluations are: Is the intervention working? and Is the intervention causing the change?

More complex experimental designs provide information on the causal effect of the intervention. Did the client system improve because of the intervention? What aspects of the intervention are most important in causing the change? Answers to such questions contribute to social work knowledge. They help document the effectiveness of various interventions with different types of clients and target problems. However, answering questions about causality and implementing experiential-type designs are beyond the level of evaluation expected for most social work practitioners. They are better addressed through research than through ongoing social work practice with clients.

As noted earlier, social workers have a responsibility to promote the well-being of clients and provide services competently (NASW, 2021). This entails, in part, assessing the effectiveness of our interventions. Is the client making progress? Does the intervention appear to be working? Is the target problem improving, getting worse, or staying the same? This section focuses only on designs that provide information on client progress. Such designs best fit social work practice. They are easy to implement with client systems, and they provide important information on the effectiveness of the work.

Components of Single-System Designs

There are a number of single-system evaluation designs. Some components are common to all of them. The basic components of single-subject designs are:

- specifying the target problem,
- developing quantitative measures of the target problem,
- establishing baseline measures of the target problem before intervention,
- measuring the target problem repeatedly throughout the intervention,
- displaying the data on a graph, and
- making comparisons across phases.

Specifying the target problem, developing measures, and displaying data on graphs were discussed earlier.

Establishing a Baseline

The *baseline* is the measure of the target problem before the worker begins the intervention. Repeated measurements prior to the intervention are necessary to establish a baseline. The baseline allows you to compare the client's target problem before and after the intervention (Bloom et al., 2009).

There are two types of baselines: concurrent and retrospective. For a concurrent baseline, data are collected while other assessment activities are taking place. Repeated measures of the target problem are collected before you implement an intervention within the client system. For a retrospective baseline, the client reconstructs measures of the target problem from an earlier time period, using memory. In many situations, delaying the intervention while a concurrent baseline is obtained is unacceptable. For example, it would be unethical to delay providing counseling services to people who experienced a traumatic event, such as a school shooting, in order to obtain baseline information on the victims' levels of traumatic stress. In such cases, using a retrospective baseline is an acceptable alternative.

A common question is how many data points or measurements are needed for the baseline. The answer is that it depends. For meaningful comparisons to be made between the preintervention (baseline) and the intervention phases, the baseline has to be stable. That is, there has to be an observable pattern of measurement scores during the baseline period. A stable baseline is one that does not contain obvious cycles or wide fluctuations in the data (Bloom et al., 2009). Fluctuations are acceptable only if they occur with some regularity (Marlow, 2011). Thus, ideally, the baseline phase does not end until the baseline is stable. How long it takes is influenced, in part, by the amount of variation among the data points. The greater the variation (range of scores), the more data points needed to achieve stability. Conversely, if the variation among points on the baseline is relatively small (similar scores), fewer data points are needed to achieve stability (Poulin, 2010).

Using an unstable baseline is problematic. If the measures of the target problem fluctuate widely and no pattern exists, it is difficult to determine what factors are affecting changes in the target problem and whether change has occurred once the intervention starts

(Bloom et al., 2009). In other words, it is unclear whether changes between the baseline and the intervention phases are due to usual fluctuations in the target problem or if change has actually taken place.

Making Comparisons

Assessing change requires making some sort of comparison. In traditional experimental evaluation designs, a treatment group is compared with a control group that does not receive treatment. In case evaluations using single-system designs, the client provides the basis for comparison. In essence, the client serves as their own control group. Is the client better after getting help than before? Without comparisons, it is impossible to assess change.

Work with clients can be divided into phases (Marlow, 2011). During the first few contacts, baseline data on the target problem may be collected; this is the assessment phase. The second phase is the next series of sessions, in which an intervention is implemented. If the first intervention did not achieve the desired results, a second intervention may be tried; this would be the third phase.

Single-system evaluations use letters to label the different phases. The letter A is used to designate the baseline phase. "Successive interventions are represented by successive letters: B for the first, C for the second, D for the third, and so on" (Royse et al., 2016). A single-system design that consists of a baseline phase followed by an intervention is called an *AB design*. An evaluation that does not have a baseline and only one intervention is called a *B design*. An ABA design is one in which a baseline (A) phase is followed by an intervention (B) phase and a second baseline (A) period. The various phases of a single-subject design are usually labeled on the line graph and represented by dashed vertical lines. Figure 14.2 is a line graph of an AB design.

The AB design is the most frequently used single-system design in service settings (Marlow, 2011). In this design, repeated measurements of the target problem are taken during the baseline (A) and intervention (B) phases. Measures of the target problem are taken before

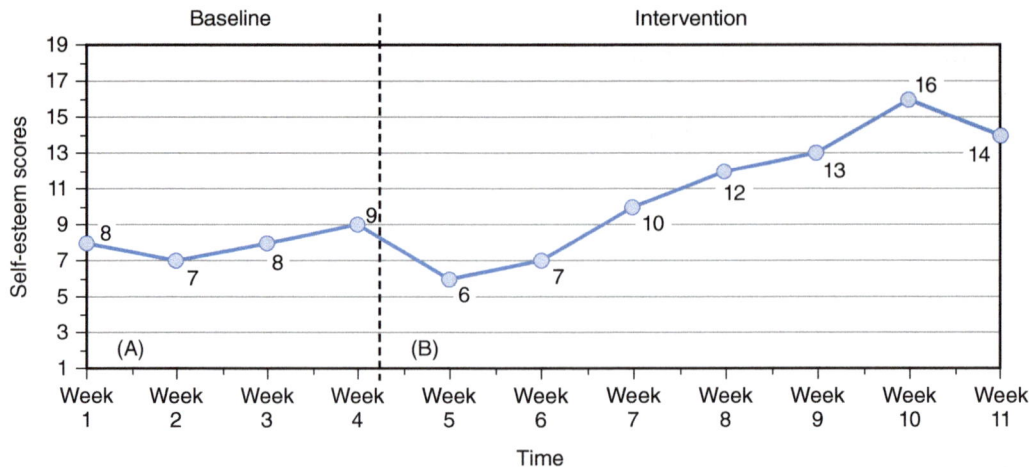

FIGURE 14.2 Sample AB design.

the intervention is implemented and throughout the intervention. As with all single-system evaluations, the findings are analyzed by plotting the data points on a chart.

The advantage of the AB design is its simplicity (Marlow, 2011). One must merely identify or develop an appropriate measurement of the target problem and then take repeated measurements during the first baseline phase and the intervention phase. This design can easily be incorporated into social work practice. It is consistent with normal practice procedures in that an assessment data-gathering phase is followed by an intervention phase (Poulin, 2010). The design usually does not compromise or hinder the development of a helping relationship and the provision of service. It fits well into most practice models, and it provides evidence of whether the intervention is working or not.

The one area of potential difficulty with the AB design is obtaining a baseline. This is a problem with all single-system designs used to evaluate ongoing practice with client systems (Poulin, 2010). Delaying the intervention while baseline data are collected is problematic when the situation warrants immediate attention. Obtaining measures of the target problem over a prolonged period of time often is not feasible or desirable. In these situations, developing a retrospective baseline is best. You and the client construct a baseline from the client's recollection of the target problem in the recent past. Although it is a compromise, a retrospective baseline provides a basis of comparison to answer the fundamental question: Is the intervention working?

The B design is the preferred option when it is necessary to intervene immediately, as in a crisis situation, without collecting baseline information or retrospective baseline information (Berlin & Marsh, 1993). It consists solely of an intervention (B) phase. Repeated measures of the target problem are taken throughout the intervention. This design is weaker than the AB design because preintervention comparison data are not available. It does, however, provide information on client progress, whether the target problem is improving, and whether the goals of the intervention have been achieved.

A third design that can be used to evaluate client progress is the ABC design. This design is an extension of the AB design. It involves the introduction of a second intervention (C) phase. If additional interventions are added beyond the second (C), they are labeled *D*, *E*, and so on. The ABC design is used when the first (B) intervention is modified or when the first intervention does not appear to be working. It does not provide information on which intervention caused change in the target problem, nor does it allow for separation of the effects of the successive interventions. It does, however, provide information on client progress. Other single-system design options are shown in Table 14.1.

Analyzing Single-System Data

Single-system design data are plotted on line graphs similar to those in Figure 14.2. Three types of significance can be used to judge change in the target problem: clinical, visual, and statistical. Clinical and visual significance are reviewed here. A review of the various approaches to calculating statistical significance is beyond the capabilities of this chapter. For a detailed discussion of the different approaches to calculating statistical significance, see Nugent's (2009) book, *Analyzing Single System Design Data*.

TABLE 14.1 OTHER SINGLE-SYSTEM DESIGNS	
Design Type	**Description of Design**
B	Measurement occurs during the intervention phase. There is no baseline data collection phase. *Example*: A client enters an inpatient drug and alcohol rehabilitation program. Upon entry into the program, he immediately begins receiving medication to treat his physical symptoms of withdrawal and begins individual cognitive behavioral therapy with a social worker. Since the social worker did not have a period of baseline prior to starting her therapeutic work with this client, all of the data collected while providing the therapy would be considered the treatment phase (B).
ABA	There is a period of baseline data collection where no intervention is given. Following the baseline phase, the intervention is administered, and data are then collected. After a period of time, the intervention is withdrawn, and another period of baseline data collection occurs. It is noteworthy that treatment carryover effects can interfere with the second baseline in this type of design. *Example*: A child with behavioral outbursts begins BHRS. During the intake process, the treatment team collects data in the forms of observations, interviews, and scales in order to determine current needs and to establish goals. This is the baseline phase (A). After collecting the baseline data, the team implements a behavior modification plan that includes reinforcements and punishments in an attempt to increase positive behaviors and eliminate undesired behaviors. While the behavior modification plan is being implemented, data are collected (B). Once the child has met the treatment goals, before discharging the child from services, the treatment team stops implementing the behavior modification plan and tracks rates of behaviors. While data are being collected after the intervention has been removed is a second baseline phase (A).
BAB	Measurement occurs during the intervention phase. The intervention is then withdrawn to collect baseline data. Following collection of baseline data, the intervention is reintroduced. *Example*: A woman with anxiety comes to a community mental health clinic for support. During her first session, the treatment begins with the social worker teaching her techniques to calm down, focus on her breath, and engage in mindfulness. The therapist asks the client to continue this intervention. Since there was no baseline period before the intervention was introduced, this case starts with the treatment phase (B). After several successful weeks using the intervention, the social worker stops the intervention and continues to collect data. Since there is no intervention being delivered, this is a baseline phase (A). The social worker eventually reintroduces the intervention, and data are collected during the second treatment phase (B).

BHRS, behavioral health rehabilitation services.

Clinical Significance

Clinical significance, also known as practical significance, is based on the client and the social worker believing that there has been meaningful change in the problem (Bloom et al., 2009). Clinical significance is achieved when the specified goal of the intervention has been reached (Marlow, 2011). Determining clinical significance is generally a subjective process that requires discussion and negotiation among the involved parties. If everyone involved agrees that the target problem has been resolved, clinical significance has been achieved.

Determining clinical significance when a goal has not been fully achieved is more difficult: How much change is clinically meaningful? There are no criteria for establishing the clinical significance of partial change in the target problem. Client change can be considered clinically significant if those involved in the helping process agree that meaningful change has occurred.

Visual Significance

Visual analysis is used for data that have been collected over time. It focuses on the trend and direction of the data. A trend occurs when data points move directionally in a relatively steady manner. A trend can be a steady increasing pattern, steady pattern of no change, or a steady decreasing pattern. Data in which there are no discernible trends or patterns are considered unstable. Unstable data show wide fluctuations in the measurement of the target problem. The interpretation of unstable data is difficult. Little can be said beyond the fact that there is no pattern and the scores vary widely (Poulin, 2010).

The visual analysis of single-system data is based primarily on a comparison of the baseline and intervention phases. For meaningful comparisons to be made, the baseline data must be stable. If they are not, interpretation of the effect of the intervention is impossible. Interpretation is also difficult if the baseline data are moving steadily in a direction that would represent improvement on the target problem. For example, if a decrease in occurrence of the target problem represents client improvement and the baseline trend shows a steady decline on the measure, it would be difficult to attribute the improved scores to the effectiveness of the intervention, because the data were already moving in the desired direction.

Calculating a celebration line helps to visually determine a trend in the data (Bloom et al., 2009). A celebration line connects the midpoints of the first and second halves of the baseline phase and extends into the intervention phase (Figure 14.3). The basic idea is that the trend

FIGURE 14.3 Line graph with celebration line.

established during the baseline phase is an estimate of what would happen if the baseline pattern were to continue and there were no intervention. The steps involved in calculating a celebration line are as follows:

1. Plot the baseline and intervention data on a line graph.
2. Divide the baseline section of the line graph in half, drawing a vertical line. If there are an even number of data points in the baseline, draw the line between the data points; if there are an odd number of points, draw the line through the midpoint number.
3. Divide each half into half by drawing dashed vertical lines on the chart.
4. Determine the mean score of the first half of the baseline by adding the scores in the half and dividing by the number of scores in the half. For baselines with an odd number of scores, omit the middle number.
5. Determine the mean score of the second half of the baseline by adding the scores in the half and dividing by the number of scores in the half. For baselines with an odd number of scores, omit the middle number.
6. Mark the dashed vertical line at the mean point for each half.
7. Draw a solid line connecting the two marks in the baseline and extend the line through the intervention phase.

> **Reflection Questions**
>
> 1. How would incorporating formal practice evaluation methods affect your social work practice with clients?
> 2. What are the advantages and disadvantages of doing so?

PROGRAM EVALUATIONS

Logic Models

A logic model is a graphic to visually represent the interrelations and connections among various parts of a program (Grinnel et al., 2010). There are numerous advantages to a logic model, including that it requires a focus on what is necessary in order for a program to meet its intended outcomes. If created in the right way, logic models can be useful for a variety of purposes. A well-constructed logic model can serve as a foundation for setting priorities within a program, evaluating and monitoring a program, and developing a strategic plan.

A variety of templates are available for creating a logic model. For program evaluations, we prefer logic models that, at a minimum, have information on program inputs, goals, activities, outputs, and outcomes. Figure 14.4 describes each element of a logic model.

Logic models are very helpful in conducting process and outcome program evaluations, both of which are discussed later in this chapter. Table 14.2 presents a logic model developed for a substance abuse program for adolescents. The substance abuse program referenced in the sample logic model is an evidence-based program called adolescent community reinforcement approach (ACRA). The program consists of 10 individual sessions with the

FIGURE 14.4 Elements of a logic model.

adolescent, two individual sessions with one or more caregivers, and two sessions with the adolescent and caregivers together. The intervention focuses on rearranging environmental contingencies so that abstaining from substances becomes more rewarding than using them. ACRA therapists teach adolescents how to find new reinforcers or enhance existing reinforcers for staying substance free, how to use existing community resources that were believed to support positive change, and how to develop a positive support system within the family. The logic model shown in Table 14.2 was used to develop the evaluation of the implementation of the program (process) and its outcome.

Process Evaluations

This type of program evaluation is sometimes called a formative evaluation. Grinnel et al. (2010) put forth that this type of evaluation serves to examine "how a program's services are delivered to clients and what administrative mechanisms exist within the program to support these services" (p. 129). Additionally, process evaluations look at routine aspects of daily operations. Within a process evaluation, activities and administration systems are explored regarding how they are organized and function. A process evaluation can be conducted at any time within an organization but often occurs early in program development. When used early in programs, process evaluations can be extremely helpful in identifying issues or glitches with the program's functioning that can be addressed and rectified.

A process evaluation seeks to determine if there is program fidelity, which means that the program is operating as it had been intended. If outcomes are not being met, it may also be quite helpful to conduct a process evaluation in order to determine if there is an issue in program implementation that is causing the unmet outcomes. As you can see, process

TABLE 14.2 SAMPLE LOGIC MODEL: ADOLESCENT SUBSTANCE ABUSE PROGRAM

Inputs (Resources)	Service or Activity	Output Objectives	Outcome Objectives
Program Resources Program director (1 FTE) Clinical director (1 FTE) Case managers (1.5 FTE) Program evaluator (0.25 FTE) Research Assistant (0.35 FTE) Three interviewers (225 hours each) Statistical consultant (25 hours) Administrative assistant (0.5 FTE) **Community Resources** Youth aid panel Magisterial district judges School district Community coalition Community hospital	**Goal 1: To decrease substance use among adolescents with histories of substance abuse.**		
	Activity 1.1. ACRA/agency case management counseling services for substance using adolescents.	**Output Objective 1.1.** To provide 12-session ACRA/agency case management services to 60 substance-using adolescents and their families during year 1. **Output Objective 1.2.** To provide 12-session ACRA/agency case management services to 75 substance-using adolescents and their families during years 2 and 3.	**Outcome Objective 1.1.** At least 50% of the adolescent alcohol users decrease the number of days of drug use during the past 30 days by 33% between intake and discharge from the 12-week ACRA/agency program as measured by the client outcomes instrument. **Outcome Objective 1.2.** At least 50% of the adolescent drug users decrease the number of days of drug use during the past 30 days by 33% between intake and discharge from the 12-week ACRA/agency program as measured by the client outcomes instrument. **Outcome Objective 1.3.** At least 33% of the adolescent alcohol users decrease the number of days of alcohol use during the past 30 days by 25% between intake and 6 months post intake into the 12-week ACRA/agency program as measured by the client outcomes instrument. **Outcome Objective 1.4.** At least 33% of the adolescent drug users decrease the number of days of drug use during the past 30 days by 25% between intake and 6 months post intake into the 12-week ACRA/agency program as measured by the client outcomes instrument.

(continued)

TABLE 14.2 SAMPLE LOGIC MODEL: ADOLESCENT SUBSTANCE ABUSE PROGRAM (CONTINUED)

Inputs (Resources)	Service or Activity	Output Objectives	Outcome Objectives
	Goal 2: To link adolescent substance users with appropriate community resources.		
	Activity 2.1. ACRA/agency case management referral/linkage services for substance-using adolescents.	**Output Objective 2.1.** To assess, each year, the service needs of 75 adolescent substance users and link those needing additional services with appropriate community resources. **Output Objective 2.2.** To provide follow-up case management referral/linkage services to all adolescent substance users referred to community resources.	**Outcome Objective 2.1.** 100% of the adolescent substance users with additional service needs will be linked with community resources as measured by the assessment instrument and client case records. **Outcome Objective 2.2.** At least 75% of the adolescent substance users referred to community resources will have followed up on the referral and contacted the community resource within 30 days of the referral as measured by the client outcomes instrument and client case records.
	Goal 3: To strengthen adolescent substance user's family support systems.		
	Activity 3.1. ACRA/agency case management family intervention services for substance using adolescents and their families.	**Output Objective 3.1.** To provide at least 2 adolescent/ family sessions to 60 substance using adolescents during year 1. **Output Objective 3.2.** To provide at least 2 adolescent/ family sessions to 75 substance using adolescents during years 2 and 3.	**Outcome Objective 3.1.** At least 50% of the adolescent substance user's scores on the Adolescent Happiness Scale will increase between initial assessment and discharge from the ACRA/agency case management program. **Outcome Objective 3.2.** At least 33% of the adolescent substance users' scores on the Adolescent Happiness Scale will increase between initial assessment and 6 months post intake in the ACRA/agency case management program.

ACRA, adolescent community reinforcement approach; FTE, full-time equivalent.

> **Reflection Questions**
> 1. Why is it important to conduct process evaluations?
> 2. In what ways are process evaluations similar to informal practice evaluations? In what ways are they different?

evaluations can be quite useful for a variety of reasons, as they not only serve to improve a program's operation but also can provide great insights into program practices and structure.

Once you decide to undertake a process evaluation, you should start by deciding what information you are hoping to gather. Once you know what information or data you would like to collect, you can then create your questions. As important as deciding what questions to ask is deciding whom you are going to ask. When conducting organizational evaluations, you need to be aware of the various stakeholders involved who may have vital information for you. *Stakeholder* is a term used to refer to those people who have an interest in your program. Stakeholders can be staff, administration, board of directors, funding sources, clients, community members, and other business or community partners.

It is important to consider from whom you are going to collect information because your approach may need to be varied for each group. When collecting data for any purpose, it is important to be sure that your data collection methods are clear and straightforward. It is also a good idea to be considerate of the participants' time. Though you may want to collect as much data as possible, it would be impossible for most people to complete surveys or interviews that ask hundreds of questions. When conducting an organizational evaluation, such as a process evaluation, you are often collecting data from staff. Be mindful that staff already have a lot on their plates, so whenever possible, try to incorporate your data collection process into the existing flow of current program operations. It can be helpful to ask the staff what they think would be a good way to collect such data. User input can be a valuable insight when conducting a process evaluation.

You will then need to collect your information and create a system to manage the incoming data. Once you have gathered your data, you will need to analyze your findings. Upon analyzing your results, you should share your findings with others. After doing all of the work associated with a process evaluation, it is important to disseminate your results to others. As we have mentioned, you should tailor the delivery of your findings to meet the needs of the stakeholder groups again. For example, you may wish to present a written report or slide show to the board of directors of the program, but clients or community members may prefer something less formal, like a conversation and handouts.

Case 14.2 describes the process evaluation for the adolescent substance abuse program outlined in the logic model in Table 14.2. In this example, the process evaluation data were used to provide ongoing feedback to the program staff to ensure program fidelity in the delivery of the ACRA program to the participating adolescents and their families.

The focus group protocol that was used for meeting with the adolescent participants of the program is shown in Exhibit 14.1. A similar focus group protocol was used to interview the parents/caregivers.

CASE 14.2 SAMPLE PROCESS EVALUATION PLAN

The process evaluation of the ACRA program will focus on two primary topics: (a) program implementation and (b) client feedback and perceptions.

Program implementation: The evaluation team will closely monitor and document all aspects of program implementation. This component of the process evaluation will address the following questions:

- How closely did the implementation match the proposed plan?
- What types of deviations from the plan occurred?
- What led to the deviations?
- What were the effects of the deviations?
- What services were provided?
- Who provided the services?
- Who received the program services?
- What was the level of service provided?
- What were the costs of the services provided?

All of the preceding questions are related to assessing program implementation. These data will be collected from program records, client records, staff interviews, and interviews with key informants from collaborating organizations. An emphasis of the implementation evaluation will be on fidelity to the ACRA model. The ACRA Global Procedure Checklist, the Therapist Skillfulness Scale, and the 15 individual ACRA Procedure Checklists will be used to access the fidelity of the implementation of the ACRA program.

Client feedback and perceptions: The second major topic of the process evaluation will focus on how clients perceive the program services and staff. This component will ascertain client feedback on all aspects of the program. The focus will be on documenting the clients' perceptions of what worked and what needs to be strengthened. These data will be collected each year from four focus groups, with approximately 10 former clients in each focus group. Two focus groups will be held at midyear with approximately 10 former adolescent clients, and two focus groups will be held with approximately 10 caregivers of former adolescent clients.

Outcome Evaluations

An outcome evaluation is a type of program evaluation that is sometimes called a summative evaluation. The primary purpose of an outcome evaluation is to determine to what extent the program is meeting its intended target by achieving its objectives. Through outcome evaluations, feedback related to program results can be given to program stakeholders, which increases the overall accountability of the program. It is beneficial to have a mechanism of providing feedback on a program in order to make program decisions, and an outcome evaluation can do just that.

Exhibit 14.1 Sample Focus Group Protocol

Directions

Please ask all of the adolescents to join you in a circle. Explain to them that you are going to ask them a few questions about the program and that you want them to be as honest as possible. Tell them that your information will not be linked to any person.

Explain that the purpose of the focus group is to get feedback to improve the program.

Ask the following questions of the group. Remember to try and get consensus about results—you do this by asking, "Does everyone agree?" and/or "Does anyone think differently?"

You need not write down every word; just capture the consensus and/or the differences in what the group answers.

Questions

1.	Tell me about your case manager.
2.	Were your individual sessions with your case manager helpful?
3.	Were the sessions with your parents/caregiver helpful?
4.	In what ways did the program help you?
5.	How did the program help you in getting along with your parents?
6.	How did the program help you better understand yourself?
7.	How did the program help you in getting along with your peers?
8.	How did the program help you in making choices about substance use?
9.	What did you like best about the program?
10.	What did you like least about the program?
11.	What should the agency do to improve the program?

The first step in conducting an outcome evaluation would be to examine the program objectives. Hopefully, the program has clearly outlined SMART objectives. SMART is an acronym used to describe objectives that are **S**pecific, **M**easurable, **A**ttainable, **R**elevant, and **T**ime-bound. It is important to understand where program objectives come from. Typically, a program begins with a mission statement. A mission statement is a written conceptual foundation that anchors the program based on what it is about and what it intends to do. From the mission statement, a vision statement can be derived. A vision statement is similar to a mission statement but focuses more on the future direction of the program. From these statements, goals are developed. Goals are broad statements that reflect the program's desired results. Then, from the goals, the objectives are created.

After exploring the program objectives, the next step in an outcome evaluation is to operationalize the variables you will be analyzing in your evaluation. You can then design your data collection and analysis processes and procedures. Then, similar to a process evaluation, you will want to be sure that you share your findings with program stakeholders. Case 14.3 is an outcome evaluation plan for the adolescent substance abuse program.

CASE 14.3 SAMPLE OUTCOME EVALUATION PLAN

Intervention outcomes: The program logic model, found elsewhere in this proposal, lists the three program goals and their associated outcome objectives. The first program goal is to have the adolescent participants abstain from substance use. Four outcomes are associated with this goal. Two deal with substance use at discharge and at 6 months post intake, and two deal with drug use at discharge and 6 months post intake. A client outcomes instrument will be used to measure the four outcomes associated with program goal 1. Program participants will be interviewed by evaluation team members using the instrument at intake, discharge, and 6 months post intake. To help meet the goal of completing follow-up interviews with at least 80% of the participants, a $20 mall certificate will be given to each adolescent who is interviewed. The participants' data will be entered into the program evaluation database that will be used to assess program outcomes.

The second program goal is to refer the adolescent participants to community resources. Three outcomes are associated with this goal. The assessment instrument and client case records will be used to measure the three outcomes related to assessment of resource needs and referral to community resources. The assessment instrument will be administered to program participants at intake and at 3, 6, and 12 months post intake by the program case managers. These data as well as information from the participants' case records will be entered into the program evaluation database that will be used to assess program outcomes.

The third program goal is to strengthen the adolescents' family support systems. Two outcomes are associated with this goal. The Perceived Social Support—Family Scale (PSS-Fa; Procidano & Heller, 1983) will be used to measure the family support outcomes listed in the logic model. The PSS-Fa will be administered by the program case managers along with the instrument. The PSS-Fa data will be entered into the program evaluation database that will be used to assess program outcomes.

Factors associated with outcomes: The second component of the outcome assessment consists of a multivariate analysis of individual, environment, and program factors that are associated with substance use, use of community resources, and family support. The data sources for these analyses will be the PSS-Fa and client case records. As noted earlier, extensive time series data on a larger number of scales and variables will be entered into an evaluation database for each adolescent participant. These data will be analyzed using SPSS for Windows. Regression analyses and analysis of variance will be used to identify the individual, environment, and program factors that are associated with the program outcomes at discharge and 6 months following intake.

DISSEMINATION

It would be near pointless to gather and analyze data and to never share the findings with others. This fruitless endeavor should be avoided. Social workers who engage in research in their practice should share their findings. There are a variety of ways to share, or disseminate, research findings. Three examples of dissemination that we explore include conference presentations, journal articles, and research reports.

Conference Presentations

Conferences are an excellent source to disseminate and to gain research information that can inform your practice. Conferences can vary in length, size, and scope. Some conferences are held with a very narrow focus on a particular topic or subject area, whereas other larger conferences have a plethora of options related to a variety of forms of practice and encourage general theoretical presentations as well as empirical findings. Conferences can be an excellent way to stay connected with other professionals and networks.

Related to disseminating research, you can submit a proposal to present at a conference. You may present a poster session, a roundtable discussion, or a more traditional lecture-style presentation. In order to submit a proposal for a conference, the guidelines are often posted on the hosting organization's website. It is very important to read the directions closely and pay particular attention to deadlines for submission. Often when submitting a proposal, you will need to submit an abstract along with three learning objectives that participants will achieve by attending your session. The abstract is simply a short summary of what you intend to present. Learning objectives often begin with the phrase "participants will" followed by short statements of what they will accomplish by participating in the presentation. A sample abstract and learning objectives are available in Exhibit 14.2.

Journal Articles

As college students, you are probably quite familiar with journal articles. Journal articles are one way that you can share your research findings with others. As you know, there are a wide variety of journals based on discipline, topic, or population. Many journal articles post a call for papers encouraging individuals to submit their own works to the journal for possible selection and publication. When considering submitting to a journal, it is

---

Exhibit 14.2 Sample Conference Abstract and Learning Objectives

Abstract

Burnout is a state of exhaustion affecting the person mentally, physically, and spiritually as the result of ongoing exposure or involvement in the helping profession. Self-care is one way to buffer against burnout. To be competent professionals, we need to engage in regular self-care. Though there is research related to the prevalence of burnout among social work professionals, research on burnout among social work faculty and students is scant. This presentation sets forth to share new research collected from social work faculty and students related to rates of burnout and self-care. The presentation also explores current self-care strategies that are being implemented in social work education programs. Participants are provided with suggestions for decreasing rates of burnout and promoting appropriate self-care for social work faculty and students.

Learning Objectives

1. Participants will be able to describe burnout as it relates to social work education for faculty and students.
2. Participants will learn how to assess for levels of burnout and self-care in their social work programs among faculty and students.
3. Participants will be able to identify self-care strategies that can be incorporated into social work education to support both faculty and students.

important to attend to the guidelines for submission, which include such things as length and other requirements.

In the case of a peer-reviewed journal, your submission will be stripped of your identifiable information and shared with two reviewers. Each reviewer will read your paper and provide feedback and possible suggestions for revision. You will hear back from the journal regarding their decision. You may hear several common responses once you have submitted your article. The first response that you may hear is that your paper has been accepted as is. This means that your paper will be published without any revisions necessary. The second response that you may hear is that your paper is provisionally accepted with revisions. Based on the comments of the reviewers and editor, you may be asked to make changes to your paper; those are the revisions the journal is looking for. At this point, you may decide that you are willing to revise your work based on the reviewers' recommendations and resubmit. The final response that you may receive is that your paper has been rejected; even if it has been rejected, there will often be detailed notes as to why. Those notes can be extremely helpful in the future, the next time you submit a paper.

Research Reports

Research reports are formal papers that outline research in an organized fashion. Many social work education programs require their students to write at least one research report during their education. Table 14.3 outlines the main parts of a research report.

TABLE 14.3 ELEMENTS OF A RESEARCH REPORT	
Title	The title of your research report should represent what your report is all about succinctly. The iAPA sets forth that titles should be no more than 12 words.
Abstract	The abstract serves as a summary of the report. A good abstract is accurate, nonevaluative, coherent and readable, and concise.
Introduction	The introduction serves to establish the foundation for your paper by demonstrating relevance.
Literature review	A review of past and current scholarship on the topic you are addressing should be presented.
Research question or hypothesis	You should explicitly state your research question or hypothesis. This serves as the bridge into your research.
Methodology	Often referred to as the methods section, this portion of your paper outlines how you planned your research, including sampling and intervention methods. You should clearly describe your research design.
Findings	The findings section is where you put forth your analyzed data results.
Discussion	The discussion allows for the findings to be explained. You should also address any limitations to your research. You can include any recommendations for future research and conclusions.
References	You should have a complete reference list that is formatted in APA style for all sources referenced in your report.

APA, American Psychological Association.

SUMMARY

This chapter focused on evaluating practice competency. The main components of this competency are evaluating practice effectiveness, which deals with the evaluation of micro social work practice with individuals, families, and groups. The second component is evaluating organization and community program outcomes.

The chapter began with a review of the NASW *Code of Ethics* (2021) values, ethical principles, and ethical standards related to practice evaluation. The chapter provided definitions of basic research, action research, and AOP social work research. We then reviewed informal approaches to evaluation of practice effectiveness through supervision and self-reflection as well as different types of worker-constructed measures that can be used in obtaining client feedback.

Evaluating program outcomes was also reviewed. The two major types of program evaluations were discussed. Process or normative evaluations are designed to collect data on the implementation of organizational and community programs. These types of evaluations are concerned with ensuring program fidelity and obtaining stakeholder feedback on what is working and not working in getting the program up and running. Program fidelity is critical if an evidence-based program is being implemented. It is important to make sure that the program is delivered in the way it was designed and empirically tested. We also reviewed developing outcome evaluations that measure the extent to which organization and community programs are achieving their stated goals and objectives.

CASE SUMMARY | UNDOCUMENTED AND HOMELESS

Practice Setting Description

Jackie is a first-year master of social work (MSW) student completing an internship at an inner-city family service agency in the Southwest. The agency is in a section of the city that has a high crime rate, gang activity, and failing schools. The area has a diverse population with many immigrants from Central and South America and a substantial African American population. The agency provides individual and family counseling services on a sliding fee scale. The agency also runs several educational and treatment groups as well as a temporary shelter for women and their children. Jackie has been assigned to work with the women and their children in the shelter. Her primary tasks are to provide concrete services and supportive counseling to the shelter residents.

Background Information

Elicia and her daughter, Maria, are undocumented immigrants from Mexico. They have been in the United States for 5 years. Elicia and Maria fled to the area from another southwestern city to escape her abusive husband approximately 2 months ago. Elicia is 25 years old, and Maria 8 years old. Elicia has a 2-year-old daughter, Sarah, who was placed in foster care because of suspected abuse in the home. Sarah is in a foster home in a small rural community in the state hundreds of miles from Elicia's current residence. Since moving to the area, Maria has not been attending school.

Elicia and Maria are currently residing in the agency's temporary shelter for families. They have been at the shelter for 2 weeks, and the agency has a 90-day limit. Prior to arriving at the shelter, Elicia and Maria were homeless and living on the streets.

(continued)

| CASE SUMMARY | UNDOCUMENTED AND HOMELESS (*CONTINUED*) |

Elicia is a high school drop-out and was a stay-at-home mother prior to leaving her husband and moving to a different part of the state. She chose to move there because she has two female cousins living in the area who are also undocumented immigrants. Elicia's native language is Spanish. She speaks some English but is not as comfortable speaking in English. Her English comprehension appears to be good. Maria speaks both English and Spanish well. When communicating with the staff, Maria acts as Elicia's interpreter since none of the staff at the shelter speak Spanish.

Maria appears to be behind academically. She struggles reading simple children's books written in English. It is unknown if her ability to read in Spanish is better than her English reading skills.

Other than her two cousins, Elicia has no other sources of support in the community. Her cousins have young families and limited resources but are well established and connected to a Latino community in the city and the local Catholic church. Her cousins refused to let Elicia and Maria live with them while she was trying to find her own place and a job. They stated that they did not have enough room and are concerned they would get in trouble with their landlord if it was found out that they were letting people stay with them. They sent her to the local church for help, and she was given the address for the agency's shelter by the priest.

Elicia has been looking for housing in the Latino community. The housing market is tight with limited options, and she has been unable to find anything that she could possibly afford. The only affordable housing she found was a room in a rundown motel that rents by the hour or by the month. It is in an area of town known for drug dealing and sex work.

On arrival in the community, Elicia found occasional work for a house cleaning company. The company hires undocumented workers, pays them very low cash wages, and threatens to turn them in to Immigration and Customs Enforcement (ICE) if they complain. The job bosses also exploit their female workers sexually, threatening to turn them in if they do not comply. Elicia was fearful about applying for other jobs because of her illegal status. She considered turning to sex work to be able to take care of her child, but her Catholic upbringing and thoughts of how this would shame her family have kept her from doing so. She is in constant fear of being detained, separated from Maria, and having her placed in foster care. She is also afraid that she will end up homeless again and forced to live on the streets or return to her abusive husband.

Elicia is extremely reluctant to sign up for any federally funded services, even those that she and her child are entitled to receive. On the suggestion that she enroll for supplemental food through the Supplemental Nutrition Assistance Program (SNAP), Elicia became nervous and refused, as she has heard that participation in SNAP services, and others like them, would draw the attention of ICE, and she had heard stories on the news of individuals being deported after signing up for such programs.

Presenting Problems

Elicia and her child are facing multiple obstacles. They need to find permanent, affordable housing and a job that pays enough to cover her housing and living expenses. In addition, Maria needs to be enrolled in school.

(*continued*)

| CASE SUMMARY | UNDOCUMENTED AND HOMELESS (*CONTINUED*) |

Additionally, Elicia is experiencing an immense amount of stress, anxiety, and possibly post-traumatic stress disorder (PTSD). She described an instance where she could not calm down her breathing and she felt lightheaded. She is very fearful of men and tries to avoid all contact with men in the community. She reports difficulty sleeping at night and feeling exhausted most of the time.

She is concerned about Maria. She has started acting out at the shelter, getting into fights with the other children, disobeying her mother, and being disrespectful and defiant to the staff and other adults. Elicia and Maria fight frequently, and when Elicia tries to discipline Maria, she throws a temper tantrum until Elicia gives up.

Elicia has many strengths. She had the strength to leave her abusive husband and move to a different city. She loves her daughter and wants desperately to keep Maria with her. She is resilient and has managed to survive and keep her daughter safe despite not having a place to stay, a job, and a limited support network. Elicia feels safe in the shelter, but she is very fearful of being caught as an illegal immigrant and is generally mistrustful of helping professionals and persons of authority.

DISCUSSION QUESTIONS

1. Jackie has been asked by the director of the community service agency to design an evaluation of the shelter program. What should she do to ensure AOP program evaluation?

2. How should she identify the goals for the evaluation to be consistent with AOP practice principles?

3. What data sources and evaluation methods would be most appropriate for an AOP evaluation?

4. What are the potential roadblocks Jackie might encounter if she follows AOP principles in designing and implementing her program evaluation?

A robust set of instructor resources designed to supplement this text is located at http://connect.springerpub.com/content/book/978-0-8261-6683-8. Qualifying instructors may request access by emailing textbook@springerpub.com.

KEY REFERENCES

Only key references appear in the print edition. To access the full reference list, visit www.springerpub.com/courseconnect. See inside front cover and tear-out card for CourseConnect details.

Bloom, M., Fischer, J., & Orme, J. (2009). *Evaluating practice: Guidelines for the accountable professional* (6th ed.). Pearson.

Boog, B. (2003). The emancipatory character of action—research, its history and the present state of the art. *Journal of Community and Applied Social Psychology, 13*(6), 426–438. https://doi.org/10.1002/casp.748

Carey, M. (2012). *Qualitative research skills for social work: Theory and practice*. Routledge.

Grinnel, R. M., Gabor, P., & Unrau, Y. A. (2010). *Program evaluation for social workers: Foundations of evidence based programs* (5th ed.). Oxford University Press.

Jordan, C., & Franklin, C. (2015). *Clinical assessment for social workers: Quantitative and qualitative methods* (4th ed.). Oxford University Press.

Maxwell, J. A. (2013). *Qualitative research design: An interactive approach* (3rd ed.). Sage.

Poulin, J., Kauffman, S., & Ingersoll, T. S. (2022). *Social work capstone projects: Demonstrating professional competencies through applied research*. Springer Publishing Company.

Reamer, F. G. (2012). Ethics in qualitative research. In R. L. Miller, W. J. Reid, & A. E. Fortune (Eds.), *Qualitative research in social work* (2nd ed., pp. 35–60). University Press.

Ruch, G., Julkunen, I., & Epstein, I. (2016). *Relationship-based research in social work: Understanding practice research*. Jessica Kingsley Publishers.

Strier, R. (2006). Anti-oppressive research in social work: A preliminary definition. *British Journal of Social Work, 1*(5), 1–15. https://www.researchgate.net/publication/228666703_Anti-Oppressive_Research_in_Social_Work_A_Preliminary_Definition

Index

ABCD. *See* asset-based community development
ableism, 93
acceptance, 220
accommodation, 260
accountability, 72
accreditation, 42–44
ACE study. *See* Adverse Childhood Experience (ACE) study
action research, 413
ADEI. *See* antiracism, diversity, equity, and inclusion
administrative supervision, 71
advancing human rights and social, racial, economic, and environmental justice, 82
   anti-oppressive practice, human rights, and social justice, 99–105
   conflict, 95–96
   global interconnections, 88–89
   justice-informed practice, 96–99
   Maslow's theory of motivation, 83–84
   National Association of Social Workers *Code of Ethics*, 82–83
   oppression, forms of, 89–94
   oppression and human rights violations, 85–88
   policy issue, 105–106
   power, types and sources of, 94–95
   social justice theories, 84–85
   social processes, 95
Adverse Childhood Experience (ACE) study, 224
advocacy, 132
affective reactions, 45
   engagement, 228
   family assessment, 295
ageism, 93–94
ambivalence, 261
anonymous participation, 147
anti-oppression assessment, 102
anti-oppressive generalist social work practice, 30–31
   collaboration, 33
   critical self-reflection, 31–32
   critically assess experiences of oppression, 34
   empowerment, 32–33
   helping process, 35–39
   minimal intervention, 35
   principles, 31–35
anti-oppressive practice (AOP), 30, 215
   community needs assessment, 387–394
   defined, 2
   generalist social work practice. *See* anti-oppressive generalist social work practice
   human rights, and social justice, 99–105
   intersectionality, 4–5
   intervention, 279–280
   oppression, 4
   policy analysis, 207
   power, 3–4
   privilege, 4
   social work research, 413–414
anti-oppressive theory, 222. *See also* oppression theory
antiracism, diversity, equity, and inclusion (ADEI), 3, 34, 112
   compa love, 120–121
   conflict theory, 115–116
   constituents as experts, 130
   critical race theory, 116–117
   cultural competence standards, 130–132
   cultural wealth, 121
   education recommendations, 136
   empathy, 133
   empowerment, 132–133
   humility, 133
   intersectionality, 117–120
   National Association of Social Workers *Code of Ethics*, 112–115
   oppression and discrimination, forms and mechanisms of, 122–125
   oppression theory, 122
   personal values and biases, 128–130

antiracism, diversity, equity, and inclusion (ADEI) (*continued*)
  policy issue, 137–138
  policy recommendations, 136
  practice recommendations, 135–136
  racial triangulation theory, 121
  research recommendations, 136
  rural diversity, 134–135
  self-awareness, 126–128
  social justice issue, 138–139
  training recommendations, 136
  workforce recommendations, 136–137
antiracist practice, 2
antisemitism, 137
AOP. *See* anti-oppressive practice
assessment. *See also specific assessments*
  contracting skills, 233
  helping process, 37–38, 233
asset
  assessment, 396
  mapping, 397
asset-based community development (ABCD), 396
assimilation, 260
attachment theory, 217–218
authenticity, 227
authority power, 94
autonomy, 255

baccalaureate social work (BSW) program, 26
baseline, 423–424
behavioral observations, 161, 163
Belmont Code, 146
biases, 100, 229
  antiracism, diversity, equity, and inclusion, 128–130
  in institution, 98
biphobia, 92
Black Lives Matter movement, 138–139
boundaries, 72
bounded rationality, 344
BRAVING acronym, 72
brief structural family therapy, 307–308
BSW program. *See* baccalaureate social work (BSW) program

campaign funding, 198–199
capitalism, 93
care, defined, 258

case management, 266
CBPR. *See* community-based participatory research
CBT. *See* cognitive behavioral therapy
change theory
  implementation stage, 347
  refreeze stage, 347–348
  unfreezing stage, 346–347
classism, 91, 115–117
client-centered therapy, 220
client change process
  action stage, 39
  being client, experience of, 40–41
  contemplation stage, 39
  discrimination and oppression, 40
  helping experience expectations, 41
  maintenance stage, 39
  precontemplation stage, 39
  preparation stage, 39
  stages of, 39–40
client feedback, ongoing, 159–160
client logs, 160–161
climate change, 177, 186–187, 190, 194
clinical significance, 426–427
coalition building, 404–405
coercive power, 94
cognitive behavioral therapy (CBT), 275–276
  connecting thoughts, behaviors, and feelings, 276
  group, 332–333
  rational emotive behavior therapy, 333
  reinforcement and punishment in, 274
  triangle, 275
cognitive processes and affective reactions, 45
cognitive theory, of group practice, 318
cohesion, 325
collaboration, 33
collaborative decision-making, 344–345
collaborative helping relationship, 37
color and low-income children, 186–187
colorblindness, 117
common good, 184
communication, 325
  interprofessional, 66
  language and, 132
community-based participatory research (CBPR), 395–396
community development theory, 379–380, 401–404
  core principles of, 380

reconciliation, 380
redistribution, 380
relocation, 379–380
community education, 361–362
  grant writing, 364–370
  planning and program development, 362–370
  program funding, 363–364
  strategic planning, 362–363
  SWOT analysis, 363
  tasks and responsibilities, 370–371
community engagement, 154, 383–385
community evaluation, 405
community intervention
  coalition building, 404–405
  community development, 401–404
  locality development model, 398–401
  social action model, 401
  social planning model, 401
community needs assessment, 385–387
  anti-oppressive practice, conducting, 387–394
  asset assessment, 396
  asset mapping, 397
  community, defining, 388–389
  community-based participatory research, 395–396
  community members' capacity assessment, 397
  community organizational capacity assessment, 397
  community resource database, 394–395
  critical self-reflection, 387
  data, analyzing, 393
  data collection, 391–393
  existing data, identify, collect and analyze, 389–391
  goals and objectives, defining, 389
  oppression, acknowledge and confront, 387–388
  purpose, defining, 388
  report and dissemination, preparing, 393–394
  resource mapping, 398
community termination, 405
community theories
  community development theory, 379–380
  conflict theory, 380–381
  critical race theory, 383
  structural functionalism, 381–383

compa love, 120–121
competence, 256
competence value, 57–58
concurrent validity, 419
conference presentations, 436
confidential participation, 147–148
confidentiality, 76, 289, 315
conflict theories, 18, 380–381
  advancing human rights and social, racial, economic, and environmental justice, 95–96
  antiracism, diversity, equity, and inclusion, 115–116
  feminist standpoint theory, 221–222
  intervention, 279
  oppression theory, 222
  trauma theory, 222–224
constituents as experts, 130
construct validity, 419
constructivist paradigm, 11–12
  conflict perspective, 18
  critical race theory, 18–19
  critical theories paradigm, 17
  ecosystems and strengths perspectives together, 17
  feminist perspectives, 19–20
  queer theory, 19
  social constructivism, 12–13
  strengths perspective, 13–14
  strengths perspective practice principles, 15–17
  strengths perspective principles, 14–15
content validity, 419
continuity of care, 235, 315
counter-transference, 127–128
CPR strengths triangle, 14
critical race theory (CRT), 18–19, 383
  antiracism, diversity, equity, and inclusion, 116–117
  good-faith critiques of, 18–19
critical self-reflection, 31–32, 37, 387
critical theories paradigm, 17
critical thinking, 45
critically assess experiences, of oppression, 34
critiquing existing research, 152–153
cross-cultural knowledge, 131
cross-cultural skills, 131
CRT. See critical race theory
culturagram, 119–120
cultural competence, 289–290

cultural competence standards, 130–132
cultural value, 61
cultural wealth, 121
culturally responsive research, 153–154
culturally sensitive practice, 122, 130–131

data
   analyzing, 393
   collection, 391–393
   existing, 389–391
data collection
   client satisfaction surveys, 392–393
   community surveys, 392
   focus groups, 393
   key informant surveys, 392
   observation data, 391–392
   survey data, 392
decision-making, 52, 58–59, 63
   collaborative, 65
   shared, 60, 66
degree of choice, 269
depressive position, 261–262
deprofessionalization, 3
descriptive knowledge, 157
descriptive policy analysis, 206
despair, 258
differentiation of self, 292
dignity, 55–56
direct practice, 27
discriminant validity, 419–420
discrimination, 5, 14, 18, 34, 37, 40, 53–56,
      53–55, 89, 97, 112–115, 114, 119, 354,
      371, 387–389
   ableism, 93
   ageism, 93
   cultural, 90
   education, employment, and housing, 92
   employment, 19
   ethnic, 86
   forms and mechanisms of, 122–125
   against LGBTQIA+ community, 137
   racial, 4, 90, 121
   religious, 137
   sexism, 91–92, 382
   systematic, 86
   transgender oppression, 92
   xenophobia and ethnocentrism, 91
disequilibrium, 8
dissemination, 435–437
distributive justice, 84–85
diversity, 132. *See also* antiracism, diversity,
      equity, and inclusion
   rural, 134–135
dominant power, 94
dual relationships, avoiding, 216

EBP. *See* evidence-based practice
ecomaps, 298–302
economic justice, 184–185
economic policy analysis, 206–207
ecosystem perspective, 9–11, 267
educational supervision, 71
ego psychology, 261
electronically protected health information
      (ePHI), 76
emotional intelligence, 360–361
empathy, 133, 220
empiricism, 148–149
empowerment, 32–33, 132–133, 319
empowerment therapy, 278–279
engagement, 36–37
   attachment theory, 217–218
   client-centered therapy, 220
   collaborative helping relationship, 37
   commonalities, 226–227
   conflict theories, 221–224
   differences, 227
   with different client systems, 226–227
   elaboration skills, 232
   empathy skills, 232
   helping process36–37, 232–234
   Helping Relationship Inventory,
      230–231
   humanistic theory, 218–219
   interprofessional collaboration, 234–236
   Maslow's theory of motivation, 219
   person-in-environment perspective,
      224–226
   personality theory, 220–221
   policy issues, 237–239
   pre-engagement stage, 36–37
   professional relationships, building, 236
   psychodynamic theories, 217–218
   relationship building, 227–229
   social constructivism, 221
   social justice issues, 239–240
   sustainment, 37
   teamwork, 236–237
Environmental Justice Screening and Mapping
      Tool, 194

ePHI. *See* electronically protected health information
equality, 184
equifinality, 291
equilibrium, 8
ETHIC acronym, 59
ethical and professional behavior, 52–53
   confidentiality and privacy, 76
   ethical dilemmas, 58–61
   ethical standards, 58
   interprofessional collaboration collaborative practice, 64–69
   professional and ethical use of technology, 75–76
   professional development, 74–75
   professional online identity, 76
   self-awareness, 73–74
   self-reflection, 73
   sharing, 71–73
   supervision, 69–71
   trust, 71–73
   value conflicts, 61–64
   values, 53–58
   vulnerability, 71–73
ethical dilemmas, 58
   ethical guidelines, 59–61
ethical standards, 58
ethnocentrism, 90–91
evaluation, 144–145
   action research, 413
   anti-oppressive practice social work research, 413–414
   applied research, 413–414
   behavioral observations, 161, 163
   client logs, 160–161
   conference presentations, 436
   designing evaluation, 422
   dissemination, 435–437
   goal attainment scales, 165–166
   helping process, 39
   informal, 158–166
   journal articles, 436–437
   logic models, 428–429
   measurement guidelines, 417–421
   measurement methods, 160–166
   National Association of Social Workers *Code of Ethics*, 147
   ongoing client feedback, 159–160
   outcome evaluations, 433–435
   practice effectiveness, 416–428
   practice-informed research and, 414–416
   process evaluations, 429, 432–433
   program evaluations, 428–438
   qualitative research, 415–416
   quantitative research, 414–415, 416
   rating scales, 162–165
   research reports, 437
   single-system data, analyzing, 425–428
   single-system designs, components of, 423–425
   social justice considerations, 166–167
   standardized measures, 421–422
   supervision and self-reflection, 158–159
evaluation design, 422
evidence-based practice (EBP), 154–155
existing research, critiquing, 152–153

family(ies)
   family systems theory, 291–293
   family triangles, addressing, 292–293
   practice with, 290–291
family assessment
   affective reactions, 295
   ecomaps, 298–302
   genograms, 302–305
   person-in-environment perspective, 296
   self, use of, 294–295
   strengths-based, 296
   strengths perspective principles, 296–298
   value conflicts, 295
family intervention
   brief structural family therapy, 307–308
   family systems therapy, 305
   functional family therapy, 305–307
   key family systems concepts, 306
   multisystemic therapy, 307
family reunification, 309
family systems theory, 291–293
family systems therapy, 305
feminist perspectives, 19–20
feminist standpoint theory, 221–222
feminist therapy, 279
FFT. *See* functional family therapy
freedom, 59, 183
Freud's stages of psychosexual development, 251
functional family therapy (FFT), 305–307
funding, campaign, 198–199

GAS. *See* goal attainment scales
gender, 117–119

generalist social work practice
   anti-oppressive, 27. *See also* anti-oppressive generalist social work practice
   client change process. *See* client change process
   defined, 26–27
   generalist interventions, 27–30
   holistic competency. *See* holistic competency
   interrelationships among competencies, 45–46
   social work competencies, 41–44
generativity, 258
generosity, 72
genograms, 302–305
genuineness, 220
geographic information system (GIS) mapping, 397
GIS mapping. *See* geographic information system (GIS) mapping
giving testimony, 200
globalization, 88
goal attainment scales (GAS), 165–166
grant writing, 364–365
   clear project or problem, developing, 366
   funding opportunity announcements (FOAs), 367
   grant source, selecting, 366–367
   notice of funding availability (NOFA), 367
   proposal, write, 368–369
   request for proposal (RFP), 367
   search engine websites, 368
   super NOFAs, 367
group(s)
   cognitive theory, 318
   development, 320–324
   dynamics, 325–327
   empowerment, 319–320
   humanism, 319
   mutual aid, 319
   practice with, 316–317
   psychodynamic theory, 318
   skills, 333–334
   structure, 324–325
   systems theory, 317–318
   types of, 320
group assessment
   group as a whole, assessing, 328
   in group therapy, 329–330
   individual group members, assessing, 328–329
   person-in-environment perspective, 327
   strengths-based, 329
   strengths perspective principles, 327–328
group culture, 326–327
group interventions
   group cognitive behavioral therapy, 332–333
   interactional group psychotherapy, 332
   mental and physical health groups, 331–332
   prevention groups, 331
   psychoeducation groups, 330–331
   rational emotive behavior therapy, 333
   social skills training groups, 332
group systems theory, 317–318
guilt, 255–256

hate crimes, 138
Health Insurance Portability and Accountability Act (HIPAA), 76
hearings, 200
helping process, 35–36
   assessment, 37–38, 233
   engagement, 36–37, 232–234
   evaluation, 39
   intervention, 38, 233–234
   termination, 234
Helping Relationship Inventory, 230
   interpersonal component, 231
   structural component, 230–231
heterosexism, 92
hierarchy of human needs, 83–84
HIPAA. *See* Health Insurance Portability and Accountability Act
historical policy analysis, 206
holistic competency, 45
   cognitive processes and affective reactions, 45
   defined, 44
   knowledge, 44
   skills, 44–45
   values, 44
homelessness, 20–22
   advancing human rights and social, racial, economic, and environmental justice, 107–109
   antiracism, diversity, equity, and inclusion, 139–141
   community assessment and intervention, 406–408
   engagement, 241–243
   ethical and professional behavior, 77–79
   evaluation, 438–440
   family assessment and intervention, 310–311

generalist social work practice, 46–48
group assessment and intervention,
    337–338
individual assessment and intervention,
    283–284
organization assessment and intervention,
    372–374
policy-informed practice, 208–210
research-informed social work practice,
    169–170
homeostasis, 8, 291
homophobia, 92
hospice team, 68
human relationships value, 56–57
    competence value, 57–58
    integrity value, 57
human rights violations, 85–88
    in Africa, 86
    in Americas, 86
    in Asia-Pacific region, 86
    in Europe and Central Asia, 87
    in Middle East and North Africa, 87
    in United States, 87
human trafficking, 54, 89
humanism, 319
humanistic theory, 218–219
humility, 133

ICCPR. *See* International Covenant on Civil
    and Political Rights
identity, 256–257
illogical reasoning, 156
individual assessment
    ego psychology, 261
    human development theories, 250–260
    object relations theory, 261–262
    policy issues, 280–281
    psychodynamic theories, 260–262
    psychosocial development theory, 252–258
    psychosocial theories, 250–251
    self-psychology, 262
    social justice issues, 281
    stage theory, 258–260
    transitions and endings, 280
individual intervention
    anti-oppressive practice, 279–280
    case management, 266
    clinical practice models, 267–280
    cognitive behavioral therapy, 275–276
    conflict theory, 279
    ecosystem perspective, 267
    empowerment therapy, 278–279
    feminist therapy, 279
    life model, 267–269
    motivational interviewing, 277–278
    narrative therapy, 271–272
    policy issues, 280–281
    rational emotive behavioral therapy, 278
    social justice issues, 281
    social learning theory, 274–275
    solution-focused brief therapy, 273–274
    stages of change, 263–265
    strengths perspective, 269–271
    supportive counseling, 266–267
    task-centered practice, 273
    transitions and endings, 280
inequities, 94, 97
    in institution, 98
inferiority, 256
informal evaluation, 158–166
initial assessment process, 37–38
initiative, sense of, 255–256
institutional approach, 177
institutional oppression, 122–123
institutional review boards (IRBs), 146
institutional supports, interprofessional
    collaboration, 67
integrity, 72, 258
integrity value, 57
interaction patterns, 325
interactional group psychotherapy, 332
interconnectedness of global economy,
    88–89
interdependent, 94–95
International Covenant on Civil and Political
    Rights (ICCPR), 106
interpersonal attraction, 325
interpersonal oppression, 122
interprofessional collaboration
    challenges, 236–237
    engagement, 234–235
    ethical and professional behavior, 64–69
    hospice team, 68
    institutional supports, 67
    roles and responsibilities, 66
    teams and teamwork, 66–67
    values and ethics for, 65–66
    working culture, 67–69
interprofessional communication, 66
intersectionality, 4–5
    antiracism, diversity, equity, and inclusion,
        117–120

intervention. *See also specific interventions*
   evaluation skills, 234
   helping process, 38, 233–234
   skills, 233
intimacy, 257–258
IRBs. *See* institutional review boards
isolation, 257–258

journal articles, 436–437
justice, defined, 184. *See also* economic justice; social justice
justice-informed practice, 96–99
juvenile detention center, 166–167

latent functions, 382–383
leadership, to advance cultural competence, 132
legitimate power, 94
letters to the editor, 201
LGBT community, 55
LGBTQIA+ community, 137
life model, 267–269
lobbying
   campaign funding, 198–199
   defined, 196
   educating, mobilizing, and organizing public, 199–200
   forms of, 196–198
locality development model, 398–401
logic models, 428–429, 430–431
logical errors, 156

macro-level generalist social work practice, 29
manifest functions, 382–383
Marx, Karl, 115
Maslow's theory of motivation, 83–84, 219, 251
master social work (MSW) program, 26
means-testing, 179
measurement guidelines
   client cooperation and consent, obtaining, 421
   data, organizing, 420–421
   good and accurate measures, using, 418–420
   information early, collecting, 418
   multiple measures, using, 417
   problems and goals, specifying, 417
   relevant information, collecting, 417
mental and physical health groups, 331–332

metatheories, 5–7
mezzo-level generalist social work practice, 28–29
MI. *See* motivational interviewing
micro generalist social work practice, 27–28
microaggressions, 123–125
midlevel theories, 5–7
minimal intervention, 35
mistrust, 253–255
motivation theory, 83–84
motivational interviewing (MI), 277–278
   empathic style of, 277
MST. *See* multisystemic therapy
MSW. *See* master social work program
multifinality, 291
multisystemic therapy (MST), 307, 308
mutual aid, 319

narrative therapy, 271–272
NASW *Code of Ethics*. *See* National Association of Social Workers (NASW) *Code of Ethics*
National Association of Social Workers (NASW) *Code of Ethics*
   advancing human rights and social, racial, economic, and environmental justice, 82–83
   antiracism, diversity, equity, and inclusion, 112–115
   community assessment and intervention, 379
   engagement, 214–216
   evaluation, 147, 412–413
   family assessment and intervention, 289–290
   group assessment and intervention, 315–316
   individual assessment and intervention, 247–249
   organization assessment and intervention, 343
   research-informed social work practice, 145–148
nonjudgment, 72
nonjudgmental attitudes, 56
Nuremberg Code, 145

object relations theory, 261–262
ongoing client feedback, 159–160
ongoing process

assessment, 38
evaluation, 39
online identity, 76
oppression, 40, 53, 54, 222
   ableism, 93
   acknowledge and confront, 387–388
   advancing human rights and social, racial, economic, and environmental justice, 85–88
   antiracism, diversity, equity, and inclusion, 122
   ageism, 93–94
   biphobia, 92
   classism, 91
   critically assess experiences of, 34
   defined, 4
   ethnocentrism, 90–91
   forms and mechanisms of, 122–125
   forms of, 89–94
   heterosexism, 92
   homophobia, 92
   institution, 122–123
   interpersonal, 122
   racism, 90
   religious, 91
   sexism, 91–92
   transgender, 92–93
   xenophobia, 90–91
organization assessment, 348–349
   foundation policies, 350–351
   internal organizational characteristics, 349–350
   internal processes, 352–353
   internal structure, 351–352
   organizational assessment variables, 353, 354, 355
   organizational environmental considerations, 353
   organizational goals and objectives, 350–351
   organizational mission and vision, 350
organization engagement, 348
organization evaluation
   adjust and revise, 371
   termination, 371–372
organization intervention, 353–354, 355
   goals and objectives, setting, 356–358
   group skills, trainings to improve, 359, 360
   intervention plan, developing, 356–358
   leadership, trainings to enhance, 359–361
   organizational and group trauma, trainings to address, 361
   productivity and technology, trainings to enhance, 358–359
organizational development theory, 345–346
organizational practice, 203–205
organizational theories
   change theory, 346–348
   organizational development theory, 345–346
   rational decision-making theory, 343–345
outcome evaluation, 39, 433–435
overgeneralization, 156

PACs. *See* political action committees
paradigms, 5–6
   constructivist, 11–12
   critical theories, 17
   positivist. *See* positivist paradigm
person-in-environment perspective, 224–226
   family assessment, 296
   group assessment, 327
person-in-environment systems, 9
personal narrative, 272
personal value, 62
   antiracism, diversity, equity, and inclusion, 128–130
personality theory, 220–221
perspectives, 5–7
PHI. *See* protected health information
physical environment, 68–69
Piaget's theory, of cognitive development, 259
policy analysis, 205, 206–207
   descriptive analysis, 206
   historical analysis, 206
   values, power, and economic analysis, 206–207
policy briefs, 200–201
policy evaluation, 204–205
policy formation, 183–188
policy foundational concepts, 183
policy implementation, 202–207
   organizational practice, 203–205
   policy analysis, 205, 206–207
   regulatory actions, 202–203

policy-informed practice
   National Association of Social Workers *Code of Ethics*, 174–175
   policies, defined, 175
   policy formation, 183–188
   policy implementation, 202–207
   policy practice, 188–189
   policy stages, 190–202
   social welfare policies. *See* social welfare policies
policy issues
   advancing human rights and social, racial, economic, and environmental justice, 105–106
   antiracism, diversity, equity, and inclusion, 137–138
   engagement, 237–239
   family assessment and intervention, 308–309
   group assessment and intervention, 335–336
   individual assessment and intervention, 280–281
policy practice, 188–189
policy stages
   political mobilization and political advocacy, 194–202
   problem characterization, 191–194
   problem identification, 190
political action committees (PACs), 198
political advocacy, 194–202
political mobilization, 194–202
positivism, 148, 150
positivist paradigm
   ecosystems perspective, 9–11
   systems theory, 7–9
postmodernism, 11
power
   authority and legitimate, 94
   coercive and dominant, 94
   and control, 326
   defined, 3–4
   policy analysis, 206–207
   privileged and interdependent, 94–95
   social structure and, 187–188
   types and sources of, 94–95
practice-informed research and research-informed practice, 144
   critiquing existing research, 152–153
   culturally responsive research, 153–154
   empiricism, 148–149
   evidence-based practice, 154–155
   multiple ways of knowing, 155–158
   National Association of Social Workers *Code of Ethics*, 145–148
   positivism, 148, 150
   research-informed practice, 151–152
   role of research, 150–151
   scientific inquiry, 149
   translating findings into practice, 158
practice wisdom, 156–157
predictive knowledge, 157
prejudices, 54, 89–91, 93–94, 115–116, 129, 138
prescriptive knowledge, 157–158
prevention groups, 331
privacy, 59, 76, 289, 315
privilege, 119
   defined, 4
   power, 94–95
problem characterization stage, of policy, 191–194
problem identification stage, of policy, 190
process evaluation, 429, 432–433
professional development, 74–75
professional education, 132
professional judgment, 45
professional online identity, 76
professional social work competencies, 41–46
professional value, 62
program funding, 363–364, 365
protected health information (PHI), 76
pseudoscience, 156
psychodynamic theories
   attachment theory, 217–218
   engagement, 217–218
   of group practice, 318
psychoeducation groups, 330–331
psychological aging, 250
psychosocial development theory
   autonomy versus shame and doubt, 255
   Erikson's theory of development, 254
   generativity versus stagnation, 258
   identity versus role confusion, 256–257
   industry versus inferiority, 256
   initiative versus guilt, 255–256
   integrity versus despair, 258
   intimacy versus isolation, 257–258
   sense of identity, developing, 256–257
   stages of, 252
   trust versus mistrust, 253–255
psychosocial theories, 250–251

qualitative research, 415–416
quantitative research, 414–415, 416
queer theory, 19

racial triangulation theory, 121
racism, 90, 91, 112–117, 115, 121
rating scales, 162–165
rational decision-making theory, 343–345
rational emotive behavioral therapy (REBT), 278
rationalism, 149
REBT. *See* rational emotive behavioral therapy
refugee resettlement programs, 309
regulatory actions, 202–203
relationship building
   affective reactions, 228
   engagement, 227–229
   professional, 236
   self-reflection and biases, 229
   trust building, 229
relationships value, 56–57
relevance, 418
reliability, 72, 418–419
religious discrimination, 137
religious oppression, 91
religious value, 61–62
research
   critiquing existing, 152–153
   culturally responsive, 153–154
   knowledge, 157–158
   role of, 150–151
research-informed practice, 151–152
   barriers to, 151
research reports, 437
research skills, 193–194
residual perspective, 177
resilience, 270–271
resource mapping, 398
resources, defined, 183
Rogerian approach, 220–221
role confusion, 256–257
rural diversity, 134–135

scientific inquiry, 149
selective observation, 156
self-awareness, 31, 73–74, 126–128, 131
self-concept, 220
self-determination, 33, 59–60, 132, 146, 289
self-efficacy, 262, 279
self-psychology, 262
self-reflection, 31–32, 37, 63, 73, 127, 158–159, 229, 348

self-regulation, 73
sensitivity, to change, 418
service delivery, 131–132
service value, 53
sexism, 91–92
sexual orientation, 92, 99, 117–118, 137
shame and doubt, 255
shared responsibility, 60
sharing, 71–73
single-system data, 425
   clinical significance, 426–427
   visual significance, 427–428
single-system designs, 423, 426
   AB design, 424–425
   baseline, establishing, 423–424
   comparisons, making, 424–425
skepticism, 149
skills dimension, 44–45
social action groups, 334–335
social action model, 401
social constructions, 191–193
social constructivism, 12–13, 221
social identity, 100–101
social influence, 325–326
social injustice, 54
social integration, 325–326
social justice, 99–105
   antiracism, diversity, equity, and inclusion, 138–139
   engagement, 239–240
   family assessment and intervention, 309
   group assessment and intervention, 336
   individual assessment and intervention, 281
   policy-informed practice, 184, 185
   practice-informed research and research-informed practice, 166–167
   value, 53–55
social justice model, of group development, 323–324
social justice theories
   advancing human rights and social, racial, economic, and environmental justice, 84–85
   distributive justice, 84–85
social learning theory, 274–275
social location, defined, 99–101
social media, 201–202
social planning model, 401
social processes, 95
social service organizations, 349
social skills training groups, 332

social structure, 187–188, 382
social value, 61
social welfare policies
   benefits, 180–182
   components of, 178–182
   defined, 175–177
   eligibility, 179–180
   reasons for caring, 182–183
   reasons for choosing, 183–188
   types of, 178
soft sciences, 149
solution-focused brief therapy, 273–274
stage theory, 258–260
stages of change, 263–265
   action, 264
   contemplation, 264
   maintenance, 264
   precontemplation, 263
   preparation, 264
   termination, 264
stagnation, 258
standardized measures, 421–422
steady state, 8
stereotypes, 89–91, 93–94, 121
strains, 122
strategic planning, 362–363
strengths perspective
   family assessment, 296
   strengths and obstacles worksheet, 298, 299–300
strengths-perspective, 13–14
   ecosystems and, 17
   group assessment, 328–330
   intervention, 269–271
   practice principles, 15–17
   principles, 14–15
strengths perspective principles
   family assessment, 296–298
   group assessment, 327–328
structural functionalism, 381
   manifest and latent functions, 382–383
   social functions, 382
   social structure, 382
summative evaluation. *See* outcome evaluation
supervision, 69, 158–159
   administrative, 71
   agreement, 70
   counseling and, 72
   domains, 70–71
   educational, 71
   purposes, 70
   support, 71
support supervision, 71
supportive counseling, 266–267
surveillance, 190
SWOT analysis, 363, 364
systems theory, 7–9
   family assessment, 291

Tarasoff ruling, 281
task-centered practice, 273
team brainstorming, 237
teams and teamwork, 66–67
teamwork, 66–67, 236–237
technology, use of, 75–76
termination
   ending skills, 234
   helping process, 234
theory of motivation, 83–84
transference, 127–128
transgender oppression, 92–93
translating findings into practice, 158
trauma theory, 222–224
   cognitive, behavioral, emotional, and physiological symptoms, 223
   risk and protective factors, 223
   trauma-informed engagement behaviors, 225
trust, 71–73, 253–255
trust building, 229
Tuckman's five stages of group development, 321–323
Tuskegee experiment, 145

UDHR. *See* Universal Declaration of Human Rights
undocumented immigrants, 20–22
   advancing human rights and social, racial, economic, and environmental justice, 107–109
   antiracism, diversity, equity, and inclusion, 139–141
   community assessment and intervention, 406–408
   engagement, 241–243
   ethical and professional behavior, 77–79
   evaluation, 438–440
   family assessment and intervention, 310–311
   generalist social work practice, 46–48

group assessment and intervention, 337–338
individual assessment and intervention, 283–284
organization assessment and intervention, 372–374
policy-informed practice, 208–210
research-informed social work practice, 169–170
Universal Declaration of Human Rights (UDHR), 86, 87
universal healthcare, 180

validity, 419
value conflicts, 61–64
   cultural value, 61
   family assessment, 295
   personal value, 62
   professional value, 62
   religious value, 61–62
   social value, 61
values, 44
   competence value, 57–58
   dignity and worth of person's value, 55–56
   human relationships value, 56–57
   and ideology, 183
   integrity value, 57
   policy analysis, 206–207
   service value, 53
   social justice value, 53–55
vault, 72
visual significance, 427–428
vulnerability, 71–73

wisdom, 258, 259
working culture, 67, 68–69
worth of the person, 55–56

xenophobia, 90–91

zero-tolerance policy, 106